Empire and the Making of Native Title

This book provides a new approach to the historical treatment of indigenous peoples' sovereignty and property rights in Australia and New Zealand. By shifting attention from the original European claims of possession to a comparison of the ways in which British players treated these matters later, Bain Attwood not only reveals some startling similarities between the Australian and New Zealand cases but revises the long-held explanations of the differences. He argues that the treatment of the sovereignty and property rights of First Nations was seldom determined by the workings of moral principle, legal doctrine, political thought or government policy. Instead, it was the highly particular historical circumstances in which the first encounters between natives and Europeans occurred and colonisation began that largely dictated whether treaties of cession were negotiated, just as a bitter political struggle determined the significance of the Treaty of Waitangi and ensured that native title was made in New Zealand.

Bain Attwood is Professor of History at Monash University and has held fellowships at the University of Cambridge and Harvard University. His book *Possession: Batman's Treaty and the Matter of History* (2009) won the 2010 Ernest Scott Prize for the most distinguished contribution to the history of Australia or New Zealand. He is the author of *Rights for Aborigines* (2003) and the co-editor of *Protection and Empire: A Global History* (2018).

Empire and the Making of Native Title

Sovereignty, Property and Indigenous People

Bain Attwood

Monash University, Victoria

 CAMBRIDGE
UNIVERSITY PRESS

CAMBRIDGE
UNIVERSITY PRESS

University Printing House, Cambridge CB2 8BS, United Kingdom

One Liberty Plaza, 20th Floor, New York, NY 10006, USA

477 Williamstown Road, Port Melbourne, VIC 3207, Australia

314–321, 3rd Floor, Plot 3, Splendor Forum, Jasola District Centre, New Delhi – 110025, India

79 Anson Road, #06–04/06, Singapore 079906

Cambridge University Press is part of the University of Cambridge.

It furthers the University's mission by disseminating knowledge in the pursuit of education, learning, and research at the highest international levels of excellence.

www.cambridge.org
Information on this title: www.cambridge.org/9781108478298
DOI: 10.1017/9781108776424

First published 2020

Printed in the United Kingdom by TJ International Ltd, Padstow Cornwall

A catalogue record for this publication is available from the British Library.

Library of Congress Cataloging-in-Publication Data
Names: Attwood, Bain, author.
Title: Empire and the making of native title : sovereignty, property and indigenous people / Bain Attwood, Monash University, Victoria.
Other titles: Sovereignty, property and indigenous people
Description: Cambridge, United Kingdom ; New York, NY : Cambridge University Press, 2020. | Includes bibliographical references and index.
Identifiers: LCCN 2020007145 (print) | LCCN 2020007146 (ebook) | ISBN 9781108478298 (hardback) | ISBN 9781108776424 (ebook)
Subjects: LCSH: Maori (New Zealand people) – Land tenure – New Zealand. | Maori (New Zealand people) – Politics and government. | Maori (New Zealand people) – Legal status, laws, etc. | Land reform – New Zealand. | New Zealand – History – 19th century.
Classification: LCC DU423.L35 A88 2020 (print) | LCC DU423.L35 (ebook) | DDC 993.01–dc23
LC record available at https://lccn.loc.gov/2020007145
LC ebook record available at https://lccn.loc.gov/2020007146

ISBN 978-1-108-47829-8 Hardback

For Claudia and Katarina

and

in memory of

Margaret Finlayson Attwood, 30 July 1926 – 27 August 2016

and

Nicholas Frederick Thomas Attwood, 25 July 2011

Contents

Acknowledgements

I have incurred many debts in researching and writing this book. Work on it was funded by grants from the Smuts Memorial Fund, Cambridge University, 2007–08; the Australian Research Council, 2008–10; and the Harvard University Australian Studies Committee, 2014–15. Research was conducted in many archives and libraries in Australia, New Zealand and the United Kingdom: Alexander Turnbull Library; Archives New Zealand/Te Rua Mahara o te Kāwanatanga; Auckland Public Library; Auckland University Library; Auckland War Memorial Museum Library; British Library; Hocken Library; Liverpool Record Office; Mitchell Library, State Library of New South Wales; National Archives of Scotland; National Archives of the United Kingdom; National Library of Australia; Royal Society of Tasmania; State Archives and Records of New South Wales; State Library of Victoria; State Records of South Australia; Tasmanian State Archives; United Kingdom Hydrographic Office Archives; University of Cambridge Library; Weston Library, University of Oxford; and the Widener Library, Harvard University. I am grateful for all the assistance that was provided to me by the librarians and archivists at these institutions. I also benefitted enormously from several digital newspaper projects – the National Library of New Zealand/Te Puna Mātuaranga o Aotearoa's *Papers Past*, the National Library of Australia's *Trove* and the British Library and Gage's *Nineteenth Century British Newspapers* – and the digital book project *Early New Zealand Books*. Several people assisted me with some of the research – Paul Hamer, Maria Johns, Philip Rainer and Fiona Viney – and Khumo Leseane drew the maps.

A number of scholars generously shared their knowledge and insights about a range of matters germane to the subject matter of the book. In particular, I am indebted to Lauren Benton, Adam Clulow, Claudia Haake, Mark Hickford, Miranda Johnson, Damen Ward and the two readers of the manuscript for Cambridge University Press. Lauren Benton, Adam Clulow, Claudia Haake, Miranda Johnson, Mark McKenna, Damen Ward and members of a research group in the

History Program at Monash University read one or more chapters, and David Chandler and Philip Rainer read the lot. Their criticisms and advice have made this a much better book than it would have been otherwise.

I also owe an enormous debt to several generations of scholars who have considered many of the questions that I address in this book, a few of whom I was fortunate enough to have as my teachers in New Zealand a long time ago. They include Peter Adams, Stuart Banner, J. C. Beaglehole, Michael Belgrave, James Belich, Lauren Benton, Judith Binney, Elizabeth Elbourne, Ned Fletcher, Mark Hickford, Don Loveridge, Paul McHugh, W. P. Morrell, Claudia Orange, David Philips, Grant Phillipson, Andrew Sharp, A. G. L. Shaw, Keith Sorrenson, Alan Ward, Damen Ward, Ian Wards and John C. Weaver.

I am grateful to the Australian Academy of the Humanities and the School of Philosophical, Historical and International Studies at Monash University for the publication subventions they granted to assist with the book's publication.

Finally, I wish to express my heartfelt thanks to my partner, Claudia Haake, and my daughter, Katarina, for putting up with my absences and absent-mindedness as I worked on this book.

Abbreviations

AJCP	Australian Joint Copying Project
APL	Auckland Public Library
ATL	Alexander Turnbull Library
AWMML	Auckland War Memorial Museum Library
BL	British Library
BPD	British Parliamentary Debates
BPP	British Parliamentary Papers
CMS	Church Missionary Society
CO	Colonial Office
HL	Hocken Library
HRA	Historical Records of Australia
HRNZ	Historical Records of New Zealand
HRV	Historical Records of Victoria
ML	Mitchell Library
MMS	Methodist Missionary Society
NANZ	National Archives of New Zealand
NZA	New Zealand Association
NZC	New Zealand Company
SACC	South Australian Colonisation Commission
SARNSW	State Archives and Records of New South Wales
SLSA	State Library of South Australia
SLV	State Library of Victoria
SRSA	State Records of South Australia
TNA	The National Archives of the United Kingdom
TSA	Tasmanian State Archives
WMS	Wesleyan Missionary Society

Principal Players

Buller, Charles (1806–1848), lawyer, politician, journalist and advocate for the New Zealand Company

Busby, James (1802–1871), British Resident in New Zealand, 1833–40

Buxton, Thomas Fowell (1786–1845), Christian humanitarian; chairman of the 1835–37 British House of Commons Select Committee inquiry into the condition of aborigines in the British colonies

Coates, Dandeson (??–1846), lay secretary of the Church Missionary Society, 1830–46

FitzRoy, Robert (1805–1865), Governor of New Zealand, 1843–45

Gipps, Sir George (1791–1847), Governor of New South Wales, 1838–46

Glenelg, Lord (1778–1866), politician; Colonial Secretary, 1835–39

Grey, Earl (see Howick, Lord)

Grey, George (1812–1898), Governor of New Zealand, 1845–53

Grey, Sir George (1799–1882), politician; parliamentary Under-Secretary for the Colonies, 1834–39

Hobson, William (1792–1842), Governor of New Zealand, 1840–42

Hope, George (1808–1863), parliamentary Under-Secretary for the Colonies, 1841–46

Howick, Lord (1802–1894), politician; parliamentary Under-Secretary for the Colonies, 1830–34; Secretary for War, 1835–39; Colonial Secretary, 1846–52

Marsden, Samuel (1765–1838), Anglican chaplain, New South Wales, and founder of the Church Missionary Society missions in New Zealand

Martin, Samuel (c. 1805?–1848), journalist and Radical

Normanby, Marquess of (1797–1863), politician; Colonial Secretary, 1839

Peel, Sir Robert (1788–1850), politician; Prime Minister, 1841–46

Ravens, Samuel (1807/1808–1888), proprietor and editor of a New Zealand Company newspaper

Russell, Lord John (1792–1878), politician; Colonial Secretary, 1839–41; Prime Minister, 1846–52

Shortland, Willoughby (1804–1869), Acting Governor of New Zealand, 1841–43

Spain, William (1803–1876), Land Claims Commissioner, 1841–45

Stanley, Lord Edward (1799–1869), politician; Colonial Secretary, 1833–44, 1841–45

Stephen, James (1789–1859), counsel for the Colonial Office, 1813–34; Assistant Under-Secretary, Colonial Office, 1834–36; Permanent Under-Secretary, Colonial Office, 1836–47

Swainson, William (1809–1884), Attorney General of New Zealand, 1841–56

Te Rauparaha (176?–1849), Ngāti Toa rangatira

Torrens, Robert (1814–1884), early advocate of colonisation of New Zealand and a director of South Australian Association; Chairman, South Australian Colonisation Commission

Wakefield, Edward Gibbon (1796–1862), political economist, author, colonial reformer and advocate for the New Zealand Association and the New Zealand Company

Wakefield, William (1803–1848), New Zealand Company's principal agent in New Zealand

Williams, Henry (1792–1867), senior Church Missionary Society missionary in New Zealand, 1823–49

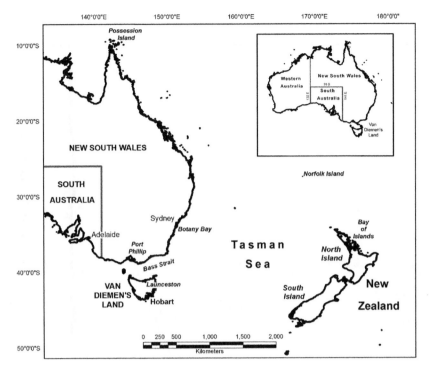

Map 1 The Australian colonies, Norfolk Island and the islands of New Zealand, showing the boundaries of the Australian colonies as they were in 1836. Significant places mentioned in the text are indicated. Cartographer: Khumo Leseane.

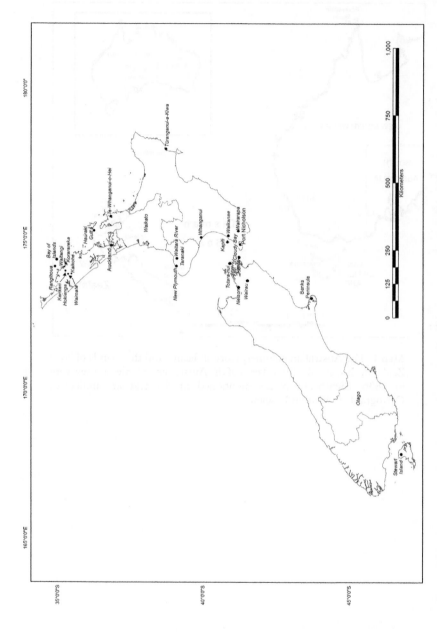

Map 2 New Zealand. Places mentioned in the text are indicated. Cartographer: Khumo Leseane.

Introduction

Over the course of many years, numerous colleagues, students, friends and relatives in New Zealand, Australia and elsewhere in the Anglophone world have asked me why New Zealand has a historic treaty – the famous Treaty of Waitangi – and Australia does not. I have assumed that what they are really asking is why the British government negotiated with the indigenous people of New Zealand (Māori) for the cession of sovereignty and title to land yet treated Australia's Aboriginal people as though they were neither sovereign nor the owners of the land. In order to answer this question satisfactorily, I have come to conclude that a particular historical approach is required. This approach has several dimensions.

Rather than being preoccupied with particular moments or events – such as James Cook's claiming possession of New Holland in 1770 or the signing of the Treaty of Waitangi in New Zealand in 1840 – that are said to have determined the foundations of Australia and New Zealand in respect of sovereignty and title to land, we must examine the treatment of these two matters over a relatively long period of time. Further, we need to pay attention to processes that were deeply historical in nature. This is so in two senses. First, the treatment of sovereignty and native title at one point in time profoundly influenced what happened later. Second, much of what took place was highly contingent and so could have been very different.

In considering these histories we must examine, especially in the New Zealand case, the role that was played by a multiplicity of players – not only government officials and the indigenous peoples themselves, but missionaries, traders, entrepreneurs, settlers, missionary societies and colonisation companies – as well as the relationships between these players. Likewise, attention must be paid to both the imperial and the colonial theatres of action, *and* to the ongoing exchanges between them.

In seeking to answer the question at the heart of this book, a comparative approach – and one that focuses on the colonies, rather than the nations that supplanted them – has been of fundamental importance. By pinpointing the differences as well as the similarities between

1

Britain's colonies in Australasia,[1] or what became Australia and New Zealand, we are better able to explain why sovereignty and rights in land were treated in the ways they were. This is so primarily because historical comparison enables us to isolate the important causal factors from the merely incidental ones.[2] The practice of comparative history can also provoke new questions. Most significantly perhaps, we can ask why the relevant historical sources or traces are slender for New South Wales (if not for all the Australian colonies), and vast for New Zealand, and what this reveals about the past. The provenance of many of the most important historical traces for New Zealand is similarly telling: they exist not only in their original manuscript form (in the imperial government's records) but also in print (in Britain's parliamentary papers), just as there is a plethora of pertinent material in the newspapers of the day. This draws our attention to the fact that both sovereignty and native title were the subject of enormous political debate in the New Zealand context, whereas in the Australian colonies this was seldom the case.

To understand the way that sovereignty and native title were treated in Britain's Australasian colonies, it is imperative that we pay a great deal of attention to claim-making, especially that of the principal British players. In so doing, we must acknowledge that claims are inherently legal or moral in nature: they are never merely a request or a demand but involve instead an appeal to some sort of imagined right or standard of justice. Moreover, they are always made with reference to somebody else and so tend to involve counterclaims and contestation, which means that making claims entails politics as individuals and groups articulate, negotiate and seek to enforce them. Finally, claim-making often requires a willingness to back up one's appeals to reason and the like with some sort of action or threat of action, and so we need to consider the power that competing parties were able to wield.[3]

Taken together, these observations make clear that in order to truly understand claims about sovereignty and property we must attend to the complex interplay that always exists between the abstract and the

---

[1] I am using *Australasia* loosely as a shorthand for Britain's colonies in what became Australia and New Zealand. Strictly speaking, in the nineteenth century the term *Australasia* tended to stand for *all* of Britain's colonies in the South Pacific. See Donald Denoon, 'Re-Membering Australasia: A Repressed Memory', *Australian Historical Studies*, vol. 34, no. 122, 2003, pp. 290–304.

[2] For some recent illuminating discussions of comparative history, see Deborah Cohen and Maura O'Connor (eds.), *Comparison and History: Europe in Cross-National Perspective*, Routledge, New York, 2004, and Philippa Levine, 'Is Comparative History Possible', *History and Theory*, vol. 53, no. 3, 2014, pp. 331–47.

[3] James J. Sheehan, 'The Problem of Sovereignty in European History', *American Historical Review*, vol. 111, no. 1, 2006, pp. 1, 3–4.

concrete, thought and practice, beliefs and ambition, principle and expediency. Consequently, we need to set aside any notion that the treatment of sovereignty and native rights in land was *determined* by particular norms, whether they be intellectual, legal, political or moral in nature,[4] though there can be no doubt that norms of this kind played an important role in the making of claims. For example, in deciding to treat with the native chiefs at Waitangi for the cession of sovereignty it is apparent that British officials were familiar with legal concepts about sovereignty that were expressed in the law of nations, but it would be simplistic as well as naïve to conclude that their course of action was dictated by those legal considerations.

Attending to claim-making requires us to pay serious attention not only to politics but to the nature of the language or languages that the principal players used in the conduct of politics. This point has several dimensions. At any one time, a number of ideas and arguments are available to political players, from which they can try to fashion a political language to do the necessary work of persuasion. In the period I examine, languages such as protection were especially important in this regard but so too was a particular kind of rights talk.

Another aspect of language concerns the words that the principal players used in referring to indigenous people, namely *natives* and *savages* (rather than *Māori* or *Aboriginal people*). These terms are writ large in the historical record. I in turn mostly use the word *native* in order to draw attention to the fact that the principal British players, especially those at the metropolitan centre, tended to perceive and portray indigenous peoples at the imperial periphery as though they belonged to a single, abstract or generic category of people. Indeed, most of these British players had little interest in the precise characteristics of these native peoples or in distinguishing between them on the basis of who they really were. (They were much more interested in themselves.) Yet there are instances in which the very real subjectivity of indigenous peoples must be registered by the historian if we are to make sense of what took place. In those moments, I use *Māori* and *Aboriginal people* as well as terms that denote

---

[4] For some time, a good deal of the relevant scholarship was characterised by this weakness, for example Anthony Pagden's *Lords of All the World: Ideologies of Empire in Spain, Britain and France c. 1500 – c. 1800* (Yale University Press, New Haven, CT, 1995). This tendency persists, especially but not only in work by intellectual historians, despite their claims to the contrary. See, for example, Andrew Fitzmaurice, *Sovereignty, Property and Empire, 1500–2000*, Cambridge University Press, Cambridge, 2014. This is not to suggest that ideas were unimportant, but the ideas that played the greatest role were those we might call lowercase 'I' ideas – that is, the kind of beliefs held by all manner of historical actors and expressed or embodied in action, rather than uppercase 'I' ideas – the arguments of a relatively small group of sophisticated theorists.

particular tribal groups and polities. (At the time the latter terms were used much more commonly than the former ones by these peoples.)

In considering the nature of the language that the principal political players used, special attention must be paid to rhetoric. The words they commonly uttered were highly functional in nature, since their speech acts were invariably designed to have consequences, namely the accomplishment of their purposes. Thus, while the principal players tended to have a variety of views about sovereignty and native title, the ones they emphasised usually depended on their assessment of what would be most useful strategically or tactically at any given moment.

Furthermore, in seeking to understand how the British actually treated sovereignty and native title, we are best to rely on historical *traces* rather than historical *sources*. A historical trace is a relic of the past that was forged as part of day-to-day life, whereas a historical source is something that was intended by its creator to stand as an account of contemporary acts and events. Traces provide a more reliable foundation for historical knowledge.[5] They tend to be found in historical relics, such as personal correspondence and minutes on official papers, that were never intended by their creators to be made public in any shape or form.[6]

It is also critical that we attend in a comprehensive manner to the particular historical contexts in which actions and statements in regard to sovereignty and rights of property in land were taken or made. In large part, this means scrutinising actions and statements in their logical place in a chronological sequence, not least because they tended to be the product of (ever-shifting) relations between political players. The kind of contextualisation I have in mind requires us to ask what actions and processes generated the traces of the past, and who created them, when and why.[7] Indeed, we cannot hope to know what the statement of any particular historical actor meant unless we clarify what precisely they were doing (or trying to do) at any given moment. This emphasis on thoroughgoing contextualisation also means that a very detailed historical narrative of events has to be provided.[8]

---

[5] Here I am drawing on Allan Megill, *Historical Knowledge, Historical Error: A Contemporary Guide to Practice*, University of Chicago Press, Chicago, 2007, pp. 25–26.

[6] For an example of what I call a 'historical source', see the memorandum penned by the Permanent Under-Secretary in the Colonial Office, James Stephen, in November 1839, which I discuss on pp. 163–64.

[7] For a discussion of this point, see T. G. Ashplant and Adrian Wilson, 'Whig History and Present-Centred History', *The Historical Journal*, vol. 31, no. 1, 1988, pp. 1–16, and 'Present-Centred History and the Problem of Historical Knowledge', *The Historical Journal*, vol. 31, no. 2, 1988, pp. 253–74.

[8] In regard to these as well as many of the points I have made so far, my approach has many similarities with what has been called the 'high politics' school of history. For an account of this body of historical scholarship, see Richard Brent, 'Butterfield's Tories: "High Politics"

As much of my discussion so far has implied, we must pay attention to the role played by individual men (and it was always men), especially but not only those who held political office. This is all the more the case because the early to mid-nineteenth century was a period when the Colonial Office (the department of government primarily responsible for overseeing the British Empire) and the colonial administrations were very small, and there were many changes among those in charge of colonial affairs at the imperial centre as well as the colonial peripheries. Furthermore, in considering the part that particular men played, we must consider not only their ideas, beliefs, values and language but also their mental states and thus the psychological forces that influenced how they felt and behaved. The political battles that took place between the most important British parties were bitterly fought largely because they aroused powerful emotions.

Finally, it is vital that we overcome the problems produced by tunnel history, that is, where a particular sub-discipline of history is allowed to dictate what counts as a historical phenomenon, as a trace or source, and as an explanation, thereby eliminating large tracts of the past from our field of vision. Here, I have sought to draw upon and integrate a number of approaches found in cross-cultural, economic, intellectual, legal and political history.

By adopting the particular historical approach that I have been describing, the historian is able to provide an explanation of the British treatment of sovereignty and native title in the Australasian colonies that is both more plausible and more reliable than the accounts currently available. Moreover, the historian can recapture much about the past that is largely unknown and hence surprising, even astounding. This enables readers to grasp that the horizon of the present is not the only horizon available to us in contemplating both the past and the future.

In this book I argue that native title[9] was *made* – or not made – in the context of British colonisation.[10] The indigenous peoples had their own ways of understanding authority and ownership of land, but legal notions

and the Writing of Modern British Political History', *The Historical Journal*, vol. 30, no. 4, 1987, pp. 943–54.

[9] I realise that many readers familiar with Australia's recent past might find my use of *native title* confusing because it has such a strong contemporary valence and because it had a very different meaning in the early to mid-nineteenth century than it does now. But *native title* is the term that was commonly used in regard to the Australian or more especially the New Zealand colonies in the 1830s and 1840s.

[10] I am not the first historian to make this argument. Mark Hickford does so in his *Lords of the Land: Indigenous Property Rights and the Jurisprudence of Empire*, Oxford University Press, Oxford, 2011, but only fleetingly.

of sovereignty and title in land did not predate colonisation. They only came into being in the course of it. This means that it is a mistake to formulate the question at the heart of this study as 'why was the sovereignty and rights in land of indigenous peoples *recognised*, or not *recognised*, by the British government', given that the word *recognised* implies that these phenomena existed in the first place.

I argue, moreover, that sovereignty and rights of property in land were made – or not made – *historically*,[11] in that they came into being only as the result of deeply historical processes, which were rarely linear in nature but halting, contingent and ultimately reliant on a large degree of chance. Hence, the story I tell in this book is largely one of unexpected events and unintended consequences. Furthermore, the historical processes involved forces that were invariably complex, occasionally incoherent, sometimes mundane, frequently base and seldom constant. As I have already suggested, central to many of those processes was the making of claims and thus contestation and conflict, not least among the principal British players, and hence a struggle for power and authority. At certain points, threats of one kind or another, including that of force, performed a crucial role in this regard. Philosophical ideas and legal concepts played a part but more often than not they are best understood as a *resource* that was drawn upon by actors in the political battles that took place.[12] Similarly, moral principles played a role in what happened but invariably they were conjoined with practical considerations.

The story of how native title was made, or not made, in Britain's Australasian colonies or at least in the New Zealand case is best told in terms of several overlapping phases.

I

In the first phase, several claims of possession were made by a British agent, James Cook, in New Holland (what was largely to become New South Wales) and the islands of New Zealand in 1769–70. These claims were relatively unimportant for how sovereignty, let alone the native people's title in land, would be treated by the British government once it decided to annex parts of these territories. While Cook unilaterally claimed possession in both places, on the basis of legal doctrines (such

---

[11] My debt to E.P. Thompson's contention that meaning tends to be made in the course of lived experience will be evident to readers familiar with his work.

[12] This argument, as much in my approach, owes a good deal to the work on 'legal politics' by socio-legal historians, especially Lauren Benton – see, for example, her 'Beyond Anachronism: Histories of International Law and Global Legal Politics', *Journal of the History of International Law*, vol. 21, no. 1, 2019, pp. 1–34.

as *discovery*), his doing so did not dictate the terms upon which the British Crown assumed sovereignty later. In the case of New Zealand, the British government disclaimed its right to dominion in the early nineteenth century and decided to negotiate cession of sovereignty with the native chiefs a few decades later, rather than assert sovereignty on the basis of Cook's claim of possession, as it did in New Holland.

II

The different ways the British government treated sovereignty in both New Holland and the islands of New Zealand are best explained by the events that took place between Cook's claiming of possession and the moment the British Crown assumed sovereignty. One factor is especially important in this regard, namely whether any informal colonisation occurred in the meantime. In the New Zealand case, beginning in the 1800s small parties of Europeans established a considerable presence – most significantly at the Bay of Islands in the far north – and entered into relationships with the local people. These relationships included treating with the natives for land.[13] The purchases (as the Europeans understood the arrangements) effectively created a notion of native title, and the Europeans who were party to these transactions in the following three decades, which included politically powerful metropolitan British players as well as Māori chiefs, would later make claims for land title on the basis of them.[14] Nothing of this kind occurred in the case of the Australian colonies.

Just as importantly, a relationship was forged in these years between Māori chiefs and representatives of the British Crown in northern New Zealand, Sydney and even London. At the heart of this relationship were ambiguous claims of protection, which comprised calls for protection as

---

[13] What happened in New Zealand has some resemblance to what the American historian Francis Jennings once called 'the deed game' in the North American context (*The Invasion of America: Indians, Colonialism, and the Cant of Conquest*, University of North Carolina Press, Chapel Hill, NC, 1975). For a more recent discussion of this, see these essays by Daniel Richter: 'Land and Words: William Penn's Letter to Kings of the Indians', in his *Trade, Land, Power: The Struggle for Eastern North America*, University of Pennsylvania Press, Philadelphia, 2013, pp. 135–54, 'The Strange Colonial North American Career of *Terra Nullius*', in Bain Attwood and Tom Griffiths (eds.), *Frontier, Race, Nation: Henry Reynolds and Australian History*, Australian Scholarly Publishing, Melbourne, 2009, pp. 159–84, and 'To "Clear the King's and Indians' Title": Seventeenth-Century Origins of North American Land Cession Treaties', in Saliha Belmessous (ed.), *Empire by Treaty: Negotiating European Expansion, 1600–1900*, Oxford University Press, New York, 2015, pp. 45–77.

[14] Stuart Banner advances a similar argument in his *Possessing the Pacific: Land, Settlers and Indigenous People from Australia to Alaska*, Harvard University Press, Cambridge, MA, 2007, 5, 43–46, 318, but he makes no reference to the role played by metropolitan forces in this claim-making and thereby overlooks the political dimensions of this matter.

well as promises of protection. These were made by several players, most importantly a churchman in Sydney seeking to found missions in northern New Zealand, governors of New South Wales, the imperial government and the chiefs themselves. They led the British government to adopt several measures in which it treated New Zealand and its native inhabitants as though they were sovereign, and this generated something like an alliance between the Crown and the Māori chiefs. This development did not occur by design. Indeed, like much of what happened, it was the result of improvisation. Nevertheless, it had profound implications for how the British government would treat the matter of sovereignty in the islands of New Zealand at the point it decided to annex New Zealand. Nothing of this kind took place in the Australian colonies or at least in the case of New South Wales.

At the point in time that the British government decided to annex New Holland and part of the islands of New Zealand, the very different histories I have just described exerted considerable influence on its decision as to whether it could, should or would seek to persuade the native people to cede sovereignty to the British Crown. In essence, imperial governments were more likely to treat with native peoples for cession of sovereignty when they realised that third parties of one kind or another were present in the territory in question or likely to be in the foreseeable future. In the case of New Holland, the British government believed there were no other such parties. Consequently, it issued the first governor of New South Wales with instructions that made no reference to the Aboriginal people other than one to conciliate them and enjoin British subjects to treat them kindly. This meant that the colony's first governor proceeded as though there was no other source of sovereignty in New South Wales than that of the British Crown. In the case of the islands of New Zealand, there *were* third parties that the British government believed it had to take into consideration. They included not only missionary societies and a colonisation company based in London – the New Zealand Association or what was to become the New Zealand Company – but also other foreign powers, France and the United States. For this reason, as well as others, the government instructed its agent to treat with the natives for a cession of sovereignty.

The way in which rights of property in land was approached by the British government at the moment it decided to annex New Holland and part of the islands of New Zealand was influenced by many of the same historical factors that impinged on its consideration of sovereignty. In the case of New Zealand, this meant it had no doubt that it had to proceed on the basis that the natives had at least some rights in land. In the case of

New South Wales, the imperial government, or least the man it appointed to be its first governor, Arthur Phillip, was unsure how to proceed.

III

In the third phase – the moment at which the colonial governments set about trying to assert their authority and acquire land – the ways in which the imperial government had treated the matter of sovereignty did not dictate how they would deal with rights of property in land in any precise sense. This means that the fact that the British government opted to make a treaty in New Zealand but not in New South Wales might be regarded as immaterial.[15] What happened during this phase was nonetheless crucial, at least for New South Wales and the rest of the Australian colonies, but this was so for a different reason.

In the case of New South Wales, Governor Phillip concluded soon after the colony was founded that there was no need to negotiate with the local people in order to acquire land. This was so because he formed the opinion that the Aboriginal people did not have the means to resist British armed might. Just as importantly, there were no other powerful forces that might have compelled him to negotiate with the Aboriginal people for land. This meant that a property regime was created in New South Wales that made no reference to the Aboriginal people's interests in land. Consequently, neither political nor legal questions about the Aboriginal people's rights of property in land ever arose in any substantive sense in the early decades of the colony. The same was true of the colonies that the British government planted in the early 1800s in Van Diemen's Land (Tasmania) and Western Australia. By the mid-1830s questions *were* raised about Aboriginal people's rights of property in land, most pointedly in the case of a treaty made with local people in the colony's Port Phillip District by Van Diemonian entrepreneurs (known as Batman's treaty) but also in the context of a new colony being founded (South Australia).

By this time, however, the British government had been granting land to settlers for nearly fifty years on the basis that the Crown was the only source of title. This arrangement would have been very difficult to

---

[15] The argument I make in this respect resembles the arguments that other historians have made recently in respect of matters of jurisdiction. See, for example, Damen Ward, 'A Means and Measure of Civilisation: Colonial Authorities and Indigenous Law in Australasia', *History Compass*, vol. 1, no. 1, 2003, pp. 1–24, Lisa Ford, *Settler Sovereignty: Jurisdiction and Indigenous People in North America and Australia, 1788–1836*, Harvard University Press, Cambridge, MA, 2010, and Shaunnagh Dorsett, *Juridical Encounters: Māori and the Colonial Courts 1840–1852*, Auckland University Press, Auckland, 2017.

overturn (though as it happened there were no British players, either at the imperial centre or the colonial periphery, who really had the wish, the will and the power to do so). Consequently, it became the law of the land. The only uncertainty that remained in New South Wales and the other Australian colonies concerned the precise legal grounds upon which the British Crown had assumed sovereignty and become the only source of title in land. The fact that the government had little need to enunciate the basis of its claim of possession at the moment it began to plant colonies in New Holland meant there were very few if any reliable historical traces to enable it to answer this question. In this context, the legal argument that the British government as well as settlers tended to prefer in order to legitimise their claims was not *terra nullius* or any doctrine that resembled it (such as *occupation*) but a historical claim the Crown had assumed sovereignty and title to all the land many years earlier, in 1788.

In the case of the islands of New Zealand, the British government instructed its agent, William Hobson, to make a treaty with the native chiefs so that the Crown could both assume sovereignty and acquire the right of pre-emption in regard to land (that is, the right to be the only purchaser of land from the natives). Yet this did not dictate the ways in which it treated sovereignty or property in subsequent years. Indeed, the treaty soon lost most of its significance, especially but not only in the eyes of the imperial government. Within a few months of it being signed, Hobson (unexpectedly) proclaimed British sovereignty over a good part of New Zealand on the grounds of Cook's claim of possession rather than the treaty alone, and several months later the imperial government confirmed Britain's claim to sovereignty on this basis. Moreover, an acrimonious political and legal fight about sovereignty and title to land broke out in Britain in 1839–40, once the government had decided to assume sovereignty by negotiating its cession with the native chiefs. The same occurred in New South Wales (under whose jurisdiction New Zealand first came) in 1840, after the treaty had been made. In these battles, the nature of native title – in the sense of the extent of the rights of property in land that the native people were deemed to have – was seldom a major consideration.

IV

In the next phase, which only occurred in the islands of New Zealand, several of the principal British players expected that the Crown and settlers would readily acquire possession of large amounts of land. This expectation, however, was confounded, not least because of native resistance to the New Zealand Company's land claims, plunging the colony into crisis. In 1839 the imperial government had realised that it had to find a way to deal with the fact that numerous British parties had purchased land from the natives on a massive scale before it assumed sovereignty in the islands. Consequently, it accepted that it would have to pay some regard to native rights in land in the course of establishing a property regime in the colony. But it never imagined the degree to which native title would become fundamental to that regime, let alone that one of the means that it adopted to deal with the claims British players made on the basis of their pre-1840 purchases – a land claims commission – would play a major role in this regard.

Just as unexpected was the fact that the crisis that had emerged in the colony by late 1843 came to focus on *both* native title and the treaty of Waitangi. There was neither rhyme nor reason why this should have occurred. It happened both incidentally and accidentally, largely because of a bitter political fight that broke out between the Colonial Office and the New Zealand Company in London, and which came to involve the missionary societies and senior political figures in Britain, and the colonial administration, missionaries, settlers and Māori in the colony.

In this conflict in 1843–44 claims and counterclaims were made in which all the parties spun stories in which claims were made about both native title and the treaty, and the two matters became entangled with one another. In the telling of these stories, both native title and the treaty – now referred to as the Treaty – acquired a remarkable significance that neither of them had previously had. The Treaty, or more specifically the first clause of its second article, by which the Crown had 'confirm[ed] and guarantee[d]' to the natives the 'possession of their lands', was interpreted anew by the Colonial Office, missionaries, the missionary societies, the New Zealand Company and its political allies. In essence, the Colonial Office's senior figures, Lord Stanley, George Hope and James Stephen, responded to an attack by the New Zealand Company's directors on the treaty by embracing it as an agreement that involved *rights* in one sense or another.[16] Indeed, they went so far as to claim that in 1840 the Crown had treated with the native chiefs at Waitangi for a cession of sovereignty on the grounds that the British government had recognised the natives' title to land and that the Crown's title to sovereignty rested on this basis alone. For its part, the Company's spokesmen reacted by claiming that both the Colonial Office and the colonial government were interpreting the first clause in the Treaty's second article to mean

---

[16] Michael Belgrave has made a somewhat similar point in contending that what he calls 'the original treaty' (of 1840) is best regarded as a treaty of relationships rather than a treaty of rights (*Historical Frictions: Maori Claims and Reinvented Histories*, Auckland University Press, Auckland, 2005, chapter 2).

that the natives had rights of property in all the land (though this was not actually the case).

The positions that the principal players adopted in regard to both sovereignty and title to land in this battle were not inconsistent with the moral, legal and political norms they espoused from time to time. But it is clear that the positions they took cannot simply be attributed to those norms, not least because in most respects their positions were forever shifting as political circumstances dictated.

V

In the last phase, beginning in 1844–45, the New Zealand Company used its considerable political power in Britain to persuade many members on both sides of the House of Commons to adopt its point of view about native title and the Treaty. They had long argued that the colony's crisis was caused by the Tory government wrongfully construing the Treaty as guaranteeing native possession of *all* the land in New Zealand and that the solution to the colony's problems lay in the establishment of a property regime that limited the rights of property the natives could claim to the lands they cultivated. Moreover, after the Whigs returned to power in 1846, a new Colonial Secretary, Earl Grey, instructed the colony's governor, George Grey, to ensure that the native title was treated in this fashion and repeated his predecessor's advice that the governor should do all he could to restore the Crown's right of pre-emption. Yet, in the end, these measures counted for very little.

Partly this was because Earl Grey's instructions led to a storm of protest by a leading churchman, a senior judge, missionaries, Māori chiefs and the missionary societies. But mostly it was because the imperial government had provided Governor Grey with funds it had withheld from his predecessors. By 1847 Governor Grey had realised that he could meet the British government's goals by purchasing large amounts of land cheaply from the natives. Moreover, he had grasped that it would be foolhardy to act on the basis of Earl Grey's abstract theories about the nature of rights of property in land. Consequently, he proceeded on the basis that Māori had rights in all of the land and that their title to it was best extinguished by acquiring their consent. Hence, native title was finally made in New Zealand. This outcome clearly owed little if anything to legal norms about the nature of native title or any political intentions on the part of the British government. Instead, it was largely the result of a long and halting historical process that had been dominated by enormous political contestation and conflict and thus a struggle for power involving the various British players as well as Māori themselves.

As readers will have already gathered, the story I am about to tell is highly particular. But I see no reason why the approach I have adopted cannot be used to analyse and explain the treatment of native people's sovereignty and rights of property in land in other imperial and colonial contexts. By the same token, I assume that the insights my approach yields can be readily applied to those situations.

1   Claiming Possession in New Holland and New Zealand, 1770s–1820s

In 1981 a novel question was addressed by an Australian historian.[1] Why had the British Crown denied – or failed to recognise – the Aboriginal people's rights in land? Alan Frost argued that this occurred because the British government acted in accordance with the international legal conventions of the mid-eighteenth century or more especially a particular legal decorum called *terra nullius*. In the 1990s, after a version of this argument had been advanced by another Australian historian, Henry Reynolds, the story of *terra nullius* swept through the country, adopted by the authors of national histories, deployed by legal and political players and presented in a startling array of cultural media. In the period since, several historians have cast doubt on the story's empirical underpinnings.[2] But its influence persists in many scholarly circles, and its uptake in the broader public realm in Australia continues unabated.[3]

In what follows I interrogate the argument that the British government's treatment of native sovereignty and rights of property in land in New South Wales, the first colony the British government planted in Australasia, is best explained in terms of the legal doctrine known as *terra nullius*. Most importantly, I will advance a very different explanation for why the British government treated these matters in the way it did. In large measure, the argument I present springs from a consideration of

[1] Forty years earlier, an Australian historian, Ernest Scott, had considered this question in 'Taking Possession of Australia: The Doctrine of "Terra Nullius" (No-Man's Land)', *Journal of the Royal Australian Historical Society*, vol. 26, pt 1, 1940, pp. 1–19, after being prompted by an American law professor (whose interest in the subject had been provoked by his own country's ambitions in the Antarctic), but no Australian historian had followed in Scott's footsteps.

[2] See, for example, Bruce Buchan, 'Traffick of Empire: Trade, Treaty and *Terra Nullius* in Australia and North America, 1750–1800', *History Compass*, vol. 5, no. 2, 2007, pp. 386–405; and Andrew Fitzmaurice, 'The Genealogy of *Terra Nullius*', *Australian Historical Studies*, vol. 38, no. 129, 2007, pp. 1–15.

[3] Alan Frost, 'New South Wales as *Terra Nullius*: The British Denial of Aboriginal Land Rights', *Historical Studies*, vol. 19, no. 77, 1981, pp. 513–23; Henry Reynolds, *The Law of the Land*, Penguin, Melbourne, 1987.

14

a sequence of events *after* James Cook laid claim to New Holland in 1770.[4]

Part I

New South Wales as Terra Nullius

I begin this chapter in a historiographical fashion in order to make clear why the contention that the British government claimed New South Wales on the basis of *terra nullius* has been brought into question in recent years. I focus on the work of Alan Frost because his approach typifies the work of many scholars who have considered claims of possession in various imperial contexts and because his argument has long been accepted by numerous historians.[5]

Frost considered the British government's treatment of native rights in land as though it was a matter determined by (international) law. By the mid-eighteenth century, he argued, a particular convention had emerged among European powers in regard to the acquisition of overseas territories. They could acquire a region that was not already in the effective possession of another imperial power in three different ways. They could do so by persuading the local people to submit themselves to its sovereignty, that is, conquest; by purchasing from those people the right to settle part(s) of their territory, that is, cession; and by asserting that they were the first to discover it and by effectively occupying the territory, that is, a unilateral claim. Frost argued that the first two conceded that native peoples had a right of possession but that the third did not. Moreover, he contended that European powers determined whether a local people had a right of possession in accordance with an amalgam of perceptions that arose from writings on the law of nature and the law of nations by writers such as Hugo Grotius, Samuel von Pufendorf and John Locke.

---

[4] This chapter comprises a revised version of my article 'Law, History and Power: The British Treatment of Aboriginal Rights in Land in New South Wales', *Journal of Commonwealth and Imperial History*, vol. 42, no. 1, 2014, pp. 171–92.

[5] See, for example, Richard Broome, *Aboriginal Australians: A History Since 1788*, Allen & Unwin, Sydney, 1982, pp. 26–27; Stuart Macintyre, *A Concise History of Australia*, 3rd edn, Cambridge University Press, Melbourne, 2009, p. 34; Stuart Banner, *Possessing the Pacific: Land, Settlers and Indigenous People from Australia to Alaska*, Harvard University Press, Cambridge, MA, 2007, pp. 16–20; Grace Karskens, *The Colony: A History of Early Sydney*, Allen & Unwin, Sydney, 2009, pp. 34–36; Ann Curthoys and Jessie Mitchell, *Taking Liberty: Indigenous Rights and Settler Self-Government in Colonial Australia, 1830–1890*, Cambridge University Press, Cambridge, 2018, p. 32. Part of my argument in this chapter is informed by Banner's *Possessing the Pacific*, but it departs in various respects from his consideration of the Australian example, not least because much of his argument echoes Frost's.

These writers held that at the beginning of the world people lived in an absolute state of nature in which they had no sense of property in land, but that they had acquired property rights once they settled in one place and enclosed and cultivated the earth. In cases where European agents realised that native peoples had established sovereignty over a territory – as a consequence of their having advanced beyond the state of nature not only by dint of mixing their labour with the soil so as to have enclosed and cultivated it but also by making roads and raising houses and towns, forming themselves into a society exhibiting systems of customs, religion and commerce, developing a code of laws and creating a polity to administer them – they had to persuade the local people to accept their overlordship. 'However', Frost continued, 'if the indigenous [people] had advanced beyond the state of nature only so far as to have developed language and the community of the family, but no further; if they had not yet mixed their labour with the earth in any permanent way; or if the region was literally uninhabited, then Europeans considered it to be *terra nullius* – that is, a land belonging to no one – to which they might gain permanent title by first discovery and effective occupation'.[6]

In accordance with this convention, Frost argued, European powers had to take two steps in order to lay claim to such a territory. They had to establish a preliminary right of possession on the basis of being the first European discoverer, which they did by performing a series of symbolic acts, such as making a formal proclamation, raising a flag and leaving proof of their presence in the form of inscriptions, cairns and the giving of gifts to the native people. But, in order to make this right real, they had to occupy the territory within a reasonable period of time by transferring a portion of its population to the region, along with its customs and laws.[7]

In the case of the first colony that the British government planted in what the Dutch had previously named Nieuw Holland, and which the British came to call New South Wales, Frost argued that the British Lords of the Admiralty had instructed Captain James Cook in 1768 'to take possession of convenient situations in the country in the name of the King of Great Britain [with the consent of the natives], or, if you find the country uninhabited, take possession for His Majesty by setting up proper marks and inscriptions, as first discoverers and possessors'. Frost contended that Cook attended to those instructions in a particular way when he reached the coast of eastern Australia on the *Endeavour* in the early months of 1770. '[H]e had to answer two questions', wrote Frost. '[H]ad a population established a right to possess the territory; or, was it a *terra nullius*? If it were a *terra nullius*, was he the first European discoverer of it?'

[6] Frost, 'New South Wales', pp. 513–15.   [7] *Ibid.*, p. 515.

In reference to the first question, Frost argued that Cook and his ship's most influential crew member, the gentleman botanist Joseph Banks, answered it in accordance with the writings on the law of nature and the law of nations. Thus, Frost claimed, 'Cook and Banks' reports ... indicated that the Aborigines had ... not reached the stages of domesticating animals or of maintaining an agriculture' and so 'had not subdued and cultivated the earth so as to obtain "dominion" over it'. Consequently, Frost concluded, in the eyes of Cook and Banks eastern New Holland was a *terra nullius*. In reference to the second question, Frost argued that Cook found no evidence of any prior European claims to discovery, and so claimed this land at intervals as he sailed up the eastern coast of Australia. Most importantly perhaps, Frost insisted: 'had [Prime Minister William] Pitt and his advisers known [in 1786] that the Aborigines were not truly nomadic, that they had indeed mixed their labour with the land, and that they lived within a complex social, political and religious framework – that is, had the British *not* seen New South Wales to be *terra nullius*, then they *would* have negotiated for the right to settle the Botany Bay area'. In other words, argued Frost, the British perception of Aboriginal people ultimately determined the grounds upon which the British Crown claimed possession of New Holland. Finally, in reference to the step that was required to confirm a claim of possession within a reasonable period of time, Frost contended that this occurred when the British began to form a colony at Botany Bay in 1788.[8]

Most scholars who have considered imperial claims of possession would concur with the general thrust of Frost's argument.[9] They have contended that by the mid-eighteenth century, if not earlier, a revolution in the sources of supranational law or inter-polity relations had occurred and that a doctrine had emerged which declared nature to be the source of the law governing the claiming of newly discovered territories. Further, they would agree that the modes of acquisition used by imperial powers included cession by native peoples. Finally, they would concur that imperial powers were increasingly asserting sovereignty over territories on the basis of a claim that they were merely taking things that belonged to no one or were void of ownership. (They have also contended that, underlying this practice, was an elaboration or rather a simplification of

---

[8] *Ibid.*, pp. 518–22, Frost's emphases.
[9] See, for example, Arthur S. Keller et al., *Creation of Rights of Sovereignty through Symbolic Acts*, Columbia University Press, New York, 1938; Anthony Pagden, *Lords of All the World: Ideologies of Empire in Spain, Britain and France c. 1500–c. 1800*, Yale University Press, New Haven, CT, 1995; Ken MacMillan, *Sovereignty and Possession in the English New World: The Legal Foundations of the English New World*, Cambridge University Press, Cambridge, 2006; and Andrew Fitzmaurice, *Sovereignty, Property and Empire, 1500–2000*, Cambridge University Press, Cambridge, 2014.

Roman property law that held that things that belonged to no one were susceptible to being acquired by someone else taking them.)

Nevertheless, recent studies have implicitly called into question several aspects of Frost's argument. Lauren Benton and Benjamin Straumann have pointed out that many scholars have invoked *terra nullius* or *res nullius* in an unduly expansive fashion, so much so that these terms have come to refer to any claim in regard to newly discovered lands, irrespective of the actual legal basis upon which those claims were made. In other words, they point out that many scholars have treated imperial claims that were actually based on a variety of rationales – such as those of discovery, improvement and settlement of lands deemed to be unoccupied – as though they were parts of a single legal principle or doctrine that they have called *terra nullius* or *res nullius*.[10]

Benton and Straumann have also argued that many scholars make a mistake in assuming that the writings of such authorities in metropolitan Europe as Grotius, Pufendorf and Locke directly or unambiguously influenced the actions of the imperial agents who were responsible for making claims of possession in the New World. They have pointed out that these agents usually had a highly imperfect understanding of legal concepts. Furthermore, they argue, those concepts are best regarded as comprising a repertoire rather than a blueprint for designing claims and they contend that imperial agents drew upon this resource in a highly pragmatic, even scattershot, fashion to meet the circumstances at hand. Most importantly, Benton and Straumann argue that imperial agents deployed legal concepts in order to make vague claims to legitimacy rather than stake claims in any strict legal sense. This was the case, they conclude, because the principal objective of imperial agents was not to lay claim to an *absolute* title but to demonstrate that their sovereign had a title to territories that was *better* than the title claimed by their imperial rivals.[11]

Frost's emphasis on the role played by *terra nullius* is further drawn into question by Benton and Straumann's contention that the legal concept that imperial agents most often referenced in the course of the long sixteenth and seventeenth centuries in making and defending claims of possession was not that, or merely that, of *occupation*, which was a mode of acquiring *res nullius*, but rather that of *possessio*. They also point out that imperial agents often assembled arguments that combined this concept with other legal concepts. *Possessio*, Benton and Straumann suggest, had certain features that made it highly attractive in imperial claim-making. In

[10] Lauren Benton and Benjamin Straumann, 'Acquiring Empire by Law: From Roman Doctrine to Early Modern European Practice', *Law and History Review*, vol. 28, no. 1, 2010, pp. 2, 6–7.

[11] *Ibid.*, pp. 3–5, 38.

Roman law it was in the first instance a claim based on fact – that is, a claim that a person who had a thing, and intended to possess it, should be regarded as its possessor – rather than a claim to ownership that was based on any entitlement, but that in due course this claim could lead to *dominium* (ownership) by way of *usucapio* (possessing some thing for a certain period without interruption). This meant, they point out, that *possessio* was highly practical in the context of imperial claim-making. A claim made on the basis of both *discovery* – that is, a claim to be a territory's first European discoverer – and *possessio* could be made and upheld more readily against an imperial rival than a claim made on the grounds of a right, because it could be evaluated more easily. This feature made it especially useful to imperial agents in circumstances where they faced particular imperial rivals or assumed they would do so. As we will see, *possessio* was also very helpful in instances where imperial agents found it difficult to negotiate cession from local peoples. By contrast, making claims to possession on the basis of *occupation* or *res nullius* could be fraught since it involved an investigation of the grounds upon which the territory could be acquired. This typically entailed answering two questions: first, whether all things in a newly discovered territory had the status of *res nullius* or whether the natives there had any property claims in those things, with the implication being that if there were any such claims those things could not be regarded as *res nullius*; and, second, in the event that there were things that were not part of anybody's property, could they be claimed as *res nullius*, or were there rights of native polities standing in the way of such claims, which was a question that required an imperial agent to find out whether the native people had anything that resembled a sovereign polity,[12] and, if so, whether this could bar the application of *res nullius*.[13]

Finally, a problem with Frost's claims in regard to *terra nullius* has been raised by the intellectual historian Andrew Fitzmaurice, namely that there was no doctrine bearing this name in early modern law and there is no evidence in the historical record of it being used in any systematic fashion until the second half of the nineteenth century. In other words, any application of the term *terra nullius* to New Holland in the late eighteenth century by historians can be said to be anachronistic. Yet it can be argued

---

[12] The instructions drawn up by the Dutch East India Company in 1642 for Abel Tasman, who was the first European to lay claim to what was later named Nova Zeelandia, seem to have required him to do this (Andrew Sharp, *The Voyages of Abel Janszoon Tasman*, Clarendon Press, Oxford, 1968, p. 39).

[13] Benton and Straumann, 'Acquiring Empire', pp. 16–17, 20, 30; Benton, 'Possessing Empire: Iberian Claims and Interpolity Law', in Saliha Belmessous (ed.), *Native Claims: Indigenous Law against Empire, 1500–1920*, Oxford University Press, New York, 2012, pp. 19–21, 26, 36.

that it is a mistake to attribute too much significance to this semantic point. After all, Benton has noted that *terra nullius* derived by analogy from the Roman law doctrine *res nullius* and that the latter had firm foundations in a body of law that predates the early modern period; and Fitzmaurice himself has observed that *terra nullius* is connected to the Roman legal doctrine of *occupatio* or *occupation*, just as he has argued that *terra nullius* approximates to that legal concept and that *occupation* was used to legitimise the dispossession of Aboriginal people in New Holland. However, the fact of the matter is that the British government did not invoke either of these two doctrines as it began to colonise New Holland. (Nor would it do so for quite some time.)[14]

Benton and Straumann's argument regarding *possessio* and the way in which imperial agents often deployed it in combination with other legal concepts seems to fit the available evidence for New Holland. In other words, it provides a much more satisfactory explanation of Cook's claim-making than does Frost's argument about *terra nullius*. Consider, for example, one of the pieces of evidence that Frost adduces for his argument, namely a passage from an account by David Collins, New South Wales' first legal officer, in which he reflected on information about the colony's boundaries that was revealed as a result of the government's commission being read publicly soon after the British landed at Botany Bay in 1788. 'By the definition of our boundaries it will be seen that we were confined along the coast of this continent to such parts of it as were navigated by Captain Cook, without infringing on what might be claimed by other nations from the right of discovery', wrote Collins. 'Of that right, however, no other [European] nation has chosen to avail itself . . . Great Britain alone has followed up the discoveries she has made in this country by at once establishing in it a regular colony and civil government'. Frost argues in part that Collins' remark reveals that the British government claimed possession on the basis that it had occupied a territory that it regarded as a *terra nullius*. But, as readers can see for themselves, it does nothing of the sort. Instead, it suggests that the government claimed possession on the basis of both *discovery* and *possessio*.[15]

Cook's Claiming

In order to assess Frost's argument in regard to *terra nullius* further, we must consider the circumstances in which claims of possession tended to

---

[14] Fitzmaurice, 'Genealogy', pp. 2–3, 10, 14; Benton and Straumann, 'Acquiring Empire', pp. 2, 18; Fitzmaurice, *Sovereignty*, pp. 5–6, 25, 302.

[15] David Collins, *An Account of the English Colony in New South Wales*, T. Cadell, London, 1798, vol. 1, p. 8; Frost, 'New South Wales', pp. 521–22.

be made by imperial agents. This can help clarify what was at stake in such claim-making and who the imperial powers regarded as stakeholders. This, in turn, can provide us with a better understanding of the significance of their original claims of possession.[16]

Scholars like Frost tend to make several erroneous assumptions about the nature of imperial claims of possession. First, they assume that these claims were necessarily concerned with *territory*. But, as several legal historians have emphasised recently, while the control of territory was often regarded as an important part of a claim to sovereignty, it was just one, often contingent aspect of it, rather than its defining element. Indeed, territorial control in many cases was merely an incidental aim in making claims of possession. Although imperial agents sometimes laid claim to vast stretches of territory, what was more important at the time they did so was the particular location or situation of the settlements that might be established later. Even then, expansive claims were usually tempered by the fact that control, where it came to be exercised at all, was asserted mainly over corridors, enclaves and irregular zones around them.[17]

Cook's claiming is a case in point. At the time the British government issued him with its instructions, it had no plans to colonise, let alone conquer Nieuw Holland or Nova Zeelandia. The point of claiming possession was merely to stake a claim in case an imperial power might want to establish an interest there at a later point in time. Moreover, as we have noted, the Lords of the Admiralty directed Cook to 'take possession of *convenient situations* in the country', that is, particular places. This is what Cook did, at least in most of his acts of claiming. For example, in the islands of New Zealand he claimed a bay – both Tūranganui-a-Kiwa (Poverty Bay) and Te-Whanganui-o-Hei (Mercury Bay) in the North Island[18] – and an inlet, Totara-nui (Queen Charlotte Sound), and its

---

[16] Benton, 'Possessing Empire', p. 19.

[17] Lauren Benton, *A Search for Sovereignty: Law and Geography in European Empires, 1400–1900*, Cambridge University Press, New York, 2009, pp. 2, 4–5, 8.

[18] In his journal Cook made no reference to claiming possession at Poverty Bay, perhaps because he was dismayed by the tumultuous clash that occurred with the natives during this, his ship's first landfall in New Zealand, but the draughtsman on board the *Endeavour*, Sydney Parkinson, did (*A Journal of a Voyage to the South Seas in His Majesty's Ship, The Endeavour*, Printed for Stanfield Parkinson, London, 1773, p. 122). Recently, an amateur historian, Margaret Cameron-Ash, has queried whether Cook actually claimed possession at either of these bays, and on the basis of very slender and rather dubious evidence about the provenance of a sentence that appears on the relevant page of the holograph version of Cook's journal (http://nla.gov.au/80/trakine/nla.obj-22 9012235), she has gone so far as to suggest that Cook might have fabricated the act of claiming at the latter place (*Lying for the Admiralty: Captain Cook's Endeavour Voyage*, Rosenberg, [Sydney], 2018, pp. 131–33).

adjacent islands, in the South Island. Neither in the proclamations he made on these occasions nor in several of the proclamations he made in New Holland did Cook see any need to specify the dimensions of the territories. Rather, he was content to make what amounted to inchoate or vague claims. Furthermore, generally speaking, the areas he claimed were nowhere as large as many historians have assumed. Certainly, Cook laid claim to a vast area on the eastern coast of New Holland in his final act of claiming, but prior to this it appears that he had only claimed the parts of the coast he actually saw,[19] and the extent of his claims in New Zealand was very limited.[20]

Many historians also make the mistake of assuming that European claims of possession necessarily encompassed not only *imperium* (sovereignty) but also *dominium* (lordship over property).[21] These terms were often imprecisely defined, especially in relation to one another, and the difference between claims to sovereignty and claims to property often tended to be blurred. But historians can often work out on the basis of the historical context what it was that imperial agents were claiming. In the case of New Holland and New Zealand, there is little evidence to suggest that Cook had any interest in making specific claims in regard to title to land, contrary to what Frost has argued. Consequently, we must be careful not to assume that the original imperial claims of possession necessarily entailed claims to property in land, let alone that they dictated how native title to land would be treated at the point that imperial governments might decide to found a colony.[22]

Scholars like Frost also tend to assume that imperial claim-making was directed at native peoples. In some cases, it was. Cook, as we have already noted, was instructed to make claims of possession with the consent of the natives unless he found the land uninhabited. But, more often than not, imperial agents made claims primarily or even solely in reference to their imperial rivals. Cook's account of his claiming of possession in New

---

[19] The record of Cook's claims of possession in New Holland is slender, to say the least. He himself made no reference to any act of claiming prior to an entry he made in his journal in regard to his claiming at Possession Island. While this is undoubtedly puzzling, I am sceptical that this means we should conclude, as Cameron-Ash has done (see *ibid.*, chapters 30, 32 and 35), that Cook made none of those claims at the time.

[20] J. C. Beaglehole (ed.), *The Journals of Captain James Cook on his Voyages of Discovery*, vol. 1, Cambridge University Press/Hakluyt Society, Cambridge, 1955, p. 207 note 10, 387; J. C. Beaglehole, *The Life of Captain James Cook*, Adam & Charles Black, London, 1974, p. 249; Bill Gammage, 'Early Boundaries of New South Wales', *Historical Studies*, vol. 19, no. 77, 1981, p. 525.

[21] For example, MacMillan, *Sovereignty and Possession*.

[22] Stuart Banner, *How the Indians Lost their Land: Law and Power on the Frontier*, Belknap Press of Harvard University Press, Cambridge, MA, 2005, pp. 2–3, 6–7, 299 note 8; Benton, *Search for Sovereignty*, pp. xi, 2–5, 8, 287–88.

Holland and New Zealand reveals that he placed markers at the top of the
highest hills, which suggests that he was primarily concerned to forestall
any claims that French and Spanish agents might make. It is also clear
that Cook was conscious of the fact that both these territories bore the
names that the Dutch empire had bestowed on them and that Abel
Tasman had previously claimed possession of parts of them. Cook's
journal also suggests that he was unable to devise a means to readily
execute the Admiralty's instruction to claim possession of convenient
situations with the consent of the natives (or to act in accordance with
the insistence of the Earl of Moreton, the President of the Royal Society,
the co-sponsor of his expedition, that the natives were 'the natural, and in
the strictest sense of the word, the legal possessors of the several regions
they inhabit'). It appears that he concluded that a claim made on the basis
of the doctrine of *discovery* would be enough to establish a preliminary
claim against another imperial power. In his final act of claiming before he
left the waters surrounding New Holland, on the island he came to call
Possession Island, Cook was relieved when an armed group of the local
people, the Kaurareg, whom he feared might oppose his landing, moved
away, enabling him to take what he called 'peaceable possession'. He was
concerned to remark that there had been no previous European discoverer, though he actually seems to have been unsure about the basis – or
the *rule*, to use his word – upon which he was claiming possession, judging
by the fact that he deleted two key passages in his journal.[23]

The record of Cook's claiming in the islands of New Zealand is ambiguous about whether he sought the consent of the natives. It also suggests
that any attempt he might have made to do this depended on whether any
natives happened to be present at the time he decided to claim possession
and what their attitude to his presence was. At Mercury Bay Cook simply
reported that his party had cut into a tree the ship's name and the date of
its landing and displayed the English flag. He did not indicate whether he
acquired the consent of the natives, but we can probably assume he would
have recorded this had he done so. At Totara-nui Cook seems to have
gone through the motions of trying to secure the consent of several native
men who happened to be there at the moment he carried a post over to an
island to set up a marker of the claim he was intent on making. The
presence of these men prompted Cook to ask his interpreter, the Tahitian
man Tupaia, to explain to the natives what he was doing and give each of
them a present. He later claimed in his journal that they had given their

[23] Earl of Morton, Hints offered to the consideration of Captain Cook, 10 August 1768,
reproduced in Beaglehole (ed.), *Journals of Cook*, p. 514; Beaglehole (ed.), *Journals of
Cook*, p. 387.

consent to his putting up the post, but he did not suggest that he had sought their consent to his claim of possession. Furthermore, it seems that Cook's gestures on this occasion were prompted largely by his determination to ensure that the natives did not pull down the post he had put up as a sign to Britain's European rivals that it had claimed possession.[24]

Frost also argues, as we have already noted, that imperial agents evaluated the culture of native peoples in order to determine whether they were sovereign polities or owners of the land. In Cook's case there is no persuasive evidence that his numerous observations about the native peoples were made with this task in mind. But even if one were to conclude that this was the case, the record of his claim-making contradicts Frost's argument that the basis of Cook's claims of possession in New Holland differed radically from the basis of those he made in New Zealand as well as his contention that this difference can be explained in terms of the way Cook perceived the native peoples. As we have just noted, in the islands of New Zealand Cook did not enter into any negotiations with the native people to secure their consent. Rather, he claimed possession on the very same grounds that he later claimed possession in New Holland, namely *discovery*. There remains the possibility that Cook concluded that the natives in neither New Zealand nor New Holland were sovereign peoples because of their very nature and that this dictated the terms on which he claimed possession. However, the evidence of claiming in other places suggests that considerations of this kind did not dictate how imperial agents acted. As Alain Beaulieu has pointed out, the British made treaties in Upper Canada with natives who were nomadic and had little political hierarchy, just as they did not make treaties with the Iroquois and the Hurons, who were sedentary, agricultural communities and had more complex political organisation.[25]

Most importantly, Frost and numerous other historians who have considered imperial claims of possession such as Cook's have erred in assuming that those claims are more significant than they really were. These claims did not determine the way in which imperial powers treated sovereignty, let alone rights of property in land, in the colonies they planted later. The New Zealand example makes this clear. Despite the claims of possession Cook made there in 1769–70, in the 1810s the

---

[24] *Ibid.*, pp. 143–44, 204, 242–43; Beaglehole, *Cook*, p. 207; J. M. R. Owens, 'New Zealand before Annexation', in W. H. Oliver with B. R. Williams (eds.), *The Oxford History of New Zealand*, Oxford University Press, Wellington, 1981, p. 30; Nicholas Thomas, *Discoveries: The Voyages of Captain Cook*, Allen Lane, London, 2003, p. 127.

[25] Alain Beaulieu, 'The Acquisition of Aboriginal Land in Canada: The Genealogy of an Ambivalent System', in Saliha Belmessous (ed.), *Empire by Treaty: Negotiating European Expansion, 1600–1900*, Oxford University Press, New York, 2015, p. 104.

British government took steps by which it more or less repudiated its claim to possession, and in the late 1830s it decided it had to negotiate cession of sovereignty with the natives before annexing the country. This means that we need to resist the temptation to conclude that imperial claims of possession were, in and of themselves, highly significant, let alone assume that they laid the foundations of settler nations. In order to understand how and why native sovereignty or property rights were treated in a particular manner in any colony, historians must investigate instead the circumstances in which an imperial power first made claims of possession and more especially the period of time that passed between that moment and the point it decided to assume sovereignty. Performing this task leads us to question the assumption that the British government's treatment of sovereignty or rights of property in land was primarily determined by legal conventions and provides us with a more satisfactory answer to the question of why the British government treated these matters in New South Wales in the way that it did.

Part II

First Encounters

To begin this investigation, we need to examine the encounters that took place between Cook and his party on the *Endeavour* and the native peoples of New Holland and New Zealand in 1769–70. For many years, scholars have placed so much emphasis on the role cultural factors played in these encounters that they have barely considered the particular histor-ical circumstances in which these peoples met.[26]

These encounters, and ways in which Cook and Banks perceived the local peoples, sprang in large part from the instructions Cook received from the British Admiralty. He was directed to make discoveries of countries previously unknown to Europeans as well as learn more about places formerly discovered but as yet poorly explored, on the premise that this would increase the prestige of Great Britain as a maritime power and advance navigation and trade. More important still, Cook was instructed to observe the nature of the land and its products, as well as the nature and number of the inhabitants, and to cultivate a friendship and alliance with the natives by giving them presents and inviting them to trade, the cultivation of trade being a long-standing purpose of such voyages of discovery. Performing these two tasks constituted a means not only of

---

[26] See, for example, Banner, *Possessing the Pacific*, pp. 5, 16–17.

making sense of the people they encountered but of facilitating relationships with them. In undertaking them, Cook and Banks tended to proceed in a comparative fashion, noting similarities and differences between the places and peoples they saw in the South Pacific. This practice was also adopted later by many government officials and settlers.[27]

The encounters that Cook and his crew had with the Aboriginal people in New Holland were strikingly few and brief, especially when compared to those they had with the local people in the Society Islands, Tahiti and New Zealand. Indeed, in New Holland, from the British mariners' point of view, scarcely any meaningful meetings took place. As Nicholas Thomas has reminded us, sound understanding is usually the result of conversation rather than observation, but most of the party on the *Endeavour* only saw rather than spoke with the Aboriginal people they encountered. As Cook himself confessed, 'we never were able to form any connections with them'. Maria Nugent suggests that Cook was partly to blame for this as he tried too hard to make contact. In the early stages of the voyage he had bided his time or allowed the locals to take the lead, but by the time he got to New Holland he was unwilling or unable to proceed in this manner.[28]

The encounters that Cook and Banks had with the Aboriginal people were not only few and fleeting. The Eora and Guugu Yimidhirr showed no interest in the goods that Cook's party offered them, they never brought anything to sell and at no point did they engage in barter of any kind. As Cook departed New Holland, he reflected: '[T]hey seemed to set no value upon any thing we gave them, nor would they ever part with any thing of their own for any one article we could offer them'. As a result, Cook and Banks concluded that the natives of this continent had no idea of trade. The Aboriginal people's response was in stark contrast with that of the native peoples Cook's party had encountered elsewhere in the Pacific, and so was all the more puzzling and troubling to Cook and Banks. Since Cook placed considerable faith in trading commodities as a means of forging relations with the native peoples, the reluctance of the Aboriginal people to engage in traffic thwarted his mission to enlarge the commerce of Great Britain by creating trading partners. More to the point, it had a considerable impact on the nature of the encounters that took place, and in turn the amount of knowledge

---

[27] Instructions issued by the Admiralty to Cook, 30 July 1768, reproduced in Beaglehole (ed.), *Journals of Cook*, pp. cclxxx; Additional Instructions, 30 July 1768, reproduced in Beaglehole (ed.), *Journals of Cook*, pp. cclxxxii–cclxxxiii.

[28] Beaglehole (ed.), *Journals of Cook*, p. 312; Thomas, *Discoveries*, 6, 51, 111, 113, 122; Maria Nugent, *Captain Cook Was Here*, Cambridge University Press, Melbourne, 2009, pp. viii, 58, 74, 100, 102.

that Cook and Banks were able to acquire about the Aboriginal people's culture. Had more trade occurred, things might well have been very different, most importantly for how the British government perceived the Aboriginal people.[29]

Representing Aborigines

Cook's encounters with Aboriginal people in New Holland played some role in the British government's decision in 1768 to assume sovereignty on the basis of Cook's claiming of possession, but the way in which these encounters came to be *represented* in British circles in the decade or so that followed was more important.

The observations of Cook and Banks that exerted the greatest influence were concerned primarily with the Aboriginal people's response to the mariners' invitation to traffic, and more especially their numbers and capacity for war. In regard to the former, Banks observed: 'These people seemed to have no idea of traffick nor could we teach them; indeed, it seemed that we had no one thing on which they set a value equal to induce them to part with the smallest trifle'. In regard to the latter, Cook concluded, after visiting Botany Bay: 'The natives do not appear to be numerous neither do they seem to live in large bodies but dispersed in small parties along by the water side'; and he repeated this observation on leaving New Holland after he had remarked: 'I do not look upon them to be a warlike people, on the contrary I think them a timorous and inoffensive race'. For his part, Banks commented at great length upon what he called 'this want of people' and these 'rank cowards', claiming that the country was 'thinly inhabited even to admiration'. He even went so far as to speculate that most of the territory was 'totally uninhabited'.[30]

Cook and Banks' impressions regarding the number of Aboriginal people and their military capacity influenced the way that New Holland and its peoples came to be seen in Britain in the course of the 1770s, as some of the remarks that they had made in their journals appeared, in a somewhat mangled form, in John Hawkesworth's popular multivolume work *An Account of the Voyages Undertaken at the Order of His Majesty for Making Discoveries in the South Pacific*, which was first published in 1773. In turn, this work

[29] Beaglehole (ed.), *Journals of Cook*, pp. 306, 312, 399; J. C. Beaglehole (ed.), *The Endeavour Journal of Joseph Banks, 1768–1771*, vol. 2, Public Library of New South Wales/Angus and Robertson, Sydney, 1962, p. 125; Thomas, *Discoveries*, pp. 111, 113.
[30] Beaglehole (ed.), *Journals of Cook*, pp. 312, 396, 399; Beaglehole (ed.), *Journal of Banks*, pp. 59, 122, 125.

informed many later accounts. For example, in 1779 a compilation paraphrasing Hawkesworth made reference to 'the small number of the human species dispersed in this extensive country'.[31]

In the same year, Banks told a House of Commons Committee on Transportation that there were 'very few natives' and that they were 'extremely cowardly'. By this time, the forty-two-year-old Banks was at the height of his powers, having been elected president of the Royal Society. More particularly, he had come to be regarded as the most authoritative source of information regarding New Holland, even though his memory of both the place and its people blurred with the passing of time, the rigour of his reportage fading as the prejudicial aspect of his opinions deepened.[32]

Most importantly, in 1785 Banks' representations of New Holland acquired political significance when he appeared before a British House of Commons committee investigating alternative sites for a convict colony in the wake of Britain's loss of colonies in North America. Part of the testimony he gave is important enough to warrant being quoted at some length:

Is the coast in general or the particular part you have mentioned [Botany Bay] much inhabited?
There are very few inhabitants.

Are they of a peaceable or hostile disposition?
Though they seemed inclined to hostilities they did not appear at all to be feared. We never saw more than 30 or 40 together.

Do you apprehend in case it was resolved to send convicts there any district of the country might be obtained by cession or purchase?
There was no probability while we were there of obtaining anything either by cession or purchase as there was nothing we could offer that they would take except provisions and those we wanted ourselves.

Have you any idea of the nature of the government under which they lived?
None whatever, nor of their language.

... Do you think that 500 men being out on shore there would meet with that obstruction from the natives which might prevent their settling there?
Certainly not – from the experience I have had of the natives of another part of the same coast I am inclined to believe they would speedily abandon the country to the newcomers.

---

[31] Jonathan Carver, *The New Universal Traveller*, printed for G. Robinson, London, 1779, p. 665.
[32] Africa, Convicts, Memorandum, undated [1779], TNA, HO 42/5.

Were the natives armed and in what manner?
They were armed with spears headed with fish bones but none of them we saw in
Botany Bay appeared at all formidable.

Historians such as Glyndwr Williams have claimed that Banks was
intent on showing that the Aborigines were 'a nomadic people with no
trace of political authority, social organisation or religious belief, and
that the east coast of New Holland was, accordingly, *terra nullius*'. Yet,
as readers of his testimony can see, Banks made no comments whatsoever about the nature of the Aboriginal people's political or social
organisation or their religious beliefs. Instead, he claimed that New
Holland was populated by a very small number of Aboriginal people,
that they were militarily weak and that the provision of a relatively small
armed force would enable the British government to form a colony
there.[33]

Perceptions of Power

It is instructive to consider how the British government approached
the matter of possession as it contemplated the establishment of new
colonies at this time (as indeed Frost has suggested). In 1784
a government official, discussing a proposal to re-establish a British
presence on the Island of Lemain on the Gambia River in north-west
Africa, stated that the land should be purchased or leased, and the
government later dispatched a representative to negotiate an agreement with the local people to buy or rent land there. In the
same year, the House of Commons Committee on Transportation
assumed that similar arrangements would be made if a colony was
founded at Das Voltas Bay in south-west Africa. Finally, in 1790 the
government instructed the captain of a warship, which it was proposing to send to Nootka Sound on the Canadian north-west coast, to
gain the local people's consent to the formation of a settlement and
purchase a grant of land from them. It appears that the British
government believed that negotiating for small parcels of land was
a sensible way of ensuring friendly relations with the natives.
Moreover, it is evident that several prominent figures assumed that
the government should do the same in the event that it chose to

---

[33] Examination of Joseph Banks, Minutes of Committee of House of Commons Respecting
a Plan for Transporting Felons to the Island of Lemain on the River Gambia,
10 May 1785, TNA, HO 7/1; Glyndwr Williams, 'Reactions on Cook's Voyage', in
Ian Donaldson and Tamsin Donaldson (eds.), *Seeing the First Australians*, George Allen
& Unwin, Sydney, 1985, p.48.

found a colony in New Holland. For example, in 1784 an advocate of founding a colony in the South Pacific, Sir John Call, suggested this course of action, and in 1785 (as I have just noted) the Commons Committee on Transportation asked Banks whether he thought any part of the country in New Holland could be acquired by such means. But in the end no official recommendations or instructions were issued to do this in the case of New Holland.[34]

In the African and North American examples it seems that the British government assumed that it would or could face competition from other European powers, that the agents of those rivals might claim possession by seeking to negotiate cession or purchase of land with the natives and/or that its own agents might encounter large groups of native people who might be able to prevent settlement. In these circumstances it made sense to negotiate with the natives. (As we will see, the absence or presence of a third party often played a decisive role in determining how native sovereignty or rights of property in land were treated.) By contrast, it appears that the British government concluded in the case of New Holland that there would be no such obstacles to its claiming possession and hence no need to negotiate cession with or to purchase land from the local people.

It is also instructive to consider what the British government might have done if it had decided to plant a colony in the islands of New Zealand in the mid-1780s – and this was suggested – or more especially in one of New Zealand's southern islands where Cook and Banks had concluded that there were few native people. Most historians tend to assume that the terms upon which the British Crown claimed possession in the New Zealand case were very different to those of New South Wales because of the way that early British agents, especially Cook and Banks, perceived and represented the native people. However, a careful reading of their journals draws this argument into question. Certainly, the encounter that the *Endeavour* had with the native people in the islands of New Zealand differed in nearly every respect from the encounter that Cook and his

---

[34] Thoughts upon the establishments to be made in the River Gambia, undated [1784], TNA, CO 267/20; Sir John Call, Proposals for Employing 600 Convicts, [August 1784], TNA, HO 42/7; John Barnes to Sir Evan Nepean, 3 January 1785, TNA, HO 42/6; Lord Sydney to the Lord Commissioners of the Treasury, 9 February 1785, TNA, HO 35/1; *BPP*, 1784–85, vol. 40, House of Commons Committee on Transportation Report, p. 1163; Examination of Banks; Nepean to Sackville Hamilton, 24 October 1786, TNA, HO 100/18; Nepean, Draft of Instructions to the Captain of the Frigate, March 1790, TNA, HO 28/61; Frost, 'New South Wales', pp. 522–23, and 'Claiming Pacific Lands: Late Eighteenth-Century and Nineteenth-Century Approaches', *Journal of Commonwealth and Postcolonial Studies*, vol. 17, no. 1, 2011, pp. 187–88.

companions later had with Aboriginal people in New Holland. Over a period of six months in what is now New Zealand, Cook's party had numerous meetings with the natives and ample opportunity to observe them. In the early months of this encounter, Cook and Banks were impressed by the numerous villages and the amount of cultivation they saw, they noted the presence of chiefs and they concluded that the country was populous. They were even more impressed by the fact that the natives embraced Cook's invitation to traffic or trade, indeed that Māori keenly wanted what Cook's party had to offer, especially iron, and that consequently there was an energetic exchange of goods. Finally, Cook and his crew encountered a good deal of hostility in many of the encounters, and they seem to have been especially awed by the arts of the Māori warriors. Yet, by the time the *Endeavour* left New Zealand, Cook and Banks had significantly revised their opinion of the natives. For example, Cook reckoned the native diet principally comprised fern roots, fish and wild fowl; both he and Banks opined that the amount of cultivation they undertook was quite limited; and Banks had formed the view that there were many fewer people than they had first thought, especially in proportion to the size of the country, and that they only inhabited the coast. Most importantly, even though they had registered the natives' arts of war, Cook and Banks were convinced of the superiority of British force. Cook asserted: 'So far as I have been able to judge of the genius of these people it doth not appear to me to be at all difficult for strangers to form a settlement in this country. They seem to be too much divided among themselves to unite in opposing'. In short, the opinion that Cook and Banks reached of the peoples of the islands of New Zealand and of the chances of the British being able to plant a colony there closely resembled the one they would form in regard to New Holland.[35]

It is useful to consider what Banks might have said if he had been asked in regard to the natives of New Zealand the questions that the House of Commons Committee on Transportation had put to him in 1785 about the natives of New Holland. We can probably assume that he would have told this committee that the coast of New Zealand was only lightly populated, that natives were well armed and could be hostile but that British arms were superior and that a force of 500 men would mean that

[35] Beaglehole (ed.), *Journals of Cook*, pp. 169–286; J. C. Beaglehole (ed.), *The Endeavour Journal of Joseph Banks, 1768–1771*, vol. 1, The Trustees of the Public Library of New South Wales in association with Angus and Robertson, Sydney, 1962, pp. 400ff; Beaglehole (ed.), *Journal of Banks*, vol. 2, pp. 11, 17–18, 26; Cook to John Walker, 13 September 1771, reproduced in Beaglehole (ed.), *Journals of Cook*, pp. 507–08; Anne Salmond, *Two Worlds: First Meeting Between Maori and Europeans 1642–1772*, Viking, Auckland, 1991, pp. 122, 265; Thomas, *Discoveries*, pp. 87, 109.

the natives would be unable to obstruct the settlement. In addition, he would probably have said that possession over a part of the country could be obtained by cession because the British had been able to trade and that there were chiefs with whom the British would be able to negotiate. However, if Banks had been asked specifically about the natives in New Zealand's southern islands, his answers would almost certainly have closely resembled the ones he provided the committee in regard to New Holland. Thus, it seems reasonable to conclude that if the British government had chosen to establish a colony somewhere in the more populous northern island of New Zealand, it would have directed its agents to negotiate a cession of sovereignty with the natives or purchase land from them, given that it had a predisposition to this mode of acquisition. By the same token, we can be relatively sure that if the British government had decided to do the same in the thinly populated South Island it would neither have negotiated cession nor purchased land from the natives. In other words, it would have proceeded on exactly the same basis as it did in New South Wales in 1788.[36]

Planning a Colony

In deciding to establish a colony in New Holland the British Home Office had two main considerations in mind. First, the imprisonment of convicts on disabled ships and gaols in Britain was proving controversial as they had become overcrowded. Consequently, officials were casting around for alternative sites, preferably islands, since these had long been regarded as useful places of exile. They finally turned to New Holland because they had concluded that the alternative sites off the African coast were unsuitable. Second, increasing rivalry between European empires and shifting patterns of maritime trade created a new interest in establishing far-flung bases. Founding a colony in New Holland could not only help to maintain

---

[36] Minutes of Committee of House of Commons Respecting a Plan for Transporting Felons to the Island of Lemain on the River Gambia, Sir Joseph Banks' evidence, 10 May 1785, TNA, HO 7/1; Alan Frost, *Convicts and Empire: A Naval Question 1776–1811*, Oxford University Press, Melbourne, 1980, pp. 15, 23. The anthropologist Anne Salmond has claimed that the British government dismissed New Zealand in the mid-1780s as a possible location for a colony because it thought that the natives were 'too numerous and too unruly', but there is no historical evidence to suggest that events such as the killing of the Frenchman Marion du Fresne and twenty-six of his men in June 1772 or the killing of ten men from one of the vessels during Cook's second voyage to the Pacific at Whareuunga Bay (Grass Cove) in Totara-nui in December 1773, or representations of those events (*Between Worlds: Early Exchanges between Maori and Europeans 1773–1815*, University of Hawai'i Press, Honolulu, 1997, pp. 25, 83, 102–05, 159–60, 182) led the British government to prefer New Holland over New Zealand as the site to plant a new colony.

Britain's maritime power by creating a base for refitting and repairing its navy and securing wood and flax (which were resources that were thought to be available in great abundance on Norfolk Island and the islands of New Zealand, situated a thousand or so miles east and southeast of New Holland) to make masts and ropes for its vessels; this could also advance British interests in the Pacific, countering any French expansion in the region by confirming the claims of possession that Cook had made.[37]

In seeking to realise these two goals, the British government had no reason to anticipate that it would need a large amount of land. A small enclave would suffice, as it would for any fort or garrison. Furthermore, the government never envisaged that there would be a regular series of shipments of convicts to this place. Moreover, as the plans to found a colony there took shape, the government realised that it could not resume the mode of transporting convicts under the control of contractors who could sell their labour assignments, as it had in North America, but would need to establish a colony in a system headed by a governor with an unusual amount of authority, not the least of which was military. Each of these factors – which can be glossed, respectively, as a plan to create a small enclave much like an island so that control over a large territory was unimportant, a plan that envisaged the shipment of a small number of convicts unlikely to grow beyond several hundred in what was believed to be a very large, sparsely populated continent and a plan for a militarily powerful system of government – probably meant, along with Banks' testimony, that the British government saw little if any need to pay attention to the sovereignty, let alone rights in land, of the native people, and so it did not.[38]

In the charter and the commission drawn up for the first governor of the new colony of New South Wales, Captain Arthur Phillip, the British Crown assumed possession of half of the continent, vested jurisdiction in this territory in the governor and his courts, and made very little provision for the conduct of relations with the Aboriginal people. These instructions are all the more striking when they are compared with the instructions about much the same matters that the British government drew up for the first consul and lieutenant governor for the islands of New

---

[37] My account in this and the next paragraph draws upon Frost, *Convicts and Empire*, chapters 1 and 2, and *Botany Bay: The Real Story*, Black Inc, Melbourne, 2011, chapters 6–10; Alan Atkinson, 'The First Plans for Governing New South Wales, 1786–87', *Australian Historical Studies*, vol. 24, no. 94, 1990, pp. 22–40, and *The Europeans in Australia*, vol. 1, Oxford University Press, Melbourne, 1997, chapter 4; Benton, *Search for Sovereignty*, chapter 4; and Emma Christopher, *A Merciless Place*, Allen & Unwin, Sydney, 2010, chapter 15.

[38] Alan Atkinson, 'The Ethics of Conquest', *Aboriginal History*, vol. 6, pt 2, 1982, p. 82.

Zealand more than fifty years later, and which played a crucial role in how the question of native sovereignty was treated there.[39]

This is not to suggest, however, that these legal instruments, any more than the events I have been discussing, determined how native rights in land were to be treated in New Holland, though it has generally been assumed by historians that that is the case. This is so for several reasons. Like the charters the British government issued in regard to the founding of colonies in North America in the sixteenth and seventeenth centuries, they should not be understood as documents that were concerned with the acquisition and possession of land. Furthermore, there is no reason to assume that any legal instrument issued by the British government for the founding of a colony dictated how land would in fact be acquired on a colonial periphery. In the North American case, the English settlers soon realised that in order to acquire land they were best to purchase it from the natives. In the case of New South Wales, Phillip was given the power to make grants of land to the settlers, but there seems to be no reason to conclude that this necessarily meant that the British government believed the Aboriginal people had no rights of property in land. On the contrary, those responsible for Phillip's instructions seem to have assumed that he might barter with the native people in New South Wales or adjacent islands since they made provision for various goods for this purpose. Furthermore, some of those who contributed to a debate in the London press about the government's plans expressed concern about the impact that British colonisation would have on the natives and one writer at least seemed to suggest that the government should acquire land by purchasing it from the local people.[40]

Finally, even though it appears the British government had ruled out the need to treat with Aboriginal people on the basis of the widely held perception that they were few in number and militarily weak, Phillip doubted that this perception of the local people was true. 'I am not of the general opinion that there are very few inhabitants in this country, at least so few as have been represented', he informed the Home Office minister, Lord Sydney, sometime in 1787, as he prepared the expedition

---

[39] Instructions to Governor Arthur Phillip, 25 April 1787, *HRA*, series 1, vol. 1, pp. 13–14; Charter of Justice, 2 April 1787, *HRA*, series 4, vol. 1, pp. 6–12.

[40] *Public Advertiser*, 28 and 30 September 1786; *English Chronicle*, 7–10 October 1786; Instructions to Governor Arthur Phillip, 25 April 1787, TNA, CO 201/1; Charter of Justice, 2 April 1787, *HRA*, series 4, vol. 1, pp. 6–12; Banner, *How the Indians*, chapter 1; Daniel Richter, 'Land and Words: William Penn's Letter to Kings of the Indians', in his *Trade, Land, Power: The Struggle for Eastern North America*, University of Pennsylvania Press, Philadelphia, 2013, pp. 135–54; James Muldoon, 'Colonial Charters: Possessory or Regulatory', *Law and History Review*, vol. 36, no. 2, 2018, pp. 359–60, 379–80.

to New South Wales. Furthermore, he remarked: 'On landing in Botany Bay, it will be necessary to throw up a slight work, as a defence against the natives, who tho[ugh] only seen in small numbers by Captain Cook, may be very numerous on other parts of the coast'. It seems unlikely, then, that Phillip had decided upon a course of action that ruled out negotiation with the Aboriginal people in regard to land.[41]

The Beginning of Colonisation

Shortly after Phillip landed in Botany Bay in 1788, he assumed sovereignty for the British Crown on the basis of Cook's claim of possession. Yet in the early months of the colony the British party's expectations regarding the natives were confounded, at least in respect of their numbers and the places they frequented. Phillip was soon telling the Home Office that he estimated there to be at least 1,500 natives in Botany Bay, Port Jackson, Broken Bay and the nearby coast and that he was in no doubt there were more inhabitants inland. Furthermore, in the course of the next couple of years, Phillip and his officers came to realise that the Aboriginal people were divided into a number of tribal groups, that each had a particular territory with known boundaries from which they took their name and that they rarely moved outside of this domain. While David Collins (whom we met earlier) could claim that the natives 'liv[ed] in that state of nature which must have been common to all men previous to their uniting in society, and acknowledging but one authority', he conceded that 'they ha[d] also their real estates'. Yet the growth of such knowledge never led Phillip to treat with the Aboriginal people at Botany Bay and Port Jackson for cession of land. This should not be construed as a matter of his repudiating the natives' rights of property in land. Rather, it was a case of his never needing to make a judgement about the matter.

This point is closely related to a striking fact that historians who have previously considered this matter have overlooked: the historical record in regard to the British government's treatment of both native sovereignty and their rights of property in land in New South Wales is remarkably sparse. This is because the government gave scant consideration to these matters when the colony was being founded. The preceding discussion has made clear why this was the case. The government never had any compelling reason to consider let alone determine the status of Aboriginal people in regard to sovereignty or title in land, and so it did not. But how

---

[41] Governor Arthur Phillip to Lord Sydney, undated [1787], TNA, CO 201/2.

might *that* be explained? Three inter-related factors seem to have been especially important.[42]

In the beginning, Phillip's party found it difficult to forge a relationship with the Aboriginal people. Indeed, several months after the British had landed, Phillip reported that the local people repeatedly avoided them. In due course, a good deal of cross-cultural exchange did in fact occur, as the archaeologist and ethnohistorian Isabel McBryde has demonstrated. But this did not radically alter Phillip and his senior officers' perceptions of the Aboriginal people because they were unable to grasp the various dimensions of that exchange. Consequently, while there were transactions between the British and the Aboriginal people of a kind that might have led to the forging of an agreement concerning resources, nothing of this kind occurred.[43]

Second, Phillip's administration never perceived any need to negotiate for access to land. This can be attributed to several factors. The colony merely comprised a small garrison settlement and so had little need for land beyond the beachhead it occupied; it was well resourced for the time being; and its administrators believed that the Aboriginal people's principal source of food lay in the waters of Botany Bay and Port Jackson rather than on the surrounding land. But most importantly, Phillip came to conclude that his party had much greater power than the Eora people. Barely nine months after landing, he informed the Home Office that less force was required to protect the colony from attacks by the local people than he had originally thought necessary. Indeed, he now claimed that he had never thought much force would be needed. A year or so later, he bluntly explained why this was so: '[the natives] are sensible of the great superiority of our arms'. It seems clear that any question as to whether the government might negotiate an agreement like a treaty in order to acquire land never arose after the founding of the colony because Phillip and his officials were convinced that they would be able to rely on the garrison's military strength to take and hold as much of the Aboriginal people's resources as they required.[44]

---

[42] Phillip to Sydney, 15 May 1788, *HRA*, series 1, vol. 1, p. 29; Phillip to Nepean, 9 July 1788, *HRA*, series 1, vol. 1, p. 56; Phillip to Sydney, 13 February 1790, *HRA*, series 1, vol. 1, p. 160; John Hunter, *An Historical Journal of the Transactions at Port Jackson and Norfolk Island*, printed for John Stockdale, London, 1793, p. 62; Collins, *Account*, pp. 544, 599.

[43] Phillip to Sydney, 9 July 1788, *HRA*, series 1, vol. 1, p. 49; Phillip to Secretary Stephens, 10 July 1788, *HRA*, series 1, vol. 1, p. 62; Phillip to Sydney, 28 September 1788, *HRA*, series 1, vol. 1, p. 76; Isabel McBryde, '"Barter ... immediately commenced to the satisfaction of both parties": Cross-Cultural Exchange at Port Jackson, 1788–1828', in Robin Torrence and Anne Clarke (eds.), *The Archaeology of Difference: Negotiating Cross-Cultural Engagements in Oceania*, Routledge, London, 2000, pp. 238–77; Karskens, *Colony*, p. 356.

[44] Phillip to Nepean, 10 July 1788, *HRA*, series 1, vol. 1, pp. 66–67; Phillip to Sydney, 28 September 1788, *HRA*, series 1, vol. 1, p. 77; Phillip to Sydney, 30 October 1788,

This conviction can in turn be attributed to several factors. New South Wales had been founded as a colony that was to be controlled by a government that had considerable authority and was backed by a good deal of military strength in the form of 200 soldiers. The nature of Aboriginal social and economic organisation meant that they had relatively limited military strength, or at least this was the belief of the government. (The scale of the resistance mounted by some Aboriginal people in later years would give colonial governments some cause to reconsider this assumption.) Finally, by the time that Phillip had expressed his view that the colony had nothing much to apprehend from attacks by the Aboriginal people, they had been devastated by a smallpox epidemic that probably killed 50 per cent of them in and around the colonial settlement and wiped out some groups completely, thereby diminishing their capacity to wage war on the British intruders.[45]

Australian historians have been unable to envisage a hypothetical situation in which the British government might have treated with the Aboriginal people as both sovereign and the owners of land. However, an American historian, Stuart Banner, has asked what might have transpired if prolonged contact between British parties and Aboriginal people had *preceded* rather than followed formal colonisation, that is, the point in time at which the British government began to exercise the sovereignty to which it had previously made a preliminary claim. To be more specific, we can ask what might have occurred if the first substantive British contact with Aboriginal people had been made by small parties of missionaries, sealers, whalers and traders, rather than a relatively large, official and militarily strong party of naval officers, soldiers and convicts, and if this contact had occurred slowly rather than in the rapid manner it did. In these circumstances, individuals who assumed the role of go-betweens or mediators would have probably emerged among both peoples. Alliances would have been forged, not least as a result of sexual relationships between European men and Aboriginal women. The Aboriginal people would have had the time to adapt to the presence of the European strangers, and the nature of their social, economic and political structures and practices would have begun to change and bear some resemblance to those of the British settlers, or they might have been

---

HRA, series 1, vol. 1, p. 96; Phillip to Sydney, 13 February 1790, HRA, series 1, vol. 1, p. 161; Phillip to W.W. Grenville, 17 June 1790, TNA, CO 201/5.

[45] Judy Campbell, *Invisible Invaders: Smallpox and Other Diseases in Aboriginal Australia, 1780–1880*, Melbourne University Press, Melbourne, 2002, pp. 88–101; John Connor, *The Australian Frontier Wars 1788–1838*, University of New South Wales Press, Sydney, 2002, pp.27, 30, 35; Banner, *Possessing the Pacific*, p. 26; Paul Irish, *Hidden from Plain View: The Aboriginal People of Coastal Sydney*, NewSouth, Sydney, 2017, p. 20.

perceived as such. At any rate, the British, unable or unwilling to seize the natives' resources by a show of superior force, would almost certainly have entered into negotiations with the Aboriginal people to obtain much-needed resources, including land. Those transactions would have led those small parties to treat with the Aboriginal people for land as though they were both sovereign and owners of it.[46]

One might also conclude that if more than one European power had wished to plant a colony in more or less the same place in New Holland, the competition between these imperial powers would have increased the need for the British to negotiate with the Aboriginal people for access to resources such as land. If, for example, the French had preceded the British and treated with Aboriginal people, the British would probably have decided that they needed to do the same. (This happened, in reverse, in respect of the islands of New Zealand.) Finally, one might speculate that if enough time had passed between settlement by some of those small parties of British settlers and the beginning of formal colonisation by the British government, a history of political and economic transactions regarding land could have developed in such a way that a significant number of settlers would have become committed to a notion of native title as the basis of *their* title to land and the government might have found it difficult to overturn this time-honoured practice. What I have just described is more or less what happened in North America, Fiji, Tonga and, as we will see later, the islands of New Zealand.

Colonial Expansion

What actually happened in New South Wales? During the first few decades of the colony, native rights of property in land had no practical or political significance from the colonial government's point of view.[47]

---

[46] Banner, *Possessing the Pacific*, pp. 26, 263.

[47] Historians of the Australian colonies have not only overlooked or failed to register the relative dearth of relevant historical traces in considering the matter of the British Crown's treatment of sovereignty or rights in land in reference to Aboriginal people; they have also misconstrued the handful of sources that exist. For example, both Frost and Reynolds claim that a legal opinion that Sir Samuel Shepherd and Sir Robert Gifford, Britain's Attorney-General and Solicitor-General respectively, prepared in 1819 for Earl Bathurst, the Colonial Secretary, constitutes evidence for the fact that British government was intent on expressing an opinion about these matters, quoting parts of the following passage to support their interpretation: '[t]hat the part of New South Wales possessed by His Majesty, not having been acquired by conquest or cession, but taken possession of by him as desert and uninhabited, and consequently colonised from this country'. But the Colonial Secretary sought this legal opinion, and the legal officers delivered it, in a context in which the authority of the Crown had been challenged by *settlers*. Consequently, the imperial government was concerned to address a question about the constitutional designation of the colony for the purposes of issuing legal

As the colony struggled to survive and maintain itself in its early years, the government required only small amounts of land, which it simply seized from the Aboriginal people. In the mid-1790s the nature of the colony began to change somewhat as soldiers, sailors and former convicts broke away from the original settlement at Port Jackson to create small holdings on the nearby Cumberland Plain. Subsequently, in the course of the next two to three decades, a relationship developed between those settlers and the Aboriginal people that was characterised by both conflict and accommodation and a blurring of the lines between the two cultures. This frontier might have resembled, albeit for a relatively brief period of time, what Richard White has famously called in the North American context a *middle ground* in the sense that neither the settlers nor the natives were able to gain their ends through force. However, the colonial government nearly always had greater power and authority than these two parties and there is little historical evidence to suggest that it felt compelled to negotiate cession of land from the Aboriginal people. To put this another way, the kind of triangular relationship between settlers, natives and government that typified other settler colonies, and which played a crucial role in the making of native title in those places, was absent in New South Wales.[48]

Beginning in the early 1820s, the nature of colonisation in New South Wales started to change dramatically, largely as a consequence of an increased British demand for commodities like wool and the imperial government's acknowledgement of the colony's potential for free enterprise. This development fuelled what James Belich has called 'explosive colonisation'. The European population increased from 24,000 in 1822 to 77,000 in 1836. Most importantly, settlers broke out from the colonial beachhead to create vast pastoral runs on the Aboriginal people's lands on the plains and slopes west of the Blue Mountains. The number of sheep

---

instruments. In other words, it was not seeking to define the basis of the Crown's claim of possession vis-à-vis the Aboriginal people, however much the passage quoted above might suggest otherwise. This is evident once the passage quoted above is restored to its historical context: 'That the part of New South Wales possessed by His Majesty, not having been acquired by conquest or cession, but taken possession of by him as desert and uninhabited, and consequently colonised from this country, *we apprehend His Majesty has not the right either by himself or through the medium of his governor to make laws ... in such colony, but that [any laws] can only, under the present circumstances of that colony, be imposed by the parliament of the United Kingdom*' (Sir Samuel Shepherd and Sir Robert Gifford to Earl Bathurst, 15 February 1819, *HRA*, series 4, vol. 1, p. 330, my emphases; Frost, 'New South Wales', p. 521; Reynolds, *Law*, p. 32). The same point can be made in regard to a legal opinion that James Stephen provided in 1822 (Counsel opinion on Statute, 20 George II, c.19, [1822], *HRA*, series 4, vol. 1, p. 414).

[48] Richard White, *The Middle Ground: Indians, Empires, and Republics in the Great Lakes Region, 1650–1815*, Cambridge University Press, New York, 1991, especially p. x; Karskens, *Colony*, pp. 14–15, 449, 454–56, 458, 462, 477, 479, 483.

grew exponentially in 1823 when the imperial government reduced tariffs on wool and again in 1828 after a parliamentary select committee declared that Australian wool was a viable substitute for German wool. The government encouraged much of this extensive occupation by granting large tracts of land to free immigrants who had sufficient capital.[49]

The seizure of the Aboriginal people's land between the early 1820s and the early to mid-1830s provoked no formal statement by the imperial or the colonial government regarding the source of its title in land. There was no occasion or circumstance that required it to do so. What is more, there was no sustained debate about native people's rights of property in land at this time, even though there was considerable awareness that Aboriginal people were being displaced and dispossessed. As settlers and Aboriginal people increasingly came into conflict on the frontiers of settlement, there was, instead, political and legal debate about matters that were largely jurisdictional in nature.[50] Could or should the Aboriginal people's attacks upon settlers and property as well as upon each other be subject to British law? What kind or degree of force could be legitimately used by settlers or the colonial government to quell Aboriginal resistance? And was the killing of Aboriginal people a crime in the eyes of British law?

There can be no doubt that some colonists believed that Aboriginal people had been the *original* possessors of the land and that consequently they had a moral duty to ensure that the natives were recompensed, largely by the provision of what was seen as the gifts of civilisation and Christianity. But there is little evidence to suggest that any serious consideration was given to upholding the Aboriginal people's rights of property in land. Once we consider in their actual historical context the examples that historians such as Henry Reynolds have cited to support their argument to the contrary, it becomes clear that the debates that did take place were primarily concerned with the question of whether the Aborigines could or should be subjected to British law or force, and whether settlers had a right to land and protection from Aboriginal attacks, rather than the question of native rights of property in land.[51]

---

[49] Wray Vamplew (ed.), *Australians: Historical Statistics*, Fairfax, Syme & Weldon, Sydney, 1987, pp. 26, 106; N. G. Butlin, *Forming a Colonial Economy, Australia 1810–1850*, Cambridge University Press, Melbourne, 1994, pp. 96, 100, 104, 115, 118–19, 127, 184, 206; James Belich, *Replenishing the Earth: The Settler Revolution and the Rise of the Anglo-World, 1783–1939*, Oxford University Press, New York, 2009, chapter 3.

[50] See Lisa Ford, *Settler Sovereignty: Jurisdiction and Indigenous People in North America and Australia, 1788–1836*, Harvard University Press, Cambridge, MA, 2010.

[51] *Sydney Gazette*, 20 May 1820, 2 June 1821, 28 June 1822, 15 November 1822, 9 January 1823, 29 July 1824, 5, 12, 19 and 26 August 1824, 9 September 1824, 14 April 1825, 29 September 1825, 12 January 1826, 11 February 1826,

Conclusion

In this chapter I have presented a very different account of how and why the British Crown treated native sovereignty and rights of property in land in New South Wales in the way it did. Following in the footsteps of recent scholarship about imperial claims of possession in other parts of the world, I have argued that imperial agents treated legal concepts as a resource rather than a script for claiming possession of overseas territories such as New Holland and New Zealand, and that they did so in order to make vague claims to legitimacy vis-à-vis their imperial rivals rather than stake strictly legal claims. More particularly, I have found no evidence to suggest that Cook claimed possession of New Holland on the basis of the legal concept of *terra nullius* — or the concept of *occupation* for that matter. I have argued, instead, that the historical record suggests that it is more likely that he relied on two other legal concepts: *discovery* and *possessio*. Furthermore, I have argued that Cook's claim-making was primarily done with a European audience in mind rather than a local one, that it was concerned with staking a preliminary claim and that this claim did not, in and of itself, determine how native sovereignty or rights of property in land were treated later.

Most importantly, in seeking to explain why the British government assumed sovereignty on the basis of Cook's claiming of possession at the point it established a colony in New Holland, I have argued that we need to shift attention away from the Cook's claim of possession and the claiming of possession more generally as a process determined merely by legal doctrines or discourses. Instead, I have argued, we need to focus on the sequence of events that began, in the case of New South Wales, with the encounters between Cook's party and the Aboriginal people, and the perceptions that Cook and Banks subsequently formed of the natives. This sequence, I have shown, continued with the way that Aboriginal people were represented in Britain as few in number and lacking in military capacity and thus unlikely to be able to oppose the British government founding a colony. Crucially, at the point that colonisation began, the colonial government, largely because it was relatively well-armed and encountered no powerful rival sources of power (indigenous or non-indigenous), never saw any need to negotiate with the local people

28 June 1826, 30 September 1826, 16 December 1826, 20 April 1827, 22 August 1827, 24 October 1828, 10 November 1828, 4 February 1830, 11 May 1830, 7 October 1830, 8 January 1831, 19 February 1831, 10, 12 and 17 March 1831, 1 and 6 September 1831, 31 December 1831, 31 July 1832, 2 August 1832, 15 December 1832, 30 November 1833, 18 January 1834, 8 May 1834; Reynolds, *Law*, chapter 3, and *This Whispering in our Hearts*, Allen & Unwin, Sydney, 1998, pp. 3–9, 60–64, 70–81.

for cession of sovereignty or the purchase of land. To put this another way, none of the factors that played a major role in persuading Europeans, either at the imperial centre or the colonial periphery, to treat local people as though they were sovereign and the owners of land were ever at play in the case of New South Wales. As a result, the British government proceeded on the basis that it was the only source of sovereignty and title in land.

2 Batman's Treaty and the Rise and Fall of Native Title, 1835–1836

It is often said that whereas the British made a treaty in New Zealand in 1840 in which they acknowledged that Māori were sovereign and recognised their rights in land, they never made such an agreement in Australia. But what really happened was much more complicated.

In recent decades we have lost sight of this past. Several factors best explain this development. Most importantly, it can be attributed to the dominance that national history has assumed in recent decades. This way of looking at the past has obscured the fact that there are some striking similarities in the way native sovereignty and rights of property were treated in Britain's Australasian colonies, or might have been treated if some of the historical circumstances in which these colonies were founded had been different. Histories framed by the nation have also hidden from view the fact that these matters were dealt with somewhat differently in each of the Australian colonies. In other words, by adopting a historical approach that returns Australia and New Zealand's pasts to the *imperial* and *colonial* contexts in which they were forged, we are able to see and understand the similarities in which the sovereignty and rights in land of the native peoples were treated in these countries as well as the differences in the way they were handled in each of the Australian colonies.

Having said this, it would be a mistake to exaggerate the similarities between the Australian and the New Zealand colonies.[1] While the imperial government authorised the making of the treaty in the case of New Zealand, it did nothing of the kind in either New South Wales or the other Australian colonies. Moreover, the treaty made in New Zealand – in which the agents of the British Crown recognised native chiefs as sovereign and acknowledged that they were in possession of their lands – *stuck*, whereas a treaty made by adventurers in one of the Australian colonies on the very

---

[1] For a recent example of this, see Saliha Belmessous, 'The Tradition of Treaty Making in Australian History', in Saliha Belmessous (ed.), *Empire by Treaty: Negotiating European Expansion, 1600–1900*, Oxford University Press, New York, 2015, pp. 186–213.

same basis quickly came unstuck, largely because it was repudiated by the British Crown. Both these phenomena need to be explained.

To begin this task I will focus in this chapter on the history of Batman's treaty.[2] Made just five years before the Treaty of Waitangi, it is the only treaty ever known to have been executed in the Australian colonies on the basis that Aboriginal people were sovereign and had rights in land in the territory in question. In June 1835 John Batman, representing a group of settlers from Van Diemen's Land (or Tasmania as it came to be known), made a treaty at Port Phillip Bay with eight chiefs representing the local Aboriginal people, the Kulin. By this agreement, which comprised two legal deeds (one now known as the Melbourne deed, the other as the Geelong deed), they acquired some 600,000 acres of land in return for a number of blankets, axes, flour and other goods, and the promise of an annual rent or tribute.

The Making of Batman's Treaty

This treaty has long been regarded as a frivolous act by a group of men who were both knaves and fools.[3] In the first place, it has been suggested, they must have known that Port Phillip Bay, which lay across the strait that separated Van Diemen's Land from the Australian mainland, was part of the sovereign territory of New South Wales rather than Van Diemen's Land and that the British government regarded itself and not the Aboriginal people as the owners of the land they purported to have purchased. In other words, it is argued, they must have realised that any attempt to grab land on the basis of a treaty with the local native people would have no legal standing and so was doomed to fail.

In fact these men, who came to form a colonisation company they soon called the Port Phillip Association, were neither knaves nor fools. Nearly all of them were part of respectable society in Hobart or Launceston, the largest towns in Van Diemen's Land. A few belonged to the colony's

---

[2] Other historians have chosen to consider the examples of the Swan River colony (or what became Western Australia), in which the making of a treaty with local people was proposed in the mid-1830s, about which the most thorough study is Ann Hunter, *A Different Kind of 'Subject': Colonial Law in Aboriginal-European Relations in Nineteenth Century Western Australia 1829–61*, Australian Scholarly Publishing, Melbourne, 2011, chapter 8, and Governor George Arthur's advocating of treaties for colonies such as South Australia, which I also discuss here. This chapter draws on the first part of my book, *Possession: Batman's Treaty and the Matter of History*, Miegunyah Press, Melbourne, 2009.

[3] See, for example, C. P. Billot, *John Batman: The Story of John Batman and the Founding of Melbourne*, Hyland House, Melbourne, 1979, p. 131; A. G. L. Shaw, *A History of the Port Phillip District: Victoria Before Separation*, Miegunyah Press, Melbourne, 1996, p. 50; Rex Harcourt, *Southern Invasion, Northern Conquest: Story of the Founding of Melbourne*, Golden Point Press, Melbourne, 2001, p. 207.

small governing elite or were closely acquainted with its principal administrators. Several were or had been public servants, or held or had held positions of considerable civic responsibility. Furthermore, a few of the key players in the Association had thought very seriously about a treaty as a mechanism to realise the Association's goals. To be more specific, Henry Arthur was the nephew of the Governor of Van Diemen's Land, Sir George Arthur, as well as being a customs officer and a Justice of the Peace; Thomas Bannister had been private secretary to Arthur and was the sheriff of Hobart, while his brother Saxe had served as the Attorney General of New South Wales between 1824 and 1826 and was well known in English circles as the author of humanitarian tracts concerning native peoples; John Thomas Collicott was postmaster general; Anthony Cottrell was a chief constable; Joseph Tice Gellibrand had been Attorney General of the colony and the proprietor of one of its newspapers; William George Sams was deputy sheriff of Launceston; James Simpson was a Commissioner of the Land Board; John Sinclair was Superintendent of Convicts in Launceston; and John Helder Wedge was a government surveyor. Several other members, such as Michael Connolly, John and William Robertson, and Charles Swanston, were merchants, financiers or pastoralists of considerable substance. What is more, several of these men invested considerable capital in this Port Phillip venture.

If we consider the factors that lay behind the Port Phillip Association's decision to make a treaty with Aboriginal people in Port Phillip, we can see that its approach was informed by a much greater degree of reason than most historians have allowed until recently. Apart from anything else, it is evident that its idea of a treaty was part and parcel of an attempt to acquire some kind of legal cover for their massive acquisition of land. A common stratagem among adventurers was simply that of taking possession of the land physically in the hope that this would enable them to acquire a legal interest in it. But the men of the Port Phillip Association opted to do more than that. They sought to clothe their land grabbing in a recognisably legal form in the belief that this would enable them to present their actions to the relevant British authorities as both worthy and legitimate. A treaty was central to this strategy for three reasons. The first, which concerns sovereignty, will be considered now. The others, which concern peace and philanthropy, will be discussed later.

The Association's treaty with the Kulin people provided it with a means of tackling an important obstacle to its venture, namely the fact that the government of New South Wales *had* asserted sovereignty over the territory at stake and denied permission to any entrepreneurs to colonise it. By recognising, or pretending to recognise, the Aboriginal people as a sovereign people, the men of the Port Phillip Association hoped that they could circumvent this obstacle. By treating the natives as though they were sovereign, they sought to disregard the very authority that the government of New South Wales claimed to exercise. The relationship between claims about sovereignty and claims to land was often fundamental in the intra-British battles that were fought in its settler colonies, as we will see. In this case, the Association invented its own fiction about the matter of sovereignty by pretending that the Governor of New South Wales had told two of their number several years earlier that Port Phillip actually lay beyond the limits of his jurisdiction. 'It is an understood fact, that these [Aboriginal] tribes are the actual possessors of the soil, and that although the land is *situate within* the limits of the British territory of New Holland, yet it is *without* the jurisdiction of New South Wales, or any other British settlement', the Association informed its principal British agent, George Mercer, shortly after Batman had made the treaty. '[T]he only ground upon which the British government can claim any right of interference with the grants obtained from the native chiefs', they ventured, 'is by a pure fiction of law, namely that the right of the soil [created] by the imaginary line defining the limits of Australia thereby vests such right in the Crown'.[4]

The Association had good reason to challenge the New South Wales government's claim of possession since it amounted to nothing more than a legal claim, or what was called 'constructive possession', rather than actual possession. The British, after all, had occupied relatively little of the territory that had been proclaimed as New South Wales. The imperial and colonial governments themselves realised that the Crown's claim of possession in areas such as Port Phillip was vulnerable to challenge by Britain's imperial rivals, if not by their own subjects. As we have seen, in the supranational or inter-polity law promulgated by European powers, claims of discovery as well as symbolic acts of possession were not regarded as sufficient to secure actual possession; occupation was required. To this end, the government of New South Wales had tried to create settlements at Port Phillip in 1803–04 and again in 1826 (as it feared French claims), only to abandon them. In these circumstances, it is hardly surprising that the Association's principal figures thought they might succeed in their venture.[5]

---

[4] John Batman and Joseph Gellibrand to Governor Ralph Darling, 11 January 1827, TNA, CO 201/247; Alex McLeay to Gellibrand and Batman, 22 March 1827, reproduced in Francis Peter Labillière, *Early History of the Colony of Victoria*, vol. 2, Sampson Low, Marston, Searle, & Rivington, London, 1879, p.35; Charles Swanston to George Mercer, 6 June and 27 August 1835, Charles Swanston Letterbooks, vol. 1, Royal Society of Tasmania, RS9/3 (i); Batman to Governor George Arthur, 25 June 1835, TNA, CO 201/247; Batman et al. to George Mercer, 27 June 1835, Port Phillip Association Papers, SLV, MS safe, their emphases.

[5] Shaw, *History*, pp. 35–36.

In Van Diemen's Land the members of the Port Phillip Association had a potentially powerful ally in assuming that they might be able to challenge the authority of the New South Wales government. Governor George Arthur had often dreamed of extending his rule to areas contiguous to Van Diemen's Land; he was confused about the territorial limits of Van Diemen's Land and New South Wales; and he assumed he had, or could establish, some form of authority in Port Phillip, which was much closer to Hobart than it was to Sydney. When it was reported that Batman had made the treaty, there was speculation about the role that Arthur might be playing in the Association's venture, so much so that it was claimed that he was one of its members. At the very least, Arthur knew the Association's foray in Port Phillip would challenge the jurisdiction of the New South Wales' government; he probably encouraged this move; he might have led the Association to believe it had his backing; and he undoubtedly hoped it would succeed. The Association would have also known that Arthur was a passionate advocate of treaty-making (for reasons I will discuss shortly).[6]

The Association's willingness to challenge the sovereignty claimed by the government of New South Wales in respect of Port Phillip undoubtedly owed much to the peculiar circumstances of its members. Van Diemonian society had a distinctive character, which included a suspicion of authority, an unwillingness to accept matters at face value, a disparagement of government and a resentment of its restraint, a rejection of any discipline and a propensity to adapt the letter of the law to their own purposes. These are characteristics often found in frontier societies where order is weak, but in the case of Van Diemen's Land they remained intact much longer and so became entrenched. This was manifest in the way that the government regulated economic and social matters, including the way it ordered land matters. The peculiar character of public life in Van Diemen's Land was especially marked in Launceston, which was where many of the Association's members came from. This

[6] Arthur to R. W. Hay, 15 November 1826, *HRA*, series 3, vol. 5, p. 435; Arthur to Hay, 24 September 1832, TNA, CO 280/35; Arthur to Thomas Fowell Buxton, 18 September 1834, Sir Thomas Fowell Buxton Papers, Weston Library, University of Oxford, MSS. Brit. Emp. S. 444, Micr. Brit. Emp. 17; Arthur to Thomas Spring Rice, 27 January 1835, TNA, CO 280/55; *Cornwall Chronicle*, 16 May and 20 June 1835; Arthur to Spring Rice, 4 July 1835, TNA, CO 280/58; Arthur to Lord Glenelg, 28 August 1835, *BPP*, 1836, Paper no. 512, Report of the Select Committee on the Disposal of Lands in the British Colonies, p. 230; Arthur to Governor Richard Bourke, 14 October 1835 and 14 January 1836, George Arthur Papers, ML, MS A1962; Arthur to Hay, 28 January 1836, reproduced in Labillière, *Early History*, p. 127; Arthur to Bourke, 25 March and 20 May 1836, *HRV*, vol. 1, pp. 23, 28; *Sydney Monitor*, 23 July 1836; *Sydney Gazette*, 4 August 1836; Shaw, *History*, p. 42; Alan Atkinson, *The Europeans in Australia: A History*, vol. 2, Oxford University Press, Melbourne, 2004, p. 77.

town had a self-regarding energy of its own, an almost republican spirit and a resentment of Arthur's authoritarian government in Hobart. In short, many Van Diemonians were accustomed to a world in which the authority of government was limited, not least in regard to claims of possession to the land. Consequently, they had become used to assuming that they could exert a considerable amount of power.[7]

The principal figures behind the Association's treaty-making were also prone to challenge the rule of law for personal reasons. Gellibrand, Wedge and Batman shared a deeply ambivalent relationship to authority. They all felt that they had been badly treated by the Van Diemonian government. Gellibrand had been dismissed from his post as Attorney General on the grounds of misconduct, and his applications for land grants had been rejected; Wedge had been passed over for promotion as a surveyor, and the land grants he thought were his due had been refused; and Batman's hopes to be a conciliator of the Aborigines had been dashed and his petitions for more government land grants rejected. Port Phillip was a place where these men could envisage themselves as kings. Indeed, one senses that many of the Association's members saw themselves as reincarnations in a far-flung land of the eponymous Highland rebels in Sir Walter Scott's *Rob Roy*. This was probably most pronounced in the native-born Batman. As many contemporaries noted, such men tended to take the law into their own hands when they felt they had been thwarted.[8]

The Association's treaty-making makes even more sense when it is considered in the broader context of the British Empire and more particularly its practices in North America. As early as the fifteenth century, European powers had concluded treaties with non-Christian peoples; throughout the seventeenth and eighteenth centuries the British had made treaties with indigenous peoples in South and West Asia, North

---

[7] Alex C. Castles, *An Australian Legal History*, Law Book Company, Sydney, 1982, pp. 288–92, and 'The Vandemonian Spirit and the Law', *Tasmanian Historical Research Association Papers and Proceedings*, vol. 83, nos. 3–4, 1991, pp. 106, 108–11, 113–14; Stefan Petrow, 'A Case of Mistaken Identity: The Vandemonian Spirit and the Law', *Tasmanian Historical Studies*, vol. 6, no. 1, 1998, p. 23; Atkinson, *Europeans*, pp. 36, 63, 145.

[8] *Tasmanian*, 15 May 1835; John Helder Wedge, Letterbook, 1824–43, ML, MS A1430, especially Wedge to W. T. Parramore, 25 April 1832, Wedge to Arthur, 23 May 1832 and 28 October 1835, and Wedge to George Frankland, [July 1832] and 30 October 1835; Wedge, Autobiographical Sketch, 1837, ML, MS A576; Batman to Major Grey, 15 June 1829, and Batman to Thomas Anstey, 12 April 1830, TSA, CSO 1/321/7578; correspondence by Batman, TSA, CSO 1/327/7578; Arthur to Bourke, 25 March and 20 May 1836, *HRV*, vol. 1, pp. 25, 28; P. C. James, 'Joseph Tice Gellibrand', *Australian Dictionary of Biography*, vol. 1, 1966, pp. 437–38; Shaw, *History*, pp. 96–98; Atkinson, *Europeans*, pp. 9, 22, 57.

Africa and North America; and during much of the nineteenth century they continued to treat with indigenous peoples in North America, Africa and the Pacific. Indeed, there were hundreds of such treaties.

The men of the Port Phillip Association must also have hoped that their venture might be granted a similar status to that bestowed upon North American adventurers. Between 1606 and 1681 the British government had granted numerous territorial charters and grants to proprietary companies and corporations, which allowed them to establish colonies in Virginia, Massachusetts, Pennsylvania and Georgia. In most of these cases, the Crown delegated governing authority and colonising responsibilities of one kind or another. This meant that the forms of colonial authority were commercial and proprietorial in nature rather than national, and it was often unclear where the authority of the imperial government ended and that of colonial authorities began. (Would-be colonisers in the Australasian colonies were familiar with the nature of these charters and grants.) Moreover, in the 1820s joint stock companies were planned to promote investment in several Australian colonies. These ventures were almost considered to be new colonies, and their promoters certainly hoped to create settlements in which the government's authority and power were limited and commercial opportunities unfettered. Among those ventures that succeeded was that of the Van Diemen's Land Company, which had secured a grant of half a million acres from the Crown. Most recently, the British government had granted a charter to the South Australian Colonisation Commission that bore some resemblance to the earlier North American charters and had unilaterally altered the boundaries of New South Wales in order to do so. Given all this, it is unremarkable that the men of the Port Phillip Association hoped that they might realise their goal of founding a new colony at Port Phillip.[9]

The Association's proposal to buy land from the native people was probably also influenced by land-grabbing practices in North America. In the decades before the imperial government's famous Royal Proclamation of 1763, direct negotiation for native people's land by settlers was commonplace. By adopting this strategy, speculators tried to secure a prior claim to grants from government. Indeed, such grants

---

[9] James Stirling and Thomas Moodie to Hay, 21 August 1828, *HRA*, series 3, vol. 6, p. 586; *Colonial Times*, 21 July 1835; Mercer to Glenelg, 16 March 1836, *HRV*, vol. 6, p. 105; Timothy J. Shannon, *Indians and Colonists at the Crossroads of Empire: The Albany Congress of 1754*, Cornell University Press, Ithaca, 2000, pp. 61, 64–65; Christopher Tomlins, 'Law's Empire: Chartering English Colonies on the American Mainland in the Seventeenth Century', in Diane Kirkby and Catharine Colebourne (eds.), *Law, History, Colonialism: The Reach of Empire*, Manchester University Press, Manchester, 2001, pp. 34–35, 37; Atkinson, *Europeans*, p. 95.

had been made over many years, some of which included settlements regarding jurisdiction. In more recent times, both before and after the American War of Independence, well-funded speculative land companies made extensive claims that were based on purchases of Indian land or sought to create independent governments in border zones. As John C. Weaver has noted, these frontiers teemed with defiance and deception as adventurers tried to grab as much as they could by hook or by crook. Their pretensions were often truly fabulous, yet they were seldom regarded as aberrant. Many of these schemes involved the leading political figures of the day, such as George Washington, Benjamin Franklin and Thomas Jefferson. They refused to be intimidated by the fact that the territory they sought to possess had already been claimed legally by one government or another. Armed with tenuous legal authority of the kind the Port Phillip Association later sought to clothe itself by making a treaty, these men expended much capital in the hope that their purchases would eventually force governments to validate their claims of possession.[10]

To summarise, the Port Phillip Association's gamble, which had a treaty with the native people at its heart, was not unusual among colonisers in the Anglophone world; indeed, what the historian Francis Jennings once called the 'deed game' was one of the principal means they used to stake out an interest. Realising that their designs for possession could be denied by government, they embraced doctrines of native sovereignty in order to proclaim their right to purchase land directly from native peoples as well as the right of those peoples to sell it to them directly. Indeed, land grabbers had long been among the most ardent champions of native sovereignty. The Port Phillip Association was no exception in this regard. Clearly, the nature of the Aboriginal people's culture did not preclude these settlers from conceiving of the natives as both sovereign and owners of the land and assuming that they could negotiate a treaty with them, contrary to what many Australian historians have long contended.[11]

---

[10] Dorothy V. Jones, *License for Empire: Colonialism by Treaty in Early America*, University of Chicago Press, Chicago, 1982, pp. 113, 115; George R. Lamplugh, *Politics on the Periphery: Factions and Parties in Georgia, 1783–1806*, University of Delaware Press, Newark, 1986, pp. 12, 31, 37, 66, 115, 199; Anthony F. C. Wallace, *Jefferson and the Indians: The Tragic Fate of the First Americans*, Belknap Press of Harvard University Press, Cambridge, MA, 1999, pp. 9–10, 21, 41, 43–44, 47; Shannon, *Indians and Colonists*, pp. 82, 115, 220, 239; John C. Weaver, *The Great Land Rush and the Making of the Modern World, 1650–1900*, McGill-Queen's University Press, Montreal and Kingston, 2003, p. 53.

[11] Francis Jennings, *The Invasion of America: Indians, Colonialism, and the Cant of Conquest*, University of North Carolina Press, Chapel Hill, NC, 1975, chapter 8; Weaver, *Land Rush*, p. 137; Stuart Banner, *How the Indians Lost Their Land: Law and Power on the*

The matter of sovereignty was not the only reason that a treaty figured in the Port Phillip Association's strategy to found a new colony. In the context of attempts to acquire native peoples' land, the most powerful meaning associated with a treaty was peace-making. So it was in this case. The Van Diemonian background of the members of Port Phillip Association played a crucial role in this respect. Indeed, it is difficult to conceive a similar group of men in New South Wales deciding to embark on a major venture in which the making of a treaty with Aboriginal people was a crucial part. Throughout much of the 1820s in Van Diemen's Land, there had been bitter conflict between the British settlers and the Aboriginal landowners. By the time this came to an end in the early 1830s, both government officials and settlers were convinced that the cost exacted by the Aboriginal people's resistance had been too high for everyone involved. This conviction deepened as some settlers gave voice to their memories of 'the black war', prompting others to consider how such a catastrophe could be prevented in the future. Several leading members of Van Diemonian society came to advocate the making of treaties. Subsequently, the Association's treaty-making in Port Phillip was welcomed in Hobart and Launceston. Several years earlier, there had been talk in Van Diemen's Land of making a treaty, but this had been rejected on the basis of a claim that the indigenous people lacked the capacity to be a sovereign power; after the war, many colonial officials and opinion-makers changed their tune in this regard.[12]

On its own, though, it is unlikely that their experience and memory of war would have led the members of the Port Phillip Association to consider making a treaty as a means of trying to ensure that colonisation in Port Phillip followed a peaceful course. By the late 1820s there was growing discussion in Britain and its colonies about the rights of citizens, the nature of Britishness, the morality of colonisation and the status of native peoples. This peaked in the mid-1830s as political changes in Britain, such as the reform of the franchise and the abolition of slavery, created an opportunity for evangelical Christians and liberals to influence government policy. Christian humanitarians became increasingly troubled by the impact of British settlement in the Cape Colony and the Australian colonies. In their eyes, British subjects were oppressing native

Frontier, Belknap Press of Harvard University Press, Cambridge, MA, 2005, pp. 12, 116; John Hirst, *Australian History in 7 Questions*, Black Inc, Melbourne, 2014, pp. 10–13, 15.
[12] *Hobart-Town Courier*, 12 April 1828; Arthur to Sir George Murray, 20 November 1830, *BPP*, 1831, Paper no. 259, Correspondence Concerning Military Operations against the Aboriginal Inhabitants of Van Diemen's Land, p. 60; Aborigines Committee report, 24 October 1831, *BPP*, 1834, Paper no. 617, Papers Relating to Aboriginal Tribes, p. 158; Arthur to Lord Goderich, 7 January 1832, *BPP*, 1834, Paper no. 617, p. 163; *Courier* (Hobart), 26 June 1835; Wedge, Autobiographical Sketch.

peoples by taking their land, killing men, women and children, exploiting their labour and spreading disease when they should have been providing for these people's physical and spiritual needs. As a result, they argued, not only were native peoples suffering; British interests were being jeopardised. As Elizabeth Elbourne has pointed out, these Christian humanitarians sought to address these problems, and so legitimise British colonisation, by promoting an agenda that would transform sinful settlers and non-Christian indigenes into moral beings, assimilate both these peoples into a civilised community and make the British nation live up to its civilising and Christianising responsibilities.[13]

By this time, then, the members of the Port Phillip Association realised that an approach to government that highlighted a concern for native people would have a greater chance of persuading the British government to accede to their claims to land. It was, they hoped, a way of distinguishing themselves from those who were derided as squatters. In its representations to the government, the Association made good use of Saxe Bannister's 1830 book *Humane Policy, or Justice to the Aborigines in New Settlements*. For example, at one point they argued: 'It is *new* to English history to seize distant countries, as has been done in Australia, without at least pretending to compensate the natives'. And, like Saxe Bannister and the British Colonial Secretary Sir George Murray, they claimed that the history of Van Diemen's Land had left an indelible stain on the character of the British government. They asserted, by way of contrast, that their approach to colonising Port Phillip offered a means of protecting Britain's name from reproach.[14]

More particularly, the Association assumed that there was much to be gained from invoking William Penn's legendary treaty of 1683, which had come to be regarded throughout the Anglophone world as the symbol of peaceable possession. In advancing their case, the members of the Association claimed that they were following in Penn's footsteps: '*We* have been guided by the *spirit* which actuated him', Thomas Bannister asserted. And on Batman's return to Van Diemen's Land after claiming to have made the treaty, he was hailed as 'The Tasmanian Penn', and it

---

[13] Elizabeth Elbourne, 'The Sin of the Settler: The 1835–36 Select Committee on Aborigines and Debates over Virtue and Conquest in the Early Nineteenth-Century British White Settler Empire', *Journal of Colonialism and Colonial History*, vol. 4, no. 3, 2003, 10.1353/cch.2004.0003, muse.jhu.edu/journals/journal_of_colonialism_and_colonial_history/v004/4.3elbourne.html.

[14] Thomas Henty and sons to Hay, March 1834, quoted by Marnie Bassett, *The Hentys: An Australian Colonial Tapestry*, Melbourne University Press, Melbourne, 1962, p. 286; Thomas Bannister to Sir Charles Burrell, 27 June 1835–3 July 1835, Port Phillip Association Papers, SLV, MS safe.

was alleged that the treaty deeds were a copy of the form adopted by 'the Great Penn'.[15]

The Association's adoption of a treaty as a means of peaceable possession also owed much to Governor Arthur. In the early 1830s, in the aftermath of the frontier war he had led in Van Diemen's Land, he had felt enormous remorse about the treatment of the Aboriginal people and was deeply troubled by the blot that he feared this had left on his governorship. Over the next few years, in the course of seeking to expand his own realm of influence, Arthur urged his superiors in London to design policies for new colonies that might prevent a repetition of the awful course of death and destruction he had witnessed in Van Diemen's Land. The recommendations Arthur put forward to the Colonial Office often included the making of treaties. He told successive colonial secretaries that he had become convinced that it was vital to make some sort of an agreement with Aboriginal people at the outset of any new colonising venture. In 1832 he advised Lord Goderich of the need to formally negotiate the purchase of the Aboriginal people's land before settlers tried to take possession of it. 'Had this system been early adopted in Van Diemen's Land, many deplorable consequences, I have no doubt, would have been adverted', he remarked. Arthur repeated this advice several months later in a memorandum he addressed to the Colonial Office's Permanent Under-Secretary, R. W. Hay. In order to conciliate the natives, it was essential that the British purchase any land they wanted to occupy. 'It was', he attested, 'a fatal error in the first settlement of Van Diemen's Land, that a treaty was not entered into with the natives, of which savages well comprehend the nature; had they received some compensation for the territory they surrendered, no matter how trifling, and had adequate laws been, from *the very first*, introduced and *enforced*, for their protection, His Majesty's government would have acquired a valuable possession, without the injurious consequences which have followed our occupation, and which must ever remain a stain upon the colonisation of Van Diemen's Land'. At the beginning of 1835 Arthur tried to persuade a recently appointed Colonial Secretary, Thomas Spring Rice, of the benefit of making such an agreement: 'On the first occupation of [this] colony, it was a great oversight that a treaty was not, at that time, made with the natives, and such compensation given to the chiefs, as they would have deemed a fair equivalent for what they surrendered; a mere trifle would have satisfied them, and that feeling of

---

[15] *Cornwall Chronicle*, 13 June 1835; *Tasmanian*, 19 June 1835; Batman to Arthur, 25 June 1835; Bannister to Burrell, 27 June 1835–3 July 1835, his emphases; *Colonial Times*, 28 July 1835.

injustice, which I am persuaded they have always entertained, would have had no existence'. Barely six weeks later, Arthur returned to the subject, telling Spring Rice: 'The great importance of the subject, and my experience of the calamities which so long flowed from the course adopted in this colony as respects the aborigines in the first years of its history, will I hope be my apology for again drawing your attention to the measures that most likely to conciliate the Aborigines of the territory about to be appropriated in Southern Australia'.[16]

Some would argue that it is unremarkable that a colonial governor would recommend treaty-making as a means of forging a peaceful course of relations between British colonisers and native landowners. As we noted earlier, British colonisers in North America had made treaties since the seventeenth century, and the British government often realised during the eighteenth century and into the nineteenth century that it could only secure peace on many frontiers in its empire by making treaties. Closer to home, in the mid-1830s government officials in the Swan River Colony (which later became Western Australia) had proposed treaties with local people after they had made attacks in the settlement so that settlers could secure the property in land that they had acquired from the Crown. As Keith Sorrenson has observed, what can be called a treaty language was generally available to colonisers, ready to be employed whenever they needed to resolve a crisis in relations with native peoples. Yet it is clear that that treaties were not made in every instance, hence my insistence here on recovering the particular historical circumstances that led the Port Phillip Association to make a treaty with Aboriginal people in Port Phillip.[17]

Promoting the Treaty

The Port Phillip Association began to lobby the government in Sydney and London for possession of land at Port Phillip shortly after they claimed to have made the treaty.[18] This campaign lasted several years.

---

[16] Arthur to Horace Twiss, 28 May 1830, TNA, CO 280/24; Arthur to Murray, 20 November 1830, *BPP*, 1831, Paper no. 259, p. 60; Arthur to Goderich, 25 October 1831 and 7 January 1832, *BPP*, 1834, Paper no. 617, pp. 154, 163; Arthur to Hay, 24 September 1832, his emphases; Arthur to Spring Rice, 27 January 1835, TNA, CO 280/55; Arthur to Spring Rice, 10 March 1835, TNA, CO 280/56; A. G. L. Shaw, *Sir George Arthur, Bart, 1784–1854*, Melbourne University Press, Melbourne, 1980, pp. 22–23, 61, 125, 128–29, 132–34.

[17] Jones, *License for Empire*, p. 9; M. P. K. Sorrenson, 'Treaties in British Colonial Policy: Precedents for Waitangi', in William Renwick (ed.), *Sovereignty and Indigenous Rights: The Treaty of Waitangi in International Contexts*, Victoria University Press, Wellington, 1991, p. 17; Hunter, *Different Kind*, pp. 158–60, 167–68.

[18] For a discussion of how the Kulin people might have understood the Treaty and its making, see my book *Possession*, pp. 52–58.

It also cost the Association a considerable amount of money as it sought legal opinions from some of the most reputable English lawyers in the field and engaged several English agents to represent it. The Association focused its lobbying on the imperial government since it assumed that London had greater political authority as well as more power than Sydney. It continued to do this, long after the Governor of New South Wales, Sir Richard Bourke, had refused in September 1835 to grant its claims to land on the basis of the treaty.

In the manner of all colonial adventurers, the Association tried to present the best possible face it could, using misinformation, exaggeration, deception and downright lies to accomplish its principal goal. In pressing its case, it frequently invoked the treaty. Yet the Association was always careful to do this in such a way that it did not make any explicit claims to having a legal right to the land that it claimed to have purchased, preferring simply to infer that it had such a right. The Association primarily couched its case in moral terms. In this register, it made several arguments, but most of them were expressed in terms of a humanitarian rhetoric of protection, in order to appeal to senior members of the Colonial Office who were Christian humanitarians. As we will see in later chapters in this book, the colonisation companies that sought to persuade the British government to allow them to colonise South Australia and New Zealand adopted the very same tactics. From the outset, the Association declared that its venture sought to combine two important objects, namely peaceful colonisation and the civilisation of the aborigines; it insisted that it had obtained the land on equitable terms; it emphasised its benevolence towards the Aboriginal people by presenting evidence of its plans to employ a catechist to spread the word of God, engage a doctor to administer to the sick, provide food and clothing, and employ only married men accompanied by their families; and it stressed the dangers of its treaty being abrogated, namely that this would deny the natives the tribute that it had promised them in perpetuity and deprive them of their country without compensation and that this would induce a sense of wrong that would lead to war. Later, the Association advanced another ground to support its claims, namely that it had improved the land at Port Phillip through its investment of capital and labour. In coming years this was one of the arguments that pastoralists in New South Wales used in a tussle with the colonial government over title to land. The Port Phillip Association, however, was unable to persuade the government at either the imperial centre or the colonial periphery to grant it any major concessions.[19]

---

[19] Members of the Port Phillip Association to Spring Rice, 27 June 1835, TNA, CO 201/
293; Mercer memo, [January 1836], enclosed with Mercer to Glenelg, 6 April 1836,

Why was the Association's venture to acquire possession of a vast tract of the indigenous people's land in Port Phillip so unsuccessful? At much the same time that the Association failed to realise its objectives, another company, the South Australian Association, succeeded in its bid to persuade the British parliament to allow it to establish a colony. How might we explain this difference? Status and location are part of the answer. The men of the South Australia Association were no mere colonials residing at the periphery of the British Empire but members of parliament, philanthropists, clergymen, merchants and company directors who lived at the metropolitan centre. They were also well connected politically. This helped to blunt the opposition that Christian humanitarians might have been presented to their undertaking, even though many of the men of the South Australian Association were no more committed to respecting Aboriginal interests than were the members of the Port Phillip Association, indeed probably less so. Furthermore, while all colonising companies at this time were dogged by the fact that many saw them as mere speculators, the South Australian Association could make a greater claim to being in the mould of systematic colonisers. It was also able to give the appearance of being a government in embryo, especially once the Association was more or less reconfigured as the South Australian Colonisation Commission, whereas the Port Phillip Association struggled to represent itself as being anything more than a group of opportunistic adventurers.

Repudiating the Treaty

In both Van Diemen's Land and New South Wales, Batman's treaty seems to have attracted considerable attention. It certainly provoked a great deal of concern among other Van Diemonian settlers wishing to acquire land in Port Phillip. Although some of these settlers welcomed the treaty as a means of preventing a repetition of the murder and mayhem of the war that they had experienced in Van Diemen's Land, most were fearful that the government might grant the Port Phillip Association land as a result of its gamble and angry that they might lose out in the rush to acquire it. Once news of the treaty became known, it was the subject of much joking in the columns of the colonial newspapers. Joking can be a serious business. In this case it came in that form of tendentious humour which often seeks to

HRA, series 1, vol. 18, p. 389; Mercer to Glenelg, 26 January and 23 April 1836, TNA, CO 201/258; Mercer to Glenelg, 16 March 1836, *HRV*, vol. 6, p. 104; Swanston, Gellibrand and Simpson to Bourke, 26 September 1836, TNA, CO 201/293.

discharge anxiety. Comic fictional stories tried to emphasise what was deemed to be the absurd nature of the treaty-making. They played on a claim that the Aboriginal headman could have had no clue about the true nature of the deal; on the discrepancy between how much the Association gave for the land and how much it was really worth; and on the fact that the headmen were treated as if they were sovereign even though it was held that they could have no such authority.[20]

In time, the outcome of the Association's treaty-making, in the sense of whether its claims to possession of the land would succeed, became the subject of serious-minded debate, and this was by no means stilled by the New South Wales government's repudiation of the treaty. Commentators could call the Association's treaty a farce and deride its claims as mere pretence, but they were actually unsure about the law of the land and thus uncertain about what might transpire. In March 1836, referring to Batman's treaty, the *Sydney Gazette* remarked: 'A weighty and a curious question will in all likelihood be at issue shortly, betwixt the subject and the crown, in respect of what constitutes a *title* to certain tracts of waste land not many hundred miles from hence'.[21]

The consideration given the treaty by newspapers such as the *Sydney Gazette* suggests that many settlers were confused about the grounds of the British Crown's claim of possession. 'Titles to land have been hitherto derived from one of other of these sources – either from right by immemorial possession or purchase – [or] by prescription or conquest', this newspaper argued in one of its editorials. The last two, it claimed, were the basis of most European titles, and so it was sceptical that the Port Phillip Association's claims on the first two grounds could succeed. The British government had taken possession of the entire country many years ago and its claim had never been abandoned by the Crown, the *Sydney Gazette* contended. But above all, it continued, the British government had what it called the 'right of superior force' and hence it could lawfully eject the Port Phillip settlers as trespassers.[22]

Several weeks after the colonial government got wind of the Association's treaty-making, Governor Bourke repudiated the treaty. '[E]very such treaty, bargain and contract with the aboriginal natives as foresaid, for the possession, title or claim to any lands, lying and being within the limits of the government of the colony of New South Wales', he declared in a proclamation, 'is void and of no effect against the rights of the Crown; and that all persons, who shall be found in possession of any

[20] *Cornwall Chronicle*, 13 and 20 June 1835; *Courier*, 26 June 1835.
[21] *Launceston Advertiser*, 10 March 1836; *Sydney Gazette*, 17 March 1836, its emphasis.
[22] *Ibid.*

such lands as aforesaid, will be considered as trespassers, and liable to dealt with in like manner as other intruders upon the Crown land within the said colony'.[23]

The treaty, it has been argued recently by Lisa Ford, shook the foundations of the British Empire in the Australian colonies since it raised fundamental questions about the Crown's authority. Certainly, the Association's claim to have purchased land from Aboriginal people in Port Phillip forced the colonial government to articulate the relationship of British sovereignty to the territory that Britain had originally claimed. Yet it appears that the Governor of New South Wales actually welcomed the opportunity to do this. The Association's treaty-making occurred at the very time that it was seeking to formulate a new conception of its authority that defined its sovereignty much more in territorial terms than had previously been the case. A year earlier, Bourke had recommended to the Colonial Office that the imperial government reverse its policy of prohibiting colonisation of lands beyond the limits of settlement in New South Wales, but his advice had been rejected. Now, the Association's treaty-making provided him with a chance to renew his case. Bourke marshalled his considerable rhetorical resources to create a story about a supposedly unbearable dilemma facing the British Crown. It went like this. The colony of New South Wales was peculiar since the basis of its wealth lay in wool; however, the poor quality of the land meant sheep and their owners had to range over it very widely; it was not only impolitic but impossible to prevent this happening; the only means to resolve this problem lay in allowing settlers to move beyond the prescribed boundaries of settlement to take up land and placing these new settlements under the government's authority. In other words, Bourke argued that the solution to the so-called crisis that the Association's treaty-making had provoked in regard to the Crown's authority lay in the government of New South Wales being allowed to extend its jurisdiction over all the colony's territory.[24]

In short, while the Association's attempt to grab land undoubtedly meant the government had to act, Bourke's administration chose to accentuate the threat posed by the treaty so that it had a pretext for consolidating its newly minted conception of the Crown's authority in New South Wales. To this end, it insisted that the Association's treaty-making was premised on a claim that Aboriginal communities were

---

[23] *New South Wales Government Gazette*, 9 September 1835.
[24] Bourke to Lord Stanley, 4 July 1834, TNA, CO 201/39; Bourke to Glenelg, 10 October 1835, TNA, CO 201/47; Lisa Ford, *Settler Sovereignty: Jurisdiction and Indigenous People in America and Australia, 1788–1836*, Harvard University Press, Cambridge, MA, 2010, p. 179.

sovereign polities; that the Association had disregarded the colonial government's authority by ignoring its prohibition on settlements beyond prescribed limits of location; that it had implied that it could create a colony that would be an *imperium et imperio*; and that it had suggested that the Crown was not in legal possession of the land. Indeed, the government claimed that the Association's treaty-making represented a flagrant infringement upon its sovereignty and so had to be rejected in the most forthright terms.[25]

In July 1835 Bourke called upon Francis Forbes, the Chief Justice of New South Wales, to provide him with advice as to how he might best deal with the Association's land-grabbing. He was told that all the lands in the territory described as New South Wales lay within the jurisdiction of the colonial government and were part of the Crown's disposable lands and that much trouble would ensue if his government was seen to tacitly acknowledge the right of the Aboriginal people to sell and settlers to buy any of this land. Forbes suggested to Bourke that the Association's treaty could be 'a good peg upon which to suspend a proclamation, defining the true limits of the Colony, within your commission as Governor, declaring that all settlements made on any land within such limits, without the previous sanction of the local government [are] illegal'. It is hardly surprising that Forbes gave Bourke this advice, given the position he had taken in the New South Wales Supreme Court in recent years. In a case heard in 1827 Forbes asserted that British sovereignty rested on the 1823 act of parliament that had established that court and its jurisdiction. There was no need to ponder whether this was right or not, he argued. 'It is sufficient for us to say that the territory is recognised as the colony of New South Wales', he told the Court. 'This is a judicial fact which comes within our knowledge; and beyond that we cannot go.' Forbes also argued that the Crown's jurisdiction in the colony extended as far as the territory it had claimed. In a case prosecuted in 1834 Forbes elaborated on the first of these two contentions. 'It is a matter of history that New South Wales was taken possession of, in the name of the King of Great Britain, about fifty-five years ago', he claimed. 'The right of the soil, and of all lands in the colony, became vested immediately upon its settlement, in his Majesty, in right of his crown, and as the representative of the British nation.' In inventing this history, Forbes had projected a new conception of sovereignty back to the beginnings of New South Wales, making it seem as though British jurisdiction had always been applied to the

---

[25] Bourke to Glenelg, 10 October 1835.

territory of the colony rather than to its subjects alone and that the Crown had always held the right of possession to all its lands.[26]

Not surprisingly, Bourke welcomed the advice Forbes gave him. This was all the more the case because during his term as acting governor of the Cape Colony he had faced a similar problem to the one the Port Phillip Association was now posing. Consequently, he was alert to the fact that settlers could try to convert their possession of Crown land into a form of title that would deprive the government of its right of possession. He was determined that this would not happen again under his watch. Bourke knew that the Association had called for recognition of its treaty on the basis of the allegedly benevolent nature of its venture, rather than any title to the land it might be presumed to convey to it, but he nonetheless recognised that this could be the thin end of the wedge and hence a threat to the authority of the Crown.[27]

The British government's repudiation of the treaty put paid to any recognition of native sovereignty and rights of property in land that the Association's treaty implied, even though it never addressed the latter in the course of its consideration of the treaty-making. How can we account for the government's response? Henry Reynolds has argued that Colonial Office repudiated the Association's treaty not on the grounds that Aboriginal people had no title and hence no right to sell the land but on the basis that the Association had no right to buy the land from anyone but the Crown. In his opinion, both the imperial and the colonial governments were simply acting in accordance with a legal doctrine called 'pre-emption', which bestowed on the Crown alone the right to buy the land of native people and which had informed practice in North America since the seventeenth century. Further, Reynolds has contended that the Colonial Office actually reiterated its support for the principle of Aboriginal rights to land in the course of considering the treaty.[28]

In regard to the first of Reynolds' contentions, it is undoubtedly true that Colonial Office chose to explain its repudiation of the treaty by reference to the Crown's right of pre-emption. It invoked the legal opinion that had been provided to the Port Phillip Association by leading English lawyers William Burge and his associates Thomas Pemberton and W. W. Follett.

---

[26] *R v Lowe*, www.law.mq.edu.au/research/colonial_case_law/nsw/cases/case_index/1827/ r_v_lowe/; *R v Steele*, www.law.mq.edu.au/research/colonial_case_law/nsw/cases/case_in dex/1834/r_v_steele/; Francis Forbes to Bourke, 26 July [1835], reproduced in J. M. Bennett (ed.), *Some Papers of Sir Francis Forbes*, Parliament of New South Wales, Sydney, 1998, p. 234.

[27] Peter Burroughs, *Britain and Australia 1831–1855: A Study in Imperial Relations and Crown Lands Administration*, Clarendon Press, Oxford, 1967, p. 147.

[28] Henry Reynolds, *The Law of the Land*, 2nd ed., Penguin, Melbourne, 1992, pp. 125–32.

They stated that the grants of land the Association had allegedly attained by dint of the treaty were null and void against the government since the right to grant land was vested in the Crown. They claimed that this forbade any settler from acquiring title by purchasing land from indigenous peoples without the government's consent. However, the Colonial Office adopted this position rather belatedly and primarily because it was strategically useful.[29]

In fact, the imperial and the colonial governments preferred to sidestep the matter of native title. This was evident from the beginning of their consideration of the treaty. For example, Spring Rice's successor as Colonial Secretary, Lord Glenelg, wrote to Governor Arthur in January 1836 to say that, rather than entering into a consideration of the question of legal principle concerning the rights possessed by the Aboriginal people, the government would focus on the practical question of whether it was *expedient* to confirm the grant of land that the treaty with the Aboriginal people had purportedly bestowed upon the Association. Likewise, Glenelg informed Bourke a few months later that he thought it was unnecessary to enter into any discussion of the principles that formed the basis upon which the disposal of lands was determined in the Australian colonies. The Colonial Office's position can probably be attributed to what Mark Hickford has called 'satisficing': this short-staffed government department, accommodated in a pair of cramped and crumbling houses at 13 and 14 Downing Street, and working under considerable pressure from the likes of colonising companies and conscientious Christians, tended to adopt courses of action that would satisfy the particular needs of any situation that it had to deal with. Yet the Colonial Office might have also chosen to put the matter of native title aside because contemplating the theft of another people's land was deeply unsettling for its senior members, who were deeply attached to Christian moral principles. Certainly, the Association's treaty was a source of embarrassment since it drew attention to the proposition that the country was the Aboriginal people's and so it cast doubt on the entire basis of the British Crown's title in land. Indeed, recognition of the treaty's terms would have been tantamount to admitting that the British claim to all the land in the Australian colonies had no moral basis. For these reasons it was best to avoid the issue altogether.[30]

---

[29] Opinion of William Burge, 16 January 1836, Opinions of Thomas Pemberton and W. W. Follett, 21 January 1836, TNA, CO 201/258; Glenelg to Bourke, 13 April 1836, TNA, CO 201/47.

[30] Glenelg to Arthur, 23 January 1836, *BPP*, 1836, Paper no. 512, p. 230; Glenelg to Bourke, 13 April 1836; Mark Hickford, 'Making "Territorial Rights of the Natives":

As for Reynolds' second contention, there seems little reason to conclude that the Colonial Office sought to uphold the Aboriginal people's rights of property in land in any real sense, however sympathetic its leading figures were in principle to protecting aboriginal peoples. Indeed, it is apparent that they saw no point in trying to do this, in fact quite to the contrary, because they believed that the Aboriginal people lacked the power that was required in order to uphold their interests in land. This belief is evident in the Colonial Office's discussion of the Association's treaty. When it repudiated the treaty in April 1836, Glenelg informed Bourke that the rights of Aboriginal people should be protected but that recognising them as sovereign polities and thus having the right to dispose of their land to those such as the adventurers of the Port Phillip Association would not be in their best interests. '[T]heir rights should be studiously defended', he observed, 'yet [I] believe that we should consult ill for the real welfare of that helpless and unfortunate race by recognising in them any right to alienate to private adventurers the land of the colony'.[31]

It is also apparent that the government's treatment of the question of the native people's rights in land that was thrown up by Batman's treaty was influenced by a factor discussed in the previous chapter. As we saw, the British Crown assumed sovereignty and asserted its authority at the outset of colonisation in New South Wales. This enabled it to determine the terms upon which the native people's land was claimed, free of any of the impediments that could arise in situations in which a government's confirmation of its preliminary claim of possession had been preceded by independent sojourners or settlers who had chosen to acquire land from the natives. This is an example of what historians like Stuart Banner have called 'path dependency', that is, once certain factors are in place, what follows continues along the trajectory that they have established. By the time that the Port Phillip Association had transacted its treaty in Port Phillip, the British government had granted title to land in all its Australian colonies as though the Crown was the only source of title. Given this, it is unremarkable that Glenelg told Bourke: 'It is indeed enough to observe that such a concession [i.e. allowing that the Aboriginal people had the right to sell land to adventurers such as the Port Phillip Association] would subvert the foundation on which all proprietary rights in New South Wales at present rest'. Hypothetically, the government could have overturned this property regime by returning

Britain and New Zealand, 1830–1847', DPhil thesis, University of Oxford, 1999, pp. 17, 103–04, 106, 160, 196, 229.
[31] Glenelg to Bourke, 13 April 1836.

Crown land to the Aboriginal people, making treaties in which it negotiated the right to purchase land and upholding its authority vis-à-vis the
settlers by insisting on its right to control any land purchasing. This would
have been relatively straightforward legally, but it would have been more
difficult politically, as the government would have had to overcome
opposition from settlers. There would also have been an economic cost
since the government would have had to buy the Aboriginal people's land
it had been granting to settlers. However, there were no forces compelling
the government to adopt this course of action. Most importantly, the
pastoralists had no interest in such a change – indeed, on the contrary,
since the source of their title or claims to land was the British Crown – and
the Aboriginal people lacked the necessary power to force the government
to make it.[32]

It might also be argued that the Port Phillip Association's failure to
make its treaty stick was partly the result of *timing*. If it had tried to
purchase land in New Zealand at this time, that is prior to the British
Crown assuming sovereignty there (and some of its principals did consider doing this), it would have stood some chance of securing title. As we
will see, the fact that New Zealand's native peoples were deemed by the
British government to have some rights of property in land was largely
a consequence of the same kind of land-grabbing tactics that were used by
the Port Phillip Association in Port Phillip Bay, but only because that
purchasing occurred *before* the Crown assumed sovereignty in the islands
of New Zealand.

Conclusion

By considering Batman's treaty we are able to put to rest the myth that
British players never seriously considered treating with Aboriginal people
for land and that the treatment of sovereignty and rights of property in
land in Britain's Australian and New Zealand colonies was like chalk and
cheese. As we have seen, the principal figures of the Port Phillip
Association acted in the same manner as many similar groups in the
British Empire, making an agreement with native people to purchase
their land (as they understood it) and physically taking possession of
territory in the hope that they could force government to concede its
claim. As we will see, the principal figures of a British colonisation
company would do the same in New Zealand and succeed.

---

[32] *Ibid.*; Gellibrand to Swanston, 14 July 1836, Port Phillip Association Papers, SLV, MS
11230; Weaver, *Land Rush*, p. 139; Stuart Banner, *Possessing the Pacific: Land, Settlers and
Indigenous People from Australia to Alaska*, Harvard University Press, Cambridge, MA,
2007, pp. 5, 43–46, 318.

By the same token – though this will only become really clear when we consider New Zealand – the Port Phillip Association's signal failure to make its treaty stick helps us to understand why in the Australian case the British government never acted in ways that would have seen it recognising the Aboriginal people's sovereignty and rights in land. By the mid-1830s, the British Crown had been granting land to settlers for nearly fifty years as though it was the only source of title. Theoretically speaking, the government could have overturned this arrangement. But the settlers, who were beginning to exert considerable power in New South Wales as pastoral occupation of native lands became the basis of the colony's economy, primarily rested their claim to title on the basis of the Crown's claim to being the only sovereign in the land.[33] They had no material interest in any claim that Aboriginal people were the real owners of the land. Indeed, they had no truck with such a claim as it threatened to undermine the legitimacy of their claims to title. In the eyes of the government, the Aboriginal people lacked the military power that was required to bring into being, let alone uphold, a property regime that recognised the native people's rights in land. Consequently, the native title that the Port Phillip Association had tentatively sought to assert by forging a treaty with Aboriginal people at Port Phillip was quickly unmade.

---

[33] For further discussion of this point, see my article 'Rights, Duties, Colonisation and Aboriginal People in New South Wales', *Australian Journal of Politics and History*, vol. 66, no. 4, 2020 forthcoming.

3 The South Australian Colonisation Commission, the Colonial Office and Aboriginal Rights in Land, 1834–1837

In this chapter we turn our attention to the Australian colony of South Australia. At the point it was founded in the mid-1830s there was a serious attempt on the part of the British government to treat native interests in land differently to the way it had treated them in New South Wales, or so several historians have contended. This argument raises the question of whether the point in time a colony was established had a substantial impact on the manner in which the British government dealt with native rights in land. It has been argued, for example, that South Australia was different to the other Australian colonies because of the influence that Christian humanitarians wielded at that moment.[1]

The way in which the apparent difference in South Australia's case has been explained by several historians is typical of the manner in which the British government's treatment of native title has been approached by an influential mode of history known as *juridical history*. This has been defined as history that seeks to construct an account of the past in order to enable a legal tribunal to redress the wrongs of the past in the present. It is a highly problematic way of representing the past, historically speaking.[2] In a classic example, *The Law of the Land*, Henry Reynolds has argued as follows. In the early to mid-1830s, evangelical abolitionists (or those he calls 'humanitarians'), having brought their crusade against slavery to a successful conclusion, turned their attention to the suffering of native people in the

---

[1] Most importantly, Henry Reynolds, *The Law of the Land*, Penguin, Melbourne, 1987, chapters 3 and 4.

[2] For critical accounts of juridical history in the Australian and New Zealand contexts, see Andrew Sharp, 'History and Sovereignty: A Case of Juridical History in New Zealand/ Aotearoa', in Michael Peters (ed.), *Cultural Politics and the University in Aotearoa/New Zealand*, Dunmore Press, Palmerston North, 1997, pp. 159–81; W. H. Oliver, 'The Future Behind Us: The Waitangi Tribunal's Retrospective Utopia', in Andrew Sharp and Paul McHugh (eds.), *Histories, Power and Loss: Uses of the Past – A New Zealand Commentary*, Bridget Williams Books, Wellington, 2001, pp. 9–29; and my '*The Law of the Land* or the Law of the Land?: History, Law and Narrative in a Settler Society', *History Compass*, vol. 2, no. 1, 2004, pp. 1–30. See also Ian Hunter, 'Natural Law, Historiography, and Aboriginal Sovereignty', *Legal History*, vol. 11, no. 2, 2007, pp. 137–67.

British Empire. Led by Thomas Fowell Buxton, the political heir of the great William Wilberforce, they became advocates for Aboriginal rights, most importantly rights of property in land. These humanitarians became very influential in official circles after the Whigs came to power in 1835 and the Colonial Office fell under the control of Lord Glenelg and Sir George Grey, respectively the Colonial Secretary and the Parliamentary Under-Secretary for the Colonies, and James Stephen, the Assistant Under-Secretary and soon to be its Permanent Under-Secretary. These men not only shared a deep moral commitment to upholding Aboriginal interests in land but were guided by well-understood legal principles regarding native title. This led them to abandon the fiction of *terra nullius* by which the British government had allegedly claimed the Australian continent in 1788, to declare that Aboriginal people actually had proprietorial rights in land and to define the precise nature of those rights. To be more specific, Glenelg insisted that the South Australian Colonisation Commission – which comprised members of a company that had promoted the founding of the colony, though it was appointed by the Colonial Office – formally recognise those rights, even making this a condition of his sanctioning the commencement of settlement. Much of the historical research conducted since the publication of *The Law of the Land* has accepted this argument of Reynolds,[3] and his account of these events continues to hold sway in the broader public realm in Australia.[4]

---

[3] There have been some notable exceptions. See, for example, David Philips, 'Evangelicals, Aborigines and "Land Rights": A Critique of Henry Reynolds on the *Select Committee on Aborigines*', *Australian Studies*, vol. 17, no. 1, 2002, pp. 147–66. See also Hannah Robert, *Paved with Good Intentions: Terra Nullius, Aboriginal Land Rights and Settler-Colonial Law*, Halstead Press, Canberra, 2016.

[4] Reynolds, *Law*, chapters 3–5. Reynolds reiterated this argument in 'South Australia: Between Van Diemen's Land and New Zealand', in Robert Foster and Paul Sendziuk (eds.), *Turning Points: Chapters in South Australian History*, Wakefield Press, Adelaide, 2012, pp. 24–32. For the influence of Reynolds' argument, see Robert Foster, 'An Imaginary Dominion: The Representation and Treatment of Aborigines in South Australia, 1834–1911', PhD thesis, University of Adelaide, 1993, chapter 1, and more especially Stuart Banner, *Possessing the Pacific: Land, Settlers and Indigenous People from Australia to Alaska*, Harvard University Press, Cambridge, MA, 2007, p.35; Ann Hunter, *A Different Kind of 'Subject': Colonial Law in Aboriginal-European Relations in Nineteenth Century Western Australia 1829–61*, Australian Scholarly Publishing, Melbourne, 2011, p. 164; Ann Curthoys and Jessie Mitchell, *Taking Liberty: Indigenous Rights and Settler Self-Government in Colonial Australia, 1830–1890*, Cambridge University Press, Cambridge, 2018, p. 61; Paul Sendziuk and Robert Foster, *A History of South Australia*, Cambridge University Press, Cambridge, 2018, pp. 15, 27–28; and Amanda Nettelbeck, *Indigenous Rights and Colonial Subjecthood: Protection and Reform in the Nineteenth-Century British Empire*, Cambridge University Press, Cambridge, 2019, pp. 47, 91–92. For evidence of the influence that Reynolds' argument continues to have in the public realm, see, for example, National Gallery of Victoria Australia, Introductory label for *The Province of South Australia 1836*, in its 2018 exhibition *Colony: Australia 1770–1861*.

By employing a different methodology to investigate the South Australian example – one that is more in keeping with the protocols of the discipline of history – we arrive at a very different account of how native rights in land were treated in this case. In what follows I seek to recover and understand the matters that the principal players were attempting to address and resolve, and the means they used to perform this work.[5]

The Planning of a New Colony

In the early 1830s a group of men in London, eager to test the principles of systematic colonisation, started to make plans to create a new colony in the southern part of the Australian continent. The members of a body known as the National Colonisation Society, led by Robert Torrens and Robert Gouger, drew up a series of proposals and presented them to the Colonial Office, where they received some encouragement from the Parliamentary Under-Secretary Lord Howick. They largely followed the political economist Edward Gibbon Wakefield's theories of colonial reform. This meant that they emphasised orderly colonisation as a means of creating a prosperous and improved Britain in the antipodes. More precisely, their plans centred upon a colonisation company controlling land sales in the colony and determining the level of emigration. Advocates of systematic colonisation believed that these measures would ensure a better balance between capital and labour, foster concentration of settlement, nurture stable institutions in which respectable free subjects would flourish and avoid the moral disorder that occurred on dispersed frontiers. To give effect to these principles, the planners insisted that the authority of the Crown to distribute land be fettered. Indeed, they sought to minimise the Crown's prerogative powers in the new colony they were proposing.[6]

In a plan that Torrens and Gouger put to the Colonial Office in the name of the South Australian Land Company in July 1832 they demanded the

---

[5] This chapter draws on my article 'Returning to the Past: The South Australian Colonisation Commission, the Colonial Office and Aboriginal Title', *Journal of Legal History*, vol. 34, no. 1, 2013, pp. 50–82.

[6] Robert Torrens et al., Memorial, 25 August 1831, TNA, CO 13/1; Torrens and Anthony Bacon, Proposal for a Colony, 15 December 1831, TNA, CO 13/1; William Whitmore, Proposal for a Colony, 26 May 1832, TNA, CO 13/1; Whitmore to Lord Goderich, 18 June 1832, TNA, CO 13/1; Douglas Pike, *Paradise of Dissent: South Australia 1829–1857*, Longmans, Green and Co, London, 1957, pp. 55, 57; Damen Ward, 'The Politics of Jurisdiction: "British" Law, Indigenous Peoples and Colonial Government in Australia and New Zealand, c. 1834–60', DPhil thesis, University of Oxford, 2003, pp. 59–60.

right to govern the colony. In fact, they sought a charter on the same basis as those charters granted to the companies that had created colonies in North America in the seventeenth century. The Colonial Office refused to sanction this request on the grounds that it was contrary to the public interest, but these self-styled 'colonial reformers' were undeterred. In November 1833 they formed a new body, the South Australian Association, to lobby the government further. One of its directors was Charles Buller, who was to play a prominent role in New Zealand's affairs some years later. To shake off the perception that they were merely speculators, the Association sought to recruit backers among liberal intellectuals and religious enthusiasts. One of the most notable to join their cause was George Fife Angas, a merchant and banker who was a fervent dissenter and a generous philanthropist. Yet the Association also won the support of parliamentarians such as Sir William Molesworth and forged links with John Shaw-Lefevre, the Parliamentary Under-Secretary for the Colonies during much of 1833–34, who kept it informed of the Colonial Office's views about the Association's plans and suggested how it might advance them.[7]

In the past, new British colonies had all been created solely by the action of the executive arm of government. However, the promoters of this venture were determined to establish the colony by a statute of parliament rather than a prerogative instrument of the Crown, in good part because they wanted to weaken the powers the imperial government could exercise in the colony. Most importantly, they not only wished to assume control over the management of land but to take public appointments out of the hands of government and deny it any power to raise revenues. At the Colonial Office, James Stephen was deeply troubled by the bill the South Australian Association drew up along these lines. In a lengthy memorandum he prepared in July 1834, Stephen emphasised the risks involved in the Association's remarkable encroachments on the Crown's prerogatives (though he made no reference whatsoever to the impact that the bill's previsions could have upon the Aboriginal people). Yet the Colonial Secretary Thomas Spring Rice, who would later admit that he had been guilty of negligence during his term in office, agreed to recommend the bill to the consideration of parliament, where it soon

---

[7] Torrens to Goderich, 9 July 1832, TNA, CO 13/1; Draft Charter, TNA, CO 13/1; James Stephen, Memorandum, 14 July 1832, TNA, CO 13/1; Robert Gouger to John George Shaw-Lefevre, 18 March 1834, TNA, CO 13/2; Shaw-Lefevre to George Grote, 15 April 1834, TNA, CO 13/2; Anon, 'George Fife Angas', *Australian Dictionary of Biography*, vol. 1, 1966, pp. 15–18; Peter Burroughs, 'Sir William Molesworth', *Oxford Dictionary of National Biography*, Oxford, 2004, www.oxforddnb.com.ezproxy.lib.monash.edu.au/view/article/189 02?docPos=1; Ward, 'Politics of Jurisdiction', pp. 61–62.

passed. The Act created a system of dual or divided control for the colony: the South Australian Colonisation Commission, which basically comprised the South Australian Association, would manage such matters as the sale of land and the recruitment of emigrants, and the colonial government would be responsible for day-to-day administration.[8]

A few weeks before the South Australia Colonisation Bill was debated in the British parliament in July and August 1834, Thomas Fowell Buxton briefly addressed the House of Commons on the subject of native tribes in the British Empire. As Reynolds has rightly observed, Buxton was the lynchpin of a Christian humanitarian network that had recently turned its attention to the plight of native peoples. Yet Reynolds has almost certainly erred in casting Buxton as a champion of native people's rights in land and more especially in arguing that his fellow humanitarians in the Colonial Office sought to uphold those rights by invoking particular legal doctrines regarding property in land. To be sure, Glenelg was the son of a leading Christian humanitarian who was a prominent supporter of the campaign to abolish the slave trade and a founder of both the Church Missionary Society and the British and Foreign Bible Society and he himself had studied at an evangelical stronghold, Magdalen College at Cambridge University. Grey's parents were pious evangelicals and his mother was a friend of the anti-slavery leader William Wilberforce, and he himself was deeply religious throughout his life. Stephen, soon to be the Colonial Office's Permanent Under-Secretary, had been brought up in the midst of a family that had played a major role in the movement against slavery, was married to a daughter of a clergyman who was a leading member of the evangelical Clapham Sect and one of the founders of the Church Missionary Society, and had played a major role in drafting the legislation that had brought about the abolition of slavery in the British Empire. All of these men were members of the Church Missionary Society. But they were also dedicated to the practical tasks of government in the service of empire. Moreover, as my account has already begun to suggest, the Colonial Office did not control the flow of events in Britain's colonies but drifted uncertainly with them instead.[9]

---

[8] Stephen to Shaw-Lefevre, 4 July 1834, TNA, CO 13/2; *Mirror of Parliament*, vol. IV, London, 1834, p. 2926; Stephen to R. W. Hay, 14 February 1835, TNA, CO 13/1; *Act 4 and 5 William IV, Cap. 95*; *Morning Post*, 19 July 1849; P. A. Howell, 'The South Australia Act, 1834', in Dean Jaensch (ed.), *The Flinders History of South Australia*, vol. 2, Wakefield Press, Adelaide, 1986, pp. 31, 39–40.

[9] Reynolds, *Law*, pp. 82–86, 97–102; John W. Cell, *British Colonial Administration in the Mid-Nineteenth Century: The Policy-Making Process*, Yale University Press, New Haven, CT, 1970, pp. xii, 24.

At the conclusion of his speech to the House of Commons in July 1834, Buxton moved a motion that the House present an address to the King to the effect that it was 'deeply impressed with the duty of acting upon the principles of justice and humanity in the intercourse and relations of this country with the native inhabitants of its colonial settlements, of affording them protection in the enjoyment of their civil rights, and of imparting to them that degree of civilisation and that religion with which Providence has blessed this nation'. He urged the King to 'take such measures, and give such directions to the governors and officers of His Majesty's colonies, settlements, and plantations, as [would] secure to the natives the due observance of justice and the protection of their rights, promote the spread of civilisation amongst them, and lead them to peaceful and voluntary reception of the Christian religion'. Reynolds has attributed enormous significance to Buxton's reference to rights in this motion. However, it seems clear that Buxton was primarily insisting that the British nation had a *duty* to employ its power in its colonies in such a way as to *protect* the interests of native peoples and to ensure the spread of both civilisation and Christianity among them. Perhaps this is unremarkable. At this time, those responsible for imperial policy placed great emphasis on the moral duties of the British state and people. Any such notion of the rights of native peoples tended to be merely derivative of those duties. In any case, Buxton was seeking to ensure that native people's *civil* rights, rather than their rights of property in land, were protected by the government.[10]

Yet there can be no doubt that Buxton and his fellow Christian humanitarians exerted some influence upon the Colonial Office, to say nothing of public discourse. In August 1834 Spring Rice directed the attention of the governors of the Australian colonies to the principles contained in Buxton's Address to the King. In the same month, some of the leading members of the South Australia Association founded the South Australia Literary Association, which proceeded to stage a couple of lectures on the subject of Aborigines. In one of those lectures the speaker expressed the hope that Britain would 'succeed in raising the natives from their present savage and wretched condition to one of civilisation and comfort'. In the case of several of the South Australia Association's members, the

---

[10] Votes and Proceedings recording Thomas Fowell Buxton's motion, House of Commons, 2 July 1834, Sir Thomas Fowell Buxton Papers, Weston Library, University of Oxford, MSS. Brit. Emp. S. 444, Micr. Brit. Emp. 17, vol. 12; *Mirror of Parliament*, vol. III, London, 1834, pp. 2561–63; Reynolds, *Law*, pp. 84–85; Knud Haakonssen, *Natural Law and Moral Philosophy: From Grotius to the Scottish Enlightenment*, Cambridge University Press, Cambridge, 1996, pp. 5–6, 314–15, 322, 326, 332, 340; Jonathan Parry, *The Politics of Patriotism: English Liberalism, National Identity and Europe, 1830–1886*, Cambridge University Press, Cambridge, 2006, p. 16.

expression of such sentiment cannot be explained merely in terms of a realisation that they needed to give their plans a benevolent gloss. They were genuinely concerned about the treatment of native people, not least because they wanted to ensure peaceful possession of the land. George Fife Angas wrote in his diary in June 1835: 'If I can get pious people sent out to that land [South Australia], the ground will be blessed for their sake; and if justice is done to the aborigines as was done by William Penn, then we shall have peace in all our borders'.[11]

In July 1835 Buxton spoke again in the House of Commons about the British treatment of native peoples in the empire. He focused on the Cape Colony, but since he had last addressed parliament on this general subject he had learned more about New South Wales and Van Diemen's Land and become deeply troubled about the destructive impact of British settlement there. At one point in his speech, he concluded: 'Thus, it would appear that British influence, wherever exerted in the colonies, was uniformly injurious to those who, upon every ground of justice and right, were entitled to protection in the possession of their lands'. Such an assertion, however, did not necessarily amount, as Reynolds has argued, to a demand that native people's rights of property in land be upheld. Buxton did not specify what protection would entail, stating instead: '[I require] no more than that we should act justly towards these people. Unless some milder and more benevolent policy were adopted, [I am] sure the time could not be far distant when these unhappy races would become wholly extinct'. Vague imprecations of this kind, Mark Hickford has pointed out, were in keeping with the nature of the demands that Buxton made in his campaign for the protection of native peoples.[12]

On this occasion, Buxton persuaded the House of Commons to form a select committee to inquire into the condition of aborigines in the British colonies. In the wake of this agreement, Sir George Grey wrote to the South Australian Colonisation Commissioners on behalf of Lord Glenelg, who had succeeded Spring Rice as Colonial Secretary, transmitting Buxton's Address and part of a dispatch in which the Governor of Van Diemen's Land, Sir George Arthur, had recommended that every effort be made 'to come to an understanding [over land] with the natives

---

[11] Thomas Spring Rice to Sir Richard Bourke, 1 August 1834, *HRA*, series 1, vol. 17, pp. 491–92; Minutes of the South Australian Literary Association, 3 October and 7 November 1834, SRSA, GRG 44/83; George Fife Angas, Diary, 4 June 1835, cited Edwin Hodder, *George Fife Angas: Father and Founder of South Australia*, Hodder and Stoughton, London, 1891, pp. 107–08; Reynolds, *Law*, pp. 100–01.

[12] *BPD*, House of Commons, 14 July 1835, columns 549–53; Mark Hickford, *Lords of the Land: Indigenous Property Rights and the Jurisprudence of Empire*, Oxford University Press, Oxford, 2011, p. 73.

of Southern Australia' before colonisation began.[13] In doing this, Reynolds has claimed, Grey urged the Colonisation Commissioners to recognise the Aboriginal people's rights in land. In fact, he did nothing of the kind. Grey merely noted that Arthur's dispatch contained some observations about conflicts between settlers and Aboriginal people and some suggestions about how they might be avoided by adopting measures of conciliation. Furthermore, contrary to what Reynolds would have us believe, the Colonisation Commissioners took this letter in their stride, responding in terms that were in keeping with those of Buxton's Address. In the following months, the Commissioners and their allies took care to speak its language of protection, and the Colonial Office saw no need to pursue the matter any further.[14]

The Colonial Office and the Matter of Restraint

Six months were to pass before the subject of the natives was raised again in any correspondence between the Colonial Office and the Colonisation Commissioners. This correspondence, and in particular the fragment of a letter that Grey sent on behalf of the Colonial Office to the Commissioners in December 1835, is central to the argument that Reynolds has made, namely that the Colonial Office's principal figures pursued the matter of Aboriginal rights in land and that they did so because they were determined to uphold these and entrench them in law.

In order to be able to assess Reynolds' argument, we have to place the Colonial Office's letter in its context, and especially in a chronological sequence of correspondence between it and the Colonisation Commission, and examine all of its text. Otherwise, we cannot hope to know what Grey meant and what he was trying to convey and why. In undertaking this work, several points must be borne in mind. The correspondence in question was part of negotiations between these two parties.

---

[13] In recent years several historians have made much of Arthur's championing of treaties with Aboriginal people, but he was actually dismissive of their claims to be sovereign polities and their rights of property in land. A couple of months after the Port Phillip Association had made their treaty, Arthur told Spring Rice that he doubted that 'a migratory savage tribe, consisting of from perhaps 30 to 40 individuals, roaming over an almost unlimited extent of country, could acquire such a property in the soil as to be able to convey it so effectually as to confer to the purchasers any right of possession which would be recognised in our courts of law' (4 July 1835, TNA, CO 280/58).

[14] Sir George Arthur to Spring Rice, 27 January 1835, TNA, CO 280/55; Sir George Grey to South Australian Colonisation Commissioners, 17 July 1835, TNA, CO 396/1; Rowland Hill to Grey, 23 July 1835, TNA, CO 13/1; Minutes of the South Australian Literary Association, 7 August 1835; *Newcastle Courant*, 26 September 1835; Minutes of the South Australian Conversazione Club, 28 October 1835, TNA, CO 386/141; Reynolds, *Law*, pp. 99, 105.

Furthermore, these negotiations were not initiated by the Colonial Office but by the Colonisation Commission, which had asked the government to issue some kind of legal instruments to give effect to the South Australia Act, establish the limits of the province and create a legislative council. Moreover, the Colonisation Commission's request was probably unnecessary; usually, legal measures of this kind *were* required, but in this case the South Australia Association had usurped the Crown's authority and gained the seal of approval it needed by securing the parliamentary statute that had founded the colony. (Consequently, Stephen was puzzled, if not irritated, by the Commission's request for some kind of legal instrument, remarking to one of his colleagues: 'What is left for His Majesty to do I cannot imagine'.) In other words, if the Colonisation Commission had not made this request, it is probable that the discussion that arose later between it and the Colonial Office regarding Aboriginal matters would never have taken place, and so the issue of Aboriginal rights in land would never have been raised. Finally, the position the Colonial Office adopted in these negotiations was influenced a good deal by the position that the Colonisation Commission was taking. This was a common occurrence. As we noted in the previous chapter, the Colonial Office's officials tended to act by *reacting* to the particular matters that were put before them, and they often did so in the same terms that their interlocutors were using.[15]

In responding to the Commission, Grey called upon it to choose the form of the legal instruments it wanted and prepare drafts of them for the consideration of the Crown's legal officers. In doing so, he urged the Commissioners to pay attention to several matters. The first substantive matter concerned the nature of the legal instruments the Commission had requested. In the past, Letters Patent under the Great Seal had always been the means by which colonies had been founded. Grey suggested that the Commissioners consider this measure. Later, we will note the significance of the fact that it was the Colonisation Commission, rather than the Colonial Office, that drafted these Letters Patent. The second matter Grey raised sprung from the fact that the South Australia Act was ambiguous in regard to the legal instruments that the Commission requested: did it presume a single act of royal authority, in which case it could never be reversed, or did it assume that there would be a succession of such acts, in which case the Crown would have the opportunity to amend the earlier ones? If it was to be the former, it was vital to consider the terms of that act now, Grey suggested. This was especially so in the case of the third matter

---

[15] SACC, Minute Book, 7 December 1835, TNA, CO 386/137; Stephen to Gordon Gairdner, 10 December 1835, TNA, CO 13/3; Grey to Torrens, 15 December 1835, TNA, CO 13/3; Ward, 'Politics of Jurisdiction', pp. 69–70.

to which he drew the Commission's attention, namely defining the boundaries of the colony. In this context Grey proceeded to make a series of remarks that were to prompt considerable conflict between the Colonisation Commission and the Colonial Office, and which lie at the heart of the claim that Reynolds has made regarding the Colonial Office's treatment of Aboriginal interests. They warrant quoting in full, as follows:

This [i.e. the importance of the matter of whether there was to be one act of royal authority or a succession of such acts] is more especially evident when it is remembered that the Act of Parliament presupposes the existence of a vacant territory, and not only recognises the dominion of the Crown but the proprietary right to the soil of the Commissioners or of those who shall purchase lands from them in any part of the territory to be comprised within the boundary lines now to be drawn. Yet *if* the utmost limits were assumed within which parliament has sanctioned the erection of the colony it would extend very far into the interior of New Holland and *might* embrace in its range numerous tribes of people whose proprietary title to the soil we have not the slightest ground for disputing. Before His Majesty can be advised to transfer to his subjects the property of the land of Australia he must have at least some reasonable assurance that he is not about to sanction any act of injustice towards the Aboriginal natives of that part of the globe. In drawing the lines of demarcation for the new province or provinces the Commissioners therefore must not proceed any further than those limits within which they can show, by some sufficient evidence, that the land is unoccupied, and that no earlier and preferable title exists.[16]

Reynolds has argued that this passage was prompted by the Colonial Office's concern about Aboriginal people's rights in land, that they had an unequivocal position on this matter, that the meaning of their remarks is unambiguous, that these were statements about rights at law and that they were seeking to uphold those rights on the basis of particular legal principles. All these contentions are difficult to sustain in the light of the available historical evidence.[17]

By considering the relevant passage in Grey's letter in the context in which it appears, we are able to grasp the nature of the matters that had provoked the Colonial Office's concerns and which had led Grey to make the remarks that Reynolds has construed in terms of *Aboriginal rights*, though Grey did not in fact use that term. These matters primarily related to two questions: where were the boundaries of the colony to be set, and who had the authority to determine them? They had troubled Stephen when the early plans for the colony had been referred to him for advice, and they remained of the utmost concern in the Colonial Office. Although the statute enabling the colony had recognised the Crown's

---

[16] Grey to Torrens, 15 December 1835, my emphases.   [17] Reynolds, *Law*, pp. 105–06.

sovereignty, it had simultaneously recognised the proprietary rights bestowed on the Commission and those who purchased the land in any part of a huge, undefined territory. This meant that the imperial government's authority and power to confine the spread of colonisation had been severely diminished. Furthermore, Buxton and his fellow humanitarians had been demanding that the government protect Aboriginal people. In this situation the Colonial Office's senior figures felt duty bound to call upon the Colonisation Commissioners to make some changes in order to ensure that the government would not be seen to be approving an act of colonisation on a scale that would be detrimental to the Aboriginal people.[18]

A careful reading of the passage at stake in Grey's letter also reveals that his references to anything that might be said to resemble Aboriginal rights were ambiguous. Grey did not positively state that Aboriginal people had title in land, let alone that all Aboriginal people might have such tenure; indeed, there is very little reliable evidence that Grey or his associates in the Colonial Office believed at this time that Aboriginal people had rights of property in land.[19] Rather, in the context of addressing the matter of

---

[18] Stephen, Memorandum, 14 July 1832.

[19] In fact, most of the evidence that Henry Reynolds has adduced for his argument that the Colonial Office believed that the Aboriginal people had rights of property in land rests upon a very small number of historical traces, most of which are merely fragments of traces. Thereby sundered from their original (con)text, they seem to support his interpretation, but they only do so because they have been inserted into a new context, namely that of Reynolds' own argument. Indeed, his interpretation of these traces can be faulted in nearly every case. Let us consider a minute that Stephen wrote in 1841: 'It is an important and *unexpected* fact that these tribes had proprietary rights in the soil – that is, in particular sections of it which were clearly defined or well understood before the occupation of their country' (14 March 1841, on Sir George Gawler to Lord John Russell, 1 August 1840, TNA, CO 13/16, my emphasis). Leaving aside for the moment the fact that Reynolds has misread the word 'unexpected', rendering it instead as 'unsuspected', he has argued: 'This was one of the most important sentences ever written in the history of white-Aboriginal relations . . . It showed how far thinking about Aboriginal land rights had gone by 1840 . . . Stephen's comment was more than an affirmation of a "proprietary [right] in the soil". It also contained a definition of what that involved – ownership of "particular sections" which were "clearly defined and understood"' (*Law*, p. 70). However, a careful consideration of Stephen's minute, and the context in which he wrote it, draws into question the historical significance Reynolds has attributed to it. Stephen scribbled this minute in the course of reading a dispatch that the Governor of South Australia, Sir George Gawler, had sent to the Colonial Secretary, Lord John Russell. In it, there appeared this phrase: 'Having ascertained very distinctly that these people [the Aborigines] possess well defined and very ancient rights of proprietary and hereditary possession of the available lands of this part at least of the territory' (Gawler to Russell, 1 August 1840). This phrase had in turn echoed a passage in a half-yearly report that Gawler had received from the Protector of the Aborigines in South Australia, Matthew Moorhouse, which he had enclosed with his dispatch. It read: 'A more extended knowledge of the language has introduced us to a more general acquaintance with the manners and customs of these people. *We find what the Europeans thought the Aborigines of*

where the boundary of the colony should be drawn, he suggested that in the event of the colony's boundaries encompassing a part of the Australian continent currently unknown to the British, it *might* be found that this area included the territory of native peoples who had title to the land of a kind that the British would have no reason to deny. It was on this basis that he told the Colonisation Commissioners that in drawing the boundaries of the new colony they must not proceed any further than those areas in which they could show there was no prior and preferable title. This suggests that Grey took for granted that there were parts of South Australia where there were Aboriginal people who had no title to land of the kind that the British government had previously recognised, and so the government conceded the Colonisation Commission's right to assume ownership there. But in seeking to persuade the Commissioners to limit the boundaries of the colony, it appears that Grey thought he might draw their bluff by invoking, in a vague manner, the possibility that there might be Aboriginal title in land that had to be respected. If this was the ploy, it worked extraordinarily well, as we will see, though not in the manner he envisaged. Finally, it is probable that if the Colonisation Commission had been willing to address the Colonial Office's concerns by agreeing to limit the new colony to an area understood to comprise Aboriginal people who had no proprietorial rights of the kind the Colonial Office was claiming it would have to respect, this would have been the end of the matter.

In the light of what we know of the approach of the Colonial Office to the expansion of settler colonies, it seems clear that its primary purpose in this South Australian matter was to try to uphold imperial order and the authority of the Crown and restrain the Colonisation Commission by limiting the boundaries of the new colony. In order to realise this long-standing government objective, Grey raised in vague and formulaic terms the possibility of Aboriginal title to land. He did this not only because it met the Colonial Office's concerns about the need to protect Aboriginal

---

Australasia did not possess – territorial rights, families owning and holding certain districts of land which pass from father to sons, never to daughters, with as much regularity as property in our own country' (Report of Matthew Moorhouse, 27 July 1840, TNA, CO 13/16, my emphasis). Quite evidently, the remark that Stephen made in his minute was prompted by the phrases that appeared in the letter he was reading, indeed he was echoing them; this, as we have seen, is how the Colonial Office's overworked staff tended to perform their work; that is, they reacted to the particular matters that were put before them by various parties and often adopted the very same terms that those interlocutors used. Most importantly, it seems clear that Stephen was *surprised* by Moorhouse's suggestion that Aboriginal people had rights in land. In other words, this was a notion he had not previously considered, rather than it being a matter that *he* knew of but which was *unsuspected* by others, as Reynolds would have it. Historians must be careful how they read historical traces lest they merely discover what they wish to find.

people and served its broader purpose of reining in British colonisation but because the Colonial Office was coming under some pressure from Christian humanitarians troubled by the catastrophic impact of that colonisation on the native peoples in the Cape Colony, New South Wales and Van Diemen's Land. This is not to argue that the interests of the Aboriginal people were unimportant to the Colonial Office, but it is to suggest that the manner in which its senior figures considered them was tempered by the approach they took to broader colonial matters and determined by pragmatic considerations rather than principle alone. As historians such as A. G. L. Shaw have argued, the Colonial Office officials not only had to think of what measures their principles might dictate; they had to weigh up what was possible and even what would be popular. In this case, it seems that Glenelg and Grey wanted to do what they thought was right, but they were uncertain what they could do. In part, this was probably because they realised, given what they knew about the relationships of power between government, settlers and natives in the Australian colonies thus far, that the imperial government's capacity to influence what happened in the new colony of South Australia was severely circumscribed. As so often, then, these government ministers were highly attuned to the limits of political possibility. We will return to this point later. For the time being, we need to consider the Colonisation Commission's response to Grey's letter.[20]

The South Australian Colonisation Commission and the Protection of Aborigines

The South Australian Colonisation Commission, or at least its chairman, Robert Torrens, misinterpreted Grey's letter. Torrens assumed that the Colonial Office was asserting that the Aboriginal people had title to land in South Australia and was demanding that the Commission draw up a plan to ensure that it would be respected. How might this mistaken assumption best be explained?

A day after the Colonisation Commission received Grey's letter, one of the inner circle of the colony's planners, John Brown, reported in his diary that Torrens was 'exceedingly depressed' and 'very nervous'. Many years later, Torrens claimed, in a report in which he recalled the circumstances of the founding of the colony, that 'the Commissioners received from the Secretary of State the startling announcement that they would not be

---

[20] A. G. L. Shaw, 'James Stephen and Colonial Policy: The Australian Experience', *Journal of Imperial and Commonwealth History*, vol. 20, no. 1, 1992, p. 23, and 'British Policy Towards the Australian Aborigines, 1830–1850', *Australian Historical Studies*, vol. 25, no. 99, 1992, pp. 266–67.

permitted to take possession of any lands in South Australia unless they should be able to prove the non-existence of a previous proprietary right on the part of any native tribe' and that '[t]his announcement amounted to a veto on the establishment of the colony'.[21] As readers have seen in the relevant passage of Grey's letter, quoted earlier, this was not the case, however much Grey might have been trying to call the Commission's bluff.

Several of the other promoters of the colony reacted to Grey's letter very differently to Torrens. For example, Brown was not overly troubled. 'There is nothing in it of any consequence but a statement that the government expect the Commission in fixing the boundaries of the province to occupy such ground only as is unoccupied by the native', he remarked in his diary. Pointing out that this matter depended upon the interpretation of the term *occupy*, Brown was confident the Commission had strong weapons to argue its case. The South Australia Act had already declared the land to be waste and unoccupied, and South Australia was not occupied by the Aborigines 'according to any law regulating possession' that a people such as the British had ever recognised, argued Brown. Furthermore, he believed that the matter of the colony's boundaries had only been raised by the Colonial Office so that it could put its opinion on record in case Buxton and his fellow humanitarians raised objections to the nature of the new colony. Most importantly, Brown not only held that the Colonial Office's putative position did not present a difficulty that could not be readily overcome by the Commissioners; he also assumed that the Commission's objectives could be accomplished by presenting to the Colonial Office a general plan for the protection of the Aborigines.[22]

Torrens' reaction to Grey's letter was in keeping with a hyperbolic account he gave in his reminiscences several years later when he recalled the character of the negotiations between the Commission and the Colonial Office: 'The Commissioners determined on making a last effort to overcome the opposition of the Colonial Department, before they relinquished their functions and abandoned the enterprise, to the accomplishment of which their exertions had been so long devoted. A respectful but earnest remonstrance was addressed to the Secretary of State. It had the desired effect. The veto [sic] against the establishment of the colony was withdrawn'. These claims as well as the remarks recorded by Brown reveal that Torrens failed to make a reasoned and hence realistic assessment of what Grey had stated on behalf of the Colonial Office. Instead, he

---

[21] John Brown, Diary, 17 December 1835, SLSA, PRG 1002/2; Robert Torrens, *Statement of the Origin and Progress of the Colony of South Australia, and of the Claims of Colonel Torrens*, The author, London, [1849], pp. 69–70.

[22] Brown, Diary, 16 and 17 December 1835.

exaggerated the problem it posed for the Commission's plans. As the historian Douglas Pike noted many years ago, Torrens was not really fitted to being the Association's or the Commission's executive officer. He was excitable, quick-tempered and prone to indulge in make-believe. Consequently, his response to Grey's letter, contrary to what Reynolds has implied, cannot be regarded as a reliable guide to the position that the Colonial Office had adopted.[23]

Three further points are in order. First, while Grey's letter undoubtedly caused some apprehension among the Colonisation Commissioners, it is hardly surprising that their concern came to focus largely on the matter of native title. Any attempt to lay claim to land on the other side of the world would have occasioned anxiety among a group of colonisers, but this was especially so when the projected land grab was on a scale as massive as the one these men envisaged. It seems reasonable to suggest that the Colonisation Commissioners were especially prone to fears that their fantasy of seizing a huge, almost boundless expanse of land would be brought to ground by some force or another, and no more so because they perceived the Colonial Office's senior figures as aligned to those Brown acerbically described as 'the saints in the House of Commons', the saints being Buxton and his fellow humanitarians. In other words, there appear to be good reasons for concluding that this was a situation in which men like Torrens were liable to misconstrue a vague and ambiguously phrased statement of the kind the Commissioners had received from a Colonial Office headed by men known to be sympathetic to these evangelicals. Second, the interpretation *Torrens* placed on Grey's letter, and indeed on all the communications that the Commission received from the Colonial Office during their negotiations, was critical in determining the Commission's reaction to the Colonial Office's requests. The Commission was a loose knit group of men, and many took no constant role in its affairs; Torrens was not only the Commission's chairman but its dominant figure; and he headed a three-man committee that oversaw the Commission's response to the Colonial Office. Third, and most importantly, the Colonisation Commissioners had envisaged a colony that was to be largely free of government oversight. Most importantly, they were to

---

[23] John Hindmarsh to George Fife Angas, 31 December 1835, George Fife Angas Papers, SLSA, PRG 174/1; Torrens, *Statement*, p. 70; Pike, *Paradise*, pp. 92–93, 98; Anon, 'Robert Torrens', *Australian Dictionary of Biography*, vol. 2, 1967, pp. 534–36; Peter Moore, 'Robert Torrens', *Oxford Dictionary of National Biography*, Oxford, 2004, www.oxforddnb.com/view/article/27565. There is further evidence for this argument: at a stage that the Colonisation Commission was actually making progress in its negotiations with the Colonial Office in January 1836, Torrens dramatically asked Shaw-Lefevre 'Should we not resign and thus throw off the responsibility from our shoulders?' (Torrens to Shaw-Le Fefevre, undated, Sir John George Shaw-Lefevre Papers, SLSA, PRG 226).

have control over the sale of all the land in a very large area. Given this, it is not surprising that the key part of Grey's letter raised a terrible spectre in the minds of Torrens and his fellow Commissioners: not simply that of the imperial government interfering in their arrangements, but more particularly of it undermining their control over the transfer of land to other parties in adjacent areas and on terms more favourable than the ones they might offer.[24]

Most of the Commissioners' response dealt with the problems Grey raised first in his letter. They were especially concerned to ensure that the colony would comprise the largest territory allowed by the Act and to guarantee the Commission's authority relative to that of the imperial government. In the case of the first of these two matters, the Commissioners were adamant that the plan of the original promoters of the colony, which proposed the founding of one large province rather than several smaller ones and encompassed the whole of the territory specified in the South Australia Act, had to be preserved. They asserted that the colony's leading principle – to sell land at a price to ensure the right balance between capital and labour – would only work if it was adopted uniformly throughout an extensive territory; they pointed out that this proposal had previously been approved by the Colonial Office; they argued that it was very important to the prosperity of the new colony; they noted that they had already procured the loan and created the fund for the purchase of the land that was required by the Act; and they claimed that considerable difficulties would result if they were only allowed to found a smaller province as one of many. In regard to the second matter Grey raised, the Commissioners insisted that it had been the intention of the parliament as well as the promoters of the colony that the legal instrument founding the colony would comprise a single act and so one that could not be amended.[25]

Only after addressing those two matters did the Commissioners turn to what they called the part of Grey's letter respecting the Aborigines. Here, they began by trying to assure the Colonial Office that they had been solicitous of the condition of the Aboriginal people since their

---

[24] Brown, Diary, 4 January 1836; Ward, 'Politics of Jurisdiction', p. 64. The Colonisation Commission originally comprised Torrens, George Fife Angas, Edward Barnard, Rowland Hill, William Hutt, John George Shaw-Lefevre, William MacKinnon, Samuel Mills, Jacob Montefiore, George Palmer, John Wright, Josiah Roberts and James Pennington. The committee appointed to handle the matters raised by the Colonial Office comprised Torrens, Shaw-Lefevre and Barnard (SACC, Minute Book, 16, 18 and 30 December 1835, 6, 8, 13, 15 and 22 January 1836, TNA, CO 386/137).

[25] Torrens to Grey, [26] December 1835; SACC, Minute Book, 30 December 1835.

appointment and especially so since Grey had transmitted Buxton's Address to the King to them. They also claimed that they had been planning for some time to submit a proposal to put into effect the wishes of the House of Commons and proceeded to sketch the principal parts of such a proposal, which they had devised in order to persuade the Colonial Office that they would implement measures that might realise the goals Buxton had articulated: 'The Commissioners have entertained the belief that by these means they may be able, in the language of the Address of the House of Commons, "to secure the natives of South Australia the due observance of justice and the preservation of their rights, and to promote the spread of civilisation amongst them, and the peaceful and voluntary reception of the Christian religion"'.[26]

In moving to address what Torrens interpreted as the Colonial Office demand that the Commission adopt measures to ensure that Aboriginal title to land was respected, the Commissioners, rather than putting forward a plan comprising general measures to protect the Aborigines, chose to present a proposal that focused specifically on rights of property in land. In doing this, they adopted a strategy that was common among many land-grabbers, namely one that deployed several legal concepts.

First, the Colonisation Commissioners implied that, while they were more than willing to conform to the Colonial Office's request that they adopt measures to protect the Aborigines in the colony since this had been endorsed by parliament, they were reluctant to accept what Torrens has construed as the Office's demand to respect Aboriginal title as this not only lacked any comparable legitimacy but flew in the face of parliament's authority. The Commissioners reminded the Colonial Office that the South Australia Act had declared that this part of Australia consisted of *waste* and *unoccupied* land. Given this, they argued, the Commissioners would be acting wrongly if they were to delay the provision of the funds necessary for founding the colony until such time as they could obtain enough evidence to prove that the Aboriginal people had no preferable title to the land. Furthermore, they pointed out, neither the parliament nor the government had made any provision for the costs involved in securing that evidence. Finally, they asserted that, having procured the funds required by the Act, the delay and uncertainty caused by such an inquiry would be regarded as a serious breach of faith by the parties who had committed themselves to settling in South Australia.[27]

Second, the Commissioners argued that the Colonial Office was making a demand that lacked the sanction of parliament and ran contrary to the rules that the British government itself had followed in the past and

[26] *Ibid.*   [27] *Ibid.*

was still following. 'In the colonisation of Australia', they reminded the Colonial Office, 'it ha[d] been invariably assumed as an established fact that the unlocated tribes ha[d] not arrived at that stage of social improvement in which a proprietary right to the soil exist[ed]'. At this point it seems evident that the Commissioners were drawing on either the works of Scottish Enlightenment philosophers such as Adam Ferguson which developed a stadial theory of history that articulated broad concepts about the nature of rights of property held by peoples at various stages of development or works on the law of nations such as Emmerich de Vattel's *Le droit des gens* (which had appeared in a new English edition in 1834) that invoked cultivation of land as a means of assessing whether or not land had been occupied in such a way as to prevent newcomers appropriating it, that is the doctrine of *occupation*. But the Commissioners appear to have placed more emphasis on a version of another legal argument, namely prescription. They insisted that the absence of proprietary rights among the Aboriginal people 'was assumed as an established fact when New South Wales and Van Diemen's Land and Western Australia were taken possession of; [and] it was assumed as the established fact when the Crown made extensive grants to the Australian and Van Diemen's Land Agricultural Companies and to the first settlers upon Swan River'. What was more, they pointed out, 'it continues to be assumed as the established fact, in all the extensive sales of public lands which are daily taking place in the remote interior of New South Wales where that colony approaches South Australia on the banks of the Murrumbidgee'. In effect, the Colonisation Commissioners argued that it was a matter of history that the British government had claimed possession of all of Australia, that this was the basis upon which it had granted or sold land to settlers and that this could not be overturned. This line of argument echoed the reasoning of New South Wales' legal officers like Chief Justice Francis Forbes in regard to the source of the Crown's title, as we noted earlier. Yet, contrary to the Commissioners' claim, there is no evidence to suggest that the British government's treatment of native title in the Australian colonies rested on the legal doctrine of *occupation*. The Colonisation Commission's argument in this regard was simply a piece of myth making.[28]

Third, the Commissioners gave a solemn undertaking that they would provide clear instructions to the land commissioners responsible for surveying and selling the land that they were not to colonise 'any district which the Aborigines *may* be found occupying, or enjoying, or possessing, any right of property in the soil'. This, they begged to suggest, would ensure that justice would be accorded to the Aboriginal people and that

[28] *Ibid.*

there was no need for the Colonial Office to decrease the size of the new colony. Here, Torrens and his fellow Commissioners had chosen their words, which all had a particular legal meaning, very carefully. They were convinced that no Aboriginal people *occupied, enjoyed* or *possessed* the land in a manner that could affect the interests of a third party, and so they assumed that the natives would never be found to have legal title to the land. Indeed, Torrens made this point clear several months later when he gave evidence to a House of Commons select committee on the disposal of lands in British colonies: 'It will be the duty of the protector of the aborigines, as I understand, to see that no land which the aborigines *really* have in possession or enjoyment (*I believe they have none*) shall be taken for settlement'.[29]

Finally, the Colonisation Commissioners offered to guarantee its undertaking to protect Aboriginal rights in land by inserting in the Letters Patent a passage 'reserving the right of the Aboriginal natives to any lands that may now be in *actual* occupation or enjoyment'. This undertaking was also worth nothing given the position the Commissioners had taken on the natives' title to land. Yet, despite the fact that it was the Commissioners who were responsible for formulating this proviso – 'nothing in these our Letters Patent contained shall affect or be construed to affect the rights of any Aboriginal Natives of the said Province to the actual occupation or enjoyment in their own persons or in the persons of their Descendants of any Lands therein now actually occupied or enjoyed by such Natives' – and that they did so on the assumption that it would ensure that no Aboriginal rights in land would be upheld, several historians and legal scholars have claimed in recent times that the Letters Patent was designed by a Colonial Office determined to secure the land rights of Aboriginal people. This is clearly nonsense.[30]

Conversations between the Colonial Office and the Colonisation Commission

Having delivered the Colonisation Commission's response to Grey's letter, Torrens was impatient for a reply. Only a few days passed before

---

[29] *Ibid.*, my emphasis; *BPP*, 1836, Paper no. 512, Report of the Select Committee on the Disposal of Lands in the British Colonies, p. 130, my emphases.

[30] Torrens to Grey, [26] December 1835, my emphasis; Draft of Letters Patent, TNA, CO 13/3; Letters Patent, 19 February 1836, Dickey and Howell (eds.), *South Australia's Foundation*, pp. 74–75; Howell, 'South Australia Act', pp. 41–42; Reynolds, *Law*, pp. 107, 110–11, 123; Shaun Berg, 'A Fractured Landscape: The Effect on Aboriginal Title to Land by the Establishment of the Province of South Australia', in Shaun Berg (ed.), *Coming to Terms: Aboriginal Title in South Australia*, Wakefield Press, Adelaide, 2010, pp. 2–3, 12.

he tried to call on Grey, and early in the new year he took himself off to the Colonial Office to see Glenelg. The colony's governor elect, John Hindmarsh, was in the Colonial Office's tiny waiting room when this meeting took place and gave a revealing account of it to Angas, which is worth quoting at length:

When [Colonel Torrens] came out to me he said the only difficulty was that Lord Glenelg insisted upon the rights of the aborigines being properly taken care of, but that he, the Colonel, did not see how to get over the difficulty. It immediately occurred to me that you had expressed some wish with respect to this subject. I therefore entreated the Colonel to go back to Glenelg and beg that you might be appointed a Commissioner [i.e. a protector] to superintend the interests of the aborigines.

The Colonel was not gone 5 minutes when he came out in high glee and his expression was that Lord Glenelg approved of the measure entirely ...

I forgot to say that Lord Glenelg calls upon the Colonel to draw up a plan for the protection of the interests of the aborigines. So you see till this discussion ends we are at a dead end still.[31]

Hindmarsh's account confirms that several matters had been in dispute between the Commission and the Colonial Office. However, it makes no reference to any Colonial Office demand for a plan that would include the protection of Aboriginal rights in land. Moreover, it suggests that the Colonial Office's concerns could be addressed relatively easily if the Commission appointed a protector who met with the Colonial Office's approval and provided a plan that set out satisfactory measures to ensure the protection of the undefined interests of the Aboriginal people.[32]

Reynolds' characterisation of this meeting is worth noting, especially as he has claimed that Glenelg made a statement during it that he has described (in his book *Why Weren't We Told*) as *the* crucial evidence for his argument that the Colonial Office recognised Aboriginal rights in land in the mid-1830s. In *The Law of the Land* Reynolds asserts that Glenelg called this meeting, but, as I just noted, it had taken place because Torrens had demanded to see Glenelg. More importantly, on the basis of the 'crucial' source that he claims Glenelg wrote, Reynolds argues that Glenelg told Torrens that the Colonial Office would not give its final approval to the Commissioners' plans until the Commission 'prepare[d] a plan for securing the rights of the Aborigines which plan should include the appointment of a Colonial Officer to be called Protector of the Aborigines *and arrangements for purchasing the lands of the natives*'. But neither Glenelg nor any member of the Colonial Office wrote the words

---

[31] Hindmarsh to Angas, 2 January 1836, Angas Papers, SLSA, PRG 174/1.
[32] SACC, Minute Book, 30 December 1835; Hindmarsh to Angas, 2 January 1836.

I have just quoted; they were penned instead by a secretary who took the minutes of a meeting of the Colonisation Commission at which Torrens claimed that this was what Glenelg had said. (It might also be noted that the minute-keeping secretary of the Colonisation Commission first scribbled 'a plan for the protection of the Aborigines' rather than 'a plan for securing the rights of the Aborigines'.) In other words, the source Reynolds has described as crucial for his argument is not a first-order historical trace containing what Glenelg might have told Torrens but merely a third-hand account. In the light of what we remarked earlier about Torrens, and given his excited state of mind at that meeting with Glenelg, there seems to be no reason to believe that his account of what Glenelg is supposed to have said at their meeting is any more reliable than his previous characterisations of the position the Colonial Office was taking in this political dispute.[33]

On 5 January, a few days after Torrens' meeting with Glenelg, several of the colony's planners – Robert Gouger, Rowland Hill, Robert Fisher and John Brown – met to devise the plan for the protection of the Aborigines that Glenelg had requested. What they prepared included these recommendations: a new position called the Protector of the Aborigines; the payment of an annual tribute to the Aborigines in the form of food and clothing, which would be equivalent to the value of the land to the Aborigines that the colonists might occupy; the limitation of surveys to land that was unoccupied by the Aborigines; and the granting of leases to any Aboriginal man who might want 'to settle as a civilised being and cultivate land'. The group believed that their proposal would have a better chance of being accepted by the Colonial Office if they placed it in the hands of William Higgins, the secretary of an organisation called the Society for the Protection of the Aborigines of South Australia, and asked him to present it.[34]

However, the next day the Board of Commissioners decided to endorse a different plan, one that Torrens had drawn up. It entailed more specific legal undertakings in regard to land than the rest of the colony's planners believed were necessary. Torrens discussed this proposal with Grey and the following day submitted to the Colonial Office a plan called 'Proposed Arrangements for Securing the Rights of the Aborigines'. It comprised a series of provisions that were ostensibly designed to protect the Aborigines' interests in land. For example, the Protector of Aborigines would be required to ascertain whether surveyed lands were in the

---

[33] SACC, Minute Book, 6 January 1836, my emphasis; Reynolds, *Law*, pp. 100–01, 115–16, my emphasis, and *Why Weren't We Told: A Personal Search for the Truth About Our History*, Viking, Melbourne, 1999, pp.198–200.

[34] Brown, Diary, 5 and 6 January 1836.

occupation or *possession* of the Aborigines before the Commissioners declared such lands open to public sale. Should he learn that such land was *occupied* or *enjoyed* by the Aborigines, the Commissioners were to negotiate a sale. And, should any Aborigines *enjoying* and *occupying* any lands within the surveyed areas decline to sell, it would be the duty of the Protector to secure their occupation and enjoyment of those lands and afford them legal redress against trespass and depredations. These undertakings, it should go without saying, were offered in the belief that the Aboriginal people did not *occupy*, *enjoy* or *possess* the land in a manner that gave them title, and so they would never be found to have any rights of property in land.[35]

Nevertheless, Torrens continued to be anxious about the appointment of the Protector: would the government claim responsibility for this, and would the appointee understand the principles upon which the colony was to be founded? Consequently, he asked Brown to try to persuade his 'religious friends' to support the appointment of someone of the Commission's choosing. More specifically, Torrens called upon Brown to 'get at Fowell Buxton about it'. Brown immediately set off for Norfolk to meet Buxton at his home. The following afternoon and evening as well as the morning of the next day, Brown worked hard to persuade Buxton that the Commissioners were disposed to use all the power they had to ensure that the Aboriginal people were treated humanely. Most importantly, he attempted to solicit Buxton's support for the appointment of a protector approved by the Commissioners. Buxton was apparently pleased by the prospect of the colony being established by a better class of settlers and commended the views that Brown expressed in regard to the treatment of the Aborigines. He refused, though, to endorse the Commission's proposal to appoint one of their own people as protector and have that figure serve under the Commissioners. Nevertheless, Buxton embraced the Commission's proposal to send out one or two protectors, telling Stephen immediately after meeting Brown: 'So strangely mad am I that I would rather carry that measure through the cabinet than be the victor of Waterloo, and I am sure it will save more lives than Waterloo destroyed'. Once again, it is apparent that the means Buxton advocated for the protection of the Aborigines were very different from those that historians such as Reynolds have attributed to him.[36]

---

[35] *Ibid.*, 7 January 1836; Torrens to Lord Glenelg, 7 January 1836, TNA, CO 13/4; SACC, Proposed Arrangements for Securing the Rights of the Aborigines Appointing a Protector with Particular Functions, TNA, CO 13/4.

[36] Brown, Diary, 4, 7, 8 and 9 January 1836; Buxton to Stephen, 9 January 1836, TNA, CO 13/5.

On 11 January Grey wrote Torrens a letter in which he told him that Glenelg was more or less satisfied by the plan the Colonisation Commissioners had put forward. Glenelg had decided that the Commissioners' proposal for the appointment of a protector (or protectors) would serve to protect the Aboriginal people's interests, though he insisted that the appointment of these protectors should be reserved to the Crown and that the protectors be independent of the land commissioners and their agents. He expressed no opinion regarding the particular nature of the Aboriginal people's interests he had in mind to protect. In other words, returning to our earlier discussion, even if Glenelg *did* tell Torrens at that meeting in early January that the Colonisation Commission had to draw up a plan that made 'arrangements for purchasing the lands of the natives', he did not call upon the Commission to draw a plan that precisely set out the nature of the natives' rights of property in land. Glenelg's position on this matter is consistent with the approach that the Colonial Office took throughout its negotiations with the Commission. Rather than seeking to uphold Aboriginal title to land, it was trying to ensure that there would be some protection of Aboriginal people and their interests from the worst ravages of colonisation.[37]

Grey's summing up in this letter to Torrens also suggests that the Colonial Office's principal objectives in its negotiations lay elsewhere, just as it reveals that the Colonial Office had decided it had to become more aggressive if it was to have any chance of realising them. After Grey stated that Glenelg wanted to incorporate, in a future statute, regulations for the protection of the Aborigines that included the ones the Colonisation Commission had crafted to ensure that Aboriginal rights in land would never be recognised, he conveyed two demands of a very different order: first, Glenelg thought provision should be made in order to revoke and renew in an amended form the various legal instruments issued under the Crown's authority; and, second, he wanted the government to have the power to reserve as much of the proceeds from the Commission's sale of lands as might be required to defray the costs of government in the colony.[38]

Not surprisingly, these demands filled Torrens with dismay. According to an entry in Brown's diary for 12 January, which was the day Torrens received Grey's letter, the chairman of the Colonisation Commission had declared that 'the colony was pretty well ended'. On this occasion, Torrens had good reason to be concerned, and all the more so because

[37] Grey, Minute, 7 January 1836, TNA, CO 13/3; Grey to Torrens, 11 January 1836, TNA, CO 13/4.
[38] *Ibid.*

the Colonial Office had implied that the draft Letters Patent would not be issued until the Commissioners agreed to changes in the current South Australia Act to address the Colonial Office's principal concerns. However, the source of Torrens' anguish was not any wish on the Colonial Office's part to secure the protection of Aboriginal rights in land, but rather its desire to lay claim to a good part of the monies from the land fund. The report that Torrens gave of this matter several months later makes this point clear. He told a select committee that what was objectionable to the Colonisation Commission was the fact that Glenelg had recommended two things: the part of the Act of Parliament which set down that the whole of the funds acquired by the sale of land would be appropriated for emigration was to be repealed so that the government had the power to appropriate a portion of the land fund for the general purposes of the colonial government, and the Commissioners were to be required to give express notice to all those to whom they had sold land that it was the intention of the government to alter the Act in this way.[39]

Torrens immediately arranged to see Grey. At this meeting he forcefully presented the Commissioners' objections. First and foremost, he told Grey that they would not countenance the government appropriating any of the land fund as this would have a fatal impact on their plans for the colony. If the Colonial Office was determined on its present course, he added, the Board of Commissioners would resign. According to Torrens, Grey was surprised by the vehemence of the Commission's opposition. He declared that the government was keen to advance the colony and allow its creation as soon as possible, expressed his opinion that the government could not legally depart from the principles of the colony as they had been set down in the South Australia Act and undertook responsibility for countering the obstacles impeding the formation of the colony.[40]

At the end of this meeting, Grey asked the Colonisation Commission to provide the Colonial Office with a summary of the government's propositions that it considered to be fatal to its plans. Significantly, the Commission's response, which Torrens prepared, explicitly stated that there was no disagreement in regard to what he called the Colonial Office's proposition concerning the arrangements for the protection of the Aborigines. This is hardly surprising. As we have seen, and as Torrens himself observed, these arrangements had been proposed by the Commissioners in the first place, and so they were only too happy to

[39] *Ibid.*; Brown, Diary, 12 January 1836; SACC, Minute Book, 13 January 1836; *BPP*, 1836, Paper no. 512, p. 123; Ward, 'Politics of Jurisdiction', p. 68 note 59.
[40] Torrens to Grey, 16 January 1836, TNA, CO 13/4.

concur with the Colonial Office's proposal to incorporate them in a future Act of Parliament. At about this time, the Commission also prepared a draft of the bill to amend the South Australia Act in which it was careful to word the parts regarding Aboriginal rights in land in the same manner as the proviso of the Letters Patent and the proposals for a protector that it had drawn up. In regard to what they called the most important feature of this part of the arrangements, the Commissioners thought it necessary to call upon the Colonial Office to exercise great care in choosing the man for the position of protector and defining his duties. At the same time, they sought to protect themselves against any encroachments by the protector by secretly passing and sealing an order of the Board of Commissioners that declared that *all* the lands in the colony would be open for public sale (even though section 6 of the South Australia Act had already bestowed upon the Commissioners the authority to do this). The Commissioners thereby revealed, yet again, that they had no intention of conceding that any of the land was in Aboriginal ownership and thus needed to be purchased before it could be sold to settlers.[41]

Once more, it is clear that what really troubled the Commissioners was the Colonial Office's proposition regarding the land fund and its proposal to allow amendments to the legal instruments issued under the Crown's authority. Both of these measures, they feared, were being advanced by the Colonial Office in order to give the imperial government the authority to define the limits of the colony, and more particularly to confine settlement within narrower bounds than those set down in the South Australia Act. The Commissioners described the former as the most important of the Colonial Office's propositions and stated categorically that they could not agree to the proceeds of the land fund being reserved for the Crown's use. They described the latter as being of vital importance and informed the Colonial Office that the opinion of a leading specialist in colonial law, Sir William Follett, supported their claim that it was the intention of parliament that the whole of South Australia be included in the colony. At the same time, the Commissioners sought to ensure that they would win their battle with the Colonial Office over these matters by providing to the press an account of the difficulties they were encountering.[42]

---

[41] Torrens to Grey, 16 January 1836; Draft of a Bill to Amend an Act to empower His Majesty to erect South Australia into a British Province or provinces, and to provide for the Colonisation and Government thereof, TNA, CO 13/5.

[42] SACC, Case for the opinion of Sir William Follett, [undated, c. 12 January 1836], TNA, CO 13/4; SACC, Minute Book, 13 and 15 January 1836; Follett, Opinion, 13 January 1836, TNA, CO 13/4; Torrens to Grey, 16 January 1836; Brown, Diary, 14, 16 and 19 January 1836, 1 February 1836.

At this point, the Colonial Office backed down. Grey expressed regret over the delay in the founding of the colony, blaming the novelty of the scheme, the peculiar nature of the legislation that governed the colony's founding and the necessity of trying to avert the kind of catastrophic impact that British settlement had had upon the Aborigines in the Australian colonies founded earlier. He reasserted the view that the protection of the interests of the Aborigines was of paramount importance to Glenelg but added that the government was content to leave the matter of defining the protector's powers to the Crown's law officers. This is telling. Had the Colonial Office wanted to uphold Aboriginal title to land, as Reynolds has claimed, it would have tried to ensure that the nature of the protector's powers was formulated in a specific manner. It did not do so. Grey claimed that the protection of the Aborigines had been its main objective in these negotiations with the Colonisation Commission. But, as we have seen, it is unlikely that this was the case. Grey's claim was, rather, a piece of myth making on the Colonial Office's part, which historians like Reynolds have embraced. It is probably significant that Grey concluded his letter to the Commissioners by reiterating the Colonial Office's concern about the matter that had troubled it from the outset, namely the sheer size of the territory the Commissioners seemed intent on colonising.[43]

Colonising

A number of scholars have pointed out that the Colonisation Commissioners had considerable power in these negotiations.[44] They had previously won the approval of the imperial government for the new colony; they could rely on the parliamentary statute they had secured; and they could exert pressure on the grounds that the government had some responsibility to honour the pledges that had already been made to investors and colonists. This is no doubt true, but, as we have seen, there appears to be little if indeed any reason to conclude that the Colonial Office's senior figures thought the Aboriginal people in the colony had any more rights in land than the Commissioners believed

---

[43] Grey to Torrens, 21 January 1836, TNA, CO 396/1; Attorney General John Campbell and Solicitor General Robert Roffe to Glenelg, 3 February 1836, and Stephen, Minute, 23 February 1836, TNA, CO 13/5.

[44] See Alex C. Castles and Michael C. Harris, *Lawmakers and Wayward Whigs: Government and Law in South Australia 1836–1986*, Wakefield Press, Adelaide, 1987, p. 8; James Crawford, 'The Appropriation of Terra Nullius: A Review Symposium', *Oceania*, vol. 59, no.3, 1989, p.228.

they had, or even that they sought changes of the kind the Commissioners proposed.[45]

It is true that the official instructions issued to Governor Hindmarsh several months later required him to 'especially take care to protect [the natives] in their persons and in the free enjoyment of their possessions'. But the Colonial Office's principal figures often used phrases such as 'the free enjoyment of their possessions', 'the original possessors of the soil' and even 'the territorial rights of the natives'. As Mark Hickford has argued, these terms were highly formulaic, and the Colonial Office seldom if ever spelled out what they meant. As we will see later when we consider the New Zealand case, invoking native title in this imprecise way served the purposes of a government engaged in political battles with a colonisation company.[46]

On arriving in the colony in December 1836, Hindmarsh issued a short proclamation in which he emphasised his resolution to extend the same protection and privileges to Aborigines as to the colony's other British subjects, expressed his determination to punish any injustices committed against the Aboriginal people and called upon settlers to assist him in promoting civilisation and Christianity among them. The Colonisation Commission had already issued instructions to its resident commissioner that included its usual caveats in respect to Aboriginal people having rights in land. It is apparent that it assumed that settlers would be able to seize whatever land they wanted because they believed that Aboriginal people were an enfeebled people. In any case, they had ensured that a small military force would accompany the first party of settlers. As it turned out, smallpox or a similar epidemic disease had already cut swathes through the Aboriginal population.[47]

---

[45] For this reason (as well as for reasons that have canvassed elsewhere in this chapter), we should be deeply sceptical about Reynolds' argument that a later Colonial Secretary, Earl Grey (formerly Lord Howick), sought to uphold native title in the context of the granting of pastoral leases in the Australian colonies during his term as Colonial Secretary (*Law*, pp. 137–46), and all the more so given the assault that he tried to launch at the very same time on native rights of property in land in New Zealand (which will be discussed in Chapter 9).

[46] Instructions to Governor John Hindmarsh, 12 July 1836, TNA, CO 381/6; Mark Hickford, 'Making "Territorial Rights of the Natives": Britain and New Zealand, 1830–1847', DPhil thesis, University of Oxford, 1999, pp. v–vi, 16, 74, 122, 162, 229–30.

[47] *Report of the Speeches Delivered at a Dinner Given to Captain John Hindmarsh . . . to Which is Appended an Answer to an Article in the Forty-Fifth Number of the Westminster Review by C. Mann*, W. Clowes and Son, London, 1835, pp. 42–43; Colonisation Commissioners for South Australia, *New Colony in South Australia*, The Commission, London, 1835, p. [2]; *South Australian Gazette and Colonial Register*, 18 June 1836; Second Letter of Instructions by the SACC to James Hurtle Fisher, Resident Commissioner in South

It was phenomena of this nature that had attracted the attention of those such as Buxton to the Australian colonies in the first place. As the Colonisation Commission prepared to colonise South Australia, the House of Commons select committee appointed at Buxton's urging began to conduct its inquiry into the condition of aborigines in the British colonies. Reynolds makes a good deal of this fact, even though the Committee only began its hearings *after* the negotiations between the Colonial Office and the Colonisation Commission had concluded. Reynolds also draws attention to the following passage in the Committee's 1837 report and claims that it referred mainly to the Australian colonies: 'It might be presumed that the native inhabitants of any land have an incontrovertible right to their own soil: a plain and sacred right, however, which seems not to have been understood. Europeans have entered their borders uninvited, and, when there, have not only acted as if they were undoubted lords of the soil, but have punished the natives as aggressors if they have evinced a disposition to live in their own country'.[48]

Yet in the part of the report in which the Committee made specific recommendations in regard to the Australian colonies, it did not demand that Aboriginal rights in land be upheld. Instead, it argued: 'Whatever may have been the injustice of th[e] encroachment [on native lands], there is no reason to suppose that either justice or humanity would now be consulted by receding from it'. Furthermore, even though the Committee had twice drawn attention to the fact that the South Australia Act had laid claim to all the lands in a territory that obviously had an aboriginal population, it recorded its satisfaction with the measures that the Colonisation Commission had taken for the founding of the new colony. Moreover, the Committee expressed opposition to the British making any treaties with native peoples on the grounds that the two parties were so unevenly matched in their negotiating power. It recommended instead that the Aboriginal people should be protected, civilised and Christianised.[49]

Australia, 8 October 1836, *BPP*, 1837–38, Paper no. 97, Second Annual Report of the Colonisation Commissioners of South Australia, p. 16; Proclamation by Hindmarsh, 28 December 1836, Dickey and Howell (eds.), *South Australia's Foundation*, p. 77; Peggy Brock, 'South Australia', in Ann McGrath (ed.), *Contested Ground: Australian Aborigines under the British Crown*, Allen & Unwin, Sydney, 1995, pp. 212–13.

[48] Reynolds, *Law*, pp. 84–86.

[49] *BPP*, 1837, Paper no. 425, Report from the Select Committee on Aborigines (British Settlements), pp. 3–5, 12, 82–84; Shaw, 'British Policy', pp. 269–70; Philips, 'Evangelicals', pp. 150–56; Elizabeth Elbourne, 'The Sin of the Settler: The 1835–36 Select Committee on Aborigines and Debates Over Virtue and Conquest in the Early Nineteenth-Century British White Settler Empire', *Journal of Colonialism and Colonial*

How might we best understand the nature of the stance that the Colonial Office adopted in regard to the Aboriginal people's interests in land in this case? A historical comparison provides us with some help in answering this question. In the same month that Glenelg sanctioned the colonisation of South Australia without seeking any guarantee that the Aboriginal people's rights in land would be respected, he directed the governor of the Cape Colony to rescind his recent annexation of the Queen Adelaide Province on the grounds that it would not only have trampled on the rights of the native people but involved an extension of British authority and thus the kind of increase in responsibility and expense that the imperial government was loath to accept. How can this difference in the Colonial Office's stance be explained? In regard to the Cape Colony, the Colonial Office could assume that the native people were powerful enough to ensure that the British government's intervention would have some effect in restraining settlers. In the case of the Australian colonies it could assume no such thing, and it never did. In October 1836 Stephen told the Colonisation Commissioners: 'In the remote part of the vast regions comprised within the range of the Australian colonies the power of the law is unavoidably feeble, when opposed by the predominant inclinations of any large body of the people'. He continued: 'In such a country unpopular regulations, unless supported by a force either of police or soldiery irresistible and overwhelming, must become little more than a dead letter'. In other words, Stephen made no reference to the possibility that Aboriginal people could help the British government restrain settler expansion. A comment he scribbled in a minute to his superior in the Colonial Office several years later explains why. 'If it were possible to make the Aborigines formidable to the Europeans ... that is, so formidable as to ensure their cautious and respectful treatment of the native race', he wrote, 'I should hold such a result to be of all others the most desirable. If they could be armed[,] disciplined, and taught to act in concert, there might be a chance for their salvation. As it is, there is none'. This is to argue that, irrespective of how the Colonial Office's senior figures might have conceived of the Aboriginal people's rights in land in principle, they saw no point in trying to uphold any such rights in a context in which they were convinced that the balance of power tilted so heavily in favour of the settlers.[50]

History, vol. 4, no. 3, 2003, 10.1353/cch.2004.0003, muse.jhu.edu/journals/journal_of_colonialism_and_colonial_history/v004/4.3elbourne.html.

[50] Stephen to South Australia Colonisation Commissioners, 27 October 1836, TNA, CO 396/1; Stephen, Minute on Sir George Gipps to Russell, 8 January 1841, TNA, CO 201/306; John S. Galbraith, *Reluctant Empire: British Policy on the South African Frontier 1834–1854*, University of California Press, Berkeley, 1963, pp. vii, 124, 128–29, 132.

Comparing the colony of South Australia with the colony of New Zealand is even more instructive. Both were founded as Crown colonies just a few years apart – 1834–36 and 1839–40 – and as a consequence of lobbying by private companies – the South Australian Association, and the New Zealand Association and its successor, the New Zealand Company. Moreover, these companies were led by men who championed the same principles of systematic colonisation and cast the colonies as enlightened projects that would create prosperous versions of Britain in the Antipodes, and they comprised many of the same men. Furthermore, their promoters and lobbyists drew upon much the same legal resources in making their claims to land. Finally, the prospect of these colonies being settled by private companies also attracted the concern of Christian humanitarians, and most of the Colonial Office officials responsible for overseeing the negotiations regarding the founding of South Australia oversaw similar kinds of negotiations in regard to New Zealand. Yet, despite these commonalities, the British government would treat native rights of property in land, to say nothing of sovereignty, very differently in the New Zealand case. Explaining this difference is the task of the following chapters.

Conclusion

This chapter has revealed that we can only really understand the nature of the positions that British parties adopted in respect of natives and the land if we do two things. First, we must grasp the fact that the matter of native people's interests in land tended to arise only incidentally – that is, as a consequence of some other matter being contested, usually one concerning the Crown's authority vis-à-vis British parties such as adventurers and land-grabbers – rather than a matter in its own right. Second, we must grapple with the fact that the positions that the key British players adopted were dialogical in nature, in the sense that they were a product of political contestation between those players.

In this chapter I have argued that there are no sound historical reasons for suggesting that the Colonial Office's senior officials sought to uphold native rights of property in land in the colony of South Australia. At most, I have argued, the Colonial Office made vague and formulaic references to the possibility that there might be native peoples in South Australia who had native title to land and that it did so in the course of trying to realise its most important goal, that of reining in the scale of colonisation proposed by the South Australia Colonisation Commission. It is naïve to attribute the position the Colonial Office adopted on matters such as native people's interests in land to its principal figures' commitment to some high-minded religious, moral or legal principles. Their stances in such matters are best understood as the result of a complex mix of principle and expediency. While the Colonial Office's major players undoubtedly believed they had a duty to protect the interests of the native peoples, they were equally convinced that there were very real political factors that circumscribed any attempt on the part of the British government to uphold the interests the Aboriginal people might be deemed to have. This conviction owed a good deal to the Colonial Office's perceptions of the relative power of the imperial and colonial government, the settlers and the Aboriginal people, and especially of the force each could or could not wield.

I have also suggested that the point in time or the historical period at which a colony was founded was relatively unimportant in shaping how the British government treated native title. There is no evidence to suggest that Christian humanitarianism, whose political influence was at a high point in the 1830s, made any substantial difference to the way native rights in land were treated in South Australia, though there can be no doubt that it helped to create a milieu in which the major British political players adopted a language of protection and that this promoted a considerable amount of talk about British duties and the rights of Aboriginal people, though it seems doubtful that these rights were ever conceived as anything more than a right to be protected.

Finally, we have seen that it was adventurers in the form of the South Australian Colonisation Commissioners, rather than humanitarians in the form of evangelical Christians or Colonial Office officials, who had recourse to legal arguments in order to contest and combat what they mistakenly took to be an attempt on the part of the Colonial Office to protect the Aboriginal people's rights of property in land. In this regard, it appears that the argument they chose to place greatest store by in their dispute with the Colonial Office was not the concept of *occupation* but the historical fact that the British government had never treated the Aboriginal people as owners of the land and proceeded instead on the basis that the Crown was the only source of title to land.

4   Protection Claims and Sovereignty in the Islands of New Zealand, 1800–1839

We will now turn our attention to New Zealand. In this case, the vast majority of scholars have argued that the British government's decision to treat with the native people, Māori, for the cession of sovereignty and acquisition of land, by means of a treaty which was signed at Waitangi in February 1840, was determined by factors that were inherently normative in nature. To be more specific, these historians have contended that one or more of the following factors were at work. Certain strands of European political thought such as stadial history or four-stage theory led the government to perceive the natives as a people who had a certain kind of political system, culture, religion and economy, and thus to regard them as sovereign and owners of the land.[1] Legal concepts found in works about the law of nations similarly led the government to maintain that these natives were sovereign and had rights in land.[2] There was a British policy or at least a practice of negotiating treaties with native peoples like Māori in regard to matters such as sovereignty, trade and land.[3] The government was influenced by powerful evangelical Christians who held that these natives were sovereign and had rights in land.[4] In a rather different vein, it is commonly assumed that the British government negotiated cession of sovereignty with Māori and recognised their rights of property in land simply because it realised that these natives were too powerful to be pushed aside.[5]

[1] See, for example, Pat Moloney, 'Savagery and Civilization: Early Victorian Notions', *New Zealand Journal of History*, vol. 35, no. 2, 2001, pp. 153–76.
[2] See, for instance, Paul McHugh, "'A Pretty Gov[ernment]": The "Confederation of United Tribes" and Britain's Quest for Imperial Order in the New Zealand Islands during the 1830s', in Lauren Benton and Richard J. Ross (eds.), *Legal Pluralism and Empires, 1500–1850*, New York University Press, New York, 2013, pp. 233–58.
[3] See, for example, M. P. K. Sorrenson, 'Treaties in British Colonial Policy: Precedents for Waitangi', in William Renwick (ed.), *Sovereignty and Indigenous Rights: The Treaty of Waitangi in International Contexts*, Victoria University Press, Wellington, 1991, pp. 15–29.
[4] See, for instance, Peter Adams, *Fatal Necessity: British Intervention in New Zealand 1830–1847*, Auckland University Press/Oxford University Press, Auckland, 1977.
[5] See, for example, Jane Burbank and Fred Cooper, *Empires in World History: Power and the Politics of Difference*, Princeton University Press, Princeton, NJ, 2010, p. 300.

There is a germ of truth in most if not all of these contentions. However, a thorough-going historical analysis reveals that they fail to grapple with and make sense of the vast and often bewildering historical archive. In what follows I argue that the decision the British government took in 1839 to treat with the native chiefs for the acquisition of sovereignty – and this *was* its primary purpose in making a treaty – sprang from a series of historical forces that were highly contingent in nature. As we will see, it is a mistake to argue that there was a single strand of imperial logic running through several decades of official responses to the islands of New Zealand. Rather, the actions or reactions of the British government tended to be improvised as well as ambiguous. Thus, what happened could have been different, indeed very different, depending on the choices that the government made.

At the heart of my account is a contention that in the three or so decades prior to a treaty being made at Waitangi, British consideration of the islands of New Zealand was dominated by protection claims, as calls *for* protection and promises *of* protection were made by a range of players, who included missionaries, traders and entrepreneurs, colonisation companies, government officials and Māori rangatira (chiefs). This argument will come as no surprise to those familiar with the long history of protection. As Lauren Benton and Adam Clulow have recently pointed out, references to protection were ubiquitous in the early modern world of empire. Few historians of New Zealand have noticed this fact, and insofar as they have done so they have failed to grasp that protection talk was comprised of several, often contradictory strands and that this talk was at work from the early 1800s to the late 1830s, rather than being confined to the 1830s and a humanitarian discourse.[6]

The story I tell in this chapter has this basic trajectory. In the 1810s Britain disavowed its claim to sovereignty on the basis of Cook's claiming of possession in 1769–70, but at the same time it projected an image of itself as a protector of the natives. In seeking to lend authority to this

---

[6] Lauren Benton and Adam Clulow, 'Webs of Protection and Interpolity Zones in the Early Modern World', in Lauren Benton et al. (eds.), *Protection and Empire: A Global History*, Cambridge University Press, Cambridge, 2018, pp. 50, 65. For studies of New Zealand, see, most recently, Tony Ballantyne, *Entanglements of the Body: Missionaries, Maori, and the Question of the Body*, Duke University Press, Durham, NC, 2014, pp. 218, 248–49; and Alan Lester and Fae Dussart, *Colonization and the Origins of Humanitarian Governance: Protecting Aborigines across the Nineteenth-Century British Empire*, Cambridge University Press, Cambridge, 2014, chapter 5. An earlier, exceptional work of historical scholarship, Adams' *Fatal Necessity*, is much more satisfactory as he recognises that protection talk played an important role both before and after the rise of a humanitarian discourse of protection in the 1830s. In this regard, see also W. Ross Johnston, *Sovereignty and Protection: A Study of British Jurisdictional Imperialism in the Late Nineteenth Century*, Duke University Press, Durham, NC, 1973.

ambiguous position – by which the islands could be said to have acquired a dual status, in the sense of being a place that might and might not be a foreign sovereign territory – British agents treated Māori *as though* they were sovereign. During the next two decades this practice generated a relationship with the natives that served to constitute them as something like an ally of the British Crown. At the same time, the imperial government repelled demands from various players, most especially missionary organisations and entrepreneurs, that it provide greater protection to the natives as well as British subjects, by claiming that it had to respect the fact that the islands did not fall within the dominion of the British Crown. Indeed, the British government found it very useful, for reasons that were both internal and external to its empire, to maintain this ambiguous protection talk for some time. It only relinquished this reluctantly, after humanitarians and a colonisation company, deploying a very different discourse of protection, persuaded the Colonial Office that there was a crisis in the islands and that this demanded that the British Crown acquire sovereignty and thus the authority to impose order on the islands. Yet in deciding to intervene the British government adopted a hybrid form of protection talk that comprised the notion of protection it had long found useful to deal with matters of jurisdiction and the humanitarian notion of protection being advanced by metropolitan humanitarians and a colonisation company. This resulted in a sudden but by no means complete shift from a position that had cast the natives as more or less sovereign and forged a status for them as an ally of the British Crown to a position that portrayed them as a weak people who needed to cede sovereignty so they could become the subjects of the Crown and enjoy the protection it customarily afforded British subjects.

As readers will have already gathered, the islands of New Zealand during this period as well as the decade that followed amounted to a crowded stage. More to the point, the way in which the matter of sovereignty was treated by each of the competing players was often a function of the political contestation that occurred between them as they lobbied the British government. This means that the story that follows is extremely complex. With this in mind, I will now introduce the principal players, most of whom are key figures in the events I will describe in the remainder of this book. They include several departments of the imperial government: the Foreign Office, the Admiralty, the Treasury and the Colonial Office; a colonial government, that of New South Wales, or really a succession of its governors, King, Macquarie, Brisbane, Darling and Bourke; imperial agents, beginning with a figure known as a British Resident, James Busby; missionary societies based at the imperial centre, most importantly the Church Missionary Society,

headed by its lay secretary, Dandeson Coates; the agents of those societies, which included a leading churchman, Samuel Marsden, based in
Sydney; traders and entrepreneurs, principally located in London and
Sydney, who wanted to plant colonies in the islands; colonisation companies, most importantly the New Zealand Association and its successor,
the New Zealand Company; and, last, but not least, Māori, especially
rangatira like Ruatara and Hongi Hika.

Part I

Protection Claims and the Making of Allies

The manner in which the British government treated sovereignty as well
as rights of property in land in New Zealand was conditioned by a series of
inter-related factors. They included, in the first instance, the fact that it
only assumed sovereignty of the islands after three generations of contact
between Europeans and natives had passed. Furthermore, most of this
contact occurred in the Bay of Islands and the Hokianga, in the northern
part of the North Island, which was an area that was relatively densely
populated by native hapū (sub-tribes), who were very capable of defending their considerable resources. Finally, these people were the natives
most often represented in European accounts of New Zealand.

In the wake of the British government forming penal settlements both
at Port Jackson and on Norfolk Island in 1788, Britons, Americans and
Frenchmen began to be attracted to the islands of New Zealand by seals,
whales, flax, timber, food and fresh water. Their exploitation of these
resources depended on Māori participation. In fact, the local Ngā Puhi
rangatira were eager to master European agricultural skills and technology so that their hapū could grow new crops and fatten new animals and
thereby provision visiting ships and supply markets in the Australian
colonies and further afield. This development not only led to economic
changes that amounted to an agricultural revolution but also caused
substantial social and cultural shifts, which included Ngā Puhi becoming
more sedentary than they had been while hunting and gathering food.
The impact of these changes was keenly observed by European visitors.
For example, in 1807 the first book to be devoted to New Zealand
portrayed the natives as people who tilled the ground, entered into trade
with Europeans, had a hierarchical form of government and divided their
country into principalities.[7]

---

[7] John Savage, *Some Account of New Zealand: Particularly the Bay of Islands and Surrounding
Country*, J. Murray, London, 1807, pp. 3, 12, 20, 26, 34, 54; Kathleen Shawcross, 'Maoris

During these years, many Ngā Puhi rangatira, most notably Te Pahi, Ruatara, Hongi Hika and Patuone, visited Port Jackson (Sydney) or Poihākena as they called it, and even London, to obtain the skills and technology they desired. Many young Māori men also worked as crew on whaling and trading ships and found their way to Poihākena, London and numerous other ports. In doing so, they acquired considerable knowledge about the wider world, not the least of which concerned how Aboriginal people in the Australian colonies had fared in the wake of British colonisation. But the significance of their journeying as far as we are concerned primarily lay in the relationship that was forged between rangatira and representatives of the British Crown. After two young men, Tuki-tahua and Huru-kokoti (or Ngahuruhuru), had been unceremoniously kidnapped near the Bay of Islands and taken to Norfolk Island in 1793 to help instruct government officials how to manufacture flax, they were befriended by the island's Lieutenant Governor, Philip Gidley King. He treated them respectfully, provided hospitality and presented them with gifts, thereby creating a bond Ngā Puhi never forgot. This relationship was renewed after King became the governor of New South Wales in 1801 and young Ngā Puhi visited Poihākena shortly afterwards. Furthermore, in May 1805 King sought to assure leading Ngā Puhi rangatira that he would redress any illtreatment their people suffered at the hands of Europeans and issued a proclamation that warned whalers that Pacific Islanders, including those in the islands of New Zealand, had the same right to protection and redress as British subjects. The Governor treated the chiefs as important leaders while they looked to ally themselves with this significant figure. As we will see, these transactions laid the foundations of what became a mutual relationship of protection between Ngā Puhi and the British Crown. This relationship would have a profound influence on how the British government treated the matter of sovereignty in New Zealand.[8]

of the Bay of Islands: A Study of Changing Maori Responses to European Contact', MA thesis, University of Auckland, 1967, pp. 268–80; J. M. R. Owens, 'New Zealand before Annexation', in W. H. Oliver with B. R. Williams (eds.), *The Oxford History of New Zealand*, Clarendon Press/Oxford University Press, Oxford and Wellington, 1981, pp. 31, 40; Ann Salmond, *Between Worlds: Early Exchanges between Maori and Europeans 1773–1815*, University of Hawai'i Press, Honolulu, 1997, chapters 9–13; Paul Monin, *Hauraki Contested 1769–1875*, Bridget Williams Books, Wellington, 2001, pp. 33–38; Jim McAloon, 'Resource Frontiers, Environment, and Settler Capitalism, 1769–1860', in Eric Pawson and Tom Brooking (eds.), *Environmental Histories of New Zealand*, Oxford University Press, Melbourne, 2002, pp. 55, 58–59; Hazel Petrie, *Chiefs of Industry: Maori Tribal Enterprise in Early Colonial New Zealand*, Auckland University Press, Auckland, 2006, p. 56; Atholl Anderson, 'Old Ways and New Means, AD 1810–1830', in Atholl Anderson et al., *Tangata Whenua: A History*, Bridget Williams Books, Wellington, 2015, pp. 138, 146.

[8] Judith Binney, 'Tuki's Universe', in Keith Sinclair (ed.), *Tasman Relations: New Zealand and Australia, 1788–1988*, Auckland University Press, Auckland, 1987, pp. 15–19, 24–25;

As European economic penetration grew apace, natives of New Zealand were often treated badly by masters and crews of ships working in the South Pacific. Churchmen, entrepreneurs and government officials based in New South Wales began to call on the imperial government to deal with this problem. In doing so, they tended to couch their requests in the language of protection. This is hardly surprising. After all, the British government had never made good Cook's claim of possession by authorising the occupation of any part of the islands, which meant New Zealand was deemed to lie both inside and outside its dominion. This was the very kind of situation, Lauren Benton and Lisa Ford have pointed out, in which protection talk was often deployed.[9]

The first claims for protection were made in 1808 by the principal Anglican chaplain of New South Wales, Samuel Marsden, after he began to plan a mission to the native inhabitants of northern New Zealand. In order to realise his objective, Marsden knew that he had to persuade a British missionary society (the Church Missionary Society), the government of New South Wales, the imperial government and the natives themselves to provide the mission with protection. In fact, Marsden was only able to conceive of this mission by envisioning what amounted to a circle of protection. It is also apparent, as was often the case with protection talk, that it was unclear what was to be protected, who was to protect whom and to what end. Marsden, drawing on the lesson that missionaries had learned in Tonga and Tahiti, realised that he had to secure a promise of protection from a native chief or dynasty. At the same time, he directed his missionaries to try to convince Māori of British superiority by emphasising what they could offer, which included, above all else, the protection of the British king. Furthermore, Marsden increasingly saw the New Zealanders as a recipient of protection rather than merely a source of it. This prompted him to begin a political campaign for their protection from the mistreatment they were receiving at the hands of masters and crews of ships. Despite, or probably because of, this ambiguity in the relationship of protection that Marsden sought to forge, he was able to secure the promises he needed from the various parties, most importantly the Ngā Puhi rangatira whom he had first befriended in Sydney and who saw considerable advantage in assuming the position of the protectors of settlers they regarded as their pākehā (or

---

Salmond, *Between Worlds*, pp. 211–33, 316, 324–29, 343–68, 396–97; Alison Jones and Kuni Kaa Jenkins, *Tuai: A Traveller in Two Worlds*, Bridget Williams Books, Wellington, 2017, chapters 2–5.

[9] Lauren Benton and Lisa Ford, *Rage for Order: The British Empire and the Origins of International Law, 1800–1850*, Harvard University Press, Cambridge, MA, 2016, pp. 115–16.

settlers). In 1814 Marsden established a mission at Rangihoua in the Bay of Islands, primarily under Ruatara's protection; and when this rangatira died the following year, he secured the protection of Ruatara's uncle, Hongi Hika, which enabled him to form two more missions, at Waimate and Kerikeri.[10]

If Marsden's attempt to form a mission sparked the beginning of protection talk in regard to New Zealand, attempts to acquire some means of control over lawless Britons in the islands prompted a series of protection claims. In December 1813 and again in November 1814 the Governor of New South Wales, Lachlan Macquarie, responding to representations made by Marsden, issued proclamations that were designed to stop masters of ships committing offences against the natives of New Zealand as well as of other islands in the South Pacific. Protection was fundamental to these proclamations in two ways. First, Macquarie would have assumed that the British Crown was obliged to offer protection to its subjects and that those subjects were obliged to pledge obedience to the Crown. Second, while Macquarie assumed that the British government had sovereignty over the islands of New Zealand on the grounds that they were part of the territory included in his commission as governor of New South Wales, he must have been aware that the proclamations he issued involved considerable bluff. Consequently, he declared that the natives were under the protection of the British Crown. This claim was a way of imagining, and thereby conjuring up, a form of British authority that did not exist. Imperial powers had long made such protection claims in circumstances in which they enjoyed no dominion in the territory concerned but nonetheless wanted to create some form of jurisdiction. This amounts to what Lisa Ford has called *protection-as-jurisdiction*. Although some historians such as Andrew Porter would argue that Macquarie's intervention was consistent with an increasingly popular humanitarian notion that the British Empire had a duty to protect groups of vulnerable

---

[10] Samuel Marsden to Josiah Pratt, 24 March and 7 April 1808, 3 May, 25 October and 19 November 1811, CMS, London, Records Relating to the New Zealand Mission, HL, MS-0498; Minutes of the Founding Meeting of the New South Wales Society for Affording Protection to the Natives of the South Sea Islands and Promoting their Civilisation, 20 December 1813, HL, MS-0439/116; John Rawson Elder (ed.), *The Letters and Journals of Samuel Marsden 1765–1838*, Coulls Somerville Wilkie Ltd and A. H. Reed, Dunedin, 1932, pp. 64–68, 78–80, 97, 111, 125, 128, 149, 206–07, 214, 224, 292, 295, 297; Shawcross, 'Maoris', pp. 291–330, 322; Andrew Sharp, *The World, the Flesh and the Devil: The Life and Opinions of Samuel Marsden in England and the Antipodes, 1765–1838*, Auckland University Press, Auckland, 2016, pp. 220–21, 361–64, 736; Philip J. Stern, 'Limited Liabilities: The Corporation and the Political Economy of Protection in the British Empire', in Benton et al. (eds.), *Protection and Empire*, pp. 114, 127.

subjects, Macquarie made no such argument in introducing these measures.[11]

It was one thing for Macquarie to make a claim to protect, quite another to ensure that the claim had any substance. Over the next twenty years, successive New South Wales governors would pursue this object. In Macquarie's case, he sought the power he required in two sources. He called on the imperial government to introduce legislation that would bestow on his government the extraterritorial power he needed in order to subject masters and crews of ships to British law. But when he learned that this was not forthcoming, he immediately invested authority in three chiefs in northern New Zealand – Ruatara, Hongi Hika and Korokoro – to ensure the compliance of British subjects with his regulations.[12]

To make this arrangement, Macquarie had to treat Māori as though they were members of a sovereign polity. His doing so requires explanation: European powers only considered some local peoples to be capable of crude government and thus able to exercise some of the functions of a state; there was little consensus among European powers about the legal status of non-European sovereigns; and Macquarie himself knew that Māori were divided into hapū and so he must have had doubts as to whether they were truly a sovereign people. Macquarie probably chose to regard those chiefs as the representatives of a sovereign entity for two reasons. First, he desperately needed to bolster his claim to authority, and, second, the relationship of protection that Gidley King and northern rangatira had forged, and which Marsden and his missionaries and Ruatara and his kin had extended, made this a logical course of action. Macquarie might also have been influenced by British practices in India, begun by the English East India Company, through which they sought alliances with local rulers in order to create jurisdiction over small territories. Either way, there can be no doubting the significance of Macquarie's move. It meant the chiefs were treated as if they were

---

[11] Marsden to Governor Lachlan Macquarie, 1 November 1813, CMS, London, Records Relating to the New Zealand Mission, HL, MS-0498; Macquarie, Proclamation, 1 December 1813, *HRNZ*, vol. 1, pp. 316–18; Marsden to Pratt, 15 March 1814, Copy of Correspondence of Rev. Samuel Marsden 1813–1814, HL, MS-0054; Macquarie to Earl Bathurst, 17 January 1814, *HRA*, series 1, vol. 8, p. 96; J. J. Campbell to Macquarie, 9 November 1814, SARNSW, 4/1017; Macquarie, Proclamation, 9 November 1814, *HRNZ*, vol. 1, pp. 328–29; Andrew Porter, 'Trusteeship, Anti-Slavery and Humanitarianism', in Andrew Porter (ed.), *The Oxford History of the British Empire: Volume III: The Nineteenth Century*, Oxford University Press, Oxford, 1999, pp. 200–01; Benton and Ford, *Rage for Order*, chapter 4; Lisa Ford, 'Protecting the Peace on the Edges of Empire: Commissioners of Crown Lands in New South Wales', in Benton et al. (eds.), *Protection and Empire*, p. 187.

[12] Macquarie, Proclamation, 9 November 1814.

sovereign and were constituted as an ally of the British Crown. The status of the New Zealand being more or less sovereign, and the relationship this generated between the chiefs and the British Crown, was to deepen in the course of the next twenty-five years. Most importantly, while this arrangement was more a product of improvisation than design, it was to have profound implications for the terms upon which the British government would decide to intervene in the islands in 1839.[13]

Marsden and his missionaries not only played a critical role in bringing about an arrangement by which Māori were treated as though they were sovereign and allies of the British Crown. They also created a practice of treating the New Zealanders as the owners of the land. To acquire a crucial resource for his missionary endeavour, namely land for a mission site, Marsden realised that he had to negotiate with the local chiefs. Consequently, he chose to purchase 200 acres of land at Rangihoua from a Ngā Puhi chief Te Uri o Kanae, drawing up a land deed for this purpose in February 1815 (or at least this is how he saw the arrangement, whereas Ngā Puhi at the time probably understood it as a gift exchange by which the missionaries acquired a right to occupation and protection in return for an obligation to contribute to their security and well-being). It was the first of many such transactions over the next two decades as traders and settlers followed suit in the 1820s after realising that they had to negotiate with the local people to acquire land.[14]

This practice had major implications for how the New Zealanders' proprietorial interests in land would be treated by New South Wales land speculators, British colonisation companies and the Colonial Office in the mid to late 1830s. The natives were regarded as the customary owners of land and so deemed to have the capacity to convey title of a kind to foreigners or at least to British subjects.

---

[13] Macquarie to Bathurst, 17 January 1814, *HRA*, series 1, vol. 8, pp. 96, 98; Judith Binney, *The Legacy of Guilt: A Life of Thomas Kendall*, Auckland University Press, Auckland, 1968, p. 25; Robert Travers, 'A British Empire by Treaty in Eighteenth-Century India', in Saliha Belmessous (ed.), *Empire by Treaty: Negotiating European Expansion, 1600–1900*, Oxford University Press, New York, 2015, p. 138.

[14] Marsden to Secretary, CMS, 15 March 1814, Copy of Correspondence of Rev. Samuel Marsden 1813–1814, HL, MS-0054; Copy of the land deed, 24 February 1815, *BPP*, 1837–38, Paper no. 680, Report of the Select Committee of the House of Lords Appointed to Inquire into the Present State of the Islands of New Zealand (henceforth 1838 Select Committee Report), p. 117; Edward Nicolls to Bathurst, 8 November 1823, *HRNZ*, vol. 1, pp. 598–605; Baron Charles de Phillipe de Thierry to Bathurst, 23 December 1823 and 24 January 1824, *HRNZ*, vol. 1, pp. 614–15, 617–18; John George Lambton et al. to William Huskisson, undated [c. February or March 1825], William Huskisson Papers, BL, Add MS 38763; Bathurst to Edward John Littleton, 29 March 1825, *HRNZ*, vol. 1, p. 634; *The Times*, 1 April 1825; Samuel Enderby et al. to Bathurst, 24 April 1826, TNA, CO 201/221; Anne Salmond, *Tears of Rangi: Experiments Across Worlds*, Auckland University Press, Auckland, 2017, p. 92.

Crown Promises of Protection

Following Marsden's proposal to establish a mission in the Bay of Islands, several New South Wales traders and entrepreneurs, headed by Simeon Lord, petitioned the British government for a charter to enable them to form a joint stock company for the purpose of procuring and preparing hemp and flax and extracting timber in New Zealand. In doing so, they called on the government to provide them with protection, no doubt because they assumed they had a right to claim this on the grounds of the age-old understanding that the bond between British subjects and the Crown was not severed when they moved beyond its jurisdiction. Over time, such entrepreneurs typically advanced several arguments in making their claims for protection: Britain's commercial interests would be advanced; the native chiefs had expressed an interest in obtaining a protecting government; and the islands had to be placed under British protection in order to ensure that the French did not establish themselves and obtain an ascendancy that could threaten Britain's interests in the area. For their part, successive governors were keen to expand the reach of New South Wales. They supported endeavours such as Lord's in the belief that they would advance British trade and shore up the Empire's interests in the South Pacific, especially vis-à-vis the French.[15]

In response to Lord's request, Macquarie was willing to recommend to the Colonial Secretary, Earl Bathurst, that Lord and his associates be allowed to form a settlement on the condition that they obtained the permission of the native chiefs; and Bathurst only agreed to grant permission on this basis. Two years later, another important development took place in regard to the way in which Britain cast the legal status of the islands of New Zealand. Marsden had been trying to prosecute several ship captains in New South Wales courts for their maltreatment of natives, but he had failed because those courts had no jurisdiction to try British subjects for wrongs committed in the islands. Consequently, he asked the Church Missionary Society and the London Missionary Society in Britain to call upon the imperial government to enact the legislation required. In response to their representations, the government introduced a bill that made provision for the Crown to bring to trial masters and crews of ships and deserters who had committed manslaughter and

---

[15] Simeon Lord et al. to Macquarie, 3 October 1814, *HRNZ*, vol. 1, pp. 324–27; de Thierry to Bathurst, 23 December 1823, *HRNZ*, vol. 1, p. 615; Marsden to Pratt, 4 June 1824, *HRNZ*, vol. 1, p. 628; Enderby et al. to Bathurst, 24 April 1826; Robert Torrens to Lord Goderich, c. 25 January 1831, TNA, CO 201/224.

murder in Honduras and the islands of New Zealand and Tahiti once they returned to British soil.[16]

Historians have long argued that this legislation, which came to be known as the Murders Abroad Act, was an act by which the British Crown repudiated whatever claim to sovereignty it had been making in respect of New Zealand.[17] I would argue, however, that this contention rests on a misunderstanding of the nature of the move that the British government made in introducing it. While there can be no doubt the British parliament disavowed any sovereignty in the places and islands mentioned in the Act by declaring that they did not lie within His Majesty's dominions, it simultaneously implied that Britain still had some claim of possession in these territories by asserting that the local people came under the protection of the British Crown. This lent weight to the British government's attempt to forge an extraterritorial jurisdiction in the islands. There is nothing unusual about such a measure; there are many examples of imperial powers finding protection talk of this ambiguous kind invaluable when they faced a similar situation.[18] At the same time, this measure ensured that the British government would not incur any of the costly administrative responsibilities that could arise if it continued to assert its claim to sovereignty. By asserting that these islands did not lie within the dominion of the Crown, it acquired a ready means of fending off demands by British subjects that they be allowed to plant settlements there.[19]

Since its promise to protect alluded to a claim of possession, Britain was also able to shore up its interests vis-à-vis its imperial rivals. In other words, making promises to protect could work in the same manner as the imperial claim-making we noted in the opening chapter: they made vague references to possession in broadly and poorly defined territories that did not establish an absolute title to sovereignty but which might nonetheless be considered superior to any that their contenders might muster. As we will see, agents of the British government resorted to this kind of manoeuvre in regard to New Zealand on more than one occasion.[20]

---

[16] Macquarie to Bathurst, 24 June 1815, *HRA*, series 1, vol. 8, p. 561; Extract of Bathurst to Macquarie, 9 April 1816, *HRNZ*, vol. 1, p. 407; Marsden to Pratt, 15 June, 25 and 26 October and 6 November 1815, Collected Papers of and Relating to Rev. Samuel Marsden, HL, MS-0055; Marsden to Pratt, 16 March 1816, Collected Papers of and Relating to Rev. Samuel Marsden, HL, MS-0056; Memorial of the Committee of the CMS to Bathurst, undated [July 1817] and appendices, *HRNZ*, vol. 1, pp. 417–28.

[17] See, for example, E. J. Tapp, *Early New Zealand: A Dependency of New South Wales, 1788–1841*, Melbourne University Press, Melbourne, 1958, pp. 40–42.

[18] See, for example, Mary Dewhurst Lewis, *Divided Rule: Sovereignty and Empire in French Tunisia, 1881–1938*, University of California Press, Berkeley, 2014, pp. 63–64.

[19] 57 Geo III (1817) c. 53.

[20] R. Wilmot Horton to de Thierry, 10 December 1823, *HRNZ*, vol. 1, p. 615.

The imperial government was to treat the islands and peoples of New Zealand as though they had a dual status of being sovereign and not sovereign well into the late 1830s. This occurred despite the fact that it soon became apparent that extraterritorial legislation such as the Murders Abroad Act was no use in checking the behaviour of escaped convicts, castaways, sealers, whalers and adventurers. This situation prompted Marsden, the Church Missionary Society missionaries in the Bay of Islands, Sydney-based traders and New South Wales governors to make repeated calls on the imperial government to make good its promise to protect the natives by providing the necessary legal or military means.[21]

As a result, in 1823 the home government introduced legislation that included a section that extended the terms of the Murders Abroad Act by empowering courts in New South Wales to try offences committed by British subjects and British ship crews on the high seas or in places in the Indian and Pacific oceans, including New Zealand, which were not subject to the British Crown or the authority of any other state. When he learned of this legislation in May 1824, Macquarie's successor, Sir Thomas Brisbane, issued a proclamation in both English and Māori to publicise its terms, presumably in order to assure the chiefs of the goodwill of the British government. This would have reinforced the chiefs' sense of a relationship between themselves and the British Crown. It soon became apparent, however, that the British government still lacked the means required to prosecute outlaws, as this legislation, too, only made British subjects liable for prosecution once they returned to British soil.[22]

Several historians, including most recently Paul McHugh and Tony Ballantyne, have argued that the British government was constrained from intervening more in New Zealand's affairs by a series of legal rulings, such as the Murders Abroad Act of 1817, arguing that these unambiguously defined New Zealand's status by disavowing British sovereignty and pronouncing the natives to be the islands' sovereigns. However, as we have noted, in the 1817 statute the Crown implied it had some ongoing claim to possession by dint of its claim to protect natives such as the New Zealanders, and so the status of the territory was in fact ambiguous. Moreover, there is considerable evidence to suggest that the forces that

---

[21] John Bigge, Questions to CMS missionaries and their answers, 8 November 1819, *HRNZ*, vol. 1, p. 445; Marsden to Pratt, 4 June 1824, *HRNZ*, vol. 1, pp. 627–29; Marsden to Rev. E. Bickersmith, 13 March 1830, *HRNZ*, vol. 1, pp. 702–03; Marsden to Sir Ralph Darling, 2 August 1830, *HRNZ*, vol. 1, pp. 705–08.

[22] 4 Geo IV (1823) c. 96; *Sydney Gazette*, 20 May 1824; Philip Parkinson and Penelope Griffith (eds.), *Books in Maori 1815–1900: An Annotated Bibliography*, Reed, Auckland, 2004, pp. 32–33.

constrained London from intervening in New Zealand's affairs were of a rather different kind to the one these historians have emphasised.[23]

One example can suffice. In 1830 Robert Torrens (whom we met in the previous chapter) requested that the Crown bestow on him some authority over British subjects who comprised an establishment he had established in northern New Zealand. The Colonial Office asked James Stephen, at that time its legal counsel, for his opinion. Stephen began his written advice by drawing attention to what he clearly regarded as the key legal point, namely that the islands of New Zealand were not a part of His Majesty's dominions, as per the 1817 Murders Abroad Act. He then went on to speculate that Torrens might not only want to be able to keep his own men in order but also take military action against the natives, whom Stephen called 'the owners and sovereigns of the soil'. Stephen was inclined to make asides such as this, but there is little evidence to suggest that he attached any precise legal significance to them. In any case, returning to the matter at hand, he argued that, independent of any legal objections that might be raised to the British government assuming the authority in the islands of the kind Torrens was seeking, foreign states might regard this as an indirect extension of British power in the area, and he implied that the government should not act in any way that might arouse their concerns. Finally, and most importantly, Stephen argued that the real question at stake was whether the government was willing to sanction military occupation of New Zealand, given that this would, in his words, 'inevitably and shortly lead to the assumption of a permanent dominion' by it. The answer was a resounding no.[24]

On this as well as many other occasions the British government maintained that it could not afford to provide the resources required to found another colony. Indeed, it is apparent that it chose not to intervene in New Zealand's affairs for this reason as well as for political and strategic reasons. Thus, while legal arguments of the kind emphasised by Ballantyne and McHugh do occasionally appear in the relevant historical traces, they are best regarded as a resource that the British government deployed to justify its refusal to intervene in New Zealand's affairs.[25]

---

[23] Claudia Orange, *The Treaty of Waitangi*, Allen & Unwin/Port Nicholson Press, Wellington, 1987, pp. 2, 8, 21, 32, 35, 55, 60; McHugh, 'Pretty Government', pp. 237–40; Ballantyne, *Entanglements*, pp. 230–31; Shaunnagh Dorsett, 'Metropolitan Theorising: Legal Frameworks, Protectorates and Models for Maori Governance 1837–1838', *Law&History*, vol. 3, 2016, p. 8.

[24] James Stephen, Memorandum, 25 May 1830, TNA, CO 201/215.

[25] John Barrow to R. W. Hay, 24 March 1832, TNA, CO 201/228. Paul McHugh has argued that a bill known as the South Seas Islands Bill, which would have permitted the New South Wales government to establish judicial authority in New Zealand in regard to British subjects, failed to win approval because the British parliament refused to legislate

Yet the imperial government soon came under greater pressure to intervene in New Zealand's affairs. In April 1831 news reached Sydney that a leading Ngāti Toa rangatira, Te Rauparaha, and a large contingent of his people had slaughtered approximately a hundred Ngāi Tahu people on Banks Peninsula in New Zealand's South Island and had tortured and executed several of those they had taken captive. More to the point, it was learned that a British merchant ship, the *Elizabeth*, had ferried the Ngāti Toa to Banks Peninsula, that its captain had lured the principal Ngāi Tahu chief and his wife aboard the *Elizabeth*, and that the ship's mate had taken them prisoner. The news caused uproar, which only increased when the ship's captain and mate escaped punishment in the colony's courts. Marsden seized upon the incident to call on the governor of New South Wales, Sir Ralph Darling, to provide every protection to the natives against the acts of violence that British subjects committed upon them. Marsden drew upon the testimony of two young rangatira, Ahu and Wharepoaka, who had been sent to Sydney to complain about the treatment being meted out to their people by miscreant Europeans. He also mobilised his church and missionary connections in Sydney and London to extend this protest. Yet who needed protection remained ambiguous. Marsden claimed that the affair had created considerable anxiety among the natives and that they looked to the British government for redress and protection according to a promise that King George IV had apparently made to two leading northern rangatira, Waikato and Hongi Hika, when they had an audience with the King in London in 1820. But he also warned that the natives would take power into their own hands and redress the wrongs themselves unless they could be persuaded that the Crown would provide them with greater protection.[26]

for foreign territory in cases where the Crown had not previously come to some arrangement with the local sovereign. However, no Member of Parliament who spoke at the time that the government sought leave to introduce this bill made any explicit reference to the need for such an arrangement, though one member did challenge the legislation on the grounds that the government was seeking jurisdiction in a territory that did not lie within the King's dominions, and another pointed out that this meant that the House could not legislate for the islands of New Zealand. Moreover, while the government decided not to proceed with the bill after its second reading, there seems to be no reason why it could not have persuaded the parliament to pass the bill if it had really wanted to do so, given that it was able to persuade the House of Commons to pass very similar legislation four years later for the Cape Colony's adjacent territory of Natal (*BPD*, House of Commons, 7 June 1832, columns 505–06, and 13 June 1832, column 562; John S. Galbraith, *Reluctant Empire: British Policy on the South African Frontier 1834–1854*, University of California Press, Berkeley, 1963, p. 182; McHugh, 'Pretty Government', p. 239).

[26] *Sydney Gazette*, 2 April 1831; Bishop William Broughton to Darling, 14 April 1831, and an enclosure of Henry Williams to Marsden, 25 March 1831, TNA, CO 209/1; Marsden to Darling, 18 April 1831, *BPP*, 1836, Paper no. 538, Report from the Select Committee on Aborigines (British Settlements), p. 484; Marsden to Dandeson Coates, 18 April 1831,

In the closing months of 1831 further calls for protection as well as a claim of protection were made. In September a rumour circulated in Sydney that a visiting French man-of-war had designs on northern New Zealand. One of the most powerful Ngā Puhi rangatira, Rewa, and a Church Missionary Society missionary, William Yate, who were in Sydney at the time, became apprehensive that the French had designs on the Bay of Islands. Following their return home, they drew up a letter or a petition that called on the British king, William IV, to protect Māori and their country by becoming their 'friend' and 'guardian'. Thirteen of the most senior rangatira in northern New Zealand signed the letter. It seems the chiefs assumed that an appeal couched in these terms would consolidate the relationship between themselves and the British Crown that they believed Waikato and Hongi Hika had forged with King George IV in 1820, and that they saw this relationship as an alliance. But there can be little doubt that Yate and his missionary colleagues encouraged, perhaps even coached, them to cast this petition in the language of protection.[27]

In October a rumour began to circulate in Sydney that the captain of the French man-of-war had indeed claimed sovereignty by landing some men and hoisting the French flag in the Bay of Islands. The New South Wales Executive Council doubted the accuracy of the report but nonetheless took steps to foil this potential threat by asking the commander of a British naval vessel to proceed immediately to the Bay of Islands with a letter addressed to the commander of the French ship that declared that the British government had taken the islands under its protection at the request of the natives and so could not sanction the intrusion of a foreign state.[28]

HRNZ, vol. 1, pp. 715–17; Marsden to Bickersteth, 25 April 1831, *HRNZ*, vol. 1, p. 718; Binney, 'Tuki's Universe', p. 26; New Zealand History, 'Wharepoaka', https://nzhistory .govt.nz/politics/declaration/signatory/wharepoaka.

[27] Lawrence M. Rogers (ed.), *The Early Journals of Henry Williams*, Pegasus Press, Christchurch, 1961, entries for 20 and 28 September 1831, pp. 191–92; William Williams, Journal, vol. 1, 1825–31, ATL, qMS-2248, entries for 27 September and 4 October 1831; Marianne Williams to her mother-in-law, 3 October 1831, reproduced in Hugh Carleton, *The Life of Henry Williams, Archdeacon of Waimate*, Vol. 2, Wilsons & Horton, Auckland, 1877, p. 92; Warerahi et al., Petition to King William IV, undated [c. early October 1831], and William Yate to Colonial Secretary of New South Wales, 16 November 1831, *BPP*, 1840, Paper no. 238, Correspondence with the Secretary of State Relative to New Zealand, p. 7; Richard Davis to John Noble Coleman, 3 December 1831, reproduced in John Noble Coleman, *A Memoir of the Rev. Richard Davis*, James Nisbet and Co., London, 1865, p. 143; *Sydney Gazette*, 15 December 1831; Keith V. Sinclair (translator), *Laplace in New Zealand, 1831*, Heritage Press, Waikanae, 1998, pp. 42–44; Grant Phillipson, Bay of Islands Maori and the Crown 1793–1853, Treaty of Waitangi Tribunal, Wai 1040 #A1, 2005, pp. 229, 232; New Zealand History, 'Rewa', https://nzhistory.govt.nz/politics/declaration/signatory/rewa.

[28] Extract from the Minutes of the Proceedings of the New South Wales Executive Council, 31 October 1831, Miscellaneous New South Wales Archives Estrays Relating to New

A Deepening Alliance

In January 1832 the Colonial Office belatedly considered a recommendation, first made by Marsden and adopted by Darling, that a *British Resident* be appointed to New Zealand to protect British commerce and repress outrages perpetrated against the natives. The use of resident political agents was a long-established British practice in India. These officers were appointed to represent British interests in the Mughal courts as well as exert influence over British subjects, though the latter was usually done through the local sovereign. The nature of these appointments was deeply ambiguous. On the one hand, they implied that the British Crown had disavowed any claim to sovereignty, recognised the local polity as sovereign and acknowledged its power to grant or deny access to key resources. On the other hand, they provided the means whereby the Crown could assume some control over its subjects and manipulate the local polity to its own ends.[29]

In responding to demands from New South Wales that the government appoint a British Resident in the Bay of Islands, the imperial government employed a new kind of protection talk. The Colonial Secretary, Lord Goderich, informed Governor Richard Bourke that he feared that '[t]he unfortunate natives of New Zealand' would soon be added to 'those barbarous tribes' who had fallen as a result of their intercourse with 'civilised men' and asserted that there could be 'no more sacred duty than that of using every possible means to rescue the natives' from further evils and deliver Britain 'from the disgrace and crime of having either occasioned, caused or tolerated such enormities'. However, while Goderich chose to employ this rhetoric, he was actually rejecting a demand that Bourke had made. He had agreed to appoint a British Resident but was refusing to grant that officer the means he required to carry out his duties effectively, despite the fact that Bourke had pointed out that it would be useless to proceed with the appointment unless the government provided the requisite legal authority and the military power to enforce it. Goderich tried to placate Bourke, telling him that the government had obtained leave to introduce a bill (which became known as South Seas Islands Bill) that would go some way to rendering the Resident's mission effective by giving New South Wales the authority to seize, detain, prosecute and punish the perpetrators of crimes in New

Zealand 1830–45, ML, DLNAR 3; Governor Patrick Lindesay to Lord Goderich, 4 November 1831, *HRA*, series 1, vol. 16, p. 442.

[29] Michael H. Fisher, 'Diplomacy in India, 1526–1858', in H. V. Bowen et al. (eds.), *Britain's Oceanic Empire: Atlantic and Indian Ocean Worlds, c. 1550–1850*, Cambridge University Press, Cambridge, 2012, pp. 249–51, 260–63; McHugh, 'Pretty Government', p. 241.

Zealand. But he must have known that this legislation was unlikely to be approved by parliament because it had already run into opposition in the House of Commons on the grounds that the British Crown had no jurisdiction in the islands since they were not within the King's dominion.[30]

In other words, it is apparent that the imperial government had decided to continue to treat the islands of New Zealand and its peoples as though they were more or less foreign sovereigns, even though Bourke had drawn its attention to the problematic consequences of this course of action. What is more, the ambiguous status of the islands as an independent territory under the protection of the British Crown, as well as the status of the natives as a people akin to a British ally, was about to be reinforced.

Bourke was acutely aware that the imperial government had failed to furnish the thirty-one-year-old James Busby, a former New South Wales public servant, with the power and authority he needed to be able to perform the role of British Resident in northern New Zealand. He was also at something of a loss to know how he could solve this problem. Bourke delayed Busby's departure from Sydney in the hope that the House of Commons would provide the wherewithal by passing the South Seas Islands Bill, but after several months had passed he realised this support would not be forthcoming. He then seized upon a passage in a despatch Goderich had sent him in which the Colonial Office or the Lords of the Admiralty had mused: 'if the natives of New Zealand had made any approach towards a settled form of government; [and] were there any established system of jurisprudence among them, however rude, their own courts would claim and be entitled to the cognisance of all crimes committed within their territory'. Cobbling together some of these phrases, Bourke drew up instructions for Busby in which he suggested that 'some approach may be made by the natives towards a settled form of government, and that by the establishment of some form of jurisprudence among them, their courts may be able to claim the cognizance of all crimes committed within their territory; and thus may the offending subjects, of whatever state, be brought to justice'. Bourke's adoption of this course of action may have owed something to the practice of British Residents in India, discussed earlier, yet it seems more likely that he drew his inspiration from the more immediate resource he had to hand, namely Goderich's despatch. But whatever was the case, the point

---

[30] Bourke to Goderich, 23 December 1831, *HRA*, series 1, vol. 16, pp. 482–83; Goderich to Bourke, 31 January 1832, *HRA*, series 1, vol. 16, pp. 510–13; Goderich to Bourke, [2] 8 March 1832, *HRA*, series 1, vol. 16, pp. 561–63; *BPD*, House of Commons, 7 June 1832, columns 505–06; Goderich to Bourke, 14 June 1832, *HRA*, series 1, vol. 16, pp. 662–64.

is that Bourke recommended to Busby that he try to constitute the natives as a unified sovereign authority and harness their power as an ally. Busby welcomed Bourke's suggestion. This is hardly surprising. In 1831 he had submitted a memorandum to the imperial government in which he had recommended a very similar series of measures (largely on the basis of information that he had gleaned from Church Missionary Society sources).[31]

Busby arrived in the Bay of Islands in May 1833, bearing a letter in King William IV's name that comprised the British government's response to the 1831 petition in which northern rangatira had asked the King to become their protector and in which they had represented themselves in an unprecedented manner as 'the chiefs to the natives of New Zealand'. In this letter the British government figured the native chiefs as allies, since it not only promised to provide protection but also told the chiefs that it expected them to assist Busby so that he could realise the purpose of his appointment. Moreover, on his arrival, Busby arranged for a meeting to be held so that he could seek the chiefs' permission for him to assume the position of British Resident and claim the protection and privileges that were usually accorded to British subjects holding such a position in foreign states. A Church Missionary Society missionary, William Williams, who translated into Māori the address Busby gave on this occasion, reckoned that the numerous rangatira who were present did not really grasp the object for which the British Resident had been sent, reporting that one or two of them had suggested to Busby that he should have brought troops for his own protection, which was really to query how he was going to protect them when he did not even have the resources to protect himself. (As it turned out, Busby was to rely on the protection of a senior rangatira, Te Kemara, at Waitangi.) A few days later, however, another missionary, George Clarke, informed Busby that some of the rangatira in the area had begun making copies of the King's letter as well as Busby's address, in order to circulate them. This suggests that the rangatira saw Busby's appointment as a response to their petition to the King and a means of consolidating the relationship of protection with the British Crown that they believed Hongi Hika, Waikato and King George IV had initiated in 1820. Whatever the case, Busby

[31] James Busby, 'A Brief Memoir Relative to the Islands of New Zealand', [June 1831], in his *Authentic Information Relative to New South Wales and New Zealand*, Joseph Cross, London, 1832, pp. 66–70; Goderich to Bourke, 31 January 1832, *HRA*, series 1, vol. 16, p. 511; Busby to Earl of Haddington, 25 February 1833, Despatches from the British Resident 1833–70 (henceforth Busby Despatches), ATL, qMS-0352; Busby to Alexander McLeay, 19 March and 27 March 1833, Busby Despatches, qMS-0344 and qMS-0345; Bourke to Busby, 13 April 1833, *BPP*, 1840, Paper no. 238, p. 6; Bourke to Goderich, 2 May 1833, TNA, CO 209/1.

requested that 1,000 copies of the King's letter and his address be printed in English and Māori, and distributed.[32]

In the Bay of Islands Busby soon set about trying to forge a confederation of chiefs and thus a sense of national sovereignty among Māori. He took the first step by persuading northern rangatira to adopt a national flag, ostensibly in order to address a problem they had recently encountered. A Hokianga-built ship, carrying two leading Ngā Puhi rangatira, had been seized after entering a British port (Sydney) without the requisite legal proof of ownership and nationality. Busby told the rangatira that the flag would mean the vessels would remain theirs but be under the protection of the King. Later, after the imperial government had approved the flag, Busby claimed that the Crown had thereby recognised New Zealand as a sovereign country.[33]

Busby took a further step towards the formation of a permanent confederation of the chiefs in October 1835 after receiving a letter from a French émigré, Baron Charles de Thierry, in which he had set out a plan to establish at Hokianga an independent state, asserted that he had purchased the sovereignty and land from the native owners and suggested that he would come with the means to uphold this claim. Busby decided to take this adventurer at his word. He invited northern rangatira to a meeting at Waitangi to consider a 'Declaration of Independence of New Zealand' (for which he might have drawn inspiration from the American Declaration of Independence), which he had drafted and sent to the Church Missionary Society's most senior missionary in New Zealand, Henry Williams, to translate into Māori. Busby persuaded thirty-four rangatira to sign, which included not only most of the signatories to the 1831 petition to the King but also the most important of the northern chiefs, among whom were Hongi Hika, Patuone, Rewa, Te Kemara, Waikato and Wharepoaka. In the Declaration the

---

[32] Warerahi et al., Petition; Busby, Memo, 22 May 1832, *HRA*, series 1, vol. 16, p. 665; Goderich to the Chiefs of New Zealand, 14 June 1832, *BPP*, 1840, Paper no. 238, pp. 7–8; Bourke to Busby, 13 April 1833, *BPP*, 1840, Paper no. 238, p. 4; Busby, Address to Chiefs, 17 May 1833, TNA, CO 209/1; William Williams, Journal, vol. 2, entry 17 May 1833, ATL, qMS-2249; Busby to McLeay, 17 May 1833, Busby Despatches, qMS-0344; George Clarke to Busby, 24 May 1833, NANZ, BR1; Busby to McLeay, 24 May 1833, Busby Despatches, qMS-0345; McLeay to Busby, 23 July 1833, Williams Family Papers, AWMML, MS 91–75, Box 2, Folder 49; Makaore Taonui et al. to the Governor, 24 March 1856, reproduced in *Maori Messenger: Te Karere Maori*, 31 May 1856; Phillipson, Bay of Islands, p. 240.

[33] Busby, Address to the Chiefs on the Occasion of the Adoption of a Flag, 17 March 1834, NANZ, BR1/1/[56]; Busby to McLeay, 22 March 1834, Busby Despatches, qMS-0344; Busby to Hay, 3 April 1834, New Zealand Estrays Collected by Sir William Dixson, 27 March 1833–20 April 1848, ML, DLNAR 1; Busby, Address to British Subjects, 10 October 1835, TNA, CO 209/2.

rangatira proclaimed an independent state under the designation of the United Tribes of New Zealand, pronounced that all the sovereign power and authority in the territories of the United Tribes resided in this state and stated that they would not permit any other to exist unless it was by persons appointed by them and acting under the authority of laws enacted by the state. However – and this is crucial – they also agreed in the Declaration to forward it to the King and ask him to act as the parent of what they called their 'infant state' and to protect it from any challenges to its independence.[34]

In order to make sense of this greatly misunderstood document and evaluate its badly overstated historical significance,[35] we must consider the circumstances in which Busby formulated it and his understanding of its implications, grasp the nature of sovereignty and the ways in which European governments often treated it at the time, examine the British government's response to the Declaration and note the ambiguous position that the British government continued to adopt in regard to the islands.

Busby had several reasons for drawing up the Declaration, but he primarily conceived of it as a way of addressing the threat that he believed Thierry posed as the representative of a foreign power. This purpose determined the Declaration's terms and it ought to guide how we interpret it as a historical trace. Busby assumed that he had to create a fiction that New Zealand was in fact an independent state since he could assert neither British sovereignty (because he knew he lacked the authority to do so) nor native sovereignty (because he would have known that the New Zealanders were not seen as sovereign in a way that meant this status would be recognised by the agents of another European power). Consequently, he asserted that New Zealand was independent not so much because it was under a form of native sovereignty but because its status would be guaranteed by the British government by virtue of the fact that the chiefs had solemnly asked the British Crown for its protection. As we have seen, the situation in which Busby drew up the Declaration was one in which imperial agents often made claims of protection in order to

---

[34] Thierry to Busby, 14 September 1835, TNA, CO 209/2; Busby to McLeay, 10 October 1835, TNA, CO 209/2; The Declaration of Independence, 28 October 1835, TNA, CO 209/2; Orange, *Treaty*, p. 23; David Armitage, *The Declaration of Independence: A Global History*, Harvard University Press, Cambridge, 2007, p. 125.

[35] The number of historians who have misinterpreted this document are too numerous to cite. Recently, a permanent exhibition in the National Library of New Zealand has accorded the Declaration the status of being one of three constitutional documents that are said to shape Aotearoa New Zealand. See https://natlib.govt.nz/he-tohu. For a more measured discussion of the Declaration's significance, see He Whakaputanga me te Tiriti: The Declaration and the Treaty, Wai 1040, Treaty of Waitangi Tribunal Report, 2014, chapter 4.

shore up what amounted to vague claims in regard to sovereignty. In recent years, several scholars, including Paul McHugh, have sought to grapple with the position that the Declaration expressed on the matter of sovereignty. They have argued that it was by no means unusual for several reasons. Conceptions of sovereignty were much looser than they were to become later in the nineteenth century in that they allowed for the kind of plurality articulated by the Declaration; the British Empire's dealings with native polities at this time were characterised by a range of political relationships, which included the sharing of jurisdiction with local potentates in Africa, India and elsewhere; and Busby was familiar with those arrangements.[36] There is no gainsaying these points, but we should not overlook the fact that the Declaration's ambiguous expression of the status of New Zealand and its people was the product of a long chain of protection talk and consistent with the vague manner in which this status had been expressed by the British government for some time.

Busby was aware that the Declaration could be misunderstood as an act by which the British Crown recognised Māori as fully sovereign (which is the very way that it has been misunderstood in recent times). Consequently, he made it clear to his superiors that he knew that the British government could claim New Zealand as its possession on the grounds of *discovery* and settlement and that he assumed the Declaration would not prevent the government doing just that sometime in the future. Moreover, he informed the Colonial Office that he regarded the Declaration as a means by which the government could make the country a dependency of the British Crown in all but name. Finally, three months after he drew up the Declaration, Busby more or less abandoned his project of trying to turn the rangatira in northern New Zealand into a form of political authority that would produce a national sovereignty and enable them to continue to act as allies of the British government. He began instead to claim that the native chiefs would be glad to yield government of their country to the British Crown and thereby become its subjects, though in making this claim he made it clear to his superiors that they would need to give an undertaking to the chiefs to protect their people's rights, including their rights in land.[37]

---

[36] See, for example, Samuel Carpenter, Brief of Evidence in the Matter of the Treaty of Waitangi Act 1975 and in the Matter of Te Paparahi o te Taki (Northland Inquiry), Treaty of Waitangi Tribunal Wai, 1040 #A17, 2009, pp. 28, 30, 32, and McHugh, 'Pretty Government', pp. 242–43.

[37] Busby to McLeay, 10 and 11 September 1835, 31 October 1835 and 26 January 1836, Busby Despatches, qMS-0344; McLeay to Busby, 12 February 1836, TNA, CO 209/2.

In Sydney, Bourke does not seem to have regarded the Declaration as significant. He probably realised that it was in keeping with his instructions to Busby to encourage the native chiefs to take steps towards establishing a form of national government. Bourke's masters in London seem to have been more alert to the way that the Declaration might be construed legally. But, rather than registering its ambiguous assertion of native sovereignty, let alone recognising this (as many historians have claimed), the Colonial Secretary Lord Glenelg chose merely to note the chiefs' request for protection and direct Busby to assure the chiefs that the Crown would provide them with protection as far as this might be consistent with a due regard for the interests and rights of the Crown's own subjects.[38]

It seems clear that in so far as the Declaration of Independence had any significance at the metropolitan centre at the time it was made, it might have reinforced the Colonial Office's perception of the New Zealanders as a people who had a status somewhat akin to that of a sovereign power as well as a people with whom diplomatic negotiations could be conducted. For the time being, though, the Colonial Office saw no reason to change the position it had adopted in respect to the islands of New Zealand. Moreover, it maintained this position in the course of the next two years despite the fact that it received more calls to intervene and provide greater protection after it became clear that Busby lacked the necessary personal skills to project some sense of power and authority and was failing to make the best use of the meagre resources he had at his disposal.[39]

Part II

Growing Pressures to Intervene

Beginning in 1837, the imperial government came under considerable pressure from metropolitan groups to intervene in New Zealand's affairs. There was growing concern about British colonisation among Christian humanitarians; new plans to colonise the country by a colonisation

---

[38] Hay, Minute, 25 May 1836, on Busby to Hay, 2 November 1835, TNA, CO 209/1; Lord Glenelg to Bourke, 25 May 1836, *HRA*, series 1, vol. 16, p. 427.

[39] Petition of British Subjects in the Bay of Islands to His Majesty, undated [6 May 1834], TNA, CO 209/1; Bourke to Lord Stanley, 23 September 1834, *HRA*, series 1, vol. 16, p. 545; Bourke to Stanley, 6 December 1834, *HRA*, series 1, vol. 16, pp. 596–97; Bourke to Thomas Spring Rice, 1 February 1835, *HRA*, series 1, vol. 16, pp. 645–46; *BPP*, 1838, Paper no. 680, pp. 164–65, 167, 169; *Sydney Herald*, 19 January 1837; *Colonist*, 26 January 1837; Henry Williams to Edward Marsh, 28 March 1837, reproduced in Hugh Carleton, *The Life of Henry Williams, Archdeacon of Waimate*, vol. 1, Upton & Co, Auckland, 1874, p. 200; *BPP*, 1838, Paper no. 680, pp. 164–65, 167, 169; Ged Martin, 'James Busby and the Treaty of Waitangi', *British Review of New Zealand Studies*, vol. 5, 1992, pp. 15, 22; McHugh, 'Pretty Government', pp. 242–43.

company; and vigorous opposition to this proposal from missionary societies. The Colonial Office also received reports from Busby and missionaries in New Zealand that expressed alarm about cataclysmic changes that they claimed were occurring in the islands. All these parties spoke a different language of protection from the one we have seen at work so far.

In 1836 Christian humanitarians led by Thomas Fowell Buxton started to pay attention to New Zealand. The select committee, which Buxton had persuaded the House of Commons to appoint the previous year to inquire into the treatment of aborigines, not only learned about the cruel treatment of natives in Britain's colonies of settlement. It also heard about the deleterious impact that British subjects were having on native peoples in the South Pacific. In regard to New Zealand, William Yate, the Church Missionary Society missionary, and Dandeson Coates, John Beecham, and William Ellis, the secretaries of the Church Missionary Society, the Wesleyan Missionary Society (which had begun to found missions in northern New Zealand in 1823), and the London Missionary Society respectively, all gave evidence to this effect. They also repeated the calls that Marsden had been making for the British Resident and the New South Wales government to be given legal authority and military force so that more effective protection could be provided to the natives.[40]

In its final report to parliament, tabled in June 1837, this select committee asserted that the British people had a special duty towards natives, because of the ability of the British government to confer upon these peoples the most important of benefits and the inability of the natives to resist the encroachments of British subjects. 'The disparity of the parties, the strength of the one, and the incapacity of the other, to enforce the observance of their rights', it argued, 'constitutes a new and irresistible appeal to our compassionate protection'. Clearly, these claims gave protection a very different cast to the one it previously had. Natives such as the New Zealanders were now deemed to be fundamentally weak and thus a people to be regarded as subjects, rather than reckoned as more or less sovereign and capable of being allies of the British Empire. At the same time, though, these Christian humanitarians asserted that the British government had a duty to respect the rights of these natives.[41]

A month earlier, the New Zealand Association was founded in London to advocate the systematic colonisation of New Zealand. The Association was the brainchild of the 'colonial reformers' and spearheaded by Edward

[40] *BPP*, 1836, Paper no. 538, pp. iii, 188–201, 481–90, 504–13.
[41] *BPP*, 1837, Paper no. 425, Report from the Select Committee on Aborigines (British Settlements), pp. 3, 14–22, 85.

Gibbon Wakefield. Some of its principal figures had been involved in the plans to colonise South Australia a few years earlier. The Association was well connected politically, boasting among its ranks several Whig parliamentarians, the most important of whom were Benjamin Hawes, William Hutt and Francis Baring, who was joint secretary of the Treasury and first cousin of the Parliamentary Under-Secretary for the Colonies, Sir George Grey.

In order to win the Whig government's support for its scheme to colonise New Zealand, the Association assumed that it had to adopt a certain position in regard to sovereignty and rights in land. In a statement of objectives that it adopted at one of its first meetings, the Association asserted that New Zealand lay within British dominion on the grounds that the islands had been claimed by Cook, but it also argued that this only gave Britain a right of possession vis-à-vis other European nations. This meant, it went on, that the Crown had no right to colonise New Zealand unless it negotiated a cession of sovereignty with the native chiefs. In making this argument, the Association maintained that the natives in New Zealand were a people who had 'advanced beyond the savage state as to recognise property in land' and 'whose national independence ha[d] been virtually, not to say formally acknowledged by the British government'. It proposed, furthermore, that the natives be afforded protection from the aggression of British settlers as well as admitted to the rights and privileges of British subjects. In a parliamentary bill that the Association drafted at this time, it sought authority to negotiate a treaty with the native chiefs on the Crown's behalf, whereby the chiefs would cede sovereignty to the Crown.[42]

Many intellectual historians would argue that the Association adopted this position because its principal figures were influenced by the stadial theory of history. Yet in its statement of objectives the Association represented the New Zealanders as a people akin to hunter-gatherers, who were commonly deemed to lack sovereignty and rights of property in land. Moreover, the testimony that two of the Association's principal figures gave to a House of Lords select committee on New Zealand in 1838 reveals that they were of the opinion that the New Zealanders were *not* in fact a sovereign people and that Cook's claiming *did* bestow the right of sovereignty on the British government, and that they merely assumed it

[42] NZA, Minutes of Meetings, 7, 22 and 31 May 1837, NZA Minute and Letter Books, 7 May 1837–9 July 1838, ATL, Micro-MS-0459; Francis Baring to Lord Melbourne, 14 June 1837, NZA Minute and Letter Books; [New Zealand Association], *Statement of the Objects of the New Zealand Association*, Black and Armstrong, London, 1837, pp. 3–4; Abstract of a Bill of NZA, June 1837, *BPP*, 1840, Paper no. 582, Report from the Select Committee on New Zealand (henceforth 1840 Select Committee Report), p. 164.

could be useful for the Association to pretend that the natives were sovereign. One of its leading members told the Select Committee that the Association '*suppose[d]* the New Zealanders, and not Great Britain, to be in possession of the right of sovereignty' and that it had 'propose[d], accordingly, that a purchase should be made of the sovereignty', just as he emphasised that the Association was 'ready to adopt either view' on the matter. In other words, it seems clear that the position the Association chose to adopt at this stage in regard to sovereignty owed more to strategic considerations than to any philosophical ideas and that it made reference to the latter in order to lend authority to its stance.[43]

It appears that the Association adopted the position that the natives should be treated as though they were sovereign partly because it assumed that the British government subscribed to this view. It might be argued that this is unremarkable. After all, both the British Crown and parliament had declared on more than one occasion that the islands of New Zealand were not part of Britain's dominions, thereby implying that Britain had no legal right to assert sovereignty there. Yet the government had never explicitly stated that sovereignty in the islands lay with the native chiefs and that consequently there was a need for the Crown to negotiate a cession of sovereignty. In any case, the British government could readily shift its position on this matter, as the editor of *The Times* remarked in December 1838: 'Any recognition of the sovereign independence of the native chiefs that may have been extended to them by our government (and it is as vague as can well be imagined) is entirely an affair of pure grace on our part . . . which we may rightfully modify, withdraw, or regulate'.[44]

In all likelihood, the Association presumed that it had to pretend that sovereignty lay with the natives because it believed that the Colonial Office was profoundly influenced by humanitarian sentiment regarding the impact of colonisation of native peoples and so would insist that the islands could only be annexed by securing the consent of the natives (though, as we saw in the case of South Australia, the Association exaggerated the influence of Christian humanitarianism on the Colonial Office). At the hearings of the Select Committee on New Zealand in 1838, one of the Association's principal members stated: 'I hold that [Her Majesty] is the sovereign [in New Zealand], but I am afraid public opinion would not allow me to maintain that'; and one of the Association's other members echoed this remark, arguing that 'sovereign

---

[43] [New Zealand Association], *Statement*, p. 13; 1838 Select Committee Report, pp. 129–30, 132–33, 154, my emphasis.
[44] *The Times*, 26 December 1838.

rights over savage countries' had once been 'conveniently settled by allowing the priority of claim to the first discoverers' but that in recent years 'the justice of this claim ha[d] been questioned'.[45]

There are probably three other reasons why the Association was prepared, for the time being, to insist that the New Zealanders were sovereign. First, this position enabled it to claim that it would have the grounds to colonise the islands in the event that the government refused to allow it to negotiate a cession of sovereignty on the Crown's behalf. Second, it allowed the Association to pretend that the right to transfer land lay with the natives, thereby licensing any attempt it might make to acquire land before the Crown assumed sovereignty in the islands. Third, the Association's willingness to adopt the position that the natives were not only sovereign but had rights of property in land undoubtedly owed much to its knowledge of the islands' recent history. In September 1837 a magnate and prominent Whig politician, the Earl of Durham, pointed out to Edward Gibbon Wakefield that there were British subjects who were already in possession of land in New Zealand and that this meant it was 'impossible ... to follow the precedent of the South Australian Act, which declared that all the land of the province "public land"'.[46]

Once the Association's principal players had drawn up their plans for New Zealand, they assumed that the missionary societies were powerful enough to mean that they had to seek their approval. They quickly learned that Dandeson Coates, the Church Missionary Society's lay secretary, was convinced that the Association was fundamentally entrepreneurial in nature and that it was being disingenuous in adopting the humanitarian language of protection. (He was wrong on the first score but right on the second.) As soon as the Association's plans became public, the missionary societies vigorously attacked them. Coates maintained that Britain had no right to claim possession of New Zealand because he reckoned the islands were a foreign state. He also claimed that colonisation tended to inflict great wrongs on native peoples and that the Association's scheme would interrupt or even destroy the missionary societies' work of civilising and Christianising the natives of New Zealand.[47]

---

[45] 1838 Select Committee Report, pp. 129, 154; 1840 Select Committee Report, p. 5.

[46] *BPP*, 1836, Paper no. 512, Report from the Select Committee on the Disposal of Lands in the British Colonies, p. 108; [New Zealand Association], *Statement*, pp. 4, 18–19, 27; Earl of Durham to Edward Gibbon Wakefield, 3 September 1837, First Earl of Durham Papers, ATL, MS 0140, Folder 5.

[47] Resolutions of the Committee of the CMS, 6 June 1837, reproduced in Dandeson Coates, *The Present State of the New Zealand Question Considered, in a Letter to J.P. Plumptre*, Richard Watts, London, 1838, pp. 3–4; 1840 Select Committee Report, p. 4.

The Association, however, found some support for its scheme in government circles. The Secretary of State for War, Lord Howick, sounded out by one of the Association's principals, Sir H. G. Ward, was sympathetic to its ideas of systematic colonisation and saw no grounds for opposing its plans, but he warned Ward that the Colonial Office could hardly be expected to encourage or assist the Association, no doubt because he knew of the government's long-standing reluctance to assume the burden of any new colonies. This proved to be the case. James Stephen, now the Permanent Under-Secretary at the Colonial Office, was highly critical of the Association's scheme. Most of his concerns were the same as those he had had in regard to the plans of the South Australian Association, but perhaps the Colonial Office's failure to foil that association's expansive plan for South Australia made him especially determined to rein in this new scheme of Wakefield and his followers. Stephen also expressed concern that the history of colonisation suggested that the extermination of the aboriginal people would follow the founding of a British colony in New Zealand. He pointed out to Howick that Buxton's Select Committee report on aborigines was strongly opposed to any scheme to colonise New Zealand.[48]

At this point, the New Zealand Association realised that if it was going to win political support for its scheme it had to publicise the parts it had devised in the name of protecting the natives. After Wakefield recruited the Earl of Durham to join the Association's committee, become its public face and use his considerable influence with Lord Melbourne's government, Wakefield and the Association's secretary set about compiling a compendium in which they set out the Association's principles and plans in detail. Most importantly, they argued that New Zealand was already being colonised in a lawless fashion, that the natives were consequently at risk of extermination, that all the means the missionary societies and Buxton's select committee had proposed to protect the natives were inadequate, and that what was required was systematic colonisation and the assertion of British authority so that protection could be extended over all of the islands. Shortly after the publication of this volume, something of a pamphlet war broke out as both Coates and Wakefield sought to win Glenelg's ear.[49]

[48] Lord Howick to Sir H. G. Ward, 27 June 1837, Papers of Henry George, 3rd Earl Grey, University of Durham Library Special Collections (henceforth Howick Papers), GRE/B147/1; James Stephen to Howick, 1 July 1837, Howick Papers, GRE/B126/11/75; Stephen, Paper on the New Zealand Bill, 1 July 1837, Howick Papers, GRE/B126/11/80–89.

[49] NZA, Minutes of Meeting, 10 July 1837, NZA Minute and Letter Books; Durham to Wakefield, 3 September 1837; Wakefield to Durham, 30 September 1837, NZA Minute and Letter Books; [Edward Gibbon Wakefield and John Ward], *The British Colonization of New Zealand*, John W. Parker, London, 1837, pp. 30–43, 52–54, 56–58, 273–74;

The Colonial Office Responds

It was difficult for the government to ignore the lobbying of these powerful metropolitan groups, especially the New Zealand Association. In mid-
December 1837, Prime Minister Melbourne agreed to receive
a deputation from the Association. However, at this meeting tempers on
both sides became badly frayed. The deputation complained that the
Association had been badly treated by the government, telling
Melbourne that some of its members had given up their positions and
disposed of their property in anticipation of being able to form a colony in
New Zealand and that one member in particular would suffer greatly if
the government did not sanction its scheme. Melbourne, failing to realise
that this member was present, stated that he must have been mad to have
taken such a risk, whereupon this fellow leapt to his feet and declared that
he was that madman. After this meeting, Glenelg prepared
a memorandum in which he launched a comprehensive attack on the
Association's scheme. As a result, one might have expected the government to reject the Association's proposals. Yet, just five days later,
Glenelg told the Association that he was willing to accept its proposals
and offer it a charter to colonise New Zealand, albeit on certain
conditions.[50]

What caused this turnaround? Put simply, the Association had applied
enormous pressure on the government, and Melbourne found this difficult to resist as his government was dependent on the support of the
Association's chairman, the Earl of Durham, for its very survival. Hence,
Melbourne called on Howick to 'make up Glenelg's mind upon the
subject'; and Glenelg, who was notoriously indecisive, acquiesced. Not
surprisingly, Glenelg and his colleagues at the Colonial Office then
needed to find some rationale to explain its volte face. They found it in
a long report that the Office had just received from Busby. The British
Resident had painted a dramatic picture of New Zealand in a state of
crisis, due to spiralling conflict between the natives and a sharp decrease
in their numbers. This served the Colonial Office's purposes admirably.[51]

Dandeson Coates, *The Principles, Objects and Plan of the New Zealand Association
Examined*, Hatchards, London, 1837; Edward Gibbon Wakefield, *Mr Dandeson Coates
and the New Zealand Association*, Henry Hooper, London, 1837.
[50] Melbourne to Howick, 14 December 1837, Howick Papers, GRE/B115/1/85; Glenelg,
Memorandum, 15 December 1837, TNA, CO 209/2; Minutes of meeting between
Glenelg and the Association, 20 December 1837, NZA Minute and Letter Books;
Draft, Glenelg to Durham, 21 December 1837, TNA, CO 209/3; Glenelg to Durham,
29 December 1837, 1840 Select Committee Report, p. 148; 1840 Select Committee
Report, pp. 2–3, 109.
[51] Busby to Bourke, 16 June 1837, *BPP*, 1838, Paper no. 122, New Zealand: Copy of
a Despatch from Governor Sir R. Bourke to Lord Glenelg, pp. 6–12; Stephen to Jane

The government's decision to grant the Association a charter to establish a colony in the islands of New Zealand has been depicted by historians like Peter Adams as the moment it made a crucial change in its stance about the state and status of New Zealand. But there is a good deal of evidence to the contrary. Just as importantly for this study, historians have neglected to note that both sovereignty and native title would almost certainly have been treated very differently in New Zealand if the Association had accepted the charter Glenelg offered. As it turned out, the manner in which the government finally treated sovereignty and native title in the islands can be attributed in large part to the following convoluted sequence of events.[52]

In the New Year of 1838, after learning of the government's decision to offer the Association a charter, Coates furiously lobbied the Colonial Office. But it was unmoved. This prompted the Church Missionary Society and Wesleyan Missionary Society to decide that they should try to place the matter before parliament and the public, and led the secretaries of both these societies to publish pamphlets in which they set out their case. In the meantime the Association informed the Colonial Office that it could not accept two of the conditions in the charter the government had offered it: that it form a joint stock company (to ensure that its members invested their own capital in the venture) and that the colony encompass only a small part of New Zealand's territory. As a result, Glenelg effectively withdrew the government's offer. The Association then reverted to its original plan of seeking the consent of parliament to its scheme, though before doing this it tried to drum up support by securing the agreement of the House of Lords to appoint a select committee to inquire into the present state of the islands. However, after hearing a considerable amount of evidence, this committee was unable to reach agreement about what should be done and referred the matter back to the government. At this point, the Association again tried to persuade the Colonial Office to drop its requirement regarding the capital it had to subscribe, but the cabinet refused. The Association now had no

Stephen, 18 November 1837, Papers of Sir James Stephen, University of Cambridge Library, Additional MS 7888, II/122; Lord Melbourne to Howick, 14 December 1837, Howick Papers, GRE/B115/1/85; Wakefield to Durham, 15 December 1837, Durham Papers, ATL, MS 0140, Folder 2; Melbourne to Howick, 16 December 1837, Howick Papers, GRE/B115/1/107; Wakefield to Durham, 16 December 1837, and Committee of NZA, Memorial, undated, Durham Papers, ATL, MS 0140, Folders 2 and 8; Minutes of the NZA Meetings, 16 and 18 December 1837, TNA, CO 208/185; Annotations of Colonial Office officials, 18 December 1837, on Busby to Bourke, 16 June 1837, TNA, CO 209/2; Glenelg to Durham, 29 December 1837, 1840 Select Committee Report, p. 148.
[52] Adams, *Fatal Necessity*, pp. 5, 89, 101–02.

choice but to introduce its bill in parliament. By this time, the missionary societies had petitioned the House of Commons to oppose the scheme. More importantly perhaps, the influential London newspaper *The Times* had denounced what it called the Association's projects and pretences, arguing that the tendency of its proposal was to 'fleece' the natives of 'their territorial rights' and 'procure a handsome booty' for its backers. The newspaper had espied Wakefield's hand in the Company's scheming and drew attention to the role it believed his personal history was playing in it: 'The practised abductionist who has plotted this job, by the manner in which he has set his trap to catch and captivate objectors, affords abundant proof that he is perfectly master of [t]his business'. (Several years earlier, Wakefield had notoriously kidnapped a fifteen-year-old heiress to a considerable family fortune by using his considerable skills of dissimulation to persuade her to agree to a runaway marriage.) In June the Association's bill was defeated in the House of Commons after the majority of those who spoke expressed the opinion that any colonisation of New Zealand had to proceed under the protective oversight of the British Crown. Once more, the Association tried to persuade the government to waive its requirement for the subscription of capital, but it failed, sparking the Association's collapse.[53]

Glenelg was probably relieved. In any case, he seems to have anticipated that the Association's bill would be defeated and had asked Stephen to consider what course the government might adopt to meet the need for greater protection in New Zealand. Stephen outlined a proposal that had been made in a report that Governor Bourke had asked a naval officer, William Hobson, to prepare on the current state of New Zealand and the best means of securing the interests of the natives and British subjects

[53] [Dandeson Coates], *Notes for the Information of those Members of the Deputation to Lord Glenelg, Respecting the New Zealand Association, who Have not Attended the Meetings of the Committee on the Subject*, Richard Watts, London, 1837; Durham to Glenelg, 30 December 1837, 1840 Select Committee Report, pp. 149–50; Coates to Glenelg, 1 and 3 January 1838, TNA, CO 209/3; Grey to Coates, 25 January 1838, reproduced in Coates, *Present State*, pp. 6–7; Coates to Sir George Grey, 30 January 1838, TNA, CO 209/3; Coates, *Present State*, pp. 4–11, 13, 17–19, 21–22, 24; Glenelg to Durham, 5 February 1838, 1840 Select Committee Report, p. 153; John Beecham, *Colonisation: Being Remarks on Colonisation in General, with an Examination of the Proposals of the Association which has been Formed for Colonising New Zealand*, Hatchards, London, 1838, and *Remarks upon the Latest Official Documents Relating to New Zealand*, Hatchards, London, 1838; *BPD*, House of Lords, 30 March 1838, columns 152–55; 1838 Select Committee Report, passim; CMS, Petition, undated [1838], TNA, CO 209/3; *The Times*, 17 May 1838; Baring to Glenelg, 28 May 1838, TNA, 209/3; *The Times*, 29 May 1838; Glenelg to Baring, 1 June 1838, TNA, 209/3; *BPD*, House of Commons, 1 and 20 June 1838, columns 542–53 and 871–83; E. J. Ward to Melbourne, 3 July 1838, TNA, CO 209/3; Philip Temple, *A Sort of Conscience: The Wakefields*, Auckland University Press, Auckland, 2002, pp. 54–64, 89–109.

there. In this report of August 1837 Hobson had suggested that the British government should provide greater protection. Yet he also recommended that the government's intervention continue to be limited in nature: it should purchase some land from the natives to create factories or trading stations at several places (on the model of the English East India Company with which he was very familiar) and bring these within British jurisdiction as dependencies of New South Wales. In turn, Stephen suggested to Glenelg that in the event that the government decided to adopt Hobson's suggestions, it could seek to negotiate with the native chiefs a cession of the right of sovereignty in just two or three places in the islands. On receiving this report, Glenelg requested that these suggestions be kept on file, and in the following months the Colonial Office refused to countenance several new proposals for colonising New Zealand, one of which was proposed by Robert Torrens. It appears that it was increasingly of a mind to adopt Hobson's suggestion for limited intervention, but it is clear that it was in no hurry even to do that.[54]

However, in November 1838 there was an unexpected development. A very troubled Coates requested an audience with Glenelg. He had received a letter from one of the Church Missionary Society's senior missionaries in New Zealand, George Clarke, stating that none of the measures that Coates had been advocating to protect the natives there would suffice any longer, because of the increasingly lawless state of the country, the inability of the natives to form a national government and the growing volume of land sales. (Recently, transactions in land had increased spectacularly, after New South Wales entrepreneurs shifted their attention to the islands.[55]) Coates was shocked. He was still opposed to New Zealand Association's plan to colonise the country but told Glenelg that he was now willing to accept the kind of intervention by the British government that the missionary societies had been opposing tooth and nail. Perhaps Coates' representations prompted Glenelg to act. Just as likely, Glenelg now felt able to recommend that the Crown annex

[54] William Hobson to Bourke, 8 August 1837, TNA, CO 209/2; Stephen, Memo, 4 May 1838, Glenelg, undated minute on this, and Gordon Gairdner, Minute, 23 August 1838, TNA, CO 209/3; Robert Torrens, Outline of a Plan for Establishing Under the Protection of the British Crown an Independent Native Government in the Islands of New Zealand, November 1838, TNA, CO 209/3.

[55] Of the approximately 800 transactions for land (apart from those the New Zealand Company claimed to have made) considered by a land claims commission in the 1840s, 80 were made between 1823 and 1834, 70 in 1835, 80 in 1836, 50 in 1837, 110 in 1838 and 300 in 1839 (Alan Ward, Brief of Evidence in the Matter of the Treaty of Waitangi Act 1975 and in the Matter of Te Paparahi o te Taki (Northland Inquiry), Waitangi Tribunal Wai 1040 #A19, 2009, p. 52).

New Zealand since it was evident to him that the missionary societies would now endorse his recommending this course of action.[56]

For the time being, however, Glenelg merely recommended the appointment of an officer who would be vested with the powers of a British consul and directed to negotiate a cession of sovereignty in certain parts of the islands, just as Hobson had suggested. The Colonial Office decided to offer this position to the forty-six-year-old Hobson and promptly called upon him to produce a plan of how the government should proceed, much to his amazement. Much to *its* surprise, Hobson now expressed the view (which he had actually held at the time he wrote his report for Bourke in August 1837) that the only remedy for the problems in New Zealand lay in the British Crown assuming sovereignty over the whole country and promoting large-scale colonisation. Yet Glenelg was not persuaded. He proposed instead that Hobson negotiate a cession of sovereignty from the native chiefs in just those parts of New Zealand where British subjects had already settled and establish government there. He informed Hobson that he would be offered a commission as both consul and governor but that the latter commission would only take effect once he had been able to acquire sovereignty. Hobson no doubt expected that he would be instructed to leave for New Zealand soon. But in mid-February 1839 Glenelg was forced to resign (largely due to his mishandling of a crisis in the Canadian colonies), and a month later his successor, the Marquess of Normanby, seems to have decided that any decision on New Zealand should be postponed, probably because the Colonial Office had more pressing matters to deal with.[57]

By this time, several of the men who had been involved in the New Zealand Association were in the process of forming a new body that came to be called the New Zealand Land Company, and later the New Zealand Company for short. It eventually incorporated those who been involved in both the Association and a body called the New Zealand Colonisation Association, which some of the New Zealand Association members had

---

[56] Clarke to Coates, [1] March 1838, in Dandeson Coates, *Documents Exhibiting the Views of the Committee of the Church Missionary Society on the New Zealand* Question, Richard Watts, London, 1839, pp. 41–45; Coates to Glenelg, 30 November 1838, CMS Records, CH/L3, AJCP, Reel M238; Glenelg to Sir George Gipps, 1 December 1838, *BPP*, 1840, Paper no. 238, p. 19.

[57] Hobson to Eliza Hobson, 25 August 1837, William Hobson Papers, ATL, MS-Papers -0046–1; Stephen to James Backhouse, 12 December 1838, *BPP*, 1840, Paper no. 238, pp. 3–4; Draft letter to Hobson, 28 December 1838, TNA, CO 209/3; Hobson to Glenelg, 1 January 1839, TNA, CO 209/4; Hobson to Bourke, 15 January 1839, Bourke Family Papers, ML, MSS 403/3; Hobson to Glenelg, 21 January 1839, TNA, CO 209/4; Stephen, Draft Instructions for Hobson, 24 January 1839, TNA, CO 209/4; Hobson to Grey, 14 February 1839, TNA, CO 209/4; Stephen, Minute, 14 March 1839, on Memorandum of 28 February 1839, TNA, CO 209/4.

created in August the previous year. It was as well connected politically as its predecessor. In early March the New Zealand Colonisation Association advised Normanby that it had formed itself into a joint stock company and called on the government to honour the terms of the charter it had offered the New Zealand Association the previous year. The Association's chairman also sent Normanby a paper outlining the basis upon which the Association proposed to colonise New Zealand. Indeed, he tried to force Normanby's hand, claiming that the government had acknowledged what he called the independence of New Zealand in regard to territory, that the Association had already acquired a large tract of land and that American and French adventurers could threaten British interests unless British capitalists and emigrants took possession of the territory. He advised Normanby that the Association had a ship ready to depart for New Zealand and urged him to confirm the Crown's sovereignty of the islands immediately by granting the Association a charter.[58]

Normanby was reluctant to give way. A week later, he told a deputation from the Association that its aims were laudable and that he would be disposed to give them favourable consideration *if* New Zealand was a British possession, but that until such time as the government had made an arrangement with the native chiefs to acquire the right of sovereignty he could not encourage its proceedings. However, the Association's principal figures refused to accept this response. Indeed, they persuaded themselves either that they had secured the government's permission or that they could pretend that they had done so. One of its directors, William Hutt, had learned that the government intended to introduce a bill for the colonisation of New Zealand which would include a provision that stipulated that no land could be acquired unless it was purchased from the government. This meant, Hutt informed a meeting of its members, that the Association would have to pay the price the government set for land instead of the price that the natives asked, which was reckoned to be 500 per cent higher. Wakefield, asked for his opinion about what the Association should do, urged it to send off an expedition immediately: 'acquire all the land you can, and then you will find that government will see the absolute necessity of doing something'. Elaborating on the logic behind this advice, he asserted: 'Possess your selves of the soil and you are secure, but, if from *delay* you allow others to do it before you, they will succeed and you will fail'. The meeting embraced Wakefield's recommendation, probably because he had put into words what many of its members had long contemplated. A year or so

---

[58] Standish Motte to the Marquess of Normanby, 4 March 1839, *BPP*, 1840, Paper no. 238, pp. 20–21.

earlier, the Earl of Devon had suggested that the New Zealand Association should consider adopting 'the policy of shewing the disposition now manifested by bold adventurers[:] to go out under any circumstances', and one of its other members had remarked: '[Many] say we have the capital and we have the energy to do it ourselves; [so] why should we trammel ourselves with an Act of Parliament? We can go to Cook's Straits and establish a colony there under the New Zealand flag [of 1835] and be perfectly independent'. In other words, contrary to the stance that the New Zealand Association had adopted several months earlier, in which it had proceeded on the basis that it had to seek the permission of the British government to negotiate a cession of sovereignty from the native chiefs, its successor now proposed to proceed on the basis of a position that the Association had previously regarded as a fiction, namely that the chiefs were the paramount sovereign authority in New Zealand.[59]

In late April these adventurers, now acting in the name of the New Zealand Land Company, sent a deputation to the Colonial Office to tell Normanby that it was despatching an expedition to New Zealand very shortly to purchase large tracts of land as well as to establish a government. This brazen act was commonplace among land grabbers, as we observed in the context of discussing the Port Phillip Association. Many speculators who were denied government support for their designs embraced tactics like this one. Early and fast is what they sought to be, assuming that by large doses of bravado they could eventually persuade governments to be forbearing, abandon their prohibitions and grant them land.[60]

The Company's announcement that it was despatching an expedition to New Zealand caught the Colonial Office by surprise and forced its hand. It now had no choice but to assert the Crown's authority. Only by assuming or acquiring sovereignty in New Zealand could the government prevent further land purchases and investigate the validity of the ones that had occurred, thereby nipping in the bud a potential mess in both land and native affairs. The recent border wars in the Cape Colony would have

---

[59] 1838 Select Committee Report, p. 325; Normanby to William Hutt, 11 March 1839, *BPP*, 1840, Paper no. 238, pp. 21–22; NZC Minute Book, 21 March 1839, TNA, CO 208/185; 1840 Select Committee Report, pp. 12–14; Edward Betts Hopper, Diary, 1799?–1840, ATL, MS 1033, entries 14 May 1838 and 20 March 1839, original emphasis; Adams, *Fatal Necessity*, pp. 137–39.

[60] Hutt to Henry Labouchere, 29 April 1839, and enclosed Instructions of the New Zealand Land Company to Colonel William Wakefield, *BPP*, 1840, Paper no. 238, pp. 22–27; John C. Weaver, *The Great Land Rush and the Making of the Modern World, 1650–1900*, McGill-Queen's University Press, Montreal and Kingston, 2003, pp. 53, 62, 65, 73–74, 88, 104, 111, 137, 139.

reminded the Colonial Office of the problems that could erupt if it did not act. At much the same time, it appears to have accepted Hobson's advice that the Crown needed to assert sovereignty over all of New Zealand, rather than just a few small parts of it.[61]

Part III

A Cession of Sovereignty

The Colonial Office had much to do. It had to apply to parliament to secure the revenue and all the means of government required for a new colony. This process could take several months, but such a delay was unacceptable as very large amounts of land could be claimed by adventurers in the meantime. Sooner or later, someone in the Colonial Office seems to have realised that this problem could be solved by making the islands of New Zealand part and parcel of New South Wales, at least for the time being, since the authority to alter the terms of an existing colony lay within the scope of the royal prerogative and doing this would automatically give the government the powers it required.[62]

The resort to this legal mechanism would have serious implications for how the sovereignty of New Zealand would later be said to have been acquired, since it created a notional British jurisdiction in New Zealand prior to the Crown seeking to negotiate with the native chiefs a cession of sovereignty. In seeking legal advice from the Attorney General and the Solicitor General, the Colonial Office stated that the Crown would begin merely by seeking to obtain cession of sovereignty of the territories in New Zealand where British subjects had already claimed to have acquired title to land. The legal officers approved of this step, yet the relevant wording of the measure drawn up by the Colonial Office was ambiguous: the boundaries of New South Wales were said to include 'any territory [in New Zealand] which *is or may be* acquired in sovereignty' by the Crown. The Lords Commissioners of the Treasury were uneasy about this arrangement. They were only willing to approve the colony *once* the contemplated cession in sovereignty had been obtained by means of negotiation with the native chiefs. They suggested that the annexation of any part of the islands of New Zealand, and the exercise of the powers it was intended to vest in the governor and Legislative Council of New

---

[61] Labouchere to Hutt, 1 May 1839, *BPP*, 1840, Paper no. 238, pp. 27–28.
[62] Stephen to Labouchere, 18 May 1839, TNA, CO 209/4.

South Wales or the lieutenant governor of New Zealand, should be contingent upon this having been secured.[63]

To take the momentous step of assuming sovereignty in New Zealand, the Colonial Office still believed that it had to disarm the missionary societies that had long been opposed to the measure it had now decided to adopt. To perform this task the Office drew on the humanitarian language of protection. The parliamentary Under-Secretary for the Colonies, Henry Labouchere, gave a special briefing to Coates in which he led him to conclude that the government's primary object in intervening in New Zealand's affairs was not the advancement of colonisation or commerce but the protection of the interests and rights of the natives. Labouchere also told the House of Commons that the government had decided to take steps that would probably lead to the founding of a colony in New Zealand in order to protect the aboriginal people and maintain order among its inhabitants, claiming that the natives were a people quite unable to look after their own interests. But most of the work of justifying the Colonial Office's decision to intervene was performed by the preamble to the instructions that it drew up for Hobson, who was soon to become both Consul and Lieutenant Governor of New Zealand.[64]

In July the Colonial Office prepared the final version of these instructions. Although they bore Normanby's name (and will be referred to as such in later chapters of this book), they were principally the work of Stephen, its immensely influential Permanent Under-Secretary. In large part they reassembled two previous drafts that he had prepared, but they were now revised with an eye to legitimising the decision that the Colonial Office had taken. Stephen found what was needed in a form of protection talk that amounted to a hybrid of *protection-as-jurisdiction*, which the British government had long found so useful, and the humanitarian language of protection, which had been articulated by Buxton's select committee report and adopted more recently by Busby and the missionary societies.[65]

Stephen began the preamble in a highly rhetorical mode. He argued that the British government was reluctant to intervene in the islands' affairs given the impact that any colonisation would have on the natives; he claimed that the government had previously deferred to the opinion

[63] Normanby to the Attorney General, 30 May 1839, *HRNZ*, vol. 1, pp. 739–40; Letters Patent, 15 June 1839, NANZ, IA9, Box 1/2, my emphasis; G. J. Pennington to Stephen, 22 June 1839, *BPP*, 1840, Paper no. 238, pp. 33–34.

[64] Stephen to Labouchere, 15 March 1839, TNA, CO 209/4; CMS Committee, Minutes, 25 June 1839; *BPD*, House of Commons, 25 June 1839, column 829.

[65] Stephen, Drafts of Instructions to Hobson, undated and 24 January 1839, TNA, CO 209/4.

expressed by the 1837 aborigines Select Committee report that colonisation would be calamitous for the New Zealanders; and he contended that they were a people whose 'title to the soil and to the sovereignty of New Zealand [was] indisputable' and that this had been 'solemnly recognised by the British government'. Stephen went on to argue that it had become all too apparent to the government that it had to acquire sovereignty in the islands: a large number of British subjects were already dwelling permanently there, many of whom were of bad character; considerable lawlessness was occurring; great tracts of land had been purchased; an extensive settlement of British subjects would soon be established in New Zealand; and the natives would be exterminated if the government did not restrain this colonisation.[66]

Stephen turned next to discuss the matter of sovereignty more specifically. This passage warrants quoting at length, as it would be invoked in the course of a bitter clash between the Colonial Office and the New Zealand Company a few years later. 'I have already stated that we acknowledge New Zealand as a sovereign and independent state so far at least as is possible to make that acknowledgement in favour of a people composed of numerous dispersed and petty tribes, who possess few political relations to each other, and are incompetent to act or even deliberate in concert. But the admission of their rights, though inevitably qualified by this consideration, is binding on the faith of the British Crown', he asserted. 'Believing, however, that their own welfare would, under the circumstances I have mentioned, be best promoted by the surrender to Her Majesty of a right now so precarious and little more than nominal, and persuaded that the benefits of British protection and laws administered by British judges would far more than compensate for the sacrifice by the natives of a national independence which they are no longer able to maintain', Stephen continued, 'Her Majesty's Government have resolved to authorise you to treat with the aborigines of New Zealand in the recognition of Her Majesty's sovereign authority'. This was to argue that the government's apparent acknowledgement of New Zealand as a sovereign state in previous years obliged the Crown to negotiate for cession of that sovereignty, but that since the natives were now enfeebled and the authority of the chiefs fragile, it was in their best interests to cede sovereignty and thereby enjoy the benefits of British protection. In other words, to justify the government's intervention, Stephen echoed the protection talk of Buxton and his fellow humanitarians and most recently the missionary societies but he also maintained that the position the government had long adopted on the status of the

[66] Normanby to Hobson, 14 August 1839, *BPP*, 1840, Paper no. 238, p. 37.

islands and its peoples (as it pursued *protection-as-jurisdiction*) meant that it had to negotiate with the chiefs for the cession of sovereignty. Finally, Stephen, with an eye to the latter aspect of protection talk that the government had previously deployed to ward off claims to New Zealand by other foreign governments, asserted that the Crown disclaimed 'every pretension to seize on the islands of New Zealand or govern them as a part of the dominion of Great Britain' unless it could first obtain 'the free and intelligent consent' of the chiefs.[67]

This was the first time that the Colonial Office had explicitly stated that the British Crown regarded New Zealand as a sovereign and independent state, having only gestured towards this position previously. Why did it do so now? Legal scholars have contended that the British government treated the matter of acquiring the right of sovereignty in New Zealand primarily as a question of legality. The most sophisticated rendition of this argument is in the work of Paul McHugh. He has argued that the British government held that the consent of the natives was necessary because it believed that it should follow the requirements of the law of nations before it claimed sovereignty in New Zealand. In this vein McHugh draws attention to Emmerich de Vattel's famous *Le droit des gens* in which he claims that this Swiss jurist defined nations in such a way as to encompass not only non-Christian societies but most tribal societies and went so far as to equate the sovereignty of the smallest nation with that of the most powerful, and he argues that this meant that a larger state assuming sovereignty in a smaller one needed to acquire the consent of the smaller state.[68]

There is some evidence to support McHugh's contention. In Glenelg's memorandum of December 1837 (noted earlier) he referred briefly to the authority of the law of nations as well as the British government's own practice in arguing that any intervention in New Zealand's affairs had to be based upon the recognition of the native people's sovereignty as well as respect for their rights. Moreover, in July 1840 Labouchere claimed in passing that the government had been convinced, in accordance with the

---

[67] *Ibid.*, pp. 37–38.

[68] Paul McHugh, Brief of Evidence in the Matter of the Treaty of Waitangi Act 1975 and in the Matter of Te Paparahi o te Taki (Northland Inquiry), Treaty of Waitangi Tribunal, Wai 1040 #A21, 2010, pp. 12–16, 44–45, 'Pretty Government', p. 248, and '"The Most Decorous Veil which Legal Ingenuity Can Weave": The British Annexation of New Zealand (1840)', in Kelly L. Grotke and Markus J. Prutsch (eds.), *Constitutionalism, Legitimacy, and Power: Nineteenth-Century Experiences*, Oxford University Press, Oxford, 2014, pp. 300, 302–03, 306–07. Jennifer Pitts has mounted a similar argument to McHugh's in respect of the law of nations, but she contends that Vattel said little about how the law of nations might bind European powers in their dealings with peoples outside Europe ('Empire and Legal Universalisms in the Eighteenth Century', *American Historical Review*, vol. 117, no. 1, 2012, pp. 95–96, 101–04, 111).

law of nations, that it could not exercise the right of sovereignty in New Zealand unless it made some arrangement with the native inhabitants.[69]

Yet Stephen, who greatly influenced the Colonial Office's treatment of sovereignty in the islands of New Zealand, had little truck with abstract legal concepts in general and the writings of Vattel in particular (as we will see). More importantly, the fact of the matter is that the British government treated the islands of New Zealand and their peoples as both sovereign and not sovereign, as one of the passages in Stephen's instructions to Hobson, quoted above, makes clear. Moreover, the vast bulk of the historical evidence available to us suggests that the position that the British government adopted on the matter of sovereignty at this point in time is best attributed to a combination of factors that were primarily historical, moral, strategic and political in nature.

Readers will recall that the British government, as a result of simultaneously disclaiming British sovereignty over New Zealand and implying that the islands were in its possession (by promising to protect the natives), had treated the New Zealanders over the course of the previous twenty years *as though* they were sovereign. This historical practice did not necessarily dictate what the government decided to do in 1839 – the government *could* have elected to assume sovereignty on the basis of Cook's claim of possession – but it did predispose the Colonial Office towards treating with the natives.

The Colonial Office's most important figures during this period were convinced on moral grounds that treating the natives as though they were sovereign was the proper or right way to proceed. This was a consequence of the sympathies that Glenelg and Stephen had for the sentiments articulated by the Christian humanitarians, as many historians have long argued. But it was also a function of two other factors. First, as we have seen, these officials held that the history of treating the New Zealanders as though they were sovereign meant that the British Crown was bound to continue to treat the natives in this fashion. Second, these officials were outraged by the disingenuous manner in which the principal figures of the New Zealand Association and its successor pretended to adopt the principle of regarding the natives as sovereign and yet blithely assumed that they or the British Crown could lay claim to New Zealand as though it was a British territory. Moreover, they were determined to disabuse them of this notion.

Further, and probably most importantly, the Colonial Office's principal players almost certainly decided on strategic grounds that treating the natives as though they were sovereign was a useful fiction for the British

---

[69] Glenelg, Memorandum, 15 December 1837; 1840 Select Committee Report, p. 12.

government to adopt. This was primarily the case because they believed that this way of proceeding could facilitate peaceable possession.

It must be emphasised here that the Colonial Office only explicitly stated that it regarded the natives as sovereign at the point it concluded that the British government should assume sovereignty in New Zealand. In other words, it only adopted this position at the very moment it decided that the government would negotiate with the native chiefs for the *cession* of that sovereignty. In this regard, we should note a passage that historians have tended to overlook: Stephen actually instructed Hobson to treat with the native chiefs 'for the *recognition* of *British* sovereignty'. This phrasing might suggest that the Colonial Office actually held that the islands were already under the sovereign authority of the British government rather than that of the chiefs. But, whatever the case, it seems clear the Colonial Office's principal players opted to have the British government treat the natives as though they were sovereign because they believed that this would enable it to persuade the chiefs to accept the dominion that the government was now intent on asserting. There was nothing unusual in the Colonial Office adopting this inherently ambiguous position. In dealing with native peoples, imperial powers often preferred to adopt means that had the *form* of diplomacy, if not its substance.[70]

The Colonial Office almost certainly had another strategic consideration in mind in opting to adopt the position that New Zealand and its peoples had best be treated as though they were sovereign. By doing this, it put the government in a better position to deal with colonisation companies like the New Zealand Company, since it could rule that these adventurers had no right to colonise or claim land there prior to the British assumption of sovereignty. It also seems clear that the Colonial Office's principal players had foreign powers in mind in adopting this strategy.

Finally, it is worth noting that the Colonial Office could choose to treat the New Zealanders as though they were sovereign because it knew that there were parties with whom Hobson could treat, that is, the chiefs, and that it could proceed in this fashion because of the particular history of relations between the British Crown and the native chiefs that has been described in this chapter. It is also apparent that the Colonial Office assumed that its agent would be able to make a treaty in New Zealand because it realised that the kind of figures that treaty-making usually depended on, namely go-betweens or translators, were available in the

---

[70] *Sydney Gazette*, 16 and 18 September 1830 and 15 March 1832; Stephen to Labouchere, 15 March 1839; Dorothy V. Jones, *License for Empire: Colonialism by Treaty in Early America*, University of Chicago Press, Chicago, 1982, pp. xi–xii; Travers, 'British Empire', p. 134.

islands. As a result, it instructed Hobson that he would find powerful allies for his task in the form of the missionaries.[71]

Stephen went on to instruct Hobson to treat with the native chiefs for the recognition of British sovereignty 'over the whole or any part of [the] islands' that they might be willing to place under British dominion. In other words, the Colonial Office gave Hobson discretion to annex the whole country if he considered this necessary, whereas previously it had only been willing to sanction the acquisition of sovereignty in a few small places.[72]

In the final part of these instructions, Stephen provided Hobson with a considerable amount of advice about *how* he should negotiate a treaty with the chiefs, no doubt because he realised that the chiefs would be suspicious of the British government's rationale for wishing to assume sovereignty. He instructed Hobson to point out to the chiefs that it would be impossible for the British government to extend to their people any effective protection unless they ceded to the Queen the sovereignty of their country or at least parts of it. At the same time, he told him it would be necessary to induce the chiefs to agree that they would not cede their lands to anyone except the British Crown. Finally, Stephen instructed Hobson to issue a proclamation on his arrival that the Crown would not acknowledge any title to land that was not derived from or confirmed by a grant made in Her Majesty's name. In other words, he directed the Consul to exercise sovereignty, at least in respect of British subjects, *prior* to his negotiating the cession of sovereignty from the chiefs. This concluded the part of the Colonial Office's instructions to Hobson that bore upon the making of a treaty and the matter of sovereignty that lay at its heart.[73]

Hobson had several questions when he received these instructions from the Colonial Office. The first concerned sovereignty. In keeping with notions found in the law of nations and stadial history, Hobson suggested that the differences between the country's North Island and the Middle or South Island in respect of the natives' use of land and their progress towards civilisation meant that the power of the Crown could be exercised with much greater freedom in the South than in the North. In regard to the South Island, he suggested that the Crown possessed all the rights that were usually assumed by first European discoverers, whereas he noted that the British government had recognised the North Island as independent. Hobson proposed that he be permitted to claim British sovereignty over

[71] Normanby to Hobson, 14 August 1839, *BPP*, 1840, Paper no. 238, p. 38.
[72] Stephen, Drafts of Instructions to Hobson, undated, 24 January 1839 and 9 July 1839, TNA, CO 209/4; Normanby to Hobson, 14 August 1839, *BPP*, 1840, Paper no. 238, p. 38.
[73] *Ibid.*, pp. 38–39.

the South Island on the grounds of Cook being the first discoverer. (This is hardly unsurprising. Just a few months earlier, Hobson had actually recommended to the Colonial Office that the British government assume sovereignty in all of New Zealand immediately, rather than negotiate with the chiefs for its cession.) In response to Hobson's proposal, the Colonial Office allowed that he might claim sovereignty in the South Island in the event that he found it impossible to negotiate a cession of it with the chiefs. This alteration in its instructions to Hobson further reveals the degree to which the British government's approach to the matter of sovereignty was conditioned by pragmatic considerations.[74]

The Colonial Office's instructions to Hobson soon became public knowledge. This served its purposes, not least because it helped to disarm both the Church Missionary Society and the Wesleyan Missionary Society. Their secretaries, Coates and Beecham, instructed their missionaries in New Zealand to give Hobson their full support. In fact, these missionaries needed no persuading. They had come to believe that the only way to save Māori lay in the British government assuming sovereignty and taking them entirely under its protection.[75]

The treaty itself will be discussed in detail in the next chapter. For the time being, it is important to note that the notion of protection figured prominently in its final (English language) text. In its preamble the Queen (the current embodiment of the Crown) emphasised that she was anxious to protect the rights and property of the natives in the course of explaining why the British government had deemed it necessary to appoint Hobson to treat with them for a cession of sovereignty; and in its third article the Queen undertook to extend to the natives her 'royal protection' as well as impart to them 'all the rights and privileges of British subjects'.

Conclusion

In this chapter I have argued that the British government's decision in 1839 to seek the consent of native chiefs to its assumption of sovereignty

---

[74] Hobson to Glenelg, 21 January 1839; Hobson to Labouchere, [1] August 1839, *BPP*, 1840, Paper no. 238, pp. 42–43; Normanby to Hobson, 15 August 1839, *BPP*, 1840, Paper no. 238, p. 44.

[75] Remarks of the Sub-Committee on the Coates Letter to Lord Glenelg, undated [January 1839], CMS Minutes of Meetings of Missionaries, Australasian Mission (New Zealand), 3 July 1839, CMS Records, CN/04c, AJCP, Reel M214; Coates to CMS missionaries in New Zealand, 17 July 1839, quoted in Coates to Lord Stanley, 14 August 1844, *BPP*, 1844, Paper no. 641, Return to an Address of the Honourable the House of Commons, pp. 2–3; John Beecham to the Chairman of the New Zealand District, 2 September 1839, cited J. M. R. Owens, 'Missionaries and the Treaty of Waitangi', *Wesleyan Historical Society (New Zealand) Journal*, no. 49, 1986, p. 12.

in the islands of New Zealand – rather than assert it was sovereign on the basis of Cook's claim of possession seventy years earlier – cannot be explained adequately by reference to the normative factors many historians have emphasised in recent years, whether those factors be international law, European political thought or Christian humanitarianism. I have argued that the government's decision owed a great deal to strategic and political considerations and to a complex sequence of historical events that had taken place since 1769.

We have seen that the British government's decision to treat with the chiefs for sovereignty was in large part a function of a phenomenon that historians have overlooked, namely a chain of protection that was generated by a particular kind of protection talk. In the first instance, in the 1810s, claims for protection made by the churchman Marsden and his missionary backers prompted Macquarie, as the governor of New South Wales, to make a promise to protect the natives. In turn, Macquarie's lack of power and authority in the islands of New Zealand required him to treat the native chiefs as though they were sovereign, and this generated a status for Māori as being more or less an ally of Britain and brought into being a relationship of mutual protection between the chiefs and the British Crown. At the same time, the chiefs embraced this arrangement as it dovetailed with their cultural expectations and served their interests. A few years later, in 1817, the imperial government made a deliberately ambiguous move whereby it simultaneously disavowed its claims to sovereignty in the islands of New Zealand *and* maintained a claim to possession by promising to protect the natives.

In the 1820s and much of the 1830s, we have observed, the imperial government upheld its ambiguous position in regard to sovereignty in the islands, despite growing demands that it intervene in its affairs. Its stance should be attributed not so much to the influence of any particular legal convention or ruling as to the fact that this served the government's financial, political and strategic purposes. Across the same period, missionaries encouraged native chiefs to look to the British Crown as a source of protection and the chiefs found it useful to play this game as well. The appointment of Busby as a British Resident, and the major steps he took, led various parties, including, most importantly, the New Zealand Association, to assume that the British government did regard the natives as sovereign. Furthermore, the fact that small parties had negotiated with natives to purchase land from the outset of European settlement meant that later groups of European adventurers and land-grabbers followed suit.

In the late 1830s two powerful metropolitan groups – a company promoting a scheme to systematically colonise New Zealand and the missionary societies opposing such colonisation – both embraced, for different reasons, the notion that sovereignty lay with the natives. This move led them to assume or assert that any British party had to negotiate a cession of sovereignty with the natives. However, a third powerful metropolitan group – the Christian humanitarians – introduced a different kind of protection talk in considering the islands of New Zealand, and its representation of the natives as enfeebled subjects rather than powerful allies of the British Crown was eventually deployed by the New Zealand Association, Busby and the missionaries, in order to persuade the government to change its course.

Most importantly, this constellation of forces meant that at the point when the Colonial Office reluctantly accepted that the British government had to intervene and assume sovereignty, it believed that it was right, proper, sensible and advantageous to regard the natives as sovereign and treat with their chiefs for cession of it or at least their acknowledgement of British sovereignty, and so directed that this be done. It justified this principled and expedient step by utilising the two very different kinds of protection talk that we have seen at work, namely that the natives had to be treated as more or less sovereign because the Crown and parliament had historically treated them as such, but that now the natives were an enfeebled people they needed to be provided with the protection of the British Crown. Finally, we have seen how the history of protection claims had persuaded the Colonial Office's principal players that the means required to make a treaty were available in New Zealand, in the form of chiefs as interlocutors and missionaries as go-betweens or translators.

5   Making Agreements and a Struggle for Authority, 1839–1840

In recent decades the Treaty of Waitangi has dominated the story historians have told about the British government's treatment of sovereignty and native rights of property in land in the New Zealand case.[1] To grasp how these matters were treated in the early years of the colony, however, we must consider not so much the treaty made at Waitangi in the Bay of Islands but the Colonial Office's instructions to Hobson and particular developments that unfolded in London and Sydney. These developments include proclamations that were issued in regard to sovereignty and title to land both before and after the treaty was signed; contestation by the New Zealand Company of the Colonial Office's decision to treat with the natives for the cession of sovereignty rather than assume it on the basis of Cook's claim of possession; the stance the Colonial Office adopted in response to this challenge; the position the governor of New South Wales, Sir George Gipps, adopted in regard to the claims British subjects made to title on the basis of their transactions with Māori before the British Crown assumed sovereignty; the attack land claimants based in Sydney launched upon Gipps' stance; and an agreement the Colonial Office struck with the New Zealand Company that seemed to promise the Company a considerable amount of land without any reference to the natives' rights in it.

By investigating all these developments we will be able to see that the fundamental issue at stake in the period between August 1839 and November 1840 was not native rights in land (which tended to be taken for granted) but sovereignty in the sense of who had a rightful claim to be the paramount source of title to land, and thus the authority to grant land to other parties. In this period (and beyond), London and Sydney took the challenges presented to the Crown's authority very seriously. So, therefore, should we. Otherwise, we risk projecting back onto the New

---

[1] The best example of this remains Claudia Orange's *The Treaty of Waitangi*, first published in 1987.

Zealand government or state a degree of power and authority it simply did not have at the time.[2]

In what amounted to an essentially intra-British political struggle, the positions the imperial and colonial governments, individual landholders and colonisation companies adopted in respect to sovereignty were seldom predetermined. Moreover, they often shifted in the course of contestation. All the players were unsure of the rules of the game (if there were any) and consequently they improvised a good deal. In doing so, they often used the law as a resource, picking and choosing whatever legal arguments they thought would best advance their interests. Strikingly, the treaty played little if indeed any role in the tussle that took place at this time.

Part I

'An Object of the First Importance'

The British government, as we noted in the previous chapter, finally decided it had to intervene in New Zealand's affairs for several reasons, but none was more important than the need to address a looming problem in regard to land titles, which had been caused by a spectacular increase in the number of transactions that adventurers had made with Māori. Consequently, the Colonial Office not only instructed William Hobson to persuade the chiefs to agree that they would sell their land only to the Crown but also informed him that it was 'an object of the first importance' that the alienation of land be conducted upon the basis that the Crown was the only source of title to it.[3]

Yet therein lay the rub, for how was this 'object' to be achieved? In the case of the Australian colonies, the British government had found it relatively easy to insist that the Crown was the only source of title. As we have seen, the Crown's assumption of sovereignty in New Holland in 1788 took place before colonisation of any kind had occurred. Hence,

---

[2] My approach here owes something to Peter Gibbons' critique of works of national history in New Zealand (see, for example, his ' Cultural Colonisation and National Identity', *New Zealand Journal of History*, vol. 36, no. 1, 2002, pp. 5–17) as well as the work of American historians who have called for the period prior to the American War of Independence to be treated as the history of (various) British colonies rather than equate it with the future nation (see, for example, Michael Warner, 'What's Colonial about Colonial America?', in Robert Blair St George [ed.], *Possible Pasts: Becoming Colonial in Early Colonial America*, Cornell University Press, Ithaca, NY, 2000, pp. 49–70, and Donna Merwick, *Stuyvesant Bound*, University of Pennsylvania Press, Philadelphia, 2013, chapter 11).

[3] Marquess of Normanby to William Hobson, 14 August 1839, *BPP*, 1840, Paper no. 238, Correspondence with the Secretary of State Relative to New Zealand, p. 38.

there had been no private transactions for land by British subjects and so the government was readily able to insist that any later such dealings in land with the Aboriginal people, such as Batman's treaty, were null and void. But in the case of New Zealand, adopting this position was a much more difficult proposition, or so the Colonial Office believed. By the time it had decided that the British Crown should assume sovereignty, there had been several decades of informal colonisation, during which time many Britons (as well as other Europeans) had conducted numerous transactions with Māori and could lay claim to title on this basis.

The government adopted a series of measures to deal with this problem. They were outlined in the instructions that James Stephen drew up for Hobson as well as for Sir George Gipps, who had succeeded Sir Richard Bourke as the governor of New South Wales. Two of these measures were especially important. We will consider the first one here and the second (which involved a land claims commission) at greater length in the next chapter. The first measure was to comprise of a 'proclamation addressed to all the Queen's subjects in New Zealand, that Her Majesty [would] not acknowledge as valid any title to land which *either ha[d] been, or shall hereafter be acquired* in that country which [was] not either derived from or confirmed by a grant to be made in Her Majesty's name and on her behalf'. That is, the Crown asserted that it had authority not only in respect of any future transactions in land but also in regard to those transactions that had taken place *before* its acquisition of the very sovereignty that it previously suggested it did not have. By asserting now that the Crown was the only source of title in the colony, the government implied that it would proceed on the very same basis it had in the Australian colonies, that is, as though the Crown's sovereignty dated from Cook's claim of possession and rested on the doctrine of *discovery*.[4]

However, the Colonial Office assumed that it would be impossible for the government to proceed merely on these grounds, that is, by repudiating all titles to land that British subjects claimed on the basis of the purchases they had transacted with the natives before the Crown assumed sovereignty. One might argue that it is hardly surprising that the Colonial Office had such an assumption. After all, it had long given the impression – and it now explicitly stated in its instructions to Hobson – that the Crown solemnly recognised that the natives of New Zealand had an indisputable title to both sovereignty and land. This meant, logically if not legally speaking, that any British subject who acquired land from the natives before the Crown's assumption of sovereignty could be said to

---

[4] *Ibid.*, pp. 38–39, my emphasis; Normanby to Sir George Gipps, 15 August 1839, 'Papers Relative to New Zealand, Printed Solely for the Use of the Cabinet', TNA, FO 58/2.

have a valid claim to title. Moreover, the Colonial Office realised that this would be the position of those who had acquired land. In other words, it recognised that the legal fiction it had chosen in order to claim that the British Crown was the only source of title in the colony could not paper over the fact that both the Crown and parliament had declared that Britain was *not* the sovereign authority in the islands of New Zealand and that transactions in land between the natives and British subjects *had* subsequently taken place.

In these circumstances the Colonial Office entertained another assumption, which involved political calculation on its part, rather than simply being a function of what had previously happened on the ground in regard to transactions in land, as historians like Stuart Banner would be inclined to argue. It assumed that the colony's government would be unable to uphold the authority of the Crown if it ruled that *all* those transactions in land were null and void. Some concessions would have to be made. As a result, the Colonial Office inserted in Hobson's instructions, immediately after the passage quoted above, this directive: 'You will, however, at the same time, take care to dispel any apprehensions which may be created in the minds of the settlers that it is intended to dispossess the owners of any property which has been acquired on equitable conditions, and which is not upon a scale which must be prejudicial to the latent interests of the community'. Indeed, the Colonial Office ruled that those who claimed to have a form of title on the basis of their transactions with the natives prior to the Crown's assumption of sovereignty could submit their claims to a lands commission, which would investigate them and recommend to the governor whether the Crown should grant them title. This measure would have major consequences for the way native title was treated in the colony, as we will see in this chapter and indeed the rest of the book.[5]

Gipps was quick to act on these instructions, which he received on Hobson's arrival in Sydney, en route to the Bay of Islands.[6] In early January 1840 he put a stop to what was billed as the first public sale of land in New Zealand by sending a clerk to a Sydney auction house to

[5] Normanby to Hobson, 14 August 1839, *BPP*, 1840, Paper no. 238, pp. 38–39; Stuart Banner, *Possessing the Pacific: Land, Settlers and Indigenous People from Australia to Alaska*, Harvard University Press, Cambridge, MA, 2007, pp. 26, 45–47, 61.
[6] By and large, historians have neglected what occurred in Sydney during this period. Two notable exceptions are Donald M. Loveridge, The New Zealand Land Claims Act of 1840, Brief of Evidence for the Crown Law Office (Muriwhenua Land Claim), Treaty of Waitangi Tribunal, Wai 45, I2, 1993, and Ned Fletcher, 'A Praiseworthy Device for Amusing and Pacifying Savages? What the Framers Meant by the English Text of the Treaty of Waitangi', PhD thesis, University of Auckland, 2014, chapters 11, 14 and 16, but none of this research has been published.

announce that he would soon issue a proclamation that would throw into doubt whether the Crown would recognise the titles of anyone who claimed land on the basis of their transactions with the natives. This announcement provoked a great deal of concern among land claimants in Sydney. They had assumed that the British government would honour titles that had been transacted with Māori in a bona fide manner. Few seemed to have recognised that the government could rule that all their titles were null and void, or so they pretended.[7]

The editor of the Sydney newspaper the *Colonist* immediately denied that the governor had any right to interfere in the sale of land in New Zealand, arguing that the British Crown had repeatedly acknowledged the native chiefs as sovereign and recognised their right to alienate land to whomever they chose. He insisted that Gipps' intervention was arbitrary and would variously amount to contempt for the natural and inalienable rights of the natives, a claim to possession on the basis of conquest and a violation of a pledge to respect the rights of British subjects. This editorial was the first of many such editorials that appeared in the Sydney press in the next few months. At this time, land claimants quickly organised a public meeting to discuss Gipps' forthcoming proclamation. Chaired by Samuel McDonald Martin, of whom we will hear much more in the next two chapters, it decided to wait on Hobson in order to ascertain the government's intentions in regard to land titles.[8]

At this meeting Hobson was keen to reassure the land claimants but fearful of committing himself. He began by telling them that Gipps had ordered the announcement at the auction house because he was concerned that they might assume that the government was prepared to accept the validity of all titles to land that derived from purchases or grants by the natives, but then he quickly added that he had been instructed to dispel any apprehension that they would be dispossessed of lands in cases where they had acquired it on equitable terms. The deputation pressed Hobson for further information on the rules that the government would introduce for the regulation of titles. This put Hobson on the spot, as these rules had yet to be formulated. He made it clear that no claims would be deemed valid unless they were founded on a grant from the Crown, but this provoked a member of the deputation to query what right the Crown had to interfere in New Zealand's affairs given that it was a free and independent state. Hobson kept talking in general terms, claiming that it was 'the undoubted right of the sovereign [to intervene] as

---

[7] *Australian*, 2 January 1840; *Sydney Herald*, 8 January 1840; *Colonist*, 4 September 1839; *Sydney Gazette*, 14 November 1839; *Sydney Herald*, 25 and 27 November 1839; *Australian*, 7 December 1839; *Colonist*, 8 January 1840.

[8] *Ibid.*, 8 and 11 January 1840; *Sydney Herald*, 13 January 1840.

admitted by the practice of all nations and of all ages'. This statement failed to satisfy the deputation. Later in the meeting, one of its members asserted that the natives had the right to alienate their lands to whomever they chose because they were a sovereign people. This time, Hobson could not avoid the issue. His response was somewhat contradictory, reflecting the ambiguous manner in which the British government had been treating the question of sovereignty in New Zealand. He admitted that the northern chiefs had made the Declaration of Independence in 1835 but claimed they had barely understood the nature of this act. He conceded that the natives' status as sovereign had been acknowledged by the British government and that consequently his authority for the moment was merely that of a consul, but he also claimed that the natives had never been in a condition to treat with Europeans for the sale of their lands since they were no more than minors.[9] Yet, despite or perhaps because Hobson had set out the contradictory way in which the government proposed to deal with pre-existing land titles, the concerns of the land claimants seem to have been allayed.[10]

The following day, 14 January, Gipps executed a proclamation which followed closely the wording of the relevant part of the Colonial Office's instructions. He warned land claimants the Crown would not acknowledge the validity of any title that had been or could be acquired in New Zealand which was not derived from or confirmed by a grant made in Her Majesty's name; but he also reassured them that their claims would not be dismissed out of hand if they had acquired land on fair terms and on a reasonable scale. Their claims would be investigated by a lands claims commissioner who would have the responsibility of recommending to him how far any claimants might be entitled to grants from the Crown. Given the equivocal nature of this proclamation, it is unsurprising that Gipps decided to draw up two more proclamations. The first informed British subjects that the limits of New South Wales had been extended to include any territory within the islands of New Zealand that was or might be acquired in sovereignty by the Crown. The second stated that Hobson had been appointed not just as consul but as lieutenant governor in and over that territory which was or might be acquired in sovereignty by the

---

[9] For further evidence of Hobson's views about the capacity of Māori tribes to be sovereign, see a letter he wrote to Thomas Bunbury, 29 April 1840, reproduced in [Thomas Bunbury], *Reminiscences of a Veteran*, vol. 3, Charles J. Skeet, London, 1861, pp. 62–63.

[10] *Sydney Herald*, 15 and 17 January 1840; *Colonist*, 15 and 18 January 1840; Hobson to Gipps, 16 January 1840, NANZ, G36/1; *Australian*, 16 and 18 January 1840; *Australasian Chronicle*, 17 January 1840; *Sydney Monitor*, 20 January 1840; Samuel Martin, Letter IV, 25 January 1840, in his *New Zealand in a Series of Letters, Containing an Account of the Country both Before and Since its Occupation by the British Government*, Simmons & Ward, London, 1845, pp.79–80.

Crown. Gipps then held back the gazetting of these proclamations for several days, to allow Hobson time to set sail for the Bay of Islands, probably in order to ensure that word of them did not reach New Zealand before Hobson arrived and thereby provoke disaffected settlers to try to persuade the chiefs to refuse to cede sovereignty to the Crown. Gipps also dispatched Hobson with two draft proclamations that were very similar to his second and third proclamations, which Hobson could issue in the Bay of Islands.[11]

Some historians, such as Claudia Orange, have argued that these five proclamations, dated 14 and 30 January 1840 respectively, reveal that Gipps and Hobson believed that the islands of New Zealand had already fallen under the sovereign authority of the British Crown. These scholars thus draw into question the significance of the negotiations that Hobson was to undertake with the native chiefs for the cession of sovereignty. However, it seems clear that these proclamations merely *anticipated* the establishment of British sovereignty. They were made in order to declare the position that the government would adopt *once* it had acquired sovereignty, and thereby warn British subjects of the implications of this change. Moreover, the proclamations were never considered to be the basis for British sovereignty in New Zealand. Yet, as Donald Loveridge has pointed out, it is doubtful Gipps would have drawn up proclamations of this kind if he had believed he was dealing with a fully sovereign polity. In other words, these proclamations constitute further evidence of the ambiguous manner in which British officials treated the sovereignty of New Zealand and its native inhabitants.[12]

Drafting the Treaty

In the last forty or more years, an enormous amount of scholarly work has been devoted to the Treaty of Waitangi. This research has generally tended to assume that the treaty signed by a large number of rangatira

[11] Gipps, Proclamations of 14 January 1840, *BPP*, 1840, Paper no. 560, Copies or Extracts of Despatches from the Governor of New South Wales, p. 3; Gipps to Hobson, 15 January 1840, *BPP*, 1840, Paper no. 560, pp. 4–5; *Supplement to the New South Wales Government Gazette of 15 January 1840*, 18 January 1840, pp. 65–66; Hobson, Proclamations of 30 January 1840, *BPP*, 1840, Paper no. 560, pp. 8–9.

[12] Gipps to Hobson, 25 January 1840, TNA, CO 209/6; Gipps, Speech to the Legislative Council of New South Wales, 9 July 1840 (henceforth Gipps' Speech), *BPP*, 1841, Paper no. 311, Copies or Extracts of Correspondence Relative to New Zealand, p. 64; Claudia Orange, *The Treaty of Waitangi*, Allen & Unwin/Port Nicholson Press, Wellington, 1987, p. 34; Donald M. Loveridge, 'The Knot of a Thousand Difficulties': Britain and New Zealand, 1769–1840, Brief of Evidence in the Matter of the Treaty of Waitangi Act 1975 and in the Matter of Te Paparahi o te Taki (Northland Inquiry), Treaty of Waitangi Tribunal, Wai 1040, 2009, p. 189.

(more than 500), beginning at Waitangi in the Bay of Islands on 6 February 1840, played a critical role in determining how the British authorities treated sovereignty and native rights in land at the time and how they would treat, or should have treated, these matters in the years that followed. However, most if not all this scholarship mistakes the precise contemporary significance of the treaty at the time it was made, largely because it projects back onto it a significance – in the sense of both meaning and importance – that it only came to acquire later.

In order to recover the contemporary significance that the treaty had or did not have in regard to the matters of sovereignty and native title to land, we must first pay special attention to the Colonial Office's instructions to Hobson and the drafting of the English text of the treaty, rather than the Māori text (which was made by translating the English text).

The Colonial Office did not provide Hobson with any guidance regarding the actual terms of the treaty or furnish him with a draft. Nevertheless, its instructions to him spelt out the British government's requirements. Hobson was to persuade the chiefs to cede sovereignty to the British Crown and to agree that all future transactions in land would be controlled by the Crown. Further, though this was not part of the Colonial Office's specific instructions in regard to a treaty, he was to make clear to the chiefs that the government wished to provide some protection to the natives in return for the chiefs' agreeing to cede their sovereignty. As Hobson grasped, the Colonial Office regarded the treaty as a diplomatic instrument, as a means towards an end, rather than an end in itself.[13]

In recent years, scholars such as Keith Sorrenson have argued that the treaty had sources other than these instructions. In particular, they have drawn attention to the fact that the treaty is similar in most respects to treaties that the British Crown had made elsewhere in its empire, particularly in West Africa. Yet there seems to be little if indeed any reason to go beyond the Colonial Office's instructions in seeking the source of the Treaty of Waitangi, or rather Hobson's initial draft of it. (Gipps, who had also seen those instructions, drew up a treaty-like agreement in Sydney in early February that was very similar to Hobson's draft.) Moreover, doing so can distract attention from the initial draft, thereby diminishing our chances of understanding the point of the treaty in the eyes of Hobson, who was the British official primarily responsible for making it.[14]

---

[13] Normanby to Hobson, 14 August 1839, *BPP*, 1840, Paper no. 238, p. 38.

[14] Gipps, Memorandum of an Agreement, [14 February 1840], Miscellaneous New South Wales Archives Estrays relating to New Zealand 1830–45, ML, DLNAR 3; M. P. K. Sorrenson, 'Treaties in British Colonial Policy: Precedents for Waitangi' (1991), in his *Ko te Whenua te Utu/Land is the Price: Essays on Maori History, Land and Politics*, Auckland University Press, Auckland, 2014, p. 42; Paul Moon, *The Origins of the*

The initial draft of the English text of the treaty has been neglected in the immense body of historical scholarship that has been produced about the Treaty of Waitangi in recent years.[15] Yet this document, more than any other version of the treaty, reveals Hobson's understanding of what London required and what he sought to achieve. Hobson seems to have prepared this draft on the journey from Sydney to the Bay of Islands, with his clerk, James Freeman, acting as amanuensis. It finally comprised a preamble and three articles. The preamble explained why the British Crown wished to make a treaty with the chiefs: as the Queen was concerned about the present state of the islands and wished to avert the evil consequences for both natives and her own subjects that had arisen from the absence of laws and institutions, she had authorised Hobson to invite the chiefs to concur with a series of articles. The first article stated that the native chiefs would cede to the Queen 'the full sovereignty of the whole country'; the second stipulated that the chiefs yielded to the Crown 'the exclusive right of pre-emption over such waste lands as the tribes may feel disposed to alienate'; and the third extended to the natives the Queen's 'royal protection' and 'impart[ed] to them all the rights and privileges of British subjects'. As readers can see, this draft fulfilled the British government's requirements as they had been set down by the Colonial Office. As such, it is hardly surprising that it provided the basis for most, though not all, of the final version of the English text of the treaty.[16]

Having established the importance of Hobson's initial draft for the task of determining the treaty's contemporary significance for the British government, we can turn our attention to the later drafts as well as what became the final version of the English text. On 31 January or 1 February, shortly after Hobson had completed his initial draft, he fell ill. Consequently, he sent his draft to the former British Resident, James Busby, and asked for his help. Busby was of the opinion that Hobson's draft would fail to accomplish the government's objectives. He offered to prepare a further draft. Busby's draft had several marked differences to Hobson's. Only two of them need concern us. First, he suggested that this clause be added: 'Her Majesty the Queen of England confirms and guarantees to the chiefs and tribes of New Zealand and to the respective families and individuals thereof the full, exclusive and undisturbed possession of their lands and estates, forests, fisheries and other properties,

---

Treaty of Waitangi, Birdwood Publishing, Auckland, 1994, p. 117; Tom Bennion, 'Treaty-Making in the Pacific in the Nineteenth Century and the Treaty of Waitangi', *Victoria University of Wellington Law Review*, vol. 35, no. 1, 2004, p. 201.

[15] The exception to this is Fletcher's 'Praiseworthy Device'.

[16] Hobson, First Draft of the Treaty, [31 January 1840], NANZ, IA9, Box 9/10; Fletcher, 'Praiseworthy Device', chapter 1.

which they may collectively or severally possess so long as it is their wish and desire to retain the same in their possession'. Second, he suggested some changes to what became the second clause of the treaty's second article: these spelt out that the right of pre-emption the Crown was seeking was a right of purchase and specified that the natives were the proprietors of the land.[17]

Hobson accepted all of these suggestions and incorporated into a new preamble a passage that specified that the protection the British Crown was offering to the chiefs included protection of their property. The most important of Busby's suggestions became, almost unaltered, the first clause of the treaty's second article, so that it 'confirm[ed] and guarantee[d] to the chiefs and tribes of New Zealand and to the respective families and individuals thereof the full, exclusive and undisturbed possession of their lands and estates, forests, fisheries and other properties which they may collectively or individually possess so long as it is their wish and desire to retain the same in their possession'.[18]

Many historians have argued that this clause was fundamental to the treaty's significance at the time because it meant that the British Crown had undertaken to guarantee to Māori their rights of property in land. It is very doubtful that this is the case. In order to establish the contemporary significance of this clause, we need to address several questions. Why did Busby suggest this clause? What does this reveal about the nature of some of the forces that played a part in making the treaty? Why did Hobson accept this new clause? And, most importantly, what did the clause really mean? In considering these questions, it is crucial to bear in mind that the Colonial Office gave Hobson no instruction to include a guarantee to the natives regarding their land, which is why it did not figure in his initial draft.

That Busby recommended the changes he suggested is unremarkable. He had previously advised the British government that the chiefs would be willing to cede sovereignty to the Crown but that it would need to give the chiefs an undertaking that it would protect their rights, including those to property in land. Moreover, he had a personal interest in the native title implied by the clause he suggested, given that he had recently purchased a considerable amount of land from Māori.

---

[17] Busby, Draft of the Treaty, [3 February 1840], James Busby Papers, AWMML, MS 46, Box 2, Folder 6; Busby Fair Copy of the Treaty, [3 or 4 February 1840], NANZ, IA9, Box 9/10; Busby, 'Occupation of New Zealand 1833–43', c. 1865, p. 87, James Busby Papers, AWMML, MS 46, Box 6, Folder 1; Busby, *Remarks Upon a Pamphlet Entitled 'The Taranaki Question', by Sir William Martin*, Philip Kunst, Auckland, 1860, pp. 3–4.
[18] Hobson Preamble, [4 February 1840], NANZ, IA9, Box 9/10.

Busby's recommendation of the clause in question reveals the influence that local experience or practice, rather than imperial policy or preoccupations, had in drafting this part of the treaty. It seems clear that the treaty would not have included this clause were it not for the intervention of these local forces. To be more specific, Busby's draft was the product of the history of transactions in land between European and Māori, which had begun in 1815 with Marsden's purchasing and had led to a widely accepted perception among Britons in the islands that the natives of New Zealand had at least some rights of property in land. We must also note that the addition of this clause to the treaty can be regarded as the result of happenstance, namely that Hobson fell ill at a critical moment and called on Busby for help in drafting it.

We might also attribute Hobson's adoption of this clause to the influence of Church Missionary Society missionaries in the Bay of Islands, upon whose assistance the Colonial Office had told Hobson he could rely, and especially the head missionary, Henry Williams, who visited Hobson (along with other missionaries) on 3 February. In all likelihood, Williams and his fellow missionaries endorsed the inclusion of this clause in the treaty. It is well known that they had become concerned about the scale of land purchasing by Europeans and were convinced that the intervention of the British government was the only way to provide the natives with protection from land grabbing. Indeed, in March the previous year one of their number, Richard Davis, could be said to have prefigured this clause in the treaty by telling the Society's lay secretary, Dandeson Coates, 'no step [is] more likely to answer so well for the natives as the concession of the sovereignty of their country to Great Britain, retaining for themselves the possession of their lands &c'.[19]

More likely than not, Hobson accepted this clause because the missionaries as well as Busby probably told him that its addition was vital if he was to be able to persuade the chiefs to cede sovereignty and allow the Crown to assume the right of pre-emption. It is also likely that Hobson

[19] Extract of Henry Williams to Dandeson Coates, 11 January 1838, reproduced in Hugh Carleton, *The Life of Henry Williams, Archdeacon of Waimate*, vol. 1, Upton & Co, Auckland, 1874, p. 232; William Williams to Coates, 14 November 1838, CMS Records, CN/M11, AJCP, Reel 205; Henry Williams to Coates, 7 March 1839, CMS Records, CN/M11, AJCP, Reel M205; Richard Davis to Coates, 22 March 1839, CMS Records, CN/M11, AJCP, Reel M205; Henry Williams to Coates, 22 April 1839, CMS Records, CN/M11, AJCP, Reel M205; William Williams to Coates, 28 August 1839, CMS Records, CN/M11, AJCP, Reel M205; William Williams to Coates, 12 November 1839, CMS Records, CN/M11, AJCP, Reel M205; George Clarke to Coates, 20 January 1840, CMS Records, CN/M12, AJCP, Reel M205; Henry Williams to Coates, 23 January 1840, CMS Records, CN/M11, AJCP, Reel M205; Henry Williams, 'Early Recollections', reproduced in Hugh Carleton, *The Life of Henry Williams*, vol. 2, Wilsons & Horton, Auckland, 1877, p. 12; Orange, *Treaty*, p. 39.

believed that there was a considerable degree of resonance between this clause and the highly rhetorical passage in his instructions in which the Colonial Office had stated that the Crown had solemnly recognised the natives' title to the soil, not least because he was inclined to take the Colonial Office's rhetoric at face value and was concerned to comply with what he called the spirit of them.[20]

There is no evidence to suggest, however, that Hobson attached to this clause the strict legal meaning that various British players attributed to it several years later, namely that it meant the Crown had recognised that the natives had extensive rights of property in land. Indeed, it seems very unlikely that such a possibility even occurred to him. Consideration of the precise nature of native rights in land seldom if ever occurred at the point that colonisation began. In any case, as we have seen, the clause merely referred to the property that chiefs and tribes *might* possess. In other words, its reference to *possession* was no less equivocal than the reference to Aboriginal people's rights of property in land in the preamble of the South Australian Letters Patent. Likewise, there are no sound reasons for assuming that Hobson would have interpreted this clause as bestowing any *specific rights* on the natives given the absence of such language in the treaty. Finally, in the unlikely event that Hobson did construe the clause as guaranteeing to the natives whatever rights of possession they might be deemed to have, he would probably have reasoned that this signified little as it was harnessed to a clause in the same article of the treaty by which the natives had agreed to the Crown assuming the right of pre-emption. One way or another, then, it would be a mistake to conclude that Hobson attributed a great deal of significance to this clause, let alone of a legal character. In his mind, it probably did not alter the essential character of the agreement he was seeking, namely one in which he primarily sought to acquire for the Crown the right to assume sovereignty, however much its addition contributed to the way in which he represented the treaty to the chiefs as a measure of protection.

Making the Treaty at Waitangi

On 3 or 4 February Busby asked Williams to translate the treaty into Māori in time for a meeting with chiefs that was scheduled to take place at Waitangi on 5 February. In the closing decades of the twentieth century, it was commonly argued that the text of the Treaty in Māori differed in critical respects to the text in English – most importantly, the rangatira merely granted the British Crown 'te Kawanatanga katoa' or the right of

---

[20] Hobson to Bunbury, 29 April 1840, reproduced in [Bunbury], *Reminiscences*, p. 64.

government over the land, which is to say that they ceded an authority considerably less than that of sovereignty, and the Crown confirmed 'te tino rangatiratanga' or the full exercise of Maori chieftainship over their lands, which is to say that it more or less guaranteed Maori sovereignty in this respect – and that the meanings and implications of the treaty were to be found in the Māori text, not least because this was the deed that almost all the English agents and the rangatira had signed, rather than the English deed.[21] This argument still holds sway publicly, but in recent years it has been challenged by several historians, most notably Lyndsay Head and Michael Belgrave. These scholars have advanced two important arguments. First, they have argued that contemporary meanings of the key words in the two texts of the treaty did *not* differ significantly from each other, if at all. Second, they have argued that the way in which the rangatira understood the treaty at the time was a product of the *oral context* in which it was presented to them and debated, rather than their reading either its English or Māori texts, and that a consideration of the debates that took place at the treaty meetings suggests there was a large degree of common understanding between the British players and the Māori chiefs about the treaty's meaning. In effect, these scholars argue that it is a mistake to speak in terms of a distinctive Māori interpretation of the treaty that was independent of the relationship they had with Europeans, especially the missionaries, and the discussions they had about the treaty with those Europeans.[22]

In presenting the treaty to the chiefs at Waitangi on 5 February, Hobson seems to have followed his Colonial Office instructions as well as advice that Busby and the Church Missionary Society missionaries appear to have given him. At the beginning of the meeting, Hobson, with Williams translating, explained to the chiefs that he had been sent by the Queen as a governor because of her concern to protect their people as well as British subjects in New Zealand, but that he could only acquire the powers he needed to control lawlessness if they were willing to consent to the treaty he was about to propose. He reminded the chiefs that they had

---

[21] The first scholar to emphasise the significance of these differences was Ruth Ross, particularly in 'Te Tiriti o Waitangi: Texts and Translations', *New Zealand Journal of History*, vol. 6, no. 2, 1972, pp. 129–57, and her interpretation was championed by Claudia Orange in her *The Treaty of Waitangi*, especially pp. 39–43.

[22] Judith Binney, 'The Maori and the Signing of the Treaty of Waitangi', in David Green (ed.), *Towards 1990: Seven Leading Historians Examine Significant Aspects of New Zealand History*, GP Books, Wellington, 1989, especially pp. 25–27; Grant Phillipson, Bay of Islands Maori and the Crown 1793–1853, Treaty of Waitangi Tribunal, Wai 1040 #A1, 2005, pp. 263, 275, 280, 285; Michael Belgrave, *Historical Frictions: Maori Claims and Reinvented Histories*, Auckland University Press, Auckland, 2005, pp. 46–66, and Lyndsay Head, 'Land, Authority and the Forgetting of Being in Early Colonial Maori History', PhD thesis, University of Canterbury, 2006, chapter 6.

often asked the British monarch to provide them with protection and made it clear that this was what the Queen was now offering. In the course of the meeting Hobson as well as Williams and Busby sought to present the treaty in the best possible light. Hence, they not only played up the protection that the Crown was offering but downplayed the full implications of the transfer of sovereignty, suggesting that the Crown would mostly use the authority it sought to restrain its own subjects and assuring the chiefs that they would retain considerable power and independence. Hobson at the time – and Williams and Busby later – claimed that they had set out the terms of each of the treaty's clauses, but it seems doubtful that this occurred.[23]

Nevertheless, it seems that the rangatira at the meeting *more or less* grasped the gist of the treaty and that many of them welcomed it, albeit with considerable apprehension.[24] The emphasis both Hobson and Williams placed on the offer of British protection must have seemed familiar to the chiefs who had gathered at Waitangi, given the crucial role the language of protection had played in the formation of the relationship between these northern rangatira and the British Crown, most recently in the Declaration of Independence, which many of the chiefs present at this treaty meeting had signed. In other words, the ground for this treaty-making had been prepared by that protection talk. The emphasis that Hobson placed on his role as governor was similarly familiar. Over many years, Marsden, the missionaries and Busby had represented the British Crown, and thus its power and authority, in personal terms – as the king or the queen and especially governors – and many rangatira had

---

[23] William Colenso, Memoranda of the Arrival of Lieutenant Governor Hobson in New Zealand 1840, ATL, MS 1611, Folder 1; William Colenso, *The Authentic and Genuine History of the Signing of the Treaty of Waitangi*, Government Printer, Wellington, 1890, pp. 16–17; James Rutherford (ed.), *The Founding of New Zealand: The Journals of Felton Mathew*, A.H. and A.W. Reed, Dunedin, 1940, pp. 33–34; Father Louis-Catherin Servant, quoted by Peter Low, 'French Bishop, Maori Chiefs, British Treaty', in John Dunmore (ed.), *The French and the Maori*, Heritage Press, Waikanae, 1992, pp. 102–03; Williams, 'Early Recollections', reproduced in Carleton, *Henry Williams*, vol. 2, p. 12.

[24] Once historians no longer regard the Treaty as a *document* – and especially a legal document – upon which the foundations of the New Zealand nation-state rests or should rest, the agreement made at Waitangi and signed by many Māori rangatira in 1840 not only becomes less important. The need for mutual understanding that is required by any binding contract also diminishes considerably, thereby allowing us to accept the probability that the treaty was the result of process that involved a fair amount of *misunderstanding* among the parties involved in making it, or what the American historian Richard White has called a process of 'creative misunderstanding' (see *The Middle Ground: Indians, Empires, and Republics in the Great Lakes Region, 1650–1815*, Cambridge University Press, New York, 1991, especially p. x).

met governors at Port Jackson or Poihākena, and two had even met the British monarch.

More particularly, since the relationship of protection had long been figured by the British Crown and understood by the northern rangatira as something like an alliance between the two parties, many of the chiefs might have hoped that the treaty would continue to provide them with not only protection but also a certain degree of independence, and all the more so because of the way that Hobson and Williams (mis)represented it to them. Yet it seems clear that the rangatira also realised that the treaty portended a major change in the relationship between themselves and the British Crown since it must have been evident to them that the Crown's promise of protection was now contingent on their ceding at least some of their power and authority to its agent, Hobson. In fact, the debates that took place among rangatira at Waitangi as well as later treaty meetings were dominated by the question of what having a governor or a kāwana would mean in practice.

At the beginning of the meeting at Waitangi, several chiefs spoke forcefully against the treaty on the grounds that they would be subordinated to the authority of the Crown. Two examples must suffice. A senior Ngā Puhi rangatira, Te Kemara, told Hobson: 'No, no, no; I shall never say "Yes" to your staying. Were all to be on an equality, then, perhaps, Te Kemara would say "Yes"; but for the Governor to be up and Te Kemara down – Governor high up, up, up, and Te Kemara down, low, small, a worm, a crawler – No, no, no'; and another leading Ngā Puhi rangatira, Rewa, gave voice to fears that Māori would suffer the same losses that native peoples had experienced elsewhere in the wake of British colonisation, telling Hobson: 'What do native men want of a Governor? . . . I will not say "Yes" to the Governor's remaining. No, no, no; return. What! this land to become like Port Jackson and all other lands seen [or found] by the English'. By the same token, the rangatira who spoke in favour of the treaty argued that the changes that had occurred in northern New Zealand meant they had no choice but to accept some measure of British authority: 'Is [the land] not covered, all covered, with men, with strangers, foreigners . . . over whom we have no power?', Tamati Waka Nene asked his fellow rangatira. 'The Governor to go back? . . . Had you spoken thus in the old time, when the traders and grog-sellers came, had you turned them away, then you could well say to the Governor, "Go back", and it would have been correct . . . But now, as things are, no, no, no'. Indeed, in recent years the northern chiefs had begun to fear that they were failing to curb the European intrusion and had started to lose confidence in their capacity to deal with the problems of governance that had arisen. This had led them to consider whether they needed new answers to these problems and to appeal to the missionaries and Busby to provide them with a new form of law.[25]

By 1840 many northern rangatira were particularly concerned that they were losing control over their lands. This was especially pronounced in the Bay of Islands where they had lost about a quarter of their land as a result of their transactions with Europeans. Some had called for a halt to these dealings and were even seeking to prevent them; others were demanding land be returned to them. At Waitangi and the other treaty meetings that took place later in northern New Zealand, the chiefs asked Hobson what he was going to do about this problem. However, their concerns focused not so much on the loss of land but on the implications of their loss of control over it. As Lyndsay Head has argued, belonging, rather than land, still lay at the centre of the Māori world, and traditional values continued to focus on relationships of power between people, rather than on a relationship to land. This means that territorial possessions were not regarded as the foundation or the source of power but rather as a consequence of it, of a rangatira being able to demonstrate his ability to order things properly. At the treaty meeting at Waitangi the concern that the chiefs articulated in regard to land clearly focused on their loss of power and authority. This is evident in the part of the speech by Nene quoted earlier. He was not complaining that the land had gone as much as he was bemoaning the fact that it was now occupied by British subjects over whom he and his fellow rangatira had little influence.[26]

Hobson was careful at Waitangi to provide the chiefs with assurances that all lands wrongfully held by British subjects would be returned to them and that any purchases made since the proclamation he issued on his arrival would be disallowed. But there is no contemporary evidence to suggest that he saw any need to spell out what the vague promise in the

[25] Unnamed chief [Wiremu Hau] to Samuel Marsden, 14 May 1837, *BPP*, 1837–38, Paper no. 680, Report of the Select Committee of the House of Lords Appointed to Inquire into the Present State of the Islands of New Zealand (henceforth 1838 Select Committee Report), p. 272; Nōpera Panakareao to Marsden, 9 May 1837, Samuel Marsden Papers, vol. 3, ATL, Micro-MS-0743; Richard Davis to James Busby, 29 June 1839, James Busby, Official Letters to Various People, 1833–70, ATL, qMS-0352; Colenso, Memoranda; Colenso, *History*, pp. 17–27; Rutherford (ed.), *Journals of Felton Mathew*, pp. 35, 37–38; *Sydney Herald*, 21 February 1840; Binney, 'Signing', p. 25; Alan Ward, Brief of Evidence in the Matter of the Treaty of Waitangi Act 1975 and in the Matter of Te Paparahi o te Taki (Northland Inquiry), Treaty of Waitangi Tribunal, Wai 1040 #A19, 2009, pp. 22–23.

[26] Davis to CMS Secretaries, 1 June 1839 and 19 November 1839, Richard Davis, Letters and Journals, HL, MS 1211/2; Colenso, *History*, pp. 17, 20, 26; Phillipson, Bay of Islands Maori, pp. 131, 142; Head, 'Land', pp. 41, 43–44, 174–75, 180–84, 189–90, 192, 199, 219–20.

treaty that the Crown would confirm and guarantee to the natives their possession of the land might mean. There are no reliable historical traces to suggest that the missionaries saw any need to do this either. By contrast, in the context of the treaty-making, the missionaries were concerned to see the Crown secure the right of pre-emption in order to put a stop to land-grabbing. Two days after the treaty was signed, one of their number, Davis, made just one reference to the treaty's articles in writing to the Church Missionary Society's lay secretary in London: 'the natives are no longer allowed to sell their lands to private individuals but [only] to the govern-ment. This is a very judicious arrangement'. Moreover, a list of the treaty's 'principal articles' that Davis' fellow missionary, William Colenso, pro-vided to the Church Missionary Society shortly after it was signed at Waitangi did not include the first clause of its second article that ostensibly guaranteed Māori in possession of their lands. In short, the record of the treaty meetings does not suggest that the treaty had the kind of significance in regard to native title that historians have so often attributed to it and confirms that its importance lay instead in the matter of sovereignty.[27]

We cannot be sure why some rangatira agreed to sign the treaty at Waitangi. At the end of the debate on 5 February it was by no means apparent that they would do so. Hobson was apprehensive they would not. Williams urged him to allow the rangatira time to think the matter over and that evening many chiefs sought out Williams and his fellow missionaries for advice. They seemed to have reached an agreement. At any rate, the next morning about forty of them signed the treaty, including nearly all those who had spoken in opposition the previous day. As I have already stated, it is unlikely that they truly grasped the extent of the authority that the British government hoped to secure or the treaty's pre-emption clause, let alone the long-term implications of the transfer of sovereignty that the Crown had sought. In the end, it seems they decided to place their trust in the missionaries' assurances that it was in their best interests to give their consent.[28]

One final point about the treaty-making at Waitangi is required. We must be careful not to exaggerate the significance it had at the time. It had little if any bearing on how the British Crown would deal with the nitty-gritty matters that would arise in the coming years in relation to either sovereignty or native rights in land,[29] let alone how the colonial

[27] Davis to Coates, 8 February 1840, CMS Records, CN/M12, AJCP, Reel 211; Colenso to the Secretaries of the CMS, January–February 1840, William Colenso, Letters, vol. 1, ATL, qMS-0491.

[28] Williams, 'Early Recollections', reproduced in Carleton, *Henry Williams*, vol. 2, p. 14.

[29] In regard to the former, see Shaunnagh Dorsett, *Juridical Encounters: Māori and the Colonial Courts 1840–1852*, Auckland University Press, Auckland, 2017.

government would negotiate these matters with Māori. In the eyes of the new colonial administration, the treaty provided no blueprint, let alone a road map, in this regard. Besides, at the point it was signed at Waitangi, Hobson realised there was still a great deal of diplomatic work to be done in order to persuade more chiefs to sign.

Securing Native Consent?

By turning to consider some of what happened in the months that followed the initial signing of the treaty at Waitangi, we are able to examine further why the British Crown chose to assume sovereignty by treating with the Māori chiefs as well as to assess the role that the treaty ultimately played in the Crown's acquisition of sovereignty in New Zealand.

Not surprisingly, Hobson was enormously pleased with the outcome of the meeting at Waitangi as well as a treaty meeting that was held several days later at Māngungu in Hokianga. Still, he recognised that he had merely gained a cession of sovereignty in one part of New Zealand. As a result, he planned to proceed throughout the rest of the country in order to persuade more chiefs to sign the treaty, just as he proposed to issue a proclamation that announced Britain's dominion merely in the area between the North Cape at the top of the North Island and 36 degrees latitude (that is, slightly north of present-day Auckland), and to extend those limits only after he had obtained the consent of the relevant chiefs. Likewise, Hobson's superior, Gipps, by no means assumed that the task of acquiring sovereignty in New Zealand was complete as a result of the treaty signings in the country's far north.[30]

In early March Hobson suffered a stroke, but he remained committed to his plan, delegating the task to several agents, among whom were several Church Missionary Society missionaries. Gipps agreed to this course of action, as he was anxious to see British sovereignty established over all of the islands as quickly as possible, and despatched Thomas Bunbury, an army officer, for this purpose. For his part Hobson was hopeful that Bunbury would establish British authority in the South Island and Stewart Island by persuading the chiefs there to sign the treaty, even though Gipps had recommended that he simply assert British sovereignty over the South Island on the basis of the right of *discovery*. In the next few months the agents acquired more signatures to the treaty in various parts of the North Island. In the south, Bunbury proclaimed

---

[30] Rutherford (ed.), *Journals of Mathew*, p. 22; Hobson to Gipps, 5–6 February 1840, *BPP*, 1841, Paper no. 311, p. 9; Hobson to Gipps, 17 February 1840, *BPP*, 1841, Paper no. 311, p. 12; Gipps to Hobson, 31 March 1840, SRANSW, 4/1651.

British sovereignty over Stewart Island and its surrounding islands on the basis of Cook's claim of possession after he concluded that there were no chiefs with whom he could negotiate; but he sought the signatures of chiefs at Cloudy Bay in the South Island, and in mid-June he proclaimed British sovereignty over all of the South Island on the grounds of native consent.[31]

However, just a few weeks earlier, on 21 May, Hobson suddenly declared British sovereignty over all the country, that is, before the process of acquiring the consent of the chiefs to the treaty throughout the North Island had been completed and before he received any news about Bunbury's expedition in the south. Hobson issued three proclamations. In the first, he claimed the full sovereignty of the North Island on the basis of the treaty signing at Waitangi; in the second, he asserted sovereignty over the southern islands on the basis of what he called a command from Queen Victoria; and in the third, he specifically informed British subjects in Port Nicholson what he had done. Hobson drew up these proclamations in great haste, so much so that he had to correct the first two before printing them again the following month. In amending the second one, he added that he had claimed sovereignty in the southern islands on the grounds of the doctrine of *discovery*. Furthermore, in a despatch to Normanby's successor as Colonial Secretary, Lord John Russell, Hobson went to considerable lengths to justify his course of action, claiming that he had assumed sovereignty in the South Island on the basis of 'perfect knowledge of the uncivilised state of the natives' as well as Gipps' advice and obscuring the limited extent of the native consent that had been secured in the North Island at that time.[32]

Hobson no doubt felt compelled to adopt this about-turn in the way he had been trying to acquire or assume sovereignty because of the manner in which he interpreted the actions of the New Zealand Company's settlers who had begun to establish a settlement at Port Nicholson (that later became Wellington), which was several hundreds of miles south of where he had established himself. Hobson had not been especially

---

[31] Hobson to Williams, 23 March 1840, *BPP*, 1841, Paper no. 311, p. 17; Gipps to Hobson, 2 April 1840, SARNSW, 4/1651; Gipps to Hobson, 3 April 1840, TNA, CO 209/6; Hobson to Gipps, 5 April 1840, NANZ, G36/1; Hobson to Thomas Bunbury, 25 April 1840, *BPP*, 1841, Paper no. 311, pp. 17–18; Hobson to Lord John Russell, 25 May 1840, TNA, CO 209/6; Bunbury to Hobson, 28 June 1840, *BPP*, 1841, Paper no. 311, pp. 106–09, 112; Bunbury to H. Parker, 4 July 1840, *BPP*, 1841, Paper no. 311, p. 59.

[32] Hobson, Proclamations of 21 May 1840, *BPP*, 1841, Paper no. 311, pp. 18–19; Hobson to Russell, 25 May 1840; revised version of the second Proclamation of 21 May 1840, TNA, CO 209/6.

concerned about this settlement when he first heard of it, but in early May he was told that the Company's settlers had formed a provisional government, enacted laws and flown the flag of the United Chiefs (associated with the Declaration of Independence of 1835). As a naval officer accustomed to a proper observance of authority and very jealous of his own, he was particularly sensitive about acts of this kind. In his mind, they amounted to high treason.[33]

It seems Hobson was especially angered by the fact that the Company had claimed its actions were legal on the grounds that the local chiefs were the sovereign authority at Port Nicholson. To be more specific, the Company had alleged, on the basis of its examination of the proclamations Gipps had issued in mid-January, that the British Crown had disclaimed any right of sovereignty in the islands of New Zealand and had recognised every tribe as an independent foreign power. It argued that this meant that the Crown had acknowledged the rights of those chiefs to exercise authority over everyone in their territories and so every act of government in the colony had to derive its authority from their assent. In one sense, the Company's allegation was absurd since Gipps' proclamations had stated nothing of the kind. Yet those proclamations, like many of the earlier statements of the British Crown, were ambiguous about the inter-national status of New Zealand, and it is unremarkable that the Company had decided to take advantage of this ambiguity. The Company's allegation may have especially troubled Hobson because it drew his attention to the fact that the course of action he had been pursuing, namely that of treating with the chiefs in each part of the country as though they were sovereign, rested on the very same logic that the Company had sought to exploit and so was fraught with the very danger it had now exposed.[34]

At least one highly regarded scholar, Peter Adams, has argued that Hobson's proclamations of 21 May 1840 negated the point of the British government's attempt to secure the consent of the chiefs to its assumption of sovereignty and so reveals that the Treaty of Waitangi was little more than window dressing. We will return to the first of these two points later. In regard to the latter one, it is a fundamental error to interpret earlier acts in the light of later ones, just as it is wrong-headed to expect that those acts will always be consistent with one another. Had the New Zealand Company settlers at Port Nicholson not challenged the Crown's authority

---

[33] Gipps to Hobson, 3 April 1840; Hobson to Bunbury, 25 April 1840, *BPP*, 1841, Paper no. 311, p. 18; Hobson to Russell, 25 May 1840; [Bunbury], *Reminiscences*, p. 46; Guy H. Scholefield, *Captain William Hobson: First Governor of New Zealand*, Oxford University Press, Oxford, 1934, pp. 44, 77–78.

[34] *New Zealand Gazette*, 18 April 1840; *Colonial Gazette*, 16 September 1840.

or had Hobson not seen their acts as a threat to his authority, it is probable he would eventually have proclaimed British sovereignty over the three major islands of New Zealand on the basis that he and his agents had secured the consent of most of the chiefs.[35]

To further understand why the British government had been so intent on acquiring sovereignty by means of cession, it is helpful to consider what Hobson might have done if the majority of the chiefs had been unwilling to sign the treaty, especially at the beginning of his mission. We can assume he would have been reluctant to claim sovereignty over the North Island on some other ground, such as *discovery*. This is so for two reasons. First, he would have realised that he had no means to uphold this claim in the face of any resistance from natives or settlers. Hobson had been concerned about his lack of military power before taking up his appointment and had repeatedly raised the matter with the Colonial Office. Second, he would have been apprehensive that a foreign power such as the French could take exception to his proceeding in a manner that denied any need to gain native consent. In fact, unbeknown to him, the French government had decided to support the plan of a French colonisation company (the Nanto-Bordelaise Company) that hoped to acquire sovereignty over all the southern islands of New Zealand; it assumed its best chances of succeeding lay in securing this territory on the basis of native consent; and it might have challenged Hobson's declaration of sovereignty over the South Island on the grounds of *discovery* if it had not learned that some of the native chiefs had already agreed to Bunbury's request that they cede sovereignty to the British Crown. As noted previously, one of the most important reasons the imperial government was committed to assuming sovereignty by means of cession was strategic in the sense that it assumed that this was more likely to succeed than some other mode of acquisition.[36]

---

[35] Peter Adams, *Fatal Necessity: British Intervention in New Zealand 1830–1847*, Auckland University Press/Oxford University Press, Auckland, 1977, p. 161.

[36] Hobson to Governor Richard Bourke, 15 January 1839, Bourke Family Papers, ML, MSS 403/3; Hobson to Sir George Grey, 14 February 1839, TNA, CO 209/4; Hobson to Henry Labouchere, 6 June 1839, TNA, CO 209/4; Hobson to Labouchere, [1] August 1839, *BPP*, 1840, Paper no. 238, p. 44; Normanby to Hobson, 15 August 1839, *BPP*, 1840, Paper no. 238, p. 45; Stephen, Minute, 21 September 1839, TNA, CO 209/4; Hobson to Labouchere, 20 August 1839, TNA, CO 209/4; Russell to Gipps, 26 September 1839, SARNSW, 4/1017; Hobson to Gipps, 24 December 1839, NANZ, G36/1; Hobson to Gipps, 15 June 1840, NANZ, G36/1; Hobson to Russell, 15 December 1841, *BPP*, 1842, Paper no. 569, Copies of Papers and Despatches Relative to New Zealand, p. 188; Peter Tremewan, *French Akaroa: An Attempt to Colonise Southern New Zealand*, University of Canterbury Press, Christchurch, 1990, pp. 72–73, 86; Orange, *Treaty*, p. 86.

In the same vein, what would have happened in the event that Hobson had concluded that he was unable to acquire New Zealand, or at least the North Island, by cession, and had returned to Sydney to seek instructions from Gipps? It is probable that the Governor of New South Wales would have directed him to declare sovereignty over the South Island and Stewart Island on the grounds of the right of *discovery* because this step was consistent with part of the Colonial Office's instructions to Hobson. But what about the North Island? It is possible Gipps might have recommended that Hobson declare sovereignty over the areas claimed by the New Zealand Company on the grounds of a claim that the purchases of land they had made created a title in the Crown because the natives had relinquished their sovereignty by agreeing to those sales.

One way or another, it is apparent that the British government's treatment of sovereignty in the islands of New Zealand could have been very different, just as it is clear that it *was* in fact different to the way it has commonly been figured, given that Hobson did claim British sovereignty in its southern islands on the grounds of *discovery* and settlement (or *possessio*), just as Phillip had done in New Holland.

Part II

Back in London, an enormous tussle had been taking place between the New Zealand Company and the Colonial Office over the means by which the British government had chosen to assume sovereignty in New Zealand. A consideration of this conflict will reveal that the treaty of Waitangi lost a good deal of importance in the eyes of the Colonial Office once it had achieved its primary purpose.

The New Zealand Company, the Colonial Office and the Question of Sovereignty

In the wake of the Colonial Office's decision to intervene in New Zealand's affairs, the New Zealand Company assumed that the Crown would succeed in acquiring sovereignty and started to fear that entrepreneurs in New South Wales were going to beat it in the race to acquire huge amounts of land. As a result, the Company began to reposition itself on the matter of sovereignty and thus the title that British subjects sought to claim on the basis of their land purchasing. The Company soon abandoned its original stance that the natives were sovereign or should be treated as though they were, and thus its claim that bona fide purchasers could hold property on the basis of their purchases from the natives prior to the Crown assuming sovereignty. Indeed, it now attacked the Colonial

Office for its decision to disclaim sovereignty and treat with the native chiefs for its cession, and argued that the British government should simply maintain its claim to sovereignty on the grounds of Cook's discovery and thereby assert what it called its right of pre-emption in regard to land.

Near the end of August 1839 the Company started to use two of its organs, the *New Zealand Gazette* and the *Colonial Gazette*, to launch what became a relentless attack on the Colonial Office's handling of the question of sovereignty. Edward Gibbon Wakefield alleged in the *New Zealand Gazette* that the advocates of systematic colonisation, such as the New Zealand Company, had been badly treated by the Colonial Office and claimed that its ruling that the British Crown had to negotiate a cession of sovereignty from the native chiefs meant that the country was now being abandoned to missionaries, land sharks and outcasts.[37]

By the beginning of October, having seen the government's instructions to Hobson, the Company's directors had become even more concerned that its project would be foiled by a number of competitors for land. One of its principal figures, almost certainly Wakefield, writing in the *Colonial Gazette*, attacked the part of Hobson's instructions bearing on land purchasing. Noting that their main purpose was to put an end to the practice of land-sharking, he claimed that they would have the opposite effect, pointing out that while they proclaimed that the government would not acknowledge any title to land except that which was derived or confirmed from a grant made by the Crown, they simultaneously held out the promise of grants to land that had been acquired from the natives. He also argued that more uncontrolled land purchasing would occur, including by foreign subjects (in the form of French and American land sharks), in part because the instructions revealed that Hobson's power to act depended on his being able to obtain from the native chiefs a recognition of British sovereignty. Wakefield claimed that the whole affair was a complete mess and that the problem of uncontrolled colonisation and large-scale land purchasing could only be solved by the government retracing its steps and starting anew on the basis of the claim to sovereignty that had been established by Cook, thereby abandoning its acknowledgement of what he called 'the mock sovereignty of the native savage'. By doing this, he asserted, the government would 'cut the knot of a thousand difficulties'. Wakefield did not explain why he believed a claim to sovereignty on the basis of the doctrine of *discovery* would achieve this outcome. However, the evangelical clergyman John Dunmore Lang had recently argued that this course of action would allow land purchases in

---

[37] *New Zealand Gazette*, 21 August 1839. See also *Colonial Gazette*, 28 August 1839.

New Zealand to be treated as invalid on the grounds that they infringed the Crown's right of pre-emption, as he believed, following Chief Justice Marshall's ruling in *Johnson v. M'Intosh* in the United States Supreme Court in 1823, that this right was a by-product of acquiring sovereignty on the basis of *discovery*.[38]

Come November the Company's directors realised that they had not gained any traction with the Colonial Office and so tried to bypass it by appealing to the Foreign Secretary, Lord Palmerston, who was known for his aggressive championing of Britain's empire. In a letter almost certainly written by Wakefield, the Company's deputy governor, the shipping magnate Lord Joseph Somes, argued that in instructing Hobson to try to procure the cession of sovereignty to the British Crown, the government had repudiated the Crown's sovereignty in New Zealand by virtue of the fact that it had acknowledged that the natives were the sovereign there. Somes insisted that this step had encouraged the French government to entertain pretensions of obtaining sovereignty in New Zealand and asserted that it was very important that the British government prevent the establishment of French power in the midst of its colonies in Australia. He contended that Cook had taken possession of New Zealand and that this had never been questioned by any foreign power, and that this meant that Britain *had* acquired sovereignty because the law of nations recognised no other way of assuming dominion in a country where the inhabitants were 'so barbarous as to be ignorant of the meaning of the word sovereignty and therefore incapable of ceding sovereign rights'. Furthermore, Somes argued, British sovereignty had been confirmed by Phillip's commission in 1787 (because New Zealand was included within the prescribed limits of the colony of New South Wales) and proclamations of the governor of New South Wales (Macquarie) in 1814 and 1819 and an Act of Parliament of 1823, and enforced frequently by ships of war.[39]

The Company's attempt to bypass the Colonial Office seemed to have failed when Palmerston referred the matter back to the Colonial Office and asked for an explanation of its position. Yet this was a situation that required the Colonial Office to provide the best possible gloss on its decision to negotiate with native chiefs for the cession of sovereignty rather than simply assert British sovereignty on the basis of Cook's unilateral claim of possession. Stephen prepared a memorandum in which he argued in effect that the Colonial Office had acted in accordance with

---

[38] *Ibid.*, 2 October 1839.
[39] Joseph Somes to Lord Palmerston, 7 November 1839, *BPP*, 1840, Paper no. 238, pp. 66–68.

a coherent set of principles. It was simply a matter of fact, he contended, that the British Crown had repeatedly treated New Zealand as an independent state rather than a British dominion. To evidence this point, Stephen cited a series of examples that will be familiar to readers. In three legislative enactments, in 1817, 1823 and 1828, the British parliament had declared that the islands were not part of the British dominions; in replying to the northern chiefs' petition of November 1831, King William IV had declared that New Zealand was an independent state by addressing the natives as an independent people; the British parliament had rejected the South Seas Bill in June 1832 on the grounds that it could not lawfully legislate for a foreign country; Bourke's instructions to Busby in April 1833 had expressly described New Zealand as a foreign country; and the Admiralty had instructed its officers in December 1834 to acknowledge and respect the national flag of New Zealand. 'After such proceedings', Stephen stated emphatically, 'it seems to me preposterous to maintain that New Zealand is a possession of the British Crown'. Indeed, he added: 'The argument [of the Company] that to legislate at all for the trial of crimes in New Zealand renders New Zealand a British territory, or recognises it as such, would prove at little too much, for if so, the Chinese Empire, to which a precisely similar law extends, is also within Her Majesty's dominion'. Thus, he concluded, there was 'overwhelming and superabundant proof' that Britain had 'recognised New Zealand as a foreign and independent state'.[40]

In fact, Stephen's argument in this memorandum was tendentious. In none of the examples he adduced had the British state positively asserted that it regarded New Zealand as a foreign and independent state. As we have seen, the position the British government had held over many years in regard to the status of the islands was fundamentally ambiguous. The scathing tone that Stephen adopted in much of this memorandum reveals not only a certain defensiveness but also betrays the antipathy he felt towards Wakefield and the directors of the New Zealand Company, whose behaviour was unscrupulous in the extreme. At the Colonial Office, Stephen was not alone in this regard, as we will see.

By March the Company's lobbying had forced the Colonial Office to provide the Foreign Office with a copy of Stephen's memorandum and table it in parliament. But the Company did not let up. One of its principal figures, probably Wakefield, mounted a public attack on Stephen's defence of the government's handling of the matter of sovereignty.

---

[40] Stephen, Draft of Memorandum of 18 March 1840, 16 November 1839, TNA, CO 209/5; John Backhouse to Stephen, 11 March 1840, *BPP*, 1840, Paper no. 238, p. 68; [Stephen], Memorandum, 18 March 1840, *BPP*, 1840, Paper no. 238, pp. 68–69.

Once more, it was alleged that the government's course of action risked losing New Zealand to the French and undermining the systematic colonisation of the country, but now the arguments the Company presented were more sophisticated inasmuch as they drew on cases of the United States Supreme Court. Wakefield argued that the government seemed to assume that it had forfeited its claim to sovereignty in New Zealand but that a consideration of the relevant Supreme Court cases – *Johnson v. M'Intosh* (1823), *Cherokee Nation v. The State of Georgia* (1831) and *Worcester v. The State of Georgia* (1832) – demonstrated that the British Crown's right to sovereignty vis-à-vis foreign powers, which it held on the basis of prior discovery, should not have been affected by the arrangements it had made with the natives to recognise their 'distinct national character'. Wakefield quoted much of an anonymous article that had appeared in the *New Zealand Journal* a few days earlier in which the journal's proprietor and editor, Henry Chapman,[41] had made this argument.[42]

In the next few months the Company continued to harass the Colonial Office by sponsoring a large public meeting, endorsing a petition got up by London merchants, bankers and shipowners, and publishing more articles in the press. In mid-June, its directors momentarily concluded that their concerns had been put to rest as they assumed that Gipps' January proclamations meant that the Crown had finally asserted its sovereignty in New Zealand on the basis of Cook's discovery and so no foreign subject could acquire lands except by means of a Crown grant. At the same time, the Company expressed a belief that it would receive a grant from the Crown to the large amount of land that its agent had apparently acquired in the closing months of 1839, not least because it assumed that existing titles would be respected except where natives had been cheated out of their land for a mere nominal consideration. In June the previous year it seems that Normanby had told a deputation comprising figures who would become the directors of the New Zealand Company that the government would not interfere with any purchases made in a bona fide manner or equitably acquired. Certainly, this was the impression they had taken away from this meeting. Nevertheless, by early July it was apparent that the Company's directors were still deeply

---

[41] We will hear more of Chapman in the final chapter, as he was to become a judge of New Zealand's Supreme Court and write the leading judgment in an important case, *R v. Symonds*, regarding the Crown's right of pre-emption.

[42] Extract of Stephen to Backhouse, 18 March 1840, and [Stephen], Memorandum, [November 1839], *BPP*, 1840, Paper no. 238, pp. 68–69; *New Zealand Journal*, 4 April 1840; *Colonial Gazette*, 8 April 1840.

concerned about the threat they believed Australian and French entrepreneurs presented to their plans to colonise New Zealand.[43]

At this point, Lord Eliot, a director of yet another British company
planning to create a colony in New Zealand, moved a motion in the
House of Lords to establish a parliamentary select committee, largely
on the grounds that the House of Commons should consider the right of
Britain to claim sovereignty in the islands of New Zealand. In the debate
that occurred on this occasion, Eliot presented the argument that
Wakefield had been making, contending that Britain had acquired sovereignty by virtue of Cook's claiming of possession and that this meant it
had secured the sole right of acquiring the soil from the natives, citing
American Chief Justice Marshall's judgment in *Worcester* v. *The State of
Georgia*. In the course of a rambling speech, Eliot went off course,
remarking that he was at a loss to know what authority the government
had to rule that the acquisitions of land made in New Zealand were null
and void, given that it had declared the islands of New Zealand to be
independent. But he did not pursue this point any further. Instead, he
noted that Emmerich de Vattel held that title to land rested on cultivating
it, observed that this Swiss jurist had extolled Penn for purchasing land,
and suggested that New Zealand had considerable waste lands. The last
was an argument that the Company would champion in a later dispute
with the Colonial Office.[44]

In response, Lord John Russell defended the Colonial Office's handling
of the matter of sovereignty by deploying several legal arguments. He
contended that, though a right to sovereignty might accrue to the first
European discoverer, it was questionable whether that right was retained
in circumstances where the party claiming possession did not confirm it
for many years. More specifically, in the same vein as Stephen had argued
in his memorandum, Russell contended that Britain had actually relinquished rather than confirmed that right because it had made solemn
declarations on several occasions to the effect that New Zealand was
a foreign dominion. Both these considerations, he continued, made it
necessary that the government acquire a new title to the sovereignty of the
islands. After attacking the attempts of both the New Zealand Association
and the New Zealand Company to assume the prerogative of the Crown

---

[43] NZC Court of Directors, Minutes of Meetings, 13 June 1839, TNA, CO 208/180; John
Ward to Captain J. Nagle, 6 August 1839, reproduced in *Colonist*, 10 June 1840; *New
Zealand Journal*, 4 and 18 April 1840; *Spectator*, 18 April 1840; *Colonial Gazette*,
22 April 1840; *New Zealand Journal*, 20 June and 4 July 1840.

[44] *BPP*, 1840, Paper no. 582, Report of the Select Committee on New Zealand (henceforth
1840 Select Committee Report on New Zealand), p. iii; *BPD*, House of Commons,
7 July 1840, columns 523–30.

in asserting a right of sovereignty, Russell, echoing the terms in which Eliot had spoken, argued that the government had proceeded in the manner lauded by Vattel and had acted in perfect conformity with the law of nations by making an agreement with the natives to purchase their territory and land. Finally, he claimed that, while the British Crown undoubtedly had the paramount right in land, it would have been impractical for the colonial government to try to take away from the settlers all the land they had purchased from the natives since those settlers would have immediately resisted the Crown's authority.[45]

Reception of the Treaty, the 1840 Select Committee and Native Title

Just two days later, the Colonial Office received a timely despatch from Gipps. It contained the news that Hobson had been able to make a treaty. In light of the relentless attack the Company had been mounting on the Colonial Office, this news was greeted enthusiastically by the Office's senior staff. Stephen in particular felt vindicated. He immediately scribbled a minute to the parliamentary Under-Secretary for the Colonies, Vernon Smith: 'This despatch arrived this morning and [is] very opportunal [*sic*]. It seems to me to prove, if proof were wanting, how much wiser was the course [the government has] taken of negotiating for a cession of the sovereignty than would have been the course [urged by the Company] of relying on the proceedings of Captain Cook [in claiming possession of the grounds of *discovery*] or the language of Vattel [that native peoples lacked sovereignty] in opposition to our own statute book'.[46]

For his part, Smith recommended that Hobson's report be presented to parliament immediately. However, Russell directed that a collection of documents be tabled which comprised not only a copy of Hobson's report and an English text of the Treaty of Waitangi but Gipps' three proclamations of 14 January 1840 and Hobson's two proclamations of 30 January 1840. In the same vein, Russell approved of *all* the measures Gipps had adopted to give effect to the government's intention to establish British authority in New Zealand and the manner in which Hobson had executed them. Russell's actions suggest that the Colonial Office regarded the treaty as just one of the means by which the Crown had assumed sovereignty in New Zealand.[47]

Furthermore, there is nothing in the contemporary records of the Colonial Office to suggest that its key figures had examined the terms of

---

[45] *Ibid.*, columns 531–36, 545.   [46] Stephen to Russell, 9 July 1840, TNA, CO 209/6.
[47] Vernon Smith to Russell, 9 July 1840, TNA, CO 209/6; Russell to Gipps, 17 July 1840, *BPP*, 1840, Paper no. 560, p. 11.

the treaty deed closely enough to register the presence of the clause that confirmed and guaranteed to the natives the possession of their lands. In any case, even if they had scrutinised it, they would probably have concluded that all of its articles were in accordance with the spirit of Normanby's instructions to Hobson. In other words, that particular clause would not have struck them as especially significant, let alone that it carried any specific legal meaning.

As far as the Company's directors were concerned, the news that Hobson had succeeded in making the treaty was of no great significance. They had been assuming for some time that the Crown would acquire sovereignty. More to the point, they seem to have concluded that none of the treaty's terms had any particular bearing on the problems facing the Company. (They were not alone in this, as we will see.) Consequently, they pushed ahead with making their case to the parliamentary select committee that Eliot had secured and to which he was appointed chairman. The Committee's hearings were dominated by witnesses associated with the Company, especially Wakefield, who basically repeated what he had been arguing in the press in recent months. At the end of these hearings, Wakefield anonymously drafted a report in Eliot's name, but most of the committee's members refused to endorse it and directed Eliot to merely report the evidence to the House of Commons. However, in an extraordinary move, which was typical of the unscrupulous manner in which the New Zealand Company and its allies conducted themselves, Eliot disregarded this instruction and presented the report to the House as though it had been adopted by the Committee, thereby misleading many, including the influential newspaper *The Times*. A member of the committee must have leaked these shenanigans. This prompted the editor of *The Times* to declare: 'Every crafty assumption [that the Company's directors] could attempt to proceed upon – every perversion of fact they could press into their service, their intelligible biases, their unintentional misconceptions, and their usual professions of disinterestedness – all this . . . was forcibly present [in the committee's proceedings]'.[48]

Much of the report Wakefield had drafted was devoted to an attack on the government's treatment of the issue of sovereignty. No reference was made to native rights in land except in the context of an assertion of the Crown's right of pre-emption. Certainly, some members of the Committee and the members of the New Zealand Company and its supporters who gave testimony seemed to have held that there were

[48] 1840 Select Committee Report on New Zealand, pp. ii, vi, x, 5, 8–9, 38–41, 44–45, 48, 53, 97–111; *The Times*, 4 and 16 September 1840; *Devonport Independent*, 3 November 1840.

considerable waste lands in New Zealand and thus areas unencumbered by native title, but apart from an assertion to the contrary by the Church Missionary Society's lay secretary, Dandeson Coates, that 'the whole of the land [was] the property of one tribe or another', there was little if any consideration of the nature of native title. No one on the Committee seems to have regarded the matter to be important enough to warrant much discussion.[49]

Yet several historians, including Mark Hickford and Ned Fletcher, have argued to the contrary, claiming that key figures in the government expressed views at this time about the nature of native rights of property in land. One of the most important sources they have invoked is a minute that Stephen scribbled on the same day that Eliot presented his draft report to the Select Committee, probably because Vernon Smith, who was a member of the Committee, had asked Stephen for his opinion about the relevance of the United States Supreme Court rulings to the matters it had been discussing.[50] Stephen's memorandum deserves quoting at length:

The [United States Supreme Court] case of Johnson and Mackintosh proves that a grant from an Indian tribe of lands in the State of Ohio would ... confer on the grantee no valid title, in defeasance of a title derived under a grant from the United States. It shows that the whole territory over which those tribes wandered was to be regarded as the property of the British Crown in right of discovery and of conquest, and that the Indians were mere possessors of the soil on sufferance. Such is American Law. British Law in Canada is far more humane, for there, the Crown purchases of the Indians before it grants to its own subjects.

Whatever may be the ground occupied by international jurists they never forget the policy and interests of their own country. Their business is to give to rapacity and injustice the most decorous veil that legal ingenuity can weave. Seldon, in the interest of England, maintained the doctrine of what was called mare clausum. Vattel in the interest of Holland laid down the principle of open fisheries. Mr Marshall, great as he was, was still an American, and adjudicated against the rights

---

[49] 1840 Select Committee Report on New Zealand, pp. vi–ix, 51, 85, 125.

[50] See, for example, Mark Hickford, '"Decidedly the Most Interesting Savages on the Globe": An Approach to the Intellectual History of Maori Property Rights, 1837–53', *History of Political Thought*, vol. 27, no. 1, 2006, pp. 152–53, and Fletcher, 'Praiseworthy Device', pp. 841, 856–58. This minute is merely headed 28 July, and some historians have concluded that it was written in 1839 (for example, Banner, *Possessing the Pacific*, pp. 60–61, and Paul McHugh, '"The Most Decorous Veil which Legal Ingenuity Can Weave": The British Annexation of New Zealand (1840)', in Kelly L. Grotke and Markus J. Prutsch (eds.), *Constitutionalism, Legitimacy, and Power: Nineteenth-Century Experiences*, Oxford University Press, Oxford, 2014, p. 300), probably because that date has been pencilled on the folio in the Colonial Office records. For a discussion of the historical traces that suggest it was almost certainly written in 1840, see Hickford, 'Most Interesting Savages', p. 151 note 143, and Ned Fletcher, 'Praiseworthy Device', p. 141 note 363.

of the Indians. All such law is good just as long as those in power enforce it, and no longer.

Besides what is this to the case of New Zealand? The Dutch, not we, discovered it. Nearly a hundred years ago [sic] Captain Cook landed there, and claimed the sovereignty for King George the II [sic]. Nothing has ever been done to maintain and keep alive that claim. The most solemn acts have been done in repudiation and disavowal of it. Besides the New Zealanders are not wandering tribes, but bodies of men, till lately, very populous, who have a settled form of government, and who have divided and appropriated the whole territory amongst them. They are not huntsmen, but after their rude fashion, agriculturalists.

The two cases seem to me altogether dissimilar, and the decision of the Supreme Court of the United States, though it may be very good American law, is not the law we recognise and act upon on the American Continent.[51]

Stephen was keen to make a point that had been preoccupying him a good deal (because of the Company's unrelenting attack on the Colonial Office's handling of the question of sovereignty in New Zealand, for which he, rather than any Colonial Secretary, was primarily responsible), namely that the natives and not the British government were sovereign, that the British government had not maintained its claim of sovereignty but had repudiated it and that the New Zealanders did have the requisites of sovereignty and thus title in land. Consequently, as Stephen remarked, the British government had to purchase land from the natives before granting it to its own subjects. However, at this point in time, what was important to him and his colleagues in the Colonial Office was not the precise nature of native title but what Stephen called British law or we might call the principle of native consent to the extinguishment of their title to land.[52] It is crucial for us to grasp why this was so.

The Colonial Office's principal figures placed great importance on the principle of native consent in regard to acquisition of land because it was a corollary of the principle that they had adopted in regard to sovereignty. Indeed, the principles in regard to both were really one and the same. The Colonial Office's key players maintained that acknowledging the sovereignty of the natives and their title to land, and in turn acquiring the natives' consent to relinquishing them both, made the possession of foreign lands more honourable for the British nation and more just in the eyes of God – and more peaceful to boot.

---

[51] Stephen to Smith, 28 July [1840], TNA, CO 209/4.

[52] This is also apparent in Stephen's discussion of native rights in land later that year: Stephen to Smith, 28 December 1840, TNA, CO 209/8.

Part III

Contesting British Sovereignty in Sydney

At the same time that Hobson was seeking to assume sovereignty for the British Crown in New Zealand, the implications of this endeavour for claims to title to land gradually became clearer in Sydney, arousing enormous anxiety among those who had purchased land in the islands. In the debate that took place over this matter, the primary issue again was not native title per se but sovereignty, or more specifically whether the government had the right to interfere in titles to land based on transactions British subjects had made with natives prior to the Crown assuming sovereignty.

After Hobson set sail for New Zealand, the consequences of the British government's intervention in the islands' affairs for land titles claimed by British subjects had continued to be debated in the Sydney press. The editor of the *Colonist* questioned whether the government was legally warranted to establish 'the territorial sovereignty of the British Crown'. He attacked those parties who held that the government had such a right on the grounds that it could take possession by right of prior discovery and sustain that sovereignty over the entire territory, just as it had been done in colonising Australia. He also sought to counter any argument that this doctrine meant that the natives of New Zealand merely had rights of usage rather than any claim of ownership. He argued that even if one were to concede that this was the case, those native interests in land had to be recognised by the British Crown and their extinguishment negotiated, given that the British government had recognised the natives' sovereignty and proprietorship.[53]

In January a rival Sydney newspaper published an abridgement of a recent pamphlet authored by John Dunmore Lang. As noted earlier, Lang had argued that all past and future purchases of land from the New Zealanders should be disallowed on the grounds that they infringed the Crown's right of pre-emption. This seems to have raised the spectre among land claimants in Sydney that the government would rule that all their purchases of land, rather than just those deemed to be fraudulent or excessive, were null and void. An anonymous correspondent for the *Colonist*, who was probably Samuel McDonald Martin, was quick to respond. In large part, Lang had made his argument on the basis that the British Crown had already acted in this manner in regard to Batman's treaty, but Martin rejected Lang's contention that the two cases were

---

[53] *Colonist*, 22 January 1840.

comparable. He argued that for many years prior to the Port Phillip Association claiming land at Port Phillip, the British Crown had asserted her right of sovereignty over the whole continent; both her right to and the fact of her sovereignty had been acknowledged by all civilised powers; and the Port Phillip Association had acted in defiance of the British Crown's assertions of sovereignty over the country in question. By contrast, Martin contended, in New Zealand the British Crown had never tried to secure the country as a dependency and had instead acknowledged its independence by providing a national flag and appointing a British Resident. That being the case, Martin asked, was it not fair and right for British subjects to acquire land in New Zealand as well as they could in any other foreign country? Finally, he challenged the contention that the British Crown was the only legitimate source of title for British subjects, arguing that the source of title must be the country in question rather than the country they had left.[54]

At the end of January Gipps learned that purchases of land were still occurring despite his proclamations of 14 January (discussed earlier in this chapter). He had agreed to meet five Ngāi Tahu rangatira (Tūhawaiki, Tohowaki, Karetai, Kaikoreare and Tūkawa) who had been brought to Sydney by a syndicate seeking to purchase vast swathes of New Zealand's Middle or South Island. The chiefs wanted to know whether Gipps proposed to deprive particular buyers of title to the land they had sold them. Gipps, who suspected that they were really acting on behalf of the syndicate, told them that the British government had to negotiate with the chiefs for the establishment of British sovereignty before it could proceed to intervene in such cases, that these cases would be referred to a commission charged with investigating titles and that British subjects had no right to purchase the land of aboriginal people ahead of their own government. On learning this, one of the chiefs apparently shook his head and pronounced 'The Gubbanar no good'. Following this meeting, Gipps decided that he had to persuade these chiefs to sign a treaty of the same kind that Hobson was seeking to secure in New Zealand, that is, one in which the chiefs agreed to cede sovereignty and the right of pre-emption to the Crown. Consequently, at a meeting on 12 February with two of the Ngāi Tahu chiefs and five North Island chiefs, he explained the terms of such an agreement and told them that he would not confirm the titles of the land they had previously sold. The chiefs promised to return to Government House two days later with the

---

[54] John Dunmore Lang, *New Zealand in 1839, or Four Letters to the Right Hon. Earl Durham on the Colonization of that Island*, Smith, Elder and Co., London, 1839, pp. 78–79,82; *Australian*, 2, 4, 16 and 18 January 1840; *Colonist*, 22 January 1840.

other Ngāi Tahu chiefs to sign this agreement, but they never showed up, much to Gipps' annoyance. He soon learned why. A member of the syndicate who had brought the Ngāi Tahu chiefs to Sydney, John Jones, had told the chiefs that they should refuse to sign any agreement that did not secure the titles of those who had purchased land from them. To make matters worse, Jones, and his four partners, who included William Wentworth (of whom more shortly), had made an agreement with the chiefs to purchase some 20 million acres in the South Island. It is not altogether clear why they made this grandiose purchase, given that Gipps' 14 January proclamation in regard to land titles seems to have generally dissuaded potential land grabbers from making any more purchases with Māori. But, in all likelihood, the members of the syndicate, and Wentworth in particular, were keen to test the legal validity of Gipps' proclamation and thereby ascertain what claims purchasers of land such as themselves might be able to sustain in New Zealand.[55]

By mid-February unease about the British government's intentions in respect of land titles had deepened among land claimants in Sydney. A critical account of the Colonial Office's instructions to Hobson regarding the treatment of titles that rested on pre-annexation purchases (which one of the London newspapers aligned with the New Zealand Company had published in August the previous year) had reached New South Wales. Consequently, the *Sydney Herald* published an editorial in which it argued that the claimants of such titles should be very apprehensive because of the oblique manner in which the British government had treated the matter of sovereignty in New Zealand. Nevertheless, it found some reassurance in Gipps' proclamation on land claims, concluding that British subjects' rights in land on the basis of purchase from natives would not be denied but simply held in abeyance until they were confirmed by the investigation of a land claims commission. Indeed, at this time, most newspapers continued to assume that the only purchases that would be invalidated were those found not to be bona fide, or at least they pretended that this was the case.[56]

---

[55] Martin, Letter IV, 25 January 1840, in his *New Zealand*, p. 82; *Sydney Herald*, 31 January 1840; *Australian*, 1 February 1840; *Colonist*, 1 February 1840; Names of Chiefs who attended Government House belonging to the South Island, New Zealand Estrays collected by Sir William Dixson, 29 December 1830–1845, ML, DLNAR 3; Gipps, Memorandum of an Agreement, 14 February 1840; John Jones to Edward Deas Thomson, 14 February 1840, and Thomson to Gipps, 15 February 1840, reproduced in Edward Sweetman, *The Unsigned New Zealand Treaty*, Arrow Printery, Melbourne, 1939, pp. 61–62; Wentworth deed, 15 February 1840, *The Wentworth Indenture*, Nag's Head Press, Christchurch, 1979; Gipps to Russell, 16 August 1840, *BPP*, 1841, Paper no. 311, p. 63; *New Zealand Herald and Auckland Gazette*, 2 February 1842.

[56] *Colonial Gazette*, 28 August 1839; *Sydney Gazette*, 25 January 1840; *Sydney Herald*, 27 January and 19 February 1840.

At the end of February Gipps acted on Normanby's instructions to establish a commission to investigate land purchases. He directed that a lands claim bill be drafted for this purpose. He was anxious to have this legislation ready so it could be presented to the Legislative Council on the first day of the next session, though it seems that he soon decided that it would be better to postpone it until such time as Hobson was able to assume sovereignty over more of the territory of New Zealand. There was considerable speculation in the Sydney press about the policy that Gipps intended to pursue and some newspapers became increasingly critical of the measures they feared he was going to introduce. In early March the editor of the *Sydney Herald* argued in a long leader that the source of all titles in New Zealand lay in the chiefs. Shortly afterwards, Martin and Wentworth spearheaded a move by New Zealand land claimants in Sydney to form a body called the New Zealand Association in order to keep an eye on every step the government made. At its first organisational meeting, in early April, Wentworth expressed the opinion that there was nothing in English law that allowed the Crown to deny title to those who had acquired land on fair terms. Nevertheless, he recommended that the Association procure the best legal opinion available on the merits of its case. Meanwhile, debate about the fundamental question at stake continued in the pages of the Sydney press.[57]

Gipps' Land Claims Bill

In late May, at the beginning of a new session of the New South Wales Legislative Council, Gipps presented his much-anticipated Land Claims Bill. Introducing the legislation, he made it clear that he regarded the establishment of the Crown's authority in New Zealand as a matter of the greatest importance. He then proceeded to argue that the claims that British subjects had made to tracts of land on the basis of purchase or grants from natives had no foundation in either the law or the usage of imperial powers. Consequently, while he acknowledged that the Colonial Office had stated that the government would allow claims that were found to be based on equitable principles, he revealed that the preamble of this bill, which he himself had prepared, declared that *none* of the titles based on

[57] Gipps to Hobson, 15 January 1840; Memorandum of Gipps, 27 February 1840, SARNSW, 4/1017; T. C. Harington to the Attorney General of New South Wales, 29 February 1840, Miscellaneous New South Wales Archives Estrays relating to New Zealand 1830–45, ML, DLNAR 3; *Sydney Gazette*, 20 February 1840; *Colonist*, 29 February 1840; *Commercial Journal and Advertiser*, 29 February 1840; *Sydney Herald*, 9 March 1840; *Sydney Gazette*, 10 March 1840; *Australasian Chronicle*, 3 April 1840; *Australian*, 4 April 1840; *Sydney Monitor*, 20 April 1840; *Australian*, 12 May 1840; *Sydney Gazette*, 14 and 19 May 1840; *Colonist*, 20, 23 and 27 May 1840.

purchases or grants from natives were valid. Moreover, the preamble of the bill Gipps tabled not only insisted that it was the Queen's will to refuse any titles to land that did not proceed from or were not allowed by Her Majesty. It also stated that the native chiefs had no right to dispose of the territory they occupied so as to convey title to those lands. This implied that the New Zealanders had no substantive rights of property in land.[58]

It appears that Gipps believed that the challenge being made to the Crown's authority made it politically necessary for him to assume this position on native title. It is probably also the case that the stance he chose to adopt, or at least the passion with which he took it up, owed something to his hostility to Wentworth. The previous year he had bestowed on this lawyer and pastoral leaseholder the honour of being appointed to the colony's Legislative Council, but he had been outraged by the part Wentworth had played in persuading the Ngāi Tahu chiefs to reject the agreement he had sought to make with them and to accept instead Wentworth and Jones' offer to purchase much of the South Island. As Ned Fletcher has argued, Gipps was still smarting at being out-manoeuvred by Wentworth. By the same token, Wentworth had not forgiven Gipps for vetoing this purchase, which would have made him the biggest landowner in Australasia, and he nursed a personal grievance towards him.[59]

Gipps' bill provoked a furious reaction in the pages of several of the Sydney newspapers. By this time, the New Zealand Association had also released the opinions it had commissioned from two leading lawyers, William A'Beckett and J. B. Darvall. These opinions asserted that there had been no legal obstacle to British subjects purchasing land in New Zealand prior to the Crown acquiring sovereignty and that any proposal to treat those purchases as invalid was contrary to English law. Most importantly, Busby, Wentworth and a group of more than 150 land claimants (who were probably all members of the New Zealand Association) each petitioned the colony's Legislative Council for leave to address it in regard to the bill and won permission to do so.[60]

---

[58] *Votes and Proceedings of the New South Wales Legislative Council*, 1840, no. 1, p. 1; *Sydney Herald*, 29 May 1840; *Colonist*, 30 May 1840.

[59] Gipps to Hobson, 6 May and 11 June 1840, SARNSW, 4/1651; Peter Cochrane, *Colonial Ambition: Foundations of Australian Democracy*, Melbourne University Press, Melbourne, 2006, pp. 73, 78, 80, 90; Fletcher, 'Praiseworthy Device', p. 892.

[60] *Sydney Herald*, 1 June 1840; *Colonist*, 3, 4 and 6 June 1840; New Zealand Land Claims Bill, printed in *Australian*, 6 June 1840; *Australasian Chronicle*, 6 June 1840; *Australian*, 6 June 1840; *Colonist*, 13 and 17 June 1840; Busby, Petition to the Governor and the Legislative Council of New South Wales, 13 June 1840, www.parliament.nsw.gov.au/fc docs/FCDocuments/1840/02007b.pdf; *Votes and Proceedings of the New South Wales Legislative Council*, 16, 23 and 25 June 1840; *Australian*, 20 June 1840; *Australian*, 24 June 1840.

In his address to the Legislative Council, Busby claimed to speak not only as an advocate for the rights of land claimants but on behalf of the natives. Yet it is clear that he was mostly concerned with his own rights as well as those of his fellow land claimants. The arguments Busby sought to advance were concerned with the conduct of the British government and were as much historical as legal in nature. Many of these arguments had already been made in the colony by this stage, but at least one of them was novel. Busby advanced his case along three lines. First, he contended that the islands of New Zealand had been deemed by the British government to be independent of all foreign control until Hobson proclaimed British sovereignty. This meant that, unless British subjects had no right to possess lands in a foreign and independent state, the natives had the right to alienate their lands to British subjects, and those subjects had a right to such lands as they had fairly acquired them from the natives up until the time the natives ceded the right of pre-emption to the Crown. Busby argued that the position of British land claimants like him was strengthened not only by the various acts but also by the various omissions of the British government. In reference to the acts, he contended that the British government had acknowledged the natives to be independent in responding to the chiefs' adoption of a national flag and their Declaration of Independence; in regard to the omissions, he argued that the British government had acted as though the purchases were valid since it had taken no action of the kind it had taken in Port Phillip in reference to Batman's treaty. Second, Busby argued that Gipps' bill was inconsistent with various pronouncements by the British government. He pointed to Normanby's declaration in the Colonial Office's instructions to Hobson that the natives' title to sovereignty and the soil were indisputable and had been solemnly recognised by the British government, and to the Lords of the Treasury's pronouncement that any assumption of British authority should be contingent upon a territorial cession being obtained from the native chiefs. Finally – and this was Busby's distinctive intervention – he contended that Gipps' bill was inconsistent with the Treaty of Waitangi, upon which he argued that the right of the British government to interfere in New Zealand's affairs was alone founded. More specifically, he drew attention to the first clause of its second article in which he claimed that the British Crown had confirmed and guaranteed to the natives 'the entire and exclusive property in lands'. Busby argued that this meant that the natives' rights of property in land had been 'confirmed and guaranteed in the fullest sense which language could convey'. Busby also contended that the second clause of the treaty's second article, by which the chiefs had agreed to yield to the Crown the exclusive right to buy their lands, supported his interpretation.

'[I]t appears to be a necessary consequence of this clause', he asserted, 'that the right existed of conveying to others than the Queen their landed property, for why stipulate to relinquish what they did not possess?' Busby likewise argued that, even if the government did have the authority to invalidate bona fide purchases, depriving British subjects of their property would undermine the natives' confidence in 'the sacred engagement' the Crown had been entered into with them to preserve their property in land – in other words the treaty.[61]

At the conclusion of Busby's address, the governor and legislative councillors put several questions to him, but none of them touched upon the substance of his argument, let alone his particular contentions regarding the treaty. They were clearly of the view that much of his argument did not address the matter at stake: did the natives have a right to convey title to land to British subjects without the authority of the Crown? They quizzed him instead about the role he had played in devising the natives' request for a national flag and the Declaration of Independence. This line of inquiry was designed to cast doubt on whether the natives were truly a sovereign people and had the capacity to dispose of their own land to anyone other than their fellow New Zealanders.[62]

The matter under consideration was very familiar to Wentworth. In 1827 he had appeared as legal counsel in a case in the New South Wales Supreme Court that concerned the Crown's jurisdiction in relation to the Aboriginal people in the colony (*R v. Lowe*), during which he had invoked the full canon of the law of nature as well as the law of nations. In the long speech he made now, Wentworth advanced three substantive lines of argument. In the first, he contended that the proposition in the preamble of Gipps' bill that the natives were incapable of disposing of their lands to foreign subjects was erroneous. It was obviously contrary to Normanby's instructions to Hobson, because those instructions were not only rooted in the assumption that the natives had an indisputable right to the lands but they unambiguously asserted this to be the case. It was inconsistent with the British treatment of the rights of property of natives in North America, given that the history of both individuals and the government purchasing lands from the Indians showed that the absolute right of the natives to the soil had been acknowledged there. Finally, it was contrary to the law of nations, given that Vattel, whom he called the most eminent authority, had argued that 'whether the natives have the sovereignty or not, the domain belongs to them and that it is clear they only have a right to dispose of it'. Strikingly, in mounting this argument Wentworth saw no

---

[61] *Sydney Herald*, 6 July 1840.   [62] *Ibid.*

merit in invoking the treaty of Waitangi. Indeed, he explicitly stated that he would not express any opinion about it.[63]

Wentworth's second line of argument concerned the right of British subjects to found colonies as well as purchase land in a foreign country. In regard to the former, he contended that British subjects had the right to establish colonies without the concurrence of the British Crown, so long as the native people gave their consent. This right did not depend on the laws of Britain but on the laws of the country where the land was to be sold. Once more, he invoked the law of nations as well as examples from North America to support his contention. Wentworth also contested Hobson's assumption that he could claim the South Island on the ground that the British Crown had a right by virtue of the doctrine of *discovery*: this only gave a right of priority to settle in cases where the country was desert or uncultivated, which was not the case for this territory; and in any case the right of possession to a country on this basis lapsed after fifty years if the discoverer had not sought to take actual possession of that country. In reference to the right of British subjects to buy land from native peoples, Wentworth invoked a number of English legal cases, particularly the famous Calvin's case of 1608, to support his contention.[64]

Finally, Wentworth acknowledged that the Crown had previously made laws similar to Gipps' bill, but argued that they were only prospective in nature and so earlier purchases were considered to be valid. Here, like Busby, Wentworth distinguished between the case of New Zealand and that of Port Phillip in respect to Batman's treaty, noting that in the latter case the land lay within the limits of the commission of the governor of New South Wales, that the Crown's right had been asserted and never disputed, and that no land had ever been purchased from the Aboriginal people in the colony.[65]

The representatives of the 150 or so land claimants, the lawyers A'Beckett and Darvall, mounted many of the same arguments as Wentworth had. For example, A'Beckett contended that there was no law that prohibited British subjects from purchasing lands in a foreign country, and Darvall argued that the doctrine of *discovery* was irrelevant to the circumstances of New Zealand. Darvall also contended that the fact that the British government had made a treaty for the purpose of acquiring sovereignty was a tacit admission of the previous independence of the natives and that consequently it became a matter of right that all their laws

---

[63] *R v. Lowe*, www.law.mq.edu.au/research/colonial_case_law/nsw/cases/case_index/1827/ r_v_lowe/; *Sydney Herald*, 6 July 1840.
[64] *Sydney Herald*, 6 July 1840.   [65] *Ibid.*; *Colonist*, 4 July 1840.

and usages should be respected and confirmed up to the time when cession occurred. This meant that all titles acquired under the sanction of those laws and usages should be held sacred. Like Wentworth, these two lawyers made no reference to the treaty of Waitangi in making their arguments.[66]

Gipps and Native Title

A day after the last of these addresses had been presented, the news that Hobson had proclaimed British sovereignty over all of New Zealand belatedly appeared in Sydney newspapers. It seems Gipps had deliberately withheld this information until an opportune moment. More than one newspaper was quick to claim that this news put to rest the claims that the land claimants had been making. 'The Crown of England has declared its sovereignty over New Zealand by RIGHT OF DISCOVERY', the editor of the Sydney Gazette (erroneously) declared. 'Foreign nations may, if they choose, question the light of England as to her right to assume the sovereignty of New Zealand, but we cannot admit for a single instant the propriety of a few British subjects to contend against the rights and prerogatives of the sovereign, to whom they owe an unqualified allegiance'. He proceeded to spell out the logic of this argument. 'England has assumed the sovereignty of New Zealand upon the recognised plea of discovery, and by so doing the right of the native chiefs to buy or to sell lands in New Zealand is disallowed, consequently no contracts made and entered into between the subjects of Great Britain or others with the Aboriginal natives of New Zealand can be recognised'. But these newspapers were only partially correct. After all, while Hobson's proclamations made clear that sovereignty over all of the islands of New Zealand now resided in the British Crown, the question of the right of British subjects to title in land on the basis of purchases made prior to the British assumption of sovereignty was still unresolved since Hobson had claimed sovereignty over at least the North Island on the basis of cession rather than discovery. In any case, it is apparent that Gipps assumed that he still had to provide a thoroughgoing rebuttal of the arguments that had been advanced in the Legislative Council in order to legitimise his government's position and thereby uphold the Crown's authority.[67]

---

[66] Australasian Chronicle, 2 July 1840; Sydney Herald, 6 July 1840.
[67] Sydney Monitor, 3 July 1840; Sydney Gazette, 7 July 1840, original emphasis; Sydney Monitor, 13 July 1840; Australian, 14 July 1840; Loveridge, Land Claims Bill, p. 81, and Appendix, pp. 14–15.

To understand why this was so, it is helpful if we bear in mind the following points. Gipps had been charged by the British government with the responsibility of asserting the authority of the Crown in order to put a stop to further land purchasing and limit the amount of land British subjects would be granted, thereby ensuring that the colonial government had the means to advance systematic colonisation of the country and protect the natives from the ravages of uncontrolled colonisation. Like many governors, Gipps was guided in this task by what he had learned while serving in another settler colony. During his previous posting in Lower Canada, he had formed the opinion that the government's control of land was crucial to the success of colonisation, and after assuming the governorship of New South Wales he had become even more determined that property should not be surrendered willy-nilly to a small group of people as a result of his battle with a powerful group of squatters. Gipps was also conscious that considerable opposition had been expressed to his bill, both in the Legislative Council and in the press. Likewise, he realised that the British government's power to assert its authority vis-à-vis those who were laying claim to title in New Zealand was limited because the home government had refused to provide Hobson with military force and he himself lacked the means to make good this lack. This meant that he had to rely on the power of speech. It is also clear that he relished this opportunity as he was a brilliant speaker. Finally, it is apparent that Gipps had concluded that the position that the home government had previously adopted on the crucial matter of sovereignty of the islands, namely that the natives were more or less sovereign, provided a woefully inadequate basis for defending its position that all transactions in land in the territory predating the acquisition of sovereignty were invalid and that the home government had made matters worse by announcing that it would acknowledge some of those transactions as the basis for grants of land. All these considerations meant that the position Gipps adopted was over-determined. It is also the case that historians such as Judith Binney have erred, both in arguing that Gipps was deeply committed in principle to a position that the natives had barely any rights in land and in attributing this position to the way in which native rights in land had been treated in the Australian colonies. The stance Gipps adopted on native title at this moment was primarily a pragmatic one, born of a necessity that was dictated by the particular circumstances in which he found himself.[68]

---

[68] Samuel Clyde McCulloch, 'Gipps, Sir George', *Australian Dictionary of Biography*, http://adb.anu.edu/biography/gipps-sir-george-2098/text2645; Adams, *Fatal Necessity*, pp. 179–80; Binney, 'Signing', p. 25.

In a speech Gipps gave to the Legislative Council in mid-July he asserted that his Land Claims bill was founded upon three principles that he had assumed were fully recognised and indeed admitted as political axioms before he heard them being controverted by Wentworth and his fellow petitioners. First, the savage inhabitants of any country had only a qualified dominion or a right of occupancy over land. Until they had established amongst themselves a settled form of government and subjugated the ground to their own use by cultivation, they could not grant any part of it to anyone except of their own tribe. This was so for the simple reason that they had no property in it. Second, European purchasers could not buy land because the right of purchase was held exclusively by the government and could not be enjoyed by anyone without the government's consent. Third, neither individuals nor bodies of men belonging to any nation could form colonies unless they had the consent, and were under the direction and control, of their own government. Any settlement that was formed without the consent of the British Crown could be ousted legally.[69]

Gipps proceeded to argue that the first two of his three principles were supported by the opinions of acknowledged legal authorities in the United States which, he claimed, represented English law. But he also contended that the United States Supreme Court was the court of the highest judicature in the world since it adjudicated cases between sovereign states and thus reflected the law of nations or inter-national law. Hence, Gipps quoted chapter and verse from the recent commentaries of both James Kent and Joseph Story that included passages from Marshall in *Johnson v. M'Intosh*. In regard to the principle that Europeans could not purchase land because of the Crown's right of pre-emption, Gipps especially relied on passages in those commentaries that supported the position that *discovery* gave a nation absolute and exclusive title to the soil, subject only to the native right of occupancy and the authority to extinguish that right. He went so far as to tell the Legislative Council: 'It really seems to me, gentlemen, that Lord Normanby must have had these passages under his eye when he wrote his instructions, so exactly do they tally with his Lordship's description of the qualified dominion or sovereignty enjoyed by the chiefs over the territory of New Zealand'. (In light of the opinions that Stephen, who had drafted Normanby's instructions, had recently expressed about the problem of claiming New Zealand on the basis of the doctrine of discovery and the relevance of United States law, this was clearly nonsense.) In regard to the principle that the natives had no substantive rights of property in land, Gipps used the legal opinions that

[69] Gipps' Speech, pp. 63–64.

the Port Phillip Association had commissioned, which had arrived at the same conclusion.[70]

In regard to the principle about the right to form colonies, Gipps invoked a legal opinion that had been provided to the New Zealand Company in the closing months of 1839 regarding the regulations it had made prior to it sending its ships to New Zealand, which formed the basis for it setting up the government under the nominal authority of the chiefs at Port Nicholson. This opinion declared that such an act was contrary to English law and Gipps was able to quote correspondence in which the Company had been forced by the Colonial Office to concede that this was so.[71]

At this point in his speech Gipps stated that he could rest his case but that he wanted to make some further observations. The first concerned the allegation that there was a discrepancy between the provisions of his bill and Normanby's instructions to Hobson. He acknowledged that the Colonial Office had stated in those instructions that the sovereignty and ownership of land lay with the native, but he pointed out (rightly) that it was equally true that it had qualified this claim in this passage: 'as far at least as it is possible to make that acknowledgment in favour of a people composed of numerous and petty tribes, and are incompetent to act, or even to deliberate, in concert'. Moreover, Gipps claimed that this quali-fication reduced the native right of sovereignty in the Crown's estimation to nearly the same sovereign rights of the uncivilised peoples described in the pages he had quoted from Kent and Story (which was an exaggera-tion). Gipps seemed to concede that the Colonial Office had made state-ments that could be read as acknowledging the natives as sovereign, but argued that in doing so it had gone further than the facts of the case required or even supported. He contended that the independence of New Zealand had at best only been tacitly acknowledged. He also dismissed the acts that, according to some of his opponents, had supported the notion that the natives were sovereign, especially the Declaration of Independence; he argued that New Zealand had long been included in the boundaries of New South Wales and claimed that its later omission was probably an accident; and he asserted that New Zealand had in any case remained in the position of a dependency of New South Wales.[72]

In advancing his case, Gipps asserted that the Treaty of Waitangi did not have any legal import. '[S]upposing the declaration [of indepen-dence] to have been a genuine and valid one, the only effect of it would have been to prevent Captain Hobson from taking possession of the island

[70] *Ibid.*, pp. 65–72.   [71] *Ibid.*, pp. 72–74.
[72] *Colonist*, 30 May 1840; Gipps' Speech, pp. 74–75.

in which was it made [i.e. the North Island], by virtue of the right derived from the discovery of it by Captain Cook, and to make him have recourse to negotiation with the natives', he declared. 'And as this is the very course which Captain Hobson did pursue, and as Her Majesty's sovereignty has now been acknowledged by the very chiefs who signed the declaration of independence, it follows that all things are now returned to the state in which they would have been if no declaration of independence had ever been made'.[73]

Gipps also advanced a further argument to support the position he had adopted. It was civilisation and not independence that conferred upon a people the right to dispose of land in such a way as to give grantees property in it, and the New Zealanders were mere savages rather than a civilised people. Gipps drew upon the theory of stadial history as it had been articulated by the Scottish Enlightenment philosopher William Robertson in his 1777 *History of America* to support this contention. As we have seen, there was nothing unusual in this move. Glenelg had done the same in December 1837, as did his successors in the Colonial Office. But they did so in order to mount the contrary argument, that is, that the New Zealanders were savages who exhibited a degree of civilisation and thus had some claim to be sovereign. As this reveals, the way in which Māori were represented in respect of sovereignty – and the way that intellectual and legal resources were deployed to support those representations – could vary enormously, even among British officials. It all depended on the political circumstances.[74]

The members of the Legislative Council accepted the basic thrust of the position Gipps adopted, but several of them, most importantly Chief Justice Sir James Dowling and Bishop William Broughton, adopted a contrary position on the natives' capacity to own land. Dowling challenged the relevance of Gipps' consideration of this matter by pointing out that the issue at stake was *not* whether the natives had an abstract right to alienate their lands, but whether they had a particular right to alienate lands to British subjects in derogation of the sovereign rights of the Crown. Dowling also made it clear that he believed the natives had an inherent right to the soil and went so far as to argue that the government's object in asserting the sovereignty of the Crown was to maintain that very principle and thereby protect the natives. Broughton expressed similar views and made it clear that he was unwilling to assent to the preamble in Gipps' bill. Just as importantly, he, too, pointed out that the matter at stake did not require the government to deny that the natives had rights in land. 'Why', he asked, 'should the Council embarrass itself with the

[73] *Ibid.*, p. 75. [74] *Ibid.*, p. 76.

question of what a savage can or cannot do?', that is, with the abstract question of what kinds of rights of property in land the New Zealanders had.[75]

Gipps, realising that he was assured of the Legislative Council's support for the fundamentals of his bill, promptly announced that the position he had adopted on native rights of property in land could be abandoned without affecting the rest of the measure. Indeed, he revealed that he had already asked the colony's Attorney General to draft a new preamble that cast the matter in terms of the incapacity of British subjects to secure title by virtue of buying land from the natives, rather than the inability of the natives to hold title. Furthermore, he claimed that the position he had previously adopted on this matter was 'merely declaratory', intended to make clear to British subjects that they had no right to go around the world forming settlements without the sanction of the Crown. This was surely correct. Consequently, as I have already remarked, it is a mistake to read too much into the position that Gipps had assumed on native title in this political struggle with colonial land claimants.[76]

The Legislative Council's debate was reported at length in the Sydney press. Not surprisingly, several newspapers took issue with Gipps' arguments on legal grounds. For example, the editor of the *Colonist* argued that the New Zealanders had a natural right to property in the land and that the right of discovery did not extinguish it, supporting this contention by quoting passages from Marshall's judgment in *Worcester* v. *The State of Georgia*. The *Colonist*'s editor continued to maintain that the British Crown had waived the right to sovereignty it had claimed on the basis of *discovery* and that consequently its right to overturn the titles of those who had acquired land through purchases from the natives prior to British annexation rested on shaky grounds.[77]

News of Gipps' bill soon reached New Zealand. At Port Nicholson, the owner and editor of the local organ of the New Zealand Company, the *New Zealand Gazette*, was outraged by the position that the bill had adopted in regard to native rights in land. Samuel Revans would have been aware that the Company had recently adopted much the same position as Gipps, given that it claimed that New Zealand was a British possession by virtue of Cook's discovery and that the British government had erred in treating the natives as sovereign and failing to assert the Crown's right of pre-emption. Yet he pointed out that the British

---

[75] *Sydney Herald*, 13 July 1840.   [76] Gipps' Speech, pp. 76–78.
[77] *Colonist*, 4 August 1840; *Sydney Herald*, 7 August 1840; *Colonist*, 22 August and 5 November 1840.

government had allowed that the natives were sovereign and argued that this meant that the natives had the right to sell to anyone they pleased. He also contended that Gipps had no legal or constitutional authority to deny that the natives had such a right and pointed out that in North America the right of Indians to sell land and for British subjects to purchase it from them had been uniformly recognised and that consequently much of the land the settlers held derived from native title. Yet, like the Company's directors in London, Revans found it expedient to support one of the ends contemplated by the Land Claims Bill, namely that of preventing parties being granted titles to large tracts of land on the basis of their purchases from the natives. Since this meant that the Company's claims could also be disallowed, Revans had to claim that the Company's purchases differed from those of other adventurers (which was nonsense).[78]

In the Bay of Islands, the editor of the local newspaper, the *New Zealand Advertiser and Bay of Islands Gazette*, a Congregational minister, Barzillai Quaife, sought to champion the interests of those who came to be called 'the old settlers' as well as those of recent colonists whose claims rested on the notion that the natives were sovereign and therefore had rights in land. He also expressed a fear that what he called the imperial government's principal goal in claiming sovereignty, that of protecting the natives, might be defeated by the government of New South Wales. Quaife was adamant that Gipps had departed from the principles laid down by Normanby in his instructions to Hobson. Strikingly, he took these, rather than the treaty, as his point of reference. Finally, Quaife accepted that the British Crown was under no obligation to recognise the titles of British subjects in New Zealand and had the right to investigate them, but he nevertheless contended that the government could not simply take property without gaining the consent of the owners, whether they be native or European.[79]

Britons were not the only ones in New Zealand to raise their voices against the position that Gipps had adopted in his bill. A Ngā Puhi man from Kaikohe had been in the chamber of the New South Wales Legislative Council during the debate about the bill and had given an account of it on his return home. This caused great indignation among his fellow Māori, prompting several of them to wait upon the missionary Davis to ask whether it was true that the British government intended to take possession of their lands. Davis apparently told them that he believed there was no such intention and endeavoured to assure them that their property would be protected. Several months later, George Clarke, the

---

[78] *New Zealand Gazette*, 18 July 1840.
[79] *New Zealand Advertiser and Bay of Islands Gazette*, 13 August 1840. See also 10 December 1840.

former senior Church Missionary Society missionary who had assumed the role of Protector of Aborigines for New Zealand, reported that Gipps' bill had caused enormous concern among Māori at all the places he had stopped in the Hauraki Gulf and the Waikato, not least because they knew of the fate of native people in other countries colonised by European powers, such as New South Wales. At each place, Clarke sought to reassure Māori. In doing so, he repeated what Hobson had apparently told them in speeches and circulars, but most especially he invoked the treaty of Waitangi. At one place he argued that they had 'in their hands the Magna Charta of the country, securing to them everything which would make them respected. Their land and everything they had was their own, and no one could possess themselves of an inch of it without their consent'. In making such a claim in regard to the treaty, Clarke was, as we have seen, unusual as far as British authorities were concerned. But, otherwise, he was asserting the same principle that Stephen had expressed in that minute of his discussed earlier, namely that the Crown could only acquire native lands by securing the consent of the natives.[80]

Part IV

The Colonial Office, Gipps' Land Claims Act and Hobson's Proclamations

The address Gipps gave to the New South Wales Legislative Council as well as his Land Claims Act were well received by the Colonial Office when copies of them reached London six months later. Stephen drafted a despatch in which the imperial government expressed concurrence with the opinions the Governor had articulated in his address, though in the final version of this communication Russell merely commended Gipps on the able exposition of his views.[81]

It is important for us to register this reception of Gipps' speech and to understand it. This is all the more the case because historians like Peter Adams have been struck by the fact that Gipps' stance on native title differed from what they believe to be the Colonial Office's position on this matter.[82]

---

[80] George Clarke Snr, Report, 7 March 1841, *BPP*, 1842, Paper no. 569, pp. 94–98; Busby to G. W. Hope, 17 January 1845, *BPP*, 1845, Paper no. 108, Copies of Letters from Mr Shortland and Mr Busby to Lord Stanley and Mr G. W. Hope, p. 15.

[81] Stephen to Smith, 5 and 9 January 1841, Russell, Minute, 12 January 1841, and draft of Russell to Gipps, 13 January 1841, TNA, CO 209/6; Russell to Gipps, 16 January 1841, *BPP*, 1841, Paper no. 311, pp. 78–79.

[82] Adams, *Fatal Necessity*, pp. 179–80.

In seeking to explain the Colonial Office's reception, Ned Fletcher has pointed out that several technical points need to be noted. The despatches that the Colonial Office received from Gipps only comprised the bill, the Act and his speech, rather than press reports, newspaper editorials and the other speeches; consequently, it would have had little sense of the prominence that arguments about the nature of native rights in land had had in the debate about the bill. It is probable that the Colonial Office only gave Gipps' very long speech a cursory read at this time, given there are no annotations on the copy of it in the Colonial Office's records. Finally, it was only necessary for the Colonial Office to pay attention to the Land Claims Act, whose provisions did not embody the view Gipps had taken while it was a bill, namely that the natives only had what he called a right of occupancy.[83]

Yet what is more important in explaining the Colonial Office's reception is the fact that it would have been conditioned by the task it had given Gipps, that of asserting the Crown's authority so that the government could tackle the potentially dire consequences of the huge amount of land purchasing that had taken place. The opinions Gipps had expressed about native rights to property in land had no bearing on this matter, and so the Colonial Office had no reason to pay any attention to them. Instead, its officials welcomed the fact that Gipps had been able to pass legislation that promised to place very considerable limits on the Crown's recognition of pre-1840 purchases of land.[84] Indeed, they must have been surprised as well as delighted that he had been able to do this, given that they had believed it would be politically impossible for the colonial government to invalidate all the purchases made prior to the Crown assuming sovereignty.

Just as significantly, two months earlier, in October 1840, the Colonial Office had welcomed Hobson's 21 May 1840 proclamations of British sovereignty throughout New Zealand. It immediately approved and gazetted them, thereby setting the seal on British sovereignty over New Zealand, at least in its view. Moreover, its principal officers do not appear to have been troubled by the fact that Hobson had disobeyed the imperial government's orders in proclaiming British sovereignty in the North Island prior to gaining the consent of the native chiefs throughout it and in the southern islands on the basis of the doctrine of *discovery* (though they would find it useful several months later, in a very different political context, to claim that the Crown's title to sovereignty in the colony rested

---

[83] Fletcher, 'Praiseworthy Device', pp. 924–25.

[84] The Act contained an important provision: the Commission it established to investigate claims could not recommend any grant that exceeded 2,560 acres or included land of public utility.

on an act of cession from the chiefs). But the Colonial Office's response is unsurprising, for the reasons I have already canvassed. Its leading figures had favoured the making of a treaty as the best means of acquiring sovereignty for reasons that were very principled but also highly pragmatic. They were no doubt pleased that Hobson had secured the consent of at least some of the native chiefs, but at this point what was most important in their eyes was the *fact* that British sovereignty in New Zealand was now incontrovertible.[85]

In keeping with this imperative, in 1843 the Colonial Office would severely censure the colony's Attorney General, William Swainson, for questioning whether the Crown's sovereignty was absolute in New Zealand. Swainson had twice pointed out to his superiors that some native chiefs had not signed the treaty or had not properly understood its terms and he had argued that they could not be said to have agreed to cede sovereignty to the Crown. On both occasions, Russell's successor as Colonial Secretary, Lord Stanley, sent despatches to New Zealand in response saying that the British government had to deny in the most unequivocal terms such an opinion and insisting that it was a historical fact that the Crown had asserted sovereignty over New Zealand and that consequently it was incontrovertible that all of New Zealand and all persons inhabiting its territory lay within the dominion of the Crown. In each of these instances, Stephen had written unusually forthright minutes. In the first he had complained: 'the local Attorney General wholly omits to notice that by three separate commissions under the Great Seal of the United Kingdom, and by every other formal and solemn act, the Queen has *now* publicly asserted her sovereignty over the whole of the New Zealand islands'. Significantly, he went on: 'Admit, if it must be so, that this was ill-advised, unjust, a breach of faith, and so on, yet who can gainsay the fact that such are the claims of the Queen and of the nation for whom Her Majesty acts'. Here, as in the case of New South Wales, we see the British government resting its claims to sovereignty primarily on historical grounds. The treaty did not rate a mention in the Colonial Office's discussion of the matter. Nor had the Colonial Office deemed the treaty to be pertinent to the negotiations it conducted with the New Zealand Company in the closing months of 1840.[86]

---

[85] *London Gazette*, 2 October 1840, www.thegazette.co.uk/London/issue/19900/page/217 9; Russell to Hobson, 9 December 1840, *BPP*, 1841, Paper no. 311, p. 27; Draft of Stephen to Mr Stevenson, February 1841, *HRA*, series 1, vol. 21, p. 271.

[86] William Swainson, Opinion, 27 December 1842, *BPP*, 1844, Paper no. 556, Report from the Select Committee on New Zealand, Together with Minutes of Evidence, Appendix, and Index (henceforth 1844 Select Committee Report Appendices), p. 474; Stephen to Hope, 19 May [*sic*, i.e. June] 1843, TNA, CO 209/16, his emphasis; Lord Stanley to

The Colonial Office and the Company Make a Deal

The announcement in October 1840 that the British government had assumed sovereignty in all of New Zealand forced the New Zealand Company's directors to accept that they now had no choice but to try to negotiate an agreement with the Colonial Office in order to secure land in the islands. In the closing months of 1839, the Company's principal agent in New Zealand, William Wakefield, had laid claim to some 20 million acres – which encompassed much of the northern reaches of the South Island and most of what were to become the provinces of Wellington and Taranaki in the North Island – on the basis of his transactions with native chiefs, but the Colonial Office had refused to acknowledge any of these claims. Most importantly, the Company's directors realised that the colonial government was going to institute an inquiry into the titles to land of British subjects and that this would include the Company's titles. Although they claimed they had no reason to assume that the Company's titles would be found to be flawed, they were desperate to avoid this investigation into its titles by the Land Claims Commission, which Gipps' Land Claims Act had established.[87]

Just three days after the government in London confirmed Hobson's proclamations of sovereignty, the Company formed a secret committee for the task of winning over the Colonial Office. In fact, Edward Gibbon Wakefield had already concocted a plan that the committee immediately executed. In the first instance, Charles Buller, the lawyer, journalist and politician well known for his wit and charm, contrived a casual encounter with James Stephen in a London club in the hope that he could persuade him to help. Buller jokingly accused the Colonial Office's Permanent Under-Secretary of wanting to trample opponents such as the Company and claimed that the Company now acknowledged the hopelessness of its position and accepted that it was at the Colonial Office's mercy. In the weeks that followed, Buller repeatedly went to the Colonial Office seeking Stephen's help. Patricia Burns has argued that Stephen, who was intensely

William Shortland, 21 June 1843, *BPP*, 1844, 1844 Select Committee Report Appendices, p. 475; Swainson to Shortland, 13 [*sic*] July 1843, 1844 Select Committee Report Appendices, p. 167; Stephen to Hope, 28 December 1843, TNA, CO 209/22; Stanley to Governor Robert FitzRoy, 10 February 1844, 1844 Select Committee Report Appendices, p. 173.

[87] Labouchere to Lord Petre, 19 August 1839, *BPP*, 1840, Paper no. 238, p. 46; Labouchere to Robert R. Strang, 20 August 1839, *BPP*, 1840, Paper no. 238, p. 48; Stephen to G.F. Young, 19 September 1839, *BPP*, 1840, Paper no. 238, pp. 50–51; Smith to Young, 5 and 31 October 1839, *BPP*, 1840, Paper no. 238, pp. 54–55; Smith to J. Wood Beilby, 18 January 1840, *BPP*, 1840, Paper no. 238, p. 64; NZC, New Zealand Land Order, [c. January–July 1840], 1840 Select Committee Report on New Zealand, p. 162.

shy and preferred reading and writing to any face-to-face discussion, was disarmed by Buller's appeals because the Company's publicists had launched a vicious attack on him earlier in the year, accusing him of being responsible for the Colonial Office's poor treatment of the Company. Indeed, Stephen later mused: 'For aught I know, [this] flattery . . . may not have been without its effect on me. I may have been pleased with the opportunity of showing that I was utterly indifferent to the contumely and censure of which they had made me the object'. However, Burns' contention overlooks the fact that Stephen had previously recommended that the government grant the Company's predecessor a charter and had since formed the opinion that the Colonial Office had an obligation to the Company because it had tolerated (contrary to his advice) it proceeding with its colonisation plans and so had failed to warn its prospective settlers of the risks they were taking. Burns' argument also overlooks the fact that Russell had no wish to injure the Company or its settlers but was on the contrary prepared to assist. Indeed, the Colonial Secretary had recently decided that the Company could be a useful instrument for advancing the colonisation of New Zealand.[88]

Russell's decision was to have profound repercussions, as we will see. Apart from anything else, the agreement the Colonial Office and Company soon struck not only became an enormous bone of contention between these two parties in later years. It was absolutely central to an almighty tussle in regard to the native title, which much of the remaining chapters in this book will be devoted to examining.

Under the terms of this agreement, which was drafted by Stephen and Buller, the government undertook to grant the Company title to land on the basis of the amount of monies it claimed to have expended in New Zealand, mainly though not exclusively on the purchase of land. This sum was to be determined by an accountant appointed by the Colonial Office (James Pennington). Once his work was done, the Company was to receive a grant of land from the Crown for as many acres as was equal to four times the amount of money it had been found to have spent. Lastly, the grants were to be made in the parts of New Zealand that the Company had claimed on the basis of the contracts for land that William Wakefield had allegedly struck with native chiefs.[89]

---

[88] Stephen to Smith, 4 October 1840, TNA, CO 209/8; NZC Court of Directors, Minutes of Meetings, 5 October 1840, TNA, CO 208/180; Stephen, Memorandum, 15 December 1841, TNA, CO 209/11; Patricia Burns, *Fatal Success: A History of the New Zealand Company*, Heinemann Reed, Auckland, 1989, pp. 165–66; Philip Temple, *A Sort of Conscience: The Wakefields*, Auckland University Press, Auckland, 2002, p. 284.

[89] Stephen, Draft of Agreement between the British Government and the New Zealand Company, 14 October 1840, TNA, CO 209/8; NZC Court of Directors, Minutes of

Once the agreement was drafted, Stephen urged that it be finalised as soon as possible as he believed that nothing could be done towards the colonisation of New Zealand until this occurred. Russell seems to have agreed but directed that the draft agreement be examined by the government's legal advisers, albeit because he believed the Colonial Office had to be careful as he thought it was really dealing with Edward Gibbon Wakefield, whom he distrusted profoundly. (Indeed, like Stephen, Russell abhorred Wakefield.) As it turned out, the Attorney General did see a problem with what was being proposed, remarking that Gipps' Land Claims bill would annul the title of the Company to the lands that it had already purchased from the natives. This objection puzzled Stephen since in his opinion both the proposed agreement with the Company and Gipps' bill rested on the recognition of this fact, which he characterised as the invalidity of all claimants' existing title on the one hand and the need for a Crown grant to impart validity to titles on the other. Stephen therefore recommended that the Attorney General be asked to explain why he thought Gipps' bill would obstruct the agreement with the Company. However, Stephen's superiors assumed that the Attorney General was merely pointing out that a problem could arise if the home government was to guarantee a grant of land to the Company that the colonial government had already granted to an earlier purchaser. Yet it is possible that the Attorney General was troubled because whereas the terms of Gipps' bill required all land claimants to submit their claims to title to a commission that would investigate whether their purchases were bona fide, the terms of the proposed agreement with the Company implied that the government was giving the Company an undertaking to grant it titles to land without any such inquiry. Several historians, including Alan Ward, have argued that in making the agreement the Colonial Office's principal figures assumed that the Company *would* have to satisfy the Land Claims Commission that its purchases of land from the natives were bona fide. But there is no unequivocal evidence that this was so. Just as striking, though this is unremarkable in my opinion given what I have demonstrated in this chapter, the Colonial Office made no reference whatsoever to the treaty in its discussions with the Company about the agreement.[90]

Meetings, 27 October 1840, TNA, CO 208/180; Stephen, Memorandum, 15 December 1841.

[90] Stephen to Smith, 14 October 1840; Stephen, Minute, 23 October 1840, Smith, Draft of letter to Somes, 23 October 1840, Russell, Minute, 24 October 1840, Stephen to Smith, 3 November 1840, and undated Smith and Russell minutes on this, TNA, CO 209/8; Agreement between the British Government and the New Zealand Company, 18 November 1840, BPP, 1841, Paper no. 311, pp. 85–87; Adams, *Fatal Necessity*, p. 257; Michael Belgrave, 'Pre-emption, the Treaty of Waitangi and the Politics of

Not surprisingly, the Company was elated to have won this agreement, especially as it involved an extraordinary turnaround in the position the Colonial Office had been taking towards its claims, at least publicly. Wakefield excitedly told one of his disciples, William Molesworth: '[The Colonial Office has] not merely conceded what we might have gained by continuing the war, but have offered us all that we could desire'. Indeed, he went on to say: 'The satisfaction of the triumph is almost intolerable'. Wakefield's exhilaration is hardly surprising. The Company's land-grabbing gamble in New Zealand had paid off in the very way he had predicted, or so it seemed. To be more precise, the Company's directors were delighted because they had persuaded themselves that this agreement *did* exempt the Company's titles from an investigation by the Land Claims Commission. In fact, the Company's directors could hardly believe their luck.[91]

Consequently, Somes, as the Company's governor, tried to verify the nature of what its directors hoped they had secured. Necessarily, he did this in a roundabout manner, telling Russell that the Company wanted to know how the government intended to treat the titles of those like the Company that had claimed title on the basis of their land purchasing. But parliamentary Under-Secretary Smith's reply shed no light on the question that Somes was really asking, and so a month later Somes tried again, this time asking Russell for information about the general principles by which the Colonial Office proposed to be guided in its measures for the government and colonisation of New Zealand. The Colonial Office also took this inquiry at face value and responded accordingly. In doing so, Smith told Somes that all lands which had been acquired under any title other than grants made by the Crown would be subjected to an investigation by the Land Claims Commission, remarked that the basis of this inquiry would be an assertion on behalf of the Crown of a title to all lands in New Zealand that had hitherto been granted by the chiefs to British subjects and noted that Russell was unaware that any exception could arise to this principle but that if there was it would be considered on its own merits and dealt with accordingly. This failed to answer the Company's question. But its directors were keen to assume that the general principles Smith had articulated did not apply to the Company or that its claims had already been treated as one of the exceptions that he

Crown Purchase', *New Zealand Journal of History*, vol. 31, no. 1, 1997, p. 29; Alan Ward, *An Unsettled History: Treaty Claims in New Zealand Today*, Bridget Williams Books, Wellington, 1999, p. 87.
[91] Wakefield to William Molesworth, 26 October 1840, William Molesworth Correspondence with Edward Gibbon Wakefield, ATL, MSY-608; *Morning Chronicle*, 3 November 1840.

had mentioned. Consequently, they did not press the matter any further for fear this would only stir up a hornet's nest.[92]

Just a few days later, the Company's secretary, John Ward, privately informed William Wakefield: 'the arrangement with the Company is *of course* a stop to the proceedings of the Commission under the New South Wales Bill so far as regards the Company's rights'. This was wishful thinking. Yet, not surprisingly, Ward urged Wakefield to make sure he relayed this news to Hobson as soon as possible, while Somes decided to hire a fast-sailing schooner to carry a copy of the agreement to Hobson as quickly as possible.[93]

The London press was astounded that the Colonial Office had suddenly made an agreement with the Company that legalised its lawless act of colonisation. In the view of *The Times*, the Company had 'dunned the Whigs for a formal recognition of their purchases'. It attributed the agreement to what it called 'some unaccountable influence', remarking that it could not conceive what change of circumstances had occurred to induce the Colonial Office to accept the claims of a company it had previously denied, especially given that there were plenty of other parties who possessed titles in New Zealand at least as valid as the Company's. *The Times* seemed to suggest that the answer lay in the fact that the government's policy was 'fickle and indeterminate' and that those other parties were 'less able [than the Company] to propitiate the favour of the government'. A couple of months later, *The Times* returned to this matter, attacking the government for ratifying the Company's 'foul ... fortune-hunting' and expressing its amazement that any minister of the Crown could have read the evidence of the New Zealand select committee of the previous year about the Company's fraudulent bargains for lands and yet still be prepared to sanction them.[94]

Like *The Times*, we must ask why the Colonial Office was prepared to make this agreement with the Company. In all likelihood it had done so

---

[92] Somes to Russell, 22 October 1840, *BPP*, 1841, Paper no. 311, p. 21; NZC Court of Directors, Minutes of Meetings, 27 October 1840, CO 208/180; Smith to Somes, 29 October 1840, *BPP*, 1841, Paper no. 311, pp. 21–22; Somes to Russell, 19 November 1840, *BPP*, 1841, Paper no. 311, pp. 87–88; Smith to Somes, 2 December 1840, *BPP*, 1841, Paper no. 311, p. 88; NZC Court of Directors, Minutes of Meetings, 3 December 1840, CO 208/180; Somes to Russell, 4 December 1840, *BPP*, 1841, Paper no. 311, p. 89.

[93] John Ward to William Wakefield, 8 December 1840 (two letters), his emphasis, New Zealand Company, *The Twelfth Report of the Directors of the New Zealand Company*, Palmer and Clayton, London, 1844, pp. 220D–21D; Ward to Hobson, 17 December 1840, New Zealand Company, *Twelfth Report of the New Zealand Company*, p. 223D; Burns, *Fatal Success*, p. 168.

[94] *The Times*, 1 December 1840 and 18 February 1841.

for three reasons. It wished to avoid the expenditure of precious government revenue on the colonisation of these remote islands and so favoured a private company carrying out many of the tasks involved. Its principal figures believed that they had forced the Company to acknowledge the Crown's authority in regard to the matter of sovereignty and the way in which claims to land would be treated in the colony, and so they felt they could now make some concessions to it. Most importantly perhaps, its minister, Russell, was vulnerable to pressure by a company that had powerful allies in the parliament and the press. Thus, we can see just how quickly the government's handling of a critical aspect of colonisation – the granting of land – could change because of political pressure.

Conclusion

In this chapter I have argued that the significance that the Treaty of Waitangi had at the time it was signed in 1840 has consistently been misunderstood and exaggerated by historians. Nearly all the British players involved in making the treaty were preoccupied with the momentary task of persuading the chiefs to cede sovereignty to the British Crown so that the government could acquire the authority it required to impose a degree of order on this frontier, especially in regard to land, and thereby protect the natives. The inclusion in the agreement of a clause confirming the natives in the possession of their lands, which has come to be regarded by many historians as one of its most important aspects, did not spring from the instructions the British government had given Hobson, however consistent it might seem to be with those instructions. Instead, it must be attributed to the influence of local rather than metropolitan actors and forces. Without this, the treaty would never have included such a clause.

At the same time, with the exception of Busby, there is no contemporary evidence to suggest that any of the parties involved in drafting the treaty attached the significance to the first clause of its second article that they attributed to it later. The missionaries, who embraced the agreement and played a crucial role in helping to persuade Māori to sign it, welcomed that article's second clause, by which the chiefs yielded to the Crown the right of pre-emption. Nor is there any evidence that the Māori chiefs attached enormous significance to the first clause of the treaty's second article. The concerns they had about land were not so much prompted by the loss of it as territory but by the diminution of power and status this symbolised. As we will see, the significance attributed to this clause in New Zealand at the time of the treaty-making differed markedly from the meaning and importance it later came to have. This is a point historians have generally failed to grasp as they have projected back onto 1840 later understandings of the Treaty. Finally, it is clear that the inclusion of this clause in the treaty did not strike officials in London and Sydney as important.

The overriding significance that the government attached to a treaty as a diplomatic instrument to persuade the chiefs to agree to or acknowledge the British Crown's assumption of sovereignty was evident in the plans that Hobson put in place to secure this goal throughout the country. By the same token, the abrupt change in his approach to acquiring sovereignty, which was prompted by what he saw as a challenge by the New Zealand Company's settlers to the authority of the British Crown as well as his own, reveals that the way the British government and its agents treated the acquisition of sovereignty tended to be the product of pragmatic decisions that were made in particular circumstances, rather than simply the application of normative moral or legal principles. As we have noted, Hobson found it useful to change tack and claim possession of a good part, indeed the larger part of New Zealand, on the very same basis as the British government assumed possession of New South Wales in 1788, that is, the doctrine of *discovery*.

We have seen that in the period after the British government decided to intervene in the affairs of New Zealand an intense political struggle took place over the matter of sovereignty rather than native title in land per se. Adventurers such as the New Zealand Company in London challenged the very terms upon which the Colonial Office had decided to acquire sovereignty while the likes of Wentworth in Sydney raised difficult questions about the manner in which a colonial governor had decided to treat the titles that were being claimed by private British parties on the basis of purchases they had made with Māori prior to the Crown assuming sovereignty. All those players deployed legal resources like the rulings of the Marshall United States Supreme Court to support the positions they chose to adopt at any particular moment on the matter of sovereignty, upon which hung their claims to title in land. The Colonial Office and the Governor of New South Wales in turn found it necessary to employ many of the same resources in order to uphold the authority of the British Crown. In this matter, as in the making of the treaty, there were important differences of opinion between British officials in Sydney and the Bay of Islands and those in London, though for the most part neither regarded the treaty of Waitangi, least of all the first clause of its second article, as having the kind of significance it would later come to have.

Most importantly, we have seen that the way in which critical issues relating to land title were treated at the imperial centre was fundamentally a function of political power and so the way this was handled could readily change or flip according to circumstances. The Whig government, after claiming that it had to treat the claims of various parties in accordance with particular moral or legal principles, bowed to the pressure that the New Zealand Company was able to exert in parliament and the press.

None of the British parties involved in the political struggles in 1839–40 found much need to define the nature of native rights of property in land. Inasmuch as questions about native title were considered, this occurred in highly particular contexts as the result of contestation over sovereignty. By contrast, we have seen that Stephen asserted what the Colonial Office clearly saw as an important pragmatic principle regarding native title, which was a function of the equally practical principle it adopted in respect of sovereignty, namely that native rights in land should be acknowledged – and then extinguished – with their consent.

6 The Land Claims Commission and the Return of the Treaty, 1840–1843

In 1842 and 1843 native title to land became a significant matter in its own right for the first time in New Zealand, and the treaty of Waitangi returned to prominence. Neither of these events could have been predicted. In 1839–40 the precise nature of the New Zealanders' title to land had seldom been considered except as part and parcel of an intra-British struggle over sovereignty, most of the players involved in making the treaty did not regard it as being of any great lasting significance and it barely figured in any public discourse in Britain or New Zealand. Moreover, no one could have anticipated that native rights in land would rise – and the treaty of Waitangi would return – to significance *together*. The connection that was forged between them was the result of a haphazard chain of events rather than a matter of design.

Questions about the nature of the natives' rights of property in land arose largely because of an enormous fight between the New Zealand Company on the one hand and the imperial and colonial governments on the other. This tussle originated in a dispute over the November 1840 agreement between the Company and the Colonial Office, and the investigation into the Company's titles by the Land Claims Commission. Historians have previously discussed both the Commission's work and the conflict between the Company and the Colonial Office,[1] but they have failed to recognise the crucial role that their conjunction played in the treatment of native title in New Zealand. By the same token, historians have overlooked the fact that the tussle over the Commission's investigation into the Company's claims and the November 1840 agreement played a fundamental role in the chain of events that saw the treaty assume new significance, in the sense of both meaning and consequence.

---

[1] See, for example, Rosemarie V. Tonk, 'The First New Zealand Land Commissions, 1840–1845', MA thesis, University of Canterbury, 1986, in the case of the former, and J. S. Marais, *The Colonization of New Zealand* (1927), Dawsons, London, 1968, and W. P. Morrell, *British Colonial Policy in the Age of Peel and Russell*, Clarendon Press, Oxford, 1930, for the latter.

The importance that was increasingly attached to the Treaty was largely the result of a range of British players telling stories in which they put forward a novel interpretation of it. Many of these narratives flew in the face of historical fact. Nevertheless, they bestowed on the treaty a significance it did not have at the time it was made. In particular, the Company and in turn the Colonial Office came to focus on the first clause of the treaty's second article, which had confirmed the natives in any possession of land they might have, even though the presence of this clause in the treaty had previously gone unremarked in London. The Colonial Office, moreover, harnessed the treaty to a language of rights that had been absent in the discussions that took place before and during the making of the treaty in 1840.

In this chapter my account of the treaty departs from all previous historical accounts of it. Until now, no historian to my knowledge has remarked upon the fact that there was hardly any discussion about the treaty among government authorities in the two or so years after it was signed,[2] or the fact that the treaty declined in significance in 1840–41 only to return to prominence later.[3] Furthermore, whereas historians such as Peter Adams have suggested that there was a proper or correct interpretation of the treaty, I emphasise the enormous contestation that occurred over its meaning. I also reveal that interpretations shifted as the principal British parties adopted particular stances, largely as a consequence of political battles that primarily concerned matters other than native title.[4]

As in the period discussed in the previous chapter, particular players were crucial to what happened. In most of what follows, the principal players were Stephen at the Colonial Office, the Company's directors and Hobson – with whom readers are already familiar – but also the Colonial Secretary, Lord John Russell, and his successor, Lord Edward Stanley; one of the Land Claims Commissioners, William Spain; the Company's principal agent in the colony, William Wakefield; and, to a lesser degree, Willoughby Shortland, the Acting Governor of the colony after Hobson's death, William Swainson, the Attorney General, and Te Rauparaha, the Ngāti Toa rangatira. In the circumstances discussed in the closing pages

---

[2] This said, in 1999 Mark Hickford concluded that it was possible to produce 'a history concerning aboriginal title within New Zealand that is not exclusively preoccupied with a treaty initially marked at Waitangi' ('Making "Territorial Rights of the Natives": Britain and New Zealand, 1830–1847', DPhil thesis, University of Oxford, 1999, p. 308).

[3] Claudia Orange's classic study of the Treaty is a notable example in this regard.

[4] Peter Adams, *Fatal Necessity: British Intervention in New Zealand, 1830–1847*, Auckland University Press/Oxford University Press, Auckland, 1977, pp. 11, 13–15, 176, 178, 182–84, 186, 189, 208, 240; Claudia Orange, *The Treaty of Waitangi*, Allen & Unwin/Port Nicholson Press, Wellington, 1987, pp. 1, 97–99.

of this chapter, the important figures were Hobson and a group of self-styled Radicals, especially Samuel MacDonald Martin.

Part I

As we have noted, the Colonial Office's principal goal in intervening in New Zealand's affairs was to assume sovereignty and assert the authority of the British Crown, in the belief that this would enable the government to gain control over the purchasing of land and thereby ensure both imperial order and peaceful colonisation. However, the Colonial Office had made a political calculation that the Crown's authority could not be upheld at the colonial peripheries unless the British government accepted the fact that a great many transactions in land had occurred in New Zealand before the Crown assumed sovereignty and that some of the parties to those transactions had considerable power. Consequently, it had concluded that it would be unwise, if not impossible, to repudiate all the titles that British subjects claimed on the basis of their purchases from the natives prior to the Crown assuming sovereignty. Accordingly, it had instructed Gipps to establish a Land Claims Commission to investigate those claims in order to determine which ones were valid and thus the basis for a Crown land grant. In the wake of these developments, the New Zealand Company negotiated an agreement with the Colonial Office in November 1840 that the Company hoped would exempt its titles from the proposed investigation.

However, as we are about to see, the Company's expectations were dashed as a result of several interdependent factors: the flawed nature of the Company's original purchases of land from Māori chiefs and their resistance to the Company's settlers claiming possession of the land in question; a bitter disagreement between the Company and the Colonial Office about the terms of the November 1840 agreement; the procedures that the Land Claims Commission adopted; and the way in which the Commission's jurisdiction in respect of the Company's land claims was interpreted in the colony.

Flaws in the Company's Claims

In March 1839 Edward Gibbon Wakefield had urged the members of the nascent New Zealand Company to send an expedition to New Zealand to lay claim to huge amounts of land before anyone else could beat the Company to it. As a result, the Company's directors immediately adopted a plan to establish a settlement, or what amounted to a colony, in the islands, despite the fact they had no authority to do so. Like most of

Wakefield's plans, this one was truly phantastic, not least because it had to be executed at breakneck speed. In instructions he hurriedly drew up in London for his thirty-eight-year-old brother, William, who was to be the Company's principal agent and lead the expedition to New Zealand, Wakefield called for considerable diligence to be exercised in purchasing land from the natives. William was required to be especially careful that all the owners of a tract of land approved the sale of it and received a share of the purchase money; he had to ensure that the proprietors thoroughly understood the nature of these transactions; and he had to set out the boundaries of the land for any purchase not merely in words but on a map. In order for these instructions to be implemented properly, a considerable amount of time was needed, but this was something the Company did not feel it had. In fact, William Wakefield realised from the outset that it would be too difficult to carry out the Company's instructions. Indeed, he decided very early in the piece that he would not even try to do so. But this was to have far-reaching consequences.[5]

On arriving in New Zealand's waters in August 1839, William Wakefield began making deals with Māori chiefs by which he claimed millions of acres of land for the Company on both sides of Cook Strait, which was to become part of the southern district of the colony of New Zealand. On 27 September he persuaded some Te Āti Awa and other rangatira to sign a deed for Port Nicholson (or Wellington as it became) and the Heretaunga (or what the Company called the Hutt) Valley; at Kapiti on 25 October he obtained the signatures of Ngāti Toa chiefs, who included the leading rangatira Te Rauparaha, for land lying between the Mokau River on the North Taranaki Bight to 43 degrees latitude in the South Island; two weeks later, he obtained the signatures of various Te Āti Awa chiefs on a deed at Queen Charlotte Sound in regard to their interests in the land entailed in the Kapiti deed; and on 16 November he persuaded three Ngāti Hau chiefs to sign a deed for land lying between Manawatū and Pātea.[6]

The hurried way in which Wakefield conducted most of these negotiations meant they were badly flawed. What is more, he knew this at the time, because he was warned by Māori and Europeans alike. Just two weeks after he had arrived in the country, Wakefield remarked that the

---

[5] Instructions of the NZC to William Wakefield, [May 1839], *BPP*, 1840, Paper no. 238, Correspondence with the Secretary of State Relative to New Zealand, pp. 22–25; Patricia Burns, *Fatal Success: A History of the New Zealand Company*, Heinemann Reed, Auckland, 1989, pp. 89–90, 102, 105.

[6] Deeds of Purchase [1839], *BPP*, 1844, Paper no. 556, Report from the Select Committee on New Zealand, Together with Minutes of Evidence, Appendix, and Index (henceforth 1844 Select Committee Report Appendices), pp. 555–57.

laws of property among the natives in Cook Strait were very poorly defined and observed that chiefs did not necessarily have the power of absolute disposal over any land. In early October he was told by a European whaler and several Māori that the purchase deed he had negotiated in Port Nicholson was worthless unless it was ratified by Te Rauparaha. Later that month, after the signing of a deed that covered a massive amount of land lying between two degrees of latitude, Wakefield observed that some of the natives were scathing about the purchase. Finally, in November, after he had sought to make good the problems with the Port Nicholson deed by negotiating with Te Rauparaha, the Ngāti Toa chief bluntly told him that he did not intend to grant the Company millions of acres and that he had only sold him two comparatively small sections of land at the top of the South Island. Yet Wakefield brushed all these problems aside in his rush to claim land for the Company.[7]

The flaws in Wakefield's purchasing would prove especially problematic in the Company's first settlement. There were often disputes among Māori themselves regarding their respective rights to particular lands. The harbour of Port Nicholson, or what the natives called Te Whanganui-a-Tara, was no exception. In fact, it was especially complicated. In the two preceding decades, the area had been invaded several times and had changed hands twice. By 1839 Te Āti Awa, Taranaki, Ngāti Ruanui, Ngāti Tama and Ngāti Toa were regarded as the groups who held customary rights to land, but matters of ownership were still in a state of flux. Wakefield principally made his transaction at Port Nicholson with just two Te Āti Awa rangatira, Te Puni and Te Wharepouri. Several important rangatira from landowning groups in pa (villages) at Te Aro, Pipitea and Kumutoto took little if any part in these negotiations, and Te Rauparaha's kin claimed that Te Āti Awa had no right to take all the payment for it. It also seems that Te Puni and Te Wharepouri had little comprehension of the consequences of their signing Wakefield's deed.[8]

[7] William Wakefield, Journal 1839–42, entries 29 August 1839, and 5, 24 and 25 October 1839, TNA, CO 208/307; Edward Jerningham Wakefield, *Adventure in New Zealand, from 1839 to 1844, with Some Account of the Beginning of the British Colonisation of the Islands*, vol. 1, John Murray, London, 1845, p. 143; George Clarke Jnr to George Clarke Snr, 11 February 1843, Correspondence between George Clarke Snr and George Clarke Jnr, vol. 3 (1840–71), HL, MS-0062.

[8] Wakefield, *Adventure*, p. 202; Angela Ballara, 'Te Whanganui-a-Tara: Phases of Maori Occupation of Wellington Harbour c. 1800–1840', in David Hamer and Roberta Nicholls (eds.), *The Making of Wellington 1800–1914*, Victoria University Press, Wellington, 1990, pp. 9, 11, 20, 30–31, 33; Rosemarie Tonk, '"A Difficult and Complicated Question": The New Zealand Company's Wellington, Port Nicholson Claim', in Hamer and Nicholls (eds.), *Making of Wellington*, pp. 40–42, 44–45; Treaty

To make matters worse, the Company's directors had sold much of the land in question in London before Wakefield had even purchased it, and the Company's surveyors only reached Port Nicholson a few days before the first of several shiploads of settlers arrived expecting to be able to take possession of it. On the back of Wakefield's rash purchasing, early in 1840 surveyors began to survey the land as though it was in vacant possession while settlers tried to occupy lands owned by Māori who had not been involved in the negotiations with Wakefield, trampling over their homes, gardens and cemeteries in the process. Before long, Māori at Te Aro, Pipitea, Kumutoto and Tiakiwai pa asserted that they had neither sold the land in question nor received any payment for it, and retaliated against the settlers by pulling up the surveyors' pegs and obliterating their markings.[9]

Yet it took two years before the consequences of Wakefield's flawed purchases began to play themselves out politically. The reasons for this time-lag tell us a good deal about the positions that a colonial governor, Sir George Gipps, and a Colonial Secretary, Lord John Russell, could adopt on land titles in a settler colony, especially when a politically power-ful colonisation company, namely the New Zealand Company, was involved. Gipps, despite or probably because of the uncompromising position he had previously taken on the matter of titles claimed by adventurers (as discussed in Chapter 5), was prepared to compromise in order to settle the claims of the Company's settlers and thus relieve them of the problems they were encountering in trying to gain possession of land at Port Nicholson. Having been given authority by Russell to override any Colonial Office instructions he thought were impracticable or inexpedient to execute, Gipps proposed in October 1840 that the imperial government confirm the Company's settlers in the possession of some 110,000 acres of the land, subject to an inquiry by the Land Claims Commission. As we will see, measures of this kind would be improvised at several points in the coming years by both the Colonial Office and the colonial administration in New Zealand in order to put the Company's settlers into possession of lands that Wakefield had claimed to have purchased. In this instance, Russell approved Gipps' measure (in April 1841), having previously declared that the claims of settlers to title on the basis of their purchases from the natives would be disallowed.[10]

---

of Waitangi Tribunal, Te Whanganui a Tara Me Ona Takiwa: Report on the Wellington District, Wai 145, 2003, pp. xvii–viii, 56, 65, 84.

[9] Burns, *Fatal Success*, pp. 102, 131, 151–52; Tonk, 'Difficult and Complicated Question', pp. 45–46.

[10] Lord John Russell to Sir George Gipps, 4 December 1839, *BPP*, 1840, Paper no. 238, p. 49; Gipps to the Delegation, 2 October 1840, *BPP*, 1841, Paper no. 311, Copies or Extracts of Correspondence Relative to New Zealand, p. 124; Gipps to Russell, 6 October 1840, *BPP*, 1841, Paper no. 311, p. 122; Edward Deas Thomson to

At much the same time, Russell brushed aside reports from New Zealand that suggested there were considerable weaknesses in the Company's titles because they were fraudulent in one way or another. In alerting Russell to this problem on two occasions, Governor Hobson observed that the matter of the Company's titles would naturally be decided by the Land Claims Commission. But on each occasion Russell merely forwarded Hobson's reports to the Company's chairman in London, Lord Joseph Somes, for comment. On the first occasion, Somes batted the allegations away, telling Russell that the matters they raised were irrelevant in the light of the November 1840 agreement between the Colonial Office and the Company. It seems unlikely that Russell could have mistaken Somes' meaning. Somes was implying that the Company had been granted the lands in question as a result of that agreement, and consequently its titles were exempt from the investigations of the Land Claims Commission. Perhaps Russell believed that the Company's interpretation was correct. Either way, he directed Hobson to avoid becoming partisan in the matter and told Somes that he trusted that the Company would support Hobson in his endeavours to establish peaceful relations between the natives and the settlers. On the second occasion, Somes again dismissed all of the problems that Hobson had raised about the Company's purchases, but now he insisted that the Company's title to the land at Port Nicholson rested on the fact that the imperial government had delegated the authority to determine such questions about title to Gipps and that Gipps had granted the Company's settlers the land in question (as noted earlier). Russell did not demur. On the contrary, his offsider, the parliamentary Under-Secretary for the Colonies, Vernon Smith, told Hobson that the imperial government had decided to acknowledge the claims to title of any company but to refuse those of individual settlers and that this decision was irrevocable. Shortly afterwards, in the light of the Colonial Office receiving the report of the accountant, Pennington (who had been tasked to assess the amount of the Company's expenditure in order to arrive at a figure for the amount of land it would be granted under the terms of the November 1840 agreement), the Colonial Office instructed Hobson to make the necessary assignments of land.[11]

Dr G. S. Evans et al., 20 and 28 October 1840, *BPP*, 1842, Paper no. 569, Copies of Papers and Despatches Relative to New Zealand, pp. 77, 79; Russell to Gipps, 14 April 1841, *BPP*, 1841, Paper no. 311, p. 126.

[11] Dandeson Coates to Russell, 9 March 1841, *BPP*, 1841, Paper no. 311, p. 139; William Williams, Petition to the Queen, 1 February 1840, *BPP*, 1841, Paper no. 311, pp. 139–40; William Hobson to Russell, 15 October 1840, *BPP*, 1841, Paper no. 311, p. 114; Extract of Hobson to Russell, 10 November 1840, *BPP*, 1841, Paper no. 311, p. 127; Vernon Smith to Lord Joseph Somes, 19 March 1841, *BPP*, 1841, Paper

As a result, the Company's directors seem to have concluded that its titles were secure. Certainly, the Company's organ in London, the *New Zealand Journal*, claimed that no further questions about them could arise. The Company's gamble in sending William Wakefield off to New Zealand to purchase land in defiance of the imperial government seemed to have paid off handsomely. Just as Edward Gibbon Wakefield had predicted, the government had been forced to deal with the Company.[12]

Tussles in Cook Strait

In the meantime, though, Hobson's administration in New Zealand was taking a rather different view of the Company's claims. This, as we have seen, was not the first time British agents on the colonial periphery had adopted a different position from their superiors in London in regard to matters of land. Nor would it be the last. Moreover, as we will see repeatedly, the fact that communications between the colonial government and the Colonial Office in the age of sail took several months each way to reach their destination tended to diminish the force of the Colonial Office's directives to the colonial government.

Hobson proceeded along different lines to his political masters in London for several reasons. As readers will recall, the Company's settlers at Port Nicholson had mounted a fundamental challenge to his authority right from the beginning. They were by far the most important group of settlers in New Zealand in terms of their numbers, rank, wealth and the land they claimed (about a third of the country) and they continued to throw their weight around, mainly by seeking to consolidate their position territorially. Gipps had granted them promissory occupation of 110,000 acres of land around Port Nicholson on the condition that they confine themselves to this area, but they had spread themselves over lands in Whanganui, far to the north. Hobson regarded this conduct as totally subversive of his authority. Moreover, he resented what he called the Company's 'tone of dictation and authority'. This is hardly surprising. In February 1841 the editor of the Company's newspaper in Port Nicholson, Samuel Revans, threatened in its pages: 'Have we no influence at home? Our friends, rallied from all political parties, defeated

---

no. 311, p. 141; Somes to Smith, 29 March 1841, *BPP*, 1841, Paper no. 311, p. 141; Russell to Hobson, 13 April 1841, *BPP*, 1841, Paper no. 311, p. 146; Russell to Hobson, 14 April 1841, *BPP*, 1841, Paper no. 311, p. 126; Smith to Somes, 16 April 1841, *BPP*, 1841, Paper no. 311, p. 127; Smith to Russell, 23 April 1841, *BPP*, 1841, Paper no. 311, p. 146; Somes to Russell, 19 April 1841, *BPP*, 1841, Paper no. 311, pp. 128–29; Smith to Somes, 28 May 1841, *BPP*, 1842, Paper no. 569, p. 4.

[12] *New Zealand Journal*, 17 July 1841.

ministers in the House of Commons. Remember that, Captain Hobson. You have the power of annoying us for a time, but it will not be difficult to crush you'. At a public meeting the same month the Company's settlers adopted a petition to Queen Victoria demanding that Hobson be recalled.[13]

Hobson was anxious to uphold the Crown's authority. In part this was because he was apprehensive that armed conflict could break out between natives and settlers: many Māori in the neighbourhood of the Company's settlements in Port Nicholson had expressed considerable anger over the settlers' occupation of their lands, called on him to remove the intruders and threatened to evict them if he did not provide them with any redress. But there was also a personal dimension to Hobson's desire to uphold the Crown's authority. He and the Company's principal figure, William Wakefield, were very different men. Hobson was very correct, upright and cautious, while Wakefield, like his older brother, was unprincipled and given to intrigue, cunning and deceit in most of his dealings.[14]

Hobson, as we have noted, took the view that the Company's claims to title had to be subjected to the investigations of the Land Claims Commission. Wakefield probably knew that he would have to comply, but he was nonetheless unhappy about the prospect. Consequently, in August 1841, he presented a formal proposal to Hobson that was designed to circumvent the problems that an investigation of the Company's titles would cause it: the Crown would grant the Company the right to acquire a large block of land in Port Nicholson and the surrounding area and blocks of land in each of Whanganui and New Plymouth on the basis that the Company would make further payments to the native owners, while the Company agreed that it had to prove to the Commission that it had originally purchased the land in question and had thereby extinguished the natives' title to it. In other words, Wakefield's proposal rested on a premise regarding the source of the Company's title that was contrary to the one held by the Company's directors: whereas they were claiming that the Company's titles rested on the November 1840 agreement alone and so would not be subjected to the investigations of the Commission, he assumed that the validity of the Company's titles *would* be determined by the Commission.[15]

[13] Gipps to Hobson, 12 January 1841, SARNSW, 4/1651; *New Zealand Gazette*, 6, 20 and 27 February 1841; Hobson to Russell, 26 May 1841, *BPP*, 1842, Paper no. 569, pp. 112–13.

[14] *Ibid.*, p. 112; Philip Temple, *A Sort of Conscience: The Wakefields*, Auckland University Press, Auckland, 2002, pp. 275, 310, 366–67, 398.

[15] Wakefield to Ward, 27 June 1841, TNA, CO 208/99; Wakefield to Hobson, 24 August 1841, 1844 Select Committee Report Appendices, p. 544.

Hobson reluctantly accepted Wakefield's proposal after receiving advice from the colony's Attorney General, William Swainson, and its Chief Justice, William Martin, who had actually helped Wakefield to cobble the proposal together. It seems that after paying a visit to Port Nicholson, Hobson had come away more convinced than ever that the Company's lack of certainty about titles in land was retarding colonisation, causing the Company's settlers considerable hardship and endangering peaceful relations between native and settler. Moreover, the Chief Protector, George Clarke, had told him that the Māori chiefs had declared that they had never sold the land where they dwelt and that they would never sell it unless they were compelled to do so. This would not be the last time that a protector of Aborigines played a crucial role in presenting or representing native claims to a governor of the colony.[16]

It also seems likely that Hobson reconciled himself to Wakefield's proposal because it did not break the Colonial Office's cardinal principle that lands in the possession of natives could only be acquired by means of purchase, a principle that he had undoubtedly been following. He told Wakefield privately that he would sanction any fair arrangement the Company's principal agent might make with the natives, so long as Wakefield did not use any compulsion or force in trying to remove the natives from their lands. Hobson must have also known that the arrangement he had agreed to make was the same as the one adopted earlier by Gipps in respect of Port Nicholson. Nevertheless, he also realised that it amounted to a major departure from his original instructions which set down that titles claimed on the basis of purchases from the natives were to be treated by the government as null and void in instances where they were found to be faulty.[17]

As a consequence, perhaps, Hobson, given his propensity to follow instructions to the letter, did not intend this arrangement with Wakefield to have any wider application than Port Nicholson. He soon reminded him that this grant was conditional upon the findings of the Land Claims Commission. Moreover, he refused to accede to a further request from Wakefield that he grant the Company more land for a settlement in Otago (telling him that some of those lands had already been claimed by settlers who asserted that they had purchased it from the Nanto-Bordelaise

---

[16] Hobson, Intended Proclamation, 3 September 1841, 1844 Select Committee Report Appendices, p. 545; Hobson to Wakefield, 5 September 1841, *BPP*, 1842, Paper no. 569, p. 174; Wakefield to Ward, 11 September 1841, 1844 Select Committee Report Appendices, p. 543; Hobson to Russell, 20 October 1841, *BPP*, 1842, Paper no. 569, p. 162.

[17] Hobson to John Hobbs, 22 February 1841, NANZ, G36/1; Hobson to Wakefield, 5 September 1841, *BPP*, 1842, Paper no. 569, p. 175; Wakefield to Ward, 11 September 1841, 1844 Select Committee Report Appendices, p. 543.

Company and that Ngāi Tahu chiefs claimed that they had not alienated the remainder). Indeed, Hobson insisted that the Crown could not grant the Company land over which it had no rights, thereby leaving Wakefield in no doubt that he would act in accordance with his original instructions to purchase land from the natives and only make grants of land so long as they did not affect the rights of the natives to the occupation and enjoyment of their lands. Finally, Hobson explicitly told the Colonial Office that no decision on the Company's titles could or should be made until the Company's claims were considered by a Land Claims Commissioner.[18]

In April 1842, thirty-nine-year-old William Spain arrived in Port Nicholson to begin his work as a Land Claims Commissioner. Hobson immediately referred more than a hundred claims to him, the most important of which concerned the Company's titles. The manner in which Spain undertook his investigations was in keeping with instructions Gipps had issued to the Land Claims Commissioners in 1840. These created a complex process of investigation. Land claimants were required to make an application to have each of their claims heard by the Commission, appear before it, and present evidence and witnesses for each purchase. The Commissioners were tasked with investigating the circumstances of the original purchase, the payment, and the location and extent of the claim, before recommending to the governor whether an award be made and how much land should be granted (though no award was to exceed 2,560 acres unless the governor authorised it); and a protector of Aborigines (or a person appointed in his stead) as well as competent interpreters had to be present at all investigations in order to protect the rights and interests of the native vendors.[19]

Spain and his fellow Commissioners only undertook their work on the basis of these instructions because of a haphazard series of events. On becoming Colonial Secretary, Russell had formed an opinion of the Commission's role and who should perform it that departed from the views of his predecessor. Consequently, soon after the Colonial Office had struck its agreement with the Company in November 1840, he

---

[18] Wakefield to Hobson, 25 September 1841, *BPP*, 1842, Paper no. 569, p. 158; Hobson to Wakefield, 27 September 1841, *BPP*, 1842, Paper no. 569, p. 159; Wakefield to Ward, 5 November 1841, 1844 Select Committee Report Appendices, p. 547; Hobson to Russell, 13 November 1841, *BPP*, 1842, Paper no. 569, pp. 170, 174.

[19] Thomson, Questions and Answers re Administration of Land Claims Legislation, 2 October 1840, NANZ, OLC 5/1/4c; Instructions for the Land Claims Commissioners, 2 October 1840, *BPP*, 1842, Paper no. 569, pp. 80–82; Gipps to Hobson, 2 October 1840, SARNSW, 4/1651; Gipps to Russell, 9 October 1840, *BPP*, 1842, Paper no. 569, p. 79; Gipps to Russell, 5 November 1840, *BPP*, 1842, Paper no. 569, p. 82; Colonial Secretary to William Spain, 19 March 1842, NANZ, IA 4/253.

instructed Gipps to defer the execution of his Land Claims Act and thus the work of the Commission. Russell also appointed a sole commissioner from England (Spain) to replace the three commissioners Gipps had appointed and set out a new role for the Commission that seemed to envisage that it would merely arbitrate between the Crown and British subjects in order to prevent future problems, rather than investigate the validity of titles acquired in the past. However, the Colonial Office failed to inform Hobson of this change in policy. Moreover, it decided to instruct Hobson to issue Spain with very general instructions and use Gipps' Land Claims Act as his guide in doing so (contrary to advice it received from Swainson and Martin). It is clear that the Colonial Office assumed that the task it had originally assigned to the Commission would be a simple one and could be completed in a very short time and that it had failed to grasp that Gipps' instructions to the Commissioners would create a complicated and time-consuming process of investigation. As we are about to see, this chain of events was to have major consequences that were neither intended nor foreseen by the Colonial Office and the colonial government, and which they would struggle to fix.[20]

The manner in which Spain undertook his duties as a Land Claims Commissioner should not only be attributed to these instructions. It also owed something to the kind of man he was. Spain had been trained as a lawyer and was an honest, sincere and methodical man. He was also inclined to dig in his heels and insist on the propriety of his task and the authority of the colonial government when he was challenged.[21]

Most importantly, Spain agreed with Hobson that the colonial administration *was* required by the imperial government to investigate all titles to land based on purchase from the natives and that these titles included the Company's. Two months after he arrived in Port Nicholson, and in the context of a campaign that Wakefield had launched to challenge the Commission's authority to investigate the Company's titles, Spain reasoned in the following way in a letter he wrote to Hobson: 'if it had been intended by Her Majesty's Government at once to admit the Company's title to be good and the native one extinct, then surely instructions would have been sent to Your Excellency to except [i.e. exempt] that body [the Company] from the operation of the Commission, and to make them

---

[20] Russell to Gipps, 21 November 1840, *BPP*, 1841, Paper no. 311, pp. 20–21; Russell to Hobson, 9 December 1840, *BPP*, 1841, Paper no. 311, p. 30; Civil establishment, 20 January 1841, NANZ, IA 12/2; James Stephen to Smith, 19 February 1841, TNA, CO 209/6; William Martin to Russell, 10 March 1841, TNA, CO 209/13; Smith to Martin, 24 March 1841, TNA, CO 406/1; Russell to Hobson, 16 April 1841, *BPP*, 1841, Paper no. 311, p. 60.

[21] Tonk, 'Land Commissions', pp. 125, 130.

a grant of the land they were entitled to, under [accountant Pennington's] award [in accordance with the November 1840 agreement], without further inquiry'. Spain confessed he was unable to believe that this could have been the imperial government's intention because, in his words, it would be 'so totally inconsistent and irreconcilable with the profession made to [the natives]. that Her Majesty would afford equal protection to all her subjects'. Spain was taking the Colonial Office's rhetoric at face value. His doing so reveals how speech acts made in particular circumstances to serve the needs of the moment could be taken up by other parties in another context in a manner that was never intended by those who uttered them. In this case, Spain's misunderstanding of the Colonial Office's rhetoric in its instructions to Hobson (discussed above, pp. 131–32) would profoundly shape the ways in which native title would be treated by the colonial government.[22]

Spain's next interpretive move was to prove just as crucial. Having formed the impression that the imperial government intended the Land Claims Commission to investigate the Company's titles, Spain scoured the official papers he had at his disposal for confirmation of it. At the head of the numerous pieces of evidence he adduced was the first clause of the treaty of Waitangi's second article. To be more precise, it was a sequence of official papers, from which Spain constructed this line of reasoning: since Russell had acknowledged receipt of the treaty and told Gipps that the British government approved of the measures he had adopted and the way they had been carried into effect by Hobson, it was clear that the government had approved the treaty 'guaranteeing to the natives all their lands &c' (that is, quoting the first clause of the treaty's second article). This was a plausible interpretation but it is utterly unconvincing since there is no evidence to suggest that the Colonial Office even noted this particular clause in the treaty. Nonetheless, Spain's take on the treaty constituted the beginning of what became a long chain of signification about it. In effect, Spain did not simply conclude that the Company's titles had to be investigated by the Land Claims Commission. He claimed in effect that such an investigation was authorised by the treaty.[23]

After Spain took up his duties, Wakefield initially acted as though he was not unduly concerned that his purchases might be found to be flawed, even though he knew that many of them were. He assumed, or kidded himself, that the Commissioner's investigation was going to be little more than a matter of form. However, several days after Spain began his court

---

[22] Spain to Hobson, 22 June 1842, in Spain to Willoughby Shortland, 12 September 1843, 1844 Select Committee Report Appendices, p. 292.

[23] Ibid., pp. 292–94.

hearings in Port Nicholson, it became evident that he was determined to subject the Company's titles to a thorough-going investigation. As a result, Wakefield started to change his tune.[24]

In a typically crafty letter he sent to the Company's directors at the end of May, Wakefield confessed that, while he had long assumed that the Company's claims were to be omitted from the purview of the Commission as a consequence of the November 1840 agreement with the Colonial Office, he had not forgotten the assumption in that agreement that the lands had been purchased from the natives and that some passages in it had implied an investigation into the Company's titles (though it is doubtful there was any such assumption or implication). Consequently, he informed the Company's directors, he was not surprised to learn on Spain's arrival that the Commissioner had been instructed to investigate the Company's titles. He claimed that he was not apprehensive about what this investigation might reveal, remarking instead that he was merely concerned that it was going to take a very considerable period of time. Yet Wakefield went on to complain that the agreement made by a Colonial Secretary (Russell) was being made subservient to an interpretation by a colonial commissioner (Spain).[25]

Most importantly, Wakefield conjured up another scapegoat for the problems the Company was encountering in trying to acquire possession of the lands it had claimed, namely what he called Hobson's 'mischievous treaty'. 'The impression prevails here that [Spain's] instructions from the Colonial Minister [Russell] have been overruled or much modified by Hobson to meet the conditions of the treaty of Waitangi', Wakefield informed the Company's directors. 'Those conditions rendered it imperative on the government, before making any grant of land, to acquire it by purchase from the natives, and it is to be presumed that the Governor, in charging Mr Spain to investigate the Company's titles, intended only to fulfil that compact'.[26]

It is clear that Wakefield had misunderstood the treaty. Neither its terms, nor Hobson's interpretation of them, were responsible for the Company's problems. The root of its difficulties lay in the fact that Hobson believed that the imperial government's instructions to him set down that all claims to land on the basis of purchases from the natives were to be investigated by the Land Claims Commission before the Crown granted title. Yet Wakefield's (mis)interpretation of the treaty

---

[24] Wakefield, Journal of Proceedings of Commissioner's Court, 16–27 May 1842, 1844 Select Committee Report Appendices, pp. 560–62.

[25] Wakefield to Ward, 30 May 1842, 1844 Select Committee Report Appendices, pp. 558–59.

[26] *Ibid.*

added to the significance that Spain had attributed to it on the basis of *his* (mis)interpretation of it. Moreover, Wakefield's misunderstanding of the treaty was soon to have dramatic consequences for the way in which both the treaty and native title would come to be cast by the Company's directors and the Colonial Office's senior figures.

The Return of the Treaty of Waitangi and the Rise of Native Title at the Imperial Centre

William Wakefield's news took the Company's directors by surprise. They had never anticipated that the Company would find it difficult to obtain possession of the land they believed Wakefield had purchased from the natives, and they had never accepted that an investigation by the Land Claims Commission could upend its claim to land title. Yet by the time they learned in October 1842 that Hobson had ordered Spain to investigate the Company's titles and that Spain was undertaking this work in a rigorous manner, they knew they could no longer expect to receive the kind of consideration they had got from the Colonial Office during Russell's term in office.[27]

In September 1841 the Whigs had lost power to the Tories and Russell had been replaced as Colonial Secretary by Lord Edward Stanley. Much of what now took place in regard to the treatment of land titles and the treaty of Waitangi cannot be understood unless we grasp something of Stanley's character. Several historians have noted that Stanley was a sincerely religious man but that he had neither settled philosophical convictions nor the enthusiasms that characterised the Christian humanitarians. Most important to our consideration is the fact that his chief interest in politics was what the historian W. P. Morrell called 'the clash of arms in debate'. Indeed, according to Stanley's most recent biographer, Angus Hawkins, his formidable political skills were principally expressed in the impassioned assaults he made on his opponents. These personal traits are evident in Stanley's handling of New Zealand's affairs and most especially those of the New Zealand Company. As early as mid-1842 he had formed a view of the Company and how it should be treated, writing to Hobson: 'In reference to your transactions with the Company you may rely at all times on my firm and full support for your authority against any exaggerated pretensions on the part of the Company or its agents'.[28]

---

[27] For a discussion of the Company's success in wringing more concessions from Russell after they had secured the agreement of November 1840, see Burns, *Fatal Success*, pp. 173–74.

[28] Lord Stanley to Hobson, 24 June 1842, *BPP*, 1842, Paper no. 569, p. 163; Morrell, *British Colonial Policy*, pp. 32, 35; Paul Knaplund, *James Stephen and the British Colonial*

Shortly after the Company's directors learned that its titles were being investigated, Somes complained to Stanley that Spain's proceedings were founded on a misconception on Hobson's part. He insisted that the Company's titles rested exclusively on the spirit of the November 1840 agreement: the Company had been required by the government to renounce the claims to land it had made on the basis of its purchases from the natives and in return it had received a grant from the Crown. Somes argued, moreover, that the agreement itself made it clear that the grant of land the Company had received from the government was intended to be absolute and that correspondence between the Company and the Colonial Office revealed that the government had explicitly recognised the Company's right to a Crown grant and exempted its titles from the Commission's investigation. Somes called on Stanley to instruct Hobson to grant the Company the land it had been promised in the agreement.[29]

Stanley was unmoved. In a reply sent in the name of his deputy, the parliamentary Under-Secretary for the Colonies, George Hope,[30] he told Somes that the matter had to be referred to Hobson before he could rule on it. Stanley was to insist repeatedly during his term as Colonial Secretary that local governmental processes had to be allowed to take their course. This was a position that the British government commonly took in handling colonial affairs. But on this occasion Stanley decided to express an opinion regarding what he called the *principle* involved in the dispute between the Colonial Office and Company, thereby bringing into consideration a matter that both parties had set aside at the time they had forged the November 1840 agreement, namely the New Zealanders' rights in land. Stanley articulated what he claimed Somes was really saying in his letter in this way: in no case were the claims of the natives to be entertained in opposition to those of the Company in the lands covered by the November 1840 agreement; native title to those lands was to be considered as extinguished; and a grant was to be made to the Company without any regard to native interests. Having framed the Company's position in this way, Stanley declared that he could not accede to it because he could not admit that the November 1840 agreement or the correspondence connected with it would bear out the Company's construction of them.[31]

System, University of Wisconsin Press, Madison, 1953, pp. 98, 107–11; Angus Hawkins, *The Forgotten Prime Minister: The 14th Earl of Derby, Volume 1: Ascent, 1799–1851*, Oxford University Press, Oxford, 2007, pp. 262–63, 284, 419.

[29] Somes to Stanley, 24 October 1842, 1844 Select Committee Report Appendices, pp. 8–9.

[30] This letter and following letters on this matter were all sent in the name of Stanley's deputy (that is, George Hope) following the practice that Russell had adopted in sending letters to the Company's directors.

[31] Hope to Somes, 7 November 1842, 1844 Select Committee Report Appendices, p. 14.

Stanley then raised the stakes further by playing the trump card of rights. In doing so, he invoked the first clause of the treaty's second article. '[E]ven if [your] interpretation [of the agreement] could be shown to be the true one', he informed Somes, '[Lord Stanley] considers it impossible to maintain that the rights of the natives of New Zealand to the soil, which had been recognised as indisputable by Her Majesty's government in August 1839 [i.e. in Normanby's instructions to Hobson], could be thereby effected, or that the Crown either intended thereby to deprive them, or did in fact deprive them, of the "full, exclusive, and undisturbed possession of their lands and estates", which had been "confirmed and guaranteed" to them by the treaty of Waitangi'.[32]

This was the first time the Colonial Office had made a reference to the first clause of the treaty's second article, or betrayed an awareness that it was part and parcel of the treaty. Why did Stanley do so now, given that the logical source of authority for the position he was adopting did not lie in the treaty or this particular clause? It seems that the following had occurred. In mid-October the Church Missionary Society's general committee in London, responding to a concern that the missionary William Williams had raised, namely that the colonial government's Land Claims Act had stipulated that any lands deemed to be surplus by the Land Claims Commission were to be regarded as part of the Crown's demesne rather than returned to the native owners,[33] informed Stanley that the rights of the natives guaranteed by the terms of the treaty of Waitangi were in danger of being violated.[34] Then, just a week later, the Colonial Office received from Somes William Wakefield's letter of May 1842 in which he had expressed his misunderstanding of the terms of the treaty and attacked the treaty as 'mischievous'. It seems that these two letters prompted the Colonial Office to pay serious attention to the treaty for the first time and provoked the naturally combative Stanley to embrace the clause in it that the Colonial Office had never sought. Whether those letters had this effect or not, there can be no doubt that Stanley's invoking of the treaty in his letter to Somes added another link in a growing chain of signification about it.[35]

---

[32] *Ibid.*

[33] The so-called surplus lands were the result of Land Claims Commission rulings that particular purchases from the natives were invalid or that the land in question exceeded the amount that the Governor was allowed to grant.

[34] At this stage the Colonial Office was unaware of Spain's assumption that the treaty of Waitangi provided a warrant for subjecting the Company's titles to the Land Claims Commission's investigations.

[35] William Williams to CMS Secretaries, 13 November 1840, CMS Records, CN/M12, AJCP, Reel M205; Coates to Stanley, 17 October 1842, CMS Records, CH/L3, AJCP,

The Company's directors were stunned by Stanley's letter, probably because they had fooled themselves that the November 1840 agreement meant they had pulled off their attempt to acquire a fantastically large amount of land in New Zealand. At any rate, Somes (or probably Wakefield or Buller writing in Somes' name) once again tried to impress upon Stanley the Company's position on the agreement. Somes insisted that the Company's directors could find no phrase in it that suggested that the Crown's fulfilment of the grant it had promised was dependent upon the Company proving that its purchases from the natives were valid. He also argued that the Colonial Office had acted as though the Company was to be awarded land at the point the accountant (Pennington) had completed his task. Somes went on to claim that the Company had the fullest sympathy for the regard the government expressed for the natives' interests but that the duty of extinguishing native title was the government's responsibility, not the Company's.[36]

However, following a meeting with Stanley a week later, the Company's directors realised he was not going to budge. They arranged to meet him and presented a memorandum, which Somes (or Wakefield or Buller) represented shortly afterwards in a letter. In this, Somes began by suggesting that the deadlock between the Company and the Colonial Office could be solved by the Colonial Office simply instructing Hobson to make grants of land subject to the Land Claims Commission's investigation of its titles. (Clearly, the Company's directors did not grasp that this had already happened, at least in one instance.) But Somes then proceeded to raise a question about the nature of native title. He argued that the only interest in land that British law 'ha[d] ever recognised as possessed by savages [was] that of "actual occupation or enjoyment"', and that the Crown's Charter for New Zealand of November 1840 and Russell's instructions to Hobson of the following month had defined native title in this limited way. Given this, Somes argued, the land the government would need to purchase from the natives in order to settle the dispute with the Company could only amount to 'a few patches of potato ground and rude dwelling places and involve no matter of greater moment than some few hundred acres'. Consequently, he asserted, it made little sense for the government to subject the Company's titles to investigation. The position the Company was adopting amounted to a radical change in its stance regarding the nature of native title. William Wakefield had purchased land in 1839 without any regard to whether Māori actually 'occupied or enjoyed' it,

Reel M238; Somes to Stanley, 24 October 1842, 1844 Select Committee Report Appendices, pp. 8–9.

[36] Somes to Stanley, 11 November 1842, 1844 Select Committee Report Appendices, pp. 15–16.

that is, he had proceeded as though the natives had rights of ownership in all the lands in question.[37]

On receiving Somes' letter, considerable discussion took place among the Colonial Office's senior figures as to how they should deal with it. This probably occurred for two reasons. First, someone in the Colonial Office was troubled by the possibility that the Company's directors were right in a couple of important respects. An exchange of letters between Stanley's predecessor and a Company representative suggested that Russell's interpretation of the November 1840 agreement was the same as the Company's directors; and passages in both the Charter and the Royal Instructions of 1840 supported the Company's interpretation that the government had deemed that the natives' rights in land were limited to those they 'occupied or enjoyed'.[38] Second, Somes' letter had riled the Colonial Office's most senior officers. Stanley's deputy, George Hope, who took responsibility for preparing the first draft of the Colonial Office's response to Somes' letter, remarked in a covering note to James Stephen: 'Th[is] draft is much longer and more controversial than I would like but the propositions of the Company strike me as so monstrous and are advanced with so much hardihood [i.e. audacity] I did not like to leave them unnoticed'. For his part, Stephen suggested that it would be a mistake to offer the Company any concessions since he doubted that its directors were 'persons towards whom it [was] safe to be generous'.[39]

Hope and more especially Stephen's passionate views about the moral character of the Company's directors and Wakefield in particular had a considerable influence on the letter that the Colonial Office eventually prepared. Stephen intensely distrusted Wakefield, regarding him as man who suffered from a 'want of truth and honour'. (These feelings were largely a consequence of malicious public attacks that Wakefield and Buller had made on the thin-skinned Stephen in 1840, which he had found deeply hurtful and which prompted him to withdraw as much as possible from any Colonial Office business that touched on the

---

[37] NZC, Memorandum, undated [December 1842], 1844 Select Committee Report Appendices, pp. 16–18; Somes to Stanley, 21 December 1842, 1844 Select Committee Report Appendices, pp. 18–20; Somes to Stanley, 24 January 1843, 1844 Select Committee Report Appendices, p. 23.

[38] At least one historian has attributed this letter to Stanley (Mark Hickford, *Lords of the Land: Indigenous Property Rights and the Jurisprudence of Empire*, Oxford University Press, Oxford, 2011, p. 143), but as the letter makes a reference to Stanley himself it is unlikely that he wrote it.

[39] Letter to Hope, December 1842, TNA, CO 209/18; Hope to Stephen, 27 December 1842, TNA, CO 209/18; Stephen to Hope, 28 December 1842, TNA, CO 209/18.

Company's affairs.) After he read Hope's first draft and suggested a way of recasting it in a memorandum, Stephen drew his superiors' attention to the fact that his views were probably tinged with hostility towards the Company's principal figures.[40]

In the substantive part of this memorandum, Stephen recommended that the Colonial Office couch its reply to the Company largely in the form of a series of pointed historical reminders about key matters. Stephen suggested that the Colonial Office should begin this historical narrative by reminding the Company's directors that they had formed settlements in New Zealand without the consent of the government and in direct opposition to its wishes, which had sprung from the fact that the Crown had publicly and explicitly disavowed British sovereignty in the islands. Clearly, Stephen was returning here to the subject of his November 1839 memorandum on the government's handling of the matter of sovereignty (see pp. 163–64).[41]

Stephen then suggested that the Colonial Office should remind the Company's directors that the government had authorised Hobson 'to treat with the native chiefs for a cession of sovereignty *on the basis of recognising their proprietary titles to the soil,* and that *it is in virtue of the treaty so made with them,* and *on that basis alone, that Her Majesty's title to sovereignty in New Zealand at this moment rests'.* Both of these claims were tendentious. In regard to the first, the Colonial Office had decided to treat with the native chiefs for the cession of sovereignty not because it recognised their rights of property in land but because it regarded the chiefs as more or less sovereign. That Stephen made this claim now – and thereby implied that the clause of the treaty 'guaranteeing to the natives all their lands &c' was fundamental to its meaning – is best attributed to the fact that Somes had focused attention on the matter of native title and disparaged the natives' rights in land. Previously the Colonial Office had never placed so much emphasis on what Stephen was now calling the government's recognition of the natives' title to land. In doing so now, Stephen added a further link in the growing chain of significance about the treaty. In regard to Stephen's second claim, the Colonial Office had proclaimed the Crown's sovereignty over New Zealand in October 1840

---

[40] Stephen, Memorandum, 15 December 1841, TNA, CO 209/11; Stephen to Hope, 28 December 1842, TNA, CO 209/18; Stephen to Howick, February 1845, Papers of Henry George, 3rd Earl Grey, University of Durham Library Special Collections (henceforth Grey Papers), GRE/B126/11/101–04; Stephen to Howick, 16 June 1845, Grey Papers, B126/11/109–10; Stephen to Benjamin Hawes, 10 December 1846, Grey Papers, GRE/B147/38; John W. Cell, *British Colonial Administration in the Mid-Nineteenth Century: The Policy-Making Process*, Yale University Press, New Haven, CT, 1970, p. 9.

[41] Stephen to Hope, 28 December 1842.

on the basis of Hobson's May 1840 proclamations, and in those proclamations the Governor had certainly laid claim to sovereignty in the North
Island on the basis that he had (allegedly) secured the consent of all the
native chiefs in the North Island, but he had also claimed sovereignty in
the South Island on the grounds of the legal doctrine of *discovery*. Clearly,
Stephen recognised that the Colonial Office was in a jam in this dispute
with the Company and so he sought to clothe the position he wanted it to
take in an appropriate legal garb.[42]

Stephen went on to suggest that the Colonial Office should remind
the Company's directors that the government had entered into the
November 1840 agreement with the Company on the basis of the
Company's claim to have a good proprietary title to the land and to
point out that this meant that the agreement's validity rested on that
claim being true. In fact, Stephen was outraged that the Company's
directors were now arguing that it was neither here nor there that its
claims in respect of its purchases of land from the natives might turn
out to be completely untrue. (Stephen's outrage was probably all the
greater because he presumably felt some degree of culpability in what
had happened, given that he had been instrumental in making the
November 1840 agreement.) He suggested that the Colonial Office tell
the Company: 'His Lordship will not be able to admit that the Company
have such a title either as against the natives or the Crown if it shall
ultimately appear that the allegations as to their ownership were not in
point of fact true'; that it should insist: 'If at the date of the agreement the
land was not the property of the Company it must of that day have been
the property of the New Zealanders or a mere unoccupied waste. If [it had
been] the property of the New Zealanders it must belong to them still,
because nothing has ever occurred to dispossess them of it'; and that it
should point out: 'Even if it must be considered as a waste belonging to
the Crown it will not follow that the Company could strictly claim from
the Crown the execution of the agreement in respect of it because on that
supposition the government proceeded on an essential misstatement of
facts and cannot be binding on the party who was deceived by that
misstatement'.[43]

Stephen was also angered by a passage in Somes' letter that claimed
that there was a maxim common to all Christian nations that savages had
no property in the land over which they ranged. To his mind, this claim
struck at a treaty that he believed the British Crown had honourably
entered into with the natives, a treaty of which he could be said to be its
progenitor given that he was primarily responsible for drafting the

---

[42] *Ibid.*, my emphases.   [43] *Ibid.*

instructions that had directed Hobson to make it. Stephen suggested that the Colonial Office reply to the Company's claim in this way: 'Without pausing to consider the accuracy of this general statement or the propriety with which a title so sacred is connected with it, Lord Stanley observes ... that it proceeds with peculiar infelicity from a body whose contract and charter rest upon alleged purchases from those very persons whose competency to sell they now dispute and is addressed with peculiar inappropriateness to a government which derives all of its authority in New Zealand from [a compact] with the natives of which ... the proprietary rights of the natives form one of the essential bases'. Once more, we can see Stephen bestowing on the treaty of Waitangi – and one of its clauses in particular – a significance it had not previously had.[44]

Stephen's advice to his superiors in the Colonial Office is evident in much of the letter that was finally sent to the Company in January 1843. It began by expressing Stanley's astonishment that the Company had refused to acknowledge that it had known of the contents of Normanby's instructions to Hobson and would be affected by them. In those instructions, claimed Stanley, the Crown had distinctly recognised the proprietorship of the soil in the natives and disclaimed all territorial rights and any sovereignty that were not founded on a free cession by the natives. Here, Stanley was putting the treaty of Waitangi centre stage, saying he could not permit the Company to assume that the Crown, in entering into the agreement of November 1840 with the Company, could have contemplated violating the faith which it had publicly pledged to the natives (though arguably this is exactly what the government had done). Next, Stanley argued that the agreement with the Company was founded on an assumption that the Company's agents *had* purchased from the natives a proprietary right to 20 million acres of land and thereby extinguished native title. Given this, he told the Company's directors: '[I] cannot now permit it to be maintained, either that the natives had no proprietary right in the face of the Company's declaration that they had purchased those very rights, or that it is the duty of the Crown either to extinguish those rights or to set them aside in favour of the Company'. In any case, Stanley remarked, the Crown's grant was conditional upon the Company's purchases being good because if this was not the case the government had no land to grant it.[45]

Stanley went on to insist that the government was bound by law to respect the investigation that was being undertaken by the Land Claims

[44] *Ibid.*
[45] Hope to Somes, 10 January 1843, 1844 Select Committee Report Appendices, pp. 20–21.

Commission and that it had neither the will nor the power to interfere in the Commission's work. But he also asserted: 'It is the duty of that tribunal not to suffer native rights, which have been recognised by Her Majesty, to be set aside in favour of any body of settlers, however powerful'. This was also a new departure for the Colonial Office. Until now, it had conceived of the Commission as a means of investigating *settler* titles so as to meet the government's ends (of acquiring control over the market in land and learning the lands to which the Crown could claim to have title), not as a mechanism to protect native rights. Once more, we can see the Colonial Office using the language of rights, and of native rights more especially, largely because this served its current political need, namely that of advancing a case against the Company.[46]

Finally, Stanley held out an olive branch to the Company's directors, though not before he set out what he understood to be the gist of the Company's position: its directors had complained that they were being called upon to establish titles to land that no one disputed and to which no one could be proved to be entitled since most of those lands in question were waste; consequently, they proposed that Hobson be instructed to grant the Company the lands it had selected, excepting only lands which at the time of the agreement were in the actual 'occupation or enjoyment' of the natives. Strikingly, Stanley told Somes that he had no reason to doubt that much of the land might indeed be waste and that in so far as this might turn out to be the case, he was willing to put those lands at the Company's disposal. Hence, he would not object to issuing an instruction to Hobson to make a grant to the Company of those lands that was conditional upon its claims to them being established by the Land Claims Commission. In other words, Stanley accepted the proposal the Company had originally put to the Colonial Office. At the same time, however, he told Somes that he could not agree to the Company's proposition that he override all prior titles except those of the natives to land they 'occupied or enjoyed' or to even define what constituted native title. Stanley concluded by impressing upon Somes the fact that the concession he was offering was as far as he felt he could go in the light of what he called his 'duty towards others'.[47]

How might we best explain the Colonial Office's position? First, its senior figures were concerned, as they always were, with imperial order, and they believed that the government could only attain this by upholding the authority of the Crown vis-à-vis parties like the Company.

---

[46] *Ibid.*
[47] *Ibid.*, pp. 21–22; Colonial Office, Memorandum on the Twelfth Report of the Directors of the New Zealand Company, 1844 Select Committee Report Appendices, p. 2.

Second, they were committed to a principle that held that the best way to acquire land in circumstances such as New Zealand's was to treat the natives as though they were the owners of it. This meant that they were committed to a particular *process*, that of purchasing those lands from the natives. In keeping with that principle, the Colonial Office's senior figures were not inclined to hazard a definition of native title, indeed on the contrary. Doing so would weaken the Colonial Office's position, given that it probably agreed with the Company's proposition that the natives' rights were limited to the lands they 'occupied and enjoyed'. Instead, Stanley and his colleagues maintained that the matter in dispute was best dealt with on the spot by local agents grappling with the particularities of any given case. This meant that Spain should be allowed to proceed with his investigations and try to adjust any differences that existed between the parties.

Third, the Colonial Officer's senior figures wanted to assert the government's position in relation to the Company for reasons that were both moral and psychological. In regard to the former, they had strong convictions about what they believed to be *right*. It seems that this was the sense in which they primarily used the language of rights, that is, in the objective sense of something being rightfully done – rights as a standard for conduct – rather than in the subjective sense of someone having a right to something,[48] though it is apparent that they did regard the natives as having rights to protection. In regard to the latter, they wished to discipline the Company's wayward directors, or at least its principal figures, much as they might punish a wayward child.

Finally, the Colonial Office's invoking of the treaty and the natives' rights in land can be understood as a function of its senior officers' bitter political battle with the directors of the Company and their attempt to legitimise the position they had chosen to adopt in this conflict.[49]

---

[48] For a discussion of this point, see Richard Dagger, 'Rights', in Terence Ball et al. (eds.), *Political Innovation and Conceptual Change*, Cambridge University Press, New York, 1989, pp. 294, 298.

[49] Stephen to Stanley, 27 March 1845, TNA, CO 207/189. For further evidence of the Colonial Office's views on the nature of native rights in land at this time, see Stanley, Memorandum, no date [June 1843], TNA, CO 209/24; and for more evidence of its preference to deal with land matters on a case-by-case basis rather than proceed on the grounds of abstract principles, see Stephen to Hope, 9 March 1843, TNA, CO 209/40. In this paragraph my argument bears some similarity to an argument Mark Hickford has made. But I am unpersuaded by his contention that the position adopted by the Colonial Office was a result of it wanting to restraint the Company's settling activities (*Lords*, pp. 110–12). Apart from anything else, the Colonial Office would have known that those activities were already being constrained, primarily by the workings of the Land Claims Commission.

Native Title, the Treaty and the Honour of the Crown

Not surprisingly, the Company's directors regarded Stanley's January letter as inflammatory. Their response was equally intemperate. If Wakefield or Buller were not responsible for the earlier letters in Somes' name, one or other of them almost certainly wrote this one, signed by Somes, which ran to 119 pages. The Company's directors were angered by what they saw as the Colonial Office's refusal to take any notice of the grounds upon which they had asserted the Company's claim and suspected that the Colonial Office's reply had been formulated with a propagandist purpose in mind.

Somes now conceded that the Company had probably told the government that its agent had made an arrangement with the native chiefs under which they claimed 20 million acres of land in New Zealand, but he argued that it had never asserted that it could prove the validity of those purchases. In a further departure, he emphasised that it was necessary to ascertain how Russell had understood the agreement and argued that letters sent in Russell's name showed that it was impossible that he held that the November 1840 agreement was dependent on an investigation into the Company's titles.[50]

The Company's directors next took a leaf out of the Colonial Office's book by creating a narrative about the historical circumstances that bore upon the dispute. Somes began by claiming that the Company had been forced by the government's repudiation of British sovereignty to accept title to land on the basis of purchase from the natives, but that after the government had belatedly asserted sovereignty over all of New Zealand and declared that it intended to treat all purchases of land from the natives as null and void, the Company had realised that it had to come to an understanding with the government regarding its possessions. Consequently, it had asked the Colonial Office how it was going to treat the rights to land of those like itself and was offered the agreement by which, in return for consenting to forego and disclaim any pretence to title on the grounds of purchase from the natives, it was granted title on the basis that its settling of land in New Zealand was productive of public benefit. It was on these grounds that the Company had been granted title by the Crown, rather than its purchasing land from the natives.[51]

Somes dismissed Stanley's contention that the Company should have grasped the implications of Normanby's instructions. After asserting that a document of this kind had no legal standing, he argued that while the

[50] Somes to Stanley, 24 January 1843, 1844 Select Committee Report Appendices, pp. 22–26.
[51] *Ibid.*, pp. 26–28.

instructions had declared the government's intention to recognise the proprietary rights of the New Zealanders, they had stated nothing about the nature of those rights. Moreover, argued Somes, there was nothing in Normanby's consideration of this matter that gave the instructions the character of a well-considered and immutable resolve. This was all the more the case since Normanby had retracted the instructions in the wake of Hobson suggesting that he should be allowed to acquire sovereignty in the South Island by means other than cession. (There is more than a grain of historical truth in these particular arguments of Somes.)[52]

Next, Somes provided an account of the way in which he claimed the Crown had dealt with the proprietary rights of native peoples in the past. He argued that the Crown had always drawn a distinction between territories occupied by a people whose degree of civilisation meant they had established rights of property in land and those territories where there were scanty tribes who clearly had no idea of property in land; and that in the former case the Crown had respected those rights to the fullest extent but in the latter it had held that natives only had rights in the land they actually occupied and had asserted its right to the remaining land, which it regarded as unappropriated. In this context, Somes contended, Normanby's instructions to Hobson struck the Company as an anomaly that was sanctioned by no legal authority. Indeed, he went on, they seemed to be based on 'a strange medley' of the two principles applied by the Crown to those two different kinds of countries: Normanby had 'regarded the New Zealanders as a civilised people living under regular law as to recognise their property in the soil, to treat with them for the sovereignty of the country, and to respect the rights of native proprietors as guaranteed by cession', but he had also 'view[ed] them as savages in the eye of the law', declared 'all purchases from them invalid' and 'asserted the rights of the Crown over all the lands purchased from the natives'. This was the same objection that Wentworth and his fellow petitioners in New South Wales had raised. 'If the New Zealanders had no notion of proprietary rights in land, how could such rights be acknowledged by the Crown?' Somes asked. 'If they had, how could it be maintained that they had always been incapable of alienating such rights?'[53]

Somes proceeded to assert that the Company had not believed that even the Crown's power of making treaties could establish legally 'such a fiction as a native law of real property in New Zealand', given that it was apparent that Normanby's instructions had been based on a theory that could not be reconciled with either sound reason or the principles of British law. This argument led Somes to make a statement that would

[52] *Ibid.*, p. 29.   [53] *Ibid.*, pp. 29–30.

soon become notorious: 'We always have had very serious doubts whether the treaty of Waitangi, made with naked savages by a consul invested with no plenipotentiary powers, without ratification by the Crown, could be treated by lawyers as anything but *a praiseworthy device for amusing and pacifying savages* for the moment. But we thought it probable that whenever possession of New Zealand should be actually obtained by Her Majesty, the view hastily adopted by Lord Normanby would be found impracticable and abandoned'.[54]

Somes had a point. The government's primary purpose in making the treaty had been the momentary one of persuading the native chiefs to consent to the British Crown's assumption of sovereignty. Similarly, Normanby's declaration of the government's respect for native rights was vague in regard to the nature of their title to land.

Somes argued further that the Company thought it probable that once the government had actually obtained possession of New Zealand it would find the position Normanby had adopted to be impracticable and thus abandon it. Consequently, when the Colonial Office made the agreement with the Company based on the invalidity of its past purchases and dealt with the southern islands as though the Crown had unqualified ownership there, the Company had assumed that it was now prepared to assert the Crown's right to the unoccupied lands of New Zealand. This, Somes insisted, had struck the Company as the simplest way of accounting for the obvious discrepancy between Normanby's instructions and the agreement between the Colonial Office and the Company.[55]

In the same vein, Somes proceeded to assert that if there had been any omissions or misstatements in the November 1840 agreement, the fault lay with the Colonial Office, not the Company. He demanded to know whether it was reasonable for the Colonial Office to assert that the Company should have realised that the title that the Crown itself had granted was dependent on the Company having previously ensured a proper extinguishment of native title, given the nature of a couple of the instructions Normanby had given Hobson. If the Colonial Office had required the Company to show proof to the Land Claims Commission that its purchases from the natives were valid, Somes asserted, it should have stated this in the agreement, and it had not.[56]

In concluding, Somes warned the Colonial Office that in the event that it once again refused to accept the case the Company was making, he was sure that the Company could persuade a legal tribunal of its merits. In doing this, Somes returned to a point he had begun this letter, speaking the language of rights: 'We have called on your Lordship to complete our

[54] *Ibid.*, p. 30, my emphasis.   [55] *Ibid.*   [56] *Ibid.*, pp. 30–31.

legal title by the grant which your predecessor promised, because we believed it our strict right'.[57]

The Colonial Office confined itself to a brief reply to Somes' long letter. Stanley parried Somes' challenge by saying that he was happy to refer the matter to a judicial tribunal. In doing so, he again portrayed the Company as a body that was demanding that the government cast aside its duties to the natives and trample on their rights. Stanley repeated his offer to make the Company a conditional grant but insisted he could not go any further. More particularly, Stanley used the treaty as a trump card, telling the Company's directors that the government was unwilling 'to join with the Company in setting aside the treaty of Waitangi after obtaining the advantages guaranteed by it, even though it might be made with "naked savages" or though it might "be treated by lawyers as a praiseworthy device for amusing and pacifying savages for the moment"'. This would not be the only time the Company's opponents would throw this statement of the Company's back in its face. Stanley made no reference to any particular clause of the treaty now. Instead, he invoked what he called the spirit of the agreement by suggesting that the honour of the Crown was at stake: 'Lord Stanley entertains a different view of the respect due to the obligations contracted by the Crown of England; and his final answer to the demands of the Company must be that as long as he has the honour of serving the Crown he will not admit that any person, or any government, acting in the name of Her Majesty can contract a legal, moral or honorary obligation to despoil others of their lawful or equitable rights'.[58]

Stanley's positioning of the government as the protector of native rights prompted the Company's directors to insist that the matter at stake concerned the *kind* of rights in land that the natives could be said to have. Somes told Stanley that the Company still maintained that it was unreasonable for the government to recognise any native rights in land save that deriving from the legal concept of *occupation*. He also tried again to prompt the Colonial Office to declare its position on the nature of the native title. 'The only question', he told Stanley, 'is whether your Lordship asserts any other titles than that of occupancy'. Somes pointed out that Stanley had never really explained his views on the subject and urged him to limit the government's definition of native title to the lands they 'occupied and enjoyed'. Somes then repeated his argument that this definition of native title was in accordance with the principles of English common law and the position the Colonial Office itself had adopted on this matter at the time it had officially proclaimed British sovereignty in

[57] *Ibid.*, pp. 32–33.
[58] Hope to Somes, 1 February 1843, 1844 Select Committee Report Appendices, p. 36.

New Zealand, quoting the Charter of November 1840: 'Provided always that nothing in these letters patent contained shall affect, or be construed to affect, *the rights of any aboriginal natives* of the said colony of New Zealand *to the actual occupation or enjoyment of their own persons, or in the persons of their descendants,* of any lands in the said colony *now actually occupied or enjoyed by such natives'.*[59]

This line of argument led Somes to protest against Stanley's claim that the Company wished to set aside the treaty of Waitangi and to clarify its position on the agreement. 'Let Her Majesty's government observe the treaty of Waitangi religiously', he wrote. 'We only objected to its being used to defeat the clearly expressed intentions of parties making a contract in England'. As this statement reveals, the treaty had now acquired significance for both parties in this dispute. Moreover, this was primarily so because of the contestation between them.[60]

Somes proceeded to argue that the treaty did not apply to the vast extent of country over which the Company claimed the right of selection. The chiefs who signed the treaty at Waitangi neither could or did pretend to cede anything but the northern reaches of the North Island, and while it was true that Hobson had procured the agreement of chiefs further south, the agreement of the chiefs within the limits of the Company's possessions in that island rested merely on evidence that was 'far too slight and loose' to establish a fact of such 'grave public character'. In any case, Somes continued, at least half of the 20 million acres the Company had originally claimed were in the South Island, and it was obvious that its titles there could not be affected by the treaty since the Crown's title had been asserted there on the grounds of discovery and thus without any pretence of a treaty of cession. In other words, if Stanley's objection to the Company's present claim rested to any degree on the treaty, it was clear that the government could not enforce this in opposition to the Company's claims in regard to the South Island or even the southern reaches of the North Island.[61]

Finally, Somes sought clarification of the nature of the conditional grant that Stanley was offering. He was apprehensive that all adverse claims to the lands included in it would be considered by the Land Claims Commissioner, which meant that the Company would gain nothing from such an offer. By March, however, the Company's directors realised that the Company was in considerable financial trouble. In fact, they were desperate. The Crown's control over all matters concerning

---

[59] Somes to Stanley, 15 February 1843, 1844 Select Committee Report Appendices, pp. 37–39, original emphases.
[60] *Ibid.*   [61] *Ibid.*

title to land meant they had little choice but to accept Stanley's offer. In May they put to Stanley a detailed proposal for an arrangement that had these provisions: the Company would receive conditional grants for selected places; the Crown would transfer to the Company the title it was able to grant and waive its rights of pre-emption over those parts of the land that were still subject to native claims in the area of the Company's award; and the Company would be allowed to acquire Crown lands in other areas as part of their award. Under the terms of this proposal, the Company, rather than being required to substantiate its own titles, merely had to disprove the claims of other parties. Stanley accepted the proposal. The Company's directors pronounced themselves confident that this new agreement would put to rest any questions about its titles to land. But, as we will see, this confidence was misplaced.[62]

Part II

While this bitter tussle between the Colonial Office and the New Zealand Company was taking place in London, Spain pursued his investigations into the Company's claims; the Company's agents in New Zealand continued to attack the local administration and challenge the authority of the Crown; and the administration's senior figures, just like their masters in the Colonial Office, decided to repel this assault by championing the natives' rights of property in land as well as the treaty of Waitangi.

Contesting Title on the Ground (Again)

Spain's investigations into the Company's claims in Port Nicholson and its surrounds created an opportunity for Māori rangatira such as Te Rauparaha, who were required to appear as witnesses in Spain's hearings, to assert their claims to land. As a result, government officials such as the native protectors learned a great deal about the various bases of those claims – occupation, resource use, conquest, and ancestral connection – and their extensive nature. This undoubtedly played a role in helping to generate the notion of native title. More particularly, Spain learned that many of the chiefs had never consented to the Company's purchases or signed the deeds, that some of those who had agreed to sell had never received a portion of the goods they had been promised and that many had not understood the nature of the transactions properly or the use and extent of the reserves they had been

---

[62] *Ibid.*, pp. 39–40; Somes to Stanley, 8 May 1843, 1844 Select Committee Report Appendices, pp. 90–91; Hope to Somes, 12 May 1843, 1844 Select Committee Report Appendices, p. 92.

promised. Consequently, he recommended to Hobson that the Company only be granted a very small amount of the land it had claimed in Port Nicholson. At the same time, it became apparent that the Company's attempts to occupy land in Port Nicholson and more especially the Hutt Valley were increasingly being frustrated. Ngāti Toa, led by Te Rauparaha and his nephew Te Rangihaeata, were asserting their rights of ownership to the land that the Company had purchased but was yet to occupy along the banks of the Heretaunga (Hutt) River and down the valley towards the coast, by settling on it, burning off timber, planting crops and forcing the Company's settlers away.[63]

By August 1842 Wakefield realised that he was not going to be able to persuade either Spain or these Māori chiefs to accept the Company's claims. As a result, he sought to renew the terms of the agreement he had struck with Hobson the previous year, offering to compensate the natives who were disputing the Company's claims. He proposed that the amount to be paid should be decided by Spain and the Company's protector of aborigines and urged that the awards be made at the same time as Spain continued his investigation of the Company's claims. Spain welcomed this proposal in the belief that it would help settle what had clearly become a most difficult problem. He realised that his investigation into the Company's claims was going to take much longer and reveal more complications, and he feared this would have dire consequences for settlers and natives alike. He also thought the matter should be resolved sooner rather than later because he recognised that the chiefs were increasingly conscious of the value of their lands to Europeans. Willoughby Shortland, who became the colony's acting governor in September 1842 after Hobson died suddenly, agreed. In January 1843 he approved Wakefield's proposal in the belief that it would expedite a final settlement of the Company's claims (though he made some changes in terms of who would administer it). Wakefield also informed the Company's directors that he expected that this agreement would soon resolve all the differences among the Company, the natives and the government.[64]

[63] Spain to Colonial Secretary, 16 September 1842, 1844 Select Committee Report Appendices, p. 59; Spain to Colonial Secretary, 12 September 1843, 1844 Select Committee Report Appendices, pp. 295–96; Spain, Memorandum, 19 November 1843, 1844 Select Committee Report Appendices, pp. 281–82; Spain, Report on Port Nicholson, 31 March 1845, *BPP*, 1846, Paper no. 203, Copies of Despatches from the Governor of New Zealand, pp. 4–5, 7; Tonk, 'Land Commissions', pp. 170–71.

[64] Wakefield to Spain, 22 August 1842, 1844 Select Committee Report Appendices, pp. 563–64; Shortland to Wakefield, 15 September and 14 October 1842, 1844 Select Committee Report Appendices, p. 565; J. Stuart Freeman to Wakefield, 16 January 1843, 1844 Select Committee Report Appendices, p. 566; Wakefield to Shortland, 19 January 1843, 1844 Select Committee Report Appendices, p. 566; Wakefield to Ward, 28 January 1843, 1844 Select Committee Report Appendices,

Shortland and Wakefield were soon proved wrong. At Te Aro, the first of the three pa in Port Nicholson for which the government and the Company tried to implement the agreement, the Te Āti Awa chiefs agreed to accept an offer from the Company (though only after a week of tough negotiation). However, at the two other pa, Pipitea and Kumutoto, the chiefs made demands that even the government's local protector of aborigines, George Clarke Jnr, thought were exorbitant. At the end of February, Clarke provided an assessment of the value of their claims that was much lower than the chiefs were demanding, but Wakefield was flabbergasted by this new figure and declared that it was utterly impossible for the Company to proceed with any negotiations on the basis of such a sum.[65]

By May it had become evident that the Company was encountering other difficulties. At Whanganui, on the west coast of the North Island, the local people had repeatedly been denying that they had sold a significant part of the millions of acres the Company claimed to have purchased in 1839. Moreover, they were resisting the Company's attempts to take possession of those lands. In the meantime, Spain's hearings were revealing that the Company's claims had the same basic flaws as those at Port Nicholson. He nevertheless concluded that this was a case in which Wakefield could take advantage of the recent agreement and was keen that negotiations take place concurrently with his investigation into the Company's claims. But as he returned southwards and conducted an investigation of other Company claims, he was informed by Wakefield that the Company's directors did not believe that its titles rested on the validity of its purchases from the natives and that they had instructed him to postpone all negotiations regarding the compensation the Company had offered to pay for the lands at Port Nicholson. Spain was very annoyed. He refused to accept that the instructions of the Company's directors could or should apply to an agreement that had previously been struck by Wakefield and Shortland. Spain urged Wakefield to resume the negotiations but he refused.[66]

p. 565; Spain to Shortland, 12 September 1843, 1844 Select Committee Report Appendices, pp. 295–96, 305.
[65] Spain to Wakefield, 14 February 1843, 1844 Select Committee Report Appendices, pp. 307–08; Clarke to Spain, 17 and 23 February 1843, 1844 Select Committee Report Appendices, pp. 310, 312; Clarke to Wakefield, 27 February 1843, 1844 Select Committee Report Appendices, p. 322; Wakefield to Clarke, 1 March 1843, 1844 Select Committee Report Appendices, p. 322.
[66] Spain to Wakefield, 3 April 1843, BPP, 1846, Paper no. 203, p. 84; Wakefield to Spain, 8 April 1843, 1844 Select Committee Report Appendices, pp. 314–15; Spain to Jerningham Wakefield, 17 April 1843, BPP, 1846, Paper no. 203, p. 85; Spain to Wakefield, 22 May 1843, 1844 Select Committee Report Appendices, pp. 318–19; Wakefield to Spain, 24 May 1843, 1844 Select Committee Report Appendices, pp.

At the same time as these events were taking place, the Company's agents and settlers had tried to take matters into their own hands at its settlement in Nelson, at the top of the South Island, by pushing ahead with arrangements to survey the rich plains of the Wairau Valley. In March Te Rauparaha and Te Rangihaeata had visited the Company's settlement and made clear to its principal agent there, Arthur Wakefield (another one of Edward Gibbon Wakefield's brothers), that they would resist any attempt to survey the land before Spain had completed his investigation and ruled on the validity of the Company's title. Wakefield dismissed this warning and directed the Company's surveyors to begin their work. Before long, some Māori began to obstruct the survey and at the end of May Te Rauparaha and Te Rangihaeata burned down the huts of the Company's surveyors after they refused to abandon the survey. In response, Wakefield and the other leaders of the Company's settlement decided that a show of strength would settle the matter. They persuaded the police magistrate Henry Augustus Thompson, a hot-headed man prone to panic, to issue a warrant to arrest Te Rauparaha on a charge of arson and formed an armed party, which eventually numbered almost fifty men, to execute it. On 17 June this party encountered Te Rauparaha and Te Rangihaeata and a party of twenty-five or so Māori, who were also armed. Thompson demanded that Te Rauparaha surrender, but he refused. Thompson then ordered his party to seize Te Rauparaha, but as they moved forward a gun was fired and Te Rangihaeata's wife, Te Rongo, was killed. The Māori party opened fire, and Wakefield, Thompson and some of their party were forced to surrender, upon which Te Rangihaeata and his men killed several of them. Altogether, twenty-two of Thompson's party were slain in this melee.[67]

Wairau, the Crown's Authority and the Return of the Treaty of Waitangi in New Zealand

The killings at Wairau caused a huge commotion among the Company's settlers in Nelson and Port Nicholson. At a series of public meetings, and

320–21; Wakefield to Clarke, 24 May 1843, 1844 Select Committee Report Appendices, p. 326; Spain to Shortland, 12 September 1843, 1844 Select Committee Report Appendices, p. 305; Spain to Robert FitzRoy, 31 March 1845, *BPP*, 1846, Paper no. 203, pp. 76–79; Spain, Report on Nelson, 31 March 1845, *BPP*, 1846, Paper no. 203, pp. 35–36; Spain, Report on Porirua, 31 March 1845, *BPP*, 1846, Paper no. 203, pp. 93–98.

[67] Ian Wards, *The Shadow of the Land: A Study of British Policy and Racial Conflict in New Zealand 1832–1852*, Historical Publications Branch, Department of Internal Affairs, Wellington, 1968, pp. 74–78; Temple, *Conscience*, pp. 298, 316–22.

in memorials, petitions and the press, the Company and its supporters consistently characterised the events as a massacre and blamed it on the government's decision to treat the natives as independent and attribute to them the rights held by civilised states. In so doing, they made critical reference to the treaty of Waitangi, arguing that the government had all the rights that *discovery* conferred upon it by the law of nations, namely those of occupying a country, subjecting it to British sovereignty and disposing of its lands without asking permission of the natives, but had instead despoiled those rights, as a consequence of which it was now bound to protect the Company and its settlers from native claims that had 'no shadow of legal existence'. More particularly, the Company and its supporters argued that the primary cause of the events at Wairau was the government's failure to settle land claims, for which they attributed responsibility to the Land Claims Commission. The Company's spokesmen, like its directors in London, contended that the Crown's grant of land to the Company was not supposed to rest on its purchases from the natives, blamed the colonial authorities' interference in the Company's titles on the treaty, argued that it was the government's responsibility to make any payments to natives to extinguish their title, claimed that the government should insist that the natives accept the reserves provided by the terms of the Company's purchase and even called on it to follow up this demand with a show of force.[68]

In response, the colonial administration argued that the responsibility for the events at Wairau lay squarely with the Company's agents and supporters. In doing so, it emulated the Colonial Office in speaking the language of rights and invoking the first clause of the second article of the treaty, thereby, like the Company's local spokesmen, adding to the chain of signification about the treaty. Attorney General Swainson held that the events at Wairau had occurred because the Company's settlers had sought to gain undisturbed possession of the land by exercising acts of ownership upon it in opposition to natives who denied having ever sold it to them. Both Swainson and Spain believed that the settlers' actions amounted to an attempt to overthrow the Crown's authority. Shortland saw the matter in much the same way, complaining to Stanley that the Company in Cook Strait had openly acted in defiance of the government from the outset.[69]

---

[68] *New Zealand Gazette and Wellington Spectator*, 21 June and 24 June 1843, 5 and 26 July 1843, 12 August and 2 September 1843; *Nelson Examiner and New Zealand Chronicle*, 1 July 1843; Petition to the Queen, undated [July 1843], 1844 Select Committee Report Appendices, pp. 261–62; David Munro and Alfred Domett to Shortland, 16 August 1843, 1844 Select Committee Report Appendices, pp. 706–10; *Nelson Examiner and New Zealand Chronicle*, 12 August and 23 December 1843.

[69] William Swainson to Shortland, 13 [*sic*] July 1843, 1844 Select Committee Report Appendices, pp. 166–67; Shortland to Stanley, 13 July 1843, 1844 Select Committee

Unsurprisingly, the colonial government sought to discipline the Company and its settlers. In July, shortly after learning of the affray at Wairau, Swainson, who can be regarded as Shortland's mentor in many matters, persuaded him to issue a proclamation which stated emphatically that it was essential for the well-being of the colony that good feeling and confidence should continue to exist between the two races and insisted that this situation depended on 'the native owners of the soil' having 'no reason to doubt the good faith of Her Majesty's solemn assurance that their territorial rights would be recognised and respected'. In the same proclamation Shortland warned all those claiming land in cases where their claim was 'denied or disputed by the original native owners' that until the matter of ownership had been heard and determined by one of the Land Claim Commissioners they should not exercise any acts of ownership on those lands or do anything that might otherwise 'prejudic[e] the question of title' to it.[70]

In August Shortland circulated a letter in which he drew attention to this proclamation and reminded settlers of what he called the principles upon which the British government had undertaken the colonisation of the country: 'the Queen, in common with her Majesty's predecessor, disclaimed for herself and her subjects every pretension to seize upon the islands of New Zealand. That by the Treaty of Waitangi her Majesty has guaranteed to the chiefs and tribes of New Zealand the full, exclusive, and undisturbed possession of their lands; and that [in] the royal instructions under the sign manual her Majesty has distinctly established the general principle that the territorial rights of the native as owners of the soil must be recognised and respected'. In September, Shortland repeated these sentiments, quoting long passages from Stanley's fiery letter to the Company's directors of January 1843 in which the Colonial Secretary had accused the Company's directors of demanding that the government despoil the rights of the natives. Shortland declared that he, too, had no intention of setting aside the *Treaty* of Waitangi and entering into an agreement to despoil the natives of their lawful rights.[71]

Report Appendices, p. 133; Spain to Shortland, 12 September 1843, 1844 Select Committee Report Appendices, p. 301; Shortland to Stanley, 20 October and 2 December 1843, 1844 Select Committee Report Appendices, pp. 259, 278–79.

[70] Swainson to Shortland, 13 [*sic*] July 1843, 1844 Select Committee Report Appendices, p. 167 (This memorandum is incorrectly dated 13 July 1843. Its content reveals that it was written *before* Shortland's proclamation of 12 July 1843); Proclamation, 12 July 1843, *New Zealand Government Gazette*; A. H. McLintock, *Crown Colony Government in New Zealand*, Government Printer, Wellington, 1958, p.144.

[71] Swainson to Shortland, 7 August 1843, 1844 Select Committee Report Appendices, p. 177; Shortland to Munro and Domett, 9 August 1843, 1844 Select Committee Report Appendices, pp. 705–06; Shortland to William Guyton et al., 19 September 1843, 1844

Up to this point, the treaty had barely figured in any public discourse in New Zealand. There had been hardly any references to it,[72] or at least its English text,[73] in the press and no senior government official had drawn attention to the words of the first clause of its second article. Shortland's doing so now marked something of a watershed. The *treaty* had become the *Treaty*. For the rest of the decade it would be referenced frequently in the colony.[74]

Yet, even as Shortland invoked the natives' rights in land, he expressed concern that any further delay in the settlement of land claims would be ruinous to both settlers and natives. Consequently, he instructed Spain to call upon William Wakefield to resume the negotiations to pay Māori compensation in order to extinguish their title. Wakefield agreed to do so, albeit reluctantly and largely because there was growing discontent among many settlers regarding his handling of the Company's claims. However, in a manner that was typical of the Company's leading personnel, Wakefield sought to alter the terms of this arrangement by demanding that native settlements, cultivations and burial grounds be included in the lands for which compensation would be paid, though he must have known this would scupper any hope of the Company's claims being settled. He even sought to apply pressure on Spain by invoking a recent memorial in which settlers had protested about the delay in the settling of the land claims, despite the fact that it had been addressed to him. Wakefield's actions outraged Spain. He promptly closed the negotiations and began to write a report about his investigations into the Company's titles.[75]

Select Committee Report Appendices, pp. 332–33; Shortland to Stanley, 2 December 1843, 1844 Select Committee Report Appendices, p. 259.

[72] Similarly, Shaunnagh Dorsett has argued that the Treaty was only 'directly invoked' before a court on one occasion in the period up to 1852, when New Zealand ceased to be a Crown colony (*Juridical Encounters: Māori and the Colonial Courts 1840–1852*, Auckland University Press, Auckland, 2017, p. 77).

[73] Chief Protector Clarke printed the Maori text of the Treaty in one of the first issues of the government's newspaper for the natives: *Te Karere Maori*, 1 February 1842.

[74] My argument rests on a search I conducted (in May 2017) of all the New Zealand newspapers digitised by *Papers Past*, using the terms 'treaty' and 'Treaty of Waitangi'. Newspapers yet to be digitised might have made reference to the Treaty – indeed we know for example that the *Bay of Islands Observer* did (on 10 March 1842) – but it seems unlikely that a survey of those newspapers would alter the finding noted here.

[75] Shortland to Stanley, 13 July 1843, 1844 Select Committee Report Appendices, p. 134; Spain to Wakefield, 5 August 1843, 1844 Select Committee Report Appendices, pp. 326–27; Wakefield to Spain, 24 August 1843, 1844 Select Committee Report Appendices, p. 327; Wakefield to Clarke, 24 August 1843, 1844 Select Committee Report Appendices, p. 329; Spain to Wakefield, 24 August 1843, 1844 Select Committee Report Appendices, p. 329; Wakefield to Spain, 25 August 1843, 1844 Select Committee Report Appendices, p. 329; Spain to Wakefield, 25 August 1843,

'This Difficult and Complicated Question'

In what became a very long memorandum, Spain addressed three principal matters: the Land Commission's jurisdiction in respect of the Company's claims; the nature of the Company's purchasing; and the negotiations in cases where he had ruled that the Company's purchases were flawed and native title had not been extinguished. The fact that Spain decided to return to the first of these matters reveals the extent to which senior members of the colonial administration felt it necessary to counter the Company's challenge to the Crown's authority. Spain began by quoting most of his report to Hobson of June the previous year in which he had adduced numerous pieces of evidence to support his opinion that the Commission *did* have authority to investigate the Company's claims. But he invoked the Treaty of Waitangi even more than he had done on that previous occasion. He claimed that he had partly reached his opinion about the Commission's authority on the grounds that it would have been 'in direct contravention of and in utter opposition to the spirit of the treaty' for the colonial government to have agreed to grant the Company land without requiring its agents to prove that they had purchased it properly and thus extinguished native title.[76]

In regard to the second matter, Spain provided a damning assessment of the Company's transactions with Māori in 1839. All of its purchases had been made in a very casual and careless manner. Its agents had inserted into deeds of purchase descriptions and names of topographical features that they had drawn from European maps rather than learning these from the owners of the land, and they had generally done this before any negotiations had taken place. The parcels of land encompassed millions of acres and in some instances contained areas measured by degrees of latitude and longitude. The Company's agents did all this without taking the trouble to inquire, either at the time of purchase or afterwards, whether the thousands of inhabitants who occupied these vast tracts of country had consented to the sale. Moreover, Spain went on, the translation of deeds into Māori was exceedingly imperfect and tended to convey only partially the extent of territory at stake, and the explanation

1844 Select Committee Report Appendices, p. 330; *New Zealand Gazette and Wellington Spectator*, 26 August 1843; Wakefield to John Ward, 12 September 1843, New Zealand Company, *Twelfth Report of the New Zealand Company*, Palmer and Clayton, London, 1844, Appendices, pp. 80E–81E; Wakefield to Ward, 18 September 1843, 1844 Select Committee Report Appendices, p. 723.

[76] Spain to Shortland, 12 September 1843, 1844 Select Committee Report Appendices, pp. 291–96.

that the interpreters had provided of the system of reserves the Company undertook to provide was unintelligible to the Māori vendors.[77]

In reference to the third matter, Spain provided an account of the ways in which Wakefield had failed to play his part in executing the agreement to provide compensation in cases where Spain had found the Company's title to be flawed. He provided this damning criticism of Wakefield: 'I think I have now made it quite apparent that the principal agent of the Company ... has pursued one undeviating system of opposition and annoyance, and that he has done everything in his power to retard and throw every impediment in the way of my proceedings'. Spain held that the Company was morally, if not legally, bound to execute the agreement into which Wakefield had entered and was concerned about what could happen if it failed to do so. He pointed out that he had warned Wakefield of the consequences of his neglecting his duty, namely that the dashing of the natives' expectations for compensation would rebound on the settlers. Indeed, he argued that the spilling of so much blood at Wairau proved the truth of this assertion. In fact, Spain had reached the view that Wakefield had never intended to pay compensation to the natives. Furthermore, given Wakefield's tendency to overlook his own moral and legal obligations in any case involving the just claims of the natives, the prosperity of a large and respectable body of settlers and the substantial interests of the Company, Spain had concluded that it would never be safe for the government to enter into further negotiations with him. Clearly, Spain, like Stephen, Hope and Stanley, had come to regard the Company's principal representatives as totally untrustworthy.[78]

Spain concluded his report by making some suggestions for settling what he called 'this difficult and complicated question'. He ruled out the option of the government seeking to negotiate new contracts with the natives to purchase the lands in question on the grounds that they would never consent to sell at a price that was fair and reasonable, and consequently the settlement would be ruined, at great cost to both native and European. He argued that it would be better to 'complete' the existing contracts in cases where the majority of the natives who had title to lands in question had acquiesced in the sales. Indeed, Spain suggested that the government should compel the minority of those natives who had equally good titles to those lands to accept the sales, upon which they would all receive compensation, which the government would fund but which the Company would be required to reimburse.[79]

There was nothing exceptional about the drift of Spain's recommendations. As we have seen, the Colonial Office's senior figures primarily

---

[77] *Ibid.*, p. 305.   [78] *Ibid.*, pp. 296–305.   [79] *Ibid.*, pp. 306–07.

approached the general matter in question in the very same terms, that is, by emphasising the importance of treating with the natives for land because this was the best way of realising the goal of peaceable possession. This meant, at this juncture at least, that the precise nature of native title tended to be regarded by Spain as unimportant.

On receiving Spain's report, Shortland decided to terminate the agreement he had entered into with Wakefield and tell Spain to await the arrival of the colony's new governor for further instructions. At the same time, in the course of relaying Spain's report to Stanley, Shortland took the opportunity to strengthen his political master's resolve. Claiming there was a rumour that the imperial government had changed course and adopted a policy that required the natives to dispose of their lands at a fixed price, he warned Stanley that the government should never depart from 'the solemn assurances' that the local government had given the natives in the Treaty that 'their territorial rights [would] not be invaded, nor their land taken without their free consent'.[80]

The Crown's Right of Pre-emption and the Treaty of Waitangi

We can now turn to the northern parts of the islands of New Zealand, and especially the settlement of Auckland, in the period immediately following the treaty signings but more especially in 1842–43. As in Cook Strait, the colonial government faced a considerable challenge to its authority from British parties who were similarly critical of its position in regard to possession of land and title to it. But the debate about native title that took place there differed from the one in the southern parts of the colony. Here, it focused on the question of whether the natives had the right to sell land to whomsoever they chose. Likewise, the Treaty also came into play here but different parts of it were invoked, namely the second clause of its second article and its third article, rather than the first clause of its second article. This reveals that there was not a common path by which the treaty returned to significance.

Following Hobson's arrival in northern New Zealand, many rangatira were eager to sell land to the Crown in order to attract British colonists to settle nearby so they could trade with them (which was one of the reasons many chiefs wanted to sell land at this time).[81] Moreover, as a result of the

---

[80] Shortland to Stanley, 21 October 1843, 1844 Select Committee Report Appendices, pp. 290–91.

[81] For discussion of why many Māori were eager to sell land, see Ann Parsonson, 'The Pursuit of Mana', in W. H. Oliver with B. R. Williams (eds.), *The Oxford History of New Zealand*, Clarendon Press/Oxford University Press, Oxford and Wellington, 1981, pp. 140–67, and Angela Ballara, 'The Pursuit of Mana? A Re-Evaluation of the Process of

treaty meetings at Waitangi and Hokianga, these rangatira *expected* the government to buy land from them, though it appears that most took the Crown's right of pre-emption to mean that the government merely had a right of first refusal. (A few days after signing the treaty at Waitangi, one rangatira offered to sell land to a settler, and upon being told that the agreement forbade this he apparently replied: 'What! do you think I won't do as I like with my own?') However, Hobson was slow to respond to the chiefs' offers to sell land. Consequently, many of them became disgruntled. By August Hobson had purchased some of the land on offer, but in the course of the next two years the colonial government purchased very little native land, largely because it lacked the funds to do so. Moreover, most of the purchases were confined to the Tamaki isthmus or what Hobson named as Auckland (after his patron), where he had decided to form the colony's capital.[82]

During the same period, many colonists in northern New Zealand found it difficult to acquire possession of or title to land. This problem had several causes, two of which are pertinent to this discussion. First, the Land Claims Commission was slow to deal with the large number of claims submitted to it in this area – there were more than 870 of these by March 1842 – in large part because of the complicated process that Gipps had put in place to assess them (as discussed earlier). Consequently, those known as 'the old settlers' had been unable to acquire title to the land they claimed to have purchased prior to the Crown's assumption of sovereignty. Second, the Crown's assumption of the right of pre-emption, combined with the fact that the government had hardly any funds to purchase land, meant that settlers more generally were unable to acquire land.[83]

The workings of the Land Claims Commission and the Crown's right of pre-emption provoked considerable disgruntlement among the settlers. In December 1841 they began to raise their voices in the capital's press, just as land claimants in Sydney had used the press earlier to

Land Alienation by Maoris, 1840–1890', *Journal of the Polynesian Society*, vol. 91, no. 4, 1982, pp. 519–41.

[82] William Colenso to CMS Secretaries, January-February 1840, William Colenso, Letters, vol. 1, ATL, qMS-0491; Hobson to Gipps, 5 May and 15 June 1840, NANZ, G36/1; William Symonds to Colonial Secretary, 12 May 1840, TNA, CO 209/7; Hobson to Gipps, 5 and 17 November 1840, NANZ, G36/1; Donald M. Loveridge, 'An Object of the First Importance': Land Rights, Land Claims and Colonisation in New Zealand, 1839–1852, Report for the Crown Law Office for the Treaty of Waitangi Tribunal, Wai 863, 2004, pp. 66, 69.

[83] Hobson, Speech to the Legislative Council of New Zealand, 14 December 1841, *BPP*, 1843, Paper no. 323, Copies or Extracts of Any Correspondence Relative to Emigration, p. 201; Edward Godfrey and Matthew Richmond to Shortland, 12 March 1842, TNA, CO 209/14; FitzRoy to Stanley, 15 April 1844, *BPP*, 1845, Paper no. 131, p. 23; Tonk, 'Land Commissions', pp. 81–92; Loveridge, Object, pp. 77–78, 84.

express their grievances. They focused mostly on legislation that Hobson introduced along the same lines as the New South Wales Land Claims Act (after New Zealand became a colony in its own right), called the Land Claims Ordinance. In so doing, they made the same fundamental argument as land claimants and their supporters in Sydney had done in 1840 (that is, that they had a legitimate claim to title as they had purchased land from Maori at a time when they were the only sovereign in New Zealand and hence the only source of title),[84] and so there is no need for us to discuss this protest.[85]

In the course of 1842, the Crown's assumption of the right of preemption came under attack in Auckland as part and parcel of a political campaign by a group of men who cast themselves as Radicals. They took their name from a group in Upper Canada who had become famous throughout the British Empire for their advocacy of responsible government, their opposition to what they saw as the tyranny of the imperial government and their call for a violent revolution to achieve their aims. In doing so, they suggested that they might also be goaded into rebellion. These Radicals included the merchants William Brown and John Logan Campbell, and land claimants such as Walter Brodie. Their principal spokesman was Samuel McDonald Martin, who, readers will recall, played a major role in the protest against Gipps' ruling that all titles to land that rested on purchase from the natives were null and void. Martin was a well-educated, independent-minded Scot who had probably been involved in the radical politics in Britain connected with the 1832 Reform Bill. He had migrated to New South Wales in 1837 and purchased land from Māori on the Coromandel Peninsula in New Zealand two years later. Like so many who championed the rights of settlers, Martin cast himself as a defender of the sovereignty and property rights of the natives. As he had done in Sydney, he used the press to attack the government's measures in regard to land, initially as the editor of *The New Zealand Herald and Auckland Gazette*.[86]

---

[84] It might be noted that a few of these claimants took cases to court that rested, at least in part, on an argument that they had a valid claim to title on the basis of a purchase from Māori. One such case was *Snowden v. Baker* (for which see *New Zealand's Lost Cases Project*, www.victoria.ac.nz/law/nzlostcases/CaseDetails.aspx?casenumber=00023, and Bruce Kercher, 'Informal Land Titles: *Snowden v Baker* (1844)', *Victoria University of Wellington Law Review*, vol. 41, no. 3, 2010, pp. 605–21).

[85] *New Zealand Herald and Auckland Gazette*, 6, 10 and 13 November 1841, 12 January 1842; Petition of Korareka Residents, 5 December 1841, TNA, CO 209/14; Resolutions of a Meeting at Korareka, 24 December 1841, reproduced in *New Zealand Herald and Auckland Gazette*, 19 January 1842.

[86] Russell Stone, 'Auckland Political Opposition in the Crown Colony Period, 1841–53', in Len Richardson and W. David Macintyre (eds.), *Provincial Perspectives: Essays in Honour of W.J. Gardner*, University of Canterbury, Christchurch, 1980, p. 20.

In mid-1842, after he had mounted assaults on the successive bills that Hobson had introduced to replace the New South Wales Land Claims Act, Martin penned a long letter to Stanley (which was published in New Zealand simultaneously as a pamphlet) that focused in good part on the Crown's right of pre-emption. Martin argued that it deprived the natives of the right of property and claimed this was an inherent right of all men as well as British subjects. More specifically, he argued that it was anomalous for the Crown to have treated with the natives for the cession of sovereignty only to deny their right to sell land to whomsoever they chose. In doing so, he made reference to the second clause of the treaty's second article as well as its third article.[87]

Martin was not alone in his attack on the Crown's right of pre-emption. Rangatira in the northern reaches of New Zealand increasingly criticised the government's handling of land matters. In February 1843 Henry Kemp, the protector of aborigines for the Northern District, and Edward Godfrey, one of the Land Claims Commissioners, reported that several chiefs had made passionate speeches in which they objected to the government assuming authority over their possessions, insisted that they would not sell any more land to the government and declared that they would exercise their ancient rights and authority as they had done previously. Kemp assumed that the chiefs' disaffection arose from the fact that the Crown's assumption of the right of pre-emption was depriving them of the considerable amount of money they had previously received from the sale of their lands, while Godfrey believed that the source of their grievance lay partly in the fact that they were unable to dispose of their lands to whoever they pleased and that they were not together persuaded that they had surrendered the exclusive right of purchase to the Crown by signing the treaty.[88]

In June 1843 Martin became the editor of the *Daily Southern Cross*, a newspaper that had recently been founded in Auckland by his Radical ally William Brown (after the government shareholders had closed *The New Zealand Herald and Auckland Gazette* the previous year), and renewed his attack on the Crown's right of pre-emption. The editorials he wrote in the course of the next several months are worth considering for several reasons, not least because many of them were devoted to a discussion of the Treaty in which the matter of native rights as well as sovereignty was raised.

---

[87] *The New Zealand Herald and Auckland Gazette*, 29 January 1841 and 2, 5, 12, 15 and 26 February 1842; Samuel Martin, *New Zealand in 1842; or the Effects of a Bad Government on a Good Country*, John Moore, Auckland, 1842, pp. 4, 7–8, 10–11,18,20.

[88] Henry Kemp to Clarke Snr, 10 February 1843, 1844 Select Committee Report Appendices, p. 125; Godfrey to Shortland, 16 February 1843, 1844 Select Committee Report Appendices, pp. 126–27.

As we have noted, Martin had previously argued that the Crown's claiming of the right of pre-emption in the second clause of the Treaty's second article and its undertaking to protect the rights of the natives as British subjects in the Treaty's third article were utterly incompatible. Now he also claimed that this was contrary to the English constitution and the spirit of English law. Indeed, he called upon the government to honour the treaty by conferring upon the natives *all* the rights and privileges of British subjects. Moreover, he upped the ante by making two further arguments: the British Crown held no title to New Zealand other than that founded upon the Treaty and Hobson had subverted the principles upon which the government had acquired sovereignty by claiming to be governor (rather than merely consul) from the outset and by hurriedly formulating the treaty without seeking to ascertain the views of the natives. As a result of the last of these considerations, argued Martin, those chiefs who signed the treaty did not understand its meaning. To press this point home, Martin provided his readers with an English translation of the Māori text of the treaty and argued that the native chiefs had never heard of the crucial Māori word that had been used to express the notion of governorship or sovereignty – kawanatanga – and so they could not have understood the treaty. This meant, he argued, that the signatories to the treaty had not in fact agreed to concede anything tangible to the British Crown, and certainly none of their rights and privileges.[89] Martin went on to say that this meant that New Zealand no more came under the dominion of the British Empire than when Cook first landed on its shores, and consequently no act of sovereignty exercised by the Crown in New Zealand had any legal warrant. Most importantly, Martin added, the Crown could have no title to any land it had purchased from the natives unless the agreements made with the natives had stipulated the cession of sovereignty over such lands, which he doubted had been the case. 'Our position in this country', he asserted, 'is precisely that of mere subjects to the native government'. This was revolutionary talk, and all the more so because Martin had previously claimed that Britain only held her settler colonies by a very frail tenure and that the government's treatment of land claimants in New Zealand made rebellion a possibility, just as had happened in Canada.[90]

Martin also argued that the imperial government had never grasped the fact that land was of such value to the New Zealanders that the ownership of every acre of land in the country was as well known and established as it was in England. Moreover, he contended that London had failed to

---

[89] Thus, Martin anticipated arguments that were made many decades later by political players as well as the historian Ruth Ross in her famous article 'Te Tiriti o Waitangi: Texts and Translations', *New Zealand Journal of History*, vol. 6, no. 2, 1972, pp. 129–57.

[90] *Daily Southern Cross*, 3 June, 10 June, 1 July, 19 August and 26 August 1843.

realise that the natives knew their rights and were determined to protect them to the last. He also pointed out that they had the capacity to do just that. Martin went on to argue that all these factors meant that the government's plans to colonise New Zealand by acquiring possession of a large amount of native land were doomed to fail. Finally, he insisted that the only solution to the problems he had raised lay in the Crown abandoning the right of pre-emption.[91]

Martin's strongly worded editorials had an impact on the colonial administration. In a despatch Shortland sent Stanley in October 1843, shortly before his term as the acting governor came to an end, he echoed the arguments that Martin had been making about the economic impact of the Crown's right of pre-emption on the colony and suggested that the imperial government adopt Martin's remedy, that of allowing settlers to purchase land directly from the natives. More importantly, it is evident that Martin's call for the government to give up the Crown's right of pre-emption influenced Robert FitzRoy, who was about to take up the post of governor.[92]

Conclusion

In this chapter we have seen how native title became an important matter in its own right and the Treaty of Waitangi regained significance, largely as a result of a highly contingent series of events. In the southern district of the colony the mechanism that the imperial government had adopted to deal with the fact that an enormous amount of land had been purchased from the natives prior to the Crown assuming sovereignty, namely the Land Claims Commission, unwittingly set in train a process that became a Pandora's box. In what amounted to a growing chain of signification that has previously gone unremarked by historians, several parties, in the context of a fierce dispute between the New Zealand Company on the one hand and the imperial and colonial governments on the other in regard to the November 1840 agreement between the Company and the Colonial Office, formulated interpretations of what was happening or should happen that made the treaty of Waitangi important again. For the most part, the point of reference in this dispute was no longer sovereignty, which was the matter that had primarily led the British government to make the treaty, but title to land.

In this growing resignification of the treaty we noted the following steps. First, Land Claims Commissioner Spain assumed that the imperial

---

[91] *Ibid.*, 10 and 17 June 1843.
[92] Shortland to Stanley, 30 October 1843, 1844 Select Committee Report Appendices, pp. 340–41; Loveridge, Object, pp. 143–45.

government did expect the colonial administration to investigate the New Zealand Company's titles, and he found authority for his performing this task in a novel interpretation of the treaty and especially the first clause of its second article. Second, William Wakefield, as the New Zealand Company's principal agent, attributed the Company's difficulties in acquiring possession of land to what he called the mischievous treaty because he misunderstood the treaty's provisions. Third, the Company's directors relayed to the Colonial Office the letter in which Wakefield had made this attack on the treaty and this led the Colonial Office's senior officials to embrace the clause in the treaty they had not previously noticed and to harness it to a language of rights. Fourth, the Company's directors responded by arguing that the definition of native title was critically important to resolving the conflict with the Colonial Office, and in doing so it cast further aspersions on the treaty. Fifth, the Colonial Office's principal figures reacted by making the unprecedented claims that the imperial government had authorised Hobson to treat with the native chiefs for a cession of sovereignty on the basis of the Crown's recognition of the natives' title to land and that the Crown's sovereignty rested on the treaty alone. Sixth, the Company's agents and supporters in Port Nicholson and Nelson attacked the treaty in the wake of the Wairau affray. Seventh, the colonial administration, concerned to uphold the Crown's authority, mimicked the Colonial Office's recent embrace of the treaty, which saw the treaty become a subject of public commentary in New Zealand, or at least in the settler community, for the first time since it had been signed.

In regard to both land titles and the Treaty, we have seen that it mattered a great deal who was the Colonial Secretary at any particular time. Had Russell still held this position at the point that it became clear that the work of the Land Claims Commission was frustrating the Company's attempt to claim possession and putting the colonisation of the country at risk, he would almost certainly have treated the matters the Company raised very differently to the way Stanley did.

Finally, we have observed that consideration of native title arose largely as a result of the Company's directors seeking a means to resolve the impasse that had arisen between the Company and the Colonial Office. Drawing once again on various legal resources, they sought to define the natives' rights of property in land in a way that would limit those rights to the land the natives were deemed to 'occupy and enjoy'. However, the Colonial Office's principal figures, while they almost certainly shared the Company's assumption about the nature of the natives' title, refused to accept this definition of their rights in land as a means of resolving the Company's claims. In part, this was because they were committed to a principle that land was best acquired by treating with the natives for it. This meant that they maintained that land matters should be dealt with in a practical way in the colony, rather than by proceeding in accordance with an abstract theory articulated in London. Just as importantly, the Colonial Office's senior officials were determined to assert the Office's authority over what it saw as a rogue company and discipline its leading figures, whose conduct outraged them and whom they loathed.

In the last part of this chapter we saw that the Treaty similarly returned to prominence in the northern part of New Zealand and more especially Auckland, but for a very different reason than it had in the colony's southern district. There, debate focused on different clauses or articles to the one that had become the subject of controversy in Cook Strait. Self-styled political Radicals and land claimants such as Martin were eager to argue that settlers had a right to acquire title to land on the basis of the purchases they had made with the natives prior to the Crown assuming sovereignty and that they should be able to continue to buy land directly from them. This led them to launch an assault upon the second clause of the Treaty's second article, by which the government claimed that the native chiefs had agreed to the Crown assuming the right of pre-emption and to argue that this clause contradicted the treaty's third article, by which the government bestowed on the natives all the rights and privileges of British subjects.

In the light of what we have seen in this chapter, it is now evident that the way British parties treated native rights in land in New Zealand owed a great deal to the political contestation between them. It has also become apparent that the precise significance the Treaty of Waitangi came to have at this time differed according to the particular circumstances of the colony's northern and southern districts. In fact, there would be no consensus about the treaty's significance for some time to come.

7   A Colony in Crisis and a Select Committee, 1843–1844

From December 1843 there was a growing sense in many quarters that New Zealand was in a state of crisis. On arriving there, the new governor, Robert FitzRoy, had found that the colony was in deep trouble. But, to make matters worse, he made a series of moves that would provoke a barrage of criticism from the New Zealand Company's agents and allies, while in both the northern and southern districts of the colony he found Māori and settlers challenging the Crown's authority. Many of the steps FitzRoy took aroused spirited public debate in New Zealand and London about native title, the Crown's right of pre-emption and native policy more generally.

Some of the most important decisions FitzRoy made during his brief governorship sprang from his belief that the natives had greater military power than the government could marshal. His distinctive take on this matter, and the fact there was actually no consensus among the British as to whether the natives were capable of besting the British Empire in battle, gives lie to a popular historical view that the British recognised the sovereignty and rights of the New Zealanders because of the natives' military might.

As events played themselves out in New Zealand, reports of the Wairau melee reached London. These caused a hardening in the position taken by the New Zealand Company and its allies. These critics of the Colonial Office claimed that the future of the colony was at stake and that major changes were required in the way that the government was treating key matters, most especially native title. Indeed, a major public battle took place when the Company secured a parliamentary select committee inquiry into its affairs and those of the colony.

In the political contestation that took place in London in 1844, the Company and its allies as well as the Colonial Office and its supporters attributed ever greater significance to the Treaty of Waitangi. It was increasingly believed that the treaty had been fundamental to each and every step the government had taken in respect of sovereignty and land, and that a ruling about its 'true meaning' in regard to native title was critical to the colony's future. These developments have been neglected by historians, resulting in accounts that fail to consider, let alone explain, how and why the Treaty became so significant.

In this political battle, philosophical ideas, moral principles and legal concepts were invoked by the major British players at both the colonial periphery and the metropolitan centre in order to lend support to positions that they had chosen to adopt in order to serve particular goals, whether they be securing title for the Company, protecting the interests of the natives, keeping the peace, preserving the honour of the British Crown or upholding the government's course of action.

Part I

Great Expectations

In London in April 1843, the appointment of Robert FitzRoy, a thirty-nine-year-old former naval captain and member of the House of Commons, as the new governor of New Zealand was greeted enthusiastically.[1] Expectations were high, especially in the New Zealand Company's circles. One of its organs even claimed that FitzRoy had been an original member of its predecessor, the New Zealand Association. Yet the Company's arch rival, the Church Missionary Society, was similarly delighted, having suggested several years earlier (when Hobson feel ill) that FitzRoy be appointed governor.[2]

The New Zealand Company would not have been at all sanguine if it had recalled FitzRoy's appearance before the House of Lords Select Committee on New Zealand in 1838. His testimony, which was largely a product of the brief time he had spent in northern New Zealand (as captain of the *Beagle* during its famous voyage), revealed that he had a position on the colonisation of the islands akin to that of the missionary societies and that he adhered to the view expressed by the House of Commons Select Committee on aborigines in 1837, namely that British

---

[1] FitzRoy has not been well served by biographers, at least as far as his years in New Zealand are concerned. The most perceptive remarks about his term as governor of New Zealand remain those made by A. H. McClintock in his *Crown Colony Government in New Zealand*, Government Printer, Wellington, 1958, chapters 7 and 8.

[2] Dandeson Coates to James Stephen, 27 July 1840, TNA, CO 209/8; *New Zealand Journal*, 29 April 1843; John Ward to William Wakefield, 18 May 1843, TNA, CO 208/166; Coates to Robert FitzRoy, 21 June 1843, CMS Records, CH/L4, AJCP, Reel M239; Ward to Wakefield, 17 August 1843, TNA, CO 208/166; Lord Joseph Somes to Lord Stanley, 9 December 1843, *BPP*, 1844, Paper no. 556, Report from the Select Committee on New Zealand, Together with Minutes of Evidence, Appendix, and Index (henceforth 1844 Select Committee Report Appendices), pp. 127–28.

colonisation should only proceed under the control of the imperial government, as settlers could not be entrusted with any authority over native peoples. Indeed, FitzRoy had recommended that the British government adopt a measure that would maintain the authority of the native chiefs in regard to their people and leave them masters of their own property. More specifically, he categorically stated that every acre in the islands was the property of one tribe or another and that there were no unappropriated lands, even though he believed that little of it was under cultivation. FitzRoy also remarked that purchases of land from the natives required the consent of all the members of a tribe or at least a greater part of a tribe. Both of these views were to play an important role at particular moments during his governorship.[3]

On reaching New Zealand in December 1843, FitzRoy was surprised to find the colony in a critical state. The colonial administration had made relatively few grants of land, in large part because the Land Claims Commissioners in the north had been overwhelmed by the sheer number of claims that had been submitted and the complex and time-consuming investigations that they were required to undertake; it had very little land at its disposal, because the Land Claims Commission had made few recommendations for grants; and it was unable to purchase land, because the parsimonious imperial government had denied it funds. FitzRoy realised that these problems were causing considerable tension between settlers and natives, at least in the colony's southern district. As he observed warily, the New Zealand Company's settlers were clamouring to be put into possession of the land that they believed the Company had purchased and were advocating the use of force to achieve this object, while the natives were refusing to give way.[4]

FitzRoy's hands were tied to a large degree. He was starved of the money needed to buy land and was deprived of the armed force he required to lend greater moral authority to his rule. On his appointment he had raised the latter problem with the Colonial Office, but Stanley had rejected his request to double Britain's armed forces in the colony (on the grounds of cost). By the time he reached New Zealand FitzRoy was even more convinced that he lacked the physical force required to restrain both natives and settlers and thereby prevent conflict. Consequently, he seems to have decided that he should rely on one of the few powers he felt sure he

---

[3] *BPP*, 1837–38, Paper no. 680, Report of the Select Committee of the House of Lords Appointed to Inquire into the Present State of New Zealand, pp. 165–66, 168, 171–72, 175, 178, 337, 339–42.

[4] FitzRoy to Stanley, 11 January 1844, *BPP*, 1845, Paper no. 131, Papers Relative to the Affairs of New Zealand, p. 3; Extract of a Despatch of FitzRoy to Stanley, 15 January 1844, *BPP*, 1845, Paper no. 131, p. 6; FitzRoy to Stanley, 15 April 1844, *BPP*, 1845, Paper no. 131, p. 12; FitzRoy to Stanley, 15 April 1844, *BPP*, 1845, Paper no. 131, pp. 18, 21, 23–25.

had at his disposal, namely the power of speech. But by placing so much store on this, FitzRoy was inclined to overreach.[5]

Shortly after he arrived, FitzRoy hastened to Cook Strait to deal with the aftermath of the Wairau melee. In both Wellington and Nelson, the Company's settlers had high expectations that this new governor would put the matter of land titles to right, provide them with protection against native attacks, hold a judicial inquiry into the Wairau affair and force the recalcitrant natives to submit to British law. But on his way to New Zealand, FitzRoy had received copies of the Company's newspapers from both sides of Cook Strait (courtesy of William Wakefield) that carried long reports about the Wairau melee, and these had convinced him that the Company's settlers held erroneous views about causes of the clash, that its agents had been carrying out the Company's operations in an injurious manner and that together they had brought the terrible outcome of the melee upon themselves. Moreover, these reports led FitzRoy to anticipate that the Company's settlers would be a source of enormous trouble and to conceive of his task principally in terms of remedying the consequences of their recent misconduct.[6]

At a levy held in his honour shortly after he arrived in Wellington in late January 1844, FitzRoy treated the Company's agents and settlers in a high-handed manner. He attacked them for the hostile feelings he believed they harboured towards the natives, expressed his belief that the government had to protect the natives from their aggression and declared that he would not allow an inch of land belonging to the natives to be touched without their consent. Not surprisingly, this clumsy, undiplomatic speech antagonised the settlers. Indeed, they felt betrayed. To make matters worse, two days later, after a deputation of settlers had presented FitzRoy with a lengthy memorial in which they had argued that the government had to assert its absolute supremacy in order to settle the question of land titles (rather than treat the natives as though they were a sovereign power with whom it must negotiate), he gave another illjudged speech. He declared that the Wairau melee had shown the necessity of restraining the spirit of aggression that British settlers had

---

[5] FitzRoy to Stanley, 16 May 1843, 1844 Select Committee Report Appendices, pp. 388–89; FitzRoy Somerset to Stephen, 23 June 1843, and minutes by Stephen, George Hope and Stanley, TNA, WO 1/431; FitzRoy to Stanley, 15 April 1844, *BPP*, 1845, Paper no. 131, p. 19; Robert FitzRoy, *Remarks on New Zealand in February 1846*, W. and H. White, London, 1846, pp. 17–20.

[6] FitzRoy to Sir Francis Beaufort, 1 December 1843, United Kingdom Hydrographic Office Archives, LP 1857, F 191; FitzRoy to Stanley, 9 December 1843, TNA, CO 209/24; FitzRoy to Phillip P. King, 9 December 1843, Phillip Parker King Correspondence, ML, MS A3599; Extract of a Despatch from FitzRoy to Stanley, 15 January 1844, *BPP*, 1845, Paper no. 131, p. 6; FitzRoy, *Remarks*, pp. 62–63.

exhibited; that it would be difficult to induce chiefs supported by thousands of armed warriors to submit to any laws that were administered unjustly; that the adoption of coercive and harsh steps by settlers could not be justified and would lead to the destruction of the colony; that the natives should not necessarily be considered as entirely subject to British law; and that it was a dangerous error to suppose that any injustice committed by settlers would be countenanced by the British Crown.[7]

The following week, FitzRoy visited Nelson, the nearest settlement to the Wairau Valley, and spoke in much the same terms as he had in Wellington, thereby arousing further resentment among the Company's settlers. Yet it was what FitzRoy said at a meeting that he held a few days later with a large number of Māori at Waikanae, which included Te Rangihaeata and Te Rauparaha, that most alienated the settlers. He stated that 'the *pakeha*' (that is, the Māori term for foreigners) had been wrong in all they had done at Wairau and that he could not attribute as much blame to the natives. He also announced that he would neither hold an inquiry into the melee nor avenge the deaths of those who had died at the hands of Te Rauparaha and Te Rangihaeata's party. The Colonial Secretary, Lord Stanley, would take much the same position, but it was FitzRoy's remarks that became notorious among the Company's settlers. In an editorial in the Company's newspaper in Wellington, Samuel Revans complained that the new governor was clearly favouring the natives at the expense of the settlers and criticised what he saw as his cowardice.[8] In fact, the Company's agents and allies would never forgive FitzRoy for his response to the killings at Wairau, and their resentment led them to maintain a more or less constant attack on him for the duration of his governorship.[9]

---

[7] Memorial to FitzRoy, 29 January 1844, New Zealand Company, *The Fourteenth Report of the Directors of the New Zealand Company*, Stewart and Murray, London, 1844, pp. 72–82; FitzRoy's Reply to Memorial, 29 January 1844, *New Zealand Gazette and Wellington Spectator*, 31 January 1844; Wakefield to Ward, 27 January 1844, New Zealand Company, *Fourteenth Report*, pp. 67–68; *New Zealand Gazette and Wellington Spectator*, 3 February 1844; Edward Jerningham Wakefield, *Adventure in New Zealand, from 1839 to 1844, with Some Account of the Beginning of the British Colonisation of the Islands*, vol. 2, John Murray, London, 1845, pp. 505–09.

[8] Some of the missionaries were also critical of FitzRoy's handling of the matter. For example, Richard Taylor argued that he should have acted in keeping with native custom, claiming the district as compensation for the blood that had been shed. Taylor claimed that this was what the chiefs themselves had expected, that this assertion of power would have made a salutary impression upon Māori and that as a consequence of FitzRoy's failure to do this Te Rauparaha formed a very low opinion of British power, declaring that 'The Governor is soft; he is a pumpkin' (*Te Ika a Maui, or New Zealand and its Inhabitants*, Wertheim and MacIntosh, London, 1855, p. 335).

[9] *Nelson Examiner and Wellington Spectator*, 10 February 1844; Minutes of Proceedings at Waikanae on 12 February 1844, *BPP*, 1845, Paper no. 131, pp. 30–33; Stanley to

For the moment, though, FitzRoy actually proceeded to tackle the problems with the Company's title in the Wellington district and in doing so he even won the grudging approval of the Company's settlers. After giving the impression that he would grant no land to the Company until it met Spain's requirement that the Company make further payments to the natives, he persuaded William Wakefield to resume the negotiations with the natives, provide the necessary funds and accept that native settlements and cultivations would be excluded from these transactions. He then placed enormous pressure on Ngāti Toa chiefs at Te Aro, Kumutoto, Pipitea and Tiakiwai pa to accept the compensation that Wakefield was offering, telling them that this arrangement did not constitute a new purchase but was the completion of the Company's original purchase. He also refused to increase the sum on offer. The chiefs eventually accepted his terms. FitzRoy then directed Spain and another government official to assist Wakefield in buying land in the neighbouring Hutt Valley, the Wairarapa, the South Island and elsewhere of up to 400,000 acres, and to waive the Crown's right of pre-emption in favour of the Company to enable much of this purchasing. Consequently, it appeared that all the Company's land claims would soon be settled, and very much to the Company's advantage. However, in the months that followed, FitzRoy seldom acted in such a resolute fashion. Furthermore, the concessions he made to the Company made no difference to the way its agents and allies represented his deeds in the Company's newspapers on both sides of Cook Strait.[10]

FitzRoy, 10 February 1844, 1844 Select Committee Report Appendices, pp. 172–73; Francis Dillion Bell, Notes of a Meeting between FitzRoy, Te Rauparaha and Te Rangihaeata at Waikanae on 12 February 1844, New Zealand Company, *Fourteenth Report*, pp. 94–101; *New Zealand Gazette and Wellington Spectator*, 17 February 1844; *New Zealand Gazette and Wellington Spectator*, 2 March 1844; FitzRoy to Stanley, 15 April 1844, *BPP*, 1845, Paper no. 131, p. 18; Wakefield, *Adventure*, pp. 514–26.

[10] Minutes of a Conference on 29 January 1844, *BPP*, 1846, Paper no. 203, Copies of Despatches to the Governor of New Zealand, pp. 18–20; Wakefield to Ward, 29 January 1844, New Zealand Company, *Fourteenth Report*, pp. 70–72; Wakefield to Ward, 19 February 1844, 1844 Select Committee Report Appendices, p. 417; Proceedings of Meeting, 23 February 1844, *BPP*, 1845, Paper no. 131, pp. 34–35; Thomas Forsaith to George Clarke Snr, 26 February 1844, NANZ, IA1/30/34; J. W. Hamilton to Wakefield, 27 February 1844, *BPP*, 1845, Paper no. 131, p. 36; FitzRoy to William Spain, 27 February 1844, and FitzRoy to John Jermyn Symonds, 27 February 1844, *BPP*, 1845, Paper no. 131, pp. 36–37; *New Zealand Gazette and Wellington Spectator*, 6 March 1844; FitzRoy to Stanley, 15 April 1844, *BPP*, 1845, Paper no. 131, pp. 21–22.

Waiving the Crown's Right of Pre-emption

FitzRoy's proceedings in the colony's northern district would prove to be just as momentous as those in its southern district. There, too, he adopted measures that in the eyes of many of his critics made too many concessions to the natives, thereby undermining British authority. Shortly after his arrival in Auckland in December 1843, FitzRoy met groups of settlers and natives who immediately called on him to waive the Crown's right of pre-emption, thereby allowing settlers to purchase land directly from Māori. At a public meeting he was presented with an address that the Radical Samuel McDonald Martin had prepared on behalf of the settlers, in which they sought to persuade him that the colony's woes could be attributed largely to the impolitic measures the British government had adopted, especially in regard to land and the natives. Of those measures, they emphasised two. First, the government had failed to settle the land claims of the 'old settlers'. Martin did not delve into particulars of the changes he thought were needed, but he did suggest that it would be unjust for the government to take possession of the lands that the Land Claims Commission deemed to be surplus, given that the natives laid claim to those lands. Second, Martin argued that the government had to concede to the natives their full rights as British subjects, and particularly their right to sell their land to whomsoever they pleased. Discontent and dissatisfaction had spread widely among the natives, in large part because they had come to entertain feelings of suspicion and distrust about the government's conduct, he informed FitzRoy. The government could only regain the moral influence it had once enjoyed, Martin concluded, by paying scrupulous regard to the natives' rights in land.[11]

On the same day, FitzRoy received an address by Ngāti Whātua and Waikato rangatira (who had probably been guided by the Chief Protector of Aborigines, George Clarke Snr) in which they expressed apprehension about the government's failure to fulfil the promises to purchase land that they believed Hobson had made during the Treaty meeting at Waitangi. They spelled out how they understood the clause of the Treaty by which they had yielded the right of pre-emption to the Crown: in the first instance they had to offer the government any land they wanted to sell, but in the event that it was unwilling to buy they had the right to sell to whoever they chose.[12]

[11] Address from the Inhabitants of Auckland to FitzRoy, 26 December 1843, *BPP*, 1845, Paper no. 247, Copies or Extracts of Despatches from the Governor of New Zealand, pp. 20–23.

[12] Māori Addresses, *Daily Southern Cross*, 30 December 1843; *Auckland Times*, 2 January 1844.

FitzRoy welcomed these addresses by enunciating views that were contrary to his instructions from the Colonial Office. He agreed that, once all the land claims had been investigated, the lands to which the government refused to grant to claimants (the so-called surplus lands) should revert to the natives; he announced that he hoped the Crown would no longer seek to purchase land from the natives for the purpose of selling it on to the settlers; and he asserted that he had been instructed to inquire into the workings of the pre-emption system and make changes to it if this proved necessary, claiming that it had been designed solely to protect the natives from unscrupulous Europeans.[13]

FitzRoy had probably arrived in the colony determined to implement changes of this kind. Before his departure from London, he had raised some of these matters with the Colonial Office, almost certainly as a result of representations that had been made to him by the Church Missionary Society and a representative of the Auckland Radicals. Moreover, he had been told by Stanley that he could largely use his discretion in handling these matters. Nevertheless, the representations that were made on his arrival in Auckland almost certainly emboldened FitzRoy to take the steps he took. So too did the fact that the colony's capital lay in an area in which the colonists were relatively few and defenceless and Māori were numerous and well-armed as well as the main providers of its food, a valuable source of labour and a major consumer of the goods sold by its European merchants.[14]

FitzRoy wasted little time in convening the colony's Legislative Council and announcing some of the measures he proposed to introduce. One of them concerned the Crown's right of pre-emption. This announcement created expectations among both Māori and settlers. As a result, by the first week of February they had started to traffic in land in earnest, Māori as keen to sell as settlers were to buy.[15]

[13] Reply by FitzRoy to the Address from the Inhabitants of Auckland, 30 December 1844, *BPP*, 1845, Paper no. 247, pp. 23–24; FitzRoy's Reply to Address, *Daily Southern Cross*, 6 January 1844.

[14] *Auckland Times*, 9 February 1843; Hope to Coates, 27 March 1843, in Dandeson Coates (comp.), *Memoranda and Information for the Use of the Deputation to Lord Stanley in Reference to the New Zealand Mission of the Church Missionary Society*, Church Missionary Society, London, 1843, p. 17; Coates, Introduction, in Coates (comp.), *Memoranda*, pp. 6–8; FitzRoy to Stanley, 16 May 1843, 1844 Select Committee Report Appendices, pp. 387–88; FitzRoy to Stanley, 15 June 1843, 1844 Select Committee Report Appendices, p. 93; Stanley to FitzRoy, 26 June 1843, 1844 Select Committee Report Appendices, pp. 389–90; *Daily Southern Cross*, 16 September and 30 December 1843; R. C. J. Stone, *From Tamaki-Makau-Rau to Auckland*, Auckland University Press, Auckland, 2001, p. 287.

[15] Minutes of the Legislative Council, 9 January 1844, *BPP*, 1845, Paper no. 247, p. 30; *Daily Southern Cross*, 13 January 1844; Thomas Bunbury to Stanley, 12 February 1844, TNA, CO 209/27; Edward Meurant, Diary and Letters, 5, 6, 8 and 26 February 1844,

At the same time, Martin stepped up his campaign in the *Daily Southern Cross* to persuade FitzRoy to abandon the Crown's right of pre-emption. In February he published a letter that had apparently been sent to the Governor by two Ngā Puhi rangatira in which they repeated most of the claims the Ngāti Whātua and Waikato rangatira had made two months earlier: Hobson had not intimated to the Māori rangatira at the treaty-signing at Waitangi that the Queen should have the exclusive right to purchase their lands; they had understood that the government was merely to have the first right of refusal; and they did not realise that the lands they had sold to British subjects who had settled amongst them would be seized by the government. As a result, they feared that the government would turn on them next, taking their lands and killing them. In March, Martin published an editorial in which he sought to persuade FitzRoy that the Crown's right of pre-emption was a matter that not only involved a question of right but also of might: 'they [the natives] possess the MIGHT – the physical force – the basis upon which every description of right must ultimately rest'.[16]

Shortly afterwards, FitzRoy announced that he would waive the Crown's right of pre-emption in certain parts of the country on strict conditions and allow individual European settlers to directly purchase land from the natives. Moreover, in explaining these new regulations to a group of rangatira he met at Government House, he cautioned them to exercise care in selling their lands and bargain for a good price. He also stated once again that the principal reason the British government had sought the right of pre-emption was to protect the natives from rapacious Europeans. This was nonsense. The government had primarily sought a monopoly over land sales so that it could control the market in land and purchase land cheaply from the natives so it had a source of revenue to fund colonisation. FitzRoy's remark suggested that he had lost sight of the reason for this provision or even that he had repudiated the objective it was meant to serve.[17]

In April FitzRoy belatedly sent Stanley a despatch – his first in three months – in which he endeavoured to explain why he had waived the Crown's right of pre-emption in favour of the New Zealand Company in the south and individual settlers in the north. It seems clear that he had

and Meurant to Clarke Snr, 4 March 1844, Sir George Grey Special Collections, APL, NZMS 235; Clarke Snr to Andrew Sinclair, 22 March 1844, NANZ, MA 4/58.

[16] Moshes Mahe and William Barton to FitzRoy, 5 February 1844, reproduced in *Daily Southern Cross*, 17 February 1844; *Daily Southern Cross*, 2 and 9 March 1844.

[17] Extract of Minutes of the Executive Council, 22 and 25 March 1844, *BPP*, 1845, Paper no. 131, pp. 45–46; FitzRoy, Proclamation, 26 March 1844, *BPP*, 1845, Paper no. 131, p. 48; Minutes of a Meeting of Native Chiefs, 26 March 1844, *BPP*, 1845, Paper no. 131, p. 43.

postponed the performance of this task because he knew he had acted without the Colonial Office's authority. FitzRoy justified these waivers in both these instances by arguing that he had little choice. In the case of the waiver in favour of the Company, he could not purchase any land because he had neither the funds nor the authority to draw on the imperial government's coffers; the local government's failure to put settlers in possession of land was causing animosity of the kind that had provoked the Wairau melee; and if this ill-feeling was not checked it would defeat all hopes of the British colonising New Zealand in a peaceful fashion and lead to a disastrous state of hostility between native and settler that would probably result in a war of extermination. In explaining the particular terms upon which he had given permission for the Company to purchase land, FitzRoy asserted that the natives laid claim to every acre of the country, that they refused to alienate the greater part of the lands that had been claimed by the Company and that in many places they were numerous and could not be easily removed. In the case of the waiver in favour of individual settlers, FitzRoy similarly emphasised the lack of government funds but also stressed what he regarded as the exorbitant prices the natives were asking for their lands. He claimed that powerful tribes had demanded that the government buy their lands, that they had expressed great discontent that the government refused to buy or allow them to sell to the highest bidder and that they had complained that the government had previously purchased land cheaply from them, only to sell it on to settlers at a higher price. FitzRoy informed Stanley that the chiefs maintained that they had merely agreed in the Treaty of Waitangi to allow the government to have the right of first refusal to their lands and that they insisted that they had never envisaged that they would be prevented from selling their lands to the settlers if the government refused to buy them. In the light of these considerations, FitzRoy told Stanley, he had chosen to make a decision rather than seek his advice, emphasising that had he done otherwise the character of the government would have been irretrievably damaged in the natives' estimation and its moral influence lost. Not surprisingly, FitzRoy also insisted that the imperial government needed to provide him with more money and more guns.[18]

A few days before FitzRoy sent this despatch to Stanley, he wrote to a close friend in Sydney, Phillip Parker King. This private letter sheds light on how he perceived the state of the colony as well as his own position as governor. FitzRoy claimed that he had found the colony in an extraordinary state of confusion and that he was 'crippled by the

---

[18] FitzRoy to Stanley, 15 April 1844, *BPP*, 1845, Paper no. 131, pp. 18, 21–25; FitzRoy, *Remarks*, pp. 21–23.

injunctions of the home government'. More surprisingly, he confessed that he had never had a more anxious time, such, he remarked, was 'the extreme difficulty' of his position. In fact, FitzRoy seems to have been close to despair. Just as remarkably, he was preoccupied with the notion that he would be recalled, only a few months after he began his term in office. Indeed, it almost seems that FitzRoy was inviting or even willing this to happen. He mused: 'I shall probably be recalled before long for doing too much, for acting without sufficient authority, or against my instructions, but this I must risk, in such a state are public affairs'. FitzRoy's own state of mind clearly played a role in all of these assessments. Indeed, his critics would soon ask, not without reason, whether the Governor was mad.[19]

Part II

London, the Company and Native Title

As FitzRoy was about to arrive in New Zealand, news of the Wairau melee reached London. As so often, the New Zealand Company's lines of communication proved superior to those of the Colonial Office and they received the news first. The Company's constant allies were swift to blame the melee on the government. For example, the *Spectator* argued that the 'massacre' could and should have been anticipated and was largely the result of a 'hostile set of officials, [jealous] missionaries ... and ... lawless squatters' turning the natives against the Company's settlers. For their part, the Company's directors called on the government to take steps to prevent another such calamity. Most importantly, though, they seized on Wairau as an opportunity to advance the Company's position on native title, believing as they did that the best means of securing a settlement of its land claims lay in persuading the government to accept its ideas about the nature of the natives' rights of property in land.[20]

The Company began this campaign in mid-December 1843 with an anonymous letter to *The Times* contending that the Wairau melee was mainly caused by several misconceptions about native title. The author of this letter argued that it was wrong-headed to claim that natives had rights in land on the basis of either ancestry or conquest, and asserted that the natives could only hold rights in the small amount of land they occupied

---

[19] FitzRoy to King, 12 April 1844, Papers of Phillip Parker King, ML, MSS 3447/1.
[20] Somes to Stanley, 1 and 2 December 1843, 1844 Select Committee Report Appendices, pp. 128–29; *Spectator*, 16 December 1843; *Morning Chronicle*, 18 and 26 December 1843.

and cultivated. 'All property whatever amongst men exists and originates in labour', he declared. 'On this principle the New Zealand savage has no title whatsoever to the possession of wild lands'. The author accused 'well-meaning missionaries' and 'Europeans of low station' of urging the natives to make extensive claims to land, but he placed most of the blame on Spain, claiming that this Land Claims Commissioner had proceeded as though the natives owned all the land. He concluded that the government should assume the right of ownership of all the waste lands of New Zealand. In the same issue of *The Times*, however, the newspaper's editor argued that the Wairau melee had raised a highly important question of 'the *original* right to the property of the soil', condemned the anonymous letter writer's argument as the morality of thieves and contended that the British must colonise in such a manner that they did not suffer 'the reproach of robbery or perfidy'.[21]

Two days later, the Company's directors passed a series of resolutions about the Wairau melee. In the most important of these, they expressed a conviction that the natives would only respect British authority if the government provided 'an exhibition of power' and that 'all irritating questions of relative rights should be promptly and conclusively settled on just, definite and comprehensive principles'. In January the Company pressed the matter of native title further in a long article in the *New Zealand Journal*. The anonymous author, *Civilis*, who was probably Edward Gibbon Wakefield, began by arguing that the question of the natives' rights of property in land had to be decided because it lay 'at the very root of the whole matter' in New Zealand. This was a specious claim but, as we will see, it was soon accepted by some of the most powerful figures in the British parliament. *Civilis* argued that the principal writers on the subject of property rights – Grotius, Pufendorf, Locke, Blackstone and Paley – all agreed that *occupation* or appropriation by labour was the only basis for the right to possess land in such a way as to have rights of property in it, that the natives only had rights on these grounds and that all the remaining lands should be regarded as unappropriated or waste. *Civilis* attacked the imperial government for failing to act on the basis of this principle and allowing the natives to claim that they had rights in all the land, and called on it to settle the question on this basis.[22]

At the same time as this article was published, the Company's chairman, Lord Joseph Somes, sent a letter to Stanley, urging him to settle its land claims. Then, a month later, at a long meeting with Stanley and his

[21] *The Times*, 19 December 1843, my emphasis.
[22] NZC Court of Directors, Minutes of Meetings, 21 December 1843, TNA, 208/182; *New Zealand Journal*, 20 January 1844.

deputy at the Colonial Office, George Hope, a delegation of the Company's directors found it necessary to call on Stanley to make a public statement clarifying the status of the Company's claims to land and the measures that the Colonial Office would adopt for the protection of life and property in the colony. The Company was in considerable trouble; in fact, it was close to insolvency. Its financial position had been deteriorating throughout 1843, but news of the Wairau melee had severely depressed its land sales and undermined its ability to raise capital. It had to ask the government to bail it out. Stanley told the delegation that the Company had brought these problems on itself but nevertheless agreed to make public the May 1843 agreement between the Colonial Office and the Company as well as the instructions it had subsequently given FitzRoy and to consult his colleagues about providing the Company with some financial help.[23]

In late February, Somes sought to apply more pressure, sending Stanley a very long letter that was clearly designed for public consumption. In it Somes claimed that nothing but prompt and effective action by the government could prevent the Company having to suspend its operations. He also argued that the impending crisis the Company faced was principally the responsibility of the government and its officers in the colonies. Indeed, Somes claimed that all the Company's difficulties originated mainly in the fact that it had sold land in the belief that the agreement it had struck with Stanley's predecessor, Lord John Russell, in November 1840 had given it a full and unconditional grant of land, only for Stanley to interpret that agreement in such a way as to render the Company's title to land so precarious that it had had to cease all its land sales. Somes also complained that Spain's work as Land Claims Commissioner had destroyed all confidence in the Company's title and had prevented it securing a Crown grant to a single acre of land and that other colonial officials had forced its settlers to abandon any land to which the natives asserted a claim. He also argued that the treatment of the Company's land claims was the direct cause of the Wairau melee as it had led to bad blood between the natives and settlers. Somes proposed several solutions to address the Company's problems, but he clearly favoured one in which the government would lend it £100,000

---

[23] Somes to Stanley, 18 January 1844, 1844 Select Committee Report Appendices, p. 160; Hope to Somes, 1 February 1844, 1844 Select Committee Report Appendices, p. 161; William Hutt, Minutes of Deputation to Colonial Office, 17 February 1844, TNA, CO 208/182; Patricia Burns, *Fatal Success: A History of the New Zealand Company*, Heinemann Reed, Auckland, 1989, p. 252.

and appoint a special commissioner to ensure that the government and the Company would act as though they were one.[24]

The Colonial Office seemed willing to consider these proposals and a flurry of meetings took place in March between the Office, the Company and the Chancellor of the Exchequer. However, negotiations between the Company and the Colonial Office soon broke down with each party accusing the other of acting in bad faith. In early April the Company's directors decided to suspend the Company's operations and appeal to parliament to intervene. A few weeks later, on 26 April, shortly before midnight and the House of Commons rising for the evening, one of the Company's directors, a Whig MP Henry Aglionby, persuaded the House to approve a motion for a select committee to inquire into the state of the colony and the proceedings of the Company. There can be no mistaking the Company's purpose. The following day, Edward Gibbon Wakefield wrote excitedly to his sister: 'We declared war to the knife with the Colonial Office'. In the House three days later, at 1 in the morning, Aglionby announced the names of those who had agreed to serve on the select committee, most of whom were sympathetic to the Company. Stanley objected but Aglionby had outmanoeuvred him by preparing a list of names that included MPs who belonged to the government's side of the House. The best Stanley could do was persuade the House to add one of the government's senior ministers, Edward Cardwell.[25]

The 1844 Select Committee Inquiry

As soon as this committee began its hearings in mid-May, Aglionby moved to make the Company's case. Indeed, the Company's directors took the opportunity to present a recently published report in which they repeated their charge that the Company's general plan of colonisation and the whole course of its operations had been undermined by Stanley

---

[24] Somes to Stanley, 29 February 1844, 1844 Select Committee Report Appendices, pp. 233–39.

[25] Hope to Somes, 27 March 1844, 1844 Select Committee Report Appendices, p. 243; Somes to Stanley, 2 April 1844, 1844 Select Committee Report Appendices, pp. 243–47; Hope to Somes, 4 April 1844, 1844 Select Committee Report Appendices, pp. 248–29; Somes to Stanley, 18 April 1844, 1844 Select Committee Report Appendices, pp. 249–51; New Zealand Company, *Twelfth Report of the Directors of the New Zealand Company*, Palmer and Clayton, London, 1844, pp. 6, 34–35; *The Times*, 27 April 1844; Extract of Edward Gibbon Wakefield to Catherine Torlesse, 27 April 1844, Copies of Letters from Edward Gibbon Wakefield, BL, Add MS 35261; *BPD*, House of Commons, 30 April 1844, columns 516–17; *The Times*, 1 May 1844; *BPP*, 1844, Paper no. 556, Report of the 1844 Select Committee on New Zealand (henceforth 1844 Select Committee Report), p. ii; Stanley to Sir Robert Peel, 17 December 1844, 14th Earl of Derby Papers, Liverpool Record Office, 920 Der 14, 129/4/29.

setting aside the November 1840 agreement and the colonial administration insisting that the government's grant of land to the Company rested upon the outcome of the Land Claims Commission's investigations into its titles. In the press, the Company renewed its attack on the Colonial Office and more especially James Stephen.[26]

Once the Committee began its hearings, however, it became apparent that the Company was not going to get its own way, at least for the moment. Thomas McDonnell, who had once held an official position in New Zealand, damned the Wakefield system of systematic colonisation, attributed the colony's woes to the faulty manner in which the Company's principal agent in New Zealand, William Wakefield, had purchased land from the natives and claimed that it would be dangerous for the government to lay claim to waste lands without a proper inquiry into native title. At the Committee's next hearings, one of the Auckland Radicals, Walter Brodie, who had recently returned to England, gave evidence, mostly in response to questioning by Hope. He stated that the natives had settled notions of rights of property in land, asserted that every inch of the country was claimed by them, suggested that the government could not acquire any land without their consent, argued that the Crown had agreed in the Treaty of Waitangi that it would take none of their land except by means of purchase and rejected a suggestion by the Committee's chairman, Lord Howick, that the government could have laid claim to the 'waste lands' at the point it had made the Treaty, arguing that the chiefs would have refused to acquiesce.[27]

The Company's directors hastened to bring forward witnesses sympathetic to its case. They also decided to form a special political committee charged with the responsibility of preparing a statement for the Committee. However, the Colonial Office was able to persuade several more critics of the Company to appear. The most important was Theophilus Heale, who had gone to New Zealand as one of the Company's surveyors only to pen a small book in which he had challenged the Company's attempt to persuade the British public that its interests and the colony's were one and the same. Heale presented a raft of criticisms of the Company's conduct, and in responding to questions put to him by Hope he asserted that the natives' notions of tradition gave them as perfect a title to possession as any title deeds. He also claimed that the natives understood the government to have pledged itself in the Treaty of Waitangi to take their lands only with their consent and suggested that the

---

[26] 1844 Select Committee Report, p. xv; 1844 Select Committee Report Appendices, pp. 501–744; *New Zealand Journal*, 8 June 1844; 'Reform in the Colonial Office', *Fisher's Colonial Magazine*, n.s., vol. 1, no. 6, 1844, pp. 295–301.

[27] 1844 Select Committee Report, pp. 5, 9, 11, 17, 26–27, 42, 44–45.

government had to maintain the Treaty in order to retain their confidence. Finally, Heale declared that there were no waste lands in New Zealand.[28]

A month after the Committee had commenced its hearings, the Colonial Office presented a memorandum rebutting the numerous claims that the Company had made in its recent report. If there had been any chance that the Colonial Office's resolve in regard to the Company's claims might have weakened, the Company's recent attack on Stephen had put paid to this as it had angered Stanley. This memorandum began by repeating the argument that the Colonial Office had made in its correspondence with the Company in the winter of 1842–43. In other words, it argued that Russell, as Colonial Secretary, had proceeded on the assumption that the Company had in fact acquired rights in the land by virtue of its purchases and that in accordance with the rule laid down by Normanby in August 1839 that no proprietary rights of Europeans would be recognised unless confirmed by a grant from the Crown Russell had undertaken only to confirm title to those lands which the Company was found to have purchased in a proper fashion from the natives. Once again, the Colonial Office also upped the ante by playing the rights card. It argued that the proprietary rights of the natives were recognised and guaranteed by Normanby's instructions to Hobson and the Treaty of Waitangi, and that this meant that if Russell had intended to transfer those rights to the Company he must have contemplated doing so either by forcibly dispossessing the natives or by purchasing their rights in order to convey them to the Company. The memorandum went on to say that it appeared that the Company expected the former course to be followed. Furthermore, the Colonial Office threw back in the Company's face its directors' claim that the Treaty 'could not be treated by lawyers as anything but a praiseworthy device for amusing and pacifying savages for the moment' and argued that this approach would have meant that the agreement between the Crown and the Company amounted to a contract between two parties in England to 'despoil' the natives for the benefit of one of themselves.[29]

The Colonial Office also decided to bolster its position by presenting a comprehensive interpretation of the November 1840 agreement, which it had previously been reluctant to do. It likewise took the opportunity to

[28] NZC, Minutes of the Special Political Committee, 19, 21 and 24 June 1844, TNA, CO 208/188; 1844 Select Committee Report Appendices, pp. 380–86.

[29] Stanley to Stephen, 6 June 1844, Sir James Stephen Papers, University of Cambridge Library, Additional MS 7888, II/84; Colonial Office, Memorandum on the Twelfth Report of the Directors of the NZC, undated [c. 25 June 1844], 1844 Select Committee Report Appendices, p. 1.

use some correspondence that had been published in the Company's recent report to argue that the Company had once tacitly admitted that its claim to title *did* rest on its purchases from the natives. The Colonial Office suggested that the Company's directors had only changed their tune and begun to demand that the government extinguish native title after they realised that the Company would be unable to prove that its purchases were valid. It also contended that the problem the Company faced was the natural result of it having foolishly sold land before ascertaining whether it had acquired good title to it.[30]

The Colonial Office went on to rebut charges that the Company had levelled against it in its recently published report. First, in response to the Company's claim that the melee at Wairau was the consequence of the conduct of the Land Claims Commission, it suggested that the tragedy should be attributed to the indiscretion of the Company's agents in attempting to forcibly take land from the natives for which the title was in dispute, rather than waiting for Spain to investigate the justice of the Company's claim. Second, it suggested that the Company's position on the Commission's work amounted to it either denying the natives the opportunity to advocate their rights or assuming that the natives had no rights in property to advocate and argued that both merited the epithet 'shameful'. Third, it sought to counter the claim that it was hostile to the Company by pointing out the concessions it had made. Finally, it argued that the delay in settling the Company's titles was a result of William Wakefield's conduct, not Spain's.[31]

The Colonial Office concluded by arguing that, while the Company's purpose in calling the Select Committee was clearly to persuade parliament that the policy the government had adopted in regard to land title in New Zealand should be reversed, this outcome could only be realised by taking measures to forcibly dispossess the natives of their lands or by providing the colonial government with the money to acquire those lands by purchase. It suggested that the former could not be entertained for a moment and that the latter should be adopted at once if it was to be adopted at all.[32]

The tabling of this memorandum prompted the Company's directors to prepare a rebuttal, much of which was devoted to countering the Colonial Office's interpretation of the November 1840 agreement. More importantly, they asked Russell to provide a statement regarding his intentions at the time that agreement was made. Russell agreed to do so. In a letter to the Company's directors he lent enormous support to the Company's case by arguing that the foundation of the November 1840

[30] *Ibid.*, pp. 2–3. [31] *Ibid.* [32] *Ibid.*, p. 3.

agreement was the expenditure the Company had made, rather than the land it had claimed to have purchased, though he also asserted that he had understood that the Company had made large purchases of land and that he had assumed those contracts would readily enable the government to satisfy the commitments it had made in the agreement, thereby putting the Company in possession of a considerable amount of land. Russell then asked what his interpretation of the agreement would have been in the situation that had since arisen, namely that the Company's claims to land had been discovered to be unfounded. Would he have ruled that this circumstance released the Crown from its promise to the Company or that a grant of land be delayed until the Company had established its title before the Land Claims Commission? (Russell claimed that he and his colleagues had never anticipated this situation even though he had been made aware of it by Hobson, as we have seen.) In answering these questions, Russell stated that he believed that the extent of land the Crown had at its disposal was undoubtedly more than enough to satisfy the Colonial Office's undertakings to the Company because he did not suppose that the natives could establish any claim to the millions of acres of land that they neither occupied nor cultivated. By recasting the matter at stake between the Company and the Colonial Office in this way, Russell altered the terms of the dispute, shifting it away from the question of whether the government had been released from its commitments to the Company as a result of the Company's purchases being found to be flawed, or the question of whether the Company could be required to prove its claims to land before the Land Claims Commission, onto the question of how native title should be defined. In other words, Russell did exactly what the Company's directors had been trying to do for some time. Not surprisingly, they wasted no time in submitting his letter to the Select Committee's chairman, Lord Howick.[33]

The Select Committee's Resolutions

Howick had a long-established interest in colonial affairs. In the early 1830s he had served as the parliamentary Under-Secretary for the Colonies and been allowed to assume a good deal of responsibility by the easy-going Colonial Secretary, Lord Goderich. He had revised imperial land policy, partly under the influence of Edward Gibbon Wakefield's

---

[33] NZC, Memorandum, undated [c. 26 June 1844], 1844 Select Committee Report Appendices, pp. 370–78; Somes to Lord John Russell, 26 [sic, 28] June 1844, 1844 Select Committee Report Appendices, p. 411; Russell to Somes, 29 June 1844, and Somes to Viscount Howick, 4 July 1844, 1844 Select Committee Report Appendices, p. 412.

ideas about systematic colonisation. In the mid- to late 1830s he had continued to be involved in governmental deliberations about colonial matters, even though he was Secretary for War. For example, he had played an important role in persuading Glenelg to offer a charter to the New Zealand Company's predecessor. Now, as chairman of this select committee, he would play a crucial role in forging a position on the natives' rights of property in land on the basis of an unfounded assumption that the way the government had been defining those rights was the main cause of the Company's and the colony's problems.

Howick played a minor role in the Committee's hearings, but at their conclusion he moved swiftly to draft a series of resolutions. The first condemned the Company for sending out settlers in 1839 in defiance of the government, but all the remaining resolutions advanced propositions that supported the Company and its case. Before we discuss those resolutions, though, we need to consider another set of resolutions that were first presented to the Committee by Stanley's appointee, much to Howick's surprise.[34]

Cardwell proposed many of his resolutions in order to defend the position that the Colonial Office had adopted before or after the Crown had assumed sovereignty in New Zealand. His first resolution claimed that, subsequent to Cook's claim of possession, the Crown had never questioned that New Zealand was independent and had actually recognised this fact in 1832. Cardwell was undoubtedly referring to King William IV's response to the letter some northern chiefs had addressed to him (which was discussed in Chapter 4). In other resolutions, Cardwell made a series of claims about the Treaty of Waitangi. One asserted that the Treaty had been approved by the imperial government; a second argued in part that it was morally binding on the government; and a third alleged that the government had made its November 1840 agreement with the Company in conformity with the Treaty and that the agreement rested on an assumption that the Company had treated the natives as the owners of the land and had acquired good title through purchasing from them. The latter two claims were tendentious inasmuch as they ascribed to the Treaty a significance that the imperial government did not attribute to it at the time it was made. Cardwell also devoted a series of resolutions to the question of native title. In one of them he argued that while the natives' customs in regard to possession and title were undoubtedly complicated, the testimony presented to the

---

[34] Lord Howick, Journal, 8 July 1844, Papers of Henry George, 3rd Earl Grey, University of Durham Library Special Collections, Gre/V/C3/10 (henceforth Howick Journal); 1844 Select Committee Report, p. xvi.

Committee revealed that the natives did have recognisable laws in regard to land. In a second resolution he suggested that it was highly probable that much of the land in New Zealand would ultimately be vested in the Crown since it would be found that no title could be established by the natives, but that what he called a fair construction of the Treaty meant that it was impossible to limit the natives' claims to the land they occupied or cultivated at any particular time. In a third resolution, he contended that it would be unwise to proceed on any other basis than that construction of the Treaty since any attempt to put into practice an interpretation like the Company's would alienate the natives and probably lead to conflict or even a war of extermination between the races, for which British military power in the islands was completely inadequate.[35]

Cardwell also put forward a series of resolutions in which he noted that the Company had originally submitted its claims to the Land Claims Commission and had only later claimed that it had received an absolute grant of land from the Crown. He proposed further resolutions to the effect that the government had actually done what it could to put the Company in possession of land, argued that the Commission was making reasonable progress in its work and pointed out that FitzRoy had been instructed to take measures to hasten its proceedings. In the last of his resolutions Cardwell recommended that the Committee should sanction what had really been the kernel of the Colonial Office's approach to New Zealand, that of granting the colonial government considerable powers to deal with matters on the spot while it largely confined its role to the formulation of general principles.[36]

The Committee discussed Cardwell's resolutions at great length. According to Edward Gibbon Wakefield, who was following its proceedings very closely, there was a 'desperate fight' between the members of the Committee who were supporting the Company and those who were backing the government. Indeed, the Committee only agreed by a bare majority (7–6) to approve Howick's rather than Cardwell's resolutions.[37]

Howick's resolutions, like Cardwell's, were largely concerned with the Treaty. For example, in one of them he cast the treaty-making as an 'injudicious proceeding', which the majority of the Committee's members voted to sharpen by approving an amendment that claimed that the Treaty of Waitangi was part of a series of 'unwise proceedings' by the government that had begun several years prior to the signing of the Treaty.[38]

---

[35] *Ibid.*, pp. xvii–xviii.   [36] *Ibid.*, pp. xviii–xix.

[37] *Ibid.*, p. xix; Edward Gibbon Wakefield to Charles Torlesse, 9 July 1844, Letters from Other Members of the Wakefield Family, ATL, MS-Papers-9512-41.

[38] 1844 Select Committee Report, p. xvi.

Howick's third resolution turned to the matter of native title. He argued that the colonial administration's putative acknowledgement of a right of property on the part of the natives of New Zealand in all the waste lands after sovereignty had been assumed by the British Crown was contrary to all sound principles of colonial policy, that it was an error that produced some 'very injurious consequences' and that from the outset title to waste lands ought to have been vested in the Crown, thereby confining the natives' title to land they 'occupied and enjoyed'. This was the same argument the Company's directors had been making for some time. Not surprisingly, Hope moved an amendment to this resolution. He proposed that the matter of native rights in the waste lands was a question that should be determined with reference to not merely the principles of colonial policy (as Howick argued) but also the terms of the Treaty of Waitangi under which the Crown had assumed sovereignty and by which the natives were guaranteed the possession of their lands (quoting the first article of the Treaty's second clause). He also argued that, in keeping with good faith, the extent of native ownership that the natives believed the Treaty had secured for them had to be defined by inquiry on the spot or limited by an equitable settlement that was made with their agreement. Hope's proposal was narrowly defeated. The majority of the Committee agreed to amend Howick's resolution by removing his reference to the principles of colonial policy as well as his definition of native title, but they opted to assert that the local authority's so-called acknowledgement of the natives' right of property in all the wild lands after the Crown's assumption of sovereignty was 'not essential to the true construction of the Treaty of Waitangi, and was an error which has been productive of very injurious proceedings'.[39]

In attributing the colonial government's treatment of native rights in land to the way it had interpreted the Treaty, the members of the Committee bestowed on it an importance the Treaty had not had in 1840 and for some time after that. As we have seen, the way the nature of native title had come to be conceived arose haphazardly among a number of parties at the colonial peripheries and the metropolitan centre, and was the result of myriad processes, most of them deeply political in nature.

In a further resolution, Howick sought to uphold the Company's interpretation of the November 1840 agreement by proposing that it had been right to expect the government to put it in possession of the number of acres to which it had been found to have an entitlement on the basis of its expenditure and that it had this right against the Crown

---

[39] *Ibid.*, pp. xvi, xx.

without any reference to the validity or otherwise of its purchases from the natives. Hope also proposed amendments to this resolution. The most important of these would have stripped the reference to the Company having any rights. These amendments were narrowly defeated, but Hope was able to win the agreement of a bare majority to endorse a part of a subsequent resolution that stipulated that the Company could not claim any land that was not vested in the Crown. In the next resolution, Howick proposed a measure that would limit the natives' title to the lands they 'occupied and enjoyed' and thereby establish the exclusive title of the Crown to the 'waste lands'. Hope proposed an amendment to this resolution that would have gutted it, by replacing the words 'lands not actually occupied and enjoyed by natives' with the vaguer term 'waste lands', but this was narrowly defeated. Hope proposed a similar amendment to another of Howick's resolutions, but this was also lost. The Committee then proceeded to consider a series of less important resolutions proposed by Howick, though one of these called for the prohibition of any purchasing of land from natives by private persons, which is to say that it called for the Crown's right of pre-emption to be strictly enforced.[40]

Once the Committee had concluded its consideration of these resolutions, Howick began to draft a report which proved to be just as important as the resolutions. This report was highly personal in two senses. Its author regarded it as *his* report and it was very partisan. Even so, Howick's report was not original in any respect. Most of the arguments he mounted closely resembled those advanced by a Company spokesman in two articles that appeared in the *New Zealand Journal* at this time, which in turn reproduced the arguments that Wakefield or Buller had made in Somes' name during the Company's battle with the Colonial Office in the winter of 1842–43.[41]

Howick and Hope's Reports

In his report Howick created a historical narrative that mixed fact and fiction to account for the problems that the Colonial Office and the New Zealand Company had encountered in New Zealand. He began by asserting that these difficulties could be attributed principally to the fact that a set of principles by which colonisation of the country ought to have been

[40] *Ibid.*, pp. xvi, xxii–xxv.
[41] Howick, Journal, 4, 9, 10, 12, 13, 14, 15, 16, 17 and 23 July 1844; 'The Treaty of Waitangi Shown to be a Nullity from Authentic Documents', *New Zealand Journal*, 6 July 1844; 'Further Considerations on the Treaty of Waitangi', *New Zealand Journal*, 20 July 1844; Mark Hickford, *Lords of the Land: Indigenous Property Rights and the Jurisprudence of Empire*, Oxford University Press, Oxford, 2011, pp. 168, 176.

conducted had not been followed. Howick argued that these principles were the very ones that Sir George Gipps had set down in introducing his Land Claims Bill in New South Wales in 1840 (as we saw in Chapter 5): savage peoples had only a right in land they 'occupied' and they could not grant any land to anyone; the right of purchasing land or extinguishing native title belonged to the government of a colonising power; and nobody could form colonies except with the consent of their own government and under its control and direction. Observing that all these principles had been subverted by British subjects in New Zealand many years ago, and that they had been flagrantly infringed by the New Zealand Company, Howick argued that the British government of the day (of which he was a member) should have adopted more decisive measures in order to prevent the Company's original expedition sailing to New Zealand.[42]

Yet the main errors of the government, Howick proceeded to argue, just as the Company had long done, could be traced to the fact that it had chosen to disclaim British sovereignty and recognise New Zealand's independence, rather than establishing its authority at a point in the early 1830s or even the mid-1820s, and that once it belatedly decided to do this it had taken a wrong step in negotiating a treaty by which it promised to guarantee the natives in the possession of all the lands they held in return for the native chiefs' acknowledgement of British sovereignty. Howick argued that it would have been better if the British government had made no treaty whatsoever, repeated the Company's claim that the Treaty was no more than a legal fiction and asserted that it had caused very serious problems. In fact, Howick's argument resembled the argument Stanley and Hope had adopted the previous year in the sense that it too assigned to the Treaty a significance that it did not have at the time it was made. In 1840 the British government had not construed the first clause of its second article as a guarantee of the natives' rights to all the land in New Zealand. Howick went on to argue that the British government, rather than negotiating a treaty, could have assumed sovereignty over the North Island on the ground of prior discovery, just as he claimed that it had pursued this course in the southern islands and that as a consequence the Treaty of Waitangi did not extend even nominally to those islands.[43]

Howick suggested that the British government's error in negotiating a treaty had been compounded by the way it had come to define native rights of property. Indeed, this was the main argument he advanced in his report. As he remarked at one point: 'Your committee have found it

---

[42] 1844 Select Committee Report, pp. iii–iv.   [43] *Ibid.*, pp. iv–v.

necessary to enter more at length than we could have wished into the question, whether the ownership of unoccupied land ought to have been considered as vested in the Crown or in the native tribes, because, in our opinion, *all* the difficulties which have been experienced in the colonisation of New Zealand are mainly to be attributed to the erroneous view of this question which has been taken by those to whose hands the powers of government have in these islands been committed'. Throughout his report, Howick attached most of the blame for this error to the colonial administration, but at this point he argued that this mistake had originated in the Colonial Office's instructions to Hobson because they were insufficiently precise about the rights of property in land the natives could be said to have. More specifically, Howick argued that the instructions had failed to set down that all unoccupied lands were to be vested in the Crown once British sovereignty had been established, leading 'the first governor into the error of acting throughout upon the assumption that no part of the extensive and unoccupied territory of New Zealand was to be considered as belonging to the Crown, or available under its authority for the purposes of settlement until first regularly sold by natives'. Had the nature of native rights in land been clearly stated in the Treaty, Howick argued, it was likely that the Treaty would have not have caused so many problems.[44]

Yet, as we have seen, the clause in the Treaty of which Howick was complaining had not in fact been of the Colonial Office's or Hobson's making. More to the point, the Colonial Office and Hobson had never adopted a position about the precise nature of the natives' rights in land, let alone on the basis of the first clause of the Treaty's second article. Instead, in responding to the Company's demands, Hobson had merely insisted that he and the Company had to act in keeping with the Colonial Office's principle that land be acquired from the natives by means of purchase. The story Howick had chosen to tell assigned to both the Treaty and the government's putative definition of native title a degree of significance that neither actually had at the time the Company's problems had arisen.

Despite this fact, Howick went on to emphasise the significance of both the Treaty and the definition of native title still further in the rest of his report. He contended that if the first clause of the second article of the Treaty had in fact defined native title in the expansive terms it had later come to assume, it would have been immediately disallowed by the imperial government and its agents. He adduced the following evidence for this argument. At the point that both Gipps and Russell had approved

[44] *Ibid.*, pp. vi, ix–x, my emphasis.

the Treaty, neither could have grasped that it had guaranteed the natives' rights in all the land in New Zealand, since the former took the view that the natives only had rights of occupancy and the latter had heartily approved of this stance; and in the Royal Charter and instructions issued to Hobson at the point New Zealand was made a colony in its own right, Russell had clearly stated that the only land in which natives had any rights were those in their actual 'occupation and enjoyment' and that the other lands must be considered as vested in the Crown. All these facts revealed, Howick contended, that the British government could have only understood the guarantee in the first clause of the second article of the Treaty to refer to the lands the natives physically occupied and cultivated.[45]

Howick's account of the Treaty is actually difficult to gainsay. But in acknowledging this, we must grasp what Howick was doing and the historical error that lay in the larger argument he was making. By attributing the problem over land titles to an alleged flaw in the way native title had been defined (or not defined) in New Zealand, Howick overlooked or disguised the fact that the origins of the colony's or rather the Company's problems lay elsewhere.

Howick advanced his construction of the problem of native title further by arguing that if the natives' rights had only been admitted for lands they 'actually occupied and enjoyed', there would have been no difficulty in giving the settlers 'secure and quiet possession' of the land that they required and the Company would have immediately been put in possession of all the land on which they proposed establishing settlements. But this argument was also fundamentally flawed. As we have seen, the problems in regard to the Company's land titles had arisen because Hobson and Spain had insisted that they rested on the basis of purchases from Māori and were subject to the investigations of the Land Claims Commission that had been created in accordance with Normanby's instructions, and because those claims to land had been found by Spain to be badly flawed. Although limiting the definition of native title to the land that the natives 'occupied and enjoyed' might now feasibly help to solve the Company's problems – and we will return to this issue in the last chapter – the way the Crown had defined or not defined native title in the past was not the cause of those problems.[46]

Howick also took the side of the Company in its argument with the Colonial Office about the November 1840 argument. He declared that the Company *was* entitled to demand that the government put it in possession of a large amount of land without any reference to the question

[45] *Ibid.*, pp. v–vi.   [46] *Ibid.*, p. vi.

of whether its purchases from the natives had been valid. More particularly, he contended that if the view he had taken of the right of the Crown to all the unoccupied land was correct, and if this was the opinion of the Colonial Secretary at the time the agreement was made, it followed as a matter of course that the agreement was intended to give the Company a claim binding on the estate of the Crown. He also contended that one could not doubt that this conclusion was in accordance with Russell's views at the time: first, the charter under which New Zealand was created as a separate colony and the instructions to Hobson drawn up at the same time clearly implied that the ownership of the land by the natives was held to be confined to that which they actually occupied and enjoyed, and that all unoccupied land was vested in the Crown; and, second, the acknowledgement of any claim of right on the part of Europeans to land on the basis of their supposed purchases from the natives was denied in the most explicit terms. Yet, despite the fact that Howick was most emphatic in claiming that this *was* the position Russell had adopted on the nature of the natives' rights of property in land, there is a note in his private papers that suggests he actually entertained some doubt about whether this was the case. '[H]ow far this despatch [by Russell to Hobson in January 1841] *qualifies* [the] instructions [to Hobson is] very hard to understand', he mused; 'it almost seems to imply yet does not distinctly make *an admission of vague native rights to land not "in their actual occupation or enjoyment"*'.[47]

Putting aside the possibility that either Russell or Howick had such a doubt, it is clear that the particular arguments of Howick's I have just discussed were highly tendentious. First, while it seems very likely that the Colonial Office *did* assume at the time it was making the agreement with the Company that native rights of property in land were limited, there is no evidence to suggest that it saw any need to pay attention at that time to the precise nature of those rights, and so it did not. Second, while the Colonial Office denied that British subjects had title on the basis of purchases from natives, it had in fact decided that some of their claims would be allowed, hence the establishment of the Land Claims Commission (as we have noted).

Having argued that all the difficulties that had been experienced in the colonisation of New Zealand could be attributed mainly to the erroneous view that had been adopted on the question of native title by the Colonial

---

[47] Howick, 'Memoranda on New Zealand 1845 [sic, 1844]', Papers of Henry George, 3rd Earl Grey, University of Durham Library Special Collections, Gre/B161/87, my emphases; 1844 Select Committee Report, pp. ix–x; Mark Hickford, '"Vague Native Rights to Land": British Imperial Policy on Native Title and Custom in New Zealand, 1837–53', *Journal of Imperial and Commonwealth History*, vol. 38, no. 2, 2010, pp. 175–206.

Office and the colonial government, Howick acknowledged that great difficulties might arise if the government tried to change course now. Consequently, he was not prepared to recommend that the governor of the colony be ordered to assert the rights of the Crown as he believed them to exist. He proposed instead that the government explain to the governor what those rights were and the principles on which they existed, and direct him to adopt such measures as he might consider best calculated to meet the difficulties of the case, to establish the title of the Crown to all unoccupied land as soon as this could be safely accomplished and to grant legal title to the actual 'occupants' of land.[48]

In making further recommendations, Howick argued that the error the colonial administration had fallen into in failing to assert the right of the Crown to all the unoccupied land in New Zealand was very closely connected with what he called 'a want of vigour and decision in the general tone of the proceedings adopted towards the natives'. The local government had not only been overly apprehensive about infringing upon the natives' rights ownership of land, he argued; it had shown too much respect for native customs and so had failed to make the natives understand that they were now British subjects and should conduct themselves accordingly. British power and authority, contended Howick, should be resolutely exerted in order to put a stop to warfare between the natives, uphold the government's right to intervene, maintain peace and prevent native customs and practices impeding the progress of civilisation. Nevertheless, Howick realised that the British government currently lacked the power needed to pursue such a policy, and so he recommended that greater power should be placed at the governor's disposal. Yet he assumed that this power need not amount to much, since he believed that there was no reason to apprehend that the natives could overturn the power of the government by force. All that was required was that the governor be provided with enough arms so that it would be obvious to the natives that the British were militarily superior.[49]

Shortly after he completed a draft of his report, Howick showed it to the Company's directors. Wakefield excitedly informed his sister that it exculpated the Company and condemned the Colonial Office on almost every point of difference. He predicted that it would be carried by a large majority. As usual, Wakefield was getting ahead of himself. Howick was not the only one to draft a report. Hope prepared one after receiving a copy of Howick's. In it, he, like Howick, took the position that the principal question at stake concerned native title, but the argument he mounted was very different. Yet, in the course of trying to counter

[48] 1844 Select Committee Report, p. ix.   [49] *Ibid.*, pp. x, xiii.

Howick's report, Hope also bestowed on the Treaty of Waitangi enormous significance, for example by implying that the signing of the Treaty at Waitangi, rather than the proclamations of Hobson of May 1840, marked the moment at which the British Crown acquired sovereignty in New Zealand.[50]

Hope began his draft report by suggesting that the Select Committee had received a very full account of the current state of affairs in regard to the question of land titles, but that a historical approach was required in order to recall the steps by which British sovereignty was established in New Zealand and trace the nature of the rights of both native and Briton that had arisen as a consequence and were now the subject of the claims to land being made. Hope's main point was to provide a history of the treaty-making. He did so for two reasons. First, he sought to counter what he saw as Howick's faulty account of the area that the Treaty encompassed and the inferences Howick had consequently drawn. In this regard, he pointed out that the British government had asserted sovereignty over the southern islands on the basis of prior discovery only in part and argued that if it should turn out to be the case that there were many more natives in this area who were claiming rights than the government had anticipated it would only be proper that the government concede to them rights in land that the Treaty had secured in the first clause of its second article. (This resembles the argument Sir George Grey made to the South Australian Colonisation Commissioners, which we discussed in Chapter 3.) Second, choosing to side-step the question of whether or not the policy that had dictated the making of the Treaty was sound or whether or not the Treaty's terms were consistent with that policy, Hope asserted that what was now important was the fact that the Treaty was binding on the faith and honour of the Crown. Having made this point on the grounds of moral principle, Hope swiftly moved to argue that there were pragmatic reasons why the British government should uphold the Treaty: whatever confusion might exist among the natives as to the meaning of the cession of sovereignty to the islands, they clearly understood and fully relied upon the guarantee that the Treaty gave of their proprietary rights, and the government should never pretend that the natives would submit to an infringement of those rights without the most determined resistance, even if it was the Crown that made this attempt. Hope concluded: 'Your Committee, therefore, consider that the question of the extent to which the rights of natives in land in New Zealand are to be

---

[50] Wakefield to Catherine Torlesse, 4 [sic] July 1844, cited in R. Garnett, *Edward Gibbon Wakefield: The Colonization of South Australia and New Zealand*, T. Fisher Unwin, London, 1898, pp. 252–53; 1844 Select Committee Report, p. xxvi.

recognised is no longer one to be determined by reference to the general prerogative of the Crown or to sound principles of colonisation, but that it must be tried and decided upon the true construction of the Treaty only'. In other words, the natives' rights in land had been treated in New Zealand in light of the particular historical relationship that had developed between the Crown and natives as a consequence of the Treaty. This being the case, there was no point now in the government spelling out the true meaning of native title. Indeed, it would be dangerous to do so.[51]

Hope proceeded to suggest that any determination of the matter of rights in land should proceed by distinguishing between different categories of claimants. He did this partly in order to expose the fact that the picture the Company and its allies had drawn was a very partial one, since it concerned the problems that the Company had encountered more or less alone, and partly in order to reveal the fact that the problem of land titles was nowhere as great as Howick's report had suggested.[52]

Yet Hope also sought to counter the arguments that Howick had made in regard to native title. First, he argued that, even though the usages by which the natives seem to have always regulated their rights in land struck Europeans as 'obscure and complicated', the evidence provided by witnesses in the Committee's inquiry had revealed that the natives undoubtedly had rules and that those rules were not just acted upon by themselves but had been acknowledged by Europeans in the numerous transactions by which they had purchased land from the natives prior to the declaration of British sovereignty. Second, he argued that even though the Committee was not of the opinion that the natives had rights to the whole of the waste lands, it was by no means prepared to assert that the natives had no right to any of them. Third, he contended that even if it were the case that the natives had never assumed that they had rights in waste lands prior to the coming of Europeans, it could be argued that the transactions Europeans had conducted with them to transfer such lands might be considered to have created or made those rights, at least to a degree that it would now be dangerous to deny altogether that the natives had rights in such land. Fourth, he conceded that while it appeared that the amount of land the natives had in cultivation at any one point in time was very small, the natives customarily occupied those lands in rotation and so maintained rights to all of them. By mounting this general line of argument, Hope was able to assert that the Committee had been led to realise that the task of defining native title was surrounded by considerable difficulties. But more especially it enabled him to mount an

[51] *Ibid.*, pp. xxv–xxvii.   [52] *Ibid.*, p. xxvii.

argument that the Committee did not deem it prudent or right to give any decisive opinion on the extent of waste lands without an investigation that was not only fuller than the one it had undertaken but also one that could be instituted only in New Zealand.[53]

Hope agreed with Howick that it was important for the government to take steps to incorporate the natives into a community of British subjects, but suggested that this task would require upholding the Treaty and that the natives would regard any attempt to limit their rights of property in land to the places currently occupied by them as a gross violation of the agreement. Moreover, he contended that if those rights were violated it could hardly fail to lead to war. In contrast to Howick, Hope argued that any attempt to limit native rights in land could not be carried into effect against numerous, warlike and well-armed tribes except by the presence of a very considerable military force, thereby requiring an enormous increase in government expenditure.[54]

Hope's arguing, though, was to no avail. On 23 July the majority of the Committee voted to adopt Howick's report. In his diary that night, Howick expressed an enormous sense of relief that 'this very troublesome business [was] over'. This was wishful thinking.[55]

The Reception of Howick's Report

Once Howick's report was tabled in parliament in late July the Company and its allies moved quickly to trumpet its findings in the press, not least because they were apprehensive that Stanley would ignore them. '[I]t is hardly possible', the editor of the *Morning Chronicle* proclaimed, 'to conceive of a more thorough, clear, and well-reasoned condemnation both of the general policy of the government, and of its treatment of individuals'. Although the newspaper pointed out that the Committee's censure was not confined to the measures Stanley had taken, it focused on his deeds and especially the principle he had allegedly adopted with respect to the disposal of land, though it also argued that his actions sprang not so much from a particular view he held about the rights of the Crown but because he was determined to take a contrary position to that of the Company and spite it. The *Morning Chronicle* argued that the Committee had now disposed of the general principles Stanley had allegedly adopted by ruling that the natives only had rights of property in the land they 'occupied'. It also drew attention to the fact that the Committee had confirmed the Company's interpretation of the November 1840 agreement and alleged that Stanley's refusal to put an end to the Land Claims Commission's

[53] *Ibid.*, pp. xxvii–iii.   [54] *Ibid.*, pp. xxix–xxx.   [55] Howick, Journal, 23 July 1844.

work, direct the local administration to enforce the law rather than encouraging the natives to uphold their fancied rights and grant the Company its titles had led to the 'massacre' at Wairau.[56]

Shortly afterwards, the Company's directors presented a report in which they claimed they were confident that the Committee's recommendations about the Company's right to title would be accepted by the government. Just two days later, however, the *New Zealand Journal* gave voice to the Company's fear that Stanley, Stephen and Coates were going to thwart the will of parliament by opposing the Committee's resolutions. The journal devoted most of an issue to a digest of the reaction of the press to the Committee's report, which it claimed, not without reason, had joined together in condemning the policy of the government at home and the conduct of the government in New Zealand.[57]

Stanley was by no means inclined to accept the Committee's recommendations. He took refuge in the fact that it had been far from unanimous in its opinions and that some of its most important decisions had only been approved by a narrow majority. He set about trying to scuttle its report. To this end, he sent FitzRoy a long despatch in mid-August in which he told him that he was apprehensive that the principles the report had set down in regard to native title would lead to most unhappy consequences if they were implemented. Even if the question at stake was merely one of theory, Stanley declared, he doubted that he would be prepared to subscribe unhesitatingly and without reserve to the Committee's assumption that natives only had a right of occupancy in land. At the very least, he remarked, this assumption would have to be qualified heavily in the case of the natives of New Zealand. Stanley found it useful to argue, just as Glenelg had done on a previous occasion (in December 1837), that there were many gradations between 'uncivilised inhabitants', and so the nature of the rights they could claim varied. In the case of the aboriginal peoples of Australia, it was impossible to admit that they had any rights in land that could be allowed to interfere with British colonisation of a vast wilderness because they were mere wanderers who had no conception of government, barely any knowledge of religion and no notion of private property. But the New Zealanders were very different. Their main form of subsistence was agriculture, and individual and collective rights of property in land were well understood and recognised among them. 'I cannot think', Stanley concluded, 'that it would be either just or practicable to apply

---

[56] *Spectator*, 3 August 1844; *Morning Chronicle*, 5 August 1844.
[57] *Standard*, 16 August 1844; *New Zealand Journal*, 17 August 1844.

the same rule with regard to the occupation of land to classes of aborigines so widely differing from each other'.[58]

More importantly, Stanley maintained, whatever might be correct in theory or practice, the indisputable fact was that the British government *had* made such a distinction in New Zealand. In other words, he made the kind of argument the Colonial Office had made at various points in the previous five years in its fight with the Company, providing a historical account of a series of steps the British government had allegedly taken: first, prior to 1839, it had recognised the chiefs of New Zealand as the heads of an independent community; second, Normanby had asserted in 1839 that the natives' title to the land and the sovereignty of New Zealand was indisputable and that the government's previous, albeit qualified, admission of those rights was binding on the Crown, and so had instructed Hobson to negotiate the cession of sovereignty; third, by the first clause of the Treaty's second article, the Crown had confirmed and guaranteed the natives possession of their lands. Stanley told FitzRoy that he saw no point in mounting an inquiry into whether those steps had been wise or not. Instead, he argued, they had to accept that the government had taken these steps and parliament had sanctioned them, that the local legislature had since passed laws regulating titles to land and that the land commissioners had been sent out to investigate those titles. In this regard, Stanley was also able to point out that Howick had conceded that the government would encounter considerable difficulty if it were to try to change course. More particularly, he insisted that FitzRoy had to frame measures in reference to native title that were not only founded on interpretations of law and the Treaty that had been admitted by authorities at home and in the colony but also entertained by warlike and well-armed natives.[59]

Stanley proceeded to consider the nature of the native rights in land that were to be admitted by the Crown. He claimed that this was something that he and FitzRoy had discussed at great length prior to FitzRoy's departure for the colony. On that occasion, he claimed, he had taken the position in the argument about this matter between the Company and the Colonial Office that he could not authoritatively define those rights because he lacked the necessary information and because any restriction of those rights to lands occupied by natives for the purpose of cultivation struck him as quite irreconcilable with 'the large words' of the first clause of the Treaty's second article. Significantly, Stanley now added reasons

---

[58] Stanley to FitzRoy, 14 August 1844, *BPP*, 1845, Paper no. 1, Papers Relative to the Affairs of New Zealand, pp. 3–4.
[59] *Ibid.*, pp. 4–5.

for his position that he had not adduced at that time, arguing, for example, that any claim by the Crown to all the so-called unoccupied land would be at variance with Normanby's specific instruction to Hobson 'to obtain by fair and equal contracts with the natives the cession to the Crown of such waste lands as may be progressively required for the occupation of settlers resorting to New Zealand'. This said, Stanley maintained that he had assumed that FitzRoy would find on his arrival large tracts of country in New Zealand in which no tribe could assert a bona fide title and even large areas where the government would be able to purchase land from the natives cheaply and readily. Consequently, he claimed, he had anticipated in some measure the wishes of the Select Committee. He went on to emphasise, however, that he could not direct FitzRoy to establish the title of the Crown to all unoccupied land, except where this could be safely accomplished.[60]

Most importantly, Stanley declared that he did not think that Howick's report made it necessary for him to modify his instructions to FitzRoy in regard to arrangements with the Company. This was so for two reasons. First, he still held, despite the resolution of the Committee's members, that the November 1840 agreement *was* based on an assumption that the Company had purchased from the natives a large tract of land. Second, following upon the May 1843 agreement, which he had good reason to believe was acceptable to the Company, he had instructed FitzRoy to make the Company conditional grants, subject to the condition that such lands were vested in the Crown and that no other parties could establish a valid claim to them, and those instructions seemed to fulfil the intentions of the Select Committee.[61]

In the rest of this despatch Stanley called FitzRoy's attention to the Committee's recommendation that the Crown's right of pre-emption should be upheld, but he did no more than that. He did, though, urge FitzRoy to discourage the natives from making unreasonable demands for large payments for land, claiming that this would check the spread of British immigration and thus the prosperity of the country and so was not to the natives' advantage. In regard to the Committee's resolution about military protection, Stanley made it clear that FitzRoy could not expect a large increase in his forces. At the same time, he stated that even if it had been his duty to instruct him to act upon the principle laid down by the majority of the Committee in reference to native title, he would hold that a large increase in armed force was required to implement this policy and that he would look forward with apprehension to the suspicion and hostility that this measure would engender between the two races.[62]

---

[60] *Ibid.*, p. 5.   [61] *Ibid.*, pp. 5–6.   [62] *Ibid.*, pp. 6–8.

Not surprisingly, the Committee's report also provoked a sharp reaction from the missionary societies which had long been among the New Zealand Company's fiercest critics. On the same day Stanley sent his despatch to FitzRoy, Dandeson Coates wrote a long letter telling him that the Committee's resolutions in regard to the natives' land had filled his organisation with astonishment and alarm. Most importantly, he argued that the resolutions violated the provisions of the Treaty. Coates' concerns owed much to the fact that the Church Missionary Society's missionaries had played a very important role in persuading the chiefs to sign the Treaty, that they had done so knowing that they were assuming a profound responsibility in the eyes of the natives and that they were reliant on the government upholding the Treaty. Now it seemed that their worst fears, which those like the missionary Robert Maunsell had expressed at the time, were being realised.[63]

Like Stanley, Coates, rather than entering into any questions about the policy the British government had pursued, argued that the Treaty was a fact and was as substantial as any other treaty. Moreover, he contended, it was an agreement that the British government had pledged to uphold, which meant 'its provisions [could not] be violated without a breach of national faith and dishonour to the British Crown'. Later, in a pamphlet he wrote, Coates claimed that the establishment of British sovereignty in New Zealand derived exclusively from the Treaty. By quoting various documents, he also tried to show that the government had approved of the terms of the Treaty. Likewise, he dismissed the Committee's claim that the Treaty's provisions with respect to native title were unambiguous by arguing that these phrases from the first clause of the second article – 'The full, exclusive, and undisturbed possession of these lands' and the lands 'they may collectively and individually possess' – were 'so clear and explicit as to shut out all doubt as to their real import'. Coates also claimed that this was the sense that Hobson, the missionaries and the chiefs had placed upon it. Yet Coates seemed to concede that those phrases were actually imprecise as he also argued that it was an accepted principle in interpreting a document of this kind that the 'construction should be against the party using such ambiguous words' (in other words the *contra preferentum* rule).[64]

---

[63] Robert Maunsell to William Hobson, 14 April 1840, *BPP*, 1841, Paper no. 311, Copies or Extracts of Correspondence Relative to New Zealand, p. 99; Coates to Stanley, 14 August 1844, *BPP*, 1844, Paper no. 641, Copy of a Letter from the Secretary of the Church Missionary Society to Lord Stanley Relative to the Affairs of New Zealand, pp. 2–4.

[64] *Ibid.*, p. 5; Dandeson Coates, *The New Zealanders and their Lands: The Report of the Select Committee of the House of Commons on New Zealand, Considered in a Letter to Lord Stanley*, Hatchards, Seeleys, Nisbet and Co., London, 1844, pp. 17, 20–21, 25.

Like Stanley, Coates was dismissive of the Committee's claim that the Treaty was little more than a legal fiction, claiming that such an argument would not be made about any treaty made between Britain and France or the United States. He also tackled the Committee's contention that the Royal Charter, drawn up at the time New Zealand was created a colony in its own right, revealed that the British government must have understood the guarantee of native rights in land to refer only to lands they *actually occupied* and *enjoyed*. Pointing out that the Committee seemed to proceed on an assumption that these two terms were synonymous, Coates argued that it was 'clear that rights of property in land to an indefinite extent may exist, or, in other words, be "enjoyed", quite distinct from actual occupation of it'. Coates claimed that the Charter 'guard[ed] the rights of the natives "actually occupied or enjoyed by such natives" but it [did] not limit protection to such lands', contended that in 'all countries a proprietary right in land [was] enjoyed where in many cases the land [was] not really occupied for agricultural, mining and other purposes' and asserted that the right to change one's site of residence or cultivation was 'a species of "enjoyment", if not, in strictness, of "occupation"'.[65]

Coates went on to assert that the testimony of missionaries in New Zealand in recent years had made it clear that 'the universal right of ownership to the land' lay with the natives. There seems little doubt that the testimony Coates had in mind had been prompted by claims to the contrary. Indeed, Coates quoted such an example of this phenomenon: Stanley had expressed doubt as to the extent of native rights of property in land at a meeting with the Church Missionary Society in the spring of the previous year, Coates had reported this to the Society's missionaries and one of them (Rev. R. Burrowes) had replied in these terms: 'Lord Stanley's assumption that there are certain tracts of land which do not belong to any chief or tribe is without foundation; we have not been able to ascertain a single case of this kind'. In his pamphlet, Coates provided several more examples. He related a story that the missionary A.N. Brown had told which, in Coates' view, suggested that it was 'difficult to suppose any spot on the island' was not the property of 'some chief or tribe'. He also quoted several passages from a report by Chief Protector Clarke (which had been included in the appendices to the Select Committee's Report): 'From an early period, the whole of New Zealand seems to have been divided into districts accurately defined ... and must have been well known by the accurate description they have given to every little creek, valley, promontory and bay throughout the

---

[65] Coates to Stanley, 14 August 1844, *BPP*, 1844, Paper no. 641, p. 6; Coates, *New Zealanders*, p. 25.

island, the names of which have been handed down by tradition from generation to generation, and which still continue to define territorial rights of the chiefs'; 'It is ... evident that the chiefs of every tribe or "hapu", as well as the head of every family belonging to the tribe or "hapu", have distinct claims and titles to land within their respective districts'; and 'In other respects their claims and titles have become general, the "hapus" and families claiming, in common with the principal chiefs, what may be very properly termed waste lands, but even here they must be able [i.e. are able] to substantiate some sort of title'.[66]

Coates argued that all the recent Colonial Secretaries had held the same position on the natives' title to land as the Church Missionary Society. To clinch this argument, he drew attention to particular passages in their despatches. These included Normanby's instructions to Hobson in August 1839 in which he had directed him: 'It will be your duty to obtain, by fair and equal contracts with the natives, the cession to the Crown of such waste lands as may be progressively required for the occupation of settlers resorting to New Zealand'; a despatch Russell sent Hobson in December 1840 in which he argued that the natives were a people who had 'established by their own customs a division and appropriation of the soil'; and a further such despatch in January 1841 in which Russell had stated: 'Her Majesty, in the Royal Instructions under the sign manual, has distinctly established the general principle that the territorial rights of the natives, as the owners of the soil, must be recognised and respected'. The last was probably the very passage that had given Howick pause for thought as he drafted his Select Committee report, as discussed earlier.[67]

Stanley ordered that Coates' letter be printed in the parliamentary papers. Its appearance there seems to have prompted *The Times*, two weeks later, to carry a two-part editorial in which it more or less endorsed Howick's Select Committee report and more especially its argument regarding native title. This marked a significant change in the position this influential newspaper had previously taken in debates about New Zealand. It now contended that a people such as the New Zealanders could not be regarded as the owners of all of the country's lands since most of it was 'unoccupied' and there was no right of property that was not founded on *occupation*. The newspaper argued that the government had a responsibility to protect aboriginal people from unprincipled speculators, but no more than that. It also agreed with Howick's claim that the

---

[66] Coates to Stanley, 14 August 1844, *BPP*, 1844, Paper no. 641, pp. 6–7; Coates, *New Zealanders*, pp. 27–30.
[67] *Ibid.*, pp. 39–47.

Treaty was ambiguous and that Gipps and Russell had understood it as merely recognising the natives' right of occupancy. The *New Zealand Journal* wasted no time in reproducing these editorials and publishing an editorial of its own, in which it complained that Stanley was setting at nought the recommendations of the Select Committee and claimed that parties connected with the government were boasting that they did not intend to comply with them.[68]

Stanley Digs in His Heels

In the midst of this escalating political battle, Stanley and Hope showed no inclination to change direction, even though they had received FitzRoy's despatch of April 1844 in which he had revealed the radical measures he had adopted to deal with several matters concerning land. In a long despatch Stanley now sent in reply to this despatch, he expressed his general approval of the course that FitzRoy appeared to have taken and the manner in which he had dealt with various matters, commending what he called FitzRoy's strong sense of justice and earnest desire to reconcile differences. Stanley noted that FitzRoy had overstepped the letter of his instructions but declared that he was satisfied on the whole that the circumstances FitzRoy had emphasised in his report required him to adopt the steps he had taken. He also remarked that the government was aware that a governor could not discharge his duties unless he was given considerable discretion. More particularly, Stanley approved in large part of the way that FitzRoy had handled the enormous dissatisfaction regarding the question of titles to land and the consequent tensions, which included the position he had adopted in response to the Wairau melee. In regard to the all-important matter of the Company's claims, Stanley complained that the concessions FitzRoy had already made were too 'liberal' and criticised the arrangement he had made in waiving the Crown's right of pre-emption in favour of the Company in parts of the colony.[69]

In closing, Stanley turned to FitzRoy's waiving of the Crown's right of pre-emption in favour of individual settlers. He found it necessary to point out that this provision had been designed to enable the Crown to become the sole purchaser of land and thus acquire it cheaply from the native tribes, thereby providing funds for colonisation. He also drew FitzRoy's attention to the fact that the Select Committee had passed

---

[68] *BPP*, 1844, Paper no. 641, p. 1; *The Times*, 20 and 26 September 1844; *New Zealand Journal*, 28 September 1844.
[69] Stanley to FitzRoy, 30 November 1844, *BPP*, 1845, Paper no. 131, pp. 49–53.

a resolution that called for the right to be strictly upheld. However, on the grounds that the Committee had not discussed the matter in its report, he claimed that he was ignorant of the precise grounds for this resolution and so had to deal with the matter as FitzRoy had presented it to him. Thus, he accepted FitzRoy's argument that the peculiar circumstances of the colony meant that any attempt by the Crown to enforce its right of pre-emption rigidly would bring about constant conflict with the natives in dealing for land.[70]

Significantly, Stanley described those circumstances in the following terms: Europeans amounted to scarcely one-tenth of the number of natives and the natives could not be compared to the native inhabitants of other British colonies where a small number of British settlers had been able to exercise unlimited power; the natives were a people sufficiently advanced in civilisation to realise that the government had sold the land it had purchased from them at much higher prices; the natives held that their rights to the soil had been guaranteed to them by the Treaty and considered themselves to be entitled to the full value that their land would sell for in the market. In other words, Stanley stressed that the British government had to accept a situation in which there were real limits to what it could do because the natives had considerable power. Clearly, the emphasis that FitzRoy had been placing on this matter had been noted by the Colonial Office.[71]

Yet Stanley only endorsed FitzRoy's waiving of the Crown's right of pre-emption reluctantly. Moreover, he pointed out several objections to which the measure was liable and called on FitzRoy to address them. Those objections included the fact that it would encourage the natives to set even higher prices in offering land for sale and so render the Crown's acquisition of land more difficult, and that FitzRoy had gone too far in recommending to the native chiefs that they should exercise caution in disposing of their lands. Stanley also urged FitzRoy to increase the fee per acre that the government would charge settlers for purchasing the natives' land, in order to help increase the money available to finance colonisation. He noted that this measure would decrease the amount realised by the natives, but argued that it was not to their advantage to receive large payments for what he called mere waste land. He went on to remark that he saw no injustice in making such sales contribute to the support of government and emigration since it was this alone that created value in land.[72]

However, the only real sign at this stage that the Colonial Office's principal players were beginning to have a change of heart about how to

[70] *Ibid.*, pp. 54–55.   [71] *Ibid.*, p. 55.   [72] *Ibid.*, pp. 55–56.

treat the question of the New Zealanders' rights in land lies in a minute that Hope sent Stanley after being asked for views about some advice the Colonial Office had received about the Crown's right of pre-emption. Hope expressed some reservations about the fact that, whereas the Select Committee had taken the view that native rights of property were of the most limited extent, FitzRoy had adopted the opposite opinion. Hope remarked: 'I cannot but think FitzRoy pushes the doctrine of property in natives ... too far'. In other words, Hope objected to the fact that FitzRoy seemed to assume that there was no land at all that could be regarded as waste and thus be claimed by the Crown. Indeed, he told Stanley that he thought the Colonial Office should register its dissent from these views by referring FitzRoy to the position that he (Hope) had expressed in his draft report for the Select Committee: 'They are far from the opinion that rights can be established by natives to the whole wild lands in the Islands'. Yet Stanley was disinclined to take this advice, though there is no reason to believe that he disagreed with the view Hope had expressed.[73]

However, unbeknown to the Colonial Office, FitzRoy had, during the time that a debate had been raging in London about the colony, native title and the Treaty of Waitangi, adopted even bolder measures than he had previously, which would provoke even greater attacks on the government by the Company and its allies. This assault, as we will see (in the following chapter), convinced senior ministers in the government that it had to cede some ground to the Company.

Part III

Spain Changes Course

Following FitzRoy's visit to Wellington and Nelson in January 1844, Spain turned his attention to settling the Company's claims in the Hutt Valley. He soon encountered considerable opposition, especially from Te Rauparaha and Te Rangihaeata. Their resistance forced him to realise that he would have to adopt a different approach if the government was going to be able to extinguish native title and put the Company's settlers into possession of the land.[74]

At the end of March, Spain tried to put pressure on Te Rauparaha by sending him a letter (translated into Māori by the missionary Octavius

---

[73] 1844 Select Committee Report, p. xxvii; Hope to Stanley, 22 November 1844, TNA, CO 209/40.
[74] Spain to Fitzroy, 13 April 1844, *BPP*, 1846, Paper no. 203, pp. 125–26.

Hadfield). In this, he claimed that the British government had adopted a much more generous way of colonising the country than any other European nation would have done since it had treated with them for land. He also warned Te Rauparaha that if the British were to quit the country the natives would find that another colonial power would make war upon them and seize their land. Given this danger, he suggested, the natives should accept the terms that they had been offered. More specifically, Spain argued that the British government could have followed 'the established law of European nations' that held that people only had true and legal possession of land they cultivated and that Europeans deprived of land at home were lawfully entitled to take possession of lands that natives were not constantly using. In making this argument, Spain more or less quoted a passage from Joseph Chitty's 1834 edition of Vattel's *The Law of Nations*. It is important to note, however, that Spain did not suggest that the colonial government should construe native title in accordance with the legal principle of *occupation* that Vattel articulated, even though he probably regarded it as the proper basis of rights of property in land. Instead, he adopted this mode of reasoning, as he himself said, in order to effect a particular object, that of persuading Te Rauparaha to relent so that the Company's settlers could be put into possession of land and conflict between the two races averted.[75]

Once it became apparent that this strategy had failed to budge Te Rauparaha, Spain decided that the government should compel him and Te Rangihaeata to accept the compensation they had been offered by William Wakefield and cede the lands in question to the Company's settlers. In a confidential letter he sent to FitzRoy in April recommending this course of action, Spain sought to lend support to his opinion by relaying a view that Hadfield had expressed. This missionary had observed a 'great change' among natives like Te Rauparaha and Te Rangihaeata since the Wairau melee. Prior to it, they had a good opinion of the British government, feared British power and considered the British to be courageous, but since then they disbelieved the government's just intentions, ceased to fear British military strength and looked upon the British as cowards. Consequently, Hadfield believed that in order to convince the natives that the British were not to be trifled with, the government had to make a sufficient demonstration of force. Unless it could do so, it would be unable to regain its moral influence or assert the supremacy

---

[75] Emmerich de Vattel, *The Law of Nations*, edited by Joseph Chitty, S. Sweet, London, 1834, p. 100; Spain to Te Rauparaha, 21 March 1844, *BPP*, 1846, Paper no. 203, pp. 33–34; Spain to Fitzroy, 13 April 1844, *BPP*, 1846, Paper no. 203, pp. 126–27.

of British law, and a collision between the two races would occur with the loss of a great deal of blood.[76]

FitzRoy generally approved of the strategy Hadfield and Spain were recommending, but he took the view that a warning Spain had issued to the chiefs, namely that any prolonged resistance by them would be met by force, was probably stronger than the government would be able to execute. He told Spain that he had privately warned Governor Gipps that a demonstration of British military and naval strength might be required but that he had yet to officially seek his assistance. Most importantly, FitzRoy impressed upon Spain that while he could rely on his support when it was absolutely necessary, the government had 'no right to *enforce* a sale of land, vi et armis [this is, by force of arms]'. In other words, FitzRoy was unwilling to use force to try to break Te Rauparaha and Te Rangihaeata's resistance to further settlement. At this time, in instructions he drew up for Mathew Richmond, who had recently assumed a newly created position of Superintendent for the colony's southern districts, FitzRoy also emphasised that it was imperative that the utmost circumspection be exercised in dealing with Māori who refused to vacate land that had been validly purchased, even if doing this meant setting aside the legitimate interests of individual settlers. 'With so small an amount of physical force at [our] command', he declared, 'the greatest prudence, forbearance and deliberation are absolutely necessary'.[77]

Historians like W. P. Morrell have attributed this position of FitzRoy's to the high-minded principles he brought to the treatment of native matters. There is no doubt something in this, but psychological factors played a role as well. FitzRoy seems to have experienced considerable anxiety in regard to the power that a governor was required to wield. This state of mind often caused him to be unsure of himself and doubt that he had the power to persuade others to his point of view, causing him to be dogmatic at some moments (as we have observed) and to vacillate at others (as we will see). Most importantly, his anxiety about exercising authority appears to have led him unconsciously to displace the greatest source of power in the colony onto the settlers and the natives, most especially in the form of

---

[76] Minutes of Commissioner's Proceedings, 8 March 1844, *BPP*, 1846, Paper no. 203, pp. 29–31; Octavius Hadfield to Spain, 27 March 1844, *BPP*, 1845, Paper no. 369, Copies or Extracts of Despatches from the Governor of New Zealand, p. 105; Spain to FitzRoy, 12 April 1844, *BPP*, 1845, Paper no. 369, p. 104; Spain to FitzRoy, 13 April 1844, *BPP*, 1846, Paper no. 203, p. 129.

[77] FitzRoy to Spain, 3 June 1844, NANZ, G13/1, his emphasis; FitzRoy to Mathew Richmond, 4 June 1844, *BPP*, 1845, Paper no. 247, p. 20.

the armed force that the colonial government lacked, which in turn left him unduly fearful of these parties.[78]

But to return to Spain. In May he adopted much the same approach he had previously used in the Hutt Valley in order to handle a New Zealand Company claim for a 60,000-acre block of land in Taranaki. (The Company had purchased a much larger tract in this district but William Wakefield had decided to claim this land only.) It was a complicated claim. Most of this area's traditional owners, the Te Āti Awa, were absent when the Company's agents had purchased the land, having been forced off it by Ngāti Maniapoto and Waikato between the mid-1820s and the early 1830s. But between the Company's purchase and the arrival of its settlers, Te Āti Awa had begun to return and resume possession of their lands, mostly on the very same narrow coastal strip on the Waitara River that the settlers had selected. The returnees were willing to recognise the sale of lands to the Company that belonged to the forty or so of their tribe who had been present at the time Wakefield had made the purchase but they declared that their own rights could not be extinguished by those sales. They refused to give up any more land unless they received payment for it, and physically opposed settlement by adopting much the same means that had been used previously in the Wellington district.[79]

In all the previous claims that Spain had heard, he had found much to fault in Wakefield's purchasing and had ruled against the Company. It was expected that he would do the same in this case, not least by the members of the Protectorate of Aborigines who acted as his advisers and translators. After all, the purchasing Wakefield had done in this district was the most haphazard of all the transactions he had made. However, after a two-day hearing, Spain ruled that the Company had fairly purchased the land and that no further payment had to be made to the natives. In doing so, he refused to accept that the Te Āti Awa who had been conquered and forced off their lands by Ngāti Maniapoto and Waikato had any rightful claim, arguing that native custom held that a people in these circumstances had forfeited all their rights.[80]

---

[78] W. P. Morrell, *British Colonial Policy in the Age of Peel and Russell*, Clarendon Press, Oxford, 1930, p. 117; Ian Wards, *The Shadow of the Land: A Study of British Policy and Racial Conflict in New Zealand 1832–1852*, Historical Publications Branch, Department of Internal Affairs, Wellington, 1968, p. 72.

[79] Ann Parsonson, 'He Whenua Te Utu (The Payment will be Land)', PhD thesis, University of Canterbury, 1978, pp. 236–41.

[80] Minutes of the Proceedings of the Land Claims Commission at New Plymouth, 31 May 1844, 4 and 8 June 1844, *BPP*, 1846, Paper no. 203, pp. 67–69; Spain to FitzRoy, 12 June 1844, *BPP*, 1846, Paper no. 203, pp. 131–34; John Whiteley to the Secretaries of the MMS, 15 August 1844, MMS Records, Box 527, AJCP, Reel M139; Spain to FitzRoy, New Plymouth Report, 31 March 1845, *BPP*, 1846, Paper no. 203, pp. 50–52, 54, 56–58, 62–63, 68–69.

Spain was to insist that he had made this finding on legal grounds, but it seems clear that his ruling was not so much a product of his adopting any particular legal principles as it was the result of the weight he placed on several pragmatic considerations. In the course of informing FitzRoy of his ruling, he argued that if he were to admit these natives' claim that they retained rights in land they had once held, it would throw into question practically every British title in the country and this would lead to serious conflict, both between native and European and between natives. Furthermore, in a confidential memorandum that he sent FitzRoy three weeks after he had delivered his finding, he once again sought to impress upon his superior the need for resolute action in order to convince the natives of the government's power to enforce obedience to its laws. Indeed, he argued that in order to carry out the humanitarian principles that the government had stated to be its object in colonising New Zealand, it was absolutely essential that it demonstrate its power by a show of physical force. Furthermore, he contended that unless this was done the government could not hope to colonise the country extensively.[81]

Spain delivered his finding in this case in mid-June to a large crowd of Māori and settlers in New Plymouth. His decision angered the Te Āti Awa, and they immediately set out to destroy the property of settlers and drive them off the land in dispute. They were only stopped from doing so by the protector of aborigines for the southern district, George Clarke Jnr, who told them that Spain's findings merely amounted to a recommendation and that the Governor would consider their grievances sympathetically. Shortly afterwards, Te Āti Awa rangatira, led by Wiremu Kingi Te Rangitake, composed letters to FitzRoy in which they attacked Spain's decision as unrighteous, complained that they had never sold these lands, called on him to intervene and told him they would never give up the land at Waitara. Just as importantly, Clarke Jnr, his fellow protector and interpreter Thomas Forsaith, and a Methodist missionary, John Whiteley, all dissented from Spain's view of native custom regarding the rights of those forced off their lands. As their intervention reveals, missionaries as well as protectors had acquired a considerable amount of knowledge about the nature of customary laws and usages in regard to land, largely as a result of their role in the investigations of the Land Claims Commission. On this occasion, as on others, this knowledge clearly played a part in their adopting the role of the protectors of those rights. Clarke, who had worked closely with Spain in all the hearings he had conducted, was especially troubled by the Commissioner's ruling

---

[81] Spain to FitzRoy, 2 July 1844, *BPP*, 1845, Paper no. 369, pp. 106–07; Spain to FitzRoy, New Plymouth Report, 31 March 1845, *BPP*, 1846, Paper no. 203, p. 52.

because he was sure it would lead to bloodshed. He promptly sent a private letter to his father, the Chief Protector, telling him: 'If the government are determined to put the settlers in possession of lands which we cannot convince the natives or ourselves honestly that they have been alienated, they must do so at the point of the bayonet and if they once resort to violence it must end in the extermination ultimately of the natives throughout the length and breadth of the island but only after a sacrifice of life too awful to contemplate'. A few days later, Whiteley also wrote to Clarke Snr, endorsing Te Rangitake and his fellow rangatira's call upon FitzRoy to intervene. 'The law of England or the law of nations may possibly bear the Commissioner out in the award which he has given', he remarked, 'but I submit that in such a case as this the natives ought, on the strict principles of justice, to be dealt with in accordance with their own usages and laws, and not according to laws of which they [have] never heard'. He also cautioned the Chief Protector that in order to ensure peace *'we must do justice'*.[82]

Spain's finding probably took FitzRoy by surprise. At any rate, he decided to overturn it as soon as he learned of it. He confided to Whiteley: 'I will never sign a deed of grant of land to any person in New Zealand if I, in my conscience, believe that the owner of such land has not consented to convey or sell it to the proposed grantee'. FitzRoy promptly despatched a newly appointed protector of aborigines, Donald McLean, to New Plymouth to investigate. The Anglican Bishop of New Zealand, George Augustus Selwyn, also hurried there. FitzRoy followed shortly afterwards. On his arrival in early August, FitzRoy agreed to meet a deputation of settlers who had called for protection but he reacted to their concerns by blaming the events on the Company's agent. He also had no hesitation in saying that Spain had made a mistake in his ruling and that he would not and could not confirm it. FitzRoy even went so far as to assert that he thought it was absurd to presume that a people removed from their ancestral country had lost all claim to the land, though he sought to reassure the settlers they would not suffer as a consequence of his setting aside the Company's claim. On the following day, FitzRoy held a meeting that was attended by Te Āti Awa.

---

[82] Wiremu Kingi Te Rangitake et al. to FitzRoy, 10 June 1844, enclosed in Whiteley to Clarke Snr, 1 July 1844, MMS Records, Box 527, AJCP, Reel M139; George Clarke Jnr to Clarke Snr, 27 June 1844, Clarke Letters, HL, PC-0058; Whiteley to Clarke Snr, 1 July 1844, MMS Records, Box 527, AJCP, Reel M139, his emphasis; Whiteley to the Secretaries of the MMS, 15 August 1844, MMS Records, Box 527, AJCP, Reel M139; Clarke Snr, Half-Yearly Report, 1 January 1845, *BPP*, 1846, Paper no. 337, Copies or Extracts of Further Correspondence Between Lord Stanley and Governor FitzRoy and Lieutenant-Governor Grey, Relative to New Zealand, p. 11; Spain to FitzRoy, 31 March 1845, *BPP*, 1846, Paper no. 203, p. 62.

He insisted that it was up to him as the governor to decide matters like this and announced that he had decided to set aside Spain's finding and direct McLean to conduct a further investigation. He also told Te Āti Awa that he would not allow any person to take their lands unjustly and that no officer in his government would allow such injustice, though he refused to accede to demands that the Te Āti Awa chiefs made at this meeting for an immediate ruling and threatened that he could bring an armed force to put down any 'anarchy and rebellion' if this proved necessary. Privately, FitzRoy expressed the opinion that further payment would need to be paid to the Te Āti Awa to settle the dispute.[83]

It seems clear that FitzRoy was wedded to the principle that the Colonial Office had adopted at the outset of the colonisation of New Zealand, namely that it was right and proper to acquire possession of land by treating with the natives for it. Accordingly, it might be argued that it is unremarkable that he maintained that he had to uphold the rights of those natives who had not consented to this purchase, and all the more so because this position was in keeping with the opinions he had expressed in giving testimony to the House of Lords Select Committee in 1838. But it is also apparent that FitzRoy was outraged by Spain's suggestion that natives who had been forced off their lands and enslaved had lost their rights of property in land. 'Would an Englishman, after some years confinement in a French prison, or being enslaved by Africans, admit that he had forfeited his estate in England', he demanded to know. Yet, having drawn such an analogy, FitzRoy was more inclined to accept the position Whiteley had articulated, which was to emphasise the pertinence of local usages. It is also clear that he was anxious that he lacked the military means to confirm Spain's finding and put the settlers into possession of the land in question, and apprehensive that trying to uphold the finding would provoke the natives to resort to arms and that this would result in bloodshed and the probable ruin of the settlement. FitzRoy also realised that the government could actually acquire some of the land in question

---

[83] Extracts of Walter Lawry to Whiteley, 13 and 15 July 1844, Extract of Thomas Forsaith to Whiteley, 15 July 1844, FitzRoy to Whiteley, 16 July 1844, and Extract of Clarke Snr to Whiteley, 16 July 1844, MMS Records, Box 527, AJCP, Reel M139; Clarke Snr to Donald McLean, 16 July 1844, Donald McLean Papers, ATL, MS Papers 0032–0001; McLean, Minutes of Meeting, 3 August 1844, McLean Papers, ATL, MS Papers 0032–0001; John Wicksteed to Wakefield, 4 August 1844, New Zealand Company, *Seventeenth Report of the Directors of the New Zealand Company*, Stewart and Murray, London, 1845, p. 73; FitzRoy to Wakefield, 8 August 1844, *BPP*, 1846, Paper no. 203, p. 135; *New Zealand Gazette and Wellington Spectator*, 14 August 1844; Whiteley to the Secretaries of the MMS, 15 August 1844, MMS Records, Box 527, AJCP, Reel M139; FitzRoy, Memorandum on the Arrangements in Respect of the Land Question at Taranaki, 2 December 1844, *BPP*, 1845, Paper no. 369, pp. 101–02.

by making a further payment to the natives. In these circumstances, the question about the particular nature of the natives' rights of property in land, which the Company and its allies held to be crucial to the settlement of the land question, never seems to have arisen. Certainly, there was never any suggestion that the legal principle of *occupation* had any purchase in this case.[84]

Not surprisingly, the Company's agents in New Zealand were deeply unhappy that FitzRoy had chosen to set aside Spain's finding. Its local agent in New Plymouth, John Wicksteed, recognised that the decision FitzRoy had taken made good practical sense; but in the Wellington press Samuel Revans cast it as further evidence of the Governor's failure to settle land claims, warned that the native and settler populations were increasingly coming into conflict because of this, and called for an immediate and final settlement of the land question. Ten days later, Revans' off-sider in Nelson, a lawyer and poet, Alfred Domett, launched a ferocious attack on the British government's policy towards New Zealand and more particularly FitzRoy, comparing his reversal of Spain's finding with his dismissal of the settlers' concerns in the Wairau melee. After reviewing what he called the facts of the Taranaki case, Domett called on FitzRoy to weigh the consequences of 'this rash proceeding' and confirm Spain's decision if he wanted the settlers and natives to live peacefully together for any length of time.[85]

Troubles in the North

Taranaki was not the only problem that FitzRoy was facing in regard to native matters at this time. Several days before he learned of Spain's ruling and its reception by the Te Āti Awa, he had been informed about serious disturbances in the Bay of Islands. Over three days, a considerable number of well-armed Māori led by a Ngā Puhi rangatira, Hōne Wiremu Heke Pōkai, who had been one of the first to sign the Treaty at Waitangi, had entered the settlement at Kororāreka (Russell) and committed several acts of aggression that had climaxed in their hacking down the government flagstaff, which Heke regarded as a symbol of British sovereignty and the Crown taking possession of the land. Later in July, Heke would tell FitzRoy that the flagstaff belonged to him and that he had made it in order to fly the native flag, which was presumably the one that had been conceived (by Busby) in 1834 and which Heke probably associated

---

[84] *Ibid.*, p. 102; FitzRoy, *Remarks*, pp. 29–30.
[85] Wicksteed to Wakefield, 4 and 6 August 1844, New Zealand Company, *Seventeenth Report*, pp. 73, 117; *New Zealand Gazette and Wellington Spectator*, 7 and 14 August 1844; *Nelson Examiner and New Zealand Chronicle*, 24 August 1844.

with the northern chiefs' Declaration of Independence of the following year. During these assaults, one of Heke's party had declared 'war, war, war with the white people', and Heke himself had complained to the protector Henry Kemp and the missionaries William Williams and Robert Maunsell that the natives had been tricked into signing the Treaty. Thus began a conflict that would turn during the next eighteen months into a major armed confrontation between some of the northern Māori tribes and the British Crown.[86]

On learning of Heke's attacks, FitzRoy was aghast. He declared that the British had to either submit to being treated as men who were unwilling as well as unable to defend themselves and protect the British flag from dishonour, or take effective measures to restore the natives' respect for British authority. He eagerly accepted the advice of Chief Protector Clarke that this was an opportunity to demonstrate that the government could bring force to bear to maintain order and uphold British law, thereby showing the natives that they could not commit such attacks with impunity. FitzRoy quickly summoned the colony's Executive Council and won their approval for this course of action and acquired the means he needed to implement it, which involved chartering a vessel to convey himself, an officer and thirty men of a regiment to Korarāreka, after which it proceeded to Sydney to collect a ship of war, an officer and 150 soldiers, which Gipps had agreed to provide on a temporary basis.[87]

On reaching the Bay of Islands in the last week of August (after a brief visit there a month earlier), FitzRoy ordered these forces to make a demonstration of British power that he hoped would overawe natives such as Heke and encourage those who were well disposed to the government to rally to its side. However, the night before these forces were to engage Heke and his followers in battle, Clarke Snr intervened, making representations to FitzRoy on behalf of chiefs who were still friendly to the

---

[86] Thomas Beckham to Andrew Sinclair, 6 and 8 July 1844, *BPP*, 1845, Paper no. 130, Copies or Extracts from Any Recent Despatches from the Governor of New South Wales Respecting Outrages by the Natives in the Bay of Islands in New Zealand, pp. 2–4; William Clunie et al. to FitzRoy, 8 July 1844, *BPP*, 1845, Paper no. 247, pp. 88–89; C. Hector to FitzRoy, 8 July 1844, *BPP*, 1845, Paper no. 247, pp. 89–91; Hōne Heke Pokai to FitzRoy, 19 July 1844, NANZ, G30/6; [William Williams], *Plain Facts Relative to the Late War in the Northern Districts of New Zealand*, Philip Kunst, Auckland, 1847, p. 31; Clarke Snr, Half-Yearly Report, 1 January 1845, *BPP*, 1846, Paper no. 337, pp. 10–11; Heke to FitzRoy, 15 July 1845, reproduced in [Williams], *Plain Facts* p. 32.

[87] FitzRoy to Beckham, 10 July 1844, *BPP*, 1845, Paper no. 130, pp. 4–5; Executive Council Minutes, 11 July, NANZ, EC1 1; FitzRoy to Sir George Gipps, 13 July 1844, *BPP*, 1845, Paper no. 247, pp. 93–94; Gipps to FitzRoy, 3 August 1844, *BPP*, 1845, Paper no. 247, p. 94.

Crown. Those chiefs called on FitzRoy to desist from the hostilities he had planned and allow them to make amends on behalf of Heke and his supporters on the understanding that they would make themselves responsible for preventing any further outrage in the future and ensuring the peace. FitzRoy agreed to withdrew the troops to Korarāreka, and at a meeting with most of the rangatira in the area (except Heke) held several days later he gave a long address (translated by one of the missionaries) in which he emphasised the importance he attached to Heke and his party's attack on the British flag. He sought to impress upon the chiefs that the British Crown had agreed to provide them with protection but that it might have refused to do so. If this had happened, he claimed, they would have suffered the same consequences that natives had suffered at the hands of the French in Tahiti and the Marquesas Islands. It is unlikely that this bluff would have worked. In any case, FitzRoy proceeded to tell the chiefs that he could not allow acts such as Heke's to pass without some redress but that since he had received a letter of apology from him in regard to the flagstaff and an offer to erect a replacement, all he required now was for the chiefs to deliver up ten guns as an act of atonement (though the chiefs had apparently offered to give up land). After the chiefs acceded to this requirement and gave assurances of their good feeling and attachment to the Crown, FitzRoy declared that their undertakings were a sufficient guarantee for permanent tranquillity. He restored the guns to them and ordered the withdrawal of the government's troops. Furthermore, he made a further concession to the chiefs by announcing that he would remove the customs duties they were required to pay, and at a meeting the next day he promised to take steps to loosen the regulations in regard to the Crown's right of pre-emption and agreed that the so-called surplus lands should be returned to the native owners.[88]

In despatches that FitzRoy sent Gipps and Stanley shortly afterwards, he claimed that the mere appearance of the government's forces had served the purpose he had had in mind, and so there had been no need to deploy them. But, sometime later, he changed his tune, claiming that he had recognised the government's real weakness and thus the impossibility of it acting against the natives without having the support of the native chiefs well disposed to the government, and arguing that if he had defied the wishes of those chiefs and proceeded with the assault none of the troops would have returned

[88] FitzRoy to Stanley, 20 August 1844, *BPP*, 1845, Paper no. 247, p. 88; FitzRoy, Address to the Native Chiefs Assembled at Waimate on 2 September 1844, AWMML, MS-430; FitzRoy to Gipps, 4 September 1844, *BPP*, 1845, Paper no. 247, p. 95; *Daily Southern Cross*, 7 September 1844; FitzRoy, *Remarks*, pp. 32–33; Wards, *Shadow*, p. 107.

alive. One way or another, FitzRoy seems to have dreaded the prospect of armed conflict.[89]

Yet Bishop Selwyn, who had witnessed these events, also expressed the view that the forces that Gipps had provided had not materially altered the government's position and that if FitzRoy had proceeded the government would not have had a single native ally north of Auckland. *'Everything, in fact, was in the power of the native people'*, he claimed. FitzRoy also had an ally in Martin's *Daily Southern Cross*. The newspaper commended the settlement FitzRoy had made as brave and wise, claimed that a foundation had been laid for permanent friendship between the two races and argued that the Governor had proved that it was possible to govern the natives of New Zealand without the use of armed force.[90]

This, however, was not the way many of the settlers in the colony interpreted these events. In the southern district a good deal of ridicule was heaped on FitzRoy. For example, the editor of the *New Zealand Spectator and Cook's Strait Guardian*, which had recently succeeded the *New Zealand Gazette and Wellington Spectator* as the New Zealand Company's newspaper in Wellington, argued that there had been a flourish of trumpets about the supremacy of British law, the outrage to the British flag, the degradation of submitting to insults from the natives and the absolute necessity of upholding British authority, but that in the end FitzRoy had sent the troops away and accepted a mere ten guns from the natives as compensation, only to give them back. Once more, FitzRoy was deemed to be guilty of a lack of resolution in the face of native resistance to British authority.[91]

The Governor's Rash Steps

Shortly after FitzRoy returned from the Bay of Islands to Auckland in early September, he belatedly acknowledged that the colony was in deep financial trouble. He hastily sent Stanley a despatch. 'The state of this colony is unprecedented and most critical', he declared. 'We have no money.' Obviously rattled, FitzRoy then took three steps that the Colonial Office later cited as grounds for recalling him: he abolished customs duties throughout the colony, imposed a property tax and slashed the fee that the government charged settlers on purchases under

---

[89] FitzRoy to Gipps, 4 September 1844, *BPP*, 1845, Paper no. 247, p. 95; FitzRoy to Stanley, 14 September 1844, *BPP*, 1845, Paper no. 247, p. 138; FitzRoy, *Remarks*, pp. 32–33.

[90] George Augustus Selwyn to FitzRoy, November 1845, NANZ, G19/1, his emphasis; *Daily Southern Cross*, 7 and 14 September 1844.

[91] *New Zealand Spectator and Cook's Strait Guardian*, 12 October 1844.

his earlier waiver of the Crown's right of pre-emption, from 10s per acre to 1 penny an acre.[92] Only the last of these measures need concern us.[93]

What led FitzRoy to take this drastic step, which came to be known as his penny-an-acre proclamation? To begin to answer this question, we need to retrace our steps. In waiving the Crown's right of pre-emption in March that year, FitzRoy had introduced regulations that had created a cumbersome process. Consequently, little land had been granted. Moreover, the regulations had been poorly received by critics such as Martin. Even Chief Protector Clarke expressed concern that they would bar settlers from buying much land and that many natives would be dissatisfied as a result. Furthermore, Martin and his fellow Radical William Brown, whom FitzRoy had appointed as two of the three non-official members of the Legislative Council, had taken the opportunity to advance a series of resolutions and draft a report in which they argued that the system embodied in the imperial government's 1842 Land Sales Act appeared to have been devised with a view to the colonisation of countries in which the government had the power to dispose of land, but that this was clearly inappropriate in New Zealand's case, since the country had 100,000 native inhabitants (which was an exaggeration), nearly all of its 60 million acres were owned or claimed by one or more tribes or individuals, and their territorial rights as owners of that land had been guaranteed by the Treaty and distinctly recognised and respected by other acts of the British government. Further, Martin and Brown had contended that while the government had obtained the right of pre-emption and had declared that all titles not confirmed by grants from the Crown were null and void, the government did not actually have the power to prescribe the price below which lands could be sold. Finally, they argued that the system of pre-emption had already 'excited much dissatisfaction' among natives, that this was liable to increase rather than decrease and that the government could not prevent settlers from obtaining land or the temporary use of it from natives by any legislative enactment. Consequently, they suggested, British government should consider whether it might be expedient to modify the present regulations, claiming that this would lead to the peaceful and prosperous settlement of the country and put a stop to irregular and illegal dealings in land. A resolution based on the report explicitly declared that there were no waste lands in New Zealand. Both the report and the resolution were unanimously adopted by the colony's Legislative Council. What is more, the Attorney General, Swainson, had

[92] For a discussion of FitzRoy's financial measures and the part they played in his being recalled, see Jonathan Adams, 'Governor FitzRoy's Debentures and their Role in his Recall', *New Zealand Journal of History*, vol. 20, no. 1, 1986, pp. 44–63.
[93] FitzRoy to Stanley, 16 September 1844, *BPP*, 1845, Paper no. 247, pp. 140–42.

drafted the resolution, and FitzRoy had himself moved that the version of it that was approved by the Council be sent to Stanley.[94]

In the light of these developments alone, FitzRoy might have decided to change the regulations governing the conditions under which he would waive the Crown's right of pre-emption, but it seems clear that the events in the Bay of Islands in August and September prompted him to do so. In mid-October he persuaded the colony's Executive Council to approve this new measure, though several of its members expressed reservations about it.[95]

In informing Stanley of this measure, FitzRoy claimed that it was not just prudent but absolutely necessary on several grounds. He contended that in the course of the last two years there had been a growing demand on the part of the natives to dispose of their lands without government interference and control. More particularly, he argued that they had been told by settlers that in the Māori text of the Treaty they had merely granted the Queen the option of first refusal rather than the sole and exclusive right of purchase, and that the relevant part of the English text had not been translated correctly and that the natives would never have agreed to bar themselves from selling to settlers in the event that the government declined to purchase their lands. FitzRoy claimed, further-more, that settlers had drawn the natives' attention to the Treaty's third article, which imparted to them all the rights and privileges of British subjects, and told them that while they were unable to sell their own land that article was not being executed and they were no better than slaves who had no power to dispose of their own lands. Finally, FitzRoy argued once again that a failure to introduce this new measure would destroy native confidence in the government and bring on hostilities. (These arguments, as readers will have recognised, closely resembled those that Martin had made previously.)[96]

FitzRoy knew that he had no authority to adopt this measure and that he was disobeying his political master. Indeed, he went so far as to tell Stanley that he knew that he might be censured for what he had done, and even dismissed, indeed that he would not be surprised if he (Stanley)

---

[94] FitzRoy, Proclamation, 26 March 1844, *BPP*, 1845, Paper no. 131, p. 48; *Daily Southern Cross*, 6 and 20 April 1844; Clarke Snr, Half-Yearly Report, 31 July 1844, *BPP*, 1845, Paper no. 369, p. 78; Minutes of the Legislative Council Proceedings, 25 May, 6, 13 and 17 July 1844, *BPP*, 1845, Paper no. 247, pp. 41–42, 67–68, 70, 77–78; *Daily Southern Cross*, 1 June 1844, 13 and 20 July 1844; *Auckland Chronicle and New Zealand Colonist*, 1 August 1844.

[95] Clarke Snr to Sinclair, 30 September 1844, *BPP*, 1845, Paper no. 369, p. 39; Clarke Snr to FitzRoy, 9 October 1844, *BPP*, 1845, Paper no. 369, p. 26; Executive Council Minutes, 10 October 1844, *BPP*, 1845, Paper no. 369, pp. 24–25.

[96] FitzRoy to Stanley, 14 October 1844, *BPP*, 1845, Paper no. 369, pp. 20–21.

decided to do just that. Yet FitzRoy begged Stanley to dismiss any notion that it was possible to maintain peace in New Zealand without allowing the natives to sell their land to private individuals. This claim was hyperbolic, but FitzRoy seems to have believed it.[97]

In the next day or two, FitzRoy sent Stanley five despatches with numerous supporting papers, having barely kept his superior abreast of his doings in the preceding nine months, and several days later he sent another. This frenetic activity reveals his febrile state of mind at this time. FitzRoy devoted most of the last of these despatches to what he called the extreme importance of strengthening the colony's military and naval forces. He argued that it was not enough for the government to ensure that its conduct towards the natives was correct and just; it was necessary to 'maintain so large a military force in the colony that organised resistance to it may be quite hopeless'. He called for the speedy provision of such a force in order to save enormous bloodshed. In doing so, he claimed that the government was facing a new problem: there was now a possibility that the native tribes would unite and act together in the case of hostilities with Europeans. In order to ensure that the majority of the natives remained active supporters of the government, the governor needed greater military power; otherwise, they would choose to remain neutral. In all probability, FitzRoy was remembering an event he had witnessed several months earlier when 6,000 or 7,000 Māori had converged on Auckland. The Waikato tribe, led by one of the most powerful rangatira in the country, Pōtatau Te Wherowhero, and several of the local tribes had mounted an impressive demonstration of their military might. In what was the longest and most detailed despatch FitzRoy ever sent Stanley, he provided a graphic description of a mock battle in which two well-drilled forces, after forming on opposite hills a mile apart and performing a haka, had rushed thundering down the slopes towards one another.[98]

To summarise, in the course of a few short months FitzRoy had made a series of significant moves. He had rejected a ruling of Spain's that he grant land to the New Zealand Company after learning that the natives had refused to accept it; he had passed regulations that provided for a further waiving of the Crown's right of pre-emption; he had been party to a declaration that there were no waste lands in the colony and

---

[97] *Ibid.*, p. 21; FitzRoy, Memorandum on the Sale of Lands in New Zealand by the Aborigines, 14 October 1844, *BPP*, 1845, Paper no. 369, pp. 23–24.

[98] FitzRoy to Stanley, 25 May 1844, *BPP*, 1845, Paper no. 247. pp. 8–18; FitzRoy to Stanley, 14 October 1844, *BPP*, 1845, Paper no. 369, p. 27; FitzRoy to Stanley, 15 October 1844, *BPP*, 1845, Paper no. 369, pp. 28–29; FitzRoy to Stanley, 19 October 1844, *BPP*, 1845, Paper no. 369, pp. 31–33.

that the government system for further colonisation of the country should be repudiated; he appeared to have capitulated to the natives in the north after they had mounted a serious challenge to the Crown's authority; and he had abandoned a critical source of government revenue at a moment when he knew the colony was bankrupt.

As we have noted, FitzRoy argued that he had no choice but to act in this way because of the sheer power of the natives. Yet, as we will see in the final chapter, his successor as governor did not share his assessment of their power and proceeded in a very different manner with considerable success, which can only partly be attributed to the fact that the British government provided him with the increase in military forces it had denied FitzRoy. It seems fair to say that FitzRoy exaggerated the power of the natives and in so doing undermined his own capacity to make effective use of the limited resources he had. More generally, it is also clear that many of FitzRoy's acts as governor were extremely rash. Moreover, there seems to be little doubt that this can be attributed in good part to his mental state. It appears that throughout his life FitzRoy suffered long bouts of melancholy punctuated by intervals of frenetic activity. (He would eventually take his own life.) Even contemporaries who were sympathetic to FitzRoy and his values, such as Hadfield, observed that he was often incapable of appraising a situation with a calm state of mind and that this led him to act in ways that were foolish as well as foolhardy.[99]

In the closing months of 1844, FitzRoy's performance came under further attack in the southern district of the colony after he belatedly complied with a Colonial Office instruction to go there to address the Company's grievances over land matters. Prior to his arrival in Wellington in late October, a public meeting passed a resolution condemning his failure to fulfil the promise he had made seven months earlier to address the Company's difficulties. This meeting apparently concluded with three groans (rather than cheers) for the man they decried as 'the Maori Governor'. The *New Zealand Spectator and Cook's Strait Guardian* was similarly scathing in a report it carried in the first week of November that purported to be an account of the meeting FitzRoy had agreed to grant a Company deputation, not least because he apparently told the gathering that he would never consent to using force to remove natives from their land. A week later, the newspaper ran another editorial in which it attacked the terms of FitzRoy's recent proclamation about the Crown's right of pre-emption. At considerable length, it pointed out that

[99] Hadfield to Rev. H. Venn, 8 March 1847, CMS Records, CN/O48, AJCP, Reel M224; *Anglo-Maori Warder*, 24 August 1848.

the proclamation was contrary to the principles the imperial government had set down for colonising the country, since it promised to give land away for next to nothing. It predicted that FitzRoy would find that he had gone too far this time and would be dismissed from his post.[100]

After visiting Wellington, FitzRoy returned to New Plymouth where he confirmed his decision to overturn Spain's ruling and informed the settlers that all the land would have to be repurchased from the native owners. Yet he also persuaded the Te Āti Awa chiefs to sell 3,300 acres for the township of New Plymouth, waived the Crown's right of pre-emption so that the Company could negotiate the purchase of the remainder of the 60,000 acres in question and offered to advance funds for this purpose. Wicksteed, as the Company's local agent, accepted FitzRoy's decision, but William Wakefield was furious, declaring that the Governor's assumption that the Company's title in the area was defective was unfounded and that he had no right to interfere in Spain's ruling.[101]

In late November or early December, a group of the Company's settlers in Wellington sent a memorial to Stanley on the subject of FitzRoy's penny-an-acre proclamation, which was soon published in the Company's two newspapers in Cook Strait. In this carefully argued document, probably written by the lawyer Samuel Evans whose connection to the Company dated back to the founding of its predecessor, these memorialists observed that FitzRoy's proclamation had abandoned a fundamental article in the Treaty of Waitangi which had bestowed the right of pre-emption on the Crown. They contended that this measure was essential to the well-being of both natives and Europeans and complained that FitzRoy had introduced new principles for regulating the acquisition and disposal of waste lands that subverted the principles that underpinned the 1842 Waste Lands Act, thereby aggravating the problems that legislation was intended to remedy. They also contended that FitzRoy's proclamation was contrary to the law of nations and British common law, asserting that it was legally impossible for purchasers to acquire a Crown grant of land under it because the natives had no

---

[100] FitzRoy to Stanley, 16 September 1844, *BPP*, 1845, Paper no. 247, p. 139; *New Zealand Spectator and Cook's Strait Guardian*, 12 October, 2 and 9 November 1844.

[101] Wicksteed to Wakefield, 9 November 1844, New Zealand Company, *Eighteenth Report of the Directors of the New Zealand Company*, Stewart and Murray, London, 1845, pp. 87–89; FitzRoy to Wicksteed, 22 November 1844, *BPP*, 1846, Paper no. 203, p. 137; Wicksteed to Wakefield, 23 November 1844, New Zealand Company, *Supplement to the Eighteenth Report of the Directors of the New Zealand Company*, Stewart and Murray, London, 1845, pp. 26–28; Wakefield to Wicksteed, 13 December 1844, New Zealand Company, *Supplement to the Eighteenth Report*, pp. 34–39; McLean to FitzRoy, 17 December 1844, *BPP*, 1846, Paper no. 203, p. 143.

freehold in the soil. In mounting this argument, the settlers deployed much the same legal resources that the Company and its allies had used in London. But the memorialists found it necessary to claim that they regarded the Treaty of Waitangi as a fundamental law in the colony and to contend that their view of native rights in land was in no sense repugnant to the Treaty. They argued that this was so because the Treaty merely confirmed to the natives all the territorial rights as existed prior to the British Crown acquiring sovereignty, rather than conferring on them new rights they did not possess beforehand, such as a right to transfer property to British subjects. They contended that this had to be the true interpretation of the Treaty since it was clear that the Land Claims Act held that the Crown's right of pre-emption only acknowledged that the natives had a right to the occupation and use of land that they required (though this legislation made no reference to the nature of the natives' rights of property in land). Finally, the memorialists argued that FitzRoy's proclamation would destroy the capital and industry of the Company and its settlers as well as the colony's revenue and was bound to have an injurious effect on the interests of the natives.[102]

A week after the *New Zealand Spectator and Cook's Strait Guardian* published this memorial, it welcomed the news that William Wakefield and Henry Chapman, the former editor of the Company's *New Zealand Journal* and now one of the colony's principal legal officers, had received mail from London conveying the gist of Howick's Select Committee resolutions and report. It declared that in the event that the Colonial Office acted upon the Committee's recommendations, this would put an end to the system by which fictitious native claims to land had been allowed, an end to FitzRoy giving land away under his penny-an-acre proclamation, and even an end to his governorship. But the newspaper went further, asserting that FitzRoy had pursued a course that was impossible to describe with any words that were 'usually applicable to the proceedings of a rational governor'. Its editor, Revans, was hinting that FitzRoy was mad. Soon, both the Company's newspapers in New Zealand would publish statements made at public meetings on both sides of Cook Strait that suggested that the Governor was insane.[103]

For now, though, Revans argued that FitzRoy had been full of caution but had done nothing but mischief. He had not only failed to settle the

---

[102] Memorial of Port Nicholson Landowners to Stanley, undated, *BPP*, 1845, Paper no. 378, Returns of All Claims to Land in New Zealand, pp. 13–18; *New Zealand Spectator and Cook's Strait Guardian*, 7 December 1844; *Nelson Examiner and New Zealand Chronicle*, 21 December 1844.

[103] *New Zealand Spectator and Cook's Strait Guardian*, 14 and 21 December 1844, 8 February 1845; *Nelson Examiner and New Zealand Chronicle*, 8 February 1845.

land question but had rendered it more complicated; he had failed to conciliate the natives; he had failed to develop the country's resources; and he had destroyed the colony's revenues. Revans concluded that the local administration would not make any great changes for the better and so the colony's only hope was that some new men would be appointed to conduct its affairs. A week later, Revans was more specific, expressing the belief that a ship would soon arrive from England carrying reports that would leave FitzRoy no choice but to resign. As we will see, this prediction was not far from the mark.[104]

Conclusion

On his arrival in New Zealand, FitzRoy had found the colony in a critical state. The Colonial Office's assumption that the government would readily be able to acquire a good deal of cheap land, and that consequently colonisation would be rapid, had been utterly confounded. The New Zealand Company's settlers had become increasingly resentful about their failure to acquire possession of land or secure title to it, and in the wake of the Wairau melee they were urging the government to use force to assert British authority and subordinate the natives. Even the likes of Spain and the missionary Hadfield were advocating that the government make a show of force in the hope that this would persuade the natives to concede possession of the lands they had allegedly agreed to sell. For their part, many of the natives were in no mood to give ground.

In trying to address this crisis, there can be no doubt that FitzRoy had been dealt a poor hand, as the imperial government had denied him the funds to buy land and refused to agree to an increase in the colony's armed forces. But there can be no doubt that he played his hand badly. Faced with both settler aggression and native resistance, he tended to both underplay and overplay his hand. He could ill afford to do this because the Company in both New Zealand and London was able to use the power of the press to mount an assault on his handling of native title and native affairs more generally, and Māori chiefs felt emboldened to challenge British power and authority.

In time, the measures that FitzRoy saw fit to adopt, as well as the manner in which he executed them, undermined the confidence the Colonial Office had placed in him. This is hardly surprising for Stanley and his senior colleagues came to realise that he had repudiated, in one way or another, each and every one of the means that they had assumed would enable the British Crown to acquire ownership of land in the

---

[104] *New Zealand Spectator and Cook's Strait Guardian*, 14 December 1844.

colony. Even more importantly, by seeming to abandon the Crown's right of pre-emption, FitzRoy had not only drawn into question the Crown's authority but also its sovereignty – or so it seemed.

These events mattered a great deal because of the major political struggle that erupted between the New Zealand Company and the Colonial Office in London. In the wake of the news of the Wairau melee, the Company's directors were able to use the press to spin a powerful tale that claimed that its troubles were primarily the result of the so-called fact that the natives' rights of property in land had been erroneously defined by the home government and the colonial administration. Moreover, the Company was able to persuade the chairman of a parliamentary select committee to take the view that native rights in land should be limited to the lands they 'occupied or enjoyed'.

More specifically, the Company's directors and Howick came to blame the Treaty of Waitangi, or rather the first clause of its second article, for the way that the natives' rights in land had been treated by the government. The Colonial Office's senior figures followed suit in the sense that they too attributed to the Treaty a significance it had not had at the time it was made. It mattered not a jot that the historical claims that were made and the stories that were told about the Treaty's historical significance involved more fiction than fact. It was now just taken for granted that the Treaty was terribly important. Similarly, it mattered little that the claims the Company and its political allies made about the way that native title had been defined by the Colonial Office were equally fictitious.

In the course of the 1844 Select Committee's hearings, the Colonial Office's commitment to the Treaty and to native title deepened further in the face of the attack that the Company mounted on both. This might be regarded as a function of their reception of the oral and written evidence that was submitted to the Committee, which, drawing on local sources of knowledge, revealed that the natives had their own settled notions of rights of property in land and claimed every inch of the country. Yet it is apparent that at this point the nature of the position that the Colonial Office's principal players took on the Treaty began to shift. Rather than continuing to insist that it should be regarded as a legal agreement by which the Crown had confirmed and guaranteed the natives in possession of their land, they now seemed willing to concede the point the government's opponents had made, namely that the natives only had rights of property in the lands they 'occupied or enjoyed'. But, simultaneously, they returned to the kind of historical arguments that they had previously deployed in their clash with the Company's directors. They insisted that matters of native title could not be treated in accordance with abstract legal principles drawn from the law of nations and the like but had to be dealt with in the light of what had happened in the past and the facts on the ground in New Zealand. To be more specific, they contended that it was simply a matter of historical fact that the Crown had treated the natives as sovereign; that it had made a treaty that included the first clause of its second article; that this was morally binding on the government and so involved the faith and honour of the Crown; that a fair construction of the treaty meant it was impossible to limit the native claims to title to the land they occupied or enjoyed; and that it would be unwise to proceed on any other basis since this would alienate the natives and probably lead to a war for which the government lacked the necessary force.

In the wake of the Select Committee's report, Stanley upheld this position on the Treaty. He argued that, whatever might be the source of rights of property in land in theory, the fact of the matter was that the Crown had taken a series of steps by which it had recognised the natives as sovereign, had asserted that the natives' titles to land were indisputable and had directed Hobson to make a treaty by which the Crown had confirmed and guaranteed the natives possession of their lands. Moreover, he contended, the parliament had sanctioned these steps and the local government had passed laws regulating titles in keeping with them. Most importantly, he insisted that the government was morally bound by the declarations that it had made in the name of the Crown and it was clear that warlike and well-armed natives now entertained notions about their title that had been expressed in those declarations and that this meant the government would face enormous difficulties if it tried to change course.

In the colony itself, abstract legal principles and philosophical ideas played a similarly small role in the way the key British players – Spain and FitzRoy – approached the matter of native title. A mix of moral, political and strategic considerations ensured that the principle of securing native consent to the extinguishment of their interests in land continued to be upheld by the colonial administration. Even in London, where the government's opponents found it useful to deploy legal concepts and philosophical notions in order to advance their case, the major political player who was most forthright in claiming that native title was limited to the land the natives 'occupied or enjoyed', namely Howick, seems to have faltered at one point after realising that a former Colonial Secretary seemed to have conceded that the New Zealanders might have greater rights in land than he was prepared to allow.

8 The Retreat of the Government and the Rise of the Treaty, 1844–1845

In London in the winter and spring of 1844–45 the Colonial Office came under enormous pressure to acknowledge its errors and change course in its administration of New Zealand's affairs. Stanley was inclined to hold the line, but the Prime Minister Sir Robert Peel and the Home Secretary Sir James Graham called on him to reach an agreement with the New Zealand Company. In this highly charged political situation, there was extensive debate about native title in land. Moreover, the significance attributed to the Treaty of Waitangi deepened, entrenching its status as the crucial constitutional document in regard to native title and even the colony itself. The positions the different parties adopted in regard to both native title and the Treaty were largely a function of the political tussle between them. Furthermore, the more the government realised it had to concede many of the points the Company and its allies had been making in regard to native title, the more significance it attached to the Treaty. It increasingly cast the Treaty as a historical agreement that was morally binding on the British Crown and parliament.

In 1845 two important parliamentary debates took place in the House of Commons about the colony's affairs, which featured a good deal of discussion about native title and the Treaty. Several historians have noted the significance of the first of these debates but have devoted only a few paragraphs to it. They warrant careful examination. This chapter will also deal with the negotiations that took place between members of Peel's cabinet and representatives of the New Zealand Company. They reveal that the government's most senior members were keen to do a deal with the Company, even though this would have seen it set aside the principles that Stanley and the Colonial Office had been trying to uphold in their protracted battle with the Company.

Part I

Pressuring the Colonial Office, Persuading the Prime Minister

Much of the debate in this period focused on the findings of Howick's recent House of Commons Select Committee report on New Zealand. In mid-December 1844 *The Times* used the publication of the report to take issue with the Committee's explanation of the colony's troubled state of affairs. It argued that the New Zealand Company had driven the colony into its current predicament. By colonising the islands in defiance of the Crown, the Company had found it necessary to purchase land from the natives. As a result of those transactions, the Company had recognised one doctrine – purchasers such as the Company held land by virtue of a title through the natives – and established another – all the unoccupied land in the colony was the absolute property of the natives and could only be acquired by the British Crown purchasing it from them. Two weeks later, *The Times* published another editorial on this subject in order to clarify its position after a Company spokesman had misrepresented it. Its editor spelt out that the Crown had been unable to assert its authority at the outset in regard to native title because the Company had rushed ahead and purchased land, and by the time the government tried to do this it was too late. 'The mischief has been done. The natives have been already impressed with a belief, however unfounded, that the whole sovereignty of the land, occupied or *un*occupied, is of right theirs', *The Times* asserted; 'of this', its editor continued, 'it is now impossible to disabuse them, and the whole series of disorder and bloodshed of which the islands have been unhappily the scene is traceable to this source'. Yet, having made this point, *The Times* made clear its adherence to 'the fundamental doctrine' that no aboriginal tribe could claim dominion beyond the limits of their actual occupation of the land in question.[1]

This exchange of opinions between the Company and England's most influential newspaper prompted James Busby, who had recently returned to England, to write a long letter to *The Times* in which he rejected the contention that the natives only had rights of property in the land they occupied and cultivated. The former British Resident for New Zealand began this letter by advancing several well-known legal and philosophical arguments to support his contention, but he soon turned his attention to the Treaty of Waitangi. He argued that it was based on Normanby's acknowledgement of native rights to sovereignty and land, and contended that its relevant clause, namely the first clause of its second article, was

---

[1] *The Times*, 11 and 25 December 1844, its emphasis.

especially intended to confirm the natives as the owners of the land in the fullest and most extensive sense. He implied that his interpretation of this clause was correct because he had been responsible for drafting it. Busby concluded his letter with a warning that the security of British settlers and indeed the very existence of British settlement in the colony depended on the government remembering that it was bound to uphold the natives' title to land on the grounds of natural justice and national honour.[2]

Meanwhile, the Company's directors finally accepted that the Select Committee's report was not going to compel Stanley to change course. Charles Buller stepped in, pretending to play the role of the honest broker between the Company and the Colonial Office. Buller, who was regarded as one of the cleverest and most charming men in the House of Commons, sought the help of Prime Minister Sir Robert Peel. In addressing a personal letter to him, he adopted a tactic he had used before, pretending that the Company was at the mercy of the government. But he also told Peel that the Company's directors were preparing a case to bring before parliament that would seek to shift responsibility for the colony's state of affairs onto the Colonial Office, and use the Select Committee report to support their contention that the Colonial Office had violated its contracts with the Company and that successive governors had disobeyed the home government's instructions. Buller clearly hoped to persuade Peel that it was in the government's best interests for him to intervene, thereby avoiding a contest on the floor of the House of Commons. He claimed the matter had become bogged down in petty animosity between the principal actors – which was true to a degree – though he threw most of the blame for this onto Stanley.[3]

Peel was not fooled by Buller and referred his letter to Stanley. Nevertheless, the Colonial Secretary realised he had to explain himself. His reply to Peel, which took the form of a confidential letter, provides insight into the reasons he had been treating matters in New Zealand in the way he had. Stanley began this letter by confessing that he had no confidence in the Company – 'I must own that I have been disquieted by the perpetual small trickery which from first to last characterised their proceedings' – and closed it by remarking: 'The Company has been, from the first, a great bubble, the bursting of which, but for the immediate consequences to their settlers, I should rejoice at, and consider eminently advantageous to New Zealand'. Stanley, as we have seen, was not alone in

---

[2] *Ibid.*, 27 December 1844.
[3] Charles Buller to Sir Robert Peel, 14 December 1844, Sir Robert Peel Papers, BL (henceforth Peel Papers), Add MS 40555; David A. Haury, *The Origins of the Liberal Party and Liberal Imperialism: The Career of Charles Buller, 1806–1848*, Garland Publishing, New York, 1987, pp. 25, 27.

the Colonial Office in feeling uneasy about the unscrupulous behaviour of the Company's leading figures. He nevertheless insisted that he had done all in his power to settle the Company's claims. This done, he sought to explain to Peel his response to the Company's demands and the Select Committee's recommendations. 'What [the Company] ask[s], and what the [select] committee indirectly appear to recommend, *I neither can, nor will, nor dare assent to*', he wrote. As this formulation suggests, a complex series of factors lay behind Stanley's position, or at least how he chose to represent it to Peel. As he had done previously, he argued that the Crown had solemnly recognised the independence of the native chiefs prior to 1840 and that in return for the chiefs ceding sovereignty it had guaranteed to the natives 'in the most extensive terms' the possession of their 'lands, forests and fisheries', quoting the first clause of the Treaty's second article. But Stanley now argued as well that Normanby had recognised the natives' extensive claims by instructing Hobson to purchase unoccupied land. Most importantly perhaps, he complained that the Company had claimed a right to put into possession of a large amount of land 'without any reference to aboriginal title' and had dismissed the Treaty as a mere ruse to annex the land of 'naked savages'. Clearly, this stuck in the Colonial Secretary's craw.[4]

Stanley proceeded to point out to Peel that the Select Committee had maintained that the Company had a right to land. As far as he was concerned, this raised what was really the only point in dispute between the Colonial Office and the Company: what constituted the property of the Crown? It might appear at first that Stanley saw this essentially as a legal matter. 'The native titles are perfectly well understood among themselves', he asserted. 'The natives are not mere savages but men with distinct notions of the rights of property.' Yet he went on to advance an argument that suggests that pragmatic considerations were uppermost in his mind. '[The natives] are well-armed and war-like and number above 100,000. Our settlers are dispersed, not above 10,000 in number and our military force for the whole island is under 150 men', he remarked. 'With these facts I would ask if I use too strong an expression when I say, setting aside considerations of justice and good faith, I *dare* not act on the principles laid down by the Company and apparently supported by the Committee, i.e., of restricting the native claims to lands actually in occupation, and declaring all the remainder the property of the Crown'.[5]

---

[4] Peel to Lord Stanley, 15 December 1844, Fourteen Earl of Derby Papers, Liverpool Record Office, 920 DER (14) (henceforth Derby Papers), 129/4; Stanley to Peel, 17 December 1844, Derby Papers, 129/4, my emphasis.

[5] *Ibid.*, my emphasis. Perhaps the last part of Stanley's argument struck a chord with Peel. Several years later (after he had fallen from office), he stated in a private letter to George

On receiving Stanley's letter, Peel informed Buller that he was willing to grant his request for a personal interview but made it clear that his views were unlikely to depart from those of his minister. A few weeks later, Peel told Stanley he thought that he had been 'quite right throughout' and would do whatever he wished in this matter. However, pressure continued to grow on the government.[6]

At the beginning of January 1845, one of the Company's constant allies in the press, the *Spectator*, published a large supplement comprising a series of articles about New Zealand. There was little new in these reports, but the magazine told a story with all the persuasive spin that Wakefield and Buller had long been using. It advanced several lines of argument. First, it claimed that the Treaty of Waitangi was worth nothing. The government had claimed sovereignty on grounds other than the cession obtained by the Treaty, most importantly on the basis of *discovery*, as per Hobson's May 1840 proclamations. Moreover, it argued, the Treaty's terms, by which it meant the pre-emption clause, had been violated by the parties to it. Furthermore, the native signatories could not have understood the Treaty, not least because of the haste with which it was made and the difficulty of translating key concepts. In addition, *the Spectator* claimed that many chiefs had not signed the Treaty and that most had done so merely to get the presents that had been offered. Finally, it asserted that the only rights in land that the Treaty recognised were those of occupancy, and even the basis of those were slender. Second, the magazine presented the Company's interpretation of the November 1840 agreement with the government and supported this with the account that Russell had recently given of its meaning. Third, it set out the findings of Howick's Select Committee report. Finally, the *Spectator* launched an attack on Stephen, Stanley and FitzRoy. It alleged that Stephen was pro-missionary and opposed to the Company and even to colonisation, and that he held the real power in the Colonial Office; it claimed that Stanley had succumbed to particular sectional interests, was overly concerned with conducting a petty personal war with the Company and repeatedly misrepresented its case; and it asserted that FitzRoy was under the thumb of the missionary societies

---

Hope: 'If the obligations of good faith vary with the military skill and prowess to the parties to a treaty, the New Zealanders have put a claim to be respected which it has become prudent on our part to recognise' (Peel to George Hope, 19 February 1848, Papers of the Hope Family of Luffness, East Lothian, The National Archives of Scotland [henceforth Hope Papers], GD364/1/4388).

[6] Peel to Stanley, 20 December 1844, Derby Papers, 129/4; Peel to Buller, 23 December 1844, Peel Papers, Add MS 40555; Peel to Stanley, 15 January 1845, Derby Papers, 129/4.

and the protectors, and so no improvement in his administration of the colony could be expected.[7]

In mid-January Buller pressed Peel for the meeting he had been promised. Stanley warned Peel to tread cautiously: 'He is intimately connected with the Company and, I am afraid, from what I have seen of him, much more plausible than straightforward'. Ten days later, the *Spectator* urged that Stanley be removed from the Colonial Office. Macvey Napier, the editor of the influential magazine the *Edinburgh Review*, sought to refute the story that the Company was telling about New Zealand, but James Stephen despaired, telling Napier: 'Of course nothing remains but to leave [the Company] in undisputed possession of the field'.[8]

In early February the *Spectator* attacked FitzRoy again after reports reached London of his handling of Heke's rebellion and his overturning of Spain's ruling in Taranaki. Arguing that the former had diminished British authority and that the latter had annulled 'the great right of property', the magazine claimed that it appeared that the Governor's 'senses had gone' and he had become an agent for undoing the colonisation of the country. 'It is impossible', it asserted, 'that Sir Robert Peel's government can suffer such a state of matters to continue'. Two days later, Stanley, realising that the Company was planning to launch an assault on the Colonial Office's handling of New Zealand's affairs as soon as parliament resumed, sent a strongly worded despatch to FitzRoy, complaining that he had received no substantive despatches from him for more than four months even though it was apparent that he had adopted several important measures. 'It is obviously most inconvenient', Stanley complained, 'that individuals and the public should be in possession of apparently well founded reports of your proceedings during a long period in which Her Majesty's government have no information from yourself'. The next day, as the House of Commons sat for the first time for the year, Stanley had to bow to the Company's demand that he table the despatch he had sent FitzRoy in August 1844 in which he had more or less instructed him to ignore the most important of the Select Committee's resolutions.[9]

---

[7] *Spectator*, 4 January 1845. See also *Spectator*, 11 January 1845.

[8] Buller to Peel, 14 January 1845, Peel Papers, Add MS 40557; Peel to Buller, 15 January 1845, Peel Papers, Add MS 40557; Stanley to Peel, 15 January 1845, Peel Papers, Add MS 40468; *Spectator*, 25 January 1845; James Stephen to Macvey Napier, 25 January 1845, Macvey Napier Papers, BL, Add MS 34625.

[9] *Spectator*, 1 February 1845; Stanley to Robert FitzRoy, 3 February 1845, *BPP*, 1845, Paper no. 131, Return to An Address of the Honourable the House of Commons dated 11 March 1845, p. 57; *BPP*, 1845, Paper no. 1, Papers Relative to the Affairs of New Zealand.

Both the *Morning Chronicle* and *The Times* were quick to draw attention to this despatch. Several days later, the Company's directors declared that it made clear that the Company had no hope of obtaining redress of the wrongs it had suffered at the hands of the Colonial Office. Furthermore, they more or less announced that they had decided to put the Company's whole case before the House of Commons by means of a petition (though they had actually begun to draw up this petition before Stanley tabled his despatch). Buller not only continued to lobby Peel in the belief that the matter could be resolved without any further public discussion but also tried to apply pressure by telling him that the Company was drawing up this petition and would make it public very soon. In fact, Buller sent Peel a rough draft of the petition. This was a serious miscalculation. Buller had led Peel to believe that he would provide him with a private memorandum that would form the basis of confidential discussions involving Peel, Stanley and himself. Peel ticked him off and sent the petition back with its seal unbroken.[10]

Buller hurriedly prepared the memorandum Peel required. In the most important part of this document he laid out several proposals, each of which required the government to give the Company a particular undertaking. The first required the government to make an unconditional grant of land to the Company of the amount it had claimed and to take responsibility for extinguishing any native title in it; the second to sanction the formation of a separate colony that would encompass the lower part of the North Island and the South Island; the third to grant this new colony responsible government; and the fourth to take over all the property of the Company in return for £300,000 or give the Company a loan of £100,000 to enable it to realise its present property.[11]

Hope seems to have been willing to consider Buller's proposals but soon formed the opinion that they were unacceptable. Stanley was even more dismissive. He believed that Buller's first proposal went far beyond anything the Company had ever proposed and doubted that the government would contemplate buying a large amount of land and handing it over to the Company. But he was more concerned with what he saw as a suggestion that the government would give an undertaking to compel the native owners to surrender such lands. Stanley thought the second proposal was very ill advised since the colony Buller had in mind would include the district (Cook Strait) where the natives had been the most troublesome because they had been the most oppressed by the Company.

---

[10] *The Times*, 6 February 1845; *Morning Chronicle*, 6 February 1845; *Morning Post*, 14 February 1845; Buller to Peel, 3 and 7 February 1845, Peel Papers, Add MS 40559; Peel to Buller, 9 February 1845, Peel Papers, Add MS 40559.
[11] Buller to Peel, 10 February 1845, Peel Papers, Add MS 40559.

He rejected the third proposal on the grounds that the natives would be excluded from responsible government. However, Stanley welcomed part of Buller's fourth proposal, seeing it as a means of putting an end to the Company's meddling in the country's affairs and thus giving New Zealand a chance to become a valuable colony. But in the end Peel ruled that the government could not accept any of these proposals.[12]

At the beginning of March Stanley finally lost patience with FitzRoy, sending him a despatch in which he emphatically stated that the absence of any information from him about what he had been doing, and more especially the lack of any explanation of the measures he had adopted, was proving to be 'extremely embarrassing' to the government. It was vital, he observed, that the Colonial Office have FitzRoy's own account of the facts and the grounds for his conduct. Stanley listed several important measures that FitzRoy had adopted in the colony in the last eleven months which he could not sanction. One of the most troubling was FitzRoy's overturning of Spain's finding in regard to the Company's Taranaki claim. 'Whatever might be your private opinion of the merits of the case, you are aware that one of the great difficulties that the government have had to contend with is that of supporting the decisions and authority of this [Land Claims Commission]', Stanley wrote; 'but the task would become hopeless if the Governor himself should set an example of disparaging and superseding [its] authority, and thus lowering this and other courts of justice in the eyes both of British settlers and natives, between whom it is most important that you should hold an even balance'. Stanley hoped that FitzRoy had actually sent the despatches he required, but warned him that if this was not the case he would be guilty of a dereliction of duty that would warrant his being recalled.[13]

Several days later, Stanley tried to shore up the government's position by ordering that some of the correspondence the Colonial Office had recently received be tabled in the House of Commons. It included an important letter from the colony's former Colonial Secretary and Acting Governor. Willoughby Shortland had been prompted to write to Stanley after reading Howick's Select Committee report. In this letter he argued that the Committee had adopted principles that were incompatible with those upon which the British Crown had assumed sovereignty in New Zealand; he suggested that the change in policy towards the natives that the Committee had advocated would override the provisions of a treaty solemnly made with them; and he argued that the breaching of those

[12] Hope to Stanley, 11 February 1845, Derby Papers, 134/1/2; Stanley to Peel, 11 February 1845, Derby Papers, 27/5/2; Peel to Buller, 21 February 1845, Peel Papers, Add MS 40560.

[13] Stanley to FitzRoy, 1 March 1845, Peel Papers, Add MS 40571.

pledges would plunge the country into anarchy and war. More specifi-cally, Shortland claimed that the Treaty was made in accordance with the principles on which the Crown had chosen to found the colony and that the colonial government had understood the relevant clause in it, namely the first clause of its second article, in these terms and had acted accord-ingly. He challenged the Committee's claim that the natives could not have understood the significance of a transaction like the Treaty and that consequently it amounted to little more than a legal fiction. He had been present at three of the treaty meetings and had heard the native chiefs speak, he told Stanley. He had concluded that the chiefs not only under-stood the agreement but were troubled about every question concerning their lands. Shortland also argued that the chiefs would have refused to cede sovereignty to the Crown without what he called 'a reciprocal guarantee by the Crown to them of the perfect enjoyment of their terri-torial rights'.[14]

Most importantly perhaps, Shortland dismissed the Committee's claim that the colonial administration's misinterpretation of the first clause of the Treaty's second article had been responsible for a definition of native title that had deleterious consequences for the workings of the Land Claims Commission and thus the New Zealand Company. In neither the legislation nor the instructions that governed the Commission's work was there any reference to the nature of the natives' title, he pointed out. But even if the Commission had deviated from the principles embraced by the Committee's majority in regard to native title, he remarked, this could not have been the cause of the difficulties that the Company had encountered. The current disputes concerned lands that were occupied by the natives, rather than any so-called waste lands. Indeed, Shortland pointed out, the question of who was held to be the owner of what the Committee's report had called a vast and unoccupied territory was yet to require any consideration by the government since the lands that settlers were presently demanding were those generally occupied by the natives.[15]

In the same vein, Shortland drew Stanley's attention to the fact that the Company was more or less alone among those parties who had purchased land prior to British annexation in having its claims disputed by the natives. He argued that the principal cause of the difficulties the Company had experienced was the reckless way in which William Wakefield had conducted its purchasing. He also noted that the Company could have largely overcome the consequences of its own

[14] Willoughby Shortland to Stanley, 18 January 1845, *BPP*, 1845, Paper no. 108, Copies of Letters from Mr Shortland, late Acting Governor, and Mr Busby, late Resident of New Zealand, to Lord Stanley and Mr G. Hope, pp. 3–5.
[15] *Ibid.*, pp. 5–6.

misconduct if Wakefield had fulfilled the agreement he had made with Hobson (and which had been renewed by himself) to make good the Company's alleged purchases by providing a further payment to the natives. This point led him to reject the Committee's claim that the Company's difficulties owed much to the failure of the local administration to co-operate with the Company. As he observed, Hobson and his officials had always sought to help the Company but its agents had consistently acted in defiance of the Crown's authority.[16]

Much of Shortland's letter shed an unusually clear light on the matters in dispute. But material of this kind had to compete with the avalanche of Company propaganda that was presented by its directors, a considerable number of whom were MPs. They continued to concoct a badly flawed but nonetheless plausible tale about the colony's affairs, making it very difficult for accounts such as Shortland's to penetrate, let alone prevail. Consequently, much of the debate in London took place on the Company's terms.

The House of Commons Debates Begin

On 11 March the New Zealand Company's governor, Lord Joseph Somes, called on the government to table correspondence between FitzRoy and the Colonial Office on several matters relating to the colony. They included the recent outrages in the Bay of Islands, the steps FitzRoy had taken to fulfil the May 1843 agreement between the Colonial Office and the Company, his disallowance of awards recommended by Spain and his most recent waiver of the Crown's right of pre-emption. Somes knew that the Colonial Office would be unable to meet his request and so would be shown to be badly out of touch with recent events in the colony. Indeed, Hope had to plead ignorance about most of them.[17]

It soon became apparent that the Company's spokesmen in the House had a purpose beyond that of embarrassing the Colonial Office. They warned that they would not let the Select Committee's findings rest and threatened to table a petition comprising a comprehensive statement about the Colonial Office's treatment of the Company. For the time being, though, they contented themselves with mounting a full-scale attack on FitzRoy. Leading the charge, Buller alleged that he was grossly mismanaging the colony and was utterly incapable of filling his position as governor. He claimed that the government had acted improperly in appointing him, suggested that the Colonial Office ought to have sent

---

[16] *Ibid.*, pp. 7–8.
[17] *BPD*, House of Commons, 11 March 1845, columns 644–51, 654–55.

out someone to take charge of him and argued that the government should recall him. In fact, Buller was vitriolic in his assault on FitzRoy, which caused tempers in the House to fray badly.[18]

Hope (who was responsible for representing the Colonial Office in the House of Commons since Stanley had been elevated to the House of Lords) tried to foil the Company's attack by focusing on a matter about which he did have information. For several months the Company had been claiming that Stanley was guilty of a breach of faith in regard to the instructions he had given FitzRoy for the implementation of the May 1843 agreement between the Colonial Office and the Company. It had alleged that the Colonial Secretary had shown the Company one set of the instructions only to issue a different set to the Governor, and that consequently FitzRoy had not carried out the agreement. Now, one of the Company's directors, who rejoiced in the Dickensian name of Mangles, accused Stanley of gross deception. In responding to this charge, Hope tried to shift the focus of the debate onto the bigger question of the rights of the natives and to portray the Company as the despoiler of them. He pointed out that Stanley had only ever entered into an undertaking to guarantee the Company possession of land that the Crown actually owned, and that he could do no more than this since the Crown was under an obligation imposed by the Treaty of Waitangi.[19]

For his part, Peel argued that it was improper to indulge in the kind of attacks that had been made on FitzRoy, especially since they rested on newspaper reports. He also pointed out that the Company had actually welcomed FitzRoy's appointment. Nevertheless, Peel was forced to concede that some of the Governor's acts required 'very serious inquiry' and he declined to provide a full-blooded defence of them. As a result, the debate suggested that something was badly wrong with the Colonial Office's administration of New Zealand's affairs.[20]

The Company's allies in the press swiftly drew attention to this impression. Yet an editorial in *The Times* was undoubtedly more damaging to the Colonial Office, largely because it had once been the Company's sternest critic among the nation's newspapers. It argued that Stanley was answerable for the acts of those whom he had appointed to govern Britain's colonies and that it was now only a question of whether FitzRoy's conduct was bad enough to warrant his removal or whether a reprimand or disallowance of his proceedings would suffice. Most importantly, *The Times* claimed that it was little wonder that the New Zealand question was to be formally and fully brought before the House of Commons given

---

[18] *Ibid.*, columns 646, 659–75.   [19] *Ibid.*, columns 684, 689–90.
[20] *Ibid.*, columns 676–81.

the charge that Stanley had evaded the recommendations of a parliamentary select committee.[21]

The next day, Stanley sent FitzRoy a furious despatch complaining of 'the extreme inconvenience' to which the government had been put by his 'long-continued silence'. FitzRoy's failure to provide the Colonial Office with frequent and full reports meant that the Office had been unable to deal with the Company's allegations, and this had created an impression that was deeply unfavourable to the Governor and highly injurious to the government, he complained. This was not all. Stanley told FitzRoy that some of what he had learned had shaken the confidence he had placed in his discretion and that his tenure in office was at risk unless he promptly gave a full and adequate explanation of his proceedings. On the same day, Hope went to the House of Commons to try to contain the damage that the Company's allegations were causing the government. But by doing this he gave the Company's spokesmen in the House another opportunity to repeat their charges against Stanley and both Howick and Russell a chance to demand that the policy pursued in New Zealand by the Colonial Office and colonial government be the subject of a debate in the House.[22]

At the end of March the Colonial Office finally received a series of despatches in which FitzRoy had belatedly sought to explain the raft of measures he had introduced. If Stanley had not already decided to recall him, these despatches made up his mind to sacrifice FitzRoy so as to be able to shore up the Colonial Office's position. Stanley was not so much concerned by the decisions FitzRoy had made; he assumed that there might have been sound reasons for many of them. Instead, he was troubled by the fact that the Governor's assessment of the problems he encountered seemed to be extremely hasty and his decision-making rash and inconsistent. Moreover, Stanley was acutely aware that FitzRoy had adopted measures that he knew the Colonial Office had refused to sanction. Most importantly, though, the Governor had failed to explain his actions, let alone in a punctual fashion, thereby placing the government in a situation of what Stanley called 'almost inextricable embarrassment'.[23]

Many of the problems noted by Stanley concerned land and relations more generally with the natives. On the subject of land, he complained that FitzRoy had 'assumed the grave responsibility' of setting aside

---

[21] *The Times*, 13 March 1845; *Morning Chronicle*, 13 March 1845; *Spectator*, 15 March 1845.

[22] Stanley to Fitzroy, 14 March 1845, Peel Papers, Add MS 40571; *BPD*, House of Commons, 14 March 1845, columns 891–95, 900–02.

[23] Stanley, Confidential Statement, 11 April 1845, Peel Papers, Add MS 40468; Stanley to Fitzroy, 30 April 1845, Peel Papers, Add MS 40571; Stanley to Fitzroy, 14 May 1845, Peel Papers, Add MS 40571.

Spain's decision in favour of the New Zealand Company in Taranaki and had abrogated important rules in waiving the Crown's right of preemption. In regard to his handling of native matters, one of which was Heke's attacks in the Bay of Islands, he complained that FitzRoy seemed to have been motivated by a fear of offending the natives. He also professed to be unpersuaded by the vivid account that FitzRoy had given of the native military prowess he witnessed in Auckland in May 1844. Yet, as we have seen, only a few months earlier, Stanley had told Peel that the natives' military strength meant that the British government could not give way to the Company's demands. This suggests that the Colonial Office had no particular view about the natives' power or at least that it tended to represent this according to its own shifting political needs.[24]

Abortive Negotiations

In the meantime, Buller began to pursue another avenue in order to persuade the government to grant the Company's demands, that of lobbying Sir James Graham. It is worth discussing what transpired as it reveals that the government's leading members were prepared to make concessions to the Company even though this would have seen it sacrificing the principles that the Colonial Office had been trying to uphold in regard to native title and the Treaty of Waitangi.

Graham was the Home Secretary and a close friend and adviser of Peel's. He was keen to settle the conflict between the Colonial Office and Company amicably because he was concerned, not without reason, that the government was vulnerable both inside and outside the House of Commons. According to an account that Graham gave later, he and Buller chanced to meet immediately after the debate on 18 March. Given what we know of Buller, he had probably ambushed Graham, just as he had ambushed Stephen five years earlier. In any case, Buller requested a further conversation. It seems that Graham then approached Peel with a view to persuading him to put pressure on Stanley. Subsequently, one or two private meetings involving Buller, Graham and Peel took place before Graham encouraged Buller to submit a written proposal outlining his views about the best way to settle all the questions relating to New Zealand.[25]

[24] Stanley, Confidential Statement, 11 April 1845, Peel Papers, Add MS 40468; Stanley to Fitzroy, 30 April 1845, Peel Papers, Add MS 40571; Stanley to Fitzroy, 14 May 1845, Peel Papers, Add MS 40571.

[25] Sir James Graham to Peel, 9 April 1845, Peel Papers, Add MS 40451; Minutes, Secret Committee of the NZC, 1 May 1845, TNA, CO 208/188; Report presented to the Court of Directors by the Secret Committee, 28 May 1845, TNA, CO 208/188; *BPD*, House of

In this confidential proposal Buller argued that everything that had happened in New Zealand revealed that there was a 'fundamental error' in the system of colonisation that had been pursued by the government, that only a major change could address this problem and that this would make any ruling on the particular points of controversy between the Colonial Office and the Company unnecessary. Buller attributed the 'fundamental error' to 'two evils': a conflict between what he called 'the missionary system' of the government and 'the colonising system' of the Company; and the Company's flawed constitution.[26]

In respect of the first evil, Buller painted a powerful caricature of what had happened in the colony. He claimed that 'the missionary system' had tried to prevent British colonisation, uphold the 'nationality' of the natives, keep the natives apart from Europeans and maintain their rights in all of the land in New Zealand. By contrast, he argued, 'the colonising system' had sought to promote British settlement, encourage the natives to 'amalgamate' with Europeans and treat the land as unappropriated wherever it was not occupied. Buller argued that the conflict between these two systems had been aggravated by the government because it had sided with the Treaty and the missionary principle against the November 1840 agreement and the colonising principle. In respect of the second evil, Buller argued that the Company had acquired either too much or too little power at its incorporation: the government had devolved upon it the function of colonising New Zealand but had failed to delegate to it all the powers of the Crown.[27]

Buller claimed that it would be foolhardy to try to reconcile the two systems and suggested that the geopolitical circumstances of New Zealand provided the means to resolve the colony's problems. The northern part of the North Island should become one colony and no further colonisation of it should be encouraged. He characterised this area as the place where the present capital Auckland lay, the missionaries had mostly laboured and the great bulk of the natives lived, and argued that the Treaty could only have legal force there because only in this part of New Zealand could it be held that the title of the Crown was founded on cession from the natives. Buller recommended that the remainder of the North Island and all of the southern islands, which was largely

Commons, 30 May 1845, columns 1092–93; Mark Hickford, *Lords of the Land: Indigenous Property Rights and the Jurisprudence of Empire*, Oxford University Press, Oxford, 2011, p. 182.

[26] Buller, Memo, transmitted 14 or 15 April 1845, TNA, CO 208/188. Buller forwarded this memorandum to the Company on 14 or 15 April but we know he sent it to Graham several days earlier, because Graham sent it to Peel on 9 April, after both he and Stanley had read it (Graham to Peel, 9 April 1845, Peel Papers, Add MS 40451).

[27] Buller, Memo, transmitted 14 or 15 April 1845.

coterminous with the New Zealand Company's original claim and where he argued that the natives numbered no more than 9,000 and were already outnumbered by Europeans, should become a new colony and be the field of British colonisation. All the powers of government over it should be entrusted to the Company on the same terms as the proprietary charters for Pennsylvania and Maryland in the seventeenth century, and representative institutions should be granted to the settlers. He proposed that the Treaty should apply in the part of the new colony that lay in the North Island and that the Company should pay to the government a sum to purchase land, but that in the remainder of this colony the Company should assume a right of pre-emption and that all lands that were not occupied by natives or held under a grant from the government should be vested in the Company. As in earlier Company proposals, one-eleventh of all land surveyed was to be set aside as reserves for the natives and they were to enjoy the same rights and privileges as British subjects.[28]

This was a radical plan that would have seen native title treated very differently to the way it had been handled up to this point. Graham was sympathetic, and Peel was willing to countenance it. Had Stanley and Hope not been in office, the government would probably have accepted the plan. But, at least at this point in time, Stanley would not have a bar of it. Graham despaired, telling Peel: 'I had hoped that [Buller's plan] might have formed the basis of a reasonable settlement but I am afraid . . . that little hope can be entertained of an amicable adjustment of this contro- versy'. Peel seems to have agreed that Stanley had provided very cogent arguments against the government adopting Buller's proposal, but he was disinclined to accept them as this would have scuttled the negotiations. Two weeks later, a meeting took place between Stanley, Graham and Buller at which Stanley raised some of his objections to the measures that Buller had proposed, and it was agreed that Buller would draw up a new proposal to address those objections.[29]

In the last week of April Buller submitted a revised proposal to Stanley. But he had made only minor changes to it. Just as importantly, he had added a requirement that any formal proposal that might form the basis of an agreement had to come from the government rather than the Company and the government had to announce that this was the case. He also insisted that he could not postpone a motion calling for a debate in the House of Commons about the Colonial Office's treatment of the

---

[28] *Ibid.*
[29] Buller, Memo, undated, annotated by Stanley, Derby Papers, 27/5/2; Graham to Peel, 9 April 1845, Peel Papers, Add MS 40451; Peel, undated memo [c. 10 April 1845], Derby Papers, 27/5/2; Report by Buller, NZC Secret Committee, Minutes of Meetings, 1 May 1845, TNA, CO 208/188.

Company. This sly ploy was typical of the Company's advocates and agents. Not surprisingly, Stanley and Peel regarded Buller's conditions as a very serious obstacle to the government even considering his proposal. Yet Peel held that the government should continue to keep the door open for negotiations. It appears that Peel asked Graham to take Buller aside and tell him that the government objected to proceeding any further on the basis of his conditions and that he had to withdraw his motion before Stanley would have any further communication with him. Graham also told Buller that Stanley had no insuperable objection to Buller's proposal (though it is unlikely this was the case). Buller had little choice but to accede to Graham's demands.[30]

On 1 May a secret committee that the Company had formed, which included Buller, Edward Gibbon Wakefield and Henry Aglionby, agreed to submit a largely unchanged version of Buller's memorandum to Stanley. (This was done in the name of Lord Ingestre, who had succeeded Somes as the Company's chairman since he was ill and would die shortly.) On the same day Ingestre submitted this memorandum to the Colonial Office, Hope belatedly read the version of the memorandum that Buller had originally submitted. He was dismayed by its proposals and troubled that Stanley seemed to be willing to entertain them. 'I cannot return [this memorandum] to you', Hope wrote to his superior, 'without expressing my regret that any implied sanction should have been given to a plan based upon the principle which is [Buller's]'. In particular, Hope felt obliged to record his dissent from Buller's assumption that the Crown could now declare to which parts of New Zealand the Treaty of Waitangi would or would not apply. He also expressed surprise that Stanley appeared to be willing to entertain this proposal now. If the government could exempt the Company's settlements from the operation of the Treaty, he remarked, it could have done so two years ago, thereby meeting all the Company's demands and thus relieving the Colonial Office of all the problems it had had since.[31]

On 7 May Hope and Stanley met to discuss the Company's proposal. There is no record of this meeting, but it seems that Stanley tried to lean on Hope, which suggests that he might have succumbed to the pressure

---

[30] Memo, Buller to Stanley, 26 April 1845, TNA, CO 209/39; Stanley note, 27 April 1845, Derby Papers, 27/5/2, his emphasis; Peel, undated minute on Stanley note, 27 April 1845, Derby Papers, 27/5/2, his emphasis; Report by Buller, NZC Secret Committee, Minutes of Meetings, 1 May 1845, TNA, CO 208/188.

[31] NZC Secret Committee, Minutes of Meetings, 5 May 1845, TNA, CO 208/188; Lord Ingestre to Stanley, 5 May 1845, enclosing Suggestions for the Consideration of Lord Stanley, *BPP*, 1845, Paper no. 357, Return to an Address of the Honourable the House of Commons, Dated 30 May 1845, pp. 3–6; Hope to Stanley, 5 May 1845, Hope Papers, GD364/1/469.

Peel and Graham had been putting on *him*. But Hope was unwilling to
back down. The next day he reiterated to Stanley that he found it impossible to accept a proposal that assumed that the Crown had a right to set
aside the Treaty of Waitangi. Indeed, Hope declared that he would have
to resign if this was the case because he felt unable to perform the role of
presenting an about-turn in the government's position on the Treaty in
the House of Commons. '[A]s I consider the question involved will be not
one of mere policy but of principle, which as a member of parliament
I should be obliged to affirm or abandon', he emphasised, 'I need hardly
say I should not be able to give up my own views'.[32]

On 10 May Buller sent Peel a private letter begging him to intervene
and persuade Stanley to accept his proposals. He also asked Peel to pay
careful attention to the memorial that Port Nicholson settlers had sent
Stanley in December the previous year (see pp. 296–97). Buller claimed
that this memorial carried a very clear and able exposition of what
amounted to a sound interpretation of the Treaty of Waitangi and the
fatal results that had sprung from the interpretation that the British
government had put on it. He was careful to tell Peel that he was not
advocating that government abrogate or disregard the Treaty.
Nevertheless, he told him that if no effective means were taken to obviate
the interpretation that had been placed upon the first clause of its second
article, it was 'utterly hopeless to attempt any arrangement of past disputes, or ever to colonise New Zealand'. Buller claimed that this clause
had been 'interpreted to include all the territory from which each tribe
claims a right of excluding others', and that consequently the colony's
Legislative Council had declared that of 'the 60 millions of available land
in New Zealand more than 58 are the property of the 100,000 natives!'
Clearly, Buller was attributing enormous significance to the Treaty. But
this was the logical outcome of the chain of signification that had been
forged about it since 1842.[33]

On the evening of 10 May Stanley sent Graham some papers in which
he rejected the Company's proposal. But he also put forward a proposal
of his own that, according to Graham, entailed 'no unreasonable modification' of the Company's proposal. Graham saw a prospect of making
a deal with the Company. He told Peel that Hope was the stumbling
block and the matter would be settled if Stanley 'were left to himself to
negotiate with Buller'. He called on Peel to give Stanley his views about
the course that should be taken. But it seems the Prime Minister was
unwilling to do so: Stanley was one of his most senior ministers and the

[32] Hope to Stanley, 8 May 1845, Hope Papers, GD364/1/469.
[33] Buller to Peel, 10 May 1845, Peel Papers, Add MS 40566, his emphasis.

two had enjoyed a long political relationship. Certainly, Stanley was unwilling to accept the Company's proposal. Ten days later, he and Graham provided Buller with a statement of the government's reasons for rejecting it, though Stanley insisted that he was still willing to treat with the Company on the basis that the powers of the Crown and the Company would remain on their present footing or that the government would buy the Company out and dissolve it. The Company's secret committee, learning of this, concluded that there was no point in the Company making any fresh proposal to the government and that doing so would prevent it from appealing to parliament for redress during its current session.[34]

On 26 May Ingestre advised Stanley that the Company was unwilling to put forward any new proposals on the basis of either of the terms he had suggested. At the same time, he stated that the Company would be willing to consider any plan Stanley might put forward that included the government buying up the Company's interests and putting an end to its existence, so long as he guaranteed to secure the good government of their settlers and the welfare of the native race. Indeed, Ingestre told Stanley that unless the Company's secret committee could be provided with such an assurance, it could not *consent* to any further delay of the motion that Buller had undertaken to bring before the House of Commons. Not surprisingly, these shenanigans angered Stanley and he complained bitterly to Graham. Two days later, the Company's secret committee asked Buller to take the earliest opportunity to bring forward his motion on the affairs of New Zealand in the House of Commons, which he did that night. At the same time, the Company's directors released a report to the press giving a disingenuous account of the discussions that had been taking place between Buller, Graham and Stanley. In fact, it contained all the kind of falsehoods and half-truths that the Company usually traded in. But this once again proved very effective as the next morning *The Times* carried an editorial repeating these accusations.[35]

---

[34] Graham to Peel, 11 May 1845, Peel Papers, Add MS 40451; Stanley to Buller, 19 May 1845, CO 208/188; Buller to Stanley, 20 May 1845, TNA, CO 208/188; NZC Secret Committee, Minutes of Meetings, 22 May 1845, TNA, CO 208/188; Stanley to Ingestre, 23 May 1845, *BPP*, 1845, Paper no. 357, p. 8; Norman Gash, *Sir Robert Peel: The Life of Sir Robert Peel after 1830*, 2nd ed., Longman, London, 1986, pp. 86–87, 326, 450.

[35] NZC Secret Committee, Minutes of Meetings, 22 May 1845, TNA, CO 208/188; Ingestre to Stanley, 26 May 1845, *BPP*, 1845, Paper no. 357, pp. 8–9; Stephen to Hope, minute, 27 May 1845, TNA, CO 209/39; Stanley to Graham, [28 May 1845], Peel Papers, Add MS 40451; NZC Secret Committee, Minutes of Meetings, 28 May 1845, TNA, CO 208/188; *The Times*, 29 May 1845.

Graham was disgusted. He reluctantly informed Peel that his attempt to broker an amicable settlement of the dispute between the Colonial Office and the Company was at an end. The Company's directors, by claiming that the government had sought a discussion with Buller so that it might avoid his bringing forward a motion in parliament, had performed a trick by which they had sought an unfair advantage. The following day *The Times* published an editorial in which it argued that the Company had no course open to it but to appeal to the country in the present session of parliament by bringing the facts forward, and that if it had allowed any further overtures from the government it would run the danger of being entrapped by it and compromising its own character. That evening in the House of Commons Hope countered the allegation that Buller had withdrawn his motion at the request of the government. Both Buller and Graham concurred, but the latter had something else on his mind as well. He had received a note from a member of the House who described himself as the chairman of the secret committee of the New Zealand Company and which had greatly astonished him. It stated that minutes had been taken from time to time of all the conversations that had taken place between Graham and Buller, and that the Company was determined to publish them even though both Graham and Buller had treated these conversations as absolutely confidential. Aglionby, on Ingestre's behalf, had to deny that the Company ever intended to use these minutes against the government, but he repeated a canard that the government had put a proposal to the Company, rather than the other way around.[36]

Two days later, Buller officially advised Stanley that the Company's secret committee believed that the continuation of their discussions could lead to no practical result. The scene was set for a mighty battle in the House of Commons. Edward Gibbon Wakefield welcomed this development, writing to his sister: 'The whole must come out next week, and will at least have the effect of improving our position'. The Company immediately set to work lobbying MPs, and shortly before the debate began Wakefield sent a letter to Peel in which he issued this dire warning: 'Lord Stanley had chosen to go into the mire up to his neck and none can assist to pull him out without soiling himself'.[37]

---

[36] Graham to Peel, 29 May 1845, Peel Papers, Add MS 40451; *The Times*, 30 May 1845; *BPD*, House of Commons, 30 May 1845, columns 1088–93.

[37] Buller to Stanley, 2 June 1845, *BPP*, 1845, Paper no. 357, p. 10; Edward Gibbon Wakefield to Catherine Torlesse, 6 June 1845, Letters from Other Members of the Wakefield Family, ATL, MS-Papers-9512–41; Wakefield to Peel, 13 June 1845, Peel Papers, Add MS 40569.

Part II

The Great Debate

In mid-June the House of Commons debated New Zealand's affairs for the best part of three days. Buller had moved a motion that the House resolve itself into a committee to consider the state of the colony and the case of the Company, after which he would put each of the resolutions of the 1844 Select Committee report. This debate proved to be the longest the House had had about a colonial matter for some years.

Many of the speeches – and certainly those of the most important speakers – were highly erudite, which was partly a function of the fact that an enormous amount of material pertinent to the debate was readily available in printed parliamentary papers. This in turn was a consequence of the enormous political contestation that had taken place over sovereignty and native title in regard to the colony over the preceding five or six years. The principal matters in the debate – which included the government's treatment of the question of sovereignty in the islands, the nature of native title, the interpretation of the agreements between the Company and Colonial Office, the work of the Land Claims Commission, the meaning of the Treaty of Waitangi and especially the first clause of its second article, and native policy more generally – have already been discussed at length in this book, and few of the speakers articulated new lines of argument about them. Therefore, there is no need to discuss many of the speeches that were given. Yet the speeches that Howick and Russell gave were sprinkled with suggestions for changes to the government's handling of native affairs and native title that would be adopted later by the British government, especially but not only once the Whigs returned to power. It is also important to note that the points that the Colonial Office's leading critics advanced about the matters under consideration had seldom been expressed so forthrightly or eloquently. This probably played some role in persuading the government's senior ministers that they had to concede some ground, if only to save face and shore up the government's position.

For more than two days in the House, argument and counter-argument took place as the allies of the Company and the supporters of the Colonial Office traded blows. On the evening of the second day of the debate, Howick spoke. He would become Colonial Secretary after Peel's Tory government fell from power. In much of this speech he reiterated what he had stated in his Select Committee report of the previous year. But he also made a point of arguing that the real question for the House's consideration was whether the Colonial Office's policy had promoted the interests of Britain, the settlers and the natives. He argued that no one in the imperial or the colonial government since his fellow Whig Russell had quit office had understood the paramount importance of maintaining the Crown's power over all unoccupied and unused land. More especially, he claimed that if the government had upheld the Crown's right of pre-emption it could have obtained control of all the land that was unused or unoccupied by the natives for a very small consideration.[38]

Howick also contended that the colonial government had failed to ensure that British authority was respected in the colony. He blamed this problem on the colonial administration's misapprehension of the power of the natives, which he dismissed as 'absolutely ludicrous', stating: 'Had it not been found that the superior intelligence and the powers of concert and combination of civilised men invariably made them too strong to be resisted by barbarous tribes, however great the disparity of numbers?' Howick claimed that the natives of New Zealand could not be compared with those of North America. Indians were far more numerous, well skilled in their particular mode of warfare and capable of understanding the advantages of uniting against their European enemies; the New Zealanders were relatively few in number, utterly unacquainted with the rudiments of the art of war and so divided that it would hardly be possible to get two tribes to act together in concert against Europeans. Howick was talking nonsense. At about this time, Heke and other Ngā Puhi rangatira combined forces, used new pa they had built to repel British troops at Puketutu and Ōhaeawai in the Bay of Islands, and forced the British army to retreat.[39]

In concluding his speech, Howick argued that there was no hope for any real improvement in New Zealand's affairs until the House expressed an opinion on the government's policy, thereby forcing the government to abandon it and adopt a new system. He called on the government to send out the ablest man as FitzRoy's replacement, bestow on him unreserved powers and allow him to do what was required by the state of the colony. He also suggested that this new governor should have very little scruple in dismissing colonial officers such as the protectors of aborigines whom many of the speakers in the debate had blamed for the colony's present crisis.[40]

Mid-way through the debate on the third day, Graham took to his feet. It was a crucial moment as it revealed that the government's most senior

---

[38] *BPD*, House of Commons, 18 June 1845, columns 817–25.
[39] *Ibid.*, columns 841–42; James Belich, *The New Zealand Wars and the Victorian Interpretation of Racial Conflict*, Auckland University Press, Auckland, 1986, pp. 41–54.
[40] *BPD*, House of Commons, 18 June 1845, column 843.

members had decided that it had little choice but to make some admissions and concessions to its critics. In one of the shortest speeches in the three days of debate, uttered very quietly, Graham defended the Colonial Office's handling of key matters but only to the point that was required for the government to save face. He conceded that the current state of affairs in New Zealand was to be deplored and agreed that it could be attributed to the unsettled nature of rights of property in land and the absence of control over native lawlessness.[41]

Most importantly, while Graham briefly repeated the argument made by the Colonial Office's senior figures that the natives 'territorial rights' had been recognised from an early period by the government as unqualified and absolute, he expressed the opinion that Normanby's recognition of those rights had exceeded the bounds of prudence. This was a fundamental shift in the government's public position. Yet it is clear that Graham had done this in order to strengthen the government's political position. Thus he maintained that the government believed that the Treaty had bestowed on the Crown the rights of sovereignty but that in return it had to observe the engagements it had contracted with the natives in respect of the right of pre-emption and the protection of their rights of possession. 'To that [arrangement]', he told the House, 'Her Majesty's faith is bound, and I think that the Treaty must be religiously observed'.[42]

Graham proceeded to tell the House what the government was going to do next. It would ensure that an instruction it had previously issued to FitzRoy, namely to create a system that would require all claimants to prove their titles and register them within a certain time, was executed by the new governor, after which the government would assert the right of the Crown to all unregistered lands. He also suggested that the government would consider imposing a moderate tax upon waste lands. This implied that while the government was committed to upholding the Treaty's guarantee of the natives' rights of possession in land, it was planning to adopt a measure that would dispossess them. Not surprisingly, one of the Company's allies would quip shortly after the conclusion of the debate: 'The ministerial construction of the "treaty" with the savages at Waitangi is maintained in terms, but evaded; for while the proprietary rights of the natives over waste lands is asserted, those lands are to be recovered by a screw'. Graham also promised that the government would give the new governor unambiguous instructions to fulfil the

---

[41] Lord Howick, Journal, 19 June 1845, Papers of Henry George, 3rd Earl Grey, University of Durham Library Special Collections, GRE/V/C3/11; *BPD*, House of Commons, 19 June 1845, columns 915–16.

[42] *Ibid.*, columns 924–25.

May 1843 agreement by putting the Company into possession of a prima facie title subject to the proof of better title by other parties, and declared that the government was willing to provide a form of representative government to all the settlements of the New Zealand Company. He also informed the House that he was convinced that greater force should be placed at the disposal of the colonial government. Graham concluded by pointing out that the government had recalled FitzRoy because of the errors he had made, though he refused to concede that Stanley had erred in his handling of the colony's affairs. As the *Spectator* remarked at the end of the debate, there was a sense in which Graham as well as Peel tried to shield Stanley from formal censure but in order to do this 'they were obliged to surrender his policy'.[43]

At this moment in the debate it was the turn of the political figure whose deeds had been the subject of a good deal of the speeches to speak. Russell's speech is all the more worth noting because he would succeed Peel as prime minister in June the following year and oversee a government that would set about trying to introduce major changes in the way that native title was treated and the Treaty dealt with. Russell began the substantive part of his speech by insisting that the House had to bear in mind that the Treaty's second article had two parts to it. This enabled him to attack the chiefs' repudiation, and FitzRoy's abandonment, of the Crown's right of pre-emption. '[L]let us have the whole Treaty, and let us show that it is for the true interests of the New Zealanders themselves to maintain the second part of the Treaty as well as the first', he asserted. Turning to the first clause of the Treaty's second article, Russell followed a line that critics of the Colonial Office had adopted earlier in the debate in regard to native title, arguing that the House had to consider the Treaty by taking the principles of public law among European nations as its guide and following the way that the British Crown had treated this matter in its other colonies. In both cases, he contended, the aboriginal inhabitants were not regarded as having a right in all the 'waste lands'.[44]

Russell sought to rebut the government's claim that he had previously attached to the Treaty the same interpretation that it had. He pointed out that in the Royal Charter and his instructions to Hobson in late 1840 he had specifically referred to land 'in the actual occupation' of the natives and the natives 'in actual enjoyment of the land', respectively. Russell insisted that those phrases should once again guide the House in respect of the Treaty's meaning. He claimed that he had assumed during his time

---

[43] *Ibid.*, columns 925–29; *Spectator*, 21 June 1845.
[44] *BPD*, House of Commons, 19 June 1845, columns 932–33.

in office that the Treaty would present no difficulty to Hobson in carrying out his instructions. In fact, there is no evidence to suggest that Russell had paid any attention whatsoever to the Treaty at that time. Nevertheless, his claim that he had done reveals that the Treaty had come to be regarded as a crucial reference point or even *the* crucial reference point in the debate about native title. Russell also argued that the government's interpretation of the Treaty differed widely from the interpretations of any other treaty into which the British Crown had entered with native peoples and objected bluntly: '[Y]ou do this in favour of savages, and of men who are still remaining cannibals'. He insisted that the government's interpretation of the Treaty was extravagant, claiming that it maintained that there was not a single acre in New Zealand in which the natives did not have a claim.[45]

Russell turned his attention next to the November 1840 agreement, repeating what he had stated previously (in his letter to the Company's directors). He then shifted his attention to the course of action that had been pursued by the colonial government. He argued that every Colonial Secretary in recent years had realised that aboriginal peoples had suffered greatly at the hands of colonisers and that consequently they had impressed upon governors the need to pay regard to the interests of the natives. Given this, he stated, it was no wonder that senior officials in New Zealand had acted in the way they had. However, he contended, these officials had erred greatly in their judgment by 'admitting every sort of [native] claim'. Russell might have complained that Hobson and Spain had made the mistake of taking the rhetoric of Colonial Secretaries such as himself literally and thus more seriously than they were meant to do, which was certainly the case. But he no doubt realised that this would be a tactical error as it would have entailed an assault on the spirit of the Treaty. Consequently, he argued instead that it was ridiculous to treat native claims to land in the way the colonial administrators had done, since the natives were barbarians: 'if we were to write a New Zealand Blackstone, instead of the headings of title by devise [that is, title acquired under a will], title by marriage, and title by descent, we should have title by "murder", title by "massacre", title by "extermination", and title arising from other horrid circumstances'. (In fact, a good deal of title in Britain had been acquired in this fashion.) Russell claimed that Spain's proceedings as a Land Claims Commissioner had only encouraged the natives to make claims and led them to disregard British law and authority. 'This is the consequence of want of firmness in not resisting unjust demands', he asserted. 'Such conduct appears humane, and generous,

45 *Ibid.*, columns 934–35.

and kind; but it is a weak yielding to intimidation and foolish concessions which lead to absurd demands. Such is always the consequence, and especially when you are dealing with savage tribes.' The former Colonial Secretary was by no means alone in this debate in his aggressive dismissal of 'the natives'.[46]

To conclude, Russell turned to the government's plans for the future. He was very critical of its proposal to register titles as well as tax waste lands, arguing that they amounted to a 'roundabout proceeding' to take back from the natives what he reckoned they never owned. He argued that there was a much simpler way to proceed, namely by ruling that much of the land in New Zealand was waste and that the Crown had a right to dispose of that land. Finally, Russell, like Howick, suggested that the answer to New Zealand's woes lay in the government giving FitzRoy's successor absolute authority so that he could do what needed to be done.[47]

By the time Peel rose to his feet, it must have been after 1 a.m. At first, he was careful to concede that New Zealand's affairs were in a critical state and sought to assure the House that his government had adopted sound measures to address the colony's problems. It had removed FitzRoy from his post and made clear that they disapproved of his administration of New Zealand's affairs; it had appointed an able successor; and so on and so forth. Yet Peel insisted that the Crown should continue to manage the colony's affairs through the colonial government. Thus, he rejected the Company's demand that the government create a proprietary government along the lines of the charters for Britain's first North American colonies. Nevertheless, Peel struck a conciliatory tone by making clear that he thought the Company should retain its full powers in regard to settling the country and by suggesting that municipal government could be granted as the first step towards responsible government.[48]

Turning to the main question at stake in the debate, Peel refused to be drawn about what he called the proper construction of the Treaty. Instead, he insisted that the House had to remember the circumstances in which the government's connection with New Zealand had begun. To enable this recollection, Peel cleverly crafted a historical narrative in much the same vein that Stephen and Hope had done at various points. It went like this. At the time the House of Commons' relations with New Zealand had begun ten or so years earlier, 'there was a strong feeling in the parliament and the public . . . that England was chargeable with injustice in its treatment of the aborigines'. Peel referred to Thomas Fowell Buxton (who had died a few months earlier) and his 1835–37 Select Committee, and quoted this passage from its report: 'It may be presumed that the

---

[46] *Ibid.*, columns 934–44.   [47] *Ibid.*, columns 944–46.   [48] *Ibid.*, columns 948–52.

native inhabitants of any land have an incontrovertible right to their own soil – a sacred right, however, which appears not to have been understood by this country'. Peel argued that when the question had arisen as to whether Britain should intervene in New Zealand, Normanby had acted under the influence of this sentimental feeling. Moreover, he claimed that it had led Normanby to make 'improvident engagements and wr[i]te unwise despatches', thereby creating the difficulties that Stanley had had to contend with. Peel hastened to pin responsibility for this chimerical sequence of events on the House of Commons: 'you agreed to the Address to the Crown praying the Crown to protect the rights of the aborigines [moved by Buxton in 1834], you are responsible for the appointment of these [select] committees, and you are responsible for the doctrines laid down in their reports, for you adopted them'. More specifically, Peel argued that the Buxton Select Committee's assertion that the right of aborigines to their country was incontrovertible had led Normanby to state that the right of the aboriginal people of New Zealand to the soil and sovereignty of the country was indisputable, and that the parliament had in turn acknowledged New Zealand to be a sovereign and independent state. Peel's story, like any good story, was plausible, and he was able to support it by historical evidence, as we have just noted. It is also a story that has been repeated by many New Zealand historians, most recently Ned Fletcher. But, as we have seen, it is a myth nonetheless.[49]

Having framed the crucial matter in the debate in this way, Peel made several tactical moves. He told the House that it was natural it had previously acted under those sentimental public feelings, but argued that it had been wrong to do so as it had induced the Crown to adopt a course of action that had weakened its authority in New Zealand and injured the natives. Indeed, Peel went so far as to assert that it would have been better if Britain had claimed the right to New Zealand on the grounds of *discovery* than hold it by what he called 'mere cession', since he claimed that the latter was much less binding than title on the basis of the former. At this point, there were shouts of 'hear, hear' from the Company's supporters. Indeed, they probably struggled to contain their glee, since this was an argument that the Company had been making since August 1839. What Peel had to say next can only have delighted them more. 'I do not hesitate', he stated, 'to say that the Treaty of Waitangi has been a most unwise one, even for the natives'. Yet, having made this admission, Peel insisted that both the British government and parliament

---

[49] *Ibid.*, columns 954–56; Ned Fletcher, 'A Praiseworthy Device for Amusing and Pacifying Savages? What the Framers Meant by the English Text of the Treaty of Waitangi', PhD thesis, University of Auckland, 2014.

had made commitments in the Treaty that they were bound to honour. 'These [commitments] are inconvenient, I admit, but you have already sanctioned them'. This meant that it was hardly right for the House to point a finger at Stanley. He had pursued the policies that previous Colonial Secretaries had introduced and had maintained doctrines that parliament had adopted while the Whigs were in power. Peel argued that the Crown had made no claim to possession of the territory on the basis of the cession of sovereignty that it had instructed Hobson to negotiate with the chiefs and had instead instructed him to treat with the native chiefs not only for the lands they enjoyed or occupied but for all the lands that Normanby had expressly called waste lands. 'Is it not clear, then', Peel demanded to know, 'that Lord Normanby's instructions to Captain Hobson were to take the lands not by any prerogative of the Crown, but by cession from the natives?'[50]

Peel proceeded to invite the House to compare the way in which many of its members now regarded what he called the contractual obligations of the Treaty with the way they had considered those obligations a few short years ago. Quoting what had become the Company's notorious statement about the Treaty, he suggested that the House would be failing to adopt the language of statesmen if it adopted the doctrine that this statement expressed. '[A]re you now prepared', he demanded to know, 'because you find the engagements onerous and inconvenient – inconvenient not only to yourselves, but injurious to the natives even – are you prepared to disclaim and repudiate the act of statesmen, and to concur with the lawyers that the Treaty is *a mere praiseworthy device for amusing and pacifying savages?*' Peel argued that the House needed to bear in mind the 'qualifications and reserves' under which the chiefs had entered into the contract. He quoted passages from Hobson's report of the treaty-making at Waitangi in which chiefs, and one in particular – it was Tamati Waka Nene – had expressed their concern about the loss of land and had called on Hobson to protect those lands. 'Can you', asked Peel, 'resist such an appeal to your equity and honour? Do not hastily renounce that character for honour and good faith to which this native chief appealed in his eloquent address'. Peel implied that the chiefs had only signed the Treaty because Hobson had promised to ensure that the Crown would not seize land against their wishes. 'These were the circumstances under which this inconvenient Treaty was made', he insisted. Moreover, he went on: 'I will say that if ever there was a case where the stronger party

[50] *BPD*, House of Commons, 19 June 1845, columns 956–58; New Zealand Company, *A Corrected Report of the Debate in the House of Commons on the 17th, 18th, and 19th of June on the State of New Zealand and the Case of the New Zealand Company*, John Murray, London, 1845, p. 241.

was obliged by its position to respect the demands of the weaker, if ever a powerful country was bound by its engagements with a weaker, it was the engagement contracted under such circumstances with these native chiefs'. Clearly, whereas in some contexts the government found it useful to argue that the natives were formidable and had to be respected, in others, like this one, it found it convenient to argue that they were weak and needed to be protected. Peel observed that all that he had noted so far in his speech meant that the House would embark on a most inexpedient course if it was not prepared to fulfil whatever engagements it had entered into as a result of the Treaty. Likewise, in concluding his speech, he demanded to know whether the House, in contradiction of the course adopted by Stanley and by a 'manifest perversion' of the doctrines maintained by the 1835–37 Select Committee, would now affirm the 1844 Select Committee's claim that the Treaty enabled the Crown to dispossess the chiefs of all their land without full inquiry, thereby lowering the character of the House.[51]

The kernel of Peel's argument in respect of the Treaty differed from that of the Company and its allies. Their argument was based on an interpretation of the (English) *text* of the Treaty and how the nature of natives' rights of property in land had been understood by the home government and in the law of nations at the time that the Treaty was made. By contrast, Peel argued that what was important was not any strict legal interpretation of the Treaty but the fact that it *had* been made and was understood in a particular way by various parties, not least in the colony itself. In particular, there was a belief that the Crown had made a commitment to the native chiefs to respect their title to land and to acquire their land by purchase. This meant that the Crown was morally bound to uphold what amounted to a social contract. In Peel's eyes, it was especially important for the Crown to abide by this commitment because British honour was at stake. To put this another way, Peel stressed that what was crucial was the fact that the Crown had entered into a contractual *relationship* with the chiefs as a result of the *talk* that had occurred at the time the Treaty was made, though, as we have seen, the talk that had determined the way in which the Treaty had come to be understood had actually taken place several years *after* it had been signed.

At the conclusion of the debate a vote on Buller's motion was put. It was lost, but only by 50 votes (173 to 223). The Company's supporters in the press were quick to claim this as a victory. The *Morning Chronicle* asserted that the government had thrown Stanley overboard and abandoned his absolute construction of the Treaty as guaranteeing native title

[51] *BPD*, House of Commons, 19 June 1845, columns 958–61, 963, my emphasis.

to all the land. The *Spectator* declared that Stanley's colleagues had expressly or virtually conceded every point for which he had battled pertinaciously during his protracted fight with the Company, and that the era of sentiment that had thwarted colonisation had now passed away. Most importantly, *The Times* suggested that Stanley would now have to back down. Yet it soon became evident that the Company's victory was, for the time being, more apparent than real.[52]

Stanley's Resistance

In the aftermath of this debate in the House of Commons, Stanley met a Company deputation on three occasions to discuss a series of demands the Company had made. These included an immediate grant of what the Company called its lands, a request for a substantial loan from the government, an objection to the waiving of the Crown's right of pre-emption and a call for the introduction of responsible government. But Stanley was unwilling to give way. Consequently, in the first week of July Ingestre, the Company's new chairman, asked Peel to intervene but he refused, declaring that he had entire confidence in the Colonial Secretary.[53]

The next day the Company suffered another temporary blow. A member of the House of Lords presented a petition from the Church Missionary Society that maintained that the Treaty had guaranteed to the natives of New Zealand in the Treaty 'full and undisputed possession of their lands' and that the 1844 Select Committee report was contrary to this declaration and the principles of justice. The real problem for the Company, though, lay in the way Stanley responded to the tabling of this petition. He expressed surprise that anyone familiar with the policy the government had been pursuing could have imagined that it entertained the idea of avoiding or violating a treaty by which it considered itself bound. In this respect, Stanley told the House of Lords, the instructions issued to the new governor remained unaltered. 'We have told him', he announced, 'that while he should seek in every possible mode to promote the amicable settlement of the affairs of the New Zealand Company, that he should always consider it to be the paramount duty devolved upon

---

[52] *Ibid.*, column 968; *The Times*, 20 June 1845; *Morning Chronicle*, 20 and 21 June 1845; *Spectator*, 21 June 1845.

[53] Minutes of Meetings between Stanley and a Deputation of the NZC, 27 June, 1 July and 4 July 1845, *BPP*, 1845, Paper no. 571–I, Copy of all Correspondence that Passed Between Her Majesty's Government and the New Zealand Company Between 19 June and 6 July 1845, pp. 4–7; Ingestre to Peel, 5 July 1845, *BPP*, 1845, Paper no. 571–I, p. 3; Peel to Ingestre, 9 July 1845, *BPP*, 1845, Paper no. 571–I, p. 4.

him, specially and scrupulously and religiously to fulfil our solemn engagements with the natives of New Zealand'.[54]

If this was not provocative enough, after an MP sympathetic to the Company asked Stanley to state the precise nature of the construction that the government put upon the Treaty, Stanley made it clear that he had not changed his views about native title, indeed on the contrary. Stanley had not expected to be asked a question of this nature on this occasion, and he proceeded to make a series of remarks about the Treaty and native title that went far beyond any he or his colleagues in the Colonial Office had made previously. First, he claimed that all recent ministries, colonial secretaries and parliaments had placed the same construction upon the Treaty of Waitangi as he had, and that this construction had never been disputed by the member of any party until 1842. Stanley went on to claim that repeated acts of parliament between 1836 and 1842 had 'uniformly recognised' the natives' right to sell land that they did not 'occupy or enjoy'. He admitted that there might be some areas in New Zealand that were wholly waste and uncultivated, in which case they would be vested in the Crown, by virtue of the fact that the natives had ceded sovereignty. But he believed that they were few in number. Furthermore, he declared that he knew that all of the tribes in North Island had 'as perfect a knowledge of the boundaries and limits of their possessions, boundaries and limits, in some places natural, in others artificial, as satisfactory and well defined, as were, one hundred years ago, the bounds and marshes of districts occupied by great proprietors and their clans in the Highlands of Scotland'. Moreover, he insisted that in the question of title to land 'native law and custom' had to be consulted. 'By them we have agreed to be bound, and by them we must abide. These laws – these customs – and the right arising from them on the part of the Crown – we have guaranteed when we accepted the sovereignty of the islands; and be the amount at stake smaller or larger, so far as native title is proved, be the land waste or occupied, barren or enjoyed, those rights and titles the Crown of England is bound in honour to maintain.' Once more, Stanley invoked the Treaty, telling the House: '[T]he interpretation of the Treaty of Waitangi, with regard to these rights, is, that, except in the case of the intelligent consent of the natives, the Crown has no right to take possession of land, and having no right to take possession of land itself, it has no right, and so long as I am a Minister of the Crown, I shall not advise it to exercise the power of making over to another party that which it does not itself possess'.[55]

---

[54] *BPD*, House of Lords, 10 July 1845, columns 312–15.
[55] *Ibid.*, columns 315, 317–19.

It seems unlikely that Stanley believed all the things he stated in this speech. What is more important is the fact that he said them. As we know, rhetoric is a crucial part of the toolkit of any politician, and so what they state can often have a tenuous relationship with what they believe. At root, the commitments that politicians (as well as ourselves) make tend to be contingent and lack solid foundations. Nevertheless, what a politician says can be terribly important, as it was on this occasion.[56]

Not surprisingly, the Company and its supporters were outraged by Stanley's remarks or at least pretended to be. The *Morning Chronicle* declared: 'Lord Stanley has learned nothing, forgotten nothing. The three nights' debate on the affairs of New Zealand, with the narrow majority by which he missed a vote of censure, has made no impression on his Lordship's mind, except, as it would seem, to confirm him more obstinately than ever in every one of [his] errors'. Indeed, the newspaper claimed that it had never read a speech by him that contained so much mischief. In particular, it complained that Stanley was intent on detecting 'the faintest *scintilla* of title' in the natives' notions about land. Would the Prime Minister allow such 'mischievous and perilous foolery to go on', it demanded to know?[57]

The Company's directors weighed in, again calling on Peel to intervene. They also sent a circular to the ministerial members of the House of Commons, complaining of Stanley's obstinacy, calling for a further debate in order to ensure that the recommendations of the Select Committee of the previous year be carried out and demanding that the matter be treated in a non-partisan spirit. During this time, British newspapers such as *The Times* were awash with reports of further attacks that Heke had mounted in the Bay of Islands. Several days later, Buller moved a motion that the House regarded the state of affairs in New Zealand with great apprehension and claimed that this was aggravated by the want of evidence of a change in the government's policy.[58]

In order to bring before the House a matter that had been raised previously in the same session of parliament, a pretext was required. The Company found it in the recent news of the events in the Bay of Islands, even though this manoeuvre required it to change its tune about the natives' military strength. Buller now claimed that Heke's attacks amounted to a formidable insurrection in New Zealand, that it would undoubtedly be successful and that it amounted to the start of a war that

---

[56] David M. Craig, '"High Politics" and the "New Political History"', *The Historical Journal*, vol. 53, no. 2, 2010, pp. 462, 467.

[57] *Morning Chronicle*, 12 July 1845, its emphases.

[58] Henry Aglionby to Peel, 18 July 1845, TNA, CO 325/43; NZC, Circular, 11 July 1845, reproduced in *The Times*, 19 July 1845; *The Times*, 9, 15, 18, 19 and 23 July 1845.

would be carried out between the two races throughout New Zealand. In the light of the recent abortive meetings between Stanley and the Company's directors as well as Stanley's speech in the Lords, Buller demanded proof that the government was going to pursue a different course.[59]

Peel's Yielding

Many of the MPs who spoke in this two-day debate repeated what had been said previously. Yet on the first day of the debate Hope took the opportunity to assert that the recent events in the Bay of Islands demonstrated that the government had been pursuing a course founded in a policy that was sound as well as just and honourable, and to argue that any departure from it would only serve to unite the native tribes against the British and undermine the government's power. To support this claim, he quoted some remarks that Governor Sir George Gipps had made at a meeting of the New South Wales Executive Council in February (which formed part of some papers the Colonial Office had tabled in parliament several days earlier). Gipps had expressed his apprehension that it would become more difficult to keep the peace once the Select Committee report of the previous year became generally known in New Zealand. '[I]t was the opinion of every one well acquainted with the colony', Hope added, 'that if there was any question likely to unite the natives into a compact mass, it was the question as to their rights to land, denied by the Committee'. Repeating Peel's line of argument in the previous parliamentary debate, Hope contended that, however much the Whig Opposition might now say that the recognition of native rights in land was the wrong course for the government to pursue, the fact was that *they* had recognised those rights while they had been in office, which meant that the current Tory government was obliged to respect them: 'they could proceed on no other ground but a recognition of a title to the soil of New Zealand in the natives'. In fact Hope went further, more or less repeating Stanley's recent claim about the natives' ownership of the waste lands by saying that the natives 'alone owned the waste lands'.[60]

The second day of this debate was dominated by speeches by Peel and Russell. Peel argued that the only ground that could be assigned for the motion Buller had brought to the House was that the course the government had pursued since the previous debate was at variance with the

---

[59] *BPD*, House of Commons, 21 July 1845, columns 807–30.

[60] *BPP*, 1845, Paper no 517–II, Copies or Extracts of Correspondence Relative to an Attack on the British Establishment at the Bay of Islands of New Zealand, p. 5; *BPD*, House of Commons, 21 July 1845, columns 841–43.

opinions he had expressed in that debate. He proceeded to insist that this was not the case. In doing so, he adopted Stanley's take on the fundamental matter in the tussle between the government and the Company and its allies. 'I believe', Peel told the House, 'that, after all the volumes of controversy which have appeared, the question really resolves itself into this: shall the government undertake to guarantee, in this country, within certain limits in New Zealand, a certain amount of land [to the Company], without reference to the rights to that land vesting in the natives?' The Company's MPs sought to combat this framing of the matter, howling 'No, no', but Peel continued. 'We will not undertake, in the absence of surveys and local information as to the claims of the natives, to assign to you 1,000,000 or any other number of acres, and dispossess the natives by the sword'. 'Nobody ever asked for that', complained Aglionby. Peel pressed on: 'I admit that the New Zealand Company has a fair right to expect from the Crown to be put in possession of the quantity of land awarded to them at as early a period and in as satisfactory a manner as possible, with this clear reserve, that you shall not violate a compact, or infringe the rights of private property'.[61]

Next, Peel provided a more elaborate defence of the government's position than he had previously offered. Once more, this involved telling a historical tale. As in the previous debate, Peel argued that the policy that he claimed his government's predecessor, the Whigs, had pursued was a serious error. 'You should have rested your claim on the ground of discovery, and not on some cession by the natives', he told the Commons. 'Acting on the Report of the [1835–37] Aborigines' Committee, you laid down a principle which has involved you in your present difficulty; and now you are trying to make us responsible for it'. Peel went on: 'The hardness of the names connected with the subject [Howick and Russell] indispose people to pay attention to it, but if you will listen but for a quarter of an hour I will show that this difficulty is all of your own creating'.[62]

Peel argued once again that the British government and parliament had to accept the fact that the Treaty of Waitangi had been made. In the same vein as his previous speech, he claimed that the interpretation of any treaty depended on the circumstances in which a treaty was made, the impressions formed by the government and parliament of the day and the language they had instructed their representatives to use. This led Peel to state: 'It may be all very well to say this treaty was an improvident one, [just] let us get possession of the land; but I tell you there are parties in New Zealand[,] enemies to your authority, who know what passed in

[61] *Ibid.*, 23 July 1845, columns 994–1003.   [62] *Ibid.*, columns 1003–04.

1839 [*sic*, i.e. 1840], and the circumstances under which the British sovereignty was then established. I ask you to beware – first, from considerations of justice, and next by considerations of policy – how you take upon yourselves the responsibility of violating the engagements into which you have entered'.[63]

Peel proceeded to provide an interpretation of Normanby's instructions to Hobson. In doing so, he took care to argue that these were 'notorious' among the natives in New Zealand, that is, they were commonly known and highly regarded. Readers will not be surprised by the passages that Peel chose to pluck from them. He began with this one: 'The natives of New Zealand are a numerous and inoffensive people, whose title to the soil and sovereignty of New Zealand is indisputable'. What was meant by this passage, Peel asked? 'The Secretary of State [Normanby] says the title of the inhabitants to the soil of New Zealand is as perfect as their title to the sovereignty which has been solemnly recognised by the British government. Solemnly recognised!' But what was the meaning of this solemn recognition of the title of the natives to the soil? '[Normanby] says: "We acknowledge New Zealand as a sovereign and independent state. The Queen disclaims for herself and for her subjects any pretensions to seize on the islands of New Zealand, or to govern them as part of the dominions of Great Britain, unless a free and intelligent consent of the natives, expressed according to their usages, should be first obtained"'. Peel suggested to the members of the House that they now found these understandings absurd and told them that he was happy to allow that this was so. But, he insisted, 'the Secretary of State [Normanby] ought to have considered [this] before he disclaimed the right of his sovereign to exercise dominion in New Zealand unless the free and intelligent consent of the natives should have been first obtained'.[64]

Peel went on to declare that Normanby had stated: 'All dealing with the aborigines for their land must be conducted upon the same principle of sincerity, of justice, and of good faith as must govern your transactions with them for the recognition of Her Majesty's sovereignty in the island'. Observe, Peel told the House, that *you* did not claim sovereignty by right of conquest or right of discovery but by cession of the natives, and so *you* told your representative (Hobson): 'It will be your duty to obtain, by fair and equitable contracts, the cession to the Crown of such lands as may be necessarily required for the occupation of the settlers'. Peel demanded to know what construction the House would put upon these engagements. Then he tightened the screw: 'Now, observe that Lord Normanby says again: "To the natives or their chiefs much of the land of the country is of

---

[63] *Ibid.*, column 1004.   [64] *Ibid.*, columns 1004–05.

no actual use, and in their hands it possesses scarcely any exchangeable value". But first he tells you to "take no land except that which is by cession fairly granted", and he goes on to tell you that "you must be cautious that you do not take any land even by fair cession, if it could be considered that the taking of such land would interfere with their rights"'. (Both of these passages were Peel's interpretive gloss of the instructions.) And so Peel returned to the Treaty. '[I]n consequence of these instructions', he argued, 'you formed a Treaty to *this* effect: "On account of acquiring sovereignty by cession, Her Majesty the Queen of England confirms and grants to the chiefs and tribes of New Zealand, and to their respective families, the full, exclusive, undisturbed possession of their lands, forests, habitations and other property which they may collectively or individually possess, as long as they may wish or desire to retain possession of them"', quoting the first clause of the Treaty's second article; and to *this* effect: 'The native tribes and individual chiefs give to Her Majesty the exclusive right of pre-emption over such land as may be disposed of at such prices as the persons appointed on behalf of the two parties may think fair and reasonable', quoting the second clause of the Treaty's second article. These, Peel insisted, were the public engagements into which the House had entered. 'You have stipulated on the part of the Crown that, as the price and condition of your possession of sovereignty, the natives should not be called upon to relinquish their lands except by a fair cession and for a fair equivalent'.[65]

Peel moved swiftly to contend that Stanley had not argued that the natives had a claim to the whole of the waste lands of New Zealand. Rather, he had insisted, on the basis of the engagement that the British Crown had deliberately entered into with the natives, that the rights of the natives should be clearly ascertained by the government before it decided what waste lands might exist. Peel made his own position on this clear: 'I consider that the right of sovereignty which has been ceded by the natives gives to the Crown the perfect right of possession over all lands which the native tribes cannot lay a perfect claim to, [and] the tribes cannot, according to their usages, establish a right of property to certain waste lands'. This done, Peel set out what he assumed was common ground between the government and the Company: 'I admit your interest in these lands by the engagement entered into between the Crown and the natives. I admit the importance, too, of your future interests in the Colony. I admit the great advantage it would be if you could induce these natives to relinquish, by fair cession, some of these lands. I admit that to accomplish so desirable a result that every effort on our part ought to be made'. But if

---

[65] *Ibid.*, columns 1005–06, my emphasis.

Peel had previously acted on the assumption that it was necessary or useful to obscure the differences between the government and the Company, he now proceeded in the belief that the current political situation demanded the contrary. '[I]f, as I think it is, the question be whether the Crown shall, upon its own responsibility, undertake to dispossess, by force, and against the will of the inhabitants, the natives from certain lands desired by the New Zealand Company, let us, then, have no mistake upon the point, for you shall not say that I am deceiving you. I tell you at once that we are not prepared to give you any such assurance. Sir, this is the spirit in which we shall meet the question'.[66]

In his speech Russell refused to accept Peel's framing of the matter in terms of the engagements or commitments of the Crown. He argued instead that there were two great questions of paramount importance: the form of government and the purchase of land. Only the latter really need concern us here. (He opposed the granting of responsible government to the colony in the foreseeable future.) Russell argued that the question to be addressed was not whether the House was willing to violate the solemn engagements that the Crown had made in the Treaty but rather the true interpretation of the Treaty. He once again insisted that if the House attached to the Treaty the construction being put upon it by the government in respect of native title it would be 'doing that which ha[d] never before been done'. He expressed scorn for Stanley's claim in his recent speech in the Lords that the greater part of the waste lands in New Zealand were as much private property of native chiefs as the Scottish Highlands were the possessions of the Duke of Gordon or the Duke of Argyle. Perhaps the natives of New Zealand more nearly approached civilisation and had a little more knowledge of government than the aboriginal people of Australia, argued Russell, but it was 'too much to say that they should be regarded as civilised people'. He insisted that the government had to declare that the waste lands were vested in the Crown. Russell concluded his speech by arguing that there had been some progress in the course of this parliamentary debate as it had become apparent that the government adhered to a principle that the natives owned all or nearly all the lands. Now this was clear, the House could declare that the policy the government was pursuing in New Zealand was 'monstrous' and must be abandoned, and resolve that the colony must be governed according to the principles of common sense.[67]

However persuasive many members of the House might have found Russell's arguments, Peel had staked the government's position on the matter and it had the numbers. Buller's motion was lost 89 to 155. Yet

[66] *Ibid.*, columns 1006–07.   [67] *Ibid.*, columns 1014, 1017–20, 1022.

observers like *The Times* were not inclined to attach too much importance to this outcome. Its editor claimed that it was impossible to suppose that Peel really approved of Stanley's policy. Indeed, he suggested that Peel had adopted that policy in a merely nominal fashion for party purposes and argued that this no more proved that he would adhere to it, or allow it to be adhered to, than his High-Church professions had prevented him from carrying the Emancipation bill many years ago (permitting Catholics to become members of parliament) or endowing Maynooth recently (as a college for training Catholic priests). 'Sir Robert is of that class who refuse to come, but come nevertheless', the newspaper's editor remarked. 'He supports Lord Stanley against New Zealand, and yet he will take care that New Zealand shall be redressed'. Peel's majority had saved Stanley from a vote of censure, but the Prime Minister was too astute a reader of public opinion to allow the colony's problems to continue: 'We have hopes for [change in] New Zealand; the debates and disclosures have not been all in vain'. And so it proved.[68]

Conclusion

The winter and spring of 1844–45 saw debate about the nature of the New Zealanders' title to land reach a zenith in Britain. In a fierce parliamentary clash between the government and the New Zealand Company and its allies, the Treaty of Waitangi was critical as it had become *the* reference point in discussions of native title. As we have seen, this development was not a consequence of the meanings or the importance attributed to the Treaty at the time it was made in 1840. Rather, it was a result of treaty talk, that is, the claims that had been made and the stories that had been told about the Treaty by various players, beginning in 1842. Indeed, the making of claims and the telling of stories in regard to the Treaty tended to spark more claims and more stories about it. At the same time as the importance of the Treaty became commonplace, there was an enormous struggle over its meaning, especially the first clause of its second article. In fact, the Treaty's rise to prominence was the result of that very struggle over its meaning as well as the meaning of native title.

In the course of the political battle over native title, the New Zealand Company and its allies maintained their argument that the problem that the Company had encountered in acquiring possession and title to land in New Zealand was the result of the Colonial Office's erroneous interpretation of the first clause of the Treaty's second article so that the natives were deemed to have rights of property in 'waste lands'. The Company's

---

[68] *Ibid.*, column 1023; *The Times*, 24 July 1845.

relentless attack on the Colonial Office in this regard provoked the Colonial Office to embrace the Treaty more than it had ever done before but also prompted changes in the nature of the claims its senior figures tended to make about the Treaty. They continued to find rights talk useful as a means of beating up the Company and its allies and drawing the Company's character into question. But they, and more especially the government's most senior members, tended to speak less often of the Treaty in terms of the rights in land that the Crown had allegedly recognised and more in terms of the duties that the Crown had assumed as a result of the talk that had occurred at the time the Treaty was made. Consequently, they increasingly mounted arguments that emphasised considerations that were intrinsically historical, moral and pragmatic in nature. Thus, instead of insisting on any particular legal interpretation of the first clause of the Treaty's second article in respect to native title (though they sometimes reverted to doing this in the midst of heated parliamentary debates), they were more inclined to argue that Britain had to accept the fact that the Treaty had been made and was understood by various parties in New Zealand – most notably the natives – to express a particular commitment by the Crown to respect native rights of property in land. However inconvenient or improvident the executive and legislative wings of government might now regard that commitment, they had no choice but to uphold the Treaty because it had acquired the nature of a solemn contract. This was especially so, the government ministers argued, because the honour and good faith of the British nation was at stake. Yet the government also emphasised that it would be unwise to violate the commitments into which the Crown had entered because there were parties in the colony who were determined to ensure that the Treaty be upheld. Moreover, in the case of the natives, they were capable of doing this, by the use of force.

In the course of the parliamentary debates, the way that the various parties figured the natives' rights of property in land could differ markedly, but it would be a mistake to overstate the significance of this fact. The Company and its allies were keen to portray the Colonial Office as the champions of a comprehensive, even absolute, form of native title, either because they believed this to be the case or/ and because they saw political advantage in doing so. But in fact the Colonial Office was not committed to any particular definition of native title to land or to upholding any native rights in land on that basis. Rather, they were committed to upholding a local process in order to determine those rights as well as a principle that it was best to acquire possession of land by obtaining the natives' consent to the extinguishment of their title to it.

We have also observed that the way that many of the principal political players in Britain represented the natives' military power varied according to political circumstances and need, and that this tended to have little if any relationship to what was actually the case. In some circumstances these players evidently found it useful to cast the natives as a powerful force that the British government had to respect. Yet in others they obviously considered it advantageous to portray the natives as weak and to argue that the Crown had a responsibility to protect them. This manoeuvring was especially true of the government, but it was typical of the Company and its supporters as well. This draws into question the conventional wisdom that the British government respected the New Zealanders and their rights because of the simple *fact* of their might, making clear that what was more important was the way in which that power was represented and that those representations were heterogeneous as well as unstable.

9   The Making of Native Title, 1845–1850

Between 1845 and 1850 the matter of native rights of property in land in New Zealand was finally settled. This was the result of a haphazard, even contradictory process, dictated by practices and politics in the colony rather than principles articulated at the imperial metropole. For most of this period, nobody could have anticipated that the government would eventually purchase land from Māori in such a way as to confirm their title to practically all the lands of New Zealand. At the beginning, Stanley and Hope had formed the opinion that FitzRoy had conceded too much by declaring that the natives had title to all the lands, and they were concerned that the government might not be able to restore the Crown's right of pre-emption, which FitzRoy had waived under certain conditions. Moreover, half-way through this period, after Lord Howick, now Earl Grey, had assumed the position of Colonial Secretary, and Benjamin Hawes and Charles Buller were appointed to senior positions in the Colonial Office, they set about trying to realise the goals of the New Zealand Company by means that included a measure that would have seen native rights limited to the lands they 'occupied and enjoyed'.

What transpired owed much to the fact that Stanley and Hope had come to accept that the British government needed to provide the colony's new governor with the resources it had refused to grant any of his predecessors, namely more money to purchase land but also more guns to combat the challenge Māori could present to British authority. Equally important was the man that they appointed to replace FitzRoy as governor. George Grey was clever, ambitious and determined. Indeed, he has been described as 'the greatest of all the mid-nineteenth century colonial governors'. Grey would dedicate himself to making the best use of all the resources at his disposal, which included both the law and force, in order to acquire power and uphold the authority of the Crown against the other parties in the colony.[1]

---

[1] John W. Cell, 'The Imperial Conscience', in Peter Marsh (ed.), *The Conscience of the Victorian State*, Syracuse University Press, Syracuse, NY, 1979, pp. 195–96.

In particular, Grey would devote a good deal of energy to reasserting the Crown's right of pre-emption, eventually going so far as to orchestrate a legal case, which we might call *Symonds v. McIntosh*, in order to realise this objective. On the face of it, Grey's attention to this goal made perfect sense. Stanley and his successors at the Colonial Office assumed that the Crown's right of pre-emption was critical to the government's goal of acquiring land from the natives and thus being able to promote colonisation. However, restoring this right became extraordinarily important to Grey as he came to regard it as *the* symbol of the Crown's authority. This preoccupation with the Crown's right of pre-emption can be attributed partly to the status that the Treaty of Waitangi had come to have as a historical agreement. The government could use the second clause of its second article, by which it had acquired the right of pre-emption, to counter the first clause of the same article's guarantee of the natives' rights of possession, thereby turning the Treaty against itself. Historians like Peter Adams have noted this move, but hitherto no historian appears to have grasped how and why the Crown's right of pre-emption assumed so much significance at this time.[2]

The most important political struggle in this period occurred as a result of Earl Grey's attempt to address what he had claimed in his 1844 Select Committee report to be the main cause of the land problem facing the colony: that the natives had been treated from the outset as though they were the owners of land they neither 'occupied' nor 'enjoyed'. As Colonial Secretary, Earl Grey would urge Governor Grey (no relation) to treat most of the lands in New Zealand as though they were waste and hence part of the Crown's demesne. This strategy deeply troubled Bishop George Augustus Selwyn, the leading churchman in the colony, William Martin, one of the country's senior legal figures, and Church Missionary Society and Wesleyan Missionary Society missionaries such as William Williams and John Whiteley. They launched a major protest, though the fact they did so is something that cannot be taken for granted and so must be explained.

As it turned out, Earl Grey was thwarted in his attempt to treat most of the lands as though they were waste. Historians such as Stuart Banner would argue that the reasons for this lay in the fact that the natives had been treated as though they were the owners of the land prior to the British Crown's annexation of the country and the government found it difficult to overturn this practice because those who had purchased land in that period had an interest in native title as it was the basis of their

---

[2] Peter Adams, *Fatal Necessity: British Intervention in New Zealand 1830–1847*, Auckland University Press/Oxford University Press, Auckland, 1977, p. 193.

claims to title in land. But, as we will see, most of the parties involved in opposing Earl Grey's prescription in regard to native title had no such stake in the land and thus no reason to champion native rights on these grounds. Those parties included Grey himself, but also the likes of Selwyn, Martin and the Wesleyans.

Selwyn and his fellow protestors were able to mobilise connections they had in London with clergymen, a missionary society and leading politicians such as William Gladstone. As this suggests, close attention to the conduct of politics and transactions between the colony and the metropole again holds the key to our being able to understand a good deal of what happened.

Part I

A New Governor and New Instructions

At the same time that Stanley and Hope were strenuously defending the Colonial Office's handling of New Zealand's affairs against its critics in parliament in the winter and spring of 1845, they were taking steps behind closed doors to appoint a new governor and draft instructions for him that would depart from the public declamations of principle they and their senior colleagues were making. Grey's appointment as well as the instructions he was issued reveal that Stanley and Hope had finally accepted that they had to change course in order to appease the government's critics and ensure the British colonisation of New Zealand.

In choosing a new governor, the Colonial Office had two requirements: speed and experience. Both dictated the choice of thirty-three-year-old George Grey, a former captain in the British army who was currently the governor of South Australia, where he had made a name for himself as a decisive administrator. More particularly, James Stephen might have recalled that Grey had authored a paper in 1841 about the best means of promoting civilisation among the Aboriginal people of Australia, which Russell, the Colonial Secretary at the time, had much admired. Stephen or his superiors might also have remembered that this paper had been praised by the Colonial Office's critics during the 1844 Select Committee inquiry. In other words, the Colonial Office's decision to appoint Grey might well have been influenced by its belief that he had a keen and knowledgeable interest in native policy as well as a hope that his appointment might assuage its critics.[3]

---

[3] George Grey, 'Report Upon the Best Means of Promoting the Civilisation of the Aboriginal Inhabitants of Australia', *BPP*, 1841, Paper no. 311, Copies or Extracts of

In preparing its instructions for a new governor the Colonial Office realised that the crucial matter he would have to tackle was what it called the land question. The basic problem lay in the fact that the British Crown had no land at its disposal to promote colonisation. Stanley and Hope now attributed this problem to three factors. First, they held that FitzRoy, by adhering to the Treaty or more specifically an interpretation of the first clause of its second article, had erred in maintaining that the natives had rights of property in all the land in New Zealand; consequently, they maintained that he had failed to implement any of the measures by which the government had hoped to ascertain the lands in which the natives had title, thereby distinguishing those lands from the lands claimed by no one and which therefore could be classified as waste and thus be regarded as part of the Crown's demesne. In fact, the Treaty had played no role in FitzRoy forming the view that all the lands of New Zealand were the property of the natives. As we have noted, he had long held that opinion (see p. 245). Yet the Colonial Office's attribution of FitzRoy's views about native title to the terms of the Treaty testifies to the significance it had come to have. Second, the Colonial Office's senior figures believed that FitzRoy, by waiving the Crown's right of pre-emption, had allowed settlers to purchase land directly from the natives and encouraged speculation in land, thereby rendering hopeless any prospect of the government acquiring land it could sell in turn to prospective settlers. Third, and more generally, Stanley and Hope seem to have attributed the land problem to the fact that the kinds of rules in regard to property in land that might ordinarily apply in a colony could not be applied in the New Zealand case because the native population had laid claim to the whole country and the settlers were not strong enough to contend with their might. Yet they were also of the view that FitzRoy had aggravated this problem by failing to ensure that the natives had sufficient respect for British power or resolve.[4]

Stanley and Hope's analysis of the land question led them to recommend a series of measures that formed a good part of the instructions they issued to Grey. First, Stanley instructed the new governor to call upon all parties in New Zealand to register their claims to land so that the colonial administration could learn precisely which lands the natives claimed. Stanley and Hope hoped this measure would reveal that there were strict limits to the land held by the natives as well as large tracts of land to which

Correspondence Relative to New Zealand, pp. 43–47; George Hope to James Stephen, 19 May 1845, TNA, CO 209/38; *BPD*, House of Commons, 23 July 1845, column 997.

[4] Hope, Memo, 10 May 1845, TNA, CO 209/38; Stephen, Minute, 29 May 1845, TNA, CO 209/29; Lord Stanley to Grey, 13 June 1845, *BPP*, 1846, Paper no. 337, Copies or Extracts of Further Correspondence Between Lord Stanley and Governor FitzRoy and Lieutenant-Governor Grey, Relative to New Zealand, p. 70.

no one had valid title, which would mean that the Crown had in its possession a large amount of the land it required. Second, Stanley informed Grey that it was vitally important that he give consideration to re-establishing the Crown's right of pre-emption and thus prohibit any direct purchasing from the natives. This measure, as we have seen, had been a recommendation of Howick's 1844 Select Committee report. Third, Stanley informed Grey that the government maintained its long-held desire to avoid conflict with the natives but also implied that it was necessary for him to act in ways that would diminish the natives' confidence in their own strength as well as their contempt for British power.[5]

The Colonial Office's senior figures seemed to have realised, though, that these measures might not suffice. Consequently, the government gave Grey what it had withheld from his predecessors. First, Stanley placed a considerable sum of money (£10,000) at Grey's disposal and secretly authorised him, if he found it necessary, to draw on those funds to purchase land from the natives in the districts in which the New Zealand Company had claimed land. Second, Stanley sent to New Zealand a considerable military force in order to give the new governor greater power to deal with problems of the kind that Heke had been posing. Third, as part of a series of major concessions to the New Zealand Company, Stanley urged Grey to co-operate with its principal agent, William Wakefield, in order to remove the obstacles caused by unsatisfied native claims, and he appointed a special agent to assist the Company in selecting land, surveying the boundaries of those selections and assessing the reasonableness of the terms of any purchase struck with the natives.[6]

In respect of the Treaty, the Colonial Office had proposed that the government instruct Grey to 'adhere to the Treaty of Waitangi with the most exact and scrupulous fidelity', but this instruction had been over-ruled by Peel, who was no doubt apprehensive that it was too prescriptive and could prevent the new governor from realising the government's objectives, and so Grey was instructed instead to 'honourably and scrupulously fulfil the Treaty's conditions'. The only specific reference to the conditions of the Treaty came in an instruction to restore Crown's right of pre-emption so that the government could acquire more land from the natives.[7]

---

[5] Stanley to Grey, 27 June 1845, *BPP*, 1846, Paper no. 337, pp. 72–75.

[6] *Ibid.*, pp. 69–70; Stanley to Grey, 28 June 1845 (secret), TNA, CO 209/40; Stanley to Grey, 28 June 1845, *BPP*, 1846, Paper no. 337, p. 75; Stanley to Grey, 15 August 1845, *BPP*, 1846, Paper no. 337, p. 93.

[7] Sir Robert Peel, undated minute on draft of Stanley to Grey, 13 June 1845, Papers of the Hope Family of Luffness, East Lothian, National Archives of Scotland, GD364/1/461/3; Stanley to Grey, 13 June 1845, *BPP*, 1846, Paper no. 337, pp. 70, 72; Stanley to Grey, 27 June 1845, *BPP*, 1846, Paper no. 337, p. 73.

Finally, Stanley gave Grey a good deal of latitude to decide whether the measures he had been instructed to adopt were appropriate. Stephen remarked at an early stage in the drafting of these instructions that the circumstances the Colonial Office found itself in meant that they could amount to little more than the government telling him 'Go and do the best you can to give effect to the views of the government'. This was something of an exaggeration, but there can be little doubt that Stanley entrusted Grey with unusual amount of discretionary power.[8]

Grey and the Crown's Right of Pre-emption

From the moment of Grey's arrival in the colony in November 1845, he proved himself to be the most consummate of politicians.[9] He swiftly sought to allay the fears of the chiefs in the north that the government was going to lay claim to all their land. (He soon learned to speak Māori and acquired a good deal of knowledge about their culture.) Grey was no doubt aware that they had learned of the recommendations of the 1844 House of Commons Select Committee and the subsequent parliamentary debates. He told the chiefs that he had been instructed by the home government to 'most punctually and scrupulously' fulfil the conditions of the Treaty. He also remarked: 'By that treaty you have the protection of the Queen, and your possessions are made sure to you. Your lands shall certainly not be taken from you without your own consent'. This was in keeping with the principle that the Colonial Office had long maintained, namely that it was best for the government to acquire land by purchasing it from the natives. Shortly afterwards, Grey, in seeking to impress upon the settler community in the colony's north that he had been instructed to uphold the Treaty, cited the first clause of its second article. In these declarations, Grey was careful not to disclose what he thought the reference to *possessions* in that clause in the Treaty meant or what he meant by 'Your lands'. It appears that he agreed with Howick's Select Committee

---

[8] Hope to Stephen, 19 May 1845; Stephen to Hope, Minute, 21 May 1845, TNA, CO 209/38; Stanley to Grey, 13 June 1845, *BPP*, 1846, Paper no. 337, p. 72.

[9] This said, an earlier generation of scholars erred in casting Grey in overly Machiavellian terms, as Mark Francis has noted ('Writings on Colonial New Zealand: Nationalism and Intentionality', in Andrew Sharp and Paul McHugh (eds.), *Histories, Power and Loss: Uses of the Past — a New Zealand Commentary*, Bridget Williams Books, Wellington, 2001, pp. 171–78). For a discussion of more recent treatments of Grey, see Richard Price, 'Sir George Grey, Protection and the Early Nineteenth-Century Empire', in Samuel Furphy and Amanda Nettelbeck (eds.), *Aboriginal Protection and its Intermediaries in Britain's Antipodean Colonies*, Routledge, London, 2020, pp. 20–22.

report that the New Zealanders only had title in land that they 'occupied or enjoyed'.[10]

Grey bided his time before deciding what course he would pursue in regard to the land question. While he wasted no time in telling his political masters that FitzRoy's decision to waive the Crown's right of pre-emption had been most unwise, he actually took no steps to put an end to this arrangement (though he told Stanley otherwise). There are probably several reasons why the new governor was being cautious in this regard. Most importantly, he soon became aware that there was considerable opposition to the government exercising the Crown's right of pre-emption as well as views about who should be able to purchase land from the natives that were contrary to the government's.[11]

Shortly after Grey arrived in New Zealand, FitzRoy passed onto him a memorandum he had solicited from Bishop Selwyn, in which the churchman had forthrightly argued that the colony's governor should not exercise the Crown's right of pre-emption in order to create a land fund, that is, a source of revenue to fund colonisation. This was so, in Selwyn's opinion, because the governor of the colony could never convince the natives that this arrangement benefitted them given that it involved the Crown buying land cheaply from them only to resell it to the settlers at a considerable profit. Selwyn saw some advantage in the government maintaining the Crown's right of pre-emption and made it clear that he thought FitzRoy's waiving of this right was contrary to sound policy (as he believed it allowed natives to trade with settlers without any sufficient check), but he nevertheless expressed support for a system of direct purchase.[12]

At this time, there were also public attacks on the Crown's right of pre-emption. In the Auckland newspaper the *New-Zealander*, its editor, John Williamson, similarly argued that the government's use of this right to create a land fund was untenable. But he also gave voice to more fundamental objections, of the kind Samuel Martin had expressed previously.

---

[10] William Williams to CMS Secretaries, 15 November 1845, CMS Records, CN/M15, AJCP, Reel M207; Grey to Stanley, 21 November 1845, *BPP*, 1846, Paper no. 712, Papers Relative to the Affairs of New Zealand: Correspondence with Lieutenant-Governor Grey, 1845–46, p. 2; Grey to Stanley, 24 November 1845, *BPP*, 1846, Paper no. 712, p. 10; Grey, Address to Northern Chiefs, 28 November 1845, *BPP*, 1846, Paper no. 712, p. 14; Grey, Address to the Legislative Council, 12 December 1845, *New-Zealander*, 13 December 1845.

[11] Grey to Stanley, 10 December 1845, *BPP*, Paper no. 712, p. 18; Grey to Stanley, 13 December 1845, *BPP*, Paper no. 712, p. 24.

[12] George Augustus Selwyn to Robert FitzRoy, November 1845, NANZ, G19/1; Grey, Minutes on George Clarke to Grey, 30 March 1846, *BPP*, 1847, Paper no. 837, Further Papers Relative to the affairs of New Zealand: Correspondence with Governor Grey, pp. 15, 20.

Williamson maintained that the third article of the Treaty had bestowed upon the natives the rights and privileges enjoyed by all British subjects and that these included the right to dispose of their land as they saw fit. More specifically, he claimed that the natives were free to sell their lands to whoever they pleased because the government had breached the conditions of the second clause of the second article of the Treaty – the pre-emption clause – by refusing to purchase the land the natives had offered to sell. Williamson echoed Martin in claiming that any attempt by a new governor to maintain the Crown's right of pre-emption would have serious consequences because the natives would never accept that they could sell only to the Crown. He suggested that there were only two courses of action available to the government: either it extinguished native title through the use of a very considerable armed force or it governed the natives by laws that treated their rights in property in the same way it would treat the rights of other British subjects. Since Williamson believed that the former could not be adopted because of the power the natives could wield, he urged Grey to introduce a system that allowed settlers to purchase land directly from the natives.[13]

As Grey pondered how he might tackle the land question, he moved swiftly against those natives he deemed to be rebels, using the military force the government had given him. By the end of January 1846, the forces he commanded had defeated Heke and his allies in the north, and early the following month he moved south to Port Nicholson and deployed these forces to assert British law and authority and thereby put the Company's settlers into possession of the land they had claimed. Grey soon realised that the natives' military capacity was such that he had to abandon any notions of conquest, at least for the time being, but he put in place a plan to attack or arrest Te Rangihaeata and Te Rauparaha, who continued to uphold Ngāti Toa claims to land (by using guerrilla warfare).[14]

During this period Grey also sought to establish his authority in native affairs and undermine that of the chiefs and their allies more generally, by adopting two inter-related measures. One comprised the introduction of a new policy of racial 'amalgamation'[15] which Grey had pursued in South

[13] *New-Zealander*, 8 November 1845, 3, 10 and 17 January 1846, 21 and 28 March 1846.
[14] Ian Wards, *The Shadow of the Land: A Study of British Policy and Racial Conflict in New Zealand 1832–1852*, Historical Publications Branch, Department of Internal Affairs, Wellington, 1968, chapters 6–9.
[15] On this matter, see Alan Ward, *A Show of Justice: Racial 'Amalgamation' in Nineteenth-Century New Zealand*, Auckland University Press/Oxford University Press, Auckland, 1974, chapter 6, and, more recently, Shaunnagh Dorsett, *Juridical Encounters: Māori and the Colonial Courts 1840–1852*, Auckland University Press, Auckland, 2017, pp. 141–56, and Price, 'Grey', pp. 23–32.

Australia and which Buller and senior Whig politicians had recently advocated for New Zealand. The other comprised an assault on the Protectorate's officials and the missionaries who had played an important role as advisers during FitzRoy's governorship, and whom the New Zealand Company and its allies had long accused of trying to fetter British colonisation in the islands. Indeed, Grey was impatient of any authority but his own and so wasted little time in destroying the independence of the Protectorate and reducing the size of its staff. He also attacked the Chief Protector, George Clarke Snr, and censured Clarke's son. In fact, these actions marked the beginning of a vendetta by Grey against the principal officers of the Protectorate as well as leading Church Missionary Society missionaries, which included his making malicious allegations about their land purchasing. This assault undermined these missionaries' credibility as advisers on native affairs and even led to the Church Missionary Society in London dismissing Henry Williams as the head of its mission in New Zealand.[16]

In June 1846 Grey took the first of a series of steps to reassert the Crown's right of pre-emption by issuing two proclamations. In the first, he announced that he had abandoned FitzRoy's waiver system and would not accept or grant any more applications for direct purchase. In the second, he gave notice to those settlers who claimed to have purchased land under the terms of FitzRoy's second waiver that they could submit the papers connected with their claims, but made it clear that he believed that many of these claimants had evaded the regulations under which the certificates to purchase had been issued and declared that their claims would not be examined until he had ascertained the views of the imperial government.[17]

Soon after he issued these proclamations, Grey sought to justify the measures they contained to William Gladstone, who had succeeded Stanley as Colonial Secretary in December 1845. On 21 June he sent Gladstone a despatch in which he made a series of hyperbolic claims. He alleged that FitzRoy's waiving of the Crown's right of pre-emption threatened to produce 'the most disastrous consequences' for the future of the natives, the settlers and the colony. More specifically, he alleged that

---

[16] Andrew Sinclair to Clarke, 5 February 1846, NANZ, IA 4/271; Clarke to Grey, 30 March 1846, minuted by Grey, attached to Grey to Stanley, 12 June 1846, *BPP*, 1847, Paper no. 837, pp. 13–20; Grey to Stanley, 3 June 1846, *BPP*, 1847, Paper no. 837, pp. 5–6; Grey to Earl Grey, 15 November 1847, *BPP*, 1848, Paper no. 1002, p. 17; Clarke to Earl Grey, 3 August 1849, and attachment, *BPP*, 1850, Paper no. 1280, Further Papers Relative to the Affairs of New Zealand, pp. 26–27; Extract from Minutes of Correspondence, New Zealand Mission, CMS, 20 November 1849, *BPP*, 1850, Paper no. 1280, pp. 149–50.

[17] Proclamations, 15 June 1846, *BPP*, 1847, Paper no. 837, p. 22.

there were individuals who had purchased extensive tracts of land and that they would 'resort to strong efforts' to hold on to what they regarded as their rights to this land. He also claimed that a series of disputes were developing between Europeans and natives that would ultimately be impossible to settle except by 'enormous expenditure' by the British government and the introduction of 'overwhelming force'. Grey told Gladstone that he had decided it was best to take the 'decisive step' of putting a stop to FitzRoy's system rather than allow 'the seeds of irremediable disaster for both races' to be sown.[18]

Four days later, Grey sent Gladstone another despatch on this subject, which would become notorious when it was published in the colony a year later. In it Grey doubled down on the claims he had made in his previous despatch by making the outlandish claim that those men who were allegedly responsible for persuading FitzRoy to waive the Crown's right of pre-emption and laying claim to extensive tracts of land expected 'a large expenditure of British blood and money' to put them in possession of those lands. Moreover, he alleged that these men comprised several Church Missionary Society missionaries, important government officials and figures connected with the press, and that they constituted 'a very powerful party'.[19] These claims – as well as the fact that Grey was not actually proposing that the government became the only purchaser of native land but was instead planning to introduce a new scheme of direct purchase by settlers (and this remained the case for several more months) – suggest that the Crown's right of pre-emption had acquired a significance in his mind that far exceeded whatever importance it had as a means of acquiring land. In short, it had become for Grey a key marker of the Crown's authority.[20]

In November 1846 Grey introduced two further measures in the colony's Legislative Council in order to tackle what he again cast as problems that arose from FitzRoy's waiving of the Crown's right of pre-emption. The first

---

[18] Grey to William Gladstone, 21 June 1846, *BPP*, 1847, Paper no. 837, pp. 27–28.

[19] Several years later, Grey would tell Gladstone's successor this melodramatic story: 'I found that the Crown's right of pre-emption over the lands belonging to the natives had been waived; that a reckless spirit of bargaining for lands between the natives and European speculators was in progress; that rebellion prevailed in several portions of the country; that it was asserted that the natives would never submit to the Crown's resuming its right of pre-emption, and would never permit it to exercise such rights; [but] I conceived it my duty, at all hazards, to resume and enforce this right' (Grey to Earl Grey, 15 May 1848, *BPP*, 1849, Paper no. 1120, New Zealand. Further Papers Relative to the Affairs of New Zealand: Correspondence with Governor Grey, p. 23).

[20] Grey to William Gladstone, 21 June 1846, *BPP*, 1847, Paper no. 837, p. 29; Grey to Gladstone, 25 June 1846, *BPP*, 1848, Paper no. 1002, New Zealand. Further Papers Relative to the Affairs of New Zealand: Correspondence with Governor Grey, pp. 106–07; *New-Zealander*, 4 September 1847.

measure was a Native Land Claims Bill. Grey conceived of this as a means of changing the way the government dealt with the claims to land that settlers made on the basis of their purchases from the natives. He proposed to abandon the procedure that had been adopted by the Land Claims Commission, that of carefully investigating each of the settlers' purchases in order to ascertain if they were valid. Like the New Zealand Company and its allies, Grey claimed that this procedure involved too much cost and delay. Land claimants would now be induced to submit statements about the money they had expended in relation to the land they claimed to have purchased, and the government would buy them out by offering compensation in return for their agreeing to forgo their claims to land, at which point the land would be deemed to be part of the demesne land of the Crown.[21]

In introducing this bill, the colony's Colonial Secretary, Andrew Sinclair, declared that its main object was the speedy settlement of land claims, but it is apparent that Grey had a further object in mind, that of asserting the authority of the Crown as the only source of title to land in the colony. Not long before this bill was introduced, he had received a petition from settlers who claimed rights in land on the basis of the purchases they had made under FitzRoy's waiver and called on him to grant them title to those lands. While Grey knew that Stanley had directed him to recognise these purchases, he was apprehensive that this would reinforce an impression in the colony that land could be bought and sold without any reference to the rights of the Crown.[22]

Consequently, the second measure that Grey introduced on this occasion, a Native Land Purchase Bill, was devised to enable the government to prosecute settlers who had entered into agreements with the natives for the purchase or lease of their lands without the permission of the Crown. In a speech he made in introducing this bill, the Attorney General, William Swainson, claimed that it was in keeping with the imperial government's original goal of systematic colonisation and that that objective had led the government in 1839 to devise the pre-emption clause in the Treaty, to enact the Land Claims Ordinance of 1841 that had declared all purchases of lands prior to annexation null and void and to direct the colonial administration to invalidate any native alienation of land to settlers that had taken place after the proclamation of British sovereignty. Swainson argued that many of the difficulties that the colony had encountered since 1840 were the result of unrestricted and irregular

---

[21] Land Claims Bill, *New-Zealander*, 7 November 1846.

[22] Memorial, undated [c. September 1846], *New-Zealander*, 3 October 1846; Meeting of land claimants, 1 October 1846, reported *New-Zealander*, 3 October 1846; *New-Zealander*, 3 October 1846; Legislative Council Proceedings, 9 November 1846, *New-Zealander*, 14 November 1846.

settlement prior to annexation. He also claimed that FitzRoy's waivers had revived those practices and that they needed to be checked before a 'powerful class' could once again set up claims on the grounds of vested interests. Clearly, Swainson was echoing Grey's claim in his notorious despatch to Gladstone, discussed earlier.[23]

As this bill was being debated in the Legislative Council, Grey made a very telling intervention. The circumstances were as follows. A member of the Council who was critical of aspects of the bill reminded Sinclair that he had previously supported FitzRoy's waivers. This provoked the Colonial Secretary to declare that he believed that the natives had a right under the Treaty of Waitangi to sell their lands to Europeans. This remark provoked Grey in turn to complain that that principle would 'allow the natives to sell their land to whom they pleased' and to claim that its application would have the most disastrous consequences for the natives. More to the point, Sinclair's remarks seemed to have prompted Grey to sum up the bill in this way: 'it was illegal to sell, and illegal to lease, lands belonging to the natives to any other than the Crown' and that 'Nothing was more plain and incontrovertible than that doctrine'. The doctrine Grey was referring to was actually the principle of the Crown's right of pre-emption, yet the point of the legislation under consideration was to entrench the principle that the Crown was the only source of title in the colony, not to shore up the Crown's right of pre-emption. The fact that Grey could conflate these two very different principles suggests once again that in his mind the right of pre-emption stood for something much more fundamental than the Crown's right to be the only purchaser of native land,[24] namely the authority of the Crown in regard to land.[25]

Both of these bills met with considerable criticism, much of it along the lines that had been expressed earlier in the pages of the *New-Zealander* in regard to the Crown's right of pre-emption. Now, though, the editor of this newspaper was critical of the government's objects for other reasons. Williamson claimed that these bills smacked of autocracy, discerning that they were driven in large part by Grey's wish to acquire power and authority in order to realise the government's goals in regard to land.

---

[23] Native Land Purchases Bill, *New-Zealander*, 14 November 1846; Legislative Council Proceedings, 14 November 1846, *New-Zealander*, 21 November 1846.

[24] In fact, many fine historians and legal scholars have also failed to distinguish between these two principles. See, for example, Adams, *Fatal Necessity*, p. 194; Michael Belgrave, 'Pre-emption, the Treaty of Waitangi and the Politics of Crown Purchase', *New Zealand Journal of History*, vol. 31, no. 1, 1997, pp. 26–27; Bruce Kercher, 'Informal Land Titles: *Snowden v Baker* (1844)', *Victoria University of Wellington Law Review*, vol. 41, no. 3, 2010, p. 616.

[25] Legislative Council Proceedings, 14 November 1846, *New-Zealander*, 21 November 1846.

But he also claimed to have espied something even more sinister in the second of the two bills. 'This ordinance has strengthened the conviction that has been gradually forcing itself upon our mind, that His Excellency the Governor has been addressing himself to the task of carrying out the recommendation of the [1844] Select Committee of the House of Commons', Williamson remarked. What did he mean? '[T]he present measure', Williamson continued, 'must be considered as the first step towards the negation of the Treaty of Waitangi, and the adoption of the policy recommended by the [Select] Committee in the sixth resolution appended to the Report, which states, "That means ought to be forthwith adopted for establishing the exclusive title of the Crown to all land not actually occupied and enjoyed by Natives, or held under grants from the Crown"'. At a public meeting convened in order to condemn both pieces of legislation, the implications of Williamson's contention were spelt out by a speaker who argued that Grey had taken the 1842 Waste Lands Act as his guide. He objected that this earlier legislation had nothing to do with the lands belonging to natives in New Zealand: 'Were the rightful properties of the aboriginal possessors of the soil to be termed waste lands of the Crown and the terms of the Land Sales Act applied to them? If such was the case, then the Treaty of Waitangi would be violated for the natives were no longer secured the control of their own rightful possessions, which every subject of her Majesty should uninterruptedly enjoy'.[26]

At this stage, there is no evidence that Grey was planning to apply the doctrine that Howick's Select Committee report had championed – that is, to assert that the only lands in which the natives had a right of property were those they could be said to 'occupy and enjoy' – let alone that Grey saw a connection between restoring the Crown's right of pre-emption and implementing that doctrine. But back in London, as we will see in due course, the other Grey – Earl Grey – was making this very connection.

Symonds v. McIntosh *or* R v. Symonds

By April 1847 it had become apparent that very few of the settlers who claimed land under FitzRoy's waivers were willing to accept the terms of Grey's Native Land Claims Act by applying for compensation for the purchases they had made. Most of them evidently maintained that the certificates that they had been granted by FitzRoy entitled them to a land grant. In Grey's eyes, this position amounted to a claim that they already had title. He regarded this as an unacceptable challenge to the Crown's

[26] *New-Zealander*, 14, 21 and 28 November 1846.

authority and directed that the matter should be referred to the colony's highest court.[27] In deciding on this course of action, Grey claimed, as he had done in June the previous year, that the Crown's right of pre-emption had been waived over extensive tracts of land and that some of the claimants under FitzRoy's waivers were endeavouring to create fresh claims. If this purchasing was regarded as legal, he argued once again, it would create a precedent and the Crown's right of pre-emption would be deemed to have been waived over the entire colony. It was essential, he maintained, that the government acquire a ruling on the legality of FitzRoy's waiving of the Crown's right of pre-emption. Grey suggested the government should couch its case in terms of FitzRoy's waiver being a breach of the second clause of the second article of the Treaty of Waitangi.[28]

In order to mount this case, the government had to contrive a legal dispute.[29] (The famous 1823 American Supreme Court case *Johnson v. M'Intosh* had similarly been contrived,[30] though there is no evidence to suggest that Grey or his advisers were aware of this fact.) In keeping with a suggestion made by Swainson, the government issued to John Jermyn Symonds, Grey's private secretary and the protector of Aborigines, a grant of land that was already included in a certificate of one of FitzRoy's waivers that was held by Charles Hunter McIntosh, a clerk in the government's surveying office; McIntosh then petitioned the Governor to set aside the grant to Symonds on the grounds that he (McIntosh) had acquired a prior title to the land in question.[31]

The case was heard in Auckland by Chief Justice William Martin at the beginning of May 1847. Representing Symonds, Swainson took responsibility for putting the government's case. It consisted of a series of

---

[27] This was not the only legal case mounted by Grey to overturn FitzRoy's acts in regard to land title. *R v. Taylor*, for example, was another (see *R v. Taylor*, New Zealand Lost Cases Project, www.victoria.ac.nz/law/nzlostcases/CaseDetails.aspx?casenumber=00180, and Mark Hickford, '"Settling Some Very Important Principles of Colonial Law": Three "Forgotten" Cases of the 1840s', *Victoria University of Wellington Law Review*, vol. 35, no. 1, 2004, pp. 18–25).

[28] Grey to Earl Grey, 19 April 1847, *BPP*, 1847, Paper no. 892, New Zealand. Papers Relative to the Affairs of New Zealand. Correspondence with Governor Grey, p. 30; Grey Memo to William Swainson, 20 April 1847, *BPP*, 1847, Paper no. 892, pp. 32–34.

[29] It was not the only case that was contrived at this time by the government in regard to land. In 1846 the imperial government encouraged the New Zealand Company to construct a case, which became *Scott v. Grace*, in order to clarify the validity of grants that had been issued to the Company (Hickford, 'Principles of Colonial Law', p. 5).

[30] See Lindsay G. Robertson, *Conquest by Law: How the Discovery of America Dispossessed Indigenous Peoples of their Lands*, Oxford University Press, New York, 2005, pp. xi, 47.

[31] Swainson to Sinclair, 21 April 1847, *BPP*, 1847, Paper no. 892, p. 35; David V. Williams, 'The Queen v Symonds Reconsidered', *Victoria University of Wellington Law Review*, vol. 19, no. 4, 1989, pp. 388–90.

arguments focusing on the Crown's right of pre-emption, namely that FitzRoy had no authority to waive this right; that he had no power under the terms of the Treaty to transfer it to a third party (the settlers); and that, irrespective of the Treaty, this right vested in, and could only be exercised by, the Crown. McIntosh's lawyer countered with several arguments, many of which focused on the Treaty. First, he argued that the second clause of its second article did *not* bestow on the Crown the sole right to purchase land from the natives since etymologically the term *pre-emption* merely meant the right of first offer, and since this was the sense that the natives attached to the corresponding word in their own language that meaning had to be preferred against the meaning the government imputed to it (which is a species of the kind of argument that has been made in more recent times in regard to the Treaty). Second, he contended that if the natives were not allowed to sell to whomsoever they chose, and the Crown had no power to permit this and was under no obligation to purchase from the natives, the Treaty was invalid because it infringed the requirement of a contract, that of mutuality or reciprocity of obligation. Third, he argued that there were no 'express words' in the Treaty restraining the Crown from waiving the right of pre-emption and that the Crown could not be bound by a mere implication that it had no such right. Finally, he asserted that the recognition of the waivers by the relevant minister of the Crown, namely the Colonial Secretary Lord Stanley, made the acts of a governor the acts of the Crown, and that since the Crown possessed the right of waiver this meant that FitzRoy's act in waiving it was valid.[32]

At the end of the hearing, Martin reserved judgment so that he could consult his colleague Justice Henry Chapman, who was based in Wellington. At this point it seems that Grey was anxious about the outcome of the case. At any rate, at the end of May he had instructed Swainson to make the necessary preparations for an appeal to the Privy Council. This is hardly surprising, as it was by no means guaranteed that the court would rule in the government's favour.[33]

Yet the two justices did decide in favour of the government, ruling that a purchaser of land could only acquire a right to property in land if he obtained it by virtue of a grant from the Crown and that in this case McIntosh had acquired no such grant.[34] They advanced several grounds

[32] *New-Zealander*, 8 May 1847.

[33] Grey to Sinclair, 29 May 1847, Letter Book of Governor Robert FitzRoy 30 August – 11 November 1845, and of Governor George Grey 17 November 1845–15 December 1853, Sir George Grey Special Collections, APL, NZ MMS 227.

[34] This legal ruling did not preclude McIntosh from enjoying the fruits of his acquisition of the land in question. On 5 August 1847 it was recommended that he be issued with

for their judgment. First, since McIntosh's case really stood upon the fact that he had acquired a right in property from the Crown, questions about the terms of the Treaty of Waitangi had no relevance. Second, McIntosh had only been granted a certificate by which the governor consented to waive the Crown's right of pre-emption and such a certificate did not convey a legal right or title to the land. Third, in any case, the governor did not have any authority to waive the Crown's right because he lacked any express authority to do this. This authority could not be assumed on the basis of the various acts and dealings of the Crown since those acts made clear that the government had long had a policy of proscribing the sale of land by native people except to the Crown.[35]

These legal arguments alone would have determined the outcome of the case. However, the judges, or at least Chapman, were keen to address another matter, namely the source of title in the colony. This was probably because some settlers in the colony had been arguing that the natives had a right to sell land to whomsoever they chose, thereby implying that the natives rather than the Crown were the source of title to land in the colony. It seems clear that Chapman was keen to scotch this contention. Indeed, it is apparent that he believed that establishing the source of title in New Zealand was just as important a matter as the Crown's right of pre-emption. His interest in the former might have been prompted by the fact that he perceived a connection between FitzRoy holding that all lands in the colony were owned by the natives and his waiving of the Crown's right of pre-emption, and he was no doubt aware that a consideration of the source of title would serve Grey's broader objective of asserting the Crown's authority. Moreover, Chapman knew that the jurisprudence of the Marshall Supreme Court, especially in *Johnson v. M'Intosh*, had made a connection between the Crown's right of pre-emption and the notion that the Crown was the only source of title in the colony. One way or the other, much of Chapman's argumentation in what was the lead judgment in this case concerned the source of title in the colony rather than the Crown's right of pre-emption, even though it was the latter that was legally at issue.[36]

a confirmatory grant on the basis that he had been in undisputed possession of the land in question since he had purchased it and had made various improvements to it, and in October 1848 he obtained a Crown grant for it (Mark Hickford, *Lords of the Land: Indigenous Property Rights and the Jurisprudence of Empire*, Oxford University Press, Oxford, 2011, p. 205).

[35] *R v. Symonds*, *New-Zealander*, 12 June 1847.

[36] Chapman's interest in addressing broader legal matters than was required might also be attributed to the fact that he wanted to make his name as a judge and had decided that framing the case in terms of the source of title was a means of realising that ambition

At the outset of his judgment Chapman remarked: 'As this question involves principles of universal application to the respective territorial rights of the Crown, the aboriginal natives, and the European subjects of the Queen, [and] as moreover its decision may affect larger interests than even this Court is up to this moment aware of, I think it is incumbent on us to enunciate the principles upon which our conclusion is based, with more care and particularity than would, under other circumstances, be necessary'. Chapman then proceeded to argue that there were several established principles of long historical standing that were applicable to the case. The most important of those principles, he claimed, was a fundamental maxim deriving from feudal times that the Crown was the only source of title in land. (As readers might recall, this was an argument that Chapman had advanced in 1840 as the editor of the New Zealand Company's journal in London. He had contended that the British Crown's title to New Zealand rested on Cook's claim of possession on the basis of the doctrine of discovery and so there was no need for the government to negotiate with the chiefs.)[37] As a corollary of this notion, Chapman went on, colonial courts had invariably held that they could not give effect to any title that was not derived from the Crown.[38]

Chapman suggested that in ordinary circumstances this legal principle would be sufficient to decide the matter and so he could rest his case there. However, he proceeded to argue that the particulars of the case demanded that he spell out the implications of this principle for the matter that had been brought before the court. Chapman argued that it seemed clear that the principle that the Crown was the only source of title meant that no subject could acquire land from any other means or source than the Crown. Any acquisition of territory by a subject might entitle that subject to some consideration from the Crown, but it could not confer any title. Rather, the exclusive right of acquiring title in a new territory lay in the Crown. Consequently, Chapman pointed out, the Crown could lawfully oust any subject who attempted to retain possession of any lands he might have acquired. '[T]he purchases are good as against the native, but not against the Crown', he explained. Realising that this point needed more support, Chapman later suggested: 'Anciently, it seems to have been assumed that, notwithstanding the rights of the native race, and of course subject to such

(Henry Chapman to Chapman Snr, 15 and 17 June 1847, Henry Chapman Letters, ATL, qMS-0420, vol. 3).

[37] Shaunnaugh Dorsett has pointed out that Chapman's views on sovereignty 'remained virtually unchanged' across the 1840s and beyond ('Sovereignty as Governance in the Early New Zealand Crown Colony Period', in Shaunnagh Dorsett and Ian Hunter (eds.), Law and Politics in British Colonial Thought: Transpositions of Empire, Palgrave Macmillan, London, 2010, p. 211).

[38] R v. Symonds, New-Zealander, 12 June 1847.

rights, the Crown, as against its own subjects, had the full and absolute dominion over the soil as a necessary consequence of territorial jurisdiction. Strictly speaking, this is perhaps deducible from the principle of our law'.[39]

By arguing in this way, Chapman recast the Crown's right of pre-emption, thereby making it more significant than it was, technically speaking. As the legal historian Lindsay G. Roberston has pointed out, historically pre-emption had meant no more than the exclusive right to engage in the purchasing of land; in other words, this right 'had not carried with it title to the land to which the right was claimed'. However, Chapman expanded the Crown's right of pre-emption so that it comprised the Crown's right to title. By doing this, he bound together what were two distinct principles or rights – the Crown's exclusive right to purchase land, and the Crown's exclusive right to award title – and represented them in the Crown's right of pre-emption as though they were one and the same. To be more specific, Chapman had taken the Crown's right of pre-emption, which strictly speaking concerned the exclusive right of the Crown to purchase the natives' land in the future, and projected it back into that past, in order to invalidate not only titles that were based on purchases from the natives *after* the Crown assumed sovereignty but also those titles that were based on purchase *before* that had occurred, thereby rendering the Crown as the only source of title. This was a neat solution to the problem that had bedevilled the colony from the outset, and which Swainson had noted recently, namely that many British subjects had purchased land from the New Zealanders during the time that the British government had disclaimed sovereignty and acted as though the New Zealanders were the only sovereign and thus source of title in the islands. Chapman, it should be noted, was not the first to have made this move in regard to the Crown's right of pre-emption. As we have noted (pp. 162–63), the likes of his fellow New Zealand Company advocate Edward Gibbon Wakefield and John Dunmore Lang had done so in 1840, and they had copied what Chief Justice John Marshall of the United States Supreme Court had done in respect of the right of pre-emption in the 1823 case *Johnson v. M'Intosh*.[40]

In his judgment Justice Martin concurred with Chapman's argument that titles in colonies rested upon grants from the Crown. Moreover, he spelt out that this principle predated the Treaty of Waitangi and could not be altered by it. Clearly, the Treaty of Waitangi that the Colonial Office had found useful to cast as an important legal document at various points

---

[39] *Ibid.*   [40] *Ibid.*, my emphasis; Robertson, *Conquest by Law*, pp. 96, 99, 110.

in recent years was now deemed by these judges to be of no legal significance.[41]

Not surprisingly, Grey was greatly relieved to learn that the court had ruled that FitzRoy's waiving of the Crown's right of pre-emption was illegal and thus void. In a despatch to the Colonial Office he claimed that the judgment would put an end to all questioning of the government's treatment of claims to land purchased under the waivers. He argued that there could be no possibility that a governor of New Zealand could waive the Crown's right of pre-emption again, noted that the government had resumed the right several months earlier and claimed that both settlers and natives had acquiesced to this change. Yet, as Mark Hickford has pointed out, contrary to other historians like Peter Adams, securing the Crown's right of pre-emption did not in itself ensure that the government could acquire the land it needed.[42]

There is a further reason for doubting that the court's ruling was as momentous as Grey claimed it to be. In the weeks following the handing down of the court's findings, it appears that only two newspapers in the colony carried reports of both the case and the judgment. Furthermore, one of those newspapers claimed that the court's principal finding had merely reminded everyone that the Crown was the exclusive source of title and that any proper purchase from the natives was only good against parties other than the Crown; and few other newspapers reported the judgment. In any case, the colony was soon preoccupied with another matter, namely the nature of the natives' rights in land. In the same week that the court had delivered its judgment, newspapers in the colony drew attention to a new set of royal instructions and an accompanying despatch by the Colonial Secretary in London, Earl Grey, which were potentially game-changing.[43]

Part II

Earl Grey and Native Title

Earl Grey had succeeded Gladstone as Colonial Secretary in July 1846 after Peel's Tory administration had fallen from power and been replaced by a Whig administration headed by Lord John Russell. As we have seen,

---

[41] *R v. Symonds, New-Zealander*, 12 June 1847.

[42] Grey to Earl Grey, 5 July 1847, *BPP*, 1847, Paper no. 892, p. 64; Adams, *Fatal Necessity*, p. 209; Hickford, *Lords*, pp. 198–99.

[43] *New-Zealander*, 12 and 16 June 1847; *New Zealand Spectator and Cook's Strait Guardian*, 26 June 1847; *Wellington Independent*, 7, 10 and 14 July 1847; Grey, Address to the Legislative Council, 7 August 1847, *BPP*, 1848, Paper no. 1002, pp. 46–47.

in authoring the House of Commons' Select Committee report on New Zealand in 1844 and speaking in the parliamentary debates on New Zealand's affairs the following year, Earl Grey (as Lord Howick) had championed the New Zealand Company's claim that the natives of New Zealand had very limited rights of property in land. Earl Grey's appointment was not the only change that had taken place at the Colonial Office. One of the New Zealand Company's champions, Benjamin Hawes, had become the parliamentary Under-Secretary, and Charles Buller, one of the Company's principal advocates, had taken the sinecure office of Judge Advocate General on the understanding that he would play a major role in colonial affairs. Stephen was dismayed by the latter's appointment as he had come to distrust him profoundly. (Fifteen months later, he had to step down as the Colonial Office's Permanent Under-Secretary after his health collapsed, largely as a result of a nervous breakdown.) Not surprisingly, the Company was overjoyed by these three appointments. After a very long battle, it seemed that the stage was set for it to realise all its goals. Indeed, shortly after the Whigs took office, Earl Grey obligingly introduced a bill for a new constitution for New Zealand that provided for a measure of responsible government; he drew up a new royal charter whereby the colony was divided into two provinces; and he issued new instructions to Grey that included a long section on what he called the settlement of the Crown's waste lands. (Henceforth, I will refer to Grey the Governor as 'Grey', and to Grey the Colonial Secretary as 'Earl Grey' in order to avoid any confusion.) The last of these measures marked yet another shift in the position that the Colonial Office had taken towards land questions since New Zealand had begun a British colony in 1840.[44]

In those instructions, dated 23 December 1846, Earl Grey called upon Grey to create a registry of land claims in order to ascertain the extent of the land that belonged to the Crown and was thus available for future colonisation. This was no more than Stanley had previously done. But

---

[44] Directors of the NZC, Memorial to Lord John Russell, 1 July 1846, Papers of Henry George, 3rd Earl Grey (henceforth Grey Papers), University of Durham Library Special Collections, GRE/B147/19; Earl Grey, Journal, 21 October 1845–31 July 1846, entries 4 and 7 July 1846, Grey Papers, GRE/V/C3/12; James Stephen, Journal, 1846, entry 12 July 1846, Papers of Sir James Stephen, Cambridge University Library, Add MS 7888, II/118; *New Zealand Journal*, 18 July 1846; Charles Buller to Earl Grey, 3 August 1846, Grey Papers, GRE/B79/11/36–38; Buller to Earl Grey, 26 August 1846, enclosing Report of a Special Committee of the Court of the Directors of the NZC and other enclosures, Grey Papers, GRE/B147/14; New Zealand Charter, 28 December 1846, *BPP*, 1847, Paper no. 763, New Zealand. Papers Relative to the Affairs of New Zealand. Correspondence with Governor Grey, pp. 72–75, Queen's Instructions Accompanying the New Zealand Charter, *BPP*, 1847, Paper no. 763, pp. 76–87; John M. Ward, 'The Retirement of a Titan: James Stephen, 1847–50', *Journal of Modern History*, vol. 31, no. 3, 1959, pp. 189–92.

Earl Grey stipulated that no claim by the natives would be accepted unless it was established that their right had been acknowledged by some act of the Crown or that the natives actually had *occupation* of the lands in the sense that they were 'accustomed to use and enjoy' those lands 'either as places of abode, or for tillage, or the growth of crops, or for the depasturing of cattle' or more generally for the sustaining of life by 'means of labour expended'. This was the definition of the rights of property in land that the Company had been demanding for a long time and which Earl Grey had advocated in his Select Committee report.[45]

As it turned out, a long despatch, in which Earl Grey sought to provide Grey with an explanation of these instructions regarding land, proved to be more important than the instructions themselves. Earl Grey prefaced his explanatory remarks in this despatch by saying that what had happened in New Zealand had caused 'almost inextricable confusion' in regard to the respective claims and rights of various classes of people and that it was more or less impossible for the imperial government to determine what a governor's line of conduct ought to be and how far it was possible to act upon the principles to which he would otherwise have prescribed Grey's adherence. Yet, having said this, Earl Grey launched into a long account in which he sought to explain the policy that it would be right for the government to follow if it was not 'embarrassed' by past transactions, and which it still ought to adopt regarding the rights of property in land that should be acknowledged or created, most especially in regard to the natives, in so far as any freedom of choice remained to it. Earl Grey was speaking in two different and potentially contradictory registers. On the one hand, his own passionate attachment to a particular doctrine regarding the nature of rights of property in land led him to try to persuade Grey to put this into practice; on the other hand, he had enough political nous to realise that implementing this doctrine might not be possible, and so he sought to arm himself and the Governor with the means to extricate themselves from the embarrassment that such an eventuality would cause them both.[46]

In seeking to explain his instructions, Earl Grey began by claiming that there were two opinions on the natives' rights of property in land in a place such as New Zealand. The first, which was largely a straw man of his own making inasmuch as no one in government had consistently articulated it, held that the aboriginal people were the proprietors of every part of the land of which they were accustomed to assert any title. He scorned this opinion: 'This claim is represented as sacred, however ignorant such natives may be of the arts and of the habits of civilised life, however

---

[45] Queen's Instructions, 28 December 1846, *BPP*, 1847, Paper no. 763, pp. 84–85.
[46] Earl Grey to Grey, 23 December 1846, *BPP*, 1847, Paper no. 763, p. 67.

small the number of their tribes, however unsettled their abodes, and however imperfect and occasional the uses they make of the land. Whether they are nomadic tribes depasturing cattle, or hunters living by the chase, or fishermen frequenting the sea-coasts or the banks of rivers, the proprietary title in question is alike ascribed to them all'. Earl Grey made it clear that he dissented from this position entirely by enunciating what he called 'the true principle with regard to property in land'. He chose to draw this principle from the work of the Anglican clergyman and Regius Professor of History at Oxford University Dr Thomas Arnold, whose words he quoted at length. For example, 'Men were to subdue the earth, that is, to make it by their labour what it would not have been by itself, and with the labour so bestowed upon it came the right of property in it ... [S]o much does the right of property go along with labour that civilised nations have never scrupled to take possession of countries inhabited only by tribes of savages – countries which have been hunted over but never subdued or cultivated'. Earl Grey airily suggested that Arnold's reasoning had to be generally conceded and that it could hardly be denied that it was applicable to New Zealand. Thus, it was fatal to the right that had been 'claimed for the aboriginal inhabitants of those islands to the exclusive possession of the vast extent of fertile but unoccupied lands which they contain'.[47]

Earl Grey went on to spell out the implications of his main contention: 'if the savage inhabitants of New Zealand had themselves no right of property in land which they did not occupy it is obvious that they could not convey to others what they themselves did not possess, and that claims to vast tracts of waste land, founded on pretended sales from them, are altogether untenable'. Indeed, he asserted, as he had in his Select Committee report, that from the moment that British sovereignty was proclaimed in New Zealand, all lands that were not 'occupied' in the sense that he was using this legal term should have been considered as the rightful property of the Crown and the government should have then determined in what manner and according to what rules the lands that had hitherto been waste should have been assigned to the settlers.[48]

Earl Grey also argued that another consideration led to the same conclusion, namely that it had only ever been claimed that the natives held land as tribes, and since title on that basis was simply an attribute of sovereignty and that sovereignty had been transferred to the British Crown they could not be said to have retained any right in the land. He declared: 'it is clear that, according to the well-known principles of public law, while the property of individuals would have been respected, all

[47] *Ibid.*, pp. 67–68.   [48] *Ibid.*, p. 68.

public property, all rights of every description which had appertained to the previous sovereigns, would have devolved, as a matter of course, to the new sovereign who succeeded them'.[49]

These were the principles, Earl Grey told Grey, that he would have instructed him to implement if the colonisation of New Zealand was beginning now. He reiterated that he was well aware that Grey was not in a position to do this because past transactions made a strict application of those principles impracticable. Nevertheless, he made it clear that although he understood that Grey might feel compelled to depart from these principles, he still expected him to look to them as the foundation of the policy that he should pursue if he had the power to do so.[50]

What did this mean? Earl Grey acknowledged that it was too late for the Crown to assert its right to large tracts of waste land that particular tribes had been 'taught to regard as their own' and remarked that Grey had probably admitted these pretensions to a considerable extent already given that there was no apparent advantage to be gained by the government acting in a way that could be deemed to be inconsistent with good faith. Yet he proceeded to prescribe these two courses of action: 'While, however, you scrupulously fulfil whatever engagements you have contracted, and maintain those rights on the part of the native tribes to land which you have already recognised, you will avoid as much as possible any further surrender of the property of the Crown'; and 'I trust also that the evil which would otherwise arise from the concessions already made may to a great degree be neutralised by your strictly maintaining the exclusive right of the Crown to purchase land from the native tribes to which it has been assumed it belongs [i.e. the right of pre-emption]. This right, resting as it does not only upon what has been called the Treaty of Waitangi, but also upon the general and long-recognised principles of national law, is one so important that it ought almost at all hazards to be strictly enforced'. As this makes clear, Earl Grey was in effect suggesting to Grey that he use the power that the government had acquired by dint of one part of the Treaty – the clause by which it had secured the right of pre-emption for the Crown – in order to counter the consequences of the promise that many had come to hold the Crown had given to the natives in another part of it – the clause that confirmed and guaranteed to them the possession of their lands. This was probably no more than Stanley had had in mind in *his* instructions to Grey. But whereas he had merely implied that the Crown's right of pre-emption be put to this use in this way, Earl Grey now explicitly recommended this course of action.[51]

[49] *Ibid.*, pp. 68–69.   [50] *Ibid.*, p. 69.   [51] *Ibid.*

Earl Grey immediately provided a copy of his despatch to the directors of the New Zealand Company and told them they could send it to the press. Not surprisingly, the newspapers and magazines that supported the Company welcomed Grey's instructions, the despatch and the new constitution. The *Spectator* declared: 'It sweeps away the whole system of official machinery and self-impeding sophistry established by Lord Stanley – all the "treaty of Waitangi" nonsense, and all the past Downing Street plans for hindering the settlement of the islands'. *The Times* also welcomed these changes in policy, though in regard to the land question it expressed some doubt as to whether the arrangements Earl Grey had proposed would remedy the problems that had arisen. This was prescient.[52]

Grey's Purchase

By the time Earl Grey's instructions and the accompanying despatch reached Grey in April 1847, he had already embarked on a strategy in regard to native title that differed in many respects to the one Earl Grey seemed to be urging him to adopt. As we have noted, Grey had been instructed by Stanley to help the New Zealand Company to make good its claims to land. Moreover, several months later, Gladstone had impressed upon him the need to do this after the Company had complained about the colonial administration's treatment of two of its deeds in Port Nicholson. Initially, Grey delegated the task of dealing with this problem to Lieutenant-Colonel William McCleverty, the special agent who had been appointed by Stanley to assist the colonial government with the Company's acquisition of land. The instructions Grey issued to McCleverty reveal that he assumed that the natives only had rights of property in the land they cultivated. In September 1846 he directed McCleverty to proceed accordingly by seeking to buy those particular lands and treat the rest as though it was waste land. McCleverty set about doing just that. However, in the early months of 1847 he was given the role of commanding the British troops in the colony and Grey took responsibility for settling the most important of the questions relating to the Company's claims. In doing so, he ended up pursuing a very different course to the one he had instructed McCleverty to take.[53]

---

[52] *The Times*, 29 December 1846; Earl Grey to Grey, private, 31 December 1846, Sir George Grey Papers, Sir George Grey Special Collections, APL, MSS 35, Item 2; *Spectator*, 2 January 1847.

[53] Gladstone to Grey, 21 March 1846 with enclosure T.C. Harington to Gladstone, 28 February 1846, *BPP*, 1846, Paper no. 337, pp. 169–70; Grey to William McCleverty, 14 September 1846, *BPP*, 1847, Paper no. 837, pp. 63–64; Te Whanganui

Grey, as we have noted, had been authorised by Stanley to spend up to £10,000 for the purpose of buying lands required by the New Zealand Company if he found it necessary to do so, and parliament had approved a loan of £100,000 that could be drawn on for meeting the same expense. Grey now proceeded to purchase land at both Porirua and Wairau from Ngāti Toa. This not only encompassed land that was the subject of the Company's claims but also a huge amount of land which surrounded these claims. In the case of the former, Grey paid £2,000 for approximately 25,000 acres, and in the case of the latter he expended a mere £3,000 for about 3 million acres. In making these purchases, Grey made no attempt to distinguish between the lands that could be deemed to be *occupied* by the natives in the legal sense that the likes of Earl Grey understood that term, and those lands that were not. He simply purchased the lot.[54]

It is not altogether clear why Grey chose to proceed in this way. Michael Belgrave has argued that Grey had stumbled on this approach as a means of extinguishing native title. This might overstate what took place. Grey had learned from various native and missionary sources, especially the missionary Octavius Hadfield, that the natives would oppose any attempt by the government to assume ownership of their lands by claiming that they were waste, but that tribes could be willing to sell, not least because they saw government purchases of their land as confirmation that they, rather than some other tribe who claimed the same land, were its customary owners. In this particular case, Grey would have known of the competition for mana (or power) between Ngāti Toa, Ngāti Raukawa, Te Āti Awa, Ngāti Apa and other tribes in this case. He also knew that he could use military force to apply pressure on these tribes. Moreover, Grey relished making these deals, as it allowed him to play a role that he could envisage in heroic terms, that of acquiring title to a vast amount of land, which was something that none of his predecessors had been able to do (though they would probably have been able to do so had they been granted the funds the home government gave Grey).[55]

In reporting these purchases to Earl Grey in a despatch he sent in the last week of March, Grey used all of his great skills with the pen. As the historian John W. Cell once remarked, Grey's despatches were 'masterpieces of obfuscation'. In this particular despatch Grey argued that the purchases he had made would be extremely advantageous to the colony as they would meet the future needs of the government and the settlers.

---

a Tara me Ona Takiwa: Report on the Wellington District, Wai 145, Treaty of Waitangi Tribunal Report, 2003, pp. 234–35, 247.
[54] Grey to Earl Grey, 26 March 1847, *BPP*, 1847, Paper no. 892, pp. 7–8.
[55] Belgrave, 'Pre-emption', p. 36; Hickford, *Lords*, p. 200.

Indeed, he boasted that he had now disposed of every troublesome land claim in the colony except one (though this was hardly the case). Yet Grey told his superior very little about the precise nature of his purchasing. Indeed, it was only in the closing sentence of this despatch that he alluded to this: 'I have no doubt that now *the uniform system* of purchasing from [the natives] such districts in their *bona fide possession* as may be required by the government is adopted, that no further disputes or disturbances on the subject of land will take place throughout the southern portions of New Zealand'. Grey explained neither what this 'uniform system' of purchasing comprised nor what he meant by land in the natives' '*bona fide possession*', let alone how he had determined the latter. This suggests that he was reluctant to disclose to his political master precisely what he had done.[56]

This despatch would probably have been the only occasion on which Grey gave Earl Grey an explanation of his purchasing but for the fact that the purchases in question and the way in which he had conducted them came under attack in the colony. First, one of the Company's newspapers, the *New Zealand Spectator and Cook's Strait Guardian*, published a series of pseudonymous letters to the editor, the first of which might have been written by William Wakefield. In one of those letters the author argued that Grey had sacrificed a fundamental principle by purchasing such a large tract of 'waste land' at Wairau and in another the author contended that there had been no need for Grey to pay for that land except for the few acres that the natives actually occupied. Second, William Wakefield wrote personally to Grey to raise several objections, one of which included the governor's payment to natives who were not actually resident on the land at Wairau.[57]

It is also probable that Grey felt bound to provide more of an explanation for his purchasing because, sometime in the first week or so of April, he received a private letter from Earl Grey, dated 27 November 1846 (which had reached New Zealand in unusually quick time), in which the Colonial Secretary had conveyed to him drafts of the new constitution and the new instructions as well as of the accompanying despatch (that was eventually dated 27 December 1846) in which he explained those instructions. In other words, at around this time Grey learned that his superior was in good part urging him to do the opposite of what he had just done, namely to limit the government's recognition of native title to

---

[56] Grey to Earl Grey, 26 March 1847, *BPP*, 1847, Paper no. 892, pp. 7–9, my emphases; Cell, 'Imperial Conscience', p. 196.
[57] *New Zealand Spectator and Cook's Strait Guardian*, 24, 27 and 31 March 1847, 3 April 1847; William Wakefield to Grey, 25 March 1847, *BPP*, 1847, Paper no. 892, pp. 17–18.

the land that the natives could be said to occupy, and to treat the rest as waste land.[58]

On receiving Earl Grey's draft despatch, it seems that Grey sat down immediately to write another despatch to him in order to further justify his purchasing, though in doing so he pretended that he had not received Earl Grey's draft despatch. Ostensibly, Grey wrote this new despatch in order to rebut the principal objections that Wakefield had raised, which included a claim that Spain had never investigated the Company's claim to the whole of the district in question and so Ngāti Toa ownership to it had not been established. Grey claimed that Spain had in fact conducted such an investigation and had ruled that Ngāti Toa were the owners of the land, and that FitzRoy had told Stanley that these lands could not be fully occupied by settlers unless very large additional payments were made to the native owners. Turning to the Porirua block, Grey quoted part of Spain's decision in order to suggest that the Land Claims Commissioner had ruled that the natives were in 'real and bona fide possession' because 'in each and all of these places ha[d] the tribe both residences and cultivated lands', though, logically speaking, this claim did not address the probability that these lands included land that Ngāti Toa did *not* 'occupy'. Grey argued that he did not think that he could 'legally or with propriety' question Spain's rulings as this would create a bad impression among the natives. But as he went on, his prose became increasingly defensive and aggressive. For example, he complained that he was not actually required to take on such a 'difficult and ungracious task' as this purchasing but that he had felt it was his duty to do so.[59]

Grey then moved to a further objection that he claimed Wakefield had raised (though it is very doubtful the Company's principal agent had done this), writing: 'the position I understand to be adopted by the New Zealand Company's agent that if tracts of land are not in actual occupation and cultivation by natives that we have, therefore, a right to take possession of them appears to me to require one important limitation'. (Arguably, what Grey had done was to displace the source of the objection that Earl Grey had made by projecting it onto Wakefield.) Grey did not so much dispute the validity of the doctrine that he claimed Wakefield had asserted. Rather, in a deft manner, he suggested that there was a problem that had to be considered in *applying* it. The problem, as Grey described it, had two aspects. The first was a matter of definition and in turn an issue of right and wrong. Grey wrote: 'The natives do not

---

[58] Earl Grey to Grey, 27 November 1846, Sir George Grey Papers, Sir George Grey Special Collections, APL, GNZ MSS 35; Grey to Earl Grey, 9 April 1847, Grey Papers, GRE/B99/6A/1–4.

[59] Grey to Earl Grey, 7 April 1847, *BPP*, 1847, Paper no. 892, p. 16.

support themselves solely by cultivation, but from fern-root, from fishing, from eel ponds, from taking ducks, from hunting wild pigs, for which they require extensive runs, and by such like pursuits. To deprive them of their wild lands, and to limit them to lands for the purpose of cultivation, is to cut off from them some of their most important means of subsistence, and they cannot be readily and abruptly forced into becoming a solely agricultural people. Such an attempt would be unjust'. Grey was clearly asserting that there was a category of lands he called 'wild', as distinct from occupied lands and waste lands, and that the government was morally obliged to take this into consideration. He then moved to the second aspect, which raised a practical consideration. Any attempt to limit native ownership to the land that they were deemed by the government to 'occupy', he insisted, 'must, for the present, fail, because the natives would not submit to it' and their resistance would 'plunge the country into distress and war'.[60]

Warming to this theme, Grey launched into an elaborate justification of his purchasing. '[T]here seems to be no sufficient reason why such an attempt [to limit the natives' title to the land they occupied] should be made', he told Earl Grey, 'as the natives are now generally very willing to sell to the government their waste lands at a price, which, whilst it bears no proportion to the amount for which the government can resell the land, affords the natives (if paid under a judicious system) the means of rendering their position permanently far more comfortable than it was previously, when they had use of their waste lands, and thus renders them a useful and contented class of citizens, and one which will yearly become more attached to the government'. And he went on, insisting: 'I am satisfied, that to have taken the waste lands I have now purchased by any other means than those I have adopted, would once more have plunged the country into an expensive war, which, from its supposed injustice, would have aroused the sympathies of a large portion of the native population against the British government, and would thus probably have retarded for many years the settlement and civilisation of the country'.[61]

In short, Grey was arguing that a small payment to the natives for their so-called waste lands and thus an acknowledgment of their title to these lands was a way of acquiring a vast amount of land cheaply and avoiding a costly war. Grey seems to have chosen to construe Wakefield's remarks in the way he had in order to create an opportunity to challenge the

---

[60] Wakefield to Grey, 25 March 1847, *BPP*, 1847, Paper no. 892, p. 18; Grey to Earl Grey, 7 April 1847, *BPP*, 1847, Paper no. 892, p. 16.
[61] *Ibid.*, pp. 16–17.

practicality of applying the doctrine of occupation that Earl Grey had championed but without having to express his disagreement with his superior about a matter of principle, and in order to advance a rationale for the mode of proceeding that he had, somewhat but not altogether haphazardly, moved to adopt, that of large-scale purchasing of all native lands irrespective of whether they could be said to be 'occupied' or not.

The day after Grey sent Earl Grey this despatch it seems that he decided that he needed to write yet another one to him, which he marked *secret*, to provide yet more justification of his purchasing. In this despatch Grey argued that no progress had been made towards securing lands in the first fifteen months that he had been in the colony; asserted that during this period he had come to see a way of settling this most perplexing question, namely by purchasing land; and claimed that Stanley had authorised this measure. Yet all of these arguments were tendentious. Some progress had in fact been made in securing land in that period; there is no evidence that Grey had decided upon a policy of purchasing native land en masse after a long period of cogitation; and Stanley had merely authorised Grey to purchase land that was the subject of the New Zealand Company's claims. In this despatch Grey also enlarged on what the government stood to gain from his strategy: 'I cannot doubt from the value and extent of these districts that, even after the New Zealand Company have selected the land they require for their settlers, many thousand pounds will be realised by the government from the sale of the remaining portions of the waste lands and that the purchases may be regarded as a very advantageous one'. Finally, he told Earl Grey that he planned to repeat this way of proceeding in another district (Taranaki).[62]

A Crisis

News of Earl Grey's despatch to Grey of 23 December 1846 reached New Zealand in early June 1847, bearing a particular construction that a Sydney newspaper had put upon it in mid-May, namely that it actually comprised Earl Grey's instructions to Grey, and so portended much greater change in the treatment of native title than was suggested by the instructions themselves. This framing of Earl Grey's despatch influenced its reception and a good deal of what happened next, not least because several newspapers in the colony misrepresented the despatch in this way.[63]

[62] Grey to Earl Grey, 8 April 1847, TNA, CO 209/52.
[63] *Sydney Morning Herald*, 18 May 1847; *Wellington Independent*, 9 June 1847.

In the first instance newspapers like the *New Zealand Spectator and Cook's Strait Guardian* welcomed the despatch on the grounds that it set down the principles on which property in land was founded and thereby demonstrated that the natives only had a right of property in the lands they 'actually occupied and enjoyed'. They argued that these principles had long been recognised and acted upon by the British government in its intercourse with savage peoples, and claimed that there was little doubt that the Governor would revert to them as far as the circumstances of the colony made this practicable. As news of Earl Grey's despatch spread, however, it caused uneasiness in many quarters, even among those who grasped that its purpose was merely to explain the instructions that it accompanied. For example, in the eyes of Bishop Selwyn, the publication of the despatch in the colony amounted to a crisis. Indeed, an enormous controversy soon erupted as newspapers such as the *New-Zealander*, leading missionaries of the Wesleyan Missionary Society, Selwyn himself, and even Chief Justice Martin began to attack Earl Grey's principal argument in the despatch. (One might have expected the Church Missionary Society missionaries to have played a major role in this affair, but while they too were undoubtedly troubled by Earl Grey's despatch and urged their parent body in London to raise its voice, they played little part because they had lost credibility in the wake of Grey's attacks on them.)[64]

It might be argued that it is unremarkable that Earl Grey's despatch provoked a full-blooded attack in the colony. First, it was ill-conceived in many respects. Earl Grey had many fine qualities – he had considerable intellectual integrity, firm principles and extensive knowledge of colonial affairs – but he lacked sympathy for others and the insight that comes with sympathy. Moreover, he could be doctrinaire, dogmatic, arrogant and abrasive, which meant he was rather a poor politician. Many of these character flaws were apparent in this despatch. Indeed, contemporary critics remarked on this fact. For example, the editor of the *New-Zealander* observed: 'Is there not something hasty and rash in such confidence that

---

[64] *New Zealand Spectator and Cook's Strait Guardian*, 9, 12, 19 and 26 June 1847; *New-Zealander*, 16 June 1847; *Nelson Examiner and New Zealand Chronicle*, 26 June 1847; extract of a letter by Thomas Buddle to John Whiteley, quoted in Whiteley to MMS Secretaries, 28 June 1847, MMS Papers, Box 527, AJCP, Reel M140; *Nelson Examiner and New Zealand Chronicle*, 3 July 1847; *New-Zealander*, 7 July 1847; *Daily Southern Cross*, 10 July 1847; Selwyn to Gladstone, 11 July 1847, Gladstone Papers, BL, Additional MS 44299; John Morgan to CMS Secretaries, 4 August 1847, Jan Pilditch (ed.), *The Letters and Journals of Reverend John Morgan*, vol. 1, Grimsay Press in association with the University of Waikato, Glasgow, 2010, p. 226; Michael Belgrave, *Historical Frictions: Maori Claims and Reinvented Histories*, Auckland University Press, Auckland, 2005, p.150.

no latent injustice can have escaped his ken? Is there not something unpleasant, to say the least, about the cold-blooded manner in which he talks of force with reference to carrying out a measure of disputable honesty?'; and Hadfield damned what he called Earl Grey's 'painful theories and schemes on paper' and called the despatch extremely ill-judged. Second, the despatch was received in the colony in a particular context. Many of those who read or heard of it immediately recalled its author's 1844 Select Committee report. For example, the editor of the *New-Zealander* declared: '[These instructions] are not a mere crotchet of the moment, a hasty effervescence of doctrinaire ideas, but are to be traced back to the proceedings of the parliamentary committee on New Zealand in 184[4]. It would have needed little foresight, after having read the resolutions adopted by that Committee, to predict the abandonment of the Treaty of Waitangi as soon as the framer of them should find himself possessed of power to set it aside'. Furthermore, several important players knew that the despatch had already been embraced by the New Zealand Company's supporters in British newspapers as a directive that amounted to a 'sweeping away' of the Treaty. Finally, some Māori had long been apprehensive about the intentions of the British government and their missionary supporters were alive to this fact and the problems that a despatch of this kind could cause. Indeed, knowledge of the despatch spread rapidly among Māori. In the Waikato a rangatira told the missionary Alfred Brown that there was a report circulating among the natives that 'the Queen was going to take their island from them'. Brown, who was one of those who had assumed responsibility in 1840 for persuading chiefs to sign the Treaty after Hobson fell ill, had yet to learn of Grey's despatch and could only try to reassure this chief by claiming that the English nation would never violate the compact it had entered into with his fellow chiefs. At the same time, it was reported that the natives in the Bay of Islands were 'continually enquiring about the meaning of the Queen's instructions respecting waste lands'.[65]

[65] *Colonial Gazette*, 2 January 1847; *Spectator*, 2 January 1847; *New-Zealander*, 19 June 1847; Whiteley to MMS Missionaries, 28 June and 3 August 1847, MMS Papers, Box 527, AJCP, Reel M140; William Williams to Rev. Henry Venn, 12 July 1847, CMS Records, CN/O96(b), AJCP, Reel M234; Alfred Nesbit Brown, Journal, vol. 4, entry 5 August 1847, Auckland University Library, MSS and Archives A-179; *Daily Southern Cross*, 7 August 1847; E. S. Sotherby to J. B. Maxwell, 31 August 1847, *BPP*, 1847, Paper no. 899, New Zealand. Further Papers Relative to the Affairs of New Zealand. Correspondence with Governor Grey, p. 21; Octavius Hadfield to Grey, 10 September 1847, Grey New Zealand Letters, Sir George Grey Special Collections, APL, GLNZ H1.3; Robert Maunsell to Grey, 18 October 1847, *BPP*, 1848, Paper no. 1002, p. 9; Henry Williams to Grey, 1 December 1847, NANZ, IA 1/66; *Daily Southern Cross*, 20 November 1847; Thomas Chapman to the CMS Secretaries, 26 January 1848, CMS Records, CN/M18, AJCP, Reel M208; Hadfield to

It can be argued, however, that the protest that the likes of Selwyn mounted, and more especially the fact that it was prolonged, *does* require explanation. This is so for several reasons. First, many of those who read the despatch doubted that it was significant because they were not convinced that it instructed Grey to act on the basis of the principles set out in it, given that in some parts of it Earl Grey had observed that the application of those principles would be impracticable. Hadfield, for example, came to regard the despatch as 'mere waste paper'. Second, many major players assumed that these so-called instructions would never be carried out by Grey, either because they thought he would be unable to do so given the military strength of the natives, or because they believed he was too good a man or too wise a politician to try to do so. Third, several church or missionary figures discussed the despatch with Grey, and what they learned as a result suggested to them that he would not implement its 'instructions' because he had apparently formed the view that the despatch was less significant that it might first appear. According to three different parties, Grey variously stated that the so-called instructions were merely written by Earl Grey to satisfy the 'theoretical opinions to which he was pledged' and that he himself 'neither would nor could carry them into practice in New Zealand'; that Earl Grey had not in fact 'instructed him to carry [them] into execution'; that Earl Grey had 'guarantee[d] the Treaty of Waitangi as a matter of course', and that Earl Grey's views about the policy that ought to have been adopted when New Zealand was first colonised were not 'worth disputing about' since they had 'no reference to any event' that could possibly take place now or in the future; that 'there was no intention to set aside the Treaty'; and that he 'understood Earl Grey to refer exclusively to lands that ha[d] no claimants'. Fourth, reports circulated that Grey had no intention of putting the instructions into effect until he had a further directive from the Colonial Office. (Incidentally, all these parties would have been troubled to learn that Grey was of the view that the Treaty did not lay down any rule by which the government could determine what lands were the property of the natives, but this was not public knowledge.) Finally, there were parties that knew that Grey realised it was quite unnecessary to try to put Earl

Grey, 6 May 1848, Sir George Grey Papers, Sir George Grey Special Collections, APL, GLNZ H1.5; Selwyn to Grey, 1 August 1848, *BPP*, 1849, Paper no. 1120, pp. 36–37; Selwyn to Edward Coleridge, 7 October 1848, reproduced in H. W. Tucker, *Memoir of the Life and Episcopate of George Augustus Selwyn*, vol. 1, William Wells Gardner, London, 1879, pp. 274–75; William Martin to Grey, 20 October 1848, *BPP*, 1849, Paper no. 1120, p. 54; W. P. Morrell, *British Colonial Policy in the Age of Peel and Russell*, Clarendon Press, Oxford, 1930, pp. 201, 321; John M. Ward, *Earl Grey and the Australian Colonies 1846–1857: A Study of Self-Government and Self-Interest*, Melbourne University Press, 1958, pp. 3–4, 18, 20,22.

Grey's principles into action. In early July Grey told the Wesleyan missionary Thomas Buddle in the course of discussing Earl Grey's despatch: 'Why, the whole of [the natives'] waste lands might be quietly possessed by treaty [i.e. purchase] for a millionth part of what it would cost to take it by force'. Apparently, he even went so far as to claim: 'I could have large tracts of land given to me by several chiefs were I to ask it'. It is relatively easy, then, to envisage a situation in which no major protest was launched in response to Earl Grey's despatch.[66]

Yet a view soon formed among several players that a vigorous protest *was* required. The reasons for this are complex. Some involved considerable calculation, others were a product of a great deal of emotion, still others a consequence of history. First, some of the players were not reassured by what Grey had told them. What, they asked, would happen if the Governor refused to carry out Earl Grey's so-called instructions: could he be recalled and replaced by another governor who would implement them? Second, there was a belief that the expression of abstract principles about native title by a figure of authority as important as Earl Grey was an evil in itself and could have practical consequences in the future if they acquired legitimacy by tacit consent. Third, there was a conviction that unless voices were raised in protest, the moral power that the British government had acquired as a result of Māori regarding the British as true and good men would be sacrificed at a single stroke. Fourth, and most importantly perhaps, there was apprehension among some of these players that they would be parties to the wrong that would be done if they suffered Earl Grey's assertions to pass without remark. In this respect, the Anglican Church and the Church Missionary Society missionaries were anguished and aggrieved by what they construed as Earl Grey's violation of the Treaty, and they were enraged by the careless way in which he had expressed his principles. But above all else they were anxious that their own reputation, influence and work among Māori would suffer if the principles he had propounded were not repudiated and their own interpretation of the Treaty was not upheld. After all, they

---

[66] Hadfield, Letter to the Editor, 14 June 1847, *New Zealand Spectator and Cook's Strait Guardian*, 16 June 1847; Buddle to Whiteley, quoted in Whiteley to MMS, 28 June 1847; Whiteley to MMS, 28 June 1847; Earl Grey to Grey, 23 December 1846, date of receipt 30 June 1847, NANZ, G1/17; Buddle to MMS, 5 July 1847, MMS Papers, Box 527, AJCP, Reel M239; Grey to Hadfield, 24 July 1847, Octavius Hadfield: Letters from Sir George Grey, ATL, MS 89-008-09/03; Hadfield to Henry Williams, 14 August 1847, Williams Family Papers, AWMML, MS 91-75, Box 1, Folder 34, Item 205; Buddle to MMS, 2 September 1847, MMS Papers, Box 527, AJCP, Reel M140; Grey to Earl Grey, 23 August 1848, *BPP*, 1849, Paper no. 1120, p. 35; Selwyn to Edward Coleridge, 4 September 1848, reproduced in Tucker, *Memoir*, p. 273; Selwyn to Coleridge, 7 October 1848, reproduced in Tucker, *Memoir*, p. 275.

had played a major role in persuading rangatira to sign the Treaty, and in doing so they had informed them that it guaranteed them in the possession of their lands, and in the years since its signing they had repeatedly assured them that the British government would honour the Treaty. Finally, they believed that it was vital that they raise their voices in protest until such time as Grey or Earl Grey explained or repudiated the principles publicly.[67]

Protest

After the publication of Earl Grey's despatch, Hadfield was the first to take issue with it, albeit anonymously. A confidant of Grey's, he penned a letter to the *New Zealand Spectator and Cook's Strait Guardian* in which he mounted a scathing attack on the principles set forth in it. The following day, Hadfield met Grey and probably discussed the despatch with him, and later that day he sent him some remarks that he had penned in the light of their conversation, apparently in order to provide Grey with some guidance regarding the law governing sovereignty and rights in land.[68]

Very soon, Selwyn took up the cudgels. At the beginning of July, after he held several meetings with Grey and discussed the matter a great deal with his close friend Justice Martin, he decided to send a formal protest to Grey on behalf of himself and the Church Missionary Society missionaries who had been engaged by Hobson to interpret and explain the Treaty to the chiefs in 1840. In this letter Selwyn told Grey that he had decided to use all the legal and constitutional measures befitting his

[67] Whiteley to MMS, 28 June 1847; Selwyn to Henry Williams, 30 June 1847, Williams Family Papers, AWMML, MS 91-75, Box 2, Folder 68, Item 459; Buddle to WMS, 5 July 1847; Selwyn to Gladstone, 11 July 1847; Henry Williams to Selwyn, 12 July 1847; Williams Family Papers, AWMML, MS 91-75, A(i)b 55, vol. 100; Williams to Venn, 12 July 1847; Martin to Whiteley, 28 July 1847, reproduced in Whiteley to MMS, 3 August 1847; Memorial of Wesleyan Missionaries in New Zealand to MMS, 31 July 1847, MMS Papers, Box 527, AJCP, Reel M140; Hadfield to Henry Williams, 14 August 1847; Buddle to MMS, 2 September 1847; Hadfield to Grey, 10 September 1847; Maunsell to Grey, 18 October 1847, *BPP*, 1848, Paper no. 1002, pp. 9–10; Extract of John Hobbs to Martin, 22 October 1847, reproduced in William Martin, *England and the New Zealanders*, College Press, Auckland, 1847, pp. 73–74; Martin, *England and the New Zealanders*, p. 55; Henry Williams to Grey, 1 December 1847; Selwyn to Grey, 1 August 1848, *BPP*, 1849, Paper no. 1120, pp. 36–37; Selwyn to Coleridge, 4 September 1848, reproduced in Tucker, *Memoir*, p. 273; Selwyn to Coleridge, 7 October 1848, reproduced in Tucker, *Memoir*, p. 275.

[68] Hadfield to the Editor, 14 June 1847, *New Zealand Spectator and Cook's Strait Guardian*, 16 June 1847; Hadfield to Grey, 15 June 1847, Sir George Grey Papers, Sir George Grey Special Collections, APL, GLNZ H1.2; Grey to Hadfield, 24 July 1847; Christopher Lethbridge, *The Wounded Lion: Octavius Hadfield, 1814–1904*, Caxton Press, Christchurch, 1993, p. 130.

position to inform the natives of their rights and privileges as British subjects and assist them in asserting and maintaining them. At the same time, realising that no one had raised their voices in Britain to protest against Earl Grey's despatch, Selwyn sent a British lawyer, John Coleridge, a petition for presentation to the House of Commons in the event that it was required. In this petition Selwyn stated that he had felt it was his duty to deny publicly the accusations that had been brought against the British government of an intention to appropriate all the unoccupied lands of the natives without any payment. He also requested, in the event of the government setting aside the Treaty or carrying into execution any construction of it other than the one the Church Missionary Society missionaries had given in explaining it to the chiefs, that he be released from his position as an officer of the colonial government (by discontinuing the annual vote that paid his salary as the Bishop of New Zealand). Shortly afterwards, Selwyn sent Coleridge's brother a paper containing some of the arguments that he and Martin had drawn up in protest against the principles Earl Grey had articulated in his despatch.[69]

In the course of July the editors of both the *New-Zealander* and the *Daily Southern Cross* tried to put pressure on Grey to declare his position on the matter and called on Christian humanitarians in London to intervene. At the same time, the Wesleyan missionary John Whiteley persuaded twenty of his fellow missionaries to put their names to a memorial urging the Wesleyan Missionary Society in London to petition the British parliament to retract and repudiate the principles that Earl Grey had expressed. Martin had encouraged Whiteley to protest, suggested lines of argument he might use and given him permission to pass on his own views privately.[70]

Those protesting advanced a broad range of arguments in order to repudiate the principles that Earl Grey had articulated. First, they contended that a right to property in land should be founded not on any abstract principle or reasoning of the kind Earl Grey had used but on the basis of what amounted to historical possession instead. So, for example, Hadfield argued: 'The only tenable right is that of possession by prescription, modified in each particular community by the laws, whether written

---

[69] Selwyn to Grey, 1 July 1847, *BPP*, 1847, Paper no. 892, p. 82; Selwyn, undated petition, reproduced in Hugh Carleton, *The Life of Henry Williams*, vol. 2, Wilsons & Horton, Auckland, 1877, pp. 153–54; Selwyn to Gladstone, 11 July 1847; Earl Grey to Grey, 26 February 1848, Grey Papers, GRE/B99/C/19–24; Selwyn to Coleridge, 4 September 1848, reproduced in Tucker, *Memoir*, p. 272.

[70] *New-Zealander*, 3 and 10 July 1847; *Daily Southern Cross*, 10 and 17 July 1847; Martin to Whiteley, 28 July 1847, quoted in Whiteley to MMS, 3 August 1847; Memorial of Wesleyan Missionaries to MMS, 31 July 1847; Whiteley to MMS, 3 August 1847.

or unwritten, of that particular community'. Hence, he claimed, the British Crown, on obtaining the sovereignty of New Zealand, had no right to question the title of the actual possessors of property among the natives, since this was the law of the land up to that time and it was beyond the power of any later law to affect it.[71]

Second, they argued that Earl Grey's assertion that the natives had no title in so-called waste lands was at odds with the English common law, and that while the Crown had paramount or ultimate title to all lands it could only extinguish the natives' title with their consent. They claimed that the validity of these arguments had been established by both the judgments in the Symonds case. One critic argued: 'It is now quite clear, or appears from the late judgments delivered at Auckland, that in reference to Lord Grey's view of the aborigines' title to land the common law as well as the Treaty are opposed to it'. Indeed, one missionary held that '[t]he annunciation of these sentiments by the highest legal authorities in the colony just on the eve of the arrival of government instructions of so very opposite a character [could not] but [be regarded] as providential'. Particular passages in Chapman's judgment were cited word for word in support of this contention.[72]

It is worthwhile digressing briefly to discuss those passages. The Symonds case did not actually concern native rights in land, but rather the rights in land of the settlers and the Crown relative to one another. Yet Chapman in particular had discussed native title in the course of his judgment (though he was careful to avoid any examination of the nature of those rights in any detail), and he later stated privately that the principles Earl Grey had laid down in his despatch in relation to native title, which he read after he wrote his judgment, were precisely what he had asserted in his judgment.[73] More importantly, both the judges had argued that the appropriate way for the Crown to extinguish native title was by purchasing the land from the natives. 'The practice of extinguishing native titles by fair purchases is certainly more than two centuries old. It is now part of the law of the land', Chapman had written, making

[71] Hadfield, Letter to the Editor, 14 June 1847, *New Zealand Spectator and Cook's Strait Guardian*, 16 June 1847, reprinted *New-Zealander*, 14 July 1847.

[72] Whiteley to MMS Secretaries, 28 June 1847; *New-Zealander*, 10 July 1847; *Daily Southern Cross*, 10 July 1847; Hadfield, Letter to the Editor, 2 August 1847, *New Zealand Spectator and Cook's Strait Guardian*, 7 August 1847; Hadfield to Grey, 10 September 1847; Martin, *England and the New Zealanders*, pp. 25–27, 51–56; Selwyn to Grey, 1 August 1848, *BPP*, 1849, Paper no. 1120, p. 38.

[73] In notes he made for the book he contemplated, Chapman also argued that the only title to land that native peoples had was a 'mere right of occupancy' (Status of the Native Race Considered in Relation to Sovereignty, undated notes, Chapman, Legal Notes, ATL, MS-Papers-8670-047).

reference to the Marshall court's ruling in *Cherokee Nation v. State of Georgia*. 'Whatever may be the opinion of jurists as to the strength or weakness of the native title, whatsoever may have been the past vague notions of the natives of this country, whatever may be their present clearer and still growing conception of their own dominion over land, it cannot be too solemnly asserted that it is entitled to be respected; that it cannot be extinguished (at least in times of peace) otherwise than by the free consent of the native occupiers'. Martin implied the same in his judgment, as, for example, in passages like this one: 'It is everywhere assumed that where the native owners have fairly and freely parted with their lands, the same at once vest in the Crown, and become subject wholly to the disposing power of the Crown'.[74]

Third, the protestors contended that even if Earl Grey's assumption was correct in regard to legal arguments about the nature of rights of property in land, the Crown could not proceed on this basis because it had signed a treaty in which it guaranteed to the natives the possession of their lands and its representatives had affirmed that guarantee on numerous occasions since. This, as we have seen, was the argument that senior members of the Peel government had relied on in the parliamentary debate of June 1845 in calling for the Treaty to be upheld. Buddle, the Wesleyan missionary, expressed this argument thus: 'To argue the abstract question as to the truth and righteousness of the doctrine that Earl Grey has laid down in reference to the native lands is not at all necessary in this case. The question is one of contract and agreement'. This was to argue that Earl Grey's 'instructions' amounted to a fundamental breach of the Treaty of Waitangi. Various pieces of historical evidence were adduced to support this contention, as they had been by the Peel government. They included the part of Normanby's instructions in which he seemed to direct Hobson to purchase 'waste lands' from the chiefs.[75]

Fourth, the protestors explicitly argued that upholding the Treaty was a matter of national faith and honour. In the words of Henry Williams: 'To admit such an idea [as Earl Grey's] to go forth amongst the Aborigines ... it must be humiliating to every Briton so justly proud of

---

[74] *Symonds v. the Queen, New-Zealander*, 12 June 1847; Chapman to Chapman, 15 June 1847.

[75] Hadfield, Letter to the Editor, 14 June 1847, *New Zealand Spectator and Cook's Strait Guardian*, 16 June 1847; *New-Zealander*, 19 June and 14 July 1847; Selwyn to Henry Williams, 30 June 1847; *Daily Southern Cross*, 10 July 1847; Extract from a letter by Selwyn to Edward Coleridge, 24 May [*sic*] 1847, Gladstone Papers, BL, Additional MS 44137; Auckland Petition, undated [December 1847], *BPP*, 1848, Paper no. 1002, p. 79.

this nation and his sovereign to witness such dishonour put upon both'.[76]

Fifth, they argued that there were in fact no waste lands in the country. As numerous Auckland petitioners, headed by Martin and Selwyn, asserted: 'every acre of land in this country, whether occupied or not, is claimed by the aborigines; each tribe and family having its respective boundaries known, and (except in some cases of international dispute) acknowledged by all; and consequently ... there is, properly speaking, no waste land in this colony that can be appropriated to the Crown without purchase'. It was also argued that the claim that the British government had a right to seize possession of land on the grounds that they were waste could be applied with equal force to the lands many noblemen held in England and Ireland. The Church Missionary Society missionary Robert Maunsell remarked: 'England has her unoccupied territories, and no doubt Earl Grey has his unsubdued lands, ranged over by nothing else than deer or pheasant. So also has the New Zealander his bird preserves, his "runs" (the grand sources of supply to our colonial markets), his useful timbers, his valuable plants, [and] his fisheries'. Stanley had said much the same thing in the House of Lords in July 1845.[77]

Finally, the protestors argued that this matter was not merely a question of abstract rights, legal contract, moral principles or the honour of the nation, but one of whether the British government was willing to fight a war that would cost an enormous sum of money and hundreds or even thousands of British lives, and end in the extermination of the natives. It was argued that this course would be foolhardy and reckless. It was also asserted, often in tandem with this argument, that the land could be purchased very cheaply. For example, a Church Missionary Society missionary, Thomas Chapman, asked: 'Why ... should so much be risked when the government can be purchasers of land from the natives

---

[76] *New-Zealander*, 19 June 1847; Selwyn to Grey, 1 July 1847; Buddle to MMS Secretaries, 5 July 1847; *Daily Southern Cross*, 10 July 1847; Henry Williams to Selwyn, 12 July 1847; Martin to Whiteley, 28 July 1847, in Whiteley to MMS, 3 August 1847; Memorial of Wesleyan Missionaries, 31 July 1847; Morgan to CMS Secretaries, 4 August 1847, Pilditch (ed.), *Letters and Journals of Morgan*, p. 226; Buddle to MMS, 2 September 1847; Maunsell to Grey, 18 October 1847, *BPP*, 1848, Paper no. 1002, p. 9; *Daily Southern Cross*, 20 November 1847; Henry Williams to Grey, 1 December 1847.

[77] Hadfield, Letter to the Editor, 14 June 1847, *New Zealand Spectator and Cook's Strait Guardian*, 16 June 1847; Morgan to CMS Secretaries, 4 August 1847, Pilditch (ed.), *Letters and Journals of Morgan*, p. 226; Maunsell to Grey, 18 October 1847, *BPP*, 1848, Paper no. 1002, p. 10; Auckland Petition, undated [December 1847], *BPP*, 1848, Paper no. 1002, p. 79; Chapman to CMS Secretaries, 26 January 1848; Walter Lawry to MMS, 16 March 1848, reproduced in Louis Alexis Chamerovzow, *The New Zealand Question and the Rights of Aborigines*, T.C. Newby, London, 1848, pp. 417–18.

of any amount at a most trifling rate – for there are no competitors in the market – and thus avoid evils which we think will issue in active hostilities if the forcibly wresting from their "father lands" be persisted in!'; and Selwyn asserted: 'We can buy it for a farthing an acre; but millions of money and thousands of men will not enable us to take it'. In this regard they argued that since the so-called instructions had aroused suspicion and distrust among the natives, the government risked destroying the confidence and friendship that had hitherto characterised relations between the two races and so threatened to weaken the natives' attachment to the Queen and the government.[78]

In considering this protest it is crucial for us to grasp what was most at stake for those responsible for it. The most important reason they insisted that the British Crown had to respect the natives' rights of property in much of the colony's lands lay in what the secretary of the Wesleyan Missionary Society, John Beecham, would soon characterise as the principle governing 'the mode by which the Crown shall extinguish the title by which the natives h[e]ld their lands'. These players believed that it was crucial for the government, as the representative of the Crown, to *purchase* the land from the natives because by *doing* so the government would, simultaneously, recognise the rights of property that they held the natives had in the land, fulfil the promises to the natives that they believed the Crown had entered into with the chiefs in making the Treaty, uphold the honour of the British nation and acquire land peaceably. In other words, they, like Stephen in the Colonial Office, were above all else concerned that the means by which the British Crown acquired the natives' land and extinguished their title to it was one informed by the principle of native consent.[79]

Grey Responds

At the end of June Grey privately gave his consent to the protest that he knew Selwyn and Martin were getting up. Yet he chose to say nothing publicly on the subject of Earl Grey's despatch, though he must have known that doing so could have put to rest the concerns of the major

---

[78] Hadfield, Letter to the Editor, 14 June 1847, *New Zealand Spectator and Cook's Strait Guardian*, 16 June 1847; Hadfield to Grey, 15 June 1847; Buddle to MMS Secretaries, 5 July 1847; *Daily Southern Cross*, 10 and 17 July 1847; Morgan to CMS Secretaries, 4 August 1847, Pilditch (ed.), *Letters and Journals of Morgan*, p. 226; Maunsell to Grey, 18 October 1847, *BPP*, 1848, Paper no. 1002, p. 9; Auckland Petition, undated [December 1847], *BPP*, 1848, Paper no. 1002, pp. 79–80; Chapman to CMS Secretaries, 26 January 1848; Selwyn to Gladstone, 31 July 1848, Gladstone Papers, BL, Additional MS 44299.

[79] Rev. John Beecham to Earl Grey, 27 April 1848, *BPP*, 1848, no. 1002, p. 158.

parties. It seems that he was happy for Selwyn, the missionaries and other friends of the natives to raise a storm of protest, probably because he believed that this could help persuade Earl Grey that it would be very unwise for his 'instructions' to be implemented. Grey confined his official role to relaying Selwyn's petition to Earl Grey. It is also possible that Grey deliberately fuelled the flame that led to the protest by remarks that he made privately. Several years after these events took place, a story circulated that Grey had declared that Earl Grey's so-called instructions would cause bloodshed from one end of the country to the other and that if there was a vessel sailing immediately for England he would go home to remonstrate in person, that he complained to his intimates that these 'instructions' deprived him of any rest, and that he suffered a high-ranked official to remark in his presence that Earl Grey deserved to be impeached for them. No doubt this story was highly coloured. Yet Selwyn claimed at the time that Grey had confided in him that he would be unable to continue as governor if Earl Grey directed him to carry his principles into effect.[80]

Beginning in August, Grey finally sent home a series of despatches reporting the reception of Earl Grey's despatch in the colony. He sought to impress upon Earl Grey the fact that his position on the question of land was creating enormous apprehension among the natives. In the first of these despatches Grey went so far as to claim that he had received alarming reports from various parts of the North Island about the reception of the 'instructions' regarding both the new constitution and the registration of native lands that suggested that insurrection on a wide scale was on the cards. He also asserted that there could be no doubt that the country was in a very critical state. Two weeks later, Grey pulled back from this claim but nevertheless sought to impress upon Earl Grey that reports had circulated rapidly through the northern part of the North Island that the government intended to deprive the natives of all lands that were not under cultivation, and that they had excited apprehension even among the chiefs that had previously been friendly to the government and always fought on its side, which was code for saying that this was a situation fraught with danger for the colony. In late October Grey made an even greater claim in the course of forwarding to Earl Grey a strongly worded letter he had received from Robert Maunsell. Grey argued that an important part of this missionary's letter was the evidence he bore 'to the fact of the growth throughout the native

---

[80] Grey to Earl Grey, 7 July 1847, *BPP*, 1847, Paper no. 892, pp. 81–82; Selwyn to Coleridge, 4 September 1848, reproduced in Tucker, *Memoir*, pp. 272–73; *Wellington Independent*, 12 January 1853.

community of a very dangerous feeling of which he [thought] it necessary to give the government timely warning' and claimed that
Maunsell's report should be believed and that the testimony of others
confirmed the point it had made.[81]

In mid-November Grey framed another letter of protest that he forwarded to Earl Grey – this time a memorial to the Queen from several
Waikato rangatira headed by Pōtatau Te Wherowhero – in a way that
accentuated the problem that he argued the colonial government was
facing. After claiming that Te Wherowhero was probably the most influential chief in the country, Grey contended that the purpose of the
memorial was to solicit from the Crown 'a promise that the engagements
that they regard as having been formally entered into with them when they
signed the Treaty of Waitangi should be maintained inviolate', though in
fact the memorial made no reference to the Treaty whatsoever. Grey also
claimed that the chiefs had told him that 'the suspicions and jealousies of
their countrymen had been so aroused by the publication of the papers
which accompanied the new charter that some distinct declaration upon
the subject by the Queen was requisite to secure the attachment of their
countrymen to the government'. Grey drove this point home by claiming
that he had ascertained from other sources that what had excited the
chiefs' alarm was 'the fact that by the new charter and the accompanying
royal instructions the power is given to a representative legislature over
which they have no control and in which the extent and limits of the lands
of the aborigines are to be ascertained, and of assigning the limits of the
time within which all lands which have not been registered as the property
of the natives are to be forthwith regarded as the demesne lands of the
Crown'. Here, once again, Grey was clearly playing the role of
a ventriloquist in order to articulate the very objections he had to Earl
Grey's 'instructions' but which at this stage he did not want to express in
his own name. In sending all these despatches to Earl Grey, Grey would
have known that there was a very good chance that they would be made
public by virtue of being tabled in parliament (which is exactly what
happened).[82]

---

[81] Grey to Earl Grey, 20 August 1847 and enclosure of Sotheby to Maxwell,
11 August 1847, *BPP*, 1848, Paper no. 899, pp. 6–7; Grey to Earl Grey,
3 September 1847 and enclosure of Sotheby to Maxwell, 31 August 1847, *BPP*, 1848,
Paper no. 899, pp. 20–24; Grey to Earl Grey, 26 October 1847, *BPP*, 1848, Paper no.
1002, p. 8 (cf. Grey to Earl Grey, 6 November 1847, *BPP*, 1848, Paper no. 1002, p. 11).
[82] Te Wherowhero et al. to the Queen, 8 November 1847, *BPP*, 1848, Paper no. 1002,
p. 16; Grey to Earl Grey, 13 November 1847, *BPP*, 1848, Paper no. 1002, p. 15; Grey to
Earl Grey, 1 December 1847, *BPP*, 1848, Paper no. 1002, p. 120; James Rutherford, *Sir
George Grey, K.C.B., 1812–1898: A Study in Colonial Administration*, Cassell, London,
1961, p. 169.

In the closing months of 1847, the protest in New Zealand increased in scale and intensity. Some players who had previously accepted that Grey had to remain silent publicly in order to protect his position now became concerned that he might be protecting Earl Grey at the expense of protecting the Treaty. The patience of others who had hoped the governor would provide assurances, or had called upon him to do this, ran out. In November Justice Martin gave a booklet he had written in protest against Earl Grey's despatch and instructions to Selwyn to print (though this would not be completed until several months later and only a small number of copies would be distributed privately). In the same month, a petition to the Queen began to circulate in Auckland protesting against what it called Earl Grey's instructions and calling on the Queen to revoke them and provide an assurance to the chiefs that she would never permit the engagements that the Crown had entered into with them in the Treaty of Waitangi to be evaded or set aside. It was eventually signed by 410 people, among whom, Grey noted, were Martin, Selwyn and several other public officers. Leading merchants such as John Logan Campbell, and several churchmen and missionaries, were also among the signatories. The *Daily Southern Cross*, which had got wind of the protests that the missionaries were mounting, attacked Grey's dogged silence and drew attention to the petition. Finally, in early December, Henry Williams sent Grey a letter in which he attacked Earl Grey's 'instructions' and criticised Grey's silence on the subject, and shortly afterwards he sent this correspondence to a newspaper, which published it.[83]

Part III

Earl Grey Concedes Ground

In London Earl Grey was unwilling to bow to the growing chorus of complaint about his instructions or the accompanying despatch. In late November 1847 he responded angrily and haughtily to Selwyn's protest. He claimed that the Bishop had condemned the policy that he had directed Grey to pursue without taking sufficient care to ascertain what it was and insisted that Selwyn had failed altogether to grasp the purpose

---

[83] Selwyn to Coleridge, 7 October 1848, reproduced in Tucker, *Memoir*, p. 274; Martin to Grey, 20 October 1848, *BPP*, 1849, Paper no. 1120, p. 53; *Daily Southern Cross*, 13 November 1847, 20 November 1847, 4 December 1847; Petition to the Queen, undated [December 1847], NANZ, G30/14, and *BPP*, 1848, Paper no. 1002, pp. 79–80; Henry Williams to Grey, 1 December 1847; *New-Zealander*, 1 January 1848; Grey to Earl Grey, 9 March 1848, *BPP*, 1848, Paper no. 1002, p. 79; Claudia Orange, *The Treaty of Waitangi*, Allen & Unwin/Port Nicholson Press, Wellington, 1987, p.129.

of his instructions. Earl Grey maintained that his despatch, rather than calling on Grey to act upon the principle he had set forth, had stated the opposite. Yet he told Selwyn that he saw no reason to alter the opinions he had set forth and even claimed (erroneously) that the judges in the Symonds case had stated that the views he had expressed had been uniformly recognised and acted upon for 300 years.[84] Moreover, he asserted that he had endeavoured to guard against anyone supposing that he was saying that it was practicable to apply his principles to the present state of New Zealand and claimed that all he had advised Grey was this: 'that the theory of ownership by tribes of unoccupied land should not be made the foundation of any future transactions, and that what I conceive to be the rights of the Crown, that is of the public (where no engagements to the contrary have been made), should be carefully attended to in the disposal of land, wherever no property has yet been recognised'. Finally, Earl Grey argued in respect of his instructions that the 'greatest attention [had been] paid to the maintenance of everything which can be called an existing native title to land' and insisted that he could not 'imagine what portions of these instructions [could] be designated as a violation of the rights of the natives, as established by the Treaty of Waitangi, or any other agreement or authority'. As the historian John Manning Ward remarked many years ago, Earl Grey suffered from '[a] lack of political flair and a basic lack of imagination' and this 'put barriers between him and those – whether in parliament or the colonies – who had to understand or pronounce judgement on his ideas'.[85]

By this time, Selwyn's network of connections in Britain had begun to pay dividends. In the House of Commons in mid-November Gladstone had asked the government whether it was going to table Grey's answer to Earl Grey's despatch and in mid-December he pointed out that Selwyn believed that the despatch had asserted doctrines that were contrary to the Treaty of Waitangi. Most of the debate that ensued on the later occasion concerned the fact that Selwyn had protested rather than the matters he had raised, and Henry Labouchere (who represented Earl Grey since the Colonial Secretary sat in the House of Lords) merely repeated the principal claim that Earl Grey had made in responding to Selwyn. In early February 1848, however, Gladstone and his senior Peelite Tory colleagues took up the matter again.[86]

---

[84] On learning of this claim in July 1848, Martin promptly sent Earl Grey a copy of his booklet (Martin to Grey, 20 October 1848, *BPP*, 1849, Paper no. 1120, p. 53).

[85] Earl Grey to Grey, 30 November 1847, *BPP*, 1847, Paper no. 892, pp. 83–84; Ward, *Earl Grey*, p. 21.

[86] *BPD*, House of Commons, 13 December 1847, columns 1011–12 and 1028–29.

Gladstone was now well briefed with material that Selwyn and Martin had sent to Britain. The arguments he made mirrored those already advanced in New Zealand but he presented them more cogently, not least because he focused on Earl Grey's instructions rather than the accompanying despatch and pinpointed the part of them in which Earl Grey had in fact called upon Grey to implement the doctrine he had set out in his despatch. Moreover, in the arguments that Gladstone advanced, the Treaty assumed even greater primacy than it had in those made in the colony. At the heart of the speech he made on this occasion was a call upon the government to assure the House that Earl Grey's despatch and the instructions it accompanied were in conformity with the Treaty. Gladstone repeated the claim that at the time the Treaty had been made it had been universally understood that the lands in which the natives had title were not only those they had occupied and improved by labour but the lands they had used in other ways that were beneficial to themselves. By contrast, he argued, Earl Grey's instructions appeared to confine the titles of the native tribes to the lands they had improved by labour as they forbade the courts overseeing the registration of land from granting titles to the natives for any lands except those that had been improved by labour. He insisted that this limitation was not justified in the light of the way the Treaty had hitherto been interpreted. Gladstone argued that his interpretation of the instructions was confirmed by the part of Earl Grey's response to Selwyn's protest in which he had acknowledged that he had instructed Grey to ensure that in any future transactions the only lands for which the natives' title should be recognised were those they occupied and improved by labour. Gladstone argued that it was crucial that the British government acted towards the natives in good faith and that this meant that they had to adhere to the Treaty as it had been construed by all those in New Zealand that had occupied positions of authority and thus in turn the way it had been understood by the natives.[87]

As in the parliamentary debates of the previous year, the case Gladstone made did not rest only on what he called questions of justice. He also begged the House to grasp the fact that the natives were not a feeble people who could be readily overawed and overthrown by the power of the British Empire and bear in mind that Earl Grey's despatch had exposed British lives and properties to 'fearful hazard' since it could provoke the great mass of the natives to turn against the British government. Gladstone pressed this point home by quoting Grey's despatch of August the previous year in which he had claimed that the country was in

[87] *Ibid.*, 9 February 1848, columns 332–38.

a critical state due to the apprehension that the natives felt about British intentions after learning of Earl Grey's despatch. Gladstone went on to say that the natives' anxiety had been allayed by representatives of the Crown in the colony who had argued that the established interpretation of the Treaty would be respected and that the only lands that would be taken from them would be those they consented to sell. (It is unclear on what basis Gladstone made this assertion, but he was probably referring to the judgments in the Symonds case.) Finally, Gladstone twice drew attention to Grey's despatch of 7 April 1847, arguing that Grey's challenge to William Wakefield's 'claim' that the natives only had title to the lands they occupied and cultivated was understood by all to be in conformity with the established understanding of the Treaty. Gladstone called upon the government to provide assurance that *this* was the doctrine upon which it intended to act.[88]

On behalf of the government, Labouchere tried valiantly to counter Gladstone's arguments but was forced in the end to make the concession that the protesters had been seeking: 'there is no intention on the part of the Colonial Office to interfere with or take any course upon the question of waste lands in New Zealand, inconsistent with the rights guaranteed to the natives of that colony under the Treaty of Waitangi'. Cardwell, the senior Tory who had played a major role in parliamentary debates about New Zealand's affairs, seized upon this declaration and drove the point home: '[Labouchere had] said, whatever might have been the instructions of Earl Grey in 1846 – whether they were consistent with the interpretation which he put upon the Treaty of Waitangi or not – that was not the question – the Government highly approved the conduct of Captain Grey in reference to that treaty, that the Government were responsible for the peace of the island, and intended to act on the principles which had been laid down by Captain Grey'. Several days later, Peel made the same point in the House. In doing so, he could not resist the temptation of pointing out that the way in which the greatly censured Stanley had construed the Treaty now appeared to have been adopted by his critics.[89]

A week later, the Committee of the Wesleyan Missionary Society in Britain presented a lengthy memorial to Earl Grey. The Committee had undoubtedly been preparing this appeal for some time and they had probably made some changes to it very recently in order to capitalise on the arguments Gladstone had made in the House of Commons. They, too, framed the matter as one concerning the correct interpretation of the Treaty and argued that what mattered was how it had been understood in

---

[88] *Ibid.*, columns 338–42.
[89] *Ibid.*, columns 342–49, 357, and 14 February 1848, columns 612–14.

New Zealand by authorities such as the governor and the missionaries and consequently presented to Māori. They also contended that Earl Grey's response to Selwyn's protest revealed that there was a discrepancy between his instructions and this interpretation of the Treaty, and that such a violation of the Treaty could provoke a costly war that would desolate if not destroy the colony. The Committee concluded by calling on Earl Grey to direct the courts overseeing the registration of lands in New Zealand to interpret the crucial section of his instructions to mean that no part of any land belonging to the natives in accordance with their own laws and customs could be alienated without their free consent.[90]

Now on the back foot, Earl Grey realised that he had to answer this memorial carefully. He directed his deputy, Benjamin Hawes, and Herman Merivale, who was shortly to succeed Stephen as the Permanent Under-Secretary at the Colonial Office, to prepare a letter. In the first place, the Wesleyan Committee was to be given the strongest assurances that the government intended to recognise the Treaty in 'the established sense' and that he had never contemplated that any land to which the natives had a valid claim according to their own usages would be taken possession of without their free consent. In the letter that was sent (in Merivale's name), Earl Grey tried to save face by claiming that there was nothing in his instructions that was inconsistent with the Treaty or calculated to excite any reasonable alarm, and claimed that he would specifically direct Governor Grey as to their true meaning simply because he was anxious to avoid the possibility of any further misapprehension of the subject. This grudging concession made, Earl Grey immediately asserted that the Crown had the exclusive right to extinguish such title by purchase, that is, by exercising the right of pre-emption. The letter sent to the Wesleyans expressed this point in these terms: 'They [the government] recognise [the Treaty] in *both* its essential stipulations', namely the guarantee it provided to natives respecting possession of their lands, and the agreement by the natives to accept the Crown's right of pre-emption.[91]

It is difficult to avoid the conclusion that Earl Grey, having been forced to acknowledge the former provision in the Treaty, was now, more than ever, determined to assert the latter provision. As we noted earlier, in preparing his despatch of 23 December 1846, Earl Grey had assumed that vigorous use of the right of pre-emption by the government could neutralise the consequences of it recognising native title to much of the

---

[90] WMS to Earl Grey, 23 February 1848, *BPP*, 1848, Paper no. 1002, pp. 144–46, 151–52.

[91] Herman Merivale to Earl Grey, 7 March 1848, TNA, CO 209/66; Earl Grey, Memo, 17 March 1848, TNA, CO 209/64; Merivale to Beecham, 13 April 1848, *BPP*, 1848, Paper no. 1002, pp. 154–55, my emphasis.

land in New Zealand. But it seems that he had now become more enamoured of this strategy. In the next directive that he issued to his associates for the drafting of the letter to the Wesleyans, Earl Grey told them to set out a discussion that argued that if the government had strictly enforced its sole right of purchase, instead of making the mistake of allowing the settlers to buy land directly from the natives, the Crown would have had no difficulty in acquiring all the land it required. The point of this discussion was made clear in the letter that was finally sent to the Wesleyans. 'I need hardly remind you that while the Treaty of Waitangi recognised the right of the native chiefs to their land, it no less distinctly recognised the right of the Crown (which existed independently of that Treaty) to be the sole purchaser of the lands', Earl Grey asserted. 'But as there is abundant evidence that the natives did not wish to prevent but on the contrary to promote the settlement of Europeans among them, and were only too ready to part, inconsiderately, with their right to land which they did not actually occupy, the Crown, in the absence of all competition, would easily have been put in possession, by purchase, at little more than a nominal price of all the land that could be required for settlers'. The latter point, of course, was the very one that Grey, Selwyn, Martin and the Wesleyan missionaries had been making for some time.[92]

Finally, in the same combative mood, Earl Grey directed his associates to explain to the Wesleyans the rationale of the government's policy in regard to the land question. In the course of this discussion Earl Grey again sought to impress upon his audience the importance of the Crown's right of pre-emption. He argued that the question to be considered was 'whether the natives of New Zealand ought to be regarded as the absolute proprietors of the land they claim[ed], with the unrestricted power of alienating them at their pleasure, or whether, on the contrary, the Crown should be held to be the general owner of the soil as trustee for the public good and more particularly a guardian of the native races'. Earl Grey was conducting an argument with a straw man since those responsible for the protest accepted that the Crown was the general owner of the soil in the sense of being the source of all title and that it had the right of pre-emption. But it is revealing that Earl Grey considered it necessary to make this argument. This point enables us to grasp further why the Crown's right of pre-emption had become so important to the senior members of the Colonial Office: they seem to have feared that without this right the Crown would be deemed to have recognised the natives as

---

[92] Earl Grey, Memo, 17 March 1848; Merivale to Beecham, 13 April 1848, *BPP*, 1848, Paper no. 1002, pp. 154–55.

having an *absolute* right of property in the lands over which they claimed dominion.[93]

Consequently, Earl Grey and his associates found it necessary to go on to state in the letter to the Wesleyans: 'I am ... to observe that [the Crown's right of pre-emption] is the rule to which the general consent of all civilised nations, for the last three centuries, has given the authority of a recognised principle, *whether by recognising this right as originally existing in the Crown, or as obtained through the Crown's exclusive power of extinguishing the native title, either view leading practically to the same result*'. The passage I have italicised here was the result of a concern that had arisen among Earl Grey, Hawes and Merivale about an aspect of the judgment in the Symonds case. Merivale had informed Hawes that he had come to the conclusion that the judgment in this case and Earl Grey's instructions and his accompanying despatch were at cross purposes to one another in regard to native title. 'The doctrine of the judges – though perhaps not absolutely necessary for the determination of the case before them – appears to me to be this', Merivale wrote in a minute. 'That (independently of treaty) there is, or may be, a native title to *all* lands, waste as well as cultivated, but that the Crown alone can extinguish that title by purchase. The doctrine of the land instructions and despatch [by contrast] I take to be that (independently of treaty) there is no native title in waste land, that it all belongs to the Crown.' Merivale believed that there was a material difference between the two doctrines because he assumed that '[i]t follow[ed] from the first that the natives can fix the price of waste land [whereas] from the second that the Crown alone can fix the compensation to which they may be equitably entitled when such land is sold to settlers'. Merivale was mistaken in assuming that the former was a doctrine held by Chapman and Martin, but his error reveals much about the Colonial Office's concerns, and all the more so because he proceeded to argue: 'This matter has been so much sifted and investigated that it seems to me this difference cannot but be noticed and that to pass it over in a letter of this kind would be an omission prejudicial to its effect'. Hawes had a similar anxiety, though its source was different to Merivale's. After expressing concern that the Treaty had recognised what he called 'a large and partial exception to or interference' with the 'abstract rights of the Crown to wild or waste land', he insisted that the executive branch of government alone could give effect to the Treaty by defining native possession and the like. Hawes also believed that the judges in the Symonds case had erred because they appeared to have ruled that the natives might have a claim under the Treaty to all waste

[93] *Ibid.*, p. 155.

lands. In response to these remarks, Merivale inserted into the draft of the letter the passage italicised above, explaining to his superiors that its object was 'to guard against the misconception which might be raised by implying that the doctrine of the Supreme Court is precisely the same as Lord Grey's, which it is not'. Earl Grey agreed that these words were 'a very important correction of the draft'. Clearly, the Crown's right of pre-emption had acquired for Earl Grey and his colleagues a significance that exceeded its original purpose, becoming a crucial symbol of the Crown's authority and power in regard to land, just as it had for Grey.[94]

While this letter to the Wesleyans was being drafted, Earl Grey called upon his staff in the Colonial Office to draw up another despatch in which he directed Grey to inform Te Wherowhero and his fellow chiefs that the Queen had commanded him to assure them that there was not the slightest foundation to the rumours to which they had alluded. The government never intended to violate the Treaty by dispossessing the natives without their consent. On the contrary, the Queen had always directed that the Treaty should be 'most scrupulously and religiously observed'. Earl Grey had begun to speak not only in the voice of Grey but also the voice of Stanley, Peel, Stephen and all those who had been attacking the principles he had enunciated in his despatch.[95]

The concessions the government made in the parliamentary debate and Earl Grey's reply to the Wesleyans' memorial reassured most of the protesters. Consequently, much of the outcry over Earl Grey's despatch was stilled. A few months later, the assistant secretary of the Aborigines Protection Society, Louis Chamerovzow, completed a very long book that revealed that he was by no means reassured by Earl Grey's concessions, while in the colony itself a small number of people, which included the missionary Whiteley and the editor of the *Daily Southern Cross*, remained similarly troubled. But their voices carried little weight.[96]

---

[94] Merivale to Benjamin Hawes, 20 March 1848, Hawes to Merivale, 21 March 1848, draft of Merivale to Beecham, 13 April 1848, Merivale to Hawes, 10 April 1848, *BPP*, 1848, Paper no. 1002, p. 155; Grey, Minute, undated, [10 or 11 April 1848], TNA, CO 209/64; Merivale to Beecham, 13 April 1848, *BPP*, 1848, Paper no. 1002, pp. 155–56; Beecham to Earl Grey, 27 April 1848, *BPP*, 1848, no. 1002, p. 158.

[95] Earl Grey, Minute, 5 April 1848, TNA, CO 209/54; Grey to Earl Grey, 3 May 1848, *BPP*, 1848, Paper no. 1002, p. 144; Rutherford, *Grey*, p. 171.

[96] Chamerovzow, *New Zealand Question*, especially pp. 391–95, 399–401; *Daily Southern Cross*, 23 September 1848; Martin to Grey, 20 October 1848, *BPP*, 1849, Paper no. 1120, p. 56; Whiteley to MMS Secretaries, 24 April 1849, MMS Society Papers, Box 528, AJCP, Reel M141; Selwyn to Grey, 14 June 1849, *BPP*, 1850, Paper no. 1136, Further Papers Relative to the Affairs of New Zealand, p. 168.

The Making of Native Title

While this debate had been taking place, Grey continued to bide his time in the hope that the remonstrations that had been sent to London would compel Earl Grey to come to his senses and accept that there was a better way of realising the government's object of acquiring a great deal of land, thereby ensuring that he did not have to implement his instructions. During this period, Grey sent no more despatches to his superior about the course he had begun to follow. He also took steps to disassociate himself from those protesting against the despatch, in order to ensure that he maintained favour with the Colonial Office. In May 1848, however, he learned that questions had been asked in the House of Commons in December the previous year about how he had dealt with Earl Grey's instructions and the accompanying despatch. He realised that he now had to explain why he had refused to act in accordance with the principles Earl Grey had set down and pursued a very different course instead.[97]

In a carefully crafted despatch, Grey made sure that he did not explicitly divulge that he had adopted a strategy that ran counter to a good part of what Earl Grey had called upon him to do in regard to native title. He began by claiming, quite disingenuously, that he had thought it unnecessary to make any observations on Earl Grey's instructions and despatch because he believed that the points in those documents that had provoked criticism in the colony were not intended by Earl Grey to be applicable at present. He also claimed that he had felt it had been his duty to deny that the tenor of those instructions was of the kind that the protesters had maintained, and that he had told them that he had been instructed to scrupulously fulfil whatever engagements had been contracted with the natives (though there is little evidence to suggest that he had done either).[98]

Grey then set about providing an explanation of the course he had been taking. He started by remarking that he had understood Earl Grey's instructions as leaving to his discretion the task of deciding how far the principles they set down were applicable to the existing state of affairs in New Zealand, and went on to make an argument that he claimed was in keeping with what Earl Grey had stated. '[T]he question which would always arise would really be', he wrote, 'would it [be] better to endeavour at all hazards to enforce a strict principle of law [which it was impossible to

---

[97] *BPD*, House of Commons, 13 December 1847, column 1011; Sinclair to Henry Williams, 7 January 1848, *BPP*, 1849, Paper no. 1120, p. 9; Grey to Earl Grey, 9 March 1848, *BPP*, 1848, Paper no. 1002, p. 79; Grey to Earl Grey, 15 May 1848, *BPP*, 1849, no. 1120, p. 22.

[98] *Ibid.*, pp. 22–23.

induce the natives to consent to], or endeavour to find out some *nearly allied principle* which should be cheerfully assented to by both parties, and which would fully secure the interests and advantages of both'. Grey asserted that this 'nearly allied principle' could be said to have been found, though he did not actually spell out what this principle was, or at least he did not do so initially. Instead, he launched into the melodramatic story about FitzRoy's waiving of the Crown's right of pre-emption and his own heroic struggles against powerful opponents to maintain this right, which we noted earlier (p. 349, note 19). The reason for Grey telling this story was unclear at first, but it soon became apparent as he proceeded to describe the situation in New Zealand in these terms: 'the native popula-tion would, to the best of their ability, resist the enforcement of the broad principles which were maintained by Dr Arnold [that is, those Earl Grey had quoted in his despatch], but ... they [would] cheerfully recognise the Crown's right of pre-emption and ... they [would] in nearly all, if not all, instances dispose, for a merely nominal consideration, of those lands which they [did] not actually require for their own subsistence'. Grey then went on to claim: 'in many cases if Her Majesty requires land ... for the *bona fide* purposes of immediately placing settlers upon [it], the natives would cheerfully give such land up to the government without any payment, if the compliment is only paid them of requesting their acquiescence in the occupation of those lands by European settlers'. In other words, Grey argued that it did not matter that his superior's prin-ciple could not be applied because the government could obtain the land it needed by acquiring it cheaply (or even for nothing) with the natives' consent, thereby extinguishing the native title absolutely, and that he had made this possible because he had ensured that the Crown's right of pre-emption had been upheld. This is the arrangement that Grey had in mind in claiming that he had found a principle that was nearly allied to Earl Grey's, though he was clearly drawing a very long bow in making this claim.[99]

To further soften the blow that his purchasing had dealt to Earl Grey's principle in regard to native title, Grey informed his political master that he did not accept the claim that he reckoned many made, namely that there were no waste lands in the North Island that could be appropriated by the Crown except by purchase. Instead, he maintained that there were large tracts of land in which tribes had no strict legal right. He also claimed that once these lands were occupied by settlers the natives would relinquish their invalid claims in return for the government reser-ving small portions of land for their use.[100]

---

[99] *Ibid.*, p. 23, my emphasis.   [100] *Ibid.*, p. 24.

Finally, Grey proceeded to provide Earl Grey with an account of how he had given effect to the relevant part of his instructions proper. First, he again emphasised that he had maintained the Crown's right of pre-emption.[101] This implied that the very instrument that Earl Grey had urged him to use to neutralise the problem caused by the government previously conceding that the natives were the owners of most of the land *was* the very means that had enabled him to acquire large amounts of land. However, contrary to what Grey claimed and historians such as Peter Adams have argued since, the restoration of the Crown's right of pre-emption was only one of the reasons he had been able to acquire vast swathes of land from the natives. Indeed, there were several more important reasons, as Michael Belgrave and Mark Hickford have pointed out. Grey had the funds to purchase the land; the government was the only party wanting to buy land in the areas he purchased and so it had no competitors; Grey was able to execute purchases by exploiting competing native claims for the Crown's recognition of their rights in land; and in the case of one of his large purchases he had captured Te Rauparaha and placed him under house arrest in Auckland (without charging him) for almost a year, and applied military pressure on Ngāti Toa. There is also another crucial reason that has been overlooked by most historians: Grey was only in a position to acquire a great deal of land because the imperial and more especially the colonial government had succeeded in upholding the principle that the Crown was the only source of title. For example, Gipps' and Hobson's proclamations in January 1840 that all the purchases made prior to that date were null and void had more or less put a stop to such purchasing; and the establishment of the Land Claims Commission the following year had prompted most of those who had purchased large amounts of land in the mid- to late 1830s to abandon their claims.[102]

In his despatch, Grey also claimed that he had decided that it was expedient to make the registration of the lands of the natives 'a work of much time rather than to hurry it too rapidly', though he had in fact shelved this process altogether. He argued that any insistence that tribes register their lands within a certain period of time would have raised the question of the territorial limit of the various tribes, and this would have

---

[101] In fact, Grey was willing to tolerate settlers continuing to deal directly with Māori for land, at least as far as leasing land was concerned (John C. Weaver, 'Frontiers into Assets: The Social Construction of Property in New Zealand, 1840–65', *Journal of Imperial and Commonwealth History*, vol. 27, no. 3, 1999, pp. 23, 28), even though he knew that settlers could try to convert those leases into titles.

[102] Grey to Earl Grey, 15 May 1848, *BPP*, 1849, no. 1120, p. 24; Adams, *Fatal Necessity*, p. 209; Belgrave, 'Pre-emption', p. 31; Belgrave, *Historical Frictions*, p. 152; Hickford, *Lords*, pp. 198–200.

aroused their suspicions about the intentions of the government. Grey also claimed that many chiefs would have regarded compliance with this requirement as a virtual renunciation of their power and rights and thus refused to comply. He also emphasised, once again, that he had taken care to keep the purchasing of land so far in advance of the wants of the settlers that he was able to buy the lands required by the government for a trifling consideration. Finally, Grey went so far as to claim that in buying land from the natives ahead of settlement he had only recognised their title in the most nominal sense. Rather than reveal that he had paid the native vendors sums of money and thereby recognised their rights of ownership to extensive areas of land, Grey only made reference to the fact that he had promised to grant them reserves. He asserted that these reserves were for the purpose of cultivation and alleged that they had been registered as the only claims to *Crown* title that the government had admitted. This implied that what he had done in such cases was in keeping with Earl Grey's insistence that the natives could only be said to have rights of property in land that they cultivated.[103]

Not surprisingly, this clever despatch from New Zealand enabled Earl Grey as well as his deputy in London to reconcile themselves to the fact that Grey had decided it would be unwise to try to put into practice the principles that the Colonial Office had recently been articulating in regard to native title. So too did the fact that Earl Grey had cast his original despatch in such a way that he was now able to claim that he had never intended Grey to act in accordance with the principles he had laid down. Hawes, who first scribbled a minute on Grey's despatch, asserted that Grey's 'dissent from the abstract principles laid down in the Despatch of December [1846] in which the authority of Dr Arnold was appealed to, [was] more in appearance than reality'. He had merely done what Earl Grey had allowed for: 'The Governor says these principles are not applicable to N.Z. – that this application must be modified by sound policy, by a regard for native rights original or conventional, which is previously the view taken by Lord Grey in the despatch in question'. Earl Grey called on his staff to send a despatch to Grey in which he pronounced: 'I have read your despatch with great satisfaction as entirely confirming the views with which I have already fully stated to you in my despatch of 3 May [in which he had conveyed his response to the Wesleyans], which was written at nearly the same period [as] your despatch now before me'. A month later, Earl Grey wrote a further despatch in which he endorsed what Grey had done in respect of purchasing by declaring that it ought to be carried out as rapidly as possible. 'The longer it is delayed the heavier will be the cost

---

[103] Grey to Earl Grey, 15 May 1848, *BPP*, 1849, no. 1120, pp. 24–25.

to be incurred', he remarked, 'while it is the utmost importance with a view to the regular settlement of the territory that the control of all the waste land it contains should be placed as completely as possible in the hands of the government'. Earl Grey was clearly trying to save face by stating that the lands in question were waste, but it is evident that his claim that the natives had no rights of property in such lands had been set at nought. In the end, he was pragmatic enough to accept that his instructions had become a dead letter.[104]

By this time, the fact that Earl Grey's doctrine regarding native title had been well and truly put aside was made clear by a purchase that took place in the South Island. Often called Kemp's Purchase, it comprised a vast expanse in the South Island, more than 20 million acres or about a third of the total area of the country. The Māori with whom the sale was negotiated, Ngāi Tahu, clearly lacked the very requisites that Earl Grey had insisted natives needed to have in order for the British government to regard them as having rights of property in land. They were relatively few in number, especially in reference to the vast area of land of which they claimed ownership, and they lived mostly by hunting and gathering. Consequently, they were regarded as less civilised than natives in the North Island who were deemed to be agriculturalists. Indeed, as we have seen, many British players, including senior Colonial Office figures, had long maintained that the South Island could or should be treated as though it had no native owners.[105]

In this case Grey had directed Edward John Eyre, whom Earl Grey had appointed in 1846 as Lieutenant Governor for the South Island at the point he had turned New Zealand into two provinces, to see that the purchase was made. In assuming this responsibility, Eyre sought to adhere to both the letter and the spirit of Earl Grey's instructions and despatch of December 1846 and had instructed his Native Secretary, Henry Tacy Kemp, whom he deputed to undertake the task, accordingly.[106]

Kemp's personal background and experience almost certainly played a part in what happened next. He had been born on one of the Church Missionary Society's missions in the Bay of Islands and had probably adopted the missionaries' understanding that the natives' title in land was

---

[104] Hawes, Minute, 24 October 1848, TNA, CO 209/60; Grey, Minute, 26 October 1848, TNA, CO 209/60; Earl Grey to Grey, 20 November 1848, *BPP*, 1849, Paper no 1120, pp. 106–07; Earl Grey to Grey, 27 December 1848, TNA, CO 209/60.

[105] Gladstone to Grey, n.d. [March 1846], William Gladstone Papers, BL, Add MS 44363; Henry Tacy Kemp to William Gisborne, 20 June 1848, *BPP*, 1849, Paper no. 1120, p. 42; Belgrave, *Historical Frictions*, p. 151.

[106] Gisborne to Kemp, 21 June 1848 and 26 June 1848, NANZ, G7/1.

comprehensive in nature. Furthermore, his understanding of the nature of Māori claims to land probably deepened during a period he spent as a sub-protector for Aborigines working as a secretary and interpreter for the Land Claims Commission. At any rate, Kemp clearly regarded the Ngāi Tahu claims as being very extensive. Consequently, rather than confining his purchase to those areas that they occupied and cultivated, as he had been instructed to do by Eyre, he purchased all the area to which they laid claim – for the mere sum of £2,000.[107]

Eyre was dismayed when he received the deed of purchase as he realised that Kemp had deviated completely from his instructions by 'apparently recognis[ing] native rights over the whole of the land'. He reprimanded Kemp, telling him that it had never been contemplated by the British government that so very few natives 'should be considered the owners or occupiers of that immense district'. Eyre pointed out that at a meeting they had had before Kemp had set out he had been particularly careful to provide him with guidance so that Kemp would not make the mistake of 'acknowledging a validity of title in a few resident natives to vast tracts, the larger portion of which had probably never even been seen and certainly never been made use of by them, and that he repeatedly and distinctly enunciated ... that it was only the rights or titles of the natives to the extent these might be found to exist in the tracts of country referred to which were to be purchased'.[108]

Kemp claimed to be nonplussed by Eyre's reprimand. He assumed that the mere fact of entering into a negotiation with the natives for the purchase of a particular piece of land implied a recognition of their rights to the whole, not least because they believed that they were the only proprietors of that land. He suggested to Eyre that the purchase could not have been made without the government conceding this fact. Furthermore, he claimed that he could not understand why Eyre was complaining since the deed of purchase made it clear that the natives had surrendered all their lands and thus their rights of ownership. This meant, he argued, that 'their title [had been] in every point of view extinguished, and no further doubt left upon the subject'. It seems clear that Kemp, who had been present at Grey's purchasing from Ngāti Toa of the Wairau and

[107] Mark Houlahan, 'Kemp, Henry Tacy', in Roger Robinson and Nelson Wattie (eds.), *Oxford Companion to New Zealand Literature*, Oxford University Press, Melbourne, 1998, online version 2006, DOI: 10.1093/acref/9780195583489.001.0001; Belgrave, *Historical Frictions*, pp. 157, 162, 165; Marjan Lousberg, 'Edward Shortland and the Protection of Aborigines in New Zealand, 1840–1846', in Samuel Furphy and Amanda Nettelbeck (eds.), *Aboriginal Protection and its Intermediaries in Britain's Antipodean Colonies*, Routledge, London, 2020, p. 124.
[108] Gisborne to Kemp, 21 June 1848.

Porirua blocks the previous year, assumed that he was acting on the basis of a precedent that this purchase had established.[109]

For his part, Grey was very pleased with Kemp's purchase, as it confirmed the merit of the approach he had adopted in March 1847.[110] By accepting in effect that the natives had rights of property in land irrespective of how they used the land, the government had been able to purchase a vast amount of land and thereby extinguish the natives' title to it. Moreover, it had done so very cheaply. In a letter informing Earl Grey of the purchase, Grey emphasised that he had been trying to accomplish an almost complete resolution of native land claims in the South Island by acquiring a vast extent of territory for the purposes of colonisation. He seems to have felt confident enough to make it known that while he regretted the fact that Kemp had departed from the instructions that had been given to him, he did not in fact view the transaction unfavourably. Two years later, Grey would admonish Eyre's refusal to ensure that a New Zealand Company bill was honoured by the government so that Māori owners were paid an instalment for land involved in another purchase, insisting that the 'whole influence and future success' of the British in the colony 'mainly depend[ed] upon ... the most scrupulous observance of [their] engagements to the natives'.[111]

Bishop Selwyn, who had met Ngāi Tahu shortly after Kemp's purchase had been completed, could not resist commenting: 'This [purchase] is a curious commentary upon the opinions first expressed by the Committee of the House of Commons in 1845 [sic, 1844] and since avowed by Earl Grey, and will tend to put an end to all further discussion on the rights of the New Zealanders, when it is seen that lands which would have cost millions to take and keep by force, are quietly ceded for less than a farthing an acre'. In fact, Selwyn was delighted: '[I]t is a great point, after all that has been said, that the right of the native owners, even to the unoccupied lands, has thus been recognised over so wide a surface'.[112]

Selwyn turned out to be right. An end had been put to any further debate about the nature of the rights of property Māori had in land. In the

---

[109] Kemp to Gisborne, 22 June 1848, NANZ, G7/1; Gisborne to Kemp, 26 June 1848.

[110] Yet this purchase of native land proved to be one of the controversial ever made in New Zealand. For a discussion of this, see the Ngai Tahu Report, Wai 27, Treaty of Waitangi Tribunal, 1991.

[111] Grey to Edward John Eyre, 8 April 1848, *BPP*, 1849, Paper no. 1120, p. 41; Grey to Earl Grey 25 August 1848, *BPP*, 1849, Paper no. 1120, p. 41; Grey to Eyre, 13 June 1850, NANZ, G31/1.

[112] George Augustus Selwyn, *A Journal of the Bishop's Visitation Tour through his Diocese*, Society for the Propagation of the Gospel, London, 1851, pp. 122–23.

future, those responsible for purchasing land would proceed on the basis that it was best to treat with Māori as though their rights of property in land were unlimited.[113] Paradoxically, native title had finally been made in these comprehensive terms because Grey grasped, as FitzRoy had before him, that this could enable the government to realise its goal of acquiring a massive amount of land. Between 1846 and 1853, the government purchased 32.6 million acres, or about half of the country, for less than half a penny an acre.[114]

Conclusion

Despite Stanley, Hope and their senior colleagues' passionate defence of the Treaty of Waitangi in the parliamentary debates in the spring of 1845, the Treaty figured little in the instructions they simultaneously gave Grey as the new governor, save for a reference to the Crown's right of pre-emption, which they assumed was a prerequisite for the government being able to purchase land cheaply. Yet they were unsure whether the measures they recommended would realise the government's objective. In the end the most important steps they took were appointing Grey as the new governor, allowing him considerable latitude and providing him with money and troops.

Grey was similarly unsure about how he would acquire more land and what role the Crown's right of pre-emption would play in this task. However, he became convinced that a basic prerequisite was the assertion of the Crown's authority, and restoring the Crown's right of pre-emption came to assume enormous significance in his mind as the key to achieving this goal. As we have seen, many of the most important struggles that were fought in regard to land centred on the matter of the government's authority rather than the nature of the natives' rights in land. This period of Grey's governorship was no exception. Grey wasted little time in attacking the sources of power and authority that he assumed had been the cause of the government's problems in the past: the natives whom he deemed to be rebels, the institutions of the Land Claims Commission and the Protectorate, and figures like the leading missionaries and members of

---

[113] It should be noted that Grey did not always proceed by purchasing land. For example, while he purchased land in Porirua (as noted earlier), he dealt with an equivalent section of land in an adjoining block in Port Nicholson very differently. He accepted the belief of Eyre and McCleverty that over 120,000 acres in this block was waste land and so comprised the demesne lands belonging to the Crown. Consequently, he endorsed their recommendation that it be granted to the New Zealand Company without the government first purchasing it from the natives (Te Whanganui, pp. 237–38, 248, 251). Yet this did not create a precedent.

[114] Rutherford, *Grey*, p. 187.

the press. Grey went to enormous lengths to assert his authority and that of the Crown, using not only the law but force as well. In the legal case he manufactured as well as the legislative measures he introduced, the Crown's right of pre-emption became increasingly entangled with the notion that the Crown was the only source of title in the colony as Grey searched for ways of limiting the government's inadvertent recognition of sweeping native rights in land.

What happened in regard to sovereignty and title to land in New Zealand owed a good deal to who was in government in Britain or more especially who held the reins of power at the Colonial Office. The period discussed in this chapter was no exception. The appointment of Lord Howick, now Earl Grey, to the position of Colonial Secretary promised the triumph of the New Zealand Company's campaign to undo the consequences of the imperial and colonial government's recognition of native title over much of the lands of the colony. (Ironically, the Company had to surrender its charter in 1850 after collapsing under a pile of debt.) In chairing the 1844 Select Committee inquiry into the affairs of the colony and the New Zealand Company, Howick had taken the Company's side in its bitter dispute with the Colonial Office and convinced himself and others that the nature of the natives' rights in land was the key to all the problems the colony faced. Once in office, he instructed Grey that he was to accept native claims to land only in cases where this had been acknowledged by some act of the Crown or in instances where they actually 'occupied' the land in the sense that they used or enjoyed the land by mixing their labour with it, and he urged him to use the Crown's right of pre-emption to neutralise the concessions the government had already made in respect of native title. But what was to prove more important, as we have seen, was the fact that Earl Grey wrote a despatch to accompany these instructions in which he championed the doctrine that natives only had rights of property in land they could be said to 'occupy'. This move was a tribute not only to Earl Grey's intellectual commitment to this principle but also to a phantasy on his part that he could overcome all obstacles by sheer willpower.

The official version of Earl Grey's despatch took somewhat longer than usual to reach New Zealand. But, as we have seen repeatedly, what had been happening in the colony in the meantime worked to subvert the prescriptions of the Colonial Office in London. Grey had already begun to act in a way that departed from what Earl Grey dearly wished, by purchasing large swathes of land from the natives in such a way that confirmed their title to it, including their title to the 'waste lands'.

Grey's purchasing was not the result of any commitment on his part to a principle that diverged from Earl Grey's in regard to the nature of the natives' title in land. Indeed, Grey shared his political master's views on this matter. That Grey proceeded in the manner he did owes much to the fact that he had realised that he could persuade native chiefs to sell a large amount of land cheaply and that it was both unwise and unnecessary for him to try to put into practice the principles Earl Grey had espoused.

Earl Grey's notorious despatch threatened to throw a spanner in Grey's works, especially once it became public knowledge. It is unremarkable that the principles Earl Grey expressed caused uneasiness among many in the colony. Māori and missionaries had been especially perturbed by the articulation of the same principles in the report of the 1844 Select Committee. But the fact that this uneasiness led to a major protest was not inevitable. Grey could have intervened, stating publicly what he had been saying privately, for example that he did not interpret Earl Grey's despatch as amounting to instructions and that in any case Earl Grey had acknowledged in parts of the despatch that he accepted that Grey should not try to put those principles into practice; those who played a major role in the protest, namely Selwyn and Martin, would have backed him. Instead, Grey chose to remain silent. By the same token, the likes of Selwyn and Martin, knowing Grey's views, might have concluded that protest was unnecessary. However, as we have seen, key figures regarded the news of Earl Grey's 'instructions' as a crisis. In part, this can be attributed to the fact that they were affronted by what they saw as Earl Grey's carelessness in urging the Governor to pursue his principles even though this would mean that the government would break the promises they believed the British Crown had entered into with the natives in making the Treaty of Waitangi and that doing this could plunge the colony into war. But more than this, Selwyn and the missionaries felt that the despatch placed them in a horribly awkward position vis-à-vis their native flock because the missionaries had persuaded many chiefs to sign the Treaty and had repeatedly assured them that the British government would uphold it. In other words, their response was heavily influenced by the historical Treaty relationship that had been forged between themselves and Māori.

There can be no doubt, though, that the protesters also believed that important principles were at stake, as was revealed by the arguments they articulated. Strikingly, many of their arguments were not strictly legal in nature. Instead, they were wedded to the principle that the government should only extinguish native title by securing the natives' consent. They also advanced a number of arguments that were inherently historical in nature. They contended that the government could not proceed in the manner that Earl Grey seemed to have urged because it had signed a treaty in which it had guaranteed to the natives the possession of their lands and its officials had affirmed that guarantee on numerous occasions.

Consequently, the implementation of Earl Grey's so-called instructions would amount to a fundamental breach of the Treaty of Waitangi as a contract, though what they had in mind was a contract that was quintessentially moral in nature. In this regard, they held that upholding the Treaty was a matter of national honour for Britain. Finally, they argued on pragmatic grounds that it made no sense to try to put into practice Earl Grey's principles as this would result in a war that would cost Britain, the colony and Māori a great deal.

It is also evident that there was consensus between Grey, the judges in the Symonds case, Selwyn and the missionaries. They agreed that the government should only acquire land in native possession with the consent of the natives and that this could be done easily as well as cheaply. Grey must have known that this was the case. Yet he was content to see protest against Earl Grey's instructions grow to considerable proportions because he realised that it could assist him in the task of persuading Earl Grey to concede that it was unwise and unnecessary to insist on his principles being put into practice. Indeed, it is apparent that Grey acted in ways that encouraged the protest, and that he spun stories in which he exaggerated the impact that news of Earl Grey's despatch had on the natives and the state of the colony.

Those responsible for much of the protest, most importantly Selwyn, were well connected in Britain, and Peel and Gladstone had an investment in besting the Whig government because of the bitter political struggle that had taken place over the Tories' handling of New Zealand's affairs in the House of Commons a few years earlier. Gladstone and Peel were able to force Earl Grey to declare that he approved of Grey's conduct in regard to the Treaty and that he would act on the principles that Grey had apparently set down in regard to native title. Finally, the cleverly crafted despatch Grey composed in response to Earl Grey's despatch made it easier for the Colonial Secretary to accept that his principles regarding native title could not be implemented in the colony.

All these outcomes reveal the role that was played by political representation in both senses of that word. To put this another way, it is clearly a mistake to argue that what transpired was merely the result of a reality on the ground – the armed might of the natives – and a historical fact – the natives had been treated as the owners of the land from the outset of colonisation and it was too difficult for the government to overturn this practice. Instead, there is abundant evidence in this period that Grey and the missionaries *chose* to represent the natives as a considerable military force because this added force to the argument they were seeking to advance. Moreover, it was the political work undertaken by Grey, the protestors and the Tories that helped to persuade a Colonial Secretary, who clearly refused to acknowledge the reality that existed in the colony or the history that had taken place, that he had to accept this situation.

Finally, we have seen that for all the talk about the importance of defining the nature of native rights of property, ideas or legal principles counted for very little in the way that native title was finally treated by the British government. In the very site that the New Zealand Company's principal figures and nearly every senior government officer had long agreed that the natives were few and were said to have no rights of property in land, namely the South Island, the government purchased a large swathe of land from the natives. In doing so, it made native title.

Conclusion

As a result of Grey's purchasing, native title was finally defined and thus conclusively made, but as a consequence Māori began to be dispossessed of most of their land, just as the Aboriginal people of Australia had been or would be.[1] It might be argued, therefore, that in the end it mattered not a jot that the British government treated Māori as though they were sovereign and the owners of the land. Yet in the last forty or so years this historical fact has come to matter a great deal.

The increase in the number of legal claims made by Maori and Aboriginal people in regard to the loss of land and the responses of government to those claims – most importantly in the form of the creation of the Treaty of Waitangi Tribunal in New Zealand and the Native Title Tribunal in Australia – demonstrate that it is not merely a matter of historical interest that the British Crown treated sovereignty and rights of property in land very differently in its Australian and New Zealand colonies. Apart from anything else, the fact that a treaty was made in New Zealand that is said to have guaranteed Māori in the possession of their lands – and even their sovereignty – has meant that iwi (tribes) have been able to present numerous claims to the Waitangi Tribunal arguing that the British Crown breached the Treaty and to win compensation as a result. Thus far, eighty-eight cases have been settled by the New Zealand government on the basis of the Tribunal's recommendations, with financial redress in the order of $2.2 billion, while approximately fifty more claims remain outstanding. By contrast, the historical absence in Australia of a treaty that came to be interpreted in the way that the Treaty of Waitangi was has meant that many Aboriginal claimants have faced insurmountable hurdles in making legal claims, especially in south-eastern Australia, where Aboriginal people suffered the most thorough-going dispossession. Consequently, the Native Title Tribunal has awarded

[1] See Alan Ward, *A Show of Justice: Racial 'Amalgamation' in Nineteenth Century New Zealand*, Auckland University Press/Oxford University Press, Auckland, 1974, Part 2, and Richard Boast, *Buying the Land, Selling the Land: Governments and Maori Land in the North Island 1865–1921*, Victoria University Press, Wellington, 2008.

compensation in only three instances and most of the remaining applications submitted to it have been dismissed or discontinued. Likewise, the crisis in moral legitimacy that indigenous claims in regard to sovereignty and rights in land have provoked in both Australia and New Zealand is proving much more difficult to resolve in the Australian case, partly because of the absence of a recognised historical treaty and its accompanying arguments about the honour of the Crown.[2]

These contemporary claims have placed a premium on the production of histories that are highly normative in the sense that they assume or argue that particular intellectual concepts, legal doctrines and moral precepts determined, or should have determined, the manner in which the British Crown treated native sovereignty and property in land. These histories have been very influential,[3] not only in the legal realm but also the public sphere. But therein has lain a problem, because many of these works have tended to resemble myth rather than history.

The work that scholarly history performs is fundamentally different from that of myth, or at least it should be. The premise of this book has been that the duty of the academic historian is to construct as accurate and truthful an understanding of the past as possible and to explain rather than to exhort, and that these tasks can only be performed by trying to understand the past on something like its own terms, attending to specific texts and contexts, grappling as much as they can with the totality of the evidence available and maintaining the delicate tension between the demands of political commitment on the one hand and scholarly detachment on the other. While mythologisers also start out with an understanding of the past, their purpose is not to enlarge upon or deepen historical understanding. Instead, they draw upon the past in a highly subjective manner in order to serve the needs of the present. Consequently, as American historian Paul A. Cohen has observed, mythologisers provide a one-dimensional view of the past, 'wrenching from the past single characteristics or traits or patterns that are then portrayed as the essence of past reality'. Their accounts of the past, he points out, often have 'genuine links to a genuine historical past', and so in some sense can be regarded as true stories. Indeed, as we have seen, philosophical ideas and legal concepts about rights of property in land and Christian humanitarian ideals about the treatment of native people *did* figure in the consideration of native title and the Treaty of Waitangi, not least because political players at some point or other found it very useful

---

[2] Communication from Te Arawhiti/The Office for Māori-Crown Relations, 27 May 2019; Communication from the National Native Title Tribunal, 4 June 2019.

[3] The prime examples are Henry Reynolds' *The Law of the Land* and Claudia Orange's *The Treaty of Waitangi*, which have been widely read.

to deploy them for some purpose or other. But any suggestion that those ideas, concepts and sentiments played the particular kind of role that has been attributed to them by mythic accounts cannot be sustained. Consequently, like other myths, the kind of truth that these accounts convey is egregiously incomplete.[4]

Does it matter that these mythic accounts cannot be said to truly describe and properly explain what actually happened, some will ask, given that they have undoubtedly helped to address and redress the wrongs of the past? Quite clearly, this book has assumed that it does. Myths are especially vulnerable to critical probing. While selective treatment of historical evidence can establish a case, it can readily endanger the credibility of such an account. In order for a history to be able to do effective work in the long term, it needs to be true to the messy complexity of the past. Besides, by more adequately recovering the past as it was, scholarly histories can provide us with more interesting accounts of the past as well as different horizons of understanding, not only of the past but the present and future as well.[5]

In endeavouring to answer the questions I posed at the beginning of this book, I have argued that we must examine the different *colonies* that Britain founded in what became Australia and New Zealand and thus their imperial context. By doing so, we have been able to see important connections – for example, between New South Wales and New Zealand – and telling commonalties – for example, the approaches adopted by the South Australian Association and the New Zealand Company. Just as importantly, a comparative approach has enabled us to pinpoint some striking similarities, for instance, that Cook claimed possession in both New Holland and the islands of New Zealand on the same basis and that treaties were made in both places.

Most importantly, it has become apparent that the different ways in which the British government treated sovereignty and title in land in its Australasian colonies cannot be attributed to some foundational moment – Cook's claiming of possession in 1770 or the Treaty of Waitangi in 1840 – as historians have so often claimed. Rather, the differences in the way in which these matters were handled were the outcome of factors that were deeply historical in nature. Indeed, they were the product of highly particular pasts. In the first place, it mattered a great deal whether any colonisation took place before the British Crown

---

[4] Paul A. Cohen, *History in Three Keys: The Boxers as Event, Experience, and Myth*, Columbia University Press, New York, 1997, pp. 213–14.

[5] Richard White, 'Using the Past: History and Native American Studies', in Russell Thornton (ed.), *Studying Native Americans: Problems and Prospects*, University of Wisconsin Press, Madison, 1998, p. 236.

assumed sovereignty. In other words, the notion of path dependency has considerable explanatory power in this context. Where indigenous people were treated as though they were sovereign and the owners of the land prior to formal colonisation, it was much more likely that their sovereignty and rights of property in land would be taken into consideration by the colonisers. Yet that history did not decide once and for all how rights of property in land would be treated. What happened *after* the British Crown assumed sovereignty played an important role as well, and even then the way in which native title was conceived and considered did not take a simple, linear course, or at least it did not do so in the New Zealand case.

Second, it is clear that what happened on the ground in the islands of New Zealand and New Holland mattered a good deal. The practices that developed as a result of the ways that British players on the colonial peripheries first treated both sovereignty and property were critically important, but so too were politics in both the metropolitan centre and the colonial periphery, at the heart of which lay political claims and counter-claims, contestation and conflict, and a play for power. As we have seen, the story of what happened in New Zealand makes sense only if we pay attention to the struggle between the imperial and colonial government on the one hand and the New Zealand Company and its allies on the other. It was in that context that native title and the Treaty of Waitangi acquired their substance and their significance.

Third, it has become evident that the ways in which sovereignty and property were treated by the British government cannot be attributed to some grand design on its part. Normative forces – moral, legal and political – undoubtedly influenced consideration of these matters, but they seldom provided a script for Britain's agents of empire. Instead, these forces often tended to be a resource that was drawn on in a scattershot fashion by a wide range of political actors who were seeking to legitimise the claims they wished to make in regard to sovereignty and rights of property in land. Moreover, the claims those players made were subject to enormous change, as circumstances dictated. The legal doctrine that has been most emphasised by historians, whether it goes by the name of *terra nullius* or *occupation*, was but one of several that were deployed in the claim-making. Moreover, it was seldom the most important, and not only because it was rarely invoked on its own. Legal norms that were deeply historical in nature proved to be much more important.

Fourth, it has become clear that the way in which sovereignty and rights of property in land were treated was influenced by power or by the perceptions that the principal players had of the power of their protagonists. So, for example, the Colonial Office had to take the claims of the New Zealand Association and its successor the New Zealand Company more seriously than many of its heads might have wished because these bodies had powerful connections in the press and parliament. Moreover, in time, but only in time, the British grasped that they had to reckon with the might of Māori, though the way that key players regarded or represented that power waxed and waned according to circumstance.

Finally, the fact that a treaty was signed by the British Crown in New Zealand *did* play a role in the making of native title in that colony. Yet it is clear that the role that the Treaty of Waitangi played in this respect cannot be attributed to the agreement that was made at Waitangi in 1840. Rather, it is best explained by the treaty talk that unexpectedly began to be spoken in the context of claims and counter-claims about the Treaty's meaning, or more especially the meaning of the ambiguous first clause of its second article. It was this deeply contested talk that bestowed historical significance on the Treaty, ensuring that it would be regarded first as a treaty of rights and later as a solemn contract between the British Crown and Māori.

Appendix: The English Text of the Treaty of Waitangi

Preamble

Her Majesty Victoria Queen of the United Kingdom of Great Britain and Ireland regarding with Her Royal Favour the Native Chiefs and Tribes of New Zealand and anxious to Protect their just Rights and Property and to secure to them the enjoyment of Peace and good order has deemed it necessary, in consequence of the great number of Her Majesty's Subjects who have already settled in New Zealand and the rapid extension of Emigration both from Europe and Australia which is still in progress, to constitute and appoint a Functionary properly authorised to Treat with the aborigines of New Zealand for the recognition of Her Majesty's Sovereign authority over the whole or any part of those Islands. Her Majesty therefore being desirous to establish a settled form of Civil Government with a view to avert the evil consequences which must result from the absence of the necessary Laws and Institutions alike to the Native Population and to Her Subjects has been graciously pleased to empower and to authorise me William Hobson a Captain in Her Majesty's Royal Navy, Consul and Lieutenant-Governor of such Parts of New Zealand as may be, or hereafter shall be, ceded to Her Majesty to invite the Confederated & Independent Chiefs of New Zealand to concur in the following articles & Conditions.

First Article

The Chiefs of the Confederation of the United Tribes of New Zealand and the separate and Independent Chiefs who have not become members of the Confederation cede to Her Majesty the Queen of England, absolutely and without reservation, all the rights and powers of Sovereignty which the said Confederation or individual chiefs respectively exercise or

406

possess, or may be supposed to exercise or to possess over their respective territories, as the sole Sovereigns thereof.

Second Article

Her Majesty the Queen of England confirms and guarantees to the Chiefs and Tribes of New Zealand and to the respective families and individuals thereof the full exclusive and undisturbed possession of their Lands and Estates, Forests Fisheries and other properties, which they may collectively or individually possess so long as it is their wish and desire to retain the same in their possession. But the chiefs of the United Tribes and the individual chiefs yield to Her Majesty the exclusive right of preemption over such lands as the proprietors thereof may be disposed to alienate at such prices as may be agreed upon between the respective proprietors and persons appointed by Her Majesty to treat with them in that behalf.

Third Article

In consideration thereof Her Majesty the Queen of England extends to the Natives of New Zealand Her Royal protection and imparts to them all the rights and privileges of British Subjects.

Now therefore we the chiefs of the Confederation of the United Tribes of New Zealand being assembled in Congress at Victoria in Waitangi, and we the Separate and Independent Chiefs of New Zealand claiming authority over the Tribes and Territories which are specified after our respective names, having been made fully to understand the provisions of the foregoing treaty, accept and enter into the same in the full spirit & meaning thereof. In witness of which we have attached our Signatures or marks at the places and dates respectively specified.

Done at Waitangi this fifth day of February in the year of our Lord One thousand Eight hundred and forty.

Source: Ned Fletcher, 'A Praiseworthy Device for Amusing and Pacifying Savages? What the Framers Meant by the English Text of the Treaty of Waitangi', PhD thesis, University of Auckland, 2014, pp. 34–35

Bibliography

Primary Sources

Archives

Archives New Zealand/Te Rua Mahara o te Kāwanatanga

G1/17 Ordinary Inwards Despatches from the Secretary of State, 2 June 1846 – 23 December 1846

G7/1 Inwards Despatches from Lieutenant-Governor Eyre, 23 July 1847 – 22 July 1848

G19/1 Inwards Letters from Bishop Selwyn and Other Clergymen

G30/6 and G30/14 Duplicate Outwards Despatches to the Secretary of State, 7 September – 31 December 1848

G36/1 Miscellaneous Outwards Correspondence (a) Despatches from Hobson to Gipps, 24 December 1839 – 10 April 1841; (b) Private Correspondence Referring to Official Matters, 13 July 1840 – 2 April 1842; (c) Miscellaneous Letters, 7 February 1841 – 3 August 1841

IA9, Box 9/10 Drafts of the Treaty of Waitangi

OLC5/1/4c Miscellaneous Papers about the First Commissioners – Instructions to Commissioners

National Archives of the United Kingdom

CO 13 Colonial Office Correspondence South Australia

CO 201 Colonial Office Correspondence New South Wales

CO 208 Colonial Office Correspondence New Zealand

CO 209 New Zealand Company Records

CO 267 Sierra Leone Original Correspondence

CO 381 Colonial Office General Entry Books

CO 386 Land and Emigration Commission

CO 396 South Australia Entry Books

HO 7/1 Minutes of House of Commons Committee respecting transportation of convicts to the West Coast of Africa

HO 28 Admiralty Correspondence

HO 35 Home Office: Treasury and Customs Correspondence

HO 42/5 Domestic Correspondence, George III, Letters and Papers

State Archives and Records of New South Wales

NRS 909 Governor's and Colonial Secretary's Minutes and Memoranda, NRS 909, Item 4/1017

Despatches to the Lieutenant Governor of New Zealand, NRS 4530, Item 4/1651

State Records of South Australia

South Australian Literary Association, Minutes, GRG 44/83

Tasmanian Archives

CSO 1/321/7578 Colonial Secretary's Office, files relating to the Aboriginals

United Kingdom Hydrographic Office Archives

LP 1857, F 191

Manuscripts

Angas, George Fife, Papers, SLSA, PRG 174/1

Arthur, George, Papers, ML, MS A1962

Bourke Family Papers, ML, MSS 403/3

Brown, Alfred Nesbit, Journal, vol. 4, Auckland University Library, MSS and Archives A-179

Brown, John Diary, SLSA, PRG 1002/2

Busby, James, Letters and Papers, AWMML, MS 46, Box 2, Folder 6, Box 6, Folder 1

Petition to the Governor and the Legislative Council of New South Wales, 13 June 1840, www.parliament.nsw.gov.au/fcdocs/FCDocuments/1840/02 007b.pdf

Buxton, Sir Thomas Fowell, Papers, Weston Library, University of Oxford, MSS Brit. Emp. S. 444, Micr. Brit. Emp. 17

Chapman, Henry, Legal Notes, ATL, MS-Papers-8670–047

Letters, ATL, qMS-0419 and qMS-0420

Church Missionary Records, CH/L3, AJCP, Reel M238; CN/M11, AJCP, Reel 205; CN/M12, AJCP, Reel M205; CN/M14, AJCP, Reel M206; CN/M15, AJCP, Reel M207; CN/M18, AJCP, Reel M208; CN/O3, AJCP, Reel M212; CN/O4 c, AJCP, Reel M214; CN/O48, AJCP, Reel M224; CN/O96(b), AJCP, Reel M234; MC/18, AJCP, Reel M181

Church Missionary Society, London: Records Relating to the New Zealand Mission, HL, MS-0498

Colenso, William, Letters, vol. 1, ATL, qMS-0491

Memoranda of the Arrival of Lieutenant Governor Hobson in New Zealand 1840, ATL, MS 1611, Folder 1

Collected Papers of and Relating to Rev. Samuel Marsden, HL, MS-0055

Copies of Letters from Edward Gibbon Wakefield, BL, Add MS 35261

Copy of Correspondence of Rev. Samuel Marsden 1813 – 14, HL, MS-0054

Correspondence between George Clarke Snr and George Clarke Jnr, vol. 3 (1840 – 71), HL, MS-0062

Despatches from the British Resident, 1833 – 70, ATL, qMS-0344, qMS-0345, and qMS-0352

First Earl of Durham Papers, ATL, MS 0140

FitzRoy, Robert, Address to the Native Chiefs Assembled at Waimate on 2 September 1844, AWMML, MS-430

14th Earl of Derby Papers, Liverpool Record Office, 920 Der 14

George, Henry, 3rd Earl Grey, Papers, University of Durham Library Special Collections

Gladstone, William, Papers, BL, Add MS 44299

Grey, Sir George, Papers, Sir George Grey Special Collections, APL, GLNZ H1.2, GLNZ H1.5, and MSS 35

Hadfield, Octavius, Letters from Sir George Grey, ATL, MS 89–008-09/03

Hobson, William, Papers, ATL, MS-Papers-0046-1

Hopper, Edward Betts, Diary, 1799? – 1840, ATL, MS 1033

Huskisson, William, Papers, BL, Add MS 38763

Johnson, John, Journal, Sir George Grey Special Collections, APL, NZMS 27

King, Phillip Parker, Correspondence, ML, MS A3599, Papers, ML, MSS 3447/1

Letterbook of Governor Robert Fitzroy, 30 August 1845 – 11 November 1845, and of Governor George Grey, 17 November 1845 – 15 December 1853, Sir George Grey Special Collections, APL, NZ MSS 27

Letters from Other Members of the Wakefield Family, ATL, MS-Papers -9512–41

Marsden, Samuel, Papers, vol. 3, ATL, Micro-MS-0743

McLean, Donald, Papers, ATL, MS Papers 0032–0001

Methodist Missionary Society Records, Boxes 527 and 528, AJCP, Reels M139, 140 and 141

Meurant, Edward, Diary and Letters, Sir George Grey Special Collections, APL, NZ MSS 235

Miscellaneous New South Wales Archives Estrays Relating to New Zealand 1830 – 45, ML, DLNAR 3

Molesworth, William, Correspondence with Edward Gibbon Wakefield, ATL, MSY-608

Napier, Macvey, Papers, BL, MS 34620, Add MS 34625

New Zealand Association Minute and Letter Books, 9 May 1837 – 9 July 1838, ATL, Micro-MS-0459

New Zealand Estrays collected by Sir William Dixson, 27 March 1833 – 20 April 1848, ML, DLNAR 1

Papers of the Hope Family of Luffness, East Lothian, National Archives of Scotland, GD364

Peel Sir Robert, Papers, BL, Add MS 40451, 40468, 40555, 40557, 40559, 40560, 40562, 40565, 40566, 40569, 40571

Port Phillip Association Papers, SLV, MS safe

Shaw-Lefevre, Sir John George, Papers, SLSA, PRG 226

Stephen, Sir James, Papers, University of Cambridge Library, Add MS 7888

Wedge, John Helder, Letterbook, 1824 – 43, ML, MS A1430

Williams, William, Journals, vols 1 and 2, ATL, qMS-2248 and qMS-2249

Williams Family Papers, AWMML, MS 91–75, Box 1, Folder 4, Box 2, Folder 49 and Box 1, Folder 34, Item 205

Printed Official Papers

Britain

British Parliamentary Debates, House of Commons and House of Lords

1784–85, House of Commons Committee on Transportation Report

1834, Paper no. 617, Papers Relating to Aboriginal Tribes

1836, Paper no. 491, First Annual Report of the Colonisation Commissioners of South Australia

1836, Paper no. 512, Report from the Select Committee on the Disposal of Lands in the British Colonies

1836, Paper no. 538, Report from the Select Committee on Aborigines (British Settlements)

1837, Paper no. 425, Report from the Select Committee on Aborigines (British Settlements)

1837–38, Paper no. 97, Second Annual Report of the Colonisation Commissioners of South Australia

1837–38, Paper no. 443, New Zealand: A Bill for the Provisional Government of the British Settlements in the Islands of New Zealand

1837–38, Paper no. 680, Report of the Select Committee of the House of Lords Appointed to Inquire into the Present State of the Islands of New Zealand

1838, Paper no. 122, New Zealand: Copy of a Despatch from Governor Sir R. Bourke to Lord Glenelg

1839, Paper no. 526, Australian Aborigines: Copies of Extracts of Despatches

1840, Paper no. 238, Correspondence with the Secretary of State Relative to New Zealand

1840, Paper no. 560, Copies or Extracts of Despatches from the Governor of New South Wales

1840, Paper no. 582, Report from the Select Committee on New Zealand

1841, Paper no. 311, Copies or Extracts of Correspondence Relative to New Zealand

1842, Paper no. 569, Copies of Papers and Despatches Relative to New Zealand

1843, Paper no. 323, Copies or Extracts of Any Correspondence Relative to Emigration

1844, Paper no. 556, Report from the Select Committee on New Zealand, Together with Minutes of Evidence, Appendix, and Index

1844, Paper no. 641, Copy of a Letter from the Secretary of the Church Missionary Society to Lord Stanley Relative to the Affairs of New Zealand

1845, Paper no. 1, Papers Relative to the Affairs of New Zealand

1845, Paper no. 108, Copies of Letters from Mr Shortland and Mr Busby to Lord Stanley and Mr G. W. Hope

1845, Paper no. 130, Copies or Extracts from Any Recent Despatches from the Governor of New South Wales Respecting Outrages by the Natives in the Bay of Islands in New Zealand

1845, Paper no. 131, Papers Relative to the Affairs of New Zealand

1845, Paper no. 246, Return to Two Addresses of the Honourable The House of Commons, dated 18 and 20 March 1845

1845, Paper no. 247, Copies or Extracts of Despatches from the Governor of New Zealand

1845, Paper no. 357, Return to an Address of the Honourable the House of Commons, dated 30 May 1845

1845, Paper no. 369, Copies or Extracts of Despatches from the Governor of New Zealand

1845, Paper no. 378, Returns of All Claims to Land in New Zealand

1845, Paper no. 571–I, Copy of all Correspondence that Passed Between Her Majesty's Government and the New Zealand Company Between 19 June and 6 July 1845

1845, Paper no 517–II, Copies or Extracts of Correspondence Relative to an Attack on the British Establishment at the Bay of Islands of New Zealand

1846, Paper no. 203, Copies of Despatches from the Governor of New Zealand

1846, Paper no. 337, Copies or Extracts of Further Correspondence Between Lord Stanley and Governor FitzRoy and Lieutenant-Governor Grey, Relative to New Zealand

1846, Paper no. 712, Papers Relative to the Affairs of New Zealand: Correspondence with Lieutenant-Governor Grey

1847, Paper no. 837, Further Papers Relative to the Affairs of New Zealand: Correspondence with Governor Grey

1847, Paper no. 892, New Zealand. Papers Relative to the Affairs of New Zealand. Correspondence with Governor Grey

1847, Paper no. 899, New Zealand. Further Papers Relative to the Affairs of New Zealand. Correspondence with Governor Grey

1848, Paper no. 1002, New Zealand. Further Papers Relative to the Affairs of New Zealand: Correspondence with Governor Grey

1849, Paper no. 1120, New Zealand. Further Papers Relative to the Affairs of New Zealand: Correspondence with Governor Grey

1850, Paper no. 1136, Further Papers Relative to the Affairs of New Zealand

1850, Paper no. 1280, Further Papers Relative to the Affairs of New Zealand

Newspapers and Magazines

Anglo-Maori Warder
Auckland Chronicle and New Zealand Colonist
Auckland Times
Australasian Chronicle
Australian
Bay of Islands Observer
Colonial Gazette
Colonial Times
Colonist
Commercial Journal and Advertiser
Cornwall Chronicle

Courier (Hobart)
Daily Southern Cross
Devonport Independent
Fisher's Colonial Magazine
London Gazette
Maori Messenger: Te Karere Maori
Morning Chronicle
Morning Post
Nelson Examiner and New Zealand Chronicle
New South Wales Government Gazette
New Zealand Advertiser and Bay of Islands Gazette
New Zealand Colonist and Port Nicholson Advertiser
New Zealand Gazette
New Zealand Gazette and Wellington Spectator
New Zealand Herald and Auckland Gazette
New Zealand Journal
New Zealand Spectator and Cook's Strait Guardian
New Zealander
Public Advertiser
South Australian Gazette and Colonial Register
Spectator
Sydney Colonist
Sydney Gazette
Sydney Herald
Sydney Monitor
Tasmanian
The Times
Wellington Independent

Books and Pamphlets

Barton, R. J. (comp.), *Earliest New Zealand: The Journals and Correspondence of the Rev. John Butler*, Palamontain & Petherick, Masterton, 1927

Beaglehole, J. C. (ed.), *The Journals of Captain James Cook on His Voyages of Discovery, Volume 1: The Voyage of the Endeavour 1768–1771*, Cambridge University Press/Hakluyt Society, Cambridge, 1955

   The Endeavour Journal of Joseph Banks, 1768–1771, 2 vols, The Trustees of the Public Library of New South Wales in association with Angus and Robertson, Sydney, 1962

Beecham, John, *Colonisation: Being Remarks on Colonisation in General, with an Examination of the Proposals of the Association which has been Formed for Colonising New Zealand*, Hatchards, London, 1838

   Remarks upon the Latest Official Documents Relating to New Zealand, Hatchards, London, 1838

Bennett, J. M. (ed.), *Some Papers of Sir Francis Forbes*, Parliament of New South Wales, Sydney, 1998

Blackstone, Sir William, *Commentaries on the Laws of England*, 18th ed., Sherwood, Jones & Co, Dublin, 1823

Bright, John, *Hand-Book for Emigrants and Others, Being a History of New Zealand, its State and Prospects*, Henry Hooper, London, 1841

[Bunbury, Thomas], *Reminiscences of a Veteran*, vol. 3, Charles J. Skeet, London, 1861

Busby, James, *Authentic Information Relative to New South Wales and New Zealand*, Joseph Cross, London, 1832

   Remarks upon a Pamphlet Entitled 'The Taranaki Question', by Sir William Martin, Philip Kunst, Auckland, 1860

Carleton, Hugh, *The Life of Henry Williams, Archdeacon of Waimate*, vol. 1, Upton & Co, Auckland, 1874, vol. 2, Wilsons & Horton, Auckland, 1877

Carver, Jonathan, *The New Universal Traveller*, printed for G. Robinson, London, 1779

Chamerovzow, Louis Alexis, *The New Zealand Question and the Rights of Aborigines*, T. C. Newby, London, 1848

Clarke, George, *Notes on Early Life in New Zealand*, J. Walch & Sons, Hobart, 1903

[Coates, Dandeson], *Notes for the Information of Those Members of the Deputation to Lord Glenelg, Respecting the New Zealand Association, Who Have Not Attended the Meetings of the Committee on the Subject*, Richard Watts, London, 1837

Coates, Dandeson, *Documents Exhibiting the Views of the Committee of the Church Missionary Society on the New Zealand Question*, Richard Watts, London, 1839

   Memoranda and Information for the Use of the Deputation to Lord Stanley in Reference to the New Zealand Mission of the Church Missionary Society, Church Missionary Society, London, 1843

   The New Zealanders and Their Lands: The Report of the Select Committee of the House of Commons on New Zealand, Considered in a Letter to Lord Stanley, Hatchards, Seeleys, Nisbet and Co., London, 1844

   The Present State of the New Zealand Question, Considered in a Letter to J.P. Plumptre, Richard Watts, London, 1838

   The Principles, Objects and Plan of the New Zealand Association, Examined in a Letter to the Right Hon. Lord Glenelg, Hatchards, London, 1837

Coleman, John Noble, *A Memoir of the Rev. Richard Davis*, James Nisbet and Co., London, 1865

Colenso, William, *The Authentic and Genuine History of the Signing of the Treaty of Waitangi*, Government Printer, Wellington, 1890

Collins, David, *An Account of the English Colony in New South Wales*, 2 vols, T. Cadell, London, 1798

Colonisation Commissioners for South Australia, *New Colony in South Australia*, The Commission, London, 1835

Dickey, Brian and Peter Howell (eds.), *South Australia's Foundation: Select Documents*, Wakefield Press, Adelaide, 1986

Elder, John Rawson (ed.), *The Letters and Journals of Samuel Marsden 1765–1838*, Coulls Somerville Wilkie Ltd and A.H. Reed, Dunedin, 1932

FitzRoy, Robert, *Remarks on New Zealand in February 1846*, W. and H. White, London, 1846

Garnett, R., *Edward Gibbon Wakefield: The Colonization of South Australia and New Zealand*, T. Fisher Unwin, London, 1898

Gouger, Robert, *South Australia in 1837 in a Series of Letters*, Harvey and Darton, London, 1838

Hanson, R. Davies, *Extracts from a Letter to Governor Hobson*, s.n., London, 1842

Heale, Theophilus, *New Zealand and the New Zealand Company*, Sherwood, Gilbert and Piper, London, 1842

Historical Records of Australia, series 1, vols 1, 8, 16–19, and 21; series 3, vols 5–7; series 4, vol. 1

Historical Records of Victoria, vols 1 and 6

Hodder, Edwin, *George Fife Angas: Father and Founder of South Australia*, Hodder and Stoughton, London, 1891

Hunter, John, *An Historical Journal of the Transactions at Port Jackson and Norfolk Island*, printed for John Stockdale, London, 1793

Kent, James, *Commentaries on American Law*, vol. 3, O. Halstead, New York, 1828

Labillière, Francis Peter, *Early History of the Colony of Victoria*, vol. 2, Sampson Low, Marston, Searle, & Rivington, London, 1879

Lang, John Dunmore, *New Zealand in 1839, or Four Letters to the Right Hon. Earl Durham on the Colonization of That Island*, Smith, Elder and Co., London, 1839, 2nd ed., J. G. O'Connor, Sydney, 1873

McNab, Robert (ed.), *Historical Records of New Zealand, Volume 1*, Government Printer, Wellington, 1908

Mann, Charles, *Report of the Speeches Delivered at a Dinner Given to Captain John Hindmarsh*, W. Clowes and Son, London, 1835

Martin, Samuel, *New Zealand in a Series of Letters, Containing an Account of the Country Both Before and since Its Occupation by the British Government*, Simmons & Ward, London, 1845

Martin, William, *England and the New Zealanders*, College Press, Auckland, 1847

Mirror of Parliament, vol. III, London, 1834

Napier, Charles James, *Colonisation, Particularly in Southern Australia*, T. & W. Boone, London, 1835

New Zealand Association, *Statement of the Objects of the New Zealand Association*, Black and Armstrong, London, 1837

New Zealand Company, *A Corrected Report of the Debate in the House of Commons on the 17th, 18th, and 19th of June on the State of New Zealand and the Case of the New Zealand Company*, John Murray, London, 1845

    The Eighteenth Report of the Directors of the New Zealand Company, Stewart and Murray, London, 1845

    The Fourteenth Report of the Directors of the New Zealand Company, Stewart and Murray, London, 1844

    The Seventeenth Report of the Directors of the New Zealand Company, Stewart and Murray, London, 1845

    Supplement to the Eighteenth Report of the Directors of the New Zealand Company, Stewart and Murray, London, 1845

    The Twelfth Report of the Directors of the New Zealand Company, Palmer and Clayton, London, 1844

O'Malley, Vincent et al. (eds.), *The Treaty of Waitangi Companion: Maori and Pakeha from Tasman to Today*, Auckland University Press, Auckland, 2010

Parkinson, Sydney, *A Journal of a Voyage to the South Seas in His Majesty's Ship, the Endeavour*, Printed for Stanfield Parkinson, London, 1773

Pilditch, Jan (ed.), *The Letters and Journals of Reverend John Morgan*, vol. 1, Grimsay Press in association with the University of Waikato, Glasgow, 2010

Power, W. Tyrone, *Sketches in New Zealand with Pen and Pencil*, Longman, Brown, Green, and Longmans, London, 1849

Report of the Speeches Delivered at a Dinner Given to Captain John Hindmarsh ... to Which is Appended an Answer to an Article in the Forty-Fifth Number of the Westminster Review by C. Mann, W. Clowes and Son, London, 1835

Rogers, Lawrence M. (ed.), *The Early Journals of Henry Williams*, Pegasus Press, Christchurch, 1961

Rutherford, James (ed.), *The Founding of New Zealand: The Journals of Felton Mathew*, A. H. and A. W. Reed, Dunedin, 1940

Savage, John, *Some Account of New Zealand: Particularly the Bay of Islands and Surrounding Country*, J. Murray, London, 1807

Selwyn, George Augustus, *A Journal of the Bishop's Visitation Tour through His Diocese*, Society for the Propagation of the Gospel, London, 1851

Sinclair, Keith V. (translator), *Laplace in New Zealand, 1831*, Heritage Press, Waikanae, 1998

Taylor, Richard, *Te Ika a Maui, or New Zealand and Its Inhabitants*, Wertheim and MacIntosh, London, 1855

Torrens, Robert, *Statement of the Origin and Progress of the Colony of South Australia, and of the Claims of Colonel Torrens*, The author, London, 1849

Tucker, H. W., *Memoir of the Life and Episcopate of George Augustus Selwyn*, vol. 1, William Wells Gardner, London, 1879

Vattel, Emmerich de, *The Law of Nations or the Principles of the Law of Nature Applied to the Conduct and Affairs of Nations and Sovereigns: A New Edition by Joseph Chitty*, S. Sweet, London, 1834

Wakefield, Edward Gibbon, *Mr Dandeson Coates and the New Zealand Association*, Henry Hooper, London, 1837

[Wakefield, Edward Gibbon and John Ward], *The British Colonization of New Zealand*, John W. Parker, London, 1837

Wakefield, Edward Jerningham, *Adventure in New Zealand, from 1839 to 1844, with Some Account of the Beginning of the British Colonisation of the Islands*, 2 vols, John Murray, London, 1845

The Wentworth Indenture, Nag's Head Press, Christchurch, 1979

Wilkes, Charles, *Narrative of the United States Exploring Exhibition During the Years, 1838, 1839, 1840, 1841, 1842*, vol. 2, Wiley and Putnam, London, 1845

[Williams, William], *Plain Facts Relative to the Late War in the Northern Districts of New Zealand*, Philip Kunst, Auckland, 1847

Secondary Sources

Books

Adams, Peter, *Fatal Necessity: British Intervention in New Zealand 1830–1847*, Auckland University Press/Oxford University Press, Auckland, 1977

Armitage, David, *The Declaration of Independence: A Global History*, Harvard University Press, Cambridge, MA, 2007

Atkinson, Alan, *The Europeans in Australia*, vols. 1 and 2, Oxford University Press, Melbourne, 1997 and 2004

Attwood, Bain, *Possession: Batman's Treaty and the Matter of History*, Miegunyah Press, Melbourne, 2009

Ballantyne, Tony, *Entanglements of the Body: Missionaries, Maori, and the Question of the Body*, Duke University Press, Durham, NC, 2014

Ballara, Angela, *Iwi: The Dynamics of Maori Tribal Organisation from c. 1769 to c. 1845*, Victoria University Press, Wellington, 1998

    Taua: 'Musket Wars', 'Land Wars' or Tikanga? Warfare in Maori Society in the Early Nineteenth Century, Penguin Books, Auckland, 2003

Banner, Stuart, *How the Indians Lost their Land: Law and Power on the Frontier*, Belknap Press of Harvard University Press, Cambridge, MA, 2005

    Possessing the Pacific: Land, Settlers and Indigenous People from Australia to Alaska, Harvard University Press, Cambridge, MA, 2007

Barwick, Diane, *Rebellion at Coranderrk*, Aboriginal History, Canberra, 1998

Beaglehole, J. C., *The Life of Captain James Cook*, Adam & Charles Black, London, 1974

Belgrave, Michael, *Historical Frictions: Maori Claims and Reinvented Histories*, Auckland University Press, Auckland, 2005

Belich, James, *The New Zealand Wars and the Victorian Interpretation of Racial Conflict*, Auckland University Press, Auckland, 1986

    Replenishing the Earth: The Settler Revolution and the Rise of the Anglo-World, 1783–1939, Oxford University Press, New York, 2009

Benton, Lauren, *Law and Colonial Cultures: Legal Regimes in World History, 1400–1900*, Cambridge University Press, Cambridge, 2002

    A Search for Sovereignty: Law and Geography in European Empires, 1400–1900, Cambridge University Press, New York, 2009

Benton, Lauren and Lisa Ford, *Rage for Order: The British Empire and the Origins of International Law, 1800–1850*, Harvard University Press, Cambridge, MA, 2016

Berg, Shaun (ed.), *Coming to Terms: Aboriginal Title in South Australia*, Wakefield Press, Adelaide, 2010

Binney, Judith, *The Legacy of Guilt: A Life of Thomas Kendall*, Auckland University Press, Auckland, 1968

Boast, Richard, *Buying the Land, Selling the Land: Governments and Maori Land in the North Island 1865–1921*, Victoria University Press/Victoria University of Wellington Law Review, Wellington, 2008

Borch, Merete Falck, *Conciliation – Compulsion – Conversion: British Attitudes towards Indigenous Peoples, 1763–1814*, Rodopi, Amsterdam, 2004

Brazendale, Graham, *John Whiteley, Land, Sovereignty and the Land Wars of the Nineteenth Century*, Wesley Historical Society (New Zealand), Auckland, 1996

Buchan, Bruce, *Empire of Political Thought: Indigenous Australians and the Language of Colonial Government*, Pickering & Chatto, London, 2008

Burbank, Jane and Fred Cooper, *Empires in World History: Power and the Politics of Difference*, Princeton University Press, Princeton, NJ, 2010

Burns, Patricia, *Fatal Success: A History of the New Zealand Company*, Heinemann Reed, Auckland, 1989

Burroughs, Peter, *Britain and Australia 1831–1855: A Study in Imperial Relations and Crown Lands Administration*, Clarendon Press, Oxford, 1967

Butlin, N. G., *Forming a Colonial Economy, Australia 1810–1850*, Cambridge University Press, Melbourne, 1994

Calloway, Colin G., *Pen and Ink Witchcraft: Treaties and Treaty Making in American Indian History*, Oxford University Press, New York, 2013

Cameron-Ash, Margaret, *Lying for the Admiralty: Captain Cook's Endeavour Voyage*, Rosenberg, Sydney, 2018

Campbell, Judy, *Invisible Invaders: Smallpox and Other Diseases in Aboriginal Australia, 1780–1880*, Melbourne University Press, Melbourne, 2002

Castles, Alex C., *An Australian Legal History*, Law Book Company, Sydney, 1982

Castles, Alex C. and Michael C. Harris, *Lawmakers and Wayward Whigs: Government and Law in South Australia 1836–1986*, Wakefield Press, Adelaide, 1987

Cell, John W., *British Colonial Administration in the Mid-Nineteenth Century: The Policy-Making Process*, Yale University Press, New Haven, CT, 1970

Christopher, Emma, *A Merciless Place*, Allen & Unwin, Sydney, 2010

Cochrane, Peter, *Colonial Ambition: Foundations of Australian Democracy*, Melbourne University Press, Melbourne, 2006

Cohen, Deborah and Maura O'Connor (eds.), *Comparison and History: Europe in Cross-National Perspective*, Routledge, New York, 2004

Cohen, Paul A., *History in Three Keys: The Boxers as Event, Experience and Myth*, Columbia University Press, New York, 1997

Connor, John, *The Australian Frontier Wars 1788–1838*, University of New South Wales Press, Sydney, 2002

Curthoys, Ann and Jessie Mitchell, *Taking Liberty: Indigenous Rights and Settler Self-Government in Colonial Australia, 1830–1890*, Cambridge University Press, Cambridge, 2018

Dorsett, Shaunnagh, *Juridical Encounters: Māori and the Colonial Courts 1840–1852*, Auckland University Press, Auckland, 2017

Finnane, Mark and Heather Douglas, *Indigenous Crime and Settler Law: White Sovereignty after Empire*, Palgrave Macmillan, London, 2012

Fitzmaurice, Andrew, *Sovereignty, Property and Empire, 1500–2000*, Cambridge University Press, Cambridge, 2014

Ford, Lisa, *Settler Sovereignty: Jurisdiction and Indigenous People in North America and Australia, 1788–1836*, Harvard University Press, Cambridge, MA, 2010

Frost, Alan, *Botany Bay: The Real Story*, Black Inc, Melbourne, 2011

    Convicts and Empire: A Naval Question 1776–1811, Oxford University Press, Melbourne, 1980

Galbraith, John S., *Reluctant Empire: British Policy on the South African Frontier 1834–1854*, University of California Press, Berkeley, 1963

Gash, Norman, *Sir Robert Peel: The Life of Sir Robert Peel after 1830*, 2nd ed., Longman, London, 1986

Haakonssen, Knud, *Natural Law and Moral Philosophy: From Grotius to the Scottish Enlightenment*, Cambridge University Press, Cambridge, 1996

Harris, Aroha (foreword), *He Whakaputanga: The Declaration of Independence 1835*, Archives New Zealand/Te Rua Mahara o te Kawantanga, National Library of New Zealand/Te Puna Matauranga o Aotearoa, Bridget Williams Books, Wellington, 2017

Haury, David A., *The Origins of the Liberal Party and Liberal Imperialism: The Career of Charles Buller, 1806–1848*, Garland Publishing, New York, 1987

Hawkins, Angus, *The Forgotten Prime Minister: The 14th Earl of Derby*, 2 vols, Oxford University Press, Oxford, 2007 and 2008

Hickford, Mark, *Lords of the Land: Indigenous Property Rights and the Jurisprudence of Empire*, Oxford University Press, Oxford, 2011

Hunter, Ann, *A Different Kind of 'Subject': Colonial Law in Aboriginal-European Relations in Nineteenth Century Western Australia 1829–61*, Australian Scholarly Publishing, Melbourne, 2011

Irish, Paul, *Hidden from Plain View: The Aboriginal People of Coastal Sydney*, NewSouth, Sydney, 2017

Jennings, Francis, *The Invasion of America: Indians, Colonialism, and the Cant of Conquest*, University of North Carolina Press, Chapel Hill, NC, 1975

Johnson, Miranda, *The Land is Our History: Indigeneity, Law, and the Settler State*, Oxford University Press, New York, 2016

Johnston, W. Ross, *Sovereignty and Protection: A Study of British Jurisdictional Imperialism in the Late Nineteenth Century*, Duke University Press, Durham, NC, 1973

Jones, Alison and Kuni Kaa Jenkins, *Tuai: A Traveller in Two Worlds*, Bridget Williams Books, Wellington, 2017

Jones, Dorothy V., *License for Empire: Colonialism by Treaty in Early America*, University of Chicago Press, Chicago, 1982

Karskens, Grace, *The Colony: A History of Early Sydney*, Allen & Unwin, Sydney, 2009

Keller, Arthur S. et al., *Creation of Rights of Sovereignty through Symbolic Acts*, Columbia University Press, New York, 1938

Knaplund, Paul, *James Stephen and the British Colonial System*, University of Wisconsin Press, Madison, 1953

Lester, Alan and Fae Dussart, *Colonization and the Origins of Humanitarian Governance: Protecting Aborigines across the Nineteenth-Century British Empire*, Cambridge University Press, Cambridge, 2014

Lethbridge, Christopher, *The Wounded Lion: Octavius Hadfield, 1814–1904*, Caxton Press, Christchurch, 1993

Lewis, Mary Dewhurst, *Divided Rule: Sovereignty and Empire in French Tunisia, 1881–1938*, University of California Press, Berkeley, 2014

McHugh, P. G., *Aboriginal Societies and the Common Law: A History of Sovereignty, Status, and Self-Determination*, Oxford University Press, Oxford, 2004

Aboriginal Title: The Modern Jurisprudence of Tribal Land Rights, Oxford University Press, Oxford, 2011

The Maori Magna Carta: New Zealand Law and the Treaty of Waitangi, Oxford University Press, New York, 1991

McLintock, A. H., *Crown Colony Government in New Zealand*, Government Printer, Wellington, 1958

MacMillan, Ken, *Sovereignty and Possession in the English New World: The Legal Foundations of the English New World*, Cambridge University Press, Cambridge, 2006

Marais, J. S., *The Colonization of New Zealand* (1927), Dawsons, London, 1968

Megill, Allan, *Historical Knowledge, Historical Error: A Contemporary Guide to Practice*, University of Chicago Press, Chicago, 2007

Merrell, James H., *Into the American Woods: Negotiators on the Pennsylvania Frontier*, W.W. Norton & Company, New York, 1999

Monin, Paul, *Hauraki Contested 1769–1875*, Bridget Williams Books, Wellington, 2001

Moon, Paul, *FitzRoy: Governor in Crisis, 1843–1845*, David Ling, Auckland, 2000

The Origins of the Treaty of Waitangi, Birdwood Publishing, Auckland, 1994

Morrell, W. P., *British Colonial Policy in the Age of Peel and Russell*, Clarendon Press, Oxford, 1930

Nettelbeck, Amanda, *Indigenous Rights and Colonial Subjecthood: Protection and Reform in the Nineteenth-Century British Empire*, Cambridge University Press, Cambridge, 2019

Nugent, Maria, *Captain Cook Was Here*, Cambridge University Press, Melbourne, 2009

O'Malley, Vincent, *The Meeting Place: Maori and Pakeha Encounters, 1642–1840*, Auckland University Press, Auckland, 2012

Orange, Claudia, *The Treaty of Waitangi*, Allen & Unwin/Port Nicholson Press, Wellington, 1987

Pagden, Anthony, *Lords of All the World: Ideologies of Empire in Spain, Britain and France c. 1500 – c. 1800*, Yale University Press, New Haven, CT, 1995

Parkinson, P. G., *'Preserved in the Archives of the Colony': The English Drafts of the Treaty of Waitangi*, New Zealand Association of Comparative Law, Wellington, 2005

Parkinson, Philip and Penelope Griffith (eds.), *Books in Maori 1815–1900: An Annotated Bibliography*, Reed, Auckland, 2004

Parry, Jonathan, *The Politics of Patriotism: English Liberalism, National Identity and Europe, 1830–1886*, Cambridge University Press, Cambridge, 2006

Petrie, Hazel, *Chiefs of Industry: Maori Tribal Enterprise in Early Colonial New Zealand*, Auckland University Press, Auckland, 2006

Raeside, J. D., *Sovereign Chief: A Biography of Baron de Thierry*, The Caxton Press, Christchurch, 1977

Reynolds, Henry, *The Law of the Land*, Penguin, Melbourne, 1987, 2nd ed., Penguin, Melbourne, 1992

Why Weren't We Told? A Personal Search for the Truth about Our History, Viking, Melbourne, 1999

Robert, Hannah, *Paved with Good Intentions: Terra Nullius, Aboriginal Land Rights and Settler-Colonial Law*, Halstead Press, Canberra, 2016

Robertson, Lindsay G., *Conquest by Law: How the Discovery of America Dispossessed Indigenous Peoples of their Lands*, Oxford University Press, New York, 2005

Rutherford, James, *Hone Heke's Rebellion 1844–1846: An Episode in the Establishment of British Rule in New Zealand*, Auckland University College Bulletin no. 34, Auckland, 1947

    Sir George Grey, K.C.B., 1812–1898: A Study in Colonial Government, Cassell, London, 1961

    The Treaty of Waitangi and the Acquisition of British Sovereignty in New Zealand, 1840, Auckland University College Bulletin no. 36, History Series no. 3, Auckland, 1949

Salmond, Anne, *Between Worlds: Early Exchanges between Maori and Europeans 1773–1815*, University of Hawai'i Press, Honolulu, 1997

    Two Worlds: First Meeting Between Maori and Europeans 1642–1772, Viking, Auckland, 1991

    Tears of Rangi: Experiments Across Worlds, Auckland University Press, Auckland, 2017

Samson, Jane, *Imperial Benevolence: Making British Authority in the Pacific Islands*, University of Hawai'i Press, Honolulu, 1998

Scholefield, Guy H., *Captain William Hobson: First Governor of New Zealand*, Oxford University Press, Oxford, 1934

Sharp, Andrew, *The Voyages of Abel Janszoon Tasman*, Clarendon Press, Oxford, 1968

Sharp, Andrew, *Justice and the Maori: Maori Claims in New Zealand Political Argument in the 1980s*, Oxford University Press, Auckland, 1990

    The World, the Flesh and the Devil: The Life and Opinions of Samuel Marsden in England and the Antipodes, 1765–1838, Auckland University Press, Auckland, 2016

Shaw, A. G. L., *Sir George Arthur, Bart, 1784–1854*, Melbourne University Press, Melbourne, 1980

    A History of the Port Phillip District: Victoria Before Separation, Miegunyah Press, Melbourne, 1996

Standfield, Rachel, *Race and Identity in the Tasman World, 1769–1840*, Pickering & Chatto, London, 2012

Stone, R. C. J., *From Tamaki-Makau-Rau to Auckland*, Auckland University Press, Auckland, 2001

Sweetman, Edward, *The Unsigned New Zealand Treaty*, Arrow Printery, Melbourne, 1939

Tapp, E. J., *Early New Zealand: A Dependency of New South Wales, 1788–1841*, Melbourne University Press, Melbourne, 1958

Temple, Philip, *A Sort of Conscience: The Wakefields*, Auckland University Press, Auckland, 2002

Thomas, Nicholas, *Discoveries: The Voyages of Captain Cook*, Allen Lane, London, 2003

Tomlins, Christopher, *Freedom Bound: Law, Labor, and Civic Identity in Colonizing English America, 1580–1865*, Cambridge University Press, New York, 2010

Tremewan, Peter, *French Akaroa: An Attempt to Colonise Southern New Zealand*, University of Canterbury Press, Christchurch, 1990

Ward, Alan, *A Show of Justice: Racial 'Amalgamation' in Nineteenth Century New Zealand*, Auckland University Press/Oxford University Press, Auckland, 1973

    An Unsettled History: Treaty Claims in New Zealand Today, Bridget Williams Books, Wellington, 1999

Ward, John M., *British Policy in the South Pacific (1786–1893): A Study of British Policy in the South Pacific Islands Prior to the Establishment of Governments by the Great Powers*, Australasian Publishing Company, Sydney, 1948

    Earl Grey and the Australian Colonies 1846–1857: A Study of Self-Government and Self-Interest, Melbourne University Press, 1958

Wards, Ian, *The Shadow of the Land: A Study of British Policy and Racial Conflict in New Zealand 1832–1852*, Historical Publications Branch, Department of Internal Affairs, Wellington, 1968

Weaver, John C., *The Great Land Rush and the Making of the Modern World, 1650–1900*, McGill-Queen's University Press, Montreal and Kingston, 2003

Webber, Jeremy and Colin M. Macleod (eds.), *Between Consenting Peoples: Political Community and the Meaning of Consent*, UBC Press, Vancouver, 2010.

White, Richard, *The Middle Ground: Indians, Empires, and Republics in the Great Lakes Region, 1650–1815*, Cambridge University Press, New York, 1991.

Journal Articles

Adams, Jonathan, 'Governor FitzRoy's Debentures and Their Role in his Recall', *New Zealand Journal of History*, vol. 20, no. 1, 1986, pp. 44–63

Ashplant, T. G. and Adrian Wilson, 'Whig History and Present-Centred History', *The Historical Journal*, vol. 31, no. 1, 1988, pp. 1–16

    'Present-Centred History and the Problem of Historical Knowledge', *The Historical Journal*, vol. 31, no. 2, 1988, pp. 253–74

Atkinson, Alan, 'The Ethics of Conquest', *Aboriginal History*, vol. 6, pt 2, 1982, pp. 82–91

    'The First Plans for Governing New South Wales, 1786–87', *Australian Historical Studies*, vol. 24, no. 94, 1990, pp. 22–40

Attwood, Bain, '*The Law of the Land* or the Law of the Land? History, Law and Narrative in a Settler Society', *History Compass*, vol. 2, no. 1, 2004, pp. 1–30

Ballara, Angela, 'The Pursuit of Mana? A Re-Evaluation of the Process of Land Alienation by Maoris, 1840–1890', *Journal of the Polynesian Society*, vol. 91, no. 4, 1982, pp. 519–41

Beaglehole, J. C., 'Captain Hobson and the New Zealand Company: A Study in Colonial Administration', *Smith College Studies in History*, vol. 13, nos 1–3, 1927–1928, pp. 7–112

Belgrave, Michael, 'Pre-Emption, the Treaty of Waitangi and the Politics of Crown Purchase', *New Zealand Journal of History*, vol. 31, no. 1, 1997, pp. 23–37

Bennion, Tom, 'Treaty-Making in the Pacific in the Nineteenth Century and the Treaty of Waitangi', *Victoria University of Wellington Law Review*, vol. 35, no. 1, 2004, pp. 165–205

Benton, Lauren, 'Beyond Anachronism: Histories of International Law and Global Legal Politics', *Journal of the History of International Law*, vol. 21, no. 1, 2019, pp. 1–34

Benton, Lauren and Benjamin Straumann, 'Acquiring Empire by Law: From Roman Doctrine to Early Modern European Practice', *Law and History Review*, vol. 28, no. 1, 2010, pp. 1–38

Borch, Merete, 'Rethinking the Origins of *Terra Nullius*', *Australian Historical Studies*, vol. 32, no. 117, 2001, pp. 222–39

Brent, Richard, 'Butterfield's Tories: "High Politics" and the Writing of Modern British Political History', *The Historical Journal*, vol. 30, no. 4, 1987, pp. 943–54

Buchan, Bruce, 'Traffick of Empire: Trade, Treaty and *Terra Nullius* in Australia and North America, 1750–1800', *History Compass*, vol. 5, no. 2, 2007, pp. 386–405

Castles, Alex C., 'The Vandemonian Spirit and the Law', *Tasmanian Historical Research Association Papers and Proceedings*, vol. 83, nos 3–4, 1991, pp.105–18

Craig, David M., '"High Politics" and the "New Political History"', *The Historical Journal*, vol. 53, no. 2, 2010, pp. 453–75

Crawford, James, 'The Appropriation of Terra Nullius: A Review Symposium', *Oceania*, vol. 59, no. 3, 1989, pp. 226–29

Denoon, Donald, 'Re-Membering Australasia: A Repressed Memory', *Australian Historical Studies*, vol. 34, no. 122, 2003, pp. 290–304

Dorsett, Shaunnagh, 'Metropolitan Theorising: Legal Frameworks, Protectorates and Models for Māori Governance 1837–1838', *Law&History*, vol. 3, 2016, pp. 39–57

'"The Precedent is India": Crime, Legal Order and Governor Hobson's 1840 Proposal for the Modification of Criminal Laws as Applied to Māori', *Law&History*, vol. 1, 2014, pp. 29–55

Elbourne, Elizabeth, 'The Sin of the Settler: The 1835–36 Select Committee on Aborigines and Debates over Virtue and Conquest in the Early Nineteenth-Century British White Settler Empire', *Journal of Colonialism and Colonial History*, vol. 4, no. 3, 2003, muse.jhu.edu/journals/journal_of_colonialism_and_colonial_history/v004/4.3elbourne.html

Fitzmaurice, Andrew, 'Context in the History of International Law', *Journal of the History of International Law*, vol. 20, no. 1, 2019, pp. 5–30

'The Genealogy of *Terra Nullius*', *Australian Historical Studies*, vol. 38, no. 129, 2007, pp. 1–15

Frost, Alan, 'Claiming Pacific Lands: Late Eighteenth-Century and Nineteenth-Century Approaches', *Journal of Commonwealth and Postcolonial Studies*, vol. 17, no. 1, 2011, pp. 178–89

'New South Wales as *Terra Nullius*: The British Denial of Aboriginal Land Rights', *Historical Studies*, vol. 19, no. 77, 1981, pp. 513–23

Gallagher, John and Roland Robinson, 'The Imperialism of Free Trade', *Economic History Review*, n.s., vol. 6, no. 1, 1953, pp. 1–15

Gammage, Bill, 'Early Boundaries of New South Wales', *Historical Studies*, vol. 19, no. 77, 1981, pp. 524–31

Gibbons, Peter, 'Cultural Colonisation and National Identity', *New Zealand Journal of History*, vol. 36, no. 1, 2002, pp. 5–17

Grew, Raymond, 'The Case for Comparing Histories', *American Historical Review*, vol. 85, no. 4, 1980, pp. 763–78

Hickford, Mark, '"Decidedly the Most Interesting Savages on the Globe": An Approach to the Intellectual History of Maori Property Rights, 1837–53', *History of Political Thought*, vol. 27, no. 1, 2006, pp. 122–67

'"Vague Native Rights to Land": British Imperial Policy on Native Title and Custom in New Zealand, 1837–53', *Journal of Imperial and Commonwealth History*, vol. 38, no. 2, 2010, pp. 175–206

Hopkins, A. G., 'Back to the Future: From National History to Imperial History', *Past and Present*, no. 164, 1999, pp. 198–243

Hunter, Ian, 'Natural Law, Historiography, and Aboriginal Sovereignty', *Legal History*, vol. 11, no. 2, 2007, pp. 137–67

Kades, Eric, 'The Dark Side of Efficiency: Johnson v M'Intosh and the Expropriation of American Indian Lands', *University of Pennsylvania Law Review*, vol. 148, no. 4, 2000, pp. 1065–190

Kercher, Bruce, 'Informal Land Titles: *Snowden v Baker* (1844)', *Victoria University of Wellington Law Review*, vol. 41, no. 3, 2010, pp. 605–21

Levine, Philippa, 'Is Comparative History Possible', *History and Theory*, vol. 53, no. 3, 2014, pp. 331–47

Low, Peter, 'Pompallier and the Treaty', *New Zealand Journal of History*, vol. 24, no. 2, 1990, pp. 190–99

McHugh, P. G., 'The Common-Law Status of Colonies and Aboriginal "Rights": How Lawyers and Historians Treat the Past', *Saskatchewan Law Review*, vol. 61, no. 2, 1998, pp. 393–429

Martin, Ged, 'James Busby and the Treaty of Waitangi', *British Review of New Zealand Studies*, vol. 5, 1992, pp. 5–22

Mein Smith, Philippa and Peter Hempenstall, 'Australia and New Zealand: Turning Shared Pasts into a Shared History', *History Compass*, vol. 1, no. 1, 2003, AU 031, pp. 1–10

Moloney, Pat, 'Savagery and Civilization: Early Victorian Notions', *New Zealand Journal of History*, vol. 35, no. 2, 2001, pp. 153–76

Montgomerie, Deborah, 'Beyond the Search for Good Imperialism: The Challenge of Comparative Ethnohistory', *New Zealand Journal of History*, vol. 31, no. 1, 1997, pp. 153–68

Muldoon, James, 'Colonial Charters: Possessory or Regulatory', *Law and History Review*, vol. 36, no. 2, 2018, pp. 355–81

Owens, J. M. R., 'Historians and the Treaty of Waitangi', *Archifacts*, no. 1, 1990, pp. 4–21

'Missionaries and the Treaty of Waitangi', *Wesleyan Historical Society (New Zealand) Journal*, no. 49, 1986, pp. 1–25

Pennell, C. R., 'The Origins of the Foreign Jurisdiction Act and the Extension of British Sovereignty', *Historical Research*, vol. 83, no. 221, 2010, pp. 465–85

Petrow, Stefan, 'A Case of Mistaken Identity: The Vandemonian Spirit and the Law', *Tasmanian Historical Studies*, vol. 6, no. 1, 1998, pp. 22–32

Philips, David, 'Evangelicals, Aborigines and "Land Rights": A Critique of Henry Reynolds on the *Select Committee on Aborigines*', *Australian Studies*, vol. 17, no. 1, 2002, pp. 147–66

Pitts, Jennifer, 'Empire and Legal Universalisms in the Eighteenth Century', *American Historical Review*, vol. 117, no. 1, 2012, pp. 92–121

Ross, Ruth, 'Te Tiriti o Waitangi: Texts and Translations', *New Zealand Journal of History*, vol. 6, no. 2, 1972, pp. 129–57

Scott, Ernest, 'Taking Possession of Australia: The Doctrine of "Terra Nullius" (No-Man's Land)', *Journal of the Royal Australian Historical Society*, vol. 26, pt 1, 1940, pp. 1–19

Shaw, A. G. L., 'British Policy Towards the Australian Aborigines, 1830–1850', *Australian Historical Studies*, vol. 25, no. 99, 1992, pp. 265–85

'James Stephen and Colonial Policy: The Australian Experience', *Journal of Imperial and Commonwealth History*, vol. 20, no. 1, 1992, pp. 11–34

Sheehan, James J., 'The Problem of Sovereignty in European History', *American Historical Review*, vol. 111, no. 1, 2006, pp. 1–15

Skinner, Quentin, 'Meaning and Understanding in the History of Ideas', *History and Theory*, vol. 8, no. 1, 1969, pp. 3–53

Springer, James Warren, 'American Indians and the Law of Real Property in Colonial New England', *American Journal of Legal History*, vol. 30, no. 1, 1986, pp. 25–58

Ward, Damen, 'A Means and Measure of Civilisation: Colonial Authorities and Indigenous Law in Australasia', *History Compass*, vol. 1, no. 1, 2003, pp. 1–24

Ward, John M., 'Retirement of a Titan: James Stephen, 1847–50', *Journal of Modern History*, vol. 31, no. 3, 1959, pp. 189–205

Weaver, John C., 'Frontiers into Assets: The Social Construction of Property in New Zealand, 1840–65', *Journal of Imperial and Commonwealth History*, vol. 27, no. 3, 1999, pp. 17–54

Williams, David V., 'The Queen v Symonds Reconsidered', *Victoria University of Wellington Law Review*, vol. 19, no. 4, 1989, pp. 385–402

Williams, Trevor, 'James Stephen and British Intervention in New Zealand, 1838–40', *Journal of Modern History*, vol. 13, no. 1, 1941, pp. 19–35

'The Treaty of Waitangi', *History*, n.s, vol. 25, no. 99, 1940, pp. 237–51

Chapters

Anderson, Atholl, 'Old Ways and New Means, AD 1810–1830', in Atholl Anderson et al., *Tangata Whenua: A History*, Bridget Williams Books, Wellington, 2015, pp. 138–63

Attwood, Bain, 'Towards a Post-Foundational History of the Treaty', in Mark Hickford and Carwyn James (eds.), *Indigenous Peoples and the State: International Perspectives on the Treaty of Waitangi*, Routledge, Oxon, 2019, pp. 94–110

Ballantyne, Tony, 'Christianity, Colonialism and Cross-Cultural Communication', in John Stenhouse (ed.), *Christianity, Modernity and Culture*, ATF Press, Adelaide, 2005, pp. 23–57

Ballara, Angela, 'Te Whanganui-a-Tara: Phases of Maori Occupation of Wellington Harbour c. 1800–1840', in David Hamer and Roberta Nicholls (eds.), *The Making of Wellington 1800–1914*, Victoria University Press, Wellington, 1990, pp. 9–34

Beaulieu, Alain, 'The Acquisition of Aboriginal Land in Canada: The Genealogy of an Ambivalent System', in Saliha Belmessous (ed.), *Empire by Treaty: Negotiating European Expansion, 1600–1900*, Oxford University Press, New York, 2015, pp. 101–31

'"Under His Majesty's Protection": The Meaning of the Conquest for the Aboriginal Peoples of Canada', in Frans De Bruyn and Shaun Regan (eds.), *The Culture of the Seven Years' War: Empire, Identity, and the Arts in the Eighteenth-Century Atlantic World*, University of Toronto Press, Toronto, 2014, pp. 91–115

Belmessous, Saliha, 'The Treaty of Waitangi in Historical Context', in Mark Hickford and Carwyn James (eds.), *Indigenous Peoples and the State: International Perspectives on the Treaty of Waitangi*, Routledge, Oxon, 2019, pp. 77–93

'The Tradition of Treaty Making in Australian History', in Saliha Belmessous (ed.), *Empire by Treaty: Negotiating European Expansion, 1600–1900*, Oxford University Press, New York, 2015, pp. 186–213

Benton, Lauren, 'Possessing Empire: Iberian Claims and Interpolity Law', in Saliha Belmessous (ed.), *Native Claims: Indigenous Law against Empire, 1500–1920*, Oxford University Press, New York, 2012, pp. 19–40

Benton, Lauren and Adam Clulow, 'Webs of Protection and Interpolity Zones in the Early Modern World', in Lauren Benton et al. (eds.), *Protection and Empire: A Global History*, Cambridge University Press, Cambridge, 2018, pp. 49–71

Binney, Judith, 'The Maori and the Signing of the Treaty of Waitangi', in David Green (ed.), *Towards 1990: Seven Leading Historians Examine Significant Aspects of New Zealand History*, GP Books, Wellington, 1989, pp. 20–31

'Stories Without End' in her *Stories Without End: Essays 1975–2010*, Bridget Williams Books, Wellington, 2010, pp. 352–68

'Tuki's Universe', in Keith Sinclair (ed.), *Tasman Relations: New Zealand and Australia, 1788–1988*, Auckland University Press, Auckland, 1987, pp. 15–33

Cell, John W., 'The Imperial Conscience', in Peter Marsh (ed.), *The Conscience of the Victorian State*, Syracuse University Press, Syracuse, NY, 1979, pp. 173–213

Dagger, Richard, 'Rights', in Terence Ball et al. (eds.), *Political Innovation and Conceptual Change*, Cambridge University Press, New York, 1989, pp. 292–308

Dalziel, Raewyn, 'The Politics of Settlement', in W. H. Oliver with B. R. Williams (eds.), *The Oxford History of New Zealand*, Clarendon Press/Oxford University Press, Oxford and Wellington, 1981, pp. 87–111

Fisher, Michael H., 'Diplomacy in India, 1526–1858', in H. V. Bowen et al. (eds.), *Britain's Oceanic Empire: Atlantic and Indian Ocean Worlds, c. 1550–1850*, Cambridge University Press, Cambridge, 2012, pp. 249–81

Fitzmaurice, Andrew, 'Moral Uncertainty in the Dispossession of Native Americans', in P. C. Mancall (ed.), *The Atlantic World and Virginia, 1550–1624*, Omohundro Institute for Early American History, Chapel Hill, 2007, pp. 383–409

Ford, Lisa, 'Protecting the Peace on the Edges of Empire: Commissioners of Crown Lands in New South Wales', in Lauren Benton et al. (eds.), *Protection and Empire: A Global History*, Cambridge University Press, Cambridge, 2018, pp. 175–93

Ford, Lisa and David Roberts, 'Expansion, 1820–50', in Alison Bashford and Stuart Macintyre (eds.), *The Cambridge History of Australia*, Cambridge University Press, Melbourne, 2013, pp. 121–48

Francis, Mark, 'Writings on Colonial New Zealand: Nationalism and Intentionality', in Andrew Sharp and Paul McHugh (eds.), *Histories, Power and Loss: Uses of the Past — a New Zealand Commentary*, Bridget Williams Books, Wellington, 2001, pp. 165–88

Fredrickson, George M., 'Comparative History', in Michael Kammen (ed.), *The Past Before Us: Contemporary Historical Writing in the United States*, Cornell University Press, Ithaca, 1980, pp. 457–73

Frost, Alan, 'Our Original Aggression: New South Wales as *Terra Nullius*', in his *Botany Bay Mirages: Illusions of Australia's Convict Beginnings*, Melbourne University Press, Melbourne, 1994, pp. 176–89

Hickford, Mark, 'Interpreting the Treaty: Questions of Native Title, Territorial Government and Searching for Constitutional Histories', in Brad Patterson et al. (eds.), *After the Treaty: The Settler State, Race Relations and the Exercise of Power in Colonial New Zealand: Essays in Honour of Ian McLean Wards*, Steele Roberts, Wellington, 2016, pp. 92–131

Howell, P. A., 'The South Australia Act, 1834', in Dean Jaensch (ed.), *The Flinders History of South Australia*, vol. 2, Wakefield Press, Adelaide, 1986, pp. 26–51

Hunter, Ian, 'Global Justice and Regional Metaphysics: On the Critical History of the Law of Nature and Nations', in Shaunnagh Dorsett and Ian Hunter (eds.), *Law and Politics in British Colonial Thought: Transpositions of Empire*, Palgrave Macmillan, London, 2010, pp. 11–29

Kercher, Bruce, 'The Recognition of Aboriginal Status and Laws in the Supreme Court of New South Wales under Forbes CJ, 1824–1836', in A. R. Buck et al. (eds.), *Land and Freedom: Law, Property Rights and the British Diaspora*, Ashgate, Dartmouth, 2001, pp. 83–102

and Jodie Young, 'Formal and Informal Law in Two New Lands: Land Law in Newfoundland and New South Wales under Francis Forbes', in Chris English (ed.), *Essays in the History of Canadian Law*, vol. 9, University of Toronto Press, Toronto, 2005, pp. 147–91

Lousberg, Marjan, 'Edward Shortland and the Protection of Aborigines in New Zealand, 1840–1846', in Samuel Furphy and Amanda Nettelbeck (eds.), *Aboriginal Protection and Its Intermediaries in Britain's Antipodean Colonies*, Routledge, London, 2020, pp. 115–32

Low, Peter, 'French Bishop, Maori Chiefs, British Treaty', in John Dunmore (ed.), *The French and the Maori*, Heritage Press, Waikanae, 1992, pp. 97–106

McAloon, Jim, 'Resource Frontiers, Environment, and Settler Capitalism, 1769–1860', in Eric Pawson and Tom Brooking (eds.), *Environmental Histories of New Zealand*, Oxford University Press, Melbourne, 2002, pp. 52–66

McBryde, Isabel, '"Barter . . . immediately commenced to the satisfaction of both parties": Cross-Cultural Exchange at Port Jackson, 1788–1828', in Robin Torrence and Anne Clarke (eds.), *The Archaeology of Difference: Negotiating Cross-Cultural Engagements in Oceania*, Routledge, London, 2000, pp. 238–77

McHugh, P. G., '"A Pretty Gov[ernment]": The "Confederation of United Tribes" and Britain's Quest for Imperial Order in the New Zealand Islands During the 1830s', in Lauren Benton and Richard J. Ross (eds.), *Legal Pluralism and Empires, 1500–1850*, New York University Press, New York, 2013, pp. 233–58

'"The Most Decorous Veil which Legal Ingenuity Can Weave": The British Annexation of New Zealand (1840)', in Kelly L. Grotke and Markus J. Prutsch (eds.), *Constitutionalism, Legitimacy, and Power: Nineteenth-Century Experiences*, Oxford University Press, Oxford, 2014, pp. 300–20

'The Politics of Historiography and the Taxonomies of the Colonial Past: Law, History and the Tribes', in Anthony Musson and Chantal Stebbings (eds.), *Making Legal History: Approaches and Methodologies*, Cambridge University Press, Cambridge, 2012, pp. 164–95

Oliver, W. H., 'The Future Behind Us: The Waitangi Tribunal's Retrospective Utopia', in Andrew Sharp and Paul McHugh (eds.), *Histories, Power and Loss: Uses of the Past – A New Zealand Commentary*, Bridget Williams Books, Wellington, 2001, pp. 9–29

Owens, J. M. R., 'New Zealand before Annexation', in W. H. Oliver with B. R. Williams (eds.), *The Oxford History of New Zealand*, Clarendon Press/Oxford University Press, Oxford and Wellington, 1981, pp. 28–53

Pagden, Anthony, 'Law, Colonisation, Legitimisation, and the European Background', in Michael Grossberg and Christopher Tomlins (eds.), *The Cambridge History of Law in America, Volume 1, Early America (1500–1815)*, Cambridge University Press, New York, 2008, pp. 1–31

Parsonson, Ann, 'The Pursuit of Mana', in W. H. Oliver with B. R. Williams (eds.), *The Oxford History of New Zealand*, Clarendon Press/Oxford University Press, Oxford and Wellington, 1981, pp. 140–67

Pedersen, Susan, 'What is Political History Now?', in David Cannadine (ed.), *What is History Now?*, Palgrave, Basingstoke, 2002, pp. 36–56

Pocock, J. G. A., 'Waitangi as Mystery of State: Consequences of the Ascription of Federative Capacity to the Maori', in Duncan Ivison et al. (eds.), *Political Theory and the Rights of Indigenous Peoples*, Cambridge University Press, Melbourne, 2000, pp. 25–35

Porter, Andrew, 'Trusteeship, Anti-Slavery and Humanitarianism', in Andrew Porter (ed.), *The Oxford History of the British Empire: Volume III: The Nineteenth Century*, Oxford University Press, Oxford, 1999, pp. 198–221

Prest, Wilfrid, 'Antipodean Blackstone', in Wilfrid Prest (ed.), *Reinterpreting Blackstone's Commentaries: A Seminal Text in National and International Contexts*, Hart Publishing, Oxford, 2014, pp. 145–65

Price, Richard, 'Culture and Politics: Sir George Grey, Protection and the Early Nineteenth-Century Empire', in Samuel Furphy and Amanda Nettelbeck (eds.), *Aboriginal Protection and its Intermediaries in Britain's Antipodean Colonies*, Routledge, London, 2020, pp. 20–37

Richter, Daniel, 'Land and Words: William Penn's Letter to Kings of the Indians', in his *Trade, Land, Power: The Struggle for Eastern North America*, University of Pennsylvania Press, Philadelphia, 2013, pp. 135–54

'The Strange Colonial North American Career of *Terra Nullius*', in Bain Attwood and Tom Griffiths (eds.), *Frontier, Race, Nation: Henry Reynolds and Australian History*, Australian Scholarly Publishing, Melbourne, 2009, pp. 159–84

'To "Clear the King's and Indians' Title": Seventeenth-Century Origins of North American Land Cession Treaties', in Saliha Belmessous (ed.), *Empire by Treaty: Negotiating European Expansion, 1600–1900*, Oxford University Press, New York, 2015, pp. 45–77

Roberts, David Andrew, '"They Would Speedily Abandon the Country to the New Comers": The Denial of Aboriginal Rights', in Martin Crotty and David Andrew Roberts (eds.), *The Great Mistakes of Australian History*, University of New South Wales Press, Sydney, 2006, pp. 14–31

Ross, Ruth, 'The Treaty on the Ground', in Guy Powles (Foreword), *The Treaty of Waitangi: Its Origins and Significance*, University Extension Publications, Wellington, 1972, pp. 16–34

Sharp, Andrew, 'History and Sovereignty: A Case of Juridical History in New Zealand/Aotearoa', in Michael Peters (ed.), *Cultural Politics and the University in Aotearoa/New Zealand*, Dunmore Press, Palmerston North, 1997, pp. 159–81

'Recent Juridical and Constitutional Histories of Maori', in Andrew Sharp and Paul McHugh (eds.), *Histories, Power and Loss: Uses of the Past – A New Zealand Commentary*, Bridget Williams Books, Wellington, 2001, pp. 31–60

Smolenksi, John, 'The Ordering of Authority in the Colonial Americas', in John Smolenksi and Thomas J. Humphrey (eds.), *New World Orders: Violence, Sanction, and Authority in the Colonial Americas*, University of Pennsylvania Press, Philadelphia, 2005, pp. 1–16

Sorrenson, M. P. K., 'Treaties in British Colonial Policy: Precedents for Waitangi', in William Renwick (ed.), *Sovereignty and Indigenous Rights: The Treaty of Waitangi in International Contexts*, Victoria University Press, Wellington, 1991, pp. 15–29 (and reproduced in his *Ko te Whenua te Utu/ Land is the Price: Essays on Maori History, Land and Politics*, Auckland University Press, Auckland, 2014, pp. 40–54)

Stern, Philip J., 'Limited Liabilities: The Corporation and the Political Economy of Protection in the British Empire', in Lauren Benton et al. (eds.), *Protection and Empire: A Global History*, Cambridge University Press, Cambridge, 2018, pp. 114–31

Stokes, Evelyn, 'Contesting Resources: Maori, Pakeha, and a Tenurial Revolution', in Eric Pawson and Tom Brooking (eds.), *Environmental Histories of New Zealand*, Oxford University Press, Melbourne, 2002, pp. 35–51

Stone, Russell, 'Auckland Political Opposition in the Crown Colony Period, 1841–53', in Len Richardson and W. David Macintyre (eds.), *Provincial Perspectives: Essays in Honour of W. J. Gardner*, University of Canterbury, Christchurch, 1980, pp. 15–35

Tonk, Rosemarie, '"A Difficult and Complicated Question": The New Zealand Company's Wellington, Port Nicholson Claim', in David Hamer and Roberta Nicholls (eds.), *The Making of Wellington 1800–1914*, Victoria University Press, Wellington, 1990, pp. 35–59

Travers, Robert, 'A British Empire by Treaty in Eighteenth-Century India', in Saliha Belmessous (ed.), *Empire by Treaty: Negotiating European Expansion, 1600–1900*, Oxford University Press, New York, 2015, pp. 132–60

van Ittersum, Martine, 'Empire by Treaty? The Role of Written Documents in European Overseas Expansion, 1500–1800', in Adam Clulow and Tristan Mostert (eds.), *The Dutch and English East India Companies: Diplomacy, Trade and Violence in Early Modern Asia*, Amsterdam University Press, Amsterdam, 2018, pp. 153–78

Warner, Michael, 'What's Colonial about Colonial America?', in Robert Blair St George (ed.), *Possible Pasts: Becoming Colonial in Early Colonial America*, Cornell University Press, Ithaca, NY, 2000, pp. 49–70

Weaver, John C., 'Concepts of Economic Improvement and the Social Construction of Property Rights: Highlights from the English Speaking World', in John A. McLaren et al. (eds.), *Despotic Dominion: Property Rights in British Settler Societies*, UBC Press, Vancouver, 2005, pp. 79–102

White, Richard, 'Using the Past: History and Native American Studies', in Russell Thornton (ed.), *Studying Native Americans: Problems and Prospects*, University of Wisconsin Press, Madison, 1998, pp. 217–43

Williams, Glyndwr, 'Reactions on Cook's Voyage', in Ian Donaldson and Tamsin Donaldson (eds.), *Seeing the First Australians*, George Allen & Unwin, Sydney, 1985, pp. 35–50

Reports

Armstrong, David Anderson, The Land Claims Commission: Practice and Procedure, 1840–1950, Treaty of Waitangi Tribunal, Wai 45, I4, 1993

Carpenter, Samuel, Brief of Evidence in the Matter of the Treaty of Waitangi Act 1975 and in the Matter of Te Paparahi o te Taki (Northland Inquiry), Treaty of Waitangi Tribunal, Wai 1040 #A17, 2009

He Whakaputanga me te Tiriti: The Declaration and the Treaty, Wai 1040, Treaty of Waitangi Tribunal Report, 2014

Loveridge, Donald M., 'The Knot of a Thousand Difficulties': Britain and New Zealand, 1769–1840, Brief of Evidence in the Matter of the Treaty of Waitangi Act 1975 and in the Matter of Te Paparahi o te Taki (Northland Inquiry), Treaty of Waitangi Tribunal, Wai 1040 #A18, 2009

The New Zealand Land Claims Act of 1840, Brief of Evidence for the Crown Law Office (Muriwhenua Land Claim), Treaty of Waitangi Tribunal, Wai 45, I2, 1993

'An Object of the First Importance': Land Rights, Land Claims and Colonisation in New Zealand, 1839–1852, Report for the Crown Law Office for the Treaty of Waitangi Tribunal, Wai 863, 2004

McHugh, Paul, Brief of Evidence in the Matter of the Treaty of Waitangi Act 1975 and in the Matter of Te Paparahi o te Taki (Northland Inquiry), Treaty of Waitangi Tribunal, Wai 1040 #A21, 2010

Moore, Duncan et al., Old Land Claims, Treaty of Waitangi Tribunal Rangahaua Whanui Series, 1997

Ngai Tahu Report, Wai 27, Treaty of Waitangi Tribunal Report, 1991

Phillipson, Grant, Bay of Islands Maori and the Crown 1793–1853, Treaty of Waitangi Tribunal, Wai 1040 #A1, 2005

Te Whanganui a Tara Me Ona Takiwa: Treaty of Waitangi Tribunal Report on the Wellington District, Wai 145, 2003

Ward, Alan, Brief of Evidence in the Matter of the Treaty of Waitangi Act 1975 and in the Matter of Te Paparahi o te Taki (Northland Inquiry), Treaty of Waitangi Tribunal, Wai 1040 #A19, 2009

Theses

Fletcher, Ned, 'A Praiseworthy Device for Amusing and Pacifying Savages? What the Framers Meant by the English Text of the Treaty of Waitangi', PhD thesis, University of Auckland, 2014

Foster, Robert, 'An Imaginary Dominion: The Representation and Treatment of Aborigines in South Australia, 1834–1911', PhD thesis, University of Adelaide, 1993

Head, Lyndsay, 'Land, Authority and the Forgetting of Being in Early Colonial Maori History', PhD thesis, University of Canterbury, 2006

Hickford, Mark, 'Making "Territorial Rights of the Natives": Britain and New Zealand, 1830–1847', DPhil thesis, University of Oxford, 1999

Parsonson, Ann, 'He Whenua Te utu (The Payment Will be Land)', PhD thesis, University of Canterbury, 1978

Tonk, Rosemarie V., 'The First New Zealand Land Commissions, 1840–1845', MA thesis, University of Canterbury, 1986

Ward, Damen, 'The Politics of Jurisdiction: "British" Law, Indigenous Peoples and Colonial Government in Australia and New Zealand, c. 1834–60', DPhil thesis, University of Oxford, 2003

Ward, Judith, 'Fact or Fiction? William Colenso's Authentic and Genuine History of the Signing of the Treaty of Waitangi', MA thesis, Massey University, 2011

Index